DIGGING UP DIRT

Then shall the dust return to the earth as it was and the spirit shall return unto God who gave it.

Ecclesiastes 12:7 KJV

THE GOLD HILL CEMETERY
GOLD HILL, COLORADO

by Chel Courtney

Tim Walter, unknown, Dode Simms
Photo Courtesy of Lynne Walter

Boulder Daily Camera 26 August 1963:

"The Gold Hill cemetery, which was established in 1866, has a new sign.

The sign was constructed by A.J. (Tim) Walter and lettered by Mr. and Mrs. H.R. Sims [sic]. It was installed near the entrance of the cemetery by residents of the community. "

This sign was destroyed by the Four Mile Canyon Fire of September 2010.

Chel Courtney, Linda Laughlin, Michael Albes,
Amy Hardy, Jack Laughlin, Bob Walter
Photo by Gretchen Diefenderfer 19 May 2013

On 19 May 2013 a new sign was built by Tim's grandson, Bob Walter, and was installed by the Gold Hill community.

Cover photo: The grave of Rebecca Pughe in the Gold Hill Cemetery. Photo by Chel Courtney, 2013.

Copyright ©2019 by Chel Courtney
ISBN 978-1-68224-037-3,
ISBN 10 1-68224-037-1

Published by Iron Gate Publishing

DEDICATED TO ALL THE GOLD HILL RESIDENTS PAST AND PRESENT

WITH SPECIAL LOVING DEDICATION TO

WILBUR DEWEY GOUDGE & ALBERT JAMES "TIM" WALTER

"The Best of Friends"

Tim & Pearl Walter (left), Wilbur (kneeling) & Leona
Goudge with friend Al O'Brien (back right) 1957

WITH SINCERE GRATITUDE TO THE THREE WHO INSPIRED ME TO CONTINUE THEIR QUEST
JAMES "JIM" COX, RAY LARNER, ROBERT "BOB" WALTER

WITH SPECIAL GRATITUDE TO ELINOR "ELLI" COX

FOR JIM'S CEMETERY RESEARCH FILES

AND TO MY "PARTNER IN CRIME" LYNNE WALTER

"OLDEST HEARSE IN THE STATE WILDWOOD LODGE DILLON, COLORADO"
Author's Collection

I wonder as I wander
Through graves of endless grief
Those that were before me
Their lives seemed all too brief.

I know not what I'll find
When searching through their past
To honor, to cherish, to treasure
Their precious memories to last.
     —Author

Chel and Bob on Rosie's bench
Photo by Phil Courtney

ACKNOWLEDGMENTS

My deepest gratitude goes towards the following people who gave unselfishly of their time to assist me in my research. Without them this book would not be possible. I am deeply sorry if I have missed anyone.

Tami Amidon-Harrison County, Iowa researcher (Cross family)

Hope Arculin (Carnegie Library for Local History)

Robin Aslin (Reedy family)

Marti Anderson (Carnegie Library for Local History)

JoAnn Bogard (Riemenschneider family)

Beth Bradford (Bradford family)

Linda Anne Bradford Ayers (Bradford family)

Wilbur Wayne "Buddy" Bradford (Bradford family)

David Brigham (Contributor and Gold Hill Cemetery Custodian)

Marie Vanderpoel Brookhart (Vanderpoel family)

Patricia Burroughs (Edwards, Pughe & Walter families)

Maxine Goudge Bush (Goudge family)

Maggie Caldwell (Reedy family)

Dina C. Carson (Research Consultant and Contributor)

Nancy Clark (Walton family)

Dr. Doris Rhea Coy (Grover family)

Elinor "Elli" Cox (Cox & Patton families and Jim Cox's Gold Hill Cemetery research notes)

Val Crist (Fred Crist)

Marjorie Dale (Boyd family)

Gretchen Diefenderfer (Contributor)

Bill & Elisabeth Demmon (Thompson family)

Linda Dickman (Harrison County Genealogy Society-Cross family)

Kim Dryer-Church (Johannes "John" Peter Noehrn)

Mary Elson (Mark Elson)

Rene Farjado (James Dussart Regnier & Richard James Dussart Regnier)

Jessie Feather (Feather family)

Lee Feather (Feather family)

Joan Few (Historic Gold Hill, Inc. & archivist Gold Hill Museum)

Daniel Gallagher (Gallagher family)

William Gallagher-via Mary Taylor (Gallagher family)

Carol Garnett (David Roger Garnett)

Kathleen Gibson (Michael Carpenter & Gibson family)

Kerry Gibson (Gibson family)

Kris Gibson (Wyatt Cole Miller & Gibson families)

Kathleen Gilgannon (Paul Edward Smith)

Bengt Granefelt (Ecklund/Eklund families)

Tara Gottula (Mary Fraser)

Sheila Goudge (Edwin Gerald "Bud" Goudge)

Wendy Hall (Carnegie Library for Local History)

Shirley Hamblin (Pughe & Walter families)

Michael B. Harrington (Stroup family)

Chris Havens (John Felix Romig)

Jan Hayzlett (Cross & Wolcott/Woolcock families)

Thomas "Tom" Huth (Anne Hollis "Holly" (*Young*) Hirsch Huth & Jonathan Reese)

Kathy Kautzman (Walton family)

Sue Kline (Pughe & Walter families)

Martha Knapp (Knapp family)

Tom Knapp (Knapp family)

Kathy Koehler (Pughe & Walter families)

Monique Sawyer Lang (Schields/Shields family)

Phyllis Lewellen (William James Kitto)

Jim Lonsdale (James Dussart Regnier family)

Leah McKin, (Coughlin, Hastings & Pittman families and *History of Gold Hill, Colorado* by Elmer Curtis Swallow)

Anne McLellan (Edwards family)

Carol McLellan McConica (Edwards family)

MaryAnn and Paul Neumann (Benjamin "Bennie" Newmann)

Kathleen O'Brien (Gus "Gussie" Holt)

Shirley Olfert (Morey/ Mowrey/Mowry family)

Mike Olivieri (Olivieri family)

Daniel J. Olsen (Bottolfson family)

Bernard Dale Peterson (Gustafson/Petersen/Peterson family)

Ida Lou Peterson (Gustafson/Petersen/Peterson family)

Silvia Pettem (Research Consultant and Contributor)

Justin Plank (Theodore & Tillie Kinsey)

Ellen Pook (Researcher & Compiler of *Gold Hill Women Volume 3*)

Ed Raines (Research Consultant and Contributor)

Robert Reedy (Reedy family)

Richard J.D. Regnier (Regnier families)

Susan Robertshaw (Cowell & Stroup families)

Digging Up Dirt

Gale Rosenquist (Romig family & James Dussart Regnier)

Gail Seeley (Hayden family)

Karen Simmons (Benjamin "Bennie" Newman & William Robert Simmons)

Maggie Simms (Simms family and Gold Hill Cemetery Custodian)

Rick Sinner (Research Consultant and Contributor)

Marilyn Soby (Bruce Richard Stebbins)

Tolliver Swallow (*History of Gold Hill, Colorado* by Elmer Curtis Swallow)

Cari Taplin (Coughlin, Hastings & Pittman families)

Amanda Trill (Lively family)

Ron Wallick (Reedy & Romig families)

Lynne Walter (Pughe & Walter families)

Robert "Bob" Walter (Pughe & Walter families and Gold Hill Cemetery Custodian)

Nikki Welles (Goudge family)

Polly Westdal (Walton family)

Donyln Whissen (Magor & Scogland families)

Pat Wills (Grace (*Victor*) Noy/Noye Trembath/Trenbath/Trinbath)

I am deeply grateful to Wendy Hall, Marti Anderson and Hope Arculin of the Carnegie Library for Local History. With smiles on their faces they have spent numerous hours helping me locate materials.

Silvia Pettem and Ed Raines were always available to answer my "stupid" questions and offer their invaluable expertise and to Dina Carson for her knowledgeable guidance on the formatting and publishing of this book.

My deepest thanks to my dear friend Mr. Robert Dale "Bob" Walter for his delightful companionship and insight. I will always treasure the times we spent together (especially on Rosie's Bench) while researching and repairing the Gold Hill Cemetery.

I give my special loving thanks to my son, Colin Courtney, for his superb artwork and to my daughter, Carrie Courtney Trujillo for her everlasting inspiration. Finally to my dear husband and soulmate, Phil, who spent numerous hours tromping around the cemetery and for his endless time on his computer engineering the Gold Hill Cemetery map along with answering gobs of annoying computer tech questions. Without his support and patience I would have given up on this project a long time ago!

Gold Hill Cemetery Committee
Bob Walter, Maggie Simms, Chel Courtney, David Brigham
Photo by Phil Courtney

INTRODUCTION

In the mid-1800s the first cemetery was located on top of Horsfal Hill near the original Townsite of Gold Hill. As a little tyke, my Grandmother (Carrie Leona Goudge) and my Mom (Maxine Bush) would bring me to this graveyard to honor the dead. I remember several visible graves piled high with white quartz rocks.

Today that cemetery has lost its luster in being somewhat recognizable. Once thought to have been an ancient Indian burial ground the locals and the elect few try to keep its location secret.

In 1866 the current location of the Gold Hill Cemetery on Dixon Road was established. It is not verified if the cemetery's property was donated to the town or if it was just designated by the town to become the cemetery. Records are not clear and any old-timers' stories were taken to the grave.

Several of my ancestors are buried in this cemetery; some in marked graves and some whose locations will never be verified. I remember my Gramps telling me that my grand uncle Alfred was buried "over there" as he pointed his finger in a distinct direction however "over there" was a pretty large section of the cemetery.

I have spent a lot of time in this Gold Hill graveyard in both my youth and also in my adulthood. I still roam around its grounds hoping to find more clues of the past to honor the dead. These aren't complete records—never will be but to me it's a never-ending adventure that I am so honored to share with my fellow cemetery caretakers Dave Brigham, Maggie Simms and the "Head Cemetery Master" of over a half century Mr. Robert Dale "Bob" Walter.

The Old White Wooden Stile 1967   Photo courtesy of Lynne Walter

My childhood was filled with grand times tromping around in this cemetery, playing on top of the old white wooden stile where, in the correct position, one's voice could echo for miles! However I think my echoes wore on Gramps' (Wilbur Dewey Goudge) nerves but he never ever yelled at me.

Map of Gold Hill Cemetery

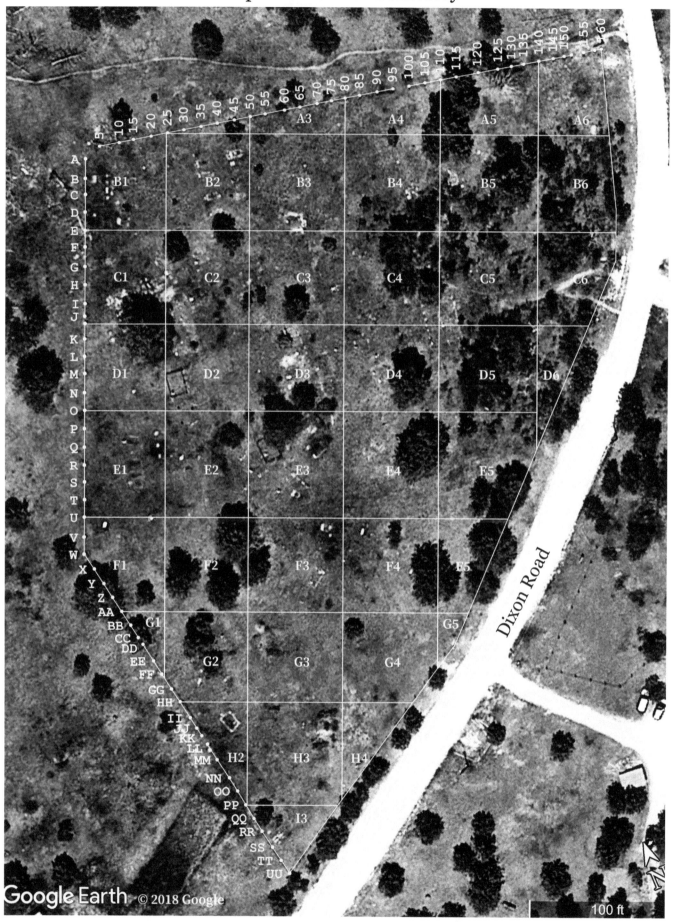

AMEN, Bernard Franklin "Bernie"

> Birth: 01/04/1951
> Death: 07/10/1984
> Cemetery Location: F4

Father: Bernard Lois Amen; Mother: Blanche (*Smith*); Wife: Vicky Linnea (maiden name might be *Matthews*) Bulla; born in (Bexar) Texas and died in Denver (Denver) Colorado at age 33 years, 6 months-extensive burns in an explosion.

Boulder Daily Camera 12 July 1984:

"Bernie Franklin Amen of 1801 Norwood Avenue died Tuesday at the University of Colorado Medical Center Burn Unit, in Denver, 25 days after receiving extensive burns in an explosion. He was 33. Mr. Amen was born in Texas, on Jan. 3, 1951, the son of Blanche and Bernie Amen Sr. He married Vicki L. Amen on Sept. 1, 1981 in Boulder. He worked for the Joseph Secor Painting Company. Mr. Amen was also an accomplished musician. He played the drums for the Second Chance Band and was a former member of the Boulder-based band Slumgullion. During his military service, he played with the Fourth Army Band. Mr. Amen is survived by his wife of Aurora, his daughter, April Amen, of Texas, his father of San Antonio, Texas, his mother and stepfather, Blanche and John Pearson, of Austin, Texas, a sister, Karen Bengch of Ransass Pass, Texas, a stepson, Casey Bulla of Denver, a stepbrother, John Person II of Austin, and a stepsister, Jenny Pearson, also of Austin. No services are scheduled. Memorial contributions may be made to the University of Colorado Medical Center, Burn Unit, 4200 E. Ninth Ave., Denver, 80220 or to Save the Whales-Greenpeace, 2029 E. 13th Ave., Denver, 80206."

[Error in newspaper article as actual record of birth states 04 January 1951]

ANDREW, Aurelia

> Birth: 01/21/1887
> Death: 03/21/1896
> Cemetery Location: D3

Father: Edwin James Andrew; Mother: Sara Jane (*Morgan*); born in Caribou (Boulder) Colorado and died in Gold Hill (Boulder) Colorado at age 9 years, 2 months, 0 days-cause of death unknown.

About the Edwin James Andrew Family

Edwin James (some records have Edward) Andrew was born in Perranzabuloe (Cornwall) England on 13 January 1860 (other sources state June of 1864); the son of Cornish natives Edwin and Margaret (*Kernick*) Andrew. Apparently his parents died early in Edwin's life as in the 1871 England census he was living with his grandparents, Peter and Mary Kemick in Perranzabuloe (Cornwall) England. Ten years later he was living with a cousin, Sarah J. Hughes and her children, in Trefeirig (Cardiganshire) Wales.

He immigrated to the United States in 1885 where he married Sarah Jane Morgan on 03 December 1885 in Gold Hill (Boulder) Colorado. She was born 09 February 1865 in Penpont, Wales; the daughter of William and Mary Ann (maiden name unknown) Morgan. This union brought forth five known children:

Aurelia: born 21 January 1887 Caribou (Boulder) Colorado and died 21 March 1896 Gold Hill (Boulder)

"Budded on earth to bloom in heaven"

Colorado; buried Gold Hill Cemetery, Gold Hill (Boulder) Colorado; see ANDREW, Aurelia

Martha Jane: born 17 October 1888 Caribou (Boulder) Colorado and died 01 July 1980 Boulder (Boulder) Colorado; buried Mountain View Cemetery, Boulder (Boulder) Colorado; married Charles Norborg Anderson

Nina: born 25 December 1890 Gold Hill (Boulder) Colorado and died 10 July 1922 Glendale (Los Angeles) California; buried Green Mountain Cemetery, Boulder (Boulder) Colorado; married Clyde Linden/Lyndon Cudebac; Green Mountain Cemetery records has birth year of 1894

Edythe A.: born 10 May 1893 Gold Hill (Boulder) Colorado and died 12 March 1978 Portland (Multnomah) Oregon; buried Willamette National Cemetery, Portland (Multnomah) Oregon; married Austin Edwin Utley

Gladys E.: born 22 January 1896 Gold Hill (Boulder) Colorado and died 29 April 1980 Los Angeles (Los Angeles) California; buried Forest Lawn Memorial Park Hollywood Hills, Los Angeles (Los Angeles) California; married Orville Garland Shaw

LaVinia: born 17 June 1903 Gold Hill (Boulder) Colorado and died 08 November 1990 Boulder (Boulder) Colorado; buried Mountain View Memorial Park, Boulder (Boulder) Colorado; married Frederick A. Carr and William J. Thomas

In 1907 the family moved down from Gold Hill to their newly purchased home at 3332 North 12th Street (*Boulder Daily Camera* 05 September 1907) and in 1909 Edwin James was operating a stage to Salina, Colorado. About 25 years later Edwin died.

Boulder Daily Camera 17 April 1934:
"Edwin James Andrew, 74, janitor of Washington school for twenty-one years, died at his home, 2935 Twelfth Street, at 12:15 p.m. today.

Mr. Andrew, widely known thruout [sic] Boulder county and highly respected by all of the pupils and teachers of Washington school, became ill last November with heart trouble. He recovered from this attack only to suffer a relapse. For the last five weeks he was bedfast.

Mr. Andrew was born in Cornwall, England, on January 19, 1889, and came to the United States 50 years ago, locating at Gold Hill in Boulder County, soon afterwards.

In Wales, England, before coming to the United States, he met Miss Sarah Jane Morgan, who came to Gold Hill 49 years ago. Her marriage to Mr. Andrew was solemnized 48 years ago.

Mr. Andrew was engaged in mining at Gold Hill until 27 years ago when he moved to Boulder. His home is opposite the school house where he spent so many years of devoted work. His son-in-law, Frederick A. Carr, has been attending to his janitor work since he became ill.

Besides Mrs. Andrew, the survivors are four daughters—Mrs. Martha Anderson, wife of Charles Anderson of Estes Park; Mrs. Edith A. Utley, wife of Austin Utley, residing in Boise, Idaho; Mrs. Gladys E. Shaw, wife of Sam Shaw, residing in Los Angeles, and Mrs. Lavinia A. Carr, wife of Frederick A. Carr, living with her parents. Another daughter, Mrs. Nina Cudebac, died some 12 years ago and is survived by a daughter, Dorothy Mae, residing with her father in Los Angeles. There are four grandchildren.

Funeral arrangements have not been completed, awaiting word from the daughters. The body is at the Howe mortuary. Rev. L.F. Reed of the Congregational church, of which Mr. Andrew was a member, will officiate. Burial will be in Green Mountain Cemetery. "

His widow, Sarah, continued to live in the family home until early 1945 when she lived with her daughter, Martha Jane. Before fall she passed away. She was buried next to her husband, Edward, in Green Mountain Cemetery, Boulder (Boulder) Colorado.

Boulder Daily Camera 21 August 1945:
"Mrs. Sarah Jane Andrew, a resident of Colorado for 60 years and of Boulder and Boulder county much of that time, died early this morning at the hospital, of shock from a fall in which she suffered a broken hip, and from a stroke.

Mrs. Andrew was the widow of Edwin James Andrew, who died April 17, 1934. He was custodian of Washington school for 21 years prior to his death and before that had been a miner.

Born in Wales, Feb. 9, 1865, daughter of Mr. and Mrs. William Morgan, she came to the United States with an older sister, Mrs. Mary Ann Boundy. She was married in 1888 to Mr. Andrew, whom she knew in Wales, the two meeting again at Gold Hill, where, he had located in 1884.

Survivors are four daughters, Mrs. W.J. Thomas, 2336 13th street, with whom she had made her home since the first of the year; Mrs. Martha Jane Anderson, wife of Charles Anderson of Estes Park; Mrs. Edythe A. Utley, Portland, Ore., and Mrs. Gladys E. Shaw of Huntington Park, Calif. The later has been here for three weeks and Mrs. Anderson much of the time [sic]. Mrs. Utley was here earlier in the year.

Besides the four daughters, six grandchildren and two great grandchildren survive.

Funeral services will be held at Howe Mortuary, probably Thursday. Rev. W.H. Bunker of the Congregational church will officiate."

B

BAISLEY, William F. "Bill"

    Birth: 06/30/1940
    Death: 02/19/1985
    Cemetery Location: G3

Father: Willard Baisley; Mother: Hazel (*Newman*); Wife: Alice (*Langer*); born in Peekskill (Westchester) New York and died in Denver (Denver) Colorado at age 44 years, 7 months, 20 days-anaphylactic reaction to a new arthritis medication

Boulder Daily Camera 20 February 1985:

    "William Bill Baisley of Salina Star Route, Gold Hill, died Tuesday at the University Hospital in Denver. He was 44. Mr. Baisley was born in Peekskill, N.Y., on June 30, 1940. He was the son of Willard and Hazel Newman Baisley. He married Alice Langer on Feb. 23, 1960, in North Carolina. Mr. Baisley worked for IBM as a facilities technician for the past 23 years. He lived in the Boulder area the past 12 years, coming from Fishkill, N.Y. He served in the U.S. Marine Corps. Survivors include his wife of Gold Hill; his father of New York; his mother, Hazel M. Rogan, of Putman Valley, N.Y., two sons, Edward F. Baisley of Gold Hill and William J. Baisley of Bozeman, Mont.; a brother, Brian Baisley of Grapevine, Texas, and two grandchildren. Visitation will be from 3-8:30 p.m. Thursday at the mortuary. Mass of Christian Burial will be celebrated at 9:30 a.m. Friday at Sacred Heart of Jesus Catholic Church, with the Rev. Michael Murray officiating. Services will conclude at Gold Hill Cemetery."

    After the 2010 Four Mile Canyon Fire the author along with Nikki Welles (sister of author) and Lynne Walter were walking through the Gold Hill Cemetery and saw the grave of Bill F. Baisley. The fire came down to the top of the Madonna figurine, split in two and traveled down each side, not burning the statue. The fire came together at the bottom of the figurine and continued on. Only the skirt of the Madonna was singed. Very eerie indeed!

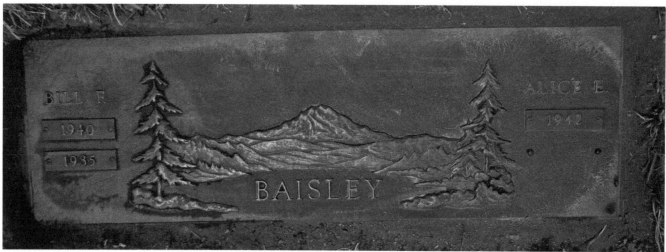

Photo by Lynne Walter

Photo by Dina C. Carson

BALSLEY, Robert Linn "Bob"

Birth: 03/25/1939
Death: 01/09/1980
Cemetery Location: D5

Father: Robert Franklin Balsley; Mother: Francis C. (*Murphy*); Wife: Shari (*Rowan*); born in Aurora (Kane) Illinois and died in Boulder (Boulder) Colorado at age 40 years, 9 months, 15 days-strep infection; author of *Early Gold Hill* May 1971

Boulder Daily Camera 11 January 1980:

"Robert Linn Balsley, 6691 Lakeview Drive, died suddenly Wednesday in Community Hospital. He was 40.

Born March 25, 1939, in Aurora, Ill., he received a bachelor's degree from Dartmouth College and a master's degree from the University of Colorado.

He and Shari Rowan were married July 30, 1960, in Aurora, Ill., and they moved to Boulder in 1961.

He was associated with the Daily Camera and was a teacher in the Boulder school district before he established the Madison Ave. West advertising agency.

Survivors include his wife; two sons, Craig and Toby; a daughter, Ami; a sister, Bunny Day, and his parents, Robert and Francis Balsley of Florida.

Memorial services will be at 11 a.m. Saturday at Sacred Heart of Mary Church with the Rev. A.B. Patterson officiating.

In lieu of flowers, contributions to an educational fund for children may be sent to Balsley Memorial Fund, Bank of Boulder, 3033 Iris Ave., Boulder, 80301."

Dartmouth Class of 1961 In Memoriam:

"Robert Linn Balsley Died: January 9, 1980...Bob died as a result of an overwhelming strep infection at the age of 40 in the Community Hospital of Boulder, Colorado, on Wednesday, January 9. He had been in the hospital less than 24 hours.

He loved Boulder. Since 1973 until his death he had headed Madison Avenue West, a local advertising agency, having spent the previous seven years as a social studies teacher at Boulder High School and getting his master's degree at the University of Colorado in 1970. In Boulder he was active in civic affairs, promoting continuing education, social studies, and social sciences programs. He was a leader of the local historical society, and was head of public relations for the Boulder Valley Educational Association.

Bob came to Dartmouth from Aurora, Illinois, where he went to high school. As a high school student, Bob was in the honor society, and active on the school newspaper, the yearbook, and dramatics. He played basketball, managed the football team, and was captain of the golf team.

At Dartmouth he majored in history, was on The Dartmouth his sophomore year, and in the outing club for four years. He designed the Carnival Poster his junior year.

Digging Up Dirt

Brett McEntagart, a classmate from Ireland, who roomed with Bob their last year, offers some remembrances of Bob, his talents, and energy. "My senior year I roomed off campus with Bob Balsley and Tom Hewitt," writes Brett. "I was particular friends with Bob, as he and I shared an interest in art. Bob was extremely talented and did some fine poster designs for the Dartmouth Winter Carnival and also a portrait of Ken Dehaven. We used to go on sketching trips together. He advised me to apply to the University of Colorado to do masters in Fine Art. He was getting married to his longtime girlfriend, Shari, after graduation and going to live in Boulder, Colorado. He said Colorado was a great place to live. He was certainly right about that."

Brett continues, "We had some great times in Boulder. Initially we stayed in a log cabin in the old mining village of Gold Hill some miles up the mountains from Boulder. The village had been abandoned years before but people had recently started to move back, people looking for a freer and more laidback lifestyle. The old post office had been renovated by the Finn family and they used to have square dancing and a keg of beer every Saturday night. It was great fun and I got to dance with Shari as Bob didn't dance! My lasting memory of the log cabin is of clouds of moths—or millers as they used to call them—flying around the lamps. I used to fill a bucket with sudsy water and hold it up to the light and they would all fly in. I was very sad to hear of his death as we had been very close in those years and he was a really talented artist."

Bob was survived by Shari, two sons, and a daughter."

BARNETT, Dora May

Birth: 03/1891
Death: 12/15/1908
Cemetery Location: D2

Father: James Barnett, Jr.; Mother: Wilmina "Minnie" (*Mayer*); born and died in Gold Hill (Boulder) Colorado at age 18 years-rheumatism; see BARNETT, James; see BARNETT, Wilmina "Minnie" (*Mayer*); see **About the James Barnett, Jr. Family**

Boulder Daily Camera 17 December 1908:
"GOLD HILL FAMILY STRICKEN—Dora, the 18 year old daughter of Mr. and Mrs. James Barnett of Gold Hill, died at her home Wednesday morning of rheumatism of the heart, after an illness of two weeks. The deceased was a very bright and attractive girl, and was born in her mountain home. The parents are heartbroken. The funeral took place this afternoon."

History of the Oscar Walton and Minnie Pearl Barnette Family (as of June 1999) sent to Jim Cox by Kathleen Kautzman 31 May 1999:

"Dora M. Barnett died at 16 [error in age], while Grandma was helping bathe her."

BARNETT, James (Jr.)

Birth: 11/01/1864
Death: 04/05/1920
Cemetery Location: D2

Father: William Henry Barnett; Mother: Mary Ann "Anna" (*Williams*); Wife: Wilmina "Minnie" (*Mayer*); born in Michigan and died in Boulder (Boulder) Colorado at age 55 years, 5 month, 4 days-influenza; error in tombstone inscription as to number of children born to James and Minnie; see BARNETT, Wilmina "Minnie" (*Mayer*); see **About the James Barnett, Jr. Family**

Boulder Daily Camera 05 April 1920:
"James Barnett of 2219 Fourteenth Street passed away at 2 o'clock this afternoon from the after effects of influenza."

Boulder Daily Camera 06 April 1920:

"JAMES BARNETT, MINING MAN OF GOLD HILL, DIES HERE...

James Barnett died April 5th, at 2 o'clock, at his home at 2219 Fourteenth Street after a two month illness following influenza. He is survived by his wife, Minnie Barnett, and two daughters, Mrs. Oscar Walton of 1734 Spruce street and Miss Myrtle R. Barnett. His mother, Mrs. Mary Ann Barnett, of Nederland, is here. The funeral will take place Thursday at one o'clock from Howe's mortuary and interment will be at Gold Hill.

The arrival of his brothers, Joseph Barnett of Casper, Wyo., George Barnett of Denver, Nailor Barnett of Nederland and his sisters, Mrs. Rose Dudley and Mrs. Lottie Schwartz of Denver, is awaited.

Mr. Barnett was born in Antenogan [sic], Mich., in 1864, and came to Colorado in 1870, living in Boulder County 45 years. He was interested in mining in Gold hill [sic] where he has many friends."

Boulder Daily Camera 08 April 1920:
"Funeral services of James Barnett were conducted from Howe's mortuary at one o'clock today by Rev. Lew C. Harris. The choir of the Christian church sang several selections. The family accompanied the remains to Gold Hill where interment took place."

BARNETT, Maud

Birth: Unknown
Death: Before 1900
Cemetery Location: D2

Father: James Barnett, Jr.; Mother: Wilmina "Minnie" (*Mayer*); born and died Gold Hill (Boulder) Colorado at age 4 years old-cause of death unknown; see BARNETT, James; see BARNETT, Wilmina "Minnie" (*Mayer*); see **About the James Barnett, Jr. Family**

BARNETT, Maud

Birth: 02/1901
Death: 02/1901
Cemetery Location: D2

Father: James Barnett, Jr.; Mother: Wilmina "Minnie" (*Mayer*); born in either Caribou or Gold Hill (Boulder) Colorado and died in Gold Hill (Boulder) Colorado at age 2 days old-cause of death unknown; see BARNETT, James; see BARNETT, Wilmina "Minnie" (*Mayer*); see **About the James Barnett, Jr. Family**

Boulder Daily Camera 22 February 1901:
"Baby Barrett [sic], idol of James Barrett's family, was buried from Trezise's undertaking parlors this afternoon."

BARNETT, Minnie

Birth: 02/1887
Death: 05/13/1887
Cemetery Location: D2

Father: James Barnett, Jr.; Mother: Wilmina "Minnie" (*Mayer*); born in Caribou (Boulder) Colorado and died in Gold Hill (Boulder) Colorado at age 3 months-cause of death unknown; no tombstone for this grave; see BARNETT, James; see BARNETT, Wilmina "Minnie" (*Mayer*); see **About the James Barnett, Jr. Family**

Boulder County Herald Weekly 18 May 1887:
    "Jas. Barnett's three-month's old girl died at Gold Hill last Friday."

BARNETT, Raymond Frederick

Birth: 12/21/1911
Death: 06/25/1912
Cemetery Location: D2

Father: James Barnett, Jr.; Mother: Wilmina "Minnie" (*Mayer*); born and died in Gold Hill (Boulder) Colorado at age 6 months, 4 days-pertussis; see BARNETT, James; see BARNETT, Wilmina "Minnie" (*Mayer*); see **About the James Barnett, Jr. Family**

Boulder Daily Camera 25 June 1912:
    "Raymond Frederick, the six-month old son of Mr. and Mrs. James Barnett of Gold Hill, died there at 1 o'clock today. The funeral will be held at Gold Hill tomorrow."

BARNETT, Sibyl Arlene

Birth: 07/11/1897
Death: 01/23/1899
Cemetery Location: E3

Father: William Howard Barnett; Mother: Ella Mae (Edna) "Lovey" (*Russell*); born and died in Gold Hill (Boulder) Colorado at age 1 year, 6 months, 12 days-cause of death unknown; see **About the James Barnett, Jr. Family**; see **About the William Howard Barnett Family**

Boulder Daily Camera 24 January 1899:
    "The two year old child of W.H. Bennetts [newspaper article error] died at Gold Hill last night. Mr. Trezise sent a casket up for the remains this morning."

Boulder County Herald Weekly 25 January 1899:
    "Barnett, son [newspaper error] of Mr. & Mrs. W.H. Barnett, died 23 January 1899 Gold Hill. Age 2 years; Trezise sent up coffin."

The James Barnett Family Plot

About the William Howard Barnett Family

Sibyl was the granddaughter of William Henry and Mary Ann "Anna" (*Williams*) Barnett; both natives of England. The family came to Gold Hill (Boulder) Colorado from Michigan about 1872 then later in Nederland (Boulder) Colorado. William, a miner, died in 1915 and Mary Ann died in 1922. Both are buried in the Nederland Cemetery (Boulder County) Colorado; see **About the James Barnett, Jr. Family.**

Sibyl's father, William Howard Barnett (brother of James Barnett Jr.) was born 16 November 1862 in Michigan; the son of William Henry and Mary Ann (*Williams*) Barnett; see BARNETT, James.

William Howard married Ella Mae/Edna "Lovey" Russell. She was born in Fontana (Miami) Kansas on 09 September 1873; the daughter of Michael L. and Mary (*Ross*) Russell. To this union two known children were born:

Hazel Marie: born 29 April 1893 Aspen (Pitkin) Colorado and died 16 May 1961 Asotin (Asotin) Washington; buried Vineland Cemetery, Clarkston (Asotin) Washington; married Binger Herman Carno/Clarneau, John W. Rivers, John A. Thomas and Albert Friedrich Luther Rehberg

Sibyl Arlene: born 11 July 1897 Gold Hill (Boulder) Colorado and died 23 January 1899 Gold Hill (Boulder) Colorado; buried Gold Hill Cemetery, Gold Hill (Boulder) Colorado; see BARNETT, Sibyl Arlene

A few years after the birth of their first child (Hazel) William Howard and Ella Mae/Edna left Aspen (Pitkin) Colorado and moved again to the Gold Hill (Boulder) Colorado area where their second daughter, Sibyl Arlene, was born in 1897.

In 1910 Ella Mae was living in (Asotin) Washington with her daughter, Hazel, niece Olive Russell and nephew Benjamin Russell. Ella is listed as being a widow however her husband, William Howard, was quite alive, living in (Shoshone) Idaho and on his second marriage to Margaret L.P. Mayer whom he married in 1909. (It is not verified that Mayer is a maiden name or a married name.)

A few years later William Howard and Margaret moved to (Jefferson) Oregon where he died 29 August

"Budded on earth to bloom in Heaven"

1915 and is buried in the Hay Creek Cemetery (Jefferson) Oregon.

After the 1930 United States census Ella Mae/Edna married her second spouse Ulysses Grant Stowell. He died on 04 March 1939 and Ella died 20 February 1952. Both are buried in the family plot in Vineland Cemetery in Clarkston (Asotin) Washington.

Unknown Newspaper from (Jefferson) Oregon September 1915:

"William H. Barnett Passes...

At his homestead, about five miles east of Hay Creek, Oregon, on Sunday evening, August 29th, 1915, the spirit of William H. Barnett took flight.

Mr. Barnett had been in poor health for several months with complications of stomach and kidney trouble. He was a native of Michigan and was born November 16th, 1862. He united with the Friend Church in 1906.

On November 16th, 1909, at Wallace, Idaho, he was married to Margaret L.P. Mayer [second wife]. He was a kind and affectionate father and a true and devoted husband. He lived a life devoted to his family and for the uplifting of the community. He spent his leisure hours in study and was ever striving for a higher and noble life.

Mr. Barnett worked in the mines of the western states for about thirty years. He has lived in this neighborhood about two years, and has made many friends here. All speak highly of him as a man and a neighbor.

Funeral services were conducted at the home at 2 o'clock, August 31st, by W.J. Jeffries, a neighbor. A large number of friends and neighbors attended, and the body was laid to rest in the Hay Creek cemetery.

Mr. Barnett leaves a widow and a daughter by a former marriage, Mrs. Hazel Klarno [Carno], of Asotin, Washington."

BARNETT, Walter

> Birth: 10/03/1904
> Death: 01/16/ 1907
> Cemetery Location: D2

Father: James Barnett, Jr.; Mother: Wilmina "Minnie" (*Mayer*); born and died in Gold Hill (Boulder) Colorado at age 2 years, 3 months, 13 days-pneumonia; see BARNETT, James; see BARNETT, Wilmina "Minnie" (*Mayer*); see **About the James Barnett, Jr. Family**

Boulder Daily Camera 16 January 1907:

"Walter Barnett, the 2 year old son of Mr. and Mrs. James Barnett of Gold Hill, died this morning of pneumonia. The funeral will take place from the home Thursday afternoon."

BARNETT, Wilmina "Minnie" (*Mayer*)

> Birth: 03/07/1869
> Death: 08/03/1940
> Cemetery Location: D2

Father: Nicholas Jacob Mayer; Mother: Caroline "Carrie" Elizabeth Dorothy (*Hertwig*); Husband: James Barnett, Jr.; born in Newark (Essex) New Jersey and died in Denver (Denver) Colorado at age 71 years, 4 months, 27 days—retroperitoneal sarcoma; error in tombstone inscription as to number of children born to James and Minnie; Holman brothers (John and Charles) dug the grave; see MAYER, Nicholas Jacob Mayer; see MAYER, Caroline "Carrie" Elizabeth Dorothy (*Hertwig*); see **About the James Barnett, Jr. Family**

Boulder Daily Camera 05 August 1940:

"Mrs. Minnie Barnett, Gold Hill Pioneer, Dies In Denver...

Mrs. Minnie Barnett, widow of James Barnett, died Saturday night at 6:30 at St. Luke's Hospital in Denver.

She was a pioneer of Colorado, living in the state 62 years. Her parents, Mr. and Mrs. Mayer, were early residents of Gold Hill and are buried there as is Mr. Barnett and other members of the family.

From Gold Hill Mrs. Barnett moved to Boulder 30 years ago and after 15-years residence in Boulder, moved to Denver. There she became a member of the Northside Woman's club and attended the Highland Christian church.

Mrs. Barnett was born in Newark, N.J., March 7, 1869. She was nine when her parents came to Colorado. She is survived by two daughters, Mrs. Pearl Walton of Boulder, and Mrs. Myrtle Grams of Denver. The latter was formerly soloist for the First Christian church of this city.

Other survivors are three granddaughters, Mrs. Pearl Milliken, Idaho Springs; Mrs. Lois Clifford, Boulder, and Miss Gwendolyn Walton of Boulder. Gerald Ray Clifford of Boulder is a great grandchild.

Funeral services will be held at Howe mortuary, Tuesday at 2:30. Rev. W.R. Ferguson, pastor of Highland Christian church, Denver, will officiate. Interment will be in the family lot in Gold Hill."

Boulder Daily Camera 06 August 1940:

"Mrs. Minnie Barnett—Services at Howe mortuary this afternoon at 2:30. Rev. W. R. Ferguson, pastor of Highland Christian church, Denver, officiated. Pallbearers were J.A. Murry, H. A. Searcy, Alex McLellan, all of Boulder, and Thomas Noland, John Kyner and Sam Kimbler, all of Denver. Mrs. William Morris sang and Mrs. H.A. Searcy played the organ. Interment Gold Hill cemetery."

About the James Barnett Family

James' father, William Henry Barnett, was born in England in 1836; coming to America in 1855. He married Mary Ann "Anna" Williams in 1860. She was born in 1846 (Cornwall) England; the daughter of Cornelius and Mary Ann (maiden name unknown) Williams. This union produced 12 known children:

William Howard: born 16 November 1862 Michigan and died 29 August 1915 near Hay Creek (Jefferson) Oregon; buried Hay Creek Cemetery, (Jefferson) Oregon; married Ella Mae/Edna "Lovey" (*Russell*) and Margaret L. P. Mayer (not known if Mayer is maiden or married name)

James: born 01 November 1864 Ontonagon (Ontonagon) Michigan and died 05 April 1920 Boulder (Boulder) Colorado; buried Gold Hill Cemetery, Gold Hill (Boulder) Colorado; married Wilmina "Minnie" Mayer; see BARNETT, James; see BARNETT, Wilmina "Minnie" (*Mayer*)

George: born 15 April 1866 Michigan and died 07 January 1927 Boulder (Boulder) Colorado; buried Nederland Cemetery, Nederland (Boulder) Colorado; married Annie E. Johnston

Rosena: born 13 October 1867 Michigan and died 31 May 1942 Casper (Natrona) Wyoming; buried Columbia Cemetery, Boulder (Boulder) Colorado; married William Edwards and Joseph Lobb Dudley; see EDWARD, William; see DUDLEY, Infant

Joseph: born 01 May 1872 Central City (Gilpin) Colorado and died 14 September 1936 Casper (Natrona) Wyoming; buried Columbia Cemetery, Boulder (Boulder) Colorado; married Francis E. "Fannie" Thompson

Lottie May: born about 1873 Colorado and died after 1953; burial unknown; married Howard C. Schultz and James E. Raymond

Albert Cornelius "Naylor": born 01 December 1885 Gold Hill (Boulder) Colorado and died 23 February 1940 Boulder (Boulder) Colorado; buried Columbia Cemetery, Boulder (Boulder) Colorado; married Lucy Bertha Harpel

The family came to Colorado around 1872, coming from Michigan. They lived in Summerville (Boulder) Colorado as early as 1876 and then moved to Gold Hill (Boulder) Colorado in the spring of 1883.

About 1907 William and Mary Ann moved to Nederland (Boulder) Colorado where William died 12 July 1915 (due to suffocation while working in a mine at the age of 82 years) and Mary Ann died 18 January 1922. Both are buried in the Nederland Cemetery in Nederland (Boulder) Colorado.

It is possible that William's son, James, was named after William's brother (James Sr.). It seems for clarification the younger James was tagged "Jr."

James Jr., first mined in Black Hawk (Gilpin) Colorado and then in Caribou (Boulder) Colorado in the very early 1870s.

James Jr., married Wilmina "Minnie" Mayer on 11 August 1886 in Gold Hill (Boulder) Colorado. She was born on 07 March 1869 in Newark (Essex) New Jersey; the daughter of Nicholas Jacob and Caroline "Carrie" Elizabeth Dorothy (*Hertwig*) Mayer; see MAYER, Caroline "Carrie" Elizabeth Dorothy (*Hertwig*) and MAYER, Nicholas Jacob. Wilmina's father (Nicholas Jacob Mayer) had to write consent statement for this marriage as Wilmina was approximately 17 ½ years of age.

Boulder County Herald Weekly 18 August 1886:

"A little episode which broke pleasantly in upon [sic] the busy activity of some of Gold Hill's citizens Wednesday was the marriage of James Barnett, Jr., and Miss Minnie Mayer. At two o'clock the relatives and special friends of bride and groom, about twenty in number, were gathered in the parlor of Mr. Barnett, Sr., and in the presence of two very attractive and hopeful people, Rev. Allen Persons, of Boulder, performed the ceremony. The guests showed their practical good sense in presenting such gifts as will be useful in the new house about to be built, and which, we hope, may be converted into a happy home."

James and Wilmina were blessed with eight known children:

Minnie: born about February 1887 Caribou (Boulder) Colorado and died 13 May 1887 Gold Hill (Boulder) Colorado; buried Gold Hill Cemetery, Gold Hill (Boulder) Colorado; no marker but assuming in the Barnett Family Plot; see BARNETT, Minnie

Minnie Pearl: born 07 May 1888 Caribou (Boulder) Colorado and died 18 January 1962 Boulder (Boulder) Colorado; buried Columbia Cemetery, Boulder (Boulder) Colorado; married Oscar L. Walton

Dora May: born March 1891 Gold Hill (Boulder) Colorado and died 15 December 1908 Gold Hill (Boulder) Colorado; buried Gold Hill Cemetery, Gold Hill (Boulder) Colorado; see BARNETT, Dora May

Maude: born in Gold Hill (Boulder) Colorado and died before 1900 in Gold Hill (Boulder) Colorado; buried Gold Hill Cemetery, Gold Hill (Boulder) Colorado; see BARNETT, Maude

Myrtle R.: born 24 July 1895 Gold Hill (Boulder) Colorado and died March 1978 Denver (Denver) Colorado; burial unknown; married Herbert L. Grams

Maude: born February 1901 either in Caribou or Gold Hill (Boulder) Colorado and died February 1901 Gold Hill (Boulder) Colorado at 2 days old); buried Gold Hill Cemetery, Gold Hill (Boulder) Colorado; see BARNETT, Maude

Raymond Frederick: born 21 December 1911 Gold Hill (Boulder) Colorado and died 25 June 1912 Gold Hill (Boulder) Colorado; buried Gold Hill Cemetery, Gold Hill (Boulder) Colorado; see BARNETT Raymond Frederick

Walter: born 03 October 1904 Gold Hill (Boulder) Colorado- died 16 January 1907 Gold Hill (Boulder) Colorado; buried Gold Hill Cemetery, Gold Hill (Boulder) Colorado; see BARNETT, Walter

By 1920 the family was living on Pine Street in Boulder (Boulder) Colorado where James was a janitor at the Methodist Church in Boulder (Boulder) Colorado. He died on 05 April 1920 in the comfort of his own home on 2219 Fourteenth Street in Boulder (Boulder) Colorado.

BENNETT(S), Infant

> Birth: 04/1889
> Death: 1889
> Cemetery Location: D3

Father: James Bennett(s); Mother: Mary Ann (*Shea*); born and died in Gold Hill (Boulder) Colorado at age less than 1 year-complications due to blood poisoning in womb; shares the same tombstone as James & Mary Ann Bennett; see BENNETT(S), James; see BENNETT(S), Mary Ann (*Shea*); see **About the James Bennett(s) Family**

BENNETT(S), James

> Birth: 06/15/1864
> Death: 07/13/1889
> Cemetery Location: D3

Father: John Thomas Bennett(s); Mother: Amelia Anne (*Johns*); Wife: Mary Ann (*Shea*); born in (Cornwall) England and died in Gold Hill (Boulder) Colorado at age 25 years, 0 months, 28 days-pneumonia; great grand uncle to author; see BENNETT(S), Mary Ann (*Shea*); see BENNETT(S), Infant; see **About the James Bennett(s) Family**

Boulder County Herald Weekly 17 July 1889:
"James Bennetts of Gold Hill died on Sunday of pneumonia. Mr. Bennetts lost his wife about three months ago."

BENNETT(S), Jane (*Bennet*) Thomas

> Birth: 12/20/1838
> Death: 03/27/1922
> Cemetery Location: E2

Father: Nicholas Bennet; Mother: Dinah (*Stephens*); 1st Husband: John Thomas; 2nd Husband: William Bennett(s); born in St. Enoder (Cornwall) England and died in Boulder (Boulder) Colorado at age of 83 years, 3 months, 7 days-senile dementia; last name spelled several ways (Bennet, Bennett, Bennets, Bennetts); tombstone has Bennet; see WALTER, Elizabeth Ann "Bessie" (*Thomas*); see THOMAS, John B.; see THOMAS, William Henry

Boulder Daily Camera 28 March 1922:
"Mrs. Jane Bennett, mother of Mrs. Walters of 2044 Marine Street and the late John B. Thomas, who died January 15, died at a local institution at 11:30 o'clock last night. For years she had been ailing with heart trouble and other complications. She was more than 80 years of age. For many years she lived at Gold Hill, in this county. The remains are at Howe's mortuary awaiting funeral arrangements."

Boulder Daily Camera 29 March 1922:
"FUNERAL OF MRS. BENNETT...The funeral of Mrs. Jane Bennett will take place Thursday at 1:30 at Howe's mortuary. Rev. J.H. Skeen will conduct the service. Interment will be in Goldhill."

About Jane (*Bennet*) Thomas Bennett(s)

Jane was born in St. Enoder (some sources state St. Agnes) (Cornwall) England on 20 December 1838; the daughter of Nicholas and Dinah (*Stephens*) Bennet. At the age of 18 years she married John Thomas, a tin miner, (age 20 years) on 15 October 1856 in Par (Cornwall) England. To this union four known children were born:

Elizabeth Ann: born 20 October 1857 England and died 27 December 1944 Boulder (Boulder) Colorado; buried Gold Hill Cemetery, Gold Hill (Boulder) Colorado; married Charles Thomas Walter; see WALTER, Elizabeth Ann "Bessie" (*Thomas*)

James: born about 1863 St. Blazey (Cornwall) England-death unknown; burial unknown (In the 1881 England census he was 18 years old and a tin miner living in the in the household of his mother, Jane, and siblings Elizabeth, John and William in St. Agnes (Cornwall) England.)

John B.: born 20 November 1868 (Cornwall) England and died 15 January 1922 Boulder (Boulder) Colorado; buried Gold Hill cemetery, Gold Hill (Boulder) Colorado; see THOMAS, John B.

William Henry: born 20 June 1869 (Cornwall) England and died 28 September 1911 Gold Hill (Boulder) Colorado); buried Gold Hill Cemetery, Gold Hill (Boulder) Colorado; see THOMAS, William Henry

Jane's husband, John Thomas, died in (Cornwall) England prior to the 1871 England census as Jane is listed as a widow with four children: Elizabeth, James, John and William. She then married William Bennetts, born about 1828 in Crantock (Cornwall) England however he died shortly after the 1891 England census.

Jane set sail for America in the early 1890s. The 1900 United States Census lists Jane, age 58 (birth year of 1841), living in Gold Hill (Boulder) Colorado (widowed)

with her son, John B. Thomas. Interesting to note the census also states she had seven children with four living (the 1910 census states eight children with four living).

Jane was living in Boulder (Boulder) Colorado with her daughter, Mrs. Elizabeth (Charles) Walter when she was taken to the University Hospital in Boulder (Boulder) Colorado. She died there on 27 March 1922 from senile dementia.

BENNETT(S), Mary Ann (*Shea*)

Birth: 04/18/1869
Death: 04/12/1889
Cemetery Location: D3

Father: Daniel Shea; Mother: Ellen (*McGlaughlin*); Husband: James Bennett(s); born in Colorado and died in Gold Hill (Boulder) Colorado at age 19 years, 11 months, 25 days-blood poisoning following childbirth; great grand aunt to author; see BENNETT(S), James; see BENNETT(S), Infant; see **About the James Bennett(s) Family**; see SHEA, Daniel

Boulder County Herald Weekly 17 April 1889:
    "Mrs. James Bennett died at Gold Hill Saturday."

Boulder News 18 April 1889:
    "Mr. Trezise sent a casket up to Gold Hill Saturday for Mrs. James Bennett."

About the James Bennett(s) Family

John Thomas Bennett(s) (father of James) was born 24 November 1829 St. Blazey (Cornwall) England; the son of Thomas Bennett(s) (mother unknown). He married Amelia Anne Johns on 25 July 1850 at the Parish of Cuby in Tregony (Cornwall) England. Amelia was born 02 December 1832 in Tregony (Cornwall) England; the daughter of William and Sarah (*Barnes*) Johns. To this union seven known children were born:

Sarah Jane: born 1852 St. Blazey (Cornwall) England-death unknown; burial unknown; married John Hobbs

Thomas Arthur: born January 1853 St. Blazey (Cornwall) England and died 15 August 1903 Denver (Denver) Colorado; buried Fairmount Cemetery, Denver (Denver) Colorado; married Rachel George; tombstone has birth year 1855 whereas mortuary records state birth year as 1854

John: born 08 April 1855 St. Blazey (Cornwall) England and died prior to the 07 April 1861 England census; burial unknown

Anne "Annie" Elizabeth: born 06 April 1857 St. Blazey (Cornwall) England and died 09 September 1930 Gold Hill (Boulder) Colorado; buried Gold Hill Cemetery, Gold Hill (Boulder) Colorado; tombstone has birth

year 1856; married Edwin David "Ned" Goudge; see GOUDGE, Annie Elizabeth (*Bennett(s)*); see GOUDGE, Edwin David "Ned"

John: born baptized 23 October 1859 St. Blazey (Cornwall) England and died prior to the 07 April 1861 England census; burial unknown

William John: baptized 23 October 1861 St. Blazey (Cornwall) England and died prior to the 26 August 1867 ship records; burial unknown

James: born 15 June 1864 St. Blazey (Cornwall) England and died 13 July 1889 Gold Hill (Boulder) Colorado; buried Gold Hill Cemetery, Gold Hill (Boulder) Colorado; married Mary Ann Shea; see BENNETT(S), James; see BENNETT(S), Mary Ann (*Shea*); see BENNETT(S), Infant

After the birth of his last born child (James) John Thomas Bennett(s), a copper miner, left for a better life in America, arriving at the Port of New York on 03 July 1866 on the ship "Pennsylvania."

A year later his wife, Amelia, and the four living children (Sarah Jane, Thomas Arthur, Annie Elizabeth and James) left their homeland to join him. They arrived at the Port of New York 26 August 1867 on the ship "City of Antwerp" however soon afterwards Amelia died as in the 1870 Mahanoy (Schuylkill) Pennsylvania census John is

listed as a widower, living with his four children (Sarah, Thomas, Annie and James). At this point John Thomas Bennett(s) seems to have vanished: no verified records have been located.

Family story goes that after the death of his wife, Amelia, John Thomas went to California Gulch in Colorado to find his fortune at mining. According to the *Boulder Daily Camera* newspaper files (in an interview with Wilbur D. Goudge, son of Edwin David "Ned and Annie Elizabeth (*Bennett(s)*) Goudge) California Gulch was a forerunner of Leadville (Lake) Colorado. The four children of John Thomas (Sarah Jane, Thomas Arthur, Annie Elizabeth and James) ended up in (Morris) New Jersey with relatives.

On 24 April 1873 the oldest child, Sarah, married John Hobbs in Randolph (Morris) New Jersey. Less than two years later in the same place her sister Annie Elizabeth married Edwin David "Ned" Goudge on 01 August 1874.

Family story says that Annie and her new husband Edwin David "Ned" Goudge (along with Annie's brothers, Thomas Arthur and James) came by train to Colorado, saying this trip was in the nature of a honeymoon for Annie and Edwin as they were to visit Annie's father, John Thomas in California Gulch. Apparently Edwin fell

"No pain, no grief no anxious fear Can reach the peaceful sleepers here."

in love with the area and persuaded Annie to stay; see GOUDGE, Annie Elizabeth (*Bennett(s)*).

Annie's brother, Thomas Arthur Bennett(s), mined in Ruby City (Gunnison) Colorado along with his brother-in-law Edwin David "Ned" Goudge before settling down in Central City (Gilpin) Colorado where he married Rachel George. Their union produced four known children before Thomas died 15 August 1903 in Denver (Denver) Colorado and was buried in the Fairmount Cemetery there. Rachel died 13 January 1919 and assumed to be buried beside her husband.

James, at sixteen years old, lived and mined at Caribou (Boulder) Colorado by 1880. Later he was living in the Gold Hill (Boulder) Colorado area where he met and married Mary Ann Shea there on the 4th of July 1888. She was born 18 April 1869; the daughter of Daniel and Ellen (*McGlaughlin*) Shea of the nearby mining town of Sunshine (Boulder) Colorado; see SHEA, Daniel.

It was a short marriage for James Bennett(s) and Mary Ann Shea. Family story goes that Mary was with child at the time of her death and the baby did not survive very long after birth. The only primary evidence to support this is an old newspaper article:

Boulder Daily Camera 27 March 1905:

"CHILDREN LOST WITHIN AS MANY YEARS AND THREE BY MATERNITY OR ITS FEAR...

Boulder County afflicted, indeed. Few families have had as sad an experience as that attending this one within the past four years. The children of Mrs. Dan Shea of Sunshine have gone quickly, though the mother, with all the sorrows of a tender heart, remains strong at 68. A son [Harry] was accidentally shot four years ago and then, quickly following, came the death of a daughter [Mary Ann (*Shea*) Bennett(s)] from blood poisoning following childbirth. Two weeks ago another daughter, Mrs. Nellie Burger, died at Cripple Creek in the same way. A third daughter, Mrs. Lagerlund, advised of the death of Mrs. Burger of the same complaint which had deprived her of another sister, passed away this morning. Her child was born February 17, but the mother had been rendered insane during pregnancy by the belief that her fate was to be that of her sisters gone before, Drs. Gilbert and Julius Jaeger contributing their best energies to save her.

Sunshine is in mourning with Mrs. Shea, widow of a well-known miner and the case presents a peculiar line of analogy in that three daughters of one household gave up their lives that others might live."

(The time-dating of Harry's death in this article was not accurate as he actually died in 1897 and the first of the three sisters to die from blood poisoning due to childbirth was Mary Ann who died in 1889.)

Unfortunately James died three months later from pneumonia on 13 July 1889 and was buried beside his wife, Mary Ann, and their baby in the Gold Hill Cemetery, Gold Hill (Boulder) Colorado.

BENNETTS, Harriet (*Tonkin*-possibility)

Birth: 04/26/1867
Death: 12/02/1934
Cemetery Location: B2

Father: Tonkin (possibly); Mother: unknown; 1st husband: Richard Ellis; 2nd husband: John Richard Bennetts; born in Penzance (Cornwall) England and died in Gold Hill (Boulder) Colorado at age 67 years, 7 months (approximately)-cause of death unknown

Boulder Daily Camera 03 December 1934:

"Harriet Bennetts, widow of John R. Bennetts, died Sunday at Gold Hill. She was 67 years of age and was a native of England. She came to the United States when she was 17. For the last 39 years she resided at Gold Hill. The funeral will be at 1p.m., on Wednesday from the Howe mortuary. She was the mother of Mrs. Jas. Kitto, with whom she made her home in Gold Hill. Three grandchildren are Mrs. Fred Walter of Gold Hill, Mrs. Edith Shayewitz and Will Kitto of Boulder. Mrs. Bennetts was employed several years ago by the Bluebird Lodge at Gold Hill."

Boulder Daily Camera 04 December 1934:

"Funeral services for Mrs. Harriet Bennetts, who died Sunday, will be held from the Howe mortuary Wednesday at one o'clock. Rev. C.O. Beckman, pastor of the Methodist church, will officiate. Burial, Gold Hill cemetery."

Boulder Daily Camera 05 December 1934:

"Funeral services were held this afternoon at 1 o'clock at the Howe mortuary for Mrs. Harriet Bennetts of Gold Hill. Rev. C.O. Beckman, pastor of the Methodist church, officiated. Pauline Darnell-Wallace sang. Pallbearers were Edward H. Smith, Paul Romig, Fred C. Walter, Ben A. Nichols, A.J. Walter and John Holman. Burial was in the Gold Hill cemetery."

Interview with Bob Boyd as told to Richard Dussart Regnier 27 July 1991:

"Jenny Kitto lived up the hill behind the Kirkbride store and her mother, Mrs. [Harriet] Bennett, passed away during a hard winter. The facilities being what they were in Gold Hill, they couldn't do too much for her. There was no mortuary, no hearse, nothing. There was no transportation large enough to put her in to get her down to Boulder. Finally, arrangements were made with the bus driver, Tim Walter, to take care of the situation. He had the largest vehicle around, the big old white bus in which he carried his passengers up and down the mountain.

Bob Boyd said that his mother had been down town visiting at one of her friends. She was walking along the road when she first heard then saw, Tim's big bus coming. Stepping off the road, she waited for it to pass. When it did she was taken back and stood there in shock as the bus passed by. There on the front seat next to Tim sat Mrs. Bennett. She knew she had died the day before, but there she was sitting next to Tim. Running up the street to their store she went inside and told her husband what she had just seen. He laughed and told her that was probably the only way Tim knew of getting her down to the mortuary... Mrs. Bennett rode all the way down the mountain sitting there beside Tim and nobody knew the difference."

About Harriet (*Tonkin*-possibility) Bennetts

Harriet Bennetts was born in Penzance (Cornwall) England; parents unknown. Her exact date of birth is somewhat in dispute. According to her petition for naturalization papers she declares she was born on 26 April 1864 however mortuary records state April of 1867 and the 1884 New York Passenger List for her immigration to the United States has age at 25 making her birth year around 1859 which is more likely.

There is a Harriet Tonkin who married a Richard James Ellis in Penzance, registered in 1876, which would be logical for the 1878 birth of their daughter:

Elizabeth Jane Harriet "Emma": born 09 January 1878 Penzance (Cornwall) England and died 14 April 1955 Boulder (Boulder) Colorado; buried Gold Hill Cemetery, Gold Hill (Boulder) Colorado; married James William Kitto; see KITTO, Elizabeth Jane Harriet "Emma" (*Ellis*)

Harriet and her daughter, Harriett Jane, came to the United States on the ship "City of Chester." Harriett Jane was about four years old when they arrived at the port of New York on the 21th day of April 1884. Even though Colorado was listed as their final destination on the New York Passengers List they traveled to Michigan to join husband Richard who had already made the voyage to America a few years prior. From there the family made the journey to Colorado.

The 1885 Colorado State Census has Harriet living in (Gilpin) Colorado with her husband, Richard, and their daughter, Jane (age nine years).

Richard James Ellis died in April of 1895 from internal injuries sustained from falling only a few feet while climbing a rope in the Richmond mine (Gold Hill mining district). Inflammation resulted followed by blood poisoning and putrefaction (decomposition of organic matter). He is buried in Columbia Cemetery, Boulder (Boulder) Colorado.

Boulder Daily Camera 08 April 1895:

"Dick" Ellis dead...This well-known miner died at his home in Gold Hill this morning after only a short illness. A few days since, he was ruptured while climbing a rope in the Richmond mine, inflammation resulted, followed by blood poison and putrefaction. Mr. Ellis left a widow and one child, a daughter aged eighteen. He was one of the best known miners in this county.

Ellis fell only a few feet, while climbing the rope, and did not tell the doctor who was called in anything about the accident. He had undoubtedly sustained internal injuries concerning which his physician was excusably ignorant."

On 28 November 1896 Harriett Ellis married John Richard Bennetts in (Boulder) Colorado. John, native of England, came to Colorado in 1866.

John Richard Bennetts was previously married in (Cornwall) England to Rebecca (*Shick/Strick*) Oats. This marriage brought forth three known children:

John R.: born 19 July 1860 (Kent) England and died 16 August 1938 Boise (Ada) Idaho; buried Morris Hill Cemetery, Boise (Ada) Idaho; never married

Anna: born 16 November 1864 (Cornwall) England and died 04 June 1940 Ipswich (Suffolk) England; burial unknown; married Henry James Berry

William Oats: born 1867 Stoke in Dameral (Devon) England and died June 1870 on ship to New York; burial at sea

This family was living in Sugar Loaf (Boulder) Colorado in the 1880 United States census. Rebecca died 18

November 1893 (age about 55 years) from pneumonia following surgery in Denver and is buried in the Columbia Cemetery, Boulder (Boulder) Colorado.

After the death of Rebecca, John Richard married Harriet Ellis on 28 November 1896 in (Boulder) Colorado. In the 1900 United States census John Richard and his son, John R., were living in King of Arizona (Yuma) Arizona Territory. John Richard is also listed with Harriet living in Gold Hill (Boulder) Colorado.

When John Richard Bennetts died on 20 March 1901 from cancer (age about 66 years) his obituary had no mention of his wife, Harriet, only that he had two children: John Bennetts and Mrs. Anna (*Bennetts*) Berry. He is buried beside his first wife, Rebecca, in the Columbia Cemetery, Boulder (Boulder) Colorado.

Boulder Daily Camera 21 March 1901:

"JACK BENNETS DEAD...

John R. Bennets, one of the best known mining men of Boulder County, died at Gold Hill last night, aged 66. He was born in England, mined in the Lake Superior district and came to Colorado in 1866. His two children, John Bennets and Mrs. Anna Berry survive him. Death was due to cancer.

The funeral will occur from the parlor of Mr. Trezise Sunday morning at to [sic] o'clock."

The 1910 census lists Harriett, 48 years old, living in Gold Hill, widowed and the mother of four children, one living (Harriett Jane) with the immigration year of 1877.

In the 1920s Harriett was a school janitor.

Boulder Tribune 07 January 1921:

"Gold Hill Woman Is Made U.S. Citizen

Seven applicants for final citizenship papers were granted their requests by Judge George H. Bradfield sitting in the district court Monday. On Tuesday he granted citizenship to David Laber, a Russian, residing in Longmont, who served with the American forces during the way. He was granted papers without being compelled to follow the usual court procedure. The citizens made Monday were Hariett Bennetts of Gold Hill, a native of Great Britain; Nicholas Peter Fante, Italian, of Boulder; John Weng, Hungarian, of Lyons; Robert T. Robinson, British, of Lafayette, Sophocles Ionanow, Greek, of Longmont; Thomas John, British, of Lafayette, and Andie Shemaski, Poland, of Superior.

Mrs. Bennetts is thot [sic] to be the only woman ever granted citizenship papers in Boulder. Her husband was applying for citizenship at the time of his death. The laws make a wife and children citizens automatically when the husband and father is awarded his papers. Mr. Bennetts has a daughter, Mrs. Fate has four children; Mr. Weng 2, Mr. Robinson 2, Mr. John 1 and Mr. Shemaski 7.

Each successful applicant was given a copy of the American creed by the Daughters of the American Revolution and a silk American flag by the W.R.C."

The 1930 census shows Harriett living with her widowed daughter, Harriett Jane, in Gold Hill (Boulder) Colorado and working as a hotel chambermaid; see KITTO, Harriet Jane (*Ellis*).

A few years later on 02 December 1934 Harriett died in Gold Hill (Boulder) Colorado.

BIGELOW, Sarah Antoinette

Birth: 09/28/1866
Death: 09/07/1939
Cemetery Location: D2

Father: Melaneton Bigelow; Mother: Sarah (*Baldwin*); born in Waterville (Oneida) New York and died in Boulder (Boulder) Colorado at age 72 years, 11 months, 10 days-arterial sclerosis; tombstone states birth year as 1868 whereas the 1900 census record and the mortuary record state 1866

Boulder Daily Camera 07 September 1939:

"Miss Antoinette Bigelow, C.U. Faculty Member 24 Years, Dies...Long Illness Fatal To Former Dean Of Women Who Came To Campus In 1910...Miss S. Antoinette Bigelow, who influenced the development of the University for 24 years as dean of women and teacher of English literature, died at 12:15 o'clock this morning at Community hospital, after an illness that has been critical since last May.

Private funeral services were held this afternoon at 2 o'clock at Riverside crematory in Denver. Interment will be Friday afternoon at Gold Hill, where she spent many summers, and memorial services will be conducted by Rev. Lucius F. Reed in the Congregational church the first week in October after friends who are now out of town return.

Miss Bigelow was taken to Community hospital last Wednesday after being critically ill since May. She had not been well, however, since a year ago this month, when she returned to Boulder from a summer in Gold Hill.

With her when she died were Miss Gertrude Angell, principal of Buffalo, N.Y., seminary and a long-time friend of Miss Bigelow who has been with her this summer, and Miss Emma Tracy of Blue Bird lodge and cottage, where Miss Bigelow has spent much time.

Came In 1910...In the years between 1910, when she came to the University as dean of women, until 1924, when she retired, Miss Bigelow led in the development of women's self-government, became the friend of men as well as coeds, and won such deep affection among "her girls" that after her retirement as dean, women graduates throughout the country honored her with a memorial scholarship fund that bears her name.

Before coming to the University Miss Bigelow's career included settlement work in the Italian district of Boston, organization of Hindman School in Kentucky where she worked among underprivileged mountaineers, and teaching in several New England schools.

Family of Pioneers...Miss Bigelow was born Sept. 28, 1866, on a farm near Sangerfield, N.Y., into a family with a long pioneer heritage. Eleven of her forefathers came to America on the Mayflower and her grandfather was one of the earliest settlers of central New York.

After attending high school and the Union School and Academy of Waterville, N.Y., she enrolled in Wellesley to study history and sociology for two years. Then she returned to Waterville to teach for two years, after which she completed work at Wellesley for her bachelor's degree in 1893.

For a time she taught in Elmwood elementary school in Buffalo, N.Y., and in Buffalo seminary, a private college preparatory school for girls. But she never gave up the comparatively easy life of a school teacher to go into Boston's Italian district, living in a settlement house herself while doing graduate work at Radcliffe College.

Went To Kentucky Mountains...Again she became a teacher, this time head of the English department at Springfield, Mass., high school. But in 1901 she deserted the New England culture for the backwoods of Kentucky. While attending Wellesley she had seen a play, "Quare Women," and was profoundly impressed by the need of mountain women and their families. And so she went to Hindman settlement, founded a few years earlier, and organized a school.

Forty-five miles from a railroad in the untraveled hills of Kentucky Miss Bigelow started a work that lives on today in the memories of residents, according to a letter recently received by Miss Angell. Kentuckians still talk of Miss Bigelow's work. "Antoinette Bigelow is a part of the Hindman heritage, the great women pioneers in this run-traveled land, "the letter said.

But Hindman also had its effect on Miss Bigelow. She never recovered, friends say, from the physical ills that resulted from the lack of proper food and care. She carried with her always afterword sympathy for the poor and a desire to right injustices in the social order.

Not strong enough to continue the arduous life, Miss Bigelow left Hindman in 1908 for Columbia university, where she obtained a master's degree in English literature and history in 1910. Then she came to the University of Colorado.

Six Women On Faculty...When Miss Bigelow first arrived in Boulder in 1910 she found a far different campus from the one she left in 1934.

Only six women were on the faculty, only about 400 coeds were enrolled, and "women's courses" such as a home economics department did not exist. There were no fine arts department, no college of music, no regular dramatics, no women's gymnasium. For the first time, physical education courses for women were to be taught that year.

Students walked on footpaths over the campus, she recalled in a talk the year she retired, and grass grew deep in the summer to feed campus horses. Commencement exercises were held at Chautauqua, and the president's office was on the first floor of Old Main.

For the first year Dean Bigelow lived in one of two women's cottages where fireplaces were hard to regulate, rooms were almost bare, girls could cook their own meals, and rent was $3 a month.

Sought Women's Dormitory...Coed, Miss Bigelow found, had little sense of solidarity, little direction, and few activities of their own. A big need, she believed, was for a women's dormitory.

So she set out to get money for a dormitory by producing yearly May fetes, which not only brought in as much as $1,400 a year but also gave women their needed central activity.

Although the funds never grew large enough to build a dormitory, it did help the University by augmenting the organ fund. And from 1912 until the World war the May fetes continued.

When the women's dormitory was build the year she retired, one hall was named, "S. Antoinette Bigelow Hall" in her honor.

During her years at the University Dean Bigelow also helped develop a women's government, which now includes a women's president, senate, House of Representatives, and self-rule, to a large degree.

As dean of women, her early students recall, she was especially interested in girls who were not well adjusted socially and who needed financial aid. Those were the days when loan funds were small, when Dean Bigelow and Dean F.B.R. Hellems often dug into their own pockets to pay a student's fees.

Taught English Classes...In addition to serving as dean, she taught such literature courses as history of English literature, American literature, Tennyson, and appreciation of poetry. Finally, upon her retirement as dean in 1928, she became a full-time member of the English literature faculty.

Never losing her interest in social problems, Miss Bigelow gave her English literature students an understanding of the common man and of society's needs along with training in the technique of poetry and the dates of literary periods.

In 1918, Miss Bigelow became ill and went to Buffalo on a leave of absence. She returned the following year, however, and taught until 1927, when regents granted her a leave of absence to travel in Greece, Crete, Italy, England, Germany, and other parts of Europe.

'An Abiding Work'...The next year, in 1928, she resigned as dean of women to devote her entire time to English literature. At that time Dean Hellems said of her, "She has done a genuinely great and abiding work."

Friends and former students in Boulder and Denver, wishing to pay a concrete tribute to their dean and friend, sent out a circular letter in 1929, describing a proposed "S. Antoinette Bigelow scholarship" to help women who, although perhaps not at the top of their class in grades, needed financial assistance.

The letter was mailed in April. On commencement day, when the fund exceeded $2, 500, Miss Bigelow was presented the scholarship and a memorial book, bound in blue suede with a hand-lettered inscription. Since then the scholarship has been presented each year to a woman student and the fund is now approximately $4,000.

Retired In 1934...In 1934 Miss Bigelow retired from active teaching, although she continued to invite students to her home for informal discussions of their problems and of campus activities.

What the University thought of Miss Bigelow was illustrated several years ago by The Silver and Gold, which was printing a series of faculty cartoons. The cartoon of Miss Bigelow showed her holding the entire University in the hollow of her hand.

Miss Bigelow was a member of Phi Beta Kappa, academic society, the American Association of University Women, the International League for Peace and Freedom, and the Congregational church.

"She is survived by a nephew, Daniel Conger, of Waterville, N.Y."

Boulder Daily Camera 08 September 1939:

"Miss S. Antoinette Bigelow—Commitment services were held at the grave in Gold Hill cemetery this afternoon. The body was cremated in Denver Thursday and short services were held there. Rev. Lucius F. Reed, pastor of the Congregational church officiated at both services. A bronze tablet is to be placed over her grave later. The Hall-Kelso mortuary was in charge."

Boulder Daily Camera 28 September 1939:

"Memorial Service Planned For Miss Bigelow Oct. 8

"Memorial services for the late Miss S. Antoinette Bigelow, who was a retired professor of English literature at the University, will be held in the Congregational church Sunday, Oct. 8—one week from this coming Sunday. The program will be at 4:30 in the afternoon.

Short addresses of appreciation of her services and lovely character, will be given by Dr. George Norlin, Miss Irene P. McKeehan, Dr. George F. Reynolds, and Dr. F.D. Bramhall. The services will be conducted by Rev. Lucius F. Reed, pastor of the church.

Mrs. A.R. Peebles will be at the organ. She will play the Pilgrim's chorus and some of the great hymns of the church that were Miss Bigelow's favorites."

BLACK, Theodore Halsey II "Ted"

Birth: 05/14/1956
Death: 08/09/2001
Cemetery Location: B4

Father: Theodore Halsey Black; Mother: Zelda (*Simmons*); Wife: Robin (*Morris*); born in New Bern (Craven) North Carolina and died in Denver (Denver) Colorado at age 45 years, 2 months, 26 days-liver transplant complications

Boulder Daily Camera 12 August 2001:

"Ted Black—Ted Black of Gold Hill died Thursday, August 9, 2001, in Denver of complications from a liver transplant. He was 45. He was born May 4, 1956, in New Bern, N.C., to Theodore Halsey Black and Zelda Simmons Black. He married Robin Morris on Sept. 7, 1987, in Gold

Hill. Mr. Black founded the Rocky Mountain Anglers fishing shop in Boulder in 1999. He previously owned Black Roofing. He graduated in 1974 from Trinity Pawling High School in Pawling, N.Y. He moved to Boulder County in the late 1970s. He enjoyed fishing, hunting, hiking and camping.

Survivors include his father and stepmother, Marilyn Black, of New Cannon, Conn.; his wife of Gold Hill; four sisters, Susan Black, Zelda Cahill and Carol McDougle, all of Nantucket, Mass., and Debbie Coldwell of Katonah, N.Y.; a daughter, Molly Ann Black of Gold Hill; and a son, T. Halsey Black III of Gold Hill. He was preceded in death by his mother.

A memorial service will be held at 10 a.m. Monday at Crist Mortuary, 3395 Penrose Place, Boulder. A reception will be at noon Monday at the Gold Hill Inn. Contributions may be made to the Gold Hill School PTO or the Gold Hill Fire Department, both at Gold Hill, CO 80302."

BLUEBELL

Birth: Unknown
Death: Unknown
Cemetery Location: E3

Marker was discovered after the 2010 Four Mile Canyon Fire; no information available

BOTTOLFSON, Anne "Annie" B. (or R.)

Birth: 01/19/1872
Death: 07/25/1879
Cemetery Location: C2

Father: Erick Bottolfson Sivlesoeen/Sivleoe; Mother: Rachel/Rachael Magnesdatter (*Langeland/Langland*);

born and died in Sunshine (Boulder) Colorado at age 6 years, 6 months, 6 days-inflammation of the bowels; U.S. Federal Census Mortality Schedules Index 1850-1889 has birth 1874 and death 1880 with the middle initial as "R."

Digging Up Dirt

About the Erick Bottolfson Family

Erick, born on 18 September 1832 in Oppheim, Hordaland Fylke, Norway; the son of Bottolf Olsson and Bridta (*Eriksdatter*) Sivlesoeen/Sivleoe-it appears that Sivlesoeen/Siveloe was omitted when he immigrated to the United States in 1847. (These are actually the names of the farms where the people were born. When the Scandinavians came to the United States sometimes they used names of the farms where they were from as surnames and sometimes they didn't.)

Erick's family and Rachel's family emigrated together from Norway the same day (28 June 1848) and on the same ship (the "Olave Kyrre" with 87 passengers) from Bergen, Norway to New York.

In Decorah (Winneshiek) Iowa Erick married Ragna/Ragne Rachel/Rachael Magnesdatter Langeland/Langland in January 1865 however other records state the marriage took place on 24 November 1870 in Canoe (Winneshiek) Iowa. She was born on 19 September of 1843 in Evanger, Hordaland, Norway, the daughter of Magne Helgesen and Gjertrud Knudsdatter "Gertie" (*Bjorgo*) Langeland/Langland. (Rachel's birth name was really "Ragna" however when the family came to America they changed it to Rachel.)

The marriage of Erick and Rachel brought forth four known children:

Cornelius: born 27 November 1865 Iowa and died 07 June 1899 Denver (Denver) Colorado; buried Greenwood Cemetery, Red Cliff (Eagle) Colorado; married Caroline Newstrom

Clifford Magne: born 11 November 1871 Gold Hill (Boulder) Colorado and died 02 July 1884 Red Cliff (Eagle) Colorado; buried Greenwood Cemetery, Red Cliff (Eagle) Colorado; died at 12 years-brain fever

Anne "Annie" B. (or R.): born 19 January 1872 Gold Hill (Boulder) Colorado and died 25 July 1879 Gold Hill (Boulder) Colorado; buried Gold Hill Cemetery, Gold Hill (Boulder) Colorado; see BOTTOLFSON, Anne "Annie" B. or R.

Bennedick O.: born 07 August 1875 (Boulder) Colorado and died 04 December 1895 Red Cliff (Eagle) Colorado; buried Greenwood Cemetery, Red Cliff (Eagle) Colorado; believed never married

Boulder County records show that Erick was in the Gold Hill area as early as April of 1864.

Denver Rocky Mountain News 15 January 1870:
"Eric Bottolfson & Co., at Gold Hill, have recently struck, on their claims on the Horsfal lode, a solid body of material nine feet thick and have not yet worked across it to the north wall. This ore was struck on the depth of 129 feet, and is said to exist many feet above that point. It yields under stamps, from $80 to $100 a cord, for the whole vein."

By 1872 the family was living in Sunshine (Boulder) Colorado and living there at the time of Annie's death. The 1880 U.S. Census has the family living in Gold Hill (Boulder) Colorado however Erick is listed again in Eagle County as a silver miner. By 1885 the entire family was living in (Eagle) Colorado where Erick was a rancher.

On 06 June 1893 Erick was naturalized in the District Court of (Eagle) Colorado with witnesses William Griner and L. R. Thomas.

On 15 March 1903 tragedy struck the Bottolfson family:

Rocky Mountain News 16 March 1903:
"DESTROYED BY FIRE...
Red Cliff, Colo., March 15—The residence of Mr. and Mrs. Erick Bottolfson, on Water Street, was totally destroyed by fire at 6 o'clock this morning, the fire originating from an over-heated stove. Nearly all the furniture and articles of any value were saved by the energetic assistance of neighbors in removing them to the street. Mr. and Mrs. Malcom Macauley, a young newly married couple, occupied the upper portion of the building. They lost all their wedding presents and a sum of money. The Bottolfson loss is about $1,000 with no insurance."

Erick died 12 January 1908 and is buried along with his sons, Cornelius, Cliff and Bennedick, in the Greenwood Cemetery in Red Cliff (Eagle) Colorado. His wife, Rachel, died 10 February 1928 in Los Angeles (Los Angeles) California and is buried in the Pomona Cemetery and Mausoleum in Pomona (Los Angeles) California.

Eagle County Blade 16 January 1908:
"Erick Bottolfson, another of the pioneers of the West, the vanguard of which is rapidly passing to the other side, died at his home on Gore creek on Sunday morning, January 12th, 1908, in his 76th year.

Mr. Bottolfson had been in failing health for several years, but an indomitable will kept him about [sic], and his death occurred peacefully while sitting in a chair at his home.

Deceased was a native of Sweden and came to the United States when a young man. He first located in Illinois but to the early days of this state came to Colorado, locating at Golden. He was one of the first of the early settlers to reach the site of the present town of Red Cliff, having arrived here in the spring of 1879. Since that time he had been actively identified with the town and the county. The Argo millsite, covering about five acres in the heart of the present town of Red Cliff, was located by Mr. Bottolfson and his partner, Smith, and was carried to final patent after a vigorous contest. Mr. Bottolfson also located and proved up on what is known as the Bottolfson ranch on Homestake creek. About four years ago a ranch was purchased on Gore creek, although Mr. Bottolfson still retained considerable town property in Red Cliff.

Mr. Bottolfson had experienced many hardships and privations and in his prime was a man of rugged physique and uncommon endurance. In the early days he has been known to carry mail and provisions on his back on snow-shoes to Holy Cross city when there was no other who would venture out on the trip. He had had a number of narrow escapes from serious accidents. Two are recalled: While warming blasting powder in the kitchen stove (a not very uncommon practice among miners) the powder exploded while Mr. Bottolfson was sitting by. The stove was blown to pieces but miraculously Mr. Bottolfson was not hurt. While working in a mine shaft on one of his claims his Shepherd dog followed him to work and while his master was at the bottom of the shaft the dog feel on him, striking Mr. Bottolfson across the back and seriously injuring him. The shaft was sixty feet deep, but Mr. Bottolfson eventually recovered from the accident.

A family of four children, three boys and a girl were born to Mr. and Mr. Bottolfson. The daughter and one son died when quite young, and other two boys, Cornelius and Ben, grew to man's estate but both died several years ago in Red Cliff. Mrs. Bottolfson survives him.

The funeral was held at the Red Cliff Congregational church on Wednesday, Rev. L.D. Jarrard conducting the services, with interment at Greenwood cemetery."

Unknown Newspaper (courtesy of Eagle Valley Library District) 16 February 1929:

(Article transcribed as written)

"One more of Eagle Counties respected citizens has joined the innumerable caravan, when Mrs. Rachel Bottolfson answered the last summons at the home of her granddaughter, Cornelia Betz, Sunday, February 10 at 2 p.m. from a 12 hour ailment resulting from hemorrhages of the stomach. Rachel Langeland Bottolfson was 85 years old the 19th day of September, 1928; and had retained her faculties and activeness till the day of death, feeling just fine on retiring Saturday night.

Much can be written of Mrs. Bottolfson, as she was a true pioneer. It was always interesting to hear her tell of many incidents, remembering some instances on board the ship, as a child of 5, she with her parents coming from Norway to American, first settling in Wisconsin, remaining there about 3 years. She told of how she and her oldest brother drove the cattle and sheep, how her father sawed and hewed 4 wheels and made sort of a wagon, and placing his house hold effects and family, with the exception of herself and brother, who walked and drove the cows and sheep, and all immigrated across the prairie, into the

wilderness and settled at Decorah, Iowa. The country being infested by Indians, in fact her aunt and family were scalped and killed in the Sippirt Lake, Iowa, massacre.

Rachel Langeland grew to womanhood at Decorah Iowa, and was engaged to be married when the Civil War broke out and two of her brothers and her sweetheart enlisted, and in the Battle of Shiloh her intended sweetheart fell, and one brother was killed at Gettysburg and one was among the unknown soldiers.

The Langeland and Bottolfson families had been neighbors in Wisconsin and Iowa, but in 1857 the Bottolfson family moved to South Dakota. In 1859 Erick Bottolfson and six other young men left Vermillion South Dakota for Colorado, coming by ox team to Denver and arriving in early summer. They then separated and started prospecting, Erick going to Boulder County. After 5 years he returned to Iowa and Rachel was wooed and won by the stalwart gold miner, and they were married January 1865.

Colorado and its gold again called and Erick was forced to leave his bride, as her mother would not consent to her braving the danger of the Indians, her fear being grounded on the massacre which had claimed her own sister. Five years later in 1870, Mrs. Bottolfson and her son came on the first train into Denver which had been finished that fall between Chicago and Denver, Mr. Bottolfson going back to Iowa after them. They then made their first home on Gold Hill, Boulder county, until 1879, when Mr. Bottolfson came to Red Cliff—Mrs. Bottolfson and the two boys coming over Loveland Pass and down the Blue Corning to Red Cliff by Eagle Park on August 7, 1880, and the [sic] Old Homestake the year following. Mrs. Bottolfson made her home in Red Cliff until 1904 when she moved to Gore Creek on a ranch until the past winter she made her home in Pomona, Cal. Coming back to Colorado for the summer amid the old haunts and her dear friends which always means so much to her.

Mrs. Bottolfson saw Red Cliff in her infancy, saw it grow to quite a camp and town, saw it recede, come back again and truly was its Guardian Angel of its earlier days, was nurse, doctor and counselor and was always called when closing the eyes of death, ably assisting doctors at bedsides of four and the first baby cry from many of our grown men and women were attended by her loving care and nursing.

One of her great desires was to see the short cut to Denver finished take an auto trip over Loveland Pass to Wheeler and come once again to Red Cliff over the same route she traveled, or for the most part walked as the hills were so steep, nearly 50 years ago; she helped to build Red Cliff, as she was an enthusiast, of schools, churches, and anything for its betterment—took part in all its activities, the auxiliary of the G.A.R. of which she was a member, of the Emerson Circle and etc. Grandma Bottolfson

31

will live long in the memories of Eagle Co. folks.

She buried her entire family, her only daughter lies buried at Gold Hill, Colo., her husband and three sons are lying in the Greenwood Cemetery, Red Cliff."

BOWMAN, George Fern

Birth 09/13/1888
Death: 02/05/1920
Cemetery Location: Unknown

Father: Alfred F. Bowman; Mother: unknown; Wife: Matilda "Tillie" (*Peterson/Petersen/Gustafson)* born in Tennessee (McDonough) Illinois and died in Boulder (Boulder) Colorado at age 32 years, 4 months, 23 days-influenza pneumonia; previous cemetery record had incorrect birth year of 1887 as well as incorrect middle initial of "T.;" no tombstone; see PETERSON/PETERSEN/ GUSTAFSON, Ida (*Burke*); see NEWLAND, Matilda "Tillie" (*Peterson/Petersen/Gustafson*)

Boulder Daily Camera 06 February 1920:

"George T. [sic] Bowman of Gold Hill died Thursday night of influenza-pneumonia at the home of W. B. Peterson at 2418 Pearl Street. Mr. Bowman was a well-known Boulder county mining man. He came to Boulder ill. His wife is the daughter of Mr. and Mrs. W. B. Peterson." [Error: W.B. Peterson and George Bowman's wife (Matilda Bowman) were siblings. They were the children of Augustus Gustof L. "Gus" and Ida (*Burke*) Gustafson/ Peterson.]

Boulder Daily Camera 07 February 1920:

"George F. Bowman, of 2418 Pearl Street, who died last Thursday, will be buried in Gold Hill Sunday afternoon. The services will be held at the cemetery, Rev. Harris officiating and the Foresters of Gold Hill taking part. The Columbine quartet will sing several selections. Mr. Tippet will leave here at 10 o'clock Sunday morning with the remains. The deceased was the son-in-law of Gus Peterson."

About George Fern Bowman

George Fern Bowman was born on 13 September 1887 in Tennessee (McDonough) Illinois; the son of Alfred Bowman. The mortuary record for George does not list his mother's name however there is an Alfred Bowman (born November of 1865 in Illinois) who married Emma J. Sparks on 01 March 1885 in (Adams) Illinois.

George was a metal miner and worked for the Gold Hill Mining Company when he married Matilda "Tillie" Peterson/Petersen/Gustafson on 14 January 1915 in Boulder (Boulder) Colorado. She was born in August of 1896 in Gold Hill (Boulder) Colorado; the daughter of Gustof L. "Gus" and Ida (*Burke*) Peterson/Petersen/

Gustafson; see PETERSON/PETERSEN/GUSTAFSON, Augustus Gustof Louis "Gus" and see PETERSON/PE-TERSEN/GUSTAFSON, Ida (*Burke*).

Both George and Matilda were living in Boulder (Boulder) Colorado at the time of their marriage. To this union one known child was born:

Gilbert William: born 09 January 1917 Boulder (Boulder) Colorado; died 13 December 1969 Longmont (Boulder) Colorado; buried Fort Logan National Cemetery, Denver (Denver) Colorado; married Helen Frand

After the death of George his wife, Matilda, married several times with the last being Alfred Newland whom she married in 1938; see NEWLAND, Matilda "Tillie" (*Peterson/Petersen/Gustafson*).

BOYD, Frank V.

Birth: 12/11/1863
Death: 05/01/1911
Cemetery Location: B2

Father: James Hamilton Boyd; Mother: Frances (*Griffith*); Wife: Mary Parker (*Kirkbride*); born in Des Moines (Polk) Iowa and died in Gold Hill (Boulder) Colorado at age 48 years, 4 months, 20 days-chronic intestinal nephritis and arteriosclerosis; Tippett Mortuary has death at 47 years, 4 months, 20 days which would make the birth date 12/11/1863; the 1900 census states birth date as December 1862; tombstone states birth date as 1862; obituary states 1863; see BOYD, Mary Parker (*Kirkbride*); see BOYD, Lillian Agnes; see **About the Frank V. Boyd Family**

Boulder County Miner 19 January 1911:

"Frank Boyd of Gold Hill is reported to be quite ill at his home in that camp."

Boulder Daily Camera 02 May 1911 and
Boulder County Tribune 05 May 1911:

"GOLD HILL MOURNS DEATH OF F BOYD... PROMINENT MERCHANT AND MINING MAN OF BOULDER COUNTY GOLD CAMP STRICKEN BY HEART TROUBLE...Frank Boyd, who has been ill for a number of years with heart and kidney trouble, died at 11:50 last night at his home at Gold Hill. He was born at Des Moines, Iowa in 1863. In 1875, he accompanied his father to this city and assisted him in building the first smelter in the county. He obtained his education in the public schools of Chicago and Boulder. For a time he was employed in his father's smelter, after which, in 1880, he went to Leadville and secured employment in the smelter there. For five years he operated the Cash mine at Gold Hill, and in 1890 he bought out George Kirkbride's mercantile store at Gold Hill. Twenty-two years ago he married Mary P. Kirkbride, of this city, whom, together with three children, he leaves to mourn his death. The children are Mrs. Bessie Scott Brown, of Denver; Donald Boyd, who has been associated with his father in running the Gold Hill store, and Archie Boyd, aged seven years. Mrs. O.M. Gilbert and Mrs. W. S. Bellman, both of this city, have gone to Gold Hill to be with their sister. Mr. Boyd has been a very prominent figure in the development of Boulder County. In 1896 he was appointed postmaster in the gold camp by President Cleveland. The funeral will be held at Gold Hill Wednesday afternoon at 2:30."

Boulder County News 04 May 1911:

"DEATH OF FRANK BOYD...Frank Boyd, one of the best known men of the mountain section and for twenty-five years a resident of Gold Hill, died of heart and kidney trouble Monday, aged 48 years. His wife is a daughter of Geo. Kirkbride of this city and he has numerous relatives. He was a man held in the highest esteem and will be greatly missed.

He was buried yesterday by Mt. Audubon lodge of Masons, of which he was a member."

BOYD, Lillian Agnes

Birth: 12/21/1892
Death: 08/18/1893
Cemetery Location: B2

Father: Frank V. Boyd; Mother: Mary Parker (*Kirkbride*); born and died in Gold Hill (Boulder) Colorado at age 7 months, 28 days-cause of death unknown; see BOYD, Frank V.; see BOYD, Mary Parker (*Kirkbride*); see **About the Frank V. Boyd Family**

Boulder News 24 August 1893:

"A little child of Frank Boyd, postmaster at Gold Hill, was buried last Friday."

BOYD, Mary Parker (*Kirkbride*)

Birth: 05/19/1869
Death: 10/23/1943
Cemetery Location: B2

Father: George Kirkbride; Mother: Jane (*Horn*); Husband: Frank V. Boyd; born in Kirkby Thore (Cumbria) England and died in Boulder (Boulder) Colorado at age 74 years, 5 months, 4 days-failing health and old age; see BOYD, Frank V.; see BOYD Lillian Agnes; see **About the Frank V. Boyd Family**

Boulder Daily Camera 25 October 1943:

"Mrs. Mary P. Boyd, Gold Hill Pioneer, Dies Suddenly...

Mrs. Mary Parker Boyd, pioneer of Boulder County, died in her sleep Saturday afternoon while visiting at the home of her daughter, Mrs. J. Scott Brown, 987 Fifteenth Street. Mrs. Boyd had been in failing health but was able to be up and around and recently moved to Boulder from Gold Hill, leasing an apartment here for the winter.

Born in Kirkbythore, England, in 1869 she was brought to the United States in that year by her parents, Mr. and Mrs. George Kirkbride. They located in Crawford County, Missouri, but in 1878 moved to Gold Hill in this county where Mr. Kirkbride was superintendent of the Prussian mine. The Kirkbrides later moved to a farm near Longmont and then to Boulder to become prominent citizens.

Miss Mary Kirkbride and the late Frank Boyd were married in Longmont Dec. 22, 1889. Mr. Boyd came to Boulder in 1875 with his father, the late Frank Boyd, Sr., who built the first mine smelter in Boulder. The son engaged in mining in the Gold Hill district and in 1896 was appointed postmaster of Gold Hill by the president. He served in that capacity for many years and operated a general store in connection with the post office. His death occurred in 1911.

Mrs. Boyd was a member of the Baptist church and of the Social Order of Beauceant. She continued to live at Gold Hill, following the death of her husband, but in recent years had spent the winters in Boulder or in Arizona.

Digging Up Dirt

Surviving Mrs. Boyd in addition to Mrs. Brown, whose husband is the able manager of the University bindery, are two sons, Don C. Boyd, a general contractor now in defense work at Fort Logan, who lives at 953 11th, and Arch F. Boyd, superintendent of the U.S. Vanadium Corporation's operations at Bishop, Calif. Because of his work, Arch Boyd will be unable to get away to come for the funeral. Seven grandchildren and two great grandchildren survive.

Mrs. O.M. Gilbert of Boulder, Mrs. William S. Bellman of Pueblo and John Kirkbride of Gold Hill are sisters and brothers of the deceased.

Funeral services will be at 2 Tuesday afternoon at Howe mortuary. Interment will be in the family lot beside Mr. Boyd in Gold Hill. The body will lie in state from 10 to 2. The casket will be closed for the services."

About the Frank V. Boyd Family

Portrait and Biographical Record of Denver and Vicinity Colorado, Chapman Publishing Company, Chicago, 1898, pgs. 238 & 239:

"Frank Boyd, postmaster at Gold Hill, Boulder County, was born in Des Moines, Iowa, in 1863, and is a son of James H. and Frances P. (Griffith) Boyd, natives respectively of Pennsylvania and Columbus, Ohio. His father, who spent some years in Iowa, removed from there in 1869 to Chicago, where he engaged in the manufacture of coffins. In 1875 he came to Colorado and settled in Boulder, where he built the first smelter in the town. He continued to operate this mill until he retired from business, since which time he has resided in Denver. He and his wife are the parents of five children, namely: Ida, Mrs. Headley, of Denver; Lincoln, who is foreman of the Philadelphia smelter in Pueblo; Frank; Mrs. Dessa Newman, of Denver; and Mrs. Lillie Foster, also of Denver.

In the public schools of Chicago and Boulder the subject of this sketch obtained a fair education. For a time he was employed in his father's smelter, after which, in 1880, he went to Leadville and secured employment in the smelter there. Afterward he operated the Cash mine in the gold district, continuing to develop it for five years. In 1890 he bought out George Kirkbride, one of the oldest merchants in the district, and embarked in the general mercantile business, which he has since conducted, having in stock a full line of dry goods, groceries and hardware.

The marriage of Mr. Boyd, in Boulder, united him with Mary P. Kirkbride, who was born in England and came to Boulder in company with her father, George Kirkbride. They are the parents of two children, Bessie and Donovan. Politically a Democrat, Mr. Boyd is active in local affairs. He is chairman of the district Democratic central committee and a member of the county central committee. In 1896 he was appointed postmaster under President Cleveland and still holds the office. Fraternally he is connected with Gold Hill Lodge of Ancient Order of United Workmen, and is a charter member of Bimetal Lodge No. 44, I.O.O.F., in which he is a past officer."

Frank V. and Mary Parker (*Kirkbride*) Boyd had four known children:

Elizabeth Irene Betty "Bessie": born 1891 Gold Hill (Boulder) Colorado and died 01 June 1968 Boulder (Boulder) Colorado; buried Green Mountain Cemetery, Boulder (Boulder) Colorado; married James Scott Brown

Lillian Agnes: born 21 December 1892 Gold Hill (Boulder) Colorado and died 18 August 1893 Gold Hill (Boulder) Colorado; buried Gold Hill Cemetery, Gold Hill (Boulder) Colorado; see BOYD, Lillian Agnes

Donovan Edison: born 25 December 1894 Gold Hill (Boulder) Colorado and died 21 April 1947 Boulder (Boulder) Colorado; buried Green Mountain Cemetery, Boulder (Boulder) Colorado; married Margaret E. Crowe

Arch Frank: born 05 April 1904 Gold Hill (Boulder) Colorado and died 10 January 1983 Grand Junction (Mesa) Colorado; buried Orchard Mesa Cemetery, Grand Junction (Mesa) Colorado; married Martha Beatrice Dunstone

Boulder County Herald Daily 01 September 1903:

"Gold Hill, Sept. 1.—Special to Herald.—The private residence of Frank W. Boyd in this city caught fire shortly after one o'clock this afternoon. Most all the men are out of town and at work in the mines, and the women had to fight the flames, which they did as best they could. The furniture in the lower part of the building was saved. The piano was gotten out but it was damaged. Many women in their efforts to save goods, suffered badly from the effect of smoke. It was impossible to get to the upper story.

It was for a while feared the school house would also go, but unless a wind starts up this will be safe. Mr. Boyd puts his loss down at $1200 with insurance at $750."

Boulder County Herald Daily 02 September 1903:

"Gold Hill, Sept. 2.—Special to Herald.-The fire at Boyd's residence yesterday afternoon set fire to the St. Clair residence but the flames were soon extinguished. At 3 o'clock this morning the wind began to blow and fanned the embers of the Boyd fire into flames again. People got up and used the hose and extinguished the blaze. Had the wind which is prevailing today been blowing yesterday, the loss would have been much greater. Mr. Boyd places his loss above his insurance at $600."

Boulder County Miner 22 April 1909:

"Mr. Frank Boyd, the noted bank leader is organizing a band which will furnish music for the Saturday night concerts which will continue throughout the summer months."

Boulder County Herald Weekly 16 March 1911:

"Miss Elizabeth Boyd, daughter of Mr. and Mrs. Frank Boyd of Gold Hill, was united in marriage last evening to J. Scott Brown of Denver. The ceremony was performed in that city, by the Rev. Frank H. Allen, of the Third Avenue Congregational church at his home, 240 West Fourth Avenue. The wedding was attended only by immediate relatives of the young couple. The bride was unattended and wore a blue traveling costume and hat to match. After a trip to various points in the state Mr. and Mrs. Brown will make their home in Denver.

The bride is very well known in this city, being a niece of Mrs. W.S. Bellman and Mrs. O.M. Gilbert. She attended the Prep school four years and has a host of friends who will wish her the greatest happiness in her married life."

Boulder Daily Camera 23 May 1935:

"Mrs. Mary P. Boyd To Spend Vacation On Coast With Her Son and Family...

Mrs. Mary P. Boyd left today for Los Angeles, Calif., where she will meet her son, A.F. Boyd, and his family of Chile, South America, who are spending a vacation in the United States. They will attend the exposition at San Diego and visit other places of interest in California.

The A.F. Boyd family will return to Boulder with Mrs. Mary P. Boyd in a few weeks and visit here with Mr. Boyd's sister, Mrs. J. Scott Brown, and his aunt, Mrs. O.M. Gilbert and family.

The Boyd family will return in September to Chile where he is employed as engineer by the Braden Copper Company. He is a graduate of Colorado School of Mines and has been with the Braden Company nine years. He has signed a contract for three more years in South America."

History of Gold Hill, Colorado by Elmer Curtis Swallow 1961 (courtesy of Tolliver Swallow, grandson of Elmer Curtis & Blanche Hastings Swallow):

"The Frank Boyd store was the oldest and largest grocery and general merchandise store at Gold Hill. This store was formerly owned by George Kirkbride, an old time resident of early Gold Hill. Mr. and Mrs. Kirkbride were parents of Mrs. Boyd."

BRADFORD, Bonnie Rae

Birth: 08/05/1928
Death: 03/29/1929
Cemetery Location: D4

Father: Harlie Elmer Bradford; Mother: Elizabeth Ann "Annie" (*Nichols*); born in Boulder (Boulder) Colorado and died in Gold Hill (Boulder) Colorado at age 7 months, 24 days-heart disease; no tombstone; cousin to author;

Linda Bradford Ayers (daughter of Mr. and Mrs. Harlie Elmer Bradford) stated that her father (Harlie) said the hardest thing he ever did was to dig the grave for his baby, Bonnie, due to lack of funds; see **About the Bradford Family**

Boulder Daily Camera 19 March 1929:

"BONNE RAE BRADFORD DIES AT GOLD HILL... Bonne [sic] Rae Bradford, the 8-month-old daughter of Mr. and Mrs. Harlie E. Bradford, of Gold Hill, died of heart disease this morning. The body was brought to Boulder by A.E. Howe. The funeral will be held at Howe's mortuary Sunday morning at 11. Interment will be at Gold Hill. Miss Billie Bradford, a special nurse, is an aunt of the deceased."

Boulder Daily Camera 30 March 1929:

"BERNICE RAE [sic]...The funeral of Bernice Rae [sic], 8-month-old daughter of Mr. and Mrs. Harie [sic] E. Bradford of Gold Hill, will be held from the Howe mortuary tomorrow morning at 11 o'clock. Rev. F.L. Greenway will officiate."

Boulder Daily Camera 01 April 1929:

"BONNIE RAE BRADFORD...Funeral services for Bonnie Rae Bradford, 8-months-old daughter of Mr. and Mrs. Harlie E. Bradford of Gold Hill, who died March 27, were held at the Howe mortuary Sunday morning at 11 o'clock. Rev. F.L. Greenway, student pastor of the Presbyterian church officiated. Miss Dorothy Stanley sang. Pallbearers were William Richards, Ray Draper, Angelo Girardo and Milton Fraser. Interment, Gold Hill cemetery."

BRADFORD, Carolyn Joy

Birth: 11/09/1953
Death: 11/09/1953
Cemetery Location: Removed

Father: Richard Charles Bradford; Mother: Shirley Ann (*Lewis*); born and died in Boulder (Boulder) Colorado-cause of death unknown; Carolyn was removed from the Gold Hill Cemetery and was laid to rest beside her sister, Cynthia Lynn Bradford (died in 1954) at Mountain View Cemetery in Boulder (Boulder) Colorado; cousin to author; Carolyn's father, Richard Charles "Dick" Bradford, was the son of Harlie Elmer and Elizabeth Ann "Annie" (*Nichols*) Bradford; see **About the Bradford Family**

Boulder Daily Camera 09 November 1953:

"Infant Dies at Birth Early Today...The infant daughter of Mr. and Mrs. Richard Bradford, 2849 Grove Street, died shortly after birth at three this morning. The father is an employee of the Dow Chemical Company at the Rocky Flats Atomic plant. Besides the parents, two sisters, Elizabeth Ann and Cynthia Lynn, survive. The paternal grandparents are Mr. and Mrs. Harlie Bradford and the maternal Mr. and Mrs. Frank Lewis, all of Boulder. Graveside services will be held Wednesday at 1:30 in the Gold Hill cemetery. Rev. William S. Avery, pastor of the United Lutheran church, will officiate. Howe Mortuary is in charge."

BRADFORD, Gerald Truman

> Birth: 02/16/1943
> Death: 04/22/1943
> Cemetery Location: D4

Father: Harlie Elmer Bradford; Mother: Elizabeth Ann "Annie" (*Nichols*); born and died in Boulder (Boulder) Colorado at age 2 months, 6 days-cause of death unknown; no tombstone; cousin to author; see **About the Bradford Family**

Boulder Daily Camera 22 April 1943:
"Gerald Truman Bradford, infant son of Mr. and Mrs. Harlie E. Bradford of 1419 Mapleton, died at Community hospital early this morning, age two months. The father is a representative of the Grand Union Tea Company in this territory and has lived in Boulder a number of years. Mrs. Bradford, formerly Elizabeth Anne Nichols, was a resident of Gold Hill before coming to Boulder. They have three sons, Richard, 12; Harlie Jr., 10; and Wilbur, 8. Also surviving is Mrs. R.J. Nichols, grandmother, who is making her home with the Bradfords. Funeral arrangements have not been completed. Howe mortuary in charge."

Boulder Daily Camera 24 April 1943:
"Gerald Truman Bradford—Infant son of Mr. and Mrs. Harlie E. Bradford of 1419 Mapleton...Funeral services were held from Howe mortuary this morning at 10. Rev. Angus C. Hull Jr., pastor of the First Baptist church, officiated. Body was buried in the Gold Hill cemetery. Pallbearers were A.J. Walters, F.E. Heitz, and Walter Gouge [sic]."

BRADFORD, Lawrence Rufus
(Previously listed as Gerald Rufus)

> Birth: 08/19/1936
> Death: 08/19/1936
> Cemetery Location: D4

Father: Harlie Elmer Bradford; Mother: Elizabeth Ann "Annie" (*Nichols*); born and died in Boulder (Boulder) Colorado-stillborn/cerebral hemorrhage; no tombstone; cousin to author; even though the mortuary record states "Gerald Rufus" Linda Bradford Ayers (daughter of Mr. and Mrs. Harlie E. Bradford) says this baby was named Lawrence Rufus, not Gerald Rufus or Rufus Gerald; see **About the Bradford Family**

Boulder Daily Camera 19 August 1936:
"GERALD RUFUS BRADFORD...Services at Howe mortuary this afternoon. Burial at Gold Hill. He died at birth this morning. His parents are Mr. and Mrs. Harlie Bradford of 836 Dewey." [error in name]

About the Bradford Family

Ethel Goudge, mother of Elizabeth Ann "Annie" (*Nichols*) Bradford, was born 15 October 1892 in Gold Hill (Boulder) Colorado; the daughter of Edwin David "Ned" and Annie (*Bennett(s)*) Goudge, early pioneers of the Gold Hill area; see GOUDGE, Edwin David "Ned" and see GOUDGE, Annie Elizabeth (*Bennett(s)*).

Ethel Goudge married Richard John Nicholls (second "L" later omitted by Ethel) on 09 April 1910 in Boulder (Boulder) Colorado. Richard John Nicholls was born on 04 December 1887 in Ophir (Tooele) Utah; the son of Henry Grenful and Elizabeth Jane (*Allen*) Nicholls. He died on 24 September 1941 in Boulder (Boulder) Colorado; buried at the Gold Hill Cemetery in Gold Hill (Boulder) Colorado; see NICHOLLS, Richard John. Their union brought forth three known children:

Edwin Grenful: born September of 1910 Gold Hill (Boulder) Colorado- died 08 December 1910 Gold Hill (Boulder) Colorado; buried Gold Hill Cemetery, Gold Hill (Boulder) Colorado; see NICHOLS, Edwin Grenful

Elizabeth Ann "Annie": born 17 December 1911 Gold Hill (Boulder) Colorado and died 01 March 1994 Louisville (Boulder) Colorado; buried Mountain View Memorial Park Cemetery, Boulder (Boulder) Colorado; married Harlie Elmer Bradford

Margaret Jean: born 11 March 1924 in Boulder (Boulder) Colorado and died 17 June 1996 Longmont (Boulder) Colorado; buried Mountain View Memorial Park Cemetery, Boulder (Boulder) Colorado; married Ernest Loyd Rapier, Stanley Allen Goff and again to Ernest Loyd Rapier

On 12 August 1927 Harlie Elmer Bradford married Elizabeth Ann Nichols in Littleton (Arapahoe) Colorado. He was born on 14 November 1909 in Bogue (Graham) Kansas; the son of Charles and Sarah (*Salmons*) Bradford. Harlie and Elizabeth Anne had eight known children:

Bonnie Rae: born 05 August 1928 Gold Hill (Boulder) Colorado and died 29 March 1929 Gold Hill (Boulder) Colorado; buried Gold Hill Cemetery, Gold Hill (Boulder) Colorado; see BRADFORD, Bonnie Rae

Lawrence Rufus (Gerald Rufus): born 19 August 1936 Boulder (Boulder) Colorado and died 19 August 1936 Boulder (Boulder) Colorado; buried Gold Hill Cemetery, Gold Hill (Boulder) Colorado; see BRADFORD, Lawrence Rufus

Gerald Truman: born 16 February 1943 Boulder (Boulder) Colorado and died 22 April 1943 Boulder (Boulder) Colorado; buried Gold Hill Cemetery, Gold Hill (Boulder) Colorado; see BRADFORD, Gerald Truman

Richard "Dick" Charles: born 12 June 1930 Boulder (Boulder) Colorado and died 16 January 1977 near Montrose (Montrose) Colorado; buried Mountain View Memorial Park, Boulder (Boulder) Colorado; married Shirley Ann Lewis, Christine Sara Saunders and Deanna (maiden name unknown); Richard was the father of Carolyn Joy Bradford; see BRADFORD, Carolyn Joy

Harlie Elmer "Bucky": born 03 February 1933 Boulder (Boulder) Colorado and died 07 January 2016 Westminster (Jefferson) Colorado; cremated-ashes scattered in Boulder (Boulder) Colorado with a memorial paver brick at the entrance to Colorado University stadium gate; married Mary Jane Schneider

Wilbur Wayne "Buddy": born 1935 Boulder (Boulder) Colorado-still living; married Marlene Evans and Joanne Rohring

Linda Anne: born 1940 Boulder (Boulder) Colorado-still living; married Richard Bruce "Dick" Ayers

Sallie Jean: born 1952 Boulder (Boulder) Colorado-still living; married Donald William Wiesmann and Rogelio Valena "Junior" Lopez

Harlie died on 01 October 1982 in Boulder (Boulder) Colorado and is buried at the Mountain View Memorial Park Cemetery in Boulder (Boulder) Colorado alongside his wife, Annie, who died on 01 March 1994 in Louisville (Boulder) Colorado.

Boulder Daily Camera 03 October 1982:
"Harlie E. Bradford of 2500 Fourth St. died Friday at Boulder Memorial Hospital He was 72.

Mr. Bradford was born in Bogue, Kan, No. 14, 1909, the son of Charles Bradford and Sarah Salmons Bradford.

He moved to Boulder from Kansas in 1917.

Mr. Bradford married Elizabeth Ann Nichols in Littleton Aug. 13, 1926.

He became a real estate broker, and was a charter member of the Board of Realtors.

He is survived by his wife of Boulder, two sons, Wilbur Bradford of Lakewood and Harlie Bradford Jr. of Arvada, two daughters, Sallie Bradford and Linda Ayers, both of Boulder, two sisters, Billy Holiday of Hygiene and Thesta La Sauzer of Miami, six grandchildren, and four great-grandchildren.

A memorial service will be held Tuesday at 3 p.m. at Howe Mortuary Chapel, with officers and members of Masonic Lodge 45 officiating.

Contributions can be made to the American Lung Association, 1600 Race St., Denver 80206."

Boulder Daily Camera 03 March 1994:
"Elizabeth Ann Bradford of Boulder died Tuesday, March 1, at Avista Hospital. She was 82.

She was born Dec. 17, 1911, in Gold Hill, the daughter of Richard John Nichols and Ethel Goudge Nichols. She married Harlie E. Bradford on Aug. 12, 1927, in Littleton.

Mrs. Bradford was a homemaker. She was a member of the First Baptist Church of Boulder and Eastern Star. She enjoyed football, gardening, flowers and collecting antiques.

She moved to Boulder from Gold Hill in 1923.

Survivors include two sons, Harlie "Buck" Bradford of Arvada and Bud Bradford of Boulder; two daughters, Linda Ayers of Boulder and Sallie Bradford of San Francisco; a sister, Jean Rapier of Longmont; eight grandchildren; and six great-grandchildren.

Services will be at 11 a.m. Saturday at Howe Mortuary, 211 11th St., Boulder. The Rev. Sheldon Schuttenberg of First Baptist Church will officiate. Services will conclude at the chapel.

Contribution may be made to the charity of the donor's choice"

Members of the Bradford family are memorialized in this location

BRADY, Emma Lou (*Hesmer*)

> Birth: 03/21/1898
> Death: 03/06/1992
> Cemetery Location: B1

Father: John Hesmer; Mother: Anna (*Tveit*); Husband: John Francis Brady; born in Marshalltown (Marshall) Iowa and died in Longmont (Boulder) Colorado at age 93 years, 11 months, 14 days-natural causes

Boulder Daily Camera 10 March 1992:

"Emma Lou Brady of 1335 Cinnamon Street Longmont, died Friday, March 6, in Longmont United Hospital. She was 93. She was born on March 21, 1898, in Marshalltown, Iowa, the daughter of John Hesmer and Anna Tveit Hesmer. She married John Francis Brady in 1923. He died in 1966. Mrs. Brady was a Boulder resident through much of the 1970s. Until 1966, she lived primarily in the Washington, D.C., and Baltimore areas. She also lived in San Jose, California, Sacramento, California and

Longmont. She was an active volunteer in the Lutheran Church. She was a potter and taught pottery at community schools in the Washington, D.C., area. Survivors include two daughters, Burnyce Larner of Gold Hill and Beverly Woodwell of Land-O-Lakes, Florida; two brothers, Selmer Hesmer of Rancho Mirage, California, and Theodore "Pete" Hesmer of Altoona, Florida; and three grandchildren. A memorial service will be held at 1p.m. Saturday at Howe Mortuary Chapel, 2121 11th Street, Boulder, with the Rev. Eugene Larson of Trinity Lutheran Church officiating. Burial will be in Gold Hill Cemetery."

BROWN, Gilbert Lewis

> Birth: 10/30/1914
> Death: 01/06/1981
> Cemetery Location: B2

Father: James Scott Brown; Mother: Elizabeth Irene (*Boyd*); Wife: Barbara (*Heaton*) born in Boulder (Boulder) Colorado and died in Boulder (Boulder) Colorado at age 60 years, 2 months, 7 days- rheumatic heart disease and cerebrovascular accident; grandson of Frank and Mary Boyd; see BOYD, Frank V., see BOYD, Mary Parker (*Kirkbride*); see CHRISTENSEN, Barbara (*Heaton*) Brown

Boulder Daily Camera 08 January 1981:

"Gilbert Lewis Brown, 2510 Grape Avenue, died Tuesday at Memorial Hospital. He was 66. He was born October 30, 1914, in Boulder, the son of James and Elizabeth Boyd Brown. He married Barbara Heaton in Denver on September 22, 1939. He graduated from the University of Colorado engineering school in 1936. Mr. Brown was a structural engineer with the Bureau of Reclamation at the Denver Federal Center for 33 years. He retired in 1969 and came to Boulder in 1978 from Denver. He is survived by his wife, of Boulder, two sons, Boyd of Boulder, and Mark of Houston, Texas; a daughter, Susan Umberger of

West Lafayette, Indiana, and five grandchildren. Memorial services will be held Friday at noon at Montview Boulevard Presbyterian Church, Denver, the Rev. Kenneth Barley and the Rev. Allen Maruyama officiating. Contributions in his memory may be made to Montview Boulevard Presbyterian Church, 1980 Dahlia, Denver, 80207, or to Boulder Memorial Hospital, 311 Mapleton, Boulder 80302. Howe Mortuary handled arrangements."

BROWN, Lawrence Conway

Birth: 07/24/1939
Death: 06/17/2015
Cemetery Location: B1

Father: Lloyd Austin Brown; Mother: Jessie (*Conway*); born in Mansfield (Richland) Ohio and died in Boulder (Boulder) Colorado at age 75 years, 10 months, 24 days-old age-heart attack

Boulder Daily Camera 22 July 2015:
"Lawrence Conway Brown of 1014 Mapleton Avenue, Boulder died Wednesday, June 17, at the age of 75. He was born July 24, 1939, in Mansfield, Ohio, the son of Lloyd Austin Brown and Jessie Conway Brown. He never married. Mr. Brown graduated from Case Institute of Technology (now part of Case Western Reserve University) in 1960 with a B.S. degree in Mathematics.

Mr. Brown retired from IBM at the end of 1991, after 32 years with IBM. He was a computer programmer, designer of programming languages, product planner and forecaster of sales. He was listed in Who's Who in Computers and Data Processing, published in 1971. He moved to Boulder in 1965. He was a member of Boulder's City Planning Board from 1966 through 1971; Vice-chairman in 1970 and Chairman in 1971. He was a member of Boulder's Library Commission from 1972 through 1974; Chairman in 1974.

Mr. Brown was a book collector interested in the history of printing. He concentrated on the fine printers of the eighteenth century and was an authority of the English printer, John Baskerville. He had been a member of the Grolier Club of New York, America's leading organization of book collectors.

Mr. Brown is survived by his brother, Charles A. Brown of Hendersonville, North Carolina."

BUCKNER, Daniel James "Buck"

Birth: 03/26/1941
Death: 10/02/2003
Cemetery Location: B5

Father: James Whitney Buckner; Mother: Margaret F. (*Perkins*); 1st Wife: Francelle Cleveland (*Clark*); 2nd Wife: Shari J. (*Robertson*); born in Los Angeles (Los Angeles)

California and died in Boulder (Boulder) Colorado at age 62 years, 6 months, 6 days-cancer

Boulder Daily Camera 04 October 2003:
"Daniel James 'Buck' Buckner—Daniel James "Buck" Buckner of Boulder died of cancer Thursday, Oct. 2, 2003, in Boulder. He was 62.

He was born March 26, 1941, in Los Angeles to James W. Buckner and Margaret F. Perkins Buckner. He married Francelle Cleveland Clark in the early 1960s. They divorced. He married Shari J. Robertson on Aug. 20, 1977, in Boulder.

Mr. Buckner owned and operated Gold Creek Photography, worked on oil rigs and was employed by the University of Colorado and the city of Boulder. He was a master of ceremonies at bluegrass festivals.

He received a bachelor's degree and attended graduate school.

His interests included performing, supporting, enjoying and teaching bluegrass music. A longtime KGNU radio disc jockey, he was named 1966 Colorado Bluegrass DJ. He was a member of the International Bluegrass Music Association, the Colorado Bluegrass Music Society and the society's committee to bring bluegrass into public schools.

Mr. Buckner lived in Gold Hill from 1970 to 1976, when he moved to Boulder.

"There will never be a replacement for Buck Buckner, but his humor, his passion for bluegrass music and his love for his family will continue on long after him," the family said.

Survivors include his wife of Boulder; three sons, Clint Buckner, Jed Buckner and Matt Buckner; two stepsons, Linden Hagans and Randal Pair; a sister, Kathleen Buckner; his former spouse; and two grandchildren.

A private burial in Gold Hill Cemetery will follow interment. A memorial service will be scheduled later.

Contributions may be made to his name to the Rock Mountain Cancer Centers, Midtown Office, 1800 Williams St., Denver, CO 80218.

Rundus Funeral Home of Broomfield is handling arrangements."

C

CARPENTER, Michael Glen

Birth: 09/24/1944
Death: 05/05/2014
Cemetery Location: F1

Father: Lawrence Glen Carpenter; Mother: Mildred May (*Parker*); Wife: Kathy (*Gibson*); born in Tucson (Pima) Arizona and died in Loveland (Larimer) Colorado at age 69 years, 7 months, 11 days-pancreatic cancer; see GIBSON, Robert Wallace; see GIBSON, Shirlee C. (*Rowan*)

About Michael Glen Carpenter

Michael graduated from the University of Arizona with a principal degree in banking and worked as a trust officer in Los Angeles (Los Angeles) California. He later moved to Vail (Eagle) Colorado and operated snow plows in the winter months and did landscaping during the summer. He moved to Boulder (Boulder) Colorado and worked for Human Resources, City of Boulder and later for the Boulder Assessor's Office. Michael earned his MRI in Residential Real Estate Appraisal and worked in the field until he retired. Michael and his wife lived in Sunset (Boulder) Colorado for 17 years and considered it home. They later moved to Loveland (Larimer) Colorado.

CELLA, Eloise (*Shearer*)

Birth: 10/03/1910
Death: 10/11/1970
Cemetery Location: E3

Michael Glen Carpenter has a natural tombstone of wood and rock.

Father: David Homer Shearer; Mother: Florence (*Humphrey*); Husband: John George Cella; born in Missouri and died in St. Louis (St. Louis) Missouri at age 60 years, 0 months, 8 days-lung cancer

Boulder Daily Camera 12 October 1970:
"Eloise S. Cella, Former Resident, Dies In St. Louis... Eloise S. Cella, former Gold Hill resident, died Sunday in St. Louis, Mo. Graveside services will be held Tuesday at 4:30 p.m. at the Gold Hill Cemetery. Memorial services will be held in St. Louis. Mrs. Cella is survived by a son, Charles J. Cella; a daughter, Mrs. Eloise C. Lipscomb, both in St. Louis; and a brother, David Shearer. Howe Mortuary is handling local arrangements."

CHRISTENSEN, Barbara (*Heaton*) Brown

Birth: 03/10/1917
Death: 05/04/2002
Cemetery Location: B2

Father: Ross Leslie Heaton; Mother: Elizabeth Blanche "Betty" (*Mott*); 1st Husband: Gilbert Lewis Brown; 2nd Husband Charles Christensen; born in Mansfield (Richland) Ohio and died in Boulder (Boulder) Colorado at age 85 years, 1 month, 24 days-lung cancer; see BROWN, Gilbert Lewis

Boulder Daily Camera 06 May 2002:
"Barbara Heaton Brown Christensen—Barbara Heaton Brown Christensen of Boulder died of lung cancer Saturday, May 4, 2002. She was 85. She was born to Ross L. Heaton and Elizabeth B. Mott Heaton on March 10, 1917, in Mansfield, Ohio. She married Gilbert L. Brown on Sept. 22, 1939, in Denver. He died Jan. 6, 1981. She married Charles Christensen on May 2, 1987, in Boulder. He died Nov. 25, 1989. She moved to Boulder in

1977 from Denver. Before that, she lived in Wyoming and California. She attended the University of Denver. Mrs. Christensen was a homemaker. She was a member of St. Andrew Presbyterian Church of Boulder and the Gold Hill Club. She was the founder of the Concern Center at St. Andrew Presbyterian Church in Boulder and was an active member of the choir. Survivors include two sons, Mark Brown of Suisun, Calif., and Boyd Brown of Gold Hill; a daughter, Susan Umberger of West Lafayette, Ind., and seven grandchildren. A memorial service will be at 4 p.m. Wednesday at St. Andrew Presbyterian Church, 3700 Baseline Road, Boulder, with the Rev. Stan Adamson officiating. Contributions may be made in her name to Historic Gold Hill, 661 Pine St., Gold Hill, CO 80302 or to the Concern Center, St. Andrew Presbyterian Church, 3700 Baseline Road, Boulder, CO 80303. M.P. Murphy & Associates Funeral Directors is in charge of arrangements."

Mountain Ear (Nederland, CO) 09 May 2002:

"Barbara Christensen—Barbara Heaton Brown Christensen 85, died on May 4, 2002, at her home in Boulder. She was born on March 10, 1917, in Mansfield, Ohio, the daughter of Ross L. Heaton and Elizabeth Blanche Mott Heaton. She attended the University of Denver and married Gilbert Lewis Brown on Sept. 22, 1939, in Denver. He preceded her in death on Jan. 6, 1981. She married Charles Christensen in Boulder on May 2, 1987. He preceded her in death on Nov. 25, 1989. She was a resident of Boulder since 1977, moving there from Denver. She formerly resided in Cody, Wyoming, and California. She was a homemaker, and was active in the Gold Hill community as a member of the Gold Hill Club. She also was a member of St. Andrew Presbyterian Church of Boulder and the founder of the Concern Center at St. Andrew Presbyterian Church in Boulder and was an active member of the choir. Survivors include two sons, Mark Brown of Suisun, Calif., and Boyd Brown of Gold Hill; a daughter, Susan

Umberger of West Lafayette, Indiana; and seven grandchildren. Services were held on May 8 at St. Andrew Presbyterian Church in Boulder, with the Rev. Stan Adamson officiating. Contributions may be made to Historic Gold Hill, 661 Pine St., Gold Hill, CO 80302; Concern Center, St. Andrew Presbyterian Church, 3700 Baseline Road, CO 80303, or Hospice of Boulder County, 2594 Trail Ridge Drive, East, Suite A, Lafayette, CO 80026. M.P. Murphy & Associates handled the arrangements."

COUGHLIN, Irene Mary
(Previously listed also as COLVIN)

> Birth: 05/04/1893
> Death: 09/19/1914
> Cemetery Location: C/D 4 & 5

Father: Daniel Coughlin; Mother: Jessie Elvia (*Hastings*); born in Gold Hill (Boulder) Colorado and died in Rowena (Boulder) Colorado at age 21 years, 4 months, 15 days-mitral pulmonary and aortic regurgitation; see **About the Daniel Coughlin Family**

Boulder Daily Camera 19 September 1914 & *Boulder County Tribune* 25 September 1914:

"THE HAND OF DEATH LAID ON MISS IRENE COUGHLIN...

While comfortably seated in a rocking chair before a warm fire in her home at Rowena this morning Miss Irene Coughlin, formally of this city, dropped dead. She had been a sufferer with heart trouble for a number of years and yesterday had a bad attack. This morning, however, she felt better and was up and around the house prior to seven o'clock when she pulled the rocking chair to the fire place and sat down. A short time later she was found dead. She died as one going to sleep, not even a grown marking the passing of her life.

Miss Coughlin was twenty-one years old and until going to Rowena two years ago was a resident of this city. She attended the Boulder public schools and the business college, and was a bright and loveable young woman. Her parents are Mr. and Mrs. John Coughlin, who during their residence in Boulder lived at 1719 Walnut. Mr. Coughlin is now working on the Cold Spring mine at Rowena.

The funeral and interment will be at Gold Hill. Besides the parents she is survived by three sisters and two brothers. The funeral services will take place Sunday at two o'clock at Gold Hill. Rev. Bowen of the Friends church will conduct the services and Undertaker A.E. Howe the funeral and interment."

Boulder Daily Herald 19 September 1914:

"Irene Coughlin Dies Suddenly At Rowena—Daughter of Mr. and Mrs. Dan Coughlin Succumbs to Heart Disease—Ill for Years...

Miss Irene Coughlin, daughter of Mr. and Mrs. Dan Coughlin of Rowena, died suddenly of heart trouble at her home in that town a few minutes after 7 o'clock, this morning. Although she had been in poor health for three years, her relatives had no idea that death was at hand. She had not been feeling well for several days, but she was able to be up and to attend to a few duties about the house.

She arose shortly before 7 o'clock this morning and was sitting in a rocking chair when the end came. Her mother and all her brothers and sisters, with one exception, were in the room when she died. Her father had just started out for work. He was called back to the house.

The deceased was born at Gold Hill, May 4, 1893. She was the oldest of seven children. The family lived in this city at 1719 Water street [sic] for several years. They moved to Rowena only last June. The surviving brothers and sisters are Elmer 17; Bertha, 15; Chester, 13; Edwin 10; Margaret, 7, and Jean, 4.

The funeral will take place Sunday afternoon, at 2:00 o'clock, from the Gold Hill church. Rev. E.V. Bowen, pastor of the Friends church of this city will officiate. Interment will be made in Gold Hill cemetery."

Boulder Daily Herald 21 September 1914:

"Many Attend Funeral of Miss Irene Coughlin…

The funeral of Miss Irene May Coughlin, daughter of Mr. and Mrs. Dan Coughlin of Rowena, who died of heart disease Saturday morning, took place yesterday afternoon at 2 o'clock from the Methodist church at Gold Hill. Rev. K.V. Bowen, pastor of the Friends church of this city, and about twenty members of the Boulder congregation attended the services, which were conducted by Mr. Dowen.

The funeral procession formed at the Coughlin residence in Rowena and proceeded in Gold Hill. Most of the residents of Rowena were present. Many beautiful flowers surrounded the casket, testifying to the deep sympathy extended to the family by their many friends.

A choir consisted of Mrs. K.V. Bowen, Miss Beulah Swallow, Miss Martha Andrew, and Edward Andrew, of Boulder; Mrs. Mary Boyd, Miss Gladys Gouge[sic], and Miss Myrtle Barnett, of Gold Hill, with T.B. Holman as organist, sang "It Is Well With My Soul," "Some Day the Silver Cord Will Be Broken," "Satisfied," "Nearer My God to Thee," "Safe in the Arms of Jesus," and "Jesus Lover of My Soul." The pallbearers were Howard Patton, Rowe Wolcott, Albert Walter, Harold Walter, Charles Holman, and William Peterson. Interment was made in Gold Hill cemetery.

Undertaker A.E. Howe of this city went to Rowena to direct the funeral.

A steamer load left yesterday at 2:00 o'clock for Gold Hill to attend the funeral of Miss Irene M. Coughlin of Rowena, but formerly of Boulder, and a member of the Golden Rule Sunday school class here. The party consisted of the following: Rev. and Mrs. K.V. Bowen, E.J. and Martha Andrew, Mrs. Mager, Mrs. Gouge [sic], Mrs. Richards, Mrs. Houseworth, Beulah Swallow, Mabel Bayless, Mary Cramer, and Mr. and Mrs. Eli Jones."

Boulder Daily Camera 21 September 1914:

"A steamer load of people left at one o'clock Sunday for Gold Hill to attend the funeral of Miss Irene M. Coughlin, a resident of Rowena but formerly of Boulder, and a member of the Golden Rule Sunday school class here. The party consisted of the following: Rev. and Mrs. K.V. Bowen, E.J. and Martha Andrew, Mrs. Gouge, Mrs. Richards, Mrs. Houseworth, Mrs. Mager, Mabel Bayless, Beulah Swallow, Mary Cramer and Mr. and Mrs. Eli Jones."

Boulder Daily Camera 21 September 1914:

"BOULDER AND GOLD HILL JOIN IN EXPRESSING GRIEF…

The funeral of Irene Mary Coughlin was held at Gold Hill Sunday afternoon. People from all over the mountains and forty Boulder relatives and friends gathered at the mountain town to pay their respects to Miss Coughlin, who died of heart disease in Rowena Saturday morning in the home of her parents, Mr. and Mrs. Dan Coughlin. The diseased was taken at the untimely age of twenty-one, after a three years courageous struggle with heart disease.

Rev. K.V. Bowen, pastor of the Friends church conducted the service and a chorus from the church—Mr. K.V. Bowen, Bulah Swallow, Martha Andrew and Edward Andrew and Mrs. Mary Boyd, Gladys Gouge and Mertle Barnett of Gold Hill sang "It Is Well With My Soul," "Some Day the Silver Chord Shall Break," "Satisfied," "Nearer My God to Thee, "Safe in the Arms of Jesus" and "Jesus Lover of My Soul."

Howard Patton, Roe Wolcott, Albert and Harold Walter, Charles Hilman, and William Peterson, former classmates of the deceased, were the pall bearers. The floral offerings were most numerous and beautiful. A.E. Howe was in charge of the funeral and interment was in Gold Hill cemetery."

Transcribed as exactly written (with spelling corrections) a three-page, handwritten letter to Blanche (Hastings) Swallow, from her sixteen-year-old niece, Irene Mary Coughlin (courtesy Leah McKin, relative):

"April 6, 1910, Goldhill, Colorado

Dear Aunt Blanch,

The time has come when I must ask a question the contemplation of which has caused me many a sleepless night, bitter tears of anguish and corresponding days of anxiety. This a subject of which I hesitate to speak to anyone as I know the whole community is upset at the present time by the same question which agitates me. Many a happy home has been broken up by this same cause. And I to thought young must share the burden of the uncouth world. I dare not even communicate my state of mind to my people as they are old fashioned about such things. In my distress I turn humbly to appeal to you for sympathy. It may surprise you to know I would consult you on such an important subject which only my own should know but like the morning dawn the whole affair must come to light. And the public must know sooner or later so I ask your friendly advice as I know you will understand me better than I can explain. I am asking a great favor of you and while you are considering this I wish you to set aside all social joys and properly consider this question. I hate to ask it bust must come to the point. DO you think it is time to put on my summer underwear? After considering this question closely, let me hear from you. Excuse blots but think of my state of mind.

As ever your loving niece

Rene."

("I really do think Irene was "pulling her Aunt's leg" with her question to her Aunt Blanche. At least, this is now the family saw it, and Irene was said to be quite the character. In fact, the Coughlin and Pittman families enjoyed pranks and jokes a great deal. Irene's little missive is one of those rare bright lights you are lucky to find in genealogy—a good laugh in the face of time passing away."-Leah McKin)

Boulder Daily Camera 24 September 1957

"At a fifty year celebration in which all the mining towns of the area chose a queen, Dan's and Jessie's seventeen-year-old daughter, Irene, was chosen from her locality."

(Snippet from "Jessie Coughlin Tells of Her Early Days in Caribou, Gold Hill, and Nederland, Later Life in Sugar Loaf")

COUGHLIN, John Henry
(Previously listed also as COLVIN)

> Birth: 06/26/1895
> Death: 04/12/1899
> Cemetery Location: C/D 4 & 5

Father: Daniel Coughlin; Mother: Jessie Elvia (*Hastings*); born in (Boulder) Colorado and died in Gold Hill (Boulder) Colorado at age 3 years, 9 months, 17 days-cause of death unknown; see **About the Daniel Coughlin Family**

Boulder Daily Camera 14 April 1899:
"The death of the four year old son of Mr. and Mrs. Dan Coughlin occurred at Gold Hill yesterday. Mr. Trezise sent up a casket and conducted the funeral at Gold Hill today."

COUGHLIN, Margaret "Mary" Ruth
(Previously listed also as COLVIN)

> Birth: 10/11/1906
> Death: 04/22/1918
> Cemetery Location: C/D 4 & 5

Father: Daniel Coughlin; Mother: Jessie Elvia (*Hastings*); born in Gold Hill (Boulder) Colorado and died in Sugarloaf (Boulder) Colorado at age 11 years, 6 months, 11 days- heart problems; tombstone has incorrect death date of 05/21/1917; see **About the Daniel Coughlin Family**

Boulder Daily Camera 23 April 1918:
"DEATH OF LITTLE RUTH, DAUGHTER OF MR. AND MRS. COUGHLIN—Margaret Ruth Coughlin, daughter of Dan and Jessie Coughlin, died at their home in Sugar Loaf [sic] at three o'clock Monday afternoon of heart trouble, age eleven years last October. The funer-

al service will be conducted by Rev. Alfred Young at the Friends church, Twelfth Street and University Avenue, Wednesday morning at 10:30. Interment will be in Gold Hill cemetery."

About the Daniel Coughlin Family

Daniel Coughlin was born 01 February 1869 in Hannock (Houghton) Michigan; the son of John and Ellen (*Tobin*) Coughlin.

In the 1880 census he was living with his family in Caribou (Boulder) Colorado.

On 16 October 1892 Daniel, at the age of 23 years, married a young seventeen year old, Jessie Elvia Hastings. She was born 17 August 1875 in Lebanon (Grafton) New Hampshire; the daughter of Henry Hiram and Emily Lorinda (*McCallister*) Hastings. To this union eight known children were born:

Irene Mary: born 04 May 1893 Gold Hill (Boulder) Colorado and died 19 September 1914 Rowena (Boulder) Colorado; buried Gold Hill Cemetery, Gold Hill (Boulder) Colorado; see COUGHLIN, Irene Mary

John Henry: born 26 June 1895 Gold Hill (Boulder) Colorado and died 12 April 1899 Gold Hill (Boulder) Colorado; buried Gold Hill Cemetery, Gold Hill (Boulder) Colorado; see COUGHLIN, John Henry

Elmer Dan "Mick": born 14 June 1897 Gold Hill (Boulder) Colorado and died 14 June 1948 Boulder (Boulder) Colorado; buried Green Mountain Cemetery, Boulder (Boulder) Colorado; married Jenny Washburn

Bertha Elva: born 14 August 1899 Gold Hill (Boulder) Colorado and died 17 February 1979 Casper (Natrona) Wyoming; buried Glenrock Cemetery, Glenrock (Converse) Wyoming; married Charles B. Perkins and Raymond Christopher Bartels

Chester Carl "Bus": born 14 July 1901 Gold Hill (Boulder) Colorado and died 03 February 1960 (Marion) Oregon); buried Belcrest Memorial Park Salem (Marion) Oregon; married Ola Juanita (*Ward*) Thompson

Edwin Lamar: born 17 July 1904 Gold Hill (Boulder) Colorado and died 01 February 1967 Denver (Denver) Colorado; buried Hampden Memorial Estates, Denver (Denver) Colorado; married Stella Marie Stewart

Margaret Ruth: born 11 October 1906 Gold Hill (Boulder) Colorado and died 22 April 1918 Gold Hill (Boulder) Colorado; buried Gold Hill Cemetery, Gold Hill (Boulder) Colorado; see COUGHLIN, Margaret Ruth

Jean Ellen: born 25 March 1910 Gold Hill (Boulder) Colorado and died 25 July 1956 Glenrock (Converse) Wyoming; buried Glenrock Cemetery, Glenrock (Converse) Wyoming; married Richard Fletcher Rogers

By the 1920 census Dan Coughlin was living in his father-in-law's (Henry Hastings) household with his family in Boulder (Boulder) Colorado where Dan was listed as a miner. Ten years later in the 1930 census Dan had moved his family to Casper (Natrona) Wyoming where he was a janitor in an electric power plant. By 1935 the Coughlin family was living in Mills (Natrona) Wyoming. It appears Dan was a proprietor of a grocery store until he died on 30 September 1941 at his home there. He was buried in the Highland Cemetery, Casper (Natrona) Wyoming.

The Casper Times (Wyoming) 02 October 1941:

"Services for Dan Coughlin to be Friday, Mills Resident Claimed Tuesday...

Funeral services for the late Daniel Coughlin, Mills, will be held Friday morning at 10 o'clock at the Gay chapel with the Castle Rock lodge No. 45, A.F. and A.M. [Ancient Free and Accepted Masons] in charge. Burial will be in Highland cemetery with the Rev. E. Lee Neal, pastor of the First Christian church, in charge of services at the grave.

The deceased died at his home in Mills Tuesday morning after a long illness. Born and raised in Hancock, Mich., he came to Wyoming 20 years ago. He was employed at Midwest for 13 years. He was a life member of the Columbia lodge No. 14, A.F. and A.M., in Boulder, Colo.

He is survived by his wife, Mrs. Jessie E. Coughlin, Mills; three sons, Elmer, Sugar Loaf, Colo., Chester, Mills, and Ed, Denver; two daughters, Mrs. Ray Bartell[sic], Parkerton, and Mrs. R.F. Rodgers, Glenrock. Also 14 grandchildren and two great-grandchildren."

Boulder Daily Camera 03 October 1941:

"Daniel Coughlin, father of Elmer (Mickey) Coughlin of Sugar Loaf, and brother of John Coughlin of Altona and Sugar Loaf, died at his home in Mills, Wyo., Tuesday morning at 11 o'clock, according to word received by relatives. He had been in failing health for two years.

Funeral services were held in Casper, Wyo., this morning at 10 o'clock. Burial in Casper cemetery.

The deceased was born at Caribou, Feb. 1, 1869. He was the son of the late Mr. and Mrs. John Coughlin, who later owned the Coughlin ranch at Sugar Loaf. He followed mining during his residence here, and was also a

mine blacksmith. Besides living at Sugar Loaf, he and his family resided in Gold Hill, and were living in Boulder when the move to Wyoming was made about the time of the close of the World War.

Mr. Coughlin and the late Jim Pittman at one time held the world's championship in double hard rock drilling, now held by his son, Elmer (Mickey), and grandson, Raymond Coughlin.

Surviving relatives besides the son and brother, are the widow, Jessie Coughlin; two sons, Chester of Mills, and Edward, of Denver; two daughters, Mrs. Bertha Bartell, wife of Ray Bartell, and Mrs. Jean Rogers, wife of Fletcher Rogers, all of Glen Rock [sic], Wyo.; nine grandchildren and two great-grandchildren, and a sister, Mrs. Kate Adams of Roseville, Calif. John Dalton of Boulder and Mrs. Paul Teets of the White Rock district, are nephew and niece of the deceased.

Mr. and Mrs. Elmer Coughlin and their son-in-law and daughter, Mr. and Mrs. Thomas Riley, all of Sugar Loaf, left Wednesday for Mills. John Coughlin, his son and daughter-in-law, Mr. and Mrs. Neil Coughlin, and Edward Coughlin, son of the deceased, and his wife, of Denver, left Thursday morning to be with the family until after the funeral services."

Boulder Daily Camera 24 September 1957:

"Jessie Coughlin Tells of Her Early Days in Caribou, Gold Hill, and Nederland, Later Life in Sugar Loaf...

The Colorado hills call Jessie Hastings Coughlin "home" each summer, where she refreshes her memories of the seventy-seven years she spent in the Boulder area. Those memories include the time she spent as a fifteen-year old waitress in the Sherman House at Caribou, and the pride she took in being the wife, mother and grandmother to champion hard rock drillers of the county. They also go even farther back to the years in the 1880's when she was sometimes allowed to drive her father's stage team down Pearl Street in Boulder, and stop the stage with a flourish at the post office where the mail for the Caribou run was ready for delivery.

Jessie's very earliest memories are of the long train ride to Boulder in 1880, when she accompanied her parents here, as a five year old child. She remembers the fascination of the strange homes she saw alongside the rails as the slow train chugged its way across the prairies. For the dugouts and soddies on the plains were far different from the stately bricks and frames of her native New Hampshire.

Jessie recalls that she and her parents settled for a time with her uncle and aunt, the I.T. McAllisters on Pine Street, while her father had employment at her Uncle Ira McAllister's saw mill here. There were few buildings in Boulder then, so that Switzer's store loomed up on the barren streets when viewed from the hills above. The

Hastings family next moved to the Barry place in the foothills near Boulder for a time. Then came another summer that looms large in Jessie's memory—the summer they lived up Left Hand Canon [sic], a half mile below the Gold Hill road.

Cloud Burst

Perhaps this summer is especially memorable, due to the terrors of the cloudburst which could have cost the Hastings' family their lives. Jessie's mother, as the waters rose higher, called to the boarder in the next room of the cabin for assistance. He knocked off a board in the partition so the children could crawl through to escape the swirling waters. Then Mrs. Hastings stood on the baby's high chair and dislodged another board in the outside wall, so the rushing waters could escape from the house. After the angry waters receded, the mud had to be scrapped from the floors and the rooms scrubbed vigorously before the house was again habitable.

Jessie's earliest schooling was at the old Central School in Boulder. The Hastings family moved to Gold Hill just prior to the building of the school house there. "Summer school" was being taught at Gold Hill in the living room of the Guise home at the time the Hastings family moved to the mountain community, but that fall the school house was built.

Stage Line

At this time, to—1884—Jessie's father, H.H. Hastings put the first stage line through between Gold Hill and Salina. Nine year old Jessie was delighted with the big bay horses, Don and Sam that pulled the cumbersome stage on the new line. But the nicest and most exciting event of her ninth year was the "birthday present" of a new little sister, Blanche (now Mrs. Curtis Swallow). After four or five years of running the Gold Hill and Salina stage, the Hastings moved back to Boulder where Jessie's father purchased another stage line, the Gold Hill and Caribou run [sic], which he operated for four years.

Jessie remembers her father's gang of stage drivers as a gay and daring crew. One particularly zealous driver, known as "The Dutchman" was wont to yell, "Get out of the way. You can't hold up the U.S. Mail!" if such obstacles as broken-down ore wagons obstructed the canon [sic].

The Sherman House

The passengers, as well as the drivers of the stage, needed to be of a vigorous nature also if they were to survive the Caribou run in inclement weather. Jessie recalls from her days at the Sherman House that passengers often declared that the icy winds on the Caribou trail had them almost frozen to their seats. The hotel keepers at Sherman House were accustomed to rushing out when the stage arrived (often at dark, after a ten a.m. start from Boulder) to rescue the chilled passengers. In spite of the protection of heavy robes, the passengers were often too chilled to move. The hotel keepers helped them to the warmth inside the Sherman House, and cared for the stage teams.

Eighteen boarders ate family style at the long tables in the dining room of Sherman House at the time Jessie was a waitress there. And one day, when the cook was unable to attend to her duties, Jessie and the daughter of the Washburns, who were the hotel's proprietors, had a busy time. They prepared the food for the large crew of boarders as well as attending to their usual tasks. But these were not tasks to dismay the young girls of Jessie's day. Nor was this Jessie's first job, even at the age of fifteen. She had had various kinds of household employment for almost as long as she can remember, both in the Hastings home and helping neighbors at the many labors essential to pioneer living.

Married in 1892

When the Hastings family moved to Nederland for a year to run the Hetzer House, Jessie became acquainted with the young hard rock miner, Dan Coughlin, whom she married in 1892. He and his partner, Jim Pittman, were expert hard rock drillers and entered the contests in that skill with enthusiasm. In the early days, the clock around the Courthouse in Boulder was roped off for this event. Hugh boulders of hard granite from Four Mile Canon [sic] were hauled in by team and wagon, for the use of the contestants, and Dan Coughlin and Jim Pittman proved their skill many times.

Drilling Contests

In 1901, in the Labor Day contest at the Boulder Chautauqua grounds, they were declared to have drilled the deepest hole ever put in hard rock. This was a skill that passed from father to son, and on down to the grandsons of the Coughlin family. Dan's and Jessie's son Elmer (Mick) and his cousin George Coughlin won trophies in later years. And Elmer with his sons, Raymond, Bill and Clyde, the latter only five and ten years of age, won in the event in a later year. So it was that the Coughlin men became famed for their prowess as hard rock drillers entering competitions at the Boulder Pow Wow and the contests at the Miners Conventions in Denver.

Mountain Entertainment

There were other mining celebrations of the early years, too, in which the family took an active part. At a fifty year celebration in which all the mining towns of the area chose a queen, Dan's and Jessie's seventeen-year-old daughter, Irene, was chosen from her locality. Some of the gay times in the early days around Sugar Loaf and Nederland where Jessie lived, were unplanned entertainment. A neighbor, feeling a sudden urge for gaiety, grabbed up whatever was convenient in the refreshment line, such as a half cake and started out. Others along the way added their bit to the evening's food. Often the group stopped at some lonely bachelor's cabin and spent a lively evening dancing to the music of Mark Dalley's accordion.

The Flu Epidemic

But there were sad times, too, in the mining towns. During the war time influenza epidemic, the theater at Nederland was turned into a morgue, and the hotel to a hospital. One dreadful week, fifty persons died of the fatal illness. The deep snows caused a great deal of hardship, too. On one occasion the snow was so deep that Jessie found it necessary to travel on snow shoes from the Coughlin cabin to Sugar Loaf where she took the stage for Boulder. She recalls that Boulder, too, was almost buried in snow, with the sidewalks still unshovelled [sic] when she arrived there.

Dan and Jessie Coughlin had eight children, three of whom are still living; Bertha (Mrs. Ray Bartell) of Glen Rock, Wyoming, Ed Coughlin of Denver, and Chester who resides in Salem, Oregon. Dan Coughlin died in 1941 and Jessie spends her winters at Glen Rock, Wyoming. But each summer she comes back to the Colorado Mountains where she spent so many years. Jessie is a still-handsome woman, looking twenty years younger than her actual age of 82. She is rather tall, with her gray hair smartly curled, and her small ears pierced by the tiny rhinestone earrings that were one of her girlhood treasures. There is an air of dignity about her that is occasionally belied by the wry smile and a brightening of her blue eyes.

Stevenson Book

Perhaps the poise she has comes from some of the ladylike, but rather vague, philosophies encased in the deerhide-bound Robert Louis Stevenson "Birthday Book" she carries about with her. The book, which once belonged to her mother, has quotations printed under its ornate page headings. One quote from "Inland Voyage" observes: "There is nothing but tit for tat in this world, though sometimes it be a little difficult to trace." Or, perhaps, Jessie's air of quietly taking life as it comes can be traced to those early years of pioneer living in Boulder and the mining towns of the area, when unexpected hardships and reverses must be met with a quiet, uncomplaining courage."

(By Jewel Maret Jenkins)

After the death of her husband Jessie moved back to Casper (Natrona) Wyoming. She died on 15 August 1963 in Thermopolis (Hot Springs) Wyoming and was buried next to her husband, Daniel, in the Highland Cemetery.

The Independent Record (Thermopolis, Wyoming) 22 August 1963:

"Jessie Coughlin Dies Thursday…
    Funeral services for Jessie Elva Coughlin, 87, were held Monday, Aug. 19 in Casper. Mrs. Coughlin died in the Memorial Hospital in Thermopolis on Aug. 15.
    She had been a resident of the Wyoming Pioneer Home for the past five years, coming to Thermopolis from Glenrock where she had lived since 1921.
    The body was sent to Casper for services and interment."

Undated Casper, Wyoming News Clipping [August 1963]:

"Services Held for Mrs. Coughlin…
    Funeral services were held Monday afternoon at 2:00 for Mrs. Jessie Coughlin, former Glenrock resident who died August 15 at Thermopolis.
    The services were held at Horstman Chapel in Casper with Rev. Roy C. Leeds of the First Christian church officiating. Burial was made in the family plot in Highland cemetery.
    Pallbearers included nephews, grandson, and a great-grandson, Allan and Jerry McKin, Tolly Swallow, Richard Watson, Richard Rogers and Carter Perkins.
    Mrs. Coughlin was born on August 17, 1875, at Lebanon, N.H. she was married October 17, 1892 to Daniel Coughlin. To this union eight children were born.
    Mrs. Coughlin, who came to Wyoming in 1921, was a member of Golden West Chapter No. 37, OES [Order of Eastern Star], and Glenella Rebekah lodge of Glenrock.
    Survivors include a daughter, Mrs. Ray Bartels of Glenrock; a son, Edwin Coughlin of Denver; one sister, Mrs. E.C. Swallow of Casper; 11 grandchildren, 27 great-grandchildren and 4 great-great-grandchildren.
    Out-of-town relatives attending services for Mrs. Jessie Coughlin in Casper Monday included Ed Coughlin of Denver, Mrs. Dale Plaster and Sandra Rogers, Richard Rogers of Great Falls, Mont., Mrs. Tom Ridley [sic], Mrs. Junie Coughlin, Mr. and Mrs. Tom Riley Jr., Mr. and Mrs. Glen Coughlin, and Mr. and Mrs. Paul Teets of Boulder, Colo., Mr. and Mrs. C.E. Schneider and Mrs. J.C. Howard of Cheyenne, Mr. Laurence Swallow, Mrs. Lois Watson and son, Dick and Mrs. Laurence [sic] Crowe of Wheatland."

COWELL, William

Birth: 11/1855
Death: 10/20/1906
Cemetery Location: E2

Father: unknown; Mother: unknown; Wife: Lillian/Lydia "Lily" (Copson) Stroup/Strupe Cowell; born in Ohio and died in Boulder (Boulder) Colorado at age 55 years-cause of death unknown

Boulder Daily Camera 22 October 1906:

"William Powell [sic] of Gold Hill died at the county hospital Sunday. Interment will be at Gold Hill after services at Buchheit's parlors tomorrow morning."

About William Cowell

William was born in November of 1855 in Ohio; parents unknown. He came to Colorado where he met Lillian/Lydia (*Copson*) Stroup/Strupe whom he married on 05 November 1898 in Boulder (Boulder) Colorado. She was born September of 1858 in the state of New York; parents unknown. She was the widow of John W. Stroup whom she married on 25 August 1881 in Boulder (Boulder) Colorado; see STROUP/STRUPE, John W.

The marriage of William and Lillian/Lydia (*Copson*) Stroup/Strupe Cowell brought forth one known child:

George Elmer: born 19 June 1899 Gold Hill (Boulder) Colorado and died 01 September 1983 Denver (Denver) Colorado; burial unknown; married Ruby C. Thompson and Jacqueline Marie (*Moser*) Pollard

After the death of William Cowell in 1906, Lillian operated a boarding house in Gold Hill (Boulder) Colorado. In 1913 she was living in Boulder (Boulder) Colorado, an employee of the University Hospital there. By 1916 she moved to Denver (Denver) Colorado.

The 1920 census has "Lily," a widow, living with her two sons, George Cowell and William Stroup. She died 06 March 1929 in Denver (Denver) Colorado from heart troubles. She is buried alongside her son, William Earl Stroup (who died in 1949) at the Crown Hill Cemetery in Wheat Ridge (Jefferson) Colorado.

Boulder Daily Camera 07 March 1929:
"FORMER GOLD HILL RESIDENT DIES OF HEART TROUBLE

Mrs. Lillian Stroup Cowell died while taking a nap at her home in Denver yesterday it was learned by Boulder friends today. She had been up and around the house as usual and had enjoyed a hearty luncheon. Afterwards she went to her room for a nap and there she was found dead by her daughters, Mrs. May Shaw and Mrs. Theo Ballou, when she failed to get up at the usual hour. Besides the two daughters, three sons, Ralph and William Stroupe and George Cowell, survive. Funeral arrangements have not been made. Boulder friends expect she will be buried at Gold Hill where both Mr. Stroup and Mr. Cowell are buried. She was a resident of Gold Hill for many years."

[buried in the Crown Hill Cemetery in Wheat Ridge (Jefferson) Colorado]

Early Days in Gold Hill by George Elmer Cowell as told to Chuck & Doll Rowan and Bob & Shirley Gibson (no date):

"My dad (William) would come up at night. He generally traveled at night because there was less traffic. They'd drive six to eight horses. When we say six to eight horses, six horses would be three teams and eight would be four teams. In them days when two teams met, they had cut-outs, and you had to pull in, let the team go by, then you'd pull out and go on. Well, if they traveled at night it was cooler traveling, they wouldn't run onto [sic] much traffic and they could keep right on a coming. He'd get as far as Salina and he'd feed his team there. Probably a four or five hour trip getting up to there, maybe 12 o'clock at night when he got there. Then he would put his team in and feed them, leave 'em rest for an hour, then he would put another team on the back and probably another team on the front, to pull the load up...I used to ride with my dad on the seat-there was a jockey box between us. A jockey box is where he kept his extra corks for the horseshoes for slippery weather, and his wrenches and hammers and things like that, and I used to sit on one side of the jockey box and him on the other in the regular seat, but he had a strap fastened across to strap me on, to keep me from being throwed [sic] off over the roads, 'cause it was pretty rough."

Interview #2-George Elmer Cowell as transcribed by Lynne Walter (no date):

"Three miles west of Gold Hill we had a freight office called Gold Hill Freight Station. They had big scales where they weighed things and they had a siding and there was always one or two boxcars sitting on this siding. My dad (William) would haul coal from these boxcars over to the mines for steam, for power, and in return he'd put on a load of ore and take it back...He would leave after supper around 7 or 8 o'clock when there was no traffic.

When I got old enough my father and I were quite close together and when I got old enough naturally love and horses and everything, I used to go with my dad every time I got a chance. Ride with him on the wagon and go to the mines and things, and there were times he would let me go to Boulder with him stay overnight and come back the next day.

My dad (William Cowell) used to drive Tally-hoes from Boulder to Boulder Falls...Then they would have a beefsteak fry. I'd go up with my dad on these excursions too. They paid him so much a night for this Tally-hoe. The thrill of it would be to come home down Boulder Canyon. My dad would unroll a big whip and start cracking it and they would come down through that Canyon 30 miles an hour just as hard as those horses could run clear from the Falls clear into Boulder. Well, that was recreation for the doctors and nurses up there. They paid a good price to have this trip."

Denver Post 11 February 1901:

"MOUNTAIN BOY'S VISIT TO DENVER

"My mother's name is 'Lilly of the Valley' and my stepfather is 'Rattlesnake Bill.' I've got two sisters, a half-brother and a whole one," said Ralph Strope, as he carefully examined the lock on the police matron's room this morning.

Ralph Strope is 14 years old and has no education. He cannot even spell his name. He was never outside of the village of Gold Hill in Boulder County until he was brought to Denver yesterday by Thomas Williams.

Williams is mining at Gold Hill and took pity on Strope and got the boy's mother to consent to him bringing the lad to Denver, where he could go to school. Williams says the boy's father is dead, and that his mother is now Mrs. "Bill" Cowell.

"Mother she [sic] has to wash to help make money," explained Ralph Strope. "Rattlesnake Bill is my stepfather, and he drives a team, but he cannot make enough to keep us, for he spends most of his money for tobacco."

Williams will ask the humane agent to take charge of the boy and place him in some institution where he can go to school."

COX, Elinor Ruth "Elli" (*Emerick*) Patton
>   Birth: 12/14/1938
>   Death: 09/16/2018
>   Cemetery Location: B1

Father: Ralph Dale Emerick; Mother: Mildred Carmen (*Radabaugh*); 1st Husband: Hager Patton; 2nd Husband: James Lee "Jim" Cox; born in Parkersburg (Wood) West Virginia and died in Boulder (Boulder) Colorado at the age of 79 years, 9 months, 2 days-cancer; no tombstone at the time of publication; see COX, James Lee "Jim;" see PATTON, Jennifer Sue; see PATTON, Sharrel "Shari" Lee

Boulder Daily Camera 19 September 2018:

"Elli Cox of Boulder died September 16th at Frasier Meadows in Boulder, Colorado. She was 79 years old. The daughter of Ralph and Mildred Emerick, she was born in 1938 in Parkersburg, West Virginia.

Elli's childhood was spent in Parkersburg and she met her first husband while attending college in West Virginia. That marriage brought the couple to Boulder, Colorado where Elli would spend the rest of her life. Following a divorce, Elli met and married James "Jim" Cox on Big Horn Mountain in Gold Hill in 1967.

The couple lived in Gold Hill for several years and remained a part of the community for the rest of their lives. They were members of the Gold Hill Club.

Her marriage to Jim led to two multi-year overseas assignments through IBM, one in Geneva, Switzerland, the other in Tokyo, Japan. The cultures of these two countries had a great impact on Eli and influenced the rest of her life.

Elli worked in a variety of departments at the University of Colorado as an executive secretary. Her last position was as the Assistant to the Academic Dean of Semester at Sea, which allowed her to travel around the world as part of the program.

While in Japan Elli was on the Board of College Women's Association of Japan, heading up the art program for Japanese children. Soon after returning to Boulder she conducted workshops for companies to give their employees a boost in their understanding of Japanese culture.

Elli studied Ikebana (Japanese flower arrangement) and Sumi-e (Japanese calligraphy), while in Japan, and upon returning to Colorado began a many years long relationship with clay. She participated in Open Studios for several years and is well known for her hand shaped pottery. Elli participated in many shows and has pieces in several local displays. She was an active member of the art community in Boulder for many years from her home at 16th and Cedar—a very close community of creative friends and neighbors.

Survivors include her son, John Andrew Cox of Denver and his girlfriend Kristy Alexander, also her brother Rodney Emerick and his wife Sally Emerick of Parkersburg, West Virginia.

She was preceded in death by her beloved Jim Cox, as well as two daughters, Jenny ad Seri.

A memorial service will be held at Crist Mortuary on Friday September 21, 2018 at 10:00 a.m.

Fond memories and expressions of sympathy may be shared at www.cristmortuary.com for the Cox family."

COX, James Lee "Jim"

Birth: 11/20/1935
Death: 05/03/2001
Cemetery Location: B1

Father: James W. Cox; Mother: Effi Pauline (*Wilson*); 1st Wife: Jodie (*LeMarr*); 2nd Wife: Elinor Ruth "Elli" (*Emerick*); born in Knoxville (Knox) Tennessee and died in Boulder (Boulder) Colorado at age 65 years, 5 months, 13 days-liver failure; James was one of three people who compiled the Gold Hill Cemetery indexes of December 1991 and June 1994; see COX, Elinor "Elli" Ruth (*Emerick*) Patton; PATTON, Jennifer Sue; see PATTON, Sharrel "Shari" Lee

James L. Cox:

"Because life is a state so unpredictable, it should be considered precious time and not taken for granted. We don't know how long we have to accomplish our goals. The challenges are to make the goals spiritually worthwhile and to use every minute of life to strive toward these goals."

Boulder Daily Camera 05 May 2001:

"James L. Cox—James L. Cox of Boulder died Thursday, May 3, 2001, at home. He was 65.

The son of James W. Cox and Effi Pauline Wilson Cox, he was born Nov. 20, 1935, in Knoxville, Tenn. He married Elinor "Elli" Emerick on April 30, 1968, in Gold Hill.

He worked for Union Carbide in Oak Ridge, Tenn., as a programmer and was one of the three non-IBM members of the six-person design team that developed the language specifications for PL/I programming language. He joined IBM in October 1964 and was systems designer for OS/360.

He was manager of the programming center, IBM Hursley Laboratory, in Hursley, England for three years. From 1968 to 1969, he was manager of advanced compiler design in Boulder. In the early 1970s, he was a professor at IBM Systems Research Institute in Geneva, Switzerland. From 1973 to 1981 he was manager and systems architect in Boulder. Between 1981 and 1985 he was with IBM Japan as manager of image product development,

architecture, and systems design products. He returned to Boulder and retired from IBM in April 1987.

Mr. Cox volunteered for the Boulder Genealogy Society and served as its librarian. He was also an active participant in the Marie Rogers Oral History Project at the Carnegie Library. In 1992 he began researching and mapping Gold Hill Cemetery and with Ray Larner and Bob Walter, and published two volumes, "Gold Hill Cemetery Records."

He and his wife were members of the Gold Hill Club.

Survivors include his wife; a son, John Andrew Cox of Denver; two daughters, Patti Cox Shellhaas of Albany, GA., and Cindy Cox Dryer of Ellicott City, MD; a stepdaughter, Jenny Patton of Texas; and six grandchildren.

He was preceded in death by a stepdaughter, Sheri Patton, in 1990.

A memorial service will be at 2 p.m. Monday at Howe Mortuary in the chapel, 2121 11th St., Boulder. His ashes will be interred at the Gold Hill Cemetery in a private family ceremony.

Flowers are welcome, and contributions can be made to Hospice of Boulder County, 2825 Marine St., Boulder, CO 80303."

[Error in the spelling of Cindy Cox Dryer-should be Dyer]

Boulder Genealogical Society Quarterly Vol. 33, No. 3, August 2001:

"James L. Cox of Boulder, Colorado, died 3 May 2001 at home. He was 65.

He was born on 20 November 1935 in Knoxville, Tennessee to James W. Cox and Effi Pauline Wilson.

Digging Up Dirt

He married first Jodie LeMarr. Their two children were Patti Cox Shellhaas and Cindy Cox Dryer. On 30 April 1968, in Gold Hill, Colorado, he married Elinor "Elli" Emerick. Elli brought two children to the marriage, Shari Patton, and Jenny Patton. Shari Patton died in 1990. Jim and Elli had one son, John Andrew Cox.

Jim attended the University of Tennessee, in Knoxville, where his major interests were mathematics and physics. He became distracted from his studies and did not get his Bachelor's degree as planned. Nevertheless, he became a full time employee at Oak Ridge national Laboratory, where he discovered a new interest—digital computers.

Jim made his career as a computer professional. In June 1956 he went to work for Union Carbide at Oak Ridge National Laboratory. While at Oak Ridge he was a member of a six person team which developed the specifications for the PL/I programming language, a major advance in the development of computer tools. He joined IBM at Poughkeepsie, New York in October 1964 and was a systems designer for OS/360. He then spent three years at the IBM Hursley Laboratory in Hursley, England. From 1968-1969 he managed advanced compiler design at the IBM facility in Boulder, Colorado. He returned to Boulder after a two-year project in Geneva, Switzerland. He worked in Japan from 1981-1985 as manager of image product development, architecture, and systems design products. He formally retired from IBM in April 1987, and opened a consulting business, working out of his home in Boulder, Colorado.

While working in Boulder he moved to Gold Hill, Colorado. Jim and Elli became active citizens of Gold Hill, an interest that continued after they moved back to Boulder in 1987. With Ray Larner and Bob Walter he mapped and researched the history of the Gold Hill Cemetery and published the *Gold Hill Cemetery Record*, published as a pamphlet, presently in its 2nd edition.

In retirement he became interested in family history, and spent much time at the Carnegie Branch Library in Boulder, Colorado. He was active in the Marie Rogers Oral History Project at the library.

Jim joined the Boulder Genealogical Society in 1994. He became a BGS volunteer for the genealogical collection at Carnegie in Boulder. In 1999 he was elected Librarian for the Society. As librarian, he purchased and set up the BGS computer; installed the appropriate software; and was well along toward inputting essential data. Because of Jim's many volunteer hours, the collection and the Boulder Genealogical Society were brought up to date with computer access to the collection, oral history information and transcriptions, as well as a growing selection of genealogically oriented CD-ROMs. In addition, Jim was instrumental in coordinating the move from the Gladden Room to another storage facility, as well as organizing the collection on new shelving.

Surviving are his wife; a son, John Andrew Cox of Denver; two daughters, Patti Cox Shellhaas of Albany, Georgia and Cindy Cox Dryer of Ellicott City, Maryland; a stepdaughter, Jenny Patton of Texas; and six grandchildren.

A memorial service was held at the Howe Mortuary Chapel in Boulder, Colorado. His ashes were interred at the Gold Hill Cemetery in a private family ceremony.

Contributions may be sent to the Boulder Genealogical Society, P.O. Box 3246, Boulder, Colorado 80307-3246. The memorial fund will be used to extend the computer resources in the Library.

The family has also specified that memorials may be sent to Hospice of Boulder County, 2825 Marine Street, Boulder, Colorado 80303 and the Marie Rogers Oral history Project at Carnegie Library, 1125 Pine, Boulder, Colorado 80305."

[Error in the spelling of Cindy Cox Dryer-should be Dyer] (The above information is a combination of materi-

al from the Boulder Camera, Boulder, Colorado obituary and direct contact with Elli, Jim's wife, by Earl Beaty)

CRIST, Fredrick Leroy "Fred"

Birth: 11/15/1934
Death: 04/21/2004
Cemetery Location: C5

Father: Muri Leroy Crist; Mother: Opal Arbutis (*Hatfield*); born between Star City and Pulaski (Pulaski) Indiana and died in Star City (Pulaski) Indiana at age 69 years, 5 months, 6 days-lymphoma

Valerie Crist (daughter of Fred Leroy Crist):

"Fredrick Leroy Crist was born on 11/15/34 of Muri Leroy and Opal Arbutis Crist. He was the second of four children, Virginia, Murlene and Jerry. He graduated from Star City High School in 1953 in a class of nine students. Their motto was "Doubt whom you will; but never yourself." This was true of Fred as he sailed through life. He was described in the class poem as "Fred Leroy Crist, with his bright red hair, would do anything just to give you a scare. He was one Mrs. Carpenter loved to tease, and he usually did exactly what he'd please;" also true words as he married and had three children, Rhonda, Eric and Valerie. During this time he explored many avenues of life learning from being an over the road truck driver hauling fruit from the south, including Florida to Indiana. He was a rancher in Wyoming. He later rode bulls in the rodeo as well as broncos. Fred owned several horses throughout his lifetime. He learned to fly a plane and worked with a friend flying oil pipeline in Oklahoma and Texas. He also worked for Ryder Technical Institute, first as an instructor teaching how to drive tractor/trailers and went on to become the operations manager for five locations across the county. Fred also taught people how to build roads with heavy equipment for the Ford Foundation in Saudi Arabia. He worked in other Arab countries and travelled

extensively during this time. Fred moved to the Gold Hill area where he became a doctor of divinity and performed many marriage ceremonies. He helped his daughter, Val, build her log home in Gold Hill. It was a learning process and labor of love. He worked on the installation of DIA airport's baggage system and then returned to live to his home state of Indiana where he then worked until contracting lymphoma. He lived a full life."

CROSS, Rowe

Birth: 03/01/1909
Death: 06/27/1909
Cemetery Location: Unknown

Father: Otto Jay Cross; Mother: Annie Elizabeth (*Woolcock/Wolcott*); born and died in Gold Hill (Boulder) Colorado at age 3 months, 26 days-poisoned by canned milk; twin to Walter Cross; no tombstone; see CROSS, Walter; see **About the Otto Jay Cross Family**

Boulder Daily Camera 28 June 1909:
"Rowe Cross, the little baby of Mr. and Mrs. Otto Cross of Gold Hill, died yesterday."

CROSS, Walter

Birth: 03/01/1909
Death: 05/24/1909
Cemetery Location: Unknown

Father: Otto Jay Cross; Mother: Annie Elizabeth (*Woolcock/Wolcott*); born and died in Gold Hill (Boulder) Colorado at age 3 months, 1 day-poisoned by canned milk; twin to Rowe Cross; no tombstone; see CROSS, Rowe; see **About the Otto Jay Cross Family**

Boulder Daily Camera 25 May 1909:
"One of the three months old twin boys of Mr. and Mrs. O. Cross of Gold Hill died Monday noon and the other child is quite ill. It is thought to have been poisoned by canned milk."

Boulder Daily Herald 27 May 1909:
"The funeral of Walter Cross, the infant son of Mr. and Mrs. O.J. Cross of Gold Hill, took place this afternoon."

About the Otto Jay Cross Family

Otto Jay Cross was born 16 July 1879 in Slayton (Murray) Minnesota; the son of Cyrus Eli and Sibyl Matilda (*Sample*) Cross. He was a brother to Curtis F. Cross; see CROSS, William Herschel.

Annie Elizabeth Woolcock/Wolcott was born 03 May 1883 in White Haven (Cumbria) England; the daughter of John and Elizabeth Jane (*Trembath*) Woolcock/Wolcott; see WOLCOTT, John.

Fred L. Crist

Dad
"Our Beloved Character"
Nov. 15, 1934 - April 21, 2004

Digging Up Dirt

Annie and her family came to the United States about 1887 when Annie was about two years old. Annie had a brother, Rowe, born in Gold Hill (Boulder) Colorado in 1888 and died in Boulder (Boulder) Colorado; buried in Columbia Cemetery Boulder (Boulder) Colorado. Annie's uncles were Edmond/Edmund and John Wolcott (Woolcock); see WOLCOTT, Edmond/Edmund; see WOLCOTT, John.

Otto and Annie were married 19 September 1908 in Boulder (Boulder) Colorado. To this union four known children were born:

Rowe: born 01 March 1909 Gold Hill (Boulder) Colorado and died 27 June 1909 Gold Hill (Boulder) Colorado; buried Gold Hill Cemetery, Gold Hill (Boulder) Colorado; see CROSS, Rowe

Walter: born 01 March 1909 Gold Hill (Boulder) Colorado and died 24 May 1909 Gold Hill (Boulder) Colorado; buried Gold Hill Cemetery, Gold Hill (Boulder) Colorado; see CROSS, Walter

Genevieve Louise: born 02 July 1910 (Boulder) Colorado and died December 1980 Albuquerque (Bernalillo) New Mexico; buried Sandia Memory Gardens, Albuquerque (Bernalillo) New Mexico; married Bernard "Bernie" Ellis Stover

Otto Jay: born 07 March 1912 Wallstreet (Boulder) Colorado and died December 1964 Bartlesville (Washington) Oklahoma; cremated (ashes scattered specifically in the Gold Hill (Boulder) Colorado area); married Catherine Burnett Seymour

In 1912, Otto Cross along with Frank Pickard, J.O. Miller and George W. Brown, took over the Black Cloud mine and mill. A lawsuit occurred in 1913:

Boulder Daily Camera 25 July 1913:

"R. J. Wolcock [sic], who was badly injured in a cave-in in the Black Cloud mine at Summerville on February 23 of this year, today began suit in the district court against J.O. Miller, Frank N. Pickard, Otto J. Cross, and George W. Brown, co-partners in the Black Cloud Mining and Leasing Co. for $10,000 damages in medical fess of $449.57 in addition to the costs of his suit. The complaint alleges negligence of Mr. Cross, superintendent of the mine, in not timbering at the point where the cave-in occurred. The left leg of Mr. Wolcott was broken in several places so that a silver wire had to be used in reducing the fractures. The ligaments of his left ankle were badly torn and he was otherwise bruised. He claims he will be a cripple for life."

Over a year later a judgement was declared:

Boulder Daily Herald 19 June 1914:

"A judgement to the amount of $2,856.95 secured against J.O. Miller in the district court on January 19, 1914, by Rowe J. Wolcock for personal injuries sustained in Miller's mine was paid in the district court this morning. They payment was made by a surety company in which Miller was insured against such suits. A lien against the judgement by Fred G. Folsom who conducted the case for Wolcock was also satisfied."

(Rowe J. Wolcock was the brother of Otto's wife, Annie)

On 27 November 1917 Annie's mother, Elizabeth Jane (*Trembath*) Woolcock/Wolcott (widow) married Benjamin Myrick Williams who was the first person to manufacture wagons and carriages in Boulder and was also at one time president of the Farmers and Andersons Ditch companies and vice-president of the Boulder Milling and Elevator Company. At the time of their marriage he was in his eighties while Elizabeth was in her fifties.

According to family member Jan Hayslett:

"Somewhere I read (and I can't remember where I found the info) that she [Elizabeth] was hired to take care of him [Ben] after his wife died in 1914 and that his relatives were absolutely furious when she married him in 1917. I think I read that they sued her, saying that he was too old and senile to be capable of making such a decision, and that she had taken advantage of an at-risk adult. Kind of the Anna Nichol Smith of Boulder...She must have won the suit because she got the house." (2205 Broadway Boulder, CO which was torn down and the Masonic Lodge was built in 1950 and now is the Museum of Boulder)

Benjamin Myrick Williams died in 1920 and Elizabeth Jane (*Trembath*) Woolcock/Wolcott Williams died 17 November 1937. Both are buried in the Columbia Cemetery, Boulder (Boulder) Colorado in different locations from each other.

In the 1930 census Otto J. and Annie Cross and children were living on Mapleton Avenue in Boulder (Boulder) Colorado where Otto was a traffic man. In the 1940 census Otto Jay was working as a mill operator in Idaho Springs (Clear Creek) Colorado (whereas his wife, Annie, was living in Ward (Boulder) Colorado with her two grown children: Genevieve and Otto Jay Jr.

Apparently Otto (Sr.) went to visit his brothers who were living in Miami (Miami-Dade) Florida and while there he was taken ill. He died on 10 December 1942 and is buried in the Graceland Memorial Park Cemetery at Coral Gables (Miami-Dade) Florida. His widow, Annie, lived about eight years more until she was taken to the Community Hospital in Boulder (Boulder) Colorado where she died on 10 August 1950 from failing health. She was buried in the city's Columbia Cemetery.

Boulder Daily Camera 11 August 1950:

"Mrs. Otto Jay Cross, Long-Time Boulder Resident, Dies

Mrs. Annie E. Cross, widow of Otto Jay Cross, who died in 1942, died at the Community Hospital Thursday night. She had been in failing health for three years and was removed to the hospital, from her home 1913 Spruce, five weeks ago.

Mrs. Cross had been a resident of Boulder County for 64 years, coming to Gold Hill, when she was but three, with her parents John and Elizabeth Jane Woolcock, frequently spelled Wolcott. She was born in White Haven, England, May 2, 1883. She made her home at Gold Hill until her marriage to Mr. Cross when they moved to Nederland, later to the Ben Williams home at Broadway and Pine, which she inherited from her mother, who had married the pioneer of Boulder Nov. 27, 1917 following the death of her husband, Mr. Woolcock. The home was sold by Mrs. Cross to the Boulder Masonic Building Association which erected a handsome Temple on the site.

[Newspaper error: birth date is 03 May 1883]

Surviving are two children, Mrs. B.V. Stover of Albuquerque, N.M., who has been with her mother since the latter became seriously ill, and a son, O.J. Cross, who is with an oil company in British Columbia. Funeral arrangements in charge of Howe Mortuary."

Boulder Daily Camera 12 August 1950:

"Mrs. Annie E. Cross, widow of Otto J. Cross—Funeral services to be held Monday at 3:30 at Howe mortuary. Rev. H.M. Walters, rector of St. John's Episcopal church, will officiate."

Boulder Daily Camera 14 August 1950:

"Mrs. Annie E. Cross—Funeral services at 3:30 this afternoon at Howe mortuary—Fred Marriott Jr. was the soloist, accompanied by F. J. Bartlett. Rev. H.M. Walters, rector of St. John's Episcopal church [sic], officiated. Pallbearers were Charles Mitchell, Fred Mitchell, Christy Plank Sr., Leroy Holubar, M.D. Bradfield. Interment was beside her husband, J.J. Cross, Columbia cemetery." [Newspaper error as J.J. Cross was buried in the Graceland Memorial Park Cemetery at Coral Gables (Miami-Dade) Florida]

CROSS, William Herschel

> Birth: 10/11/1905
> Death: 03/24/1906
> Cemetery Location: D5

Father: Curtis Frazer Cross; Mother: Bessie Florence (*Gilmore*); born and died Gold Hill (Boulder) Colorado at age 5 months, 13 days-convulsions; see **About the Curtis Frazer Cross Family**

About the Curtis Frazer Cross Family

Curtis Frazer Cross was born 06 January 1872 in Slayton (Murray) Minnesota; the son of Cyrus Eli and Sibyl Matilda (*Sample*) Cross. He was a brother to Otto Jay Cross; see **About the Otto Jay Cross Family.**

On 01 January 1903 in Onawa (Monona) Iowa he married Bessie Florence Gilmore. She was born April 1880 Little Sioux (Harrison) Iowa; the daughter of Charles Monroe and Isabelle (*Griffith*) Gilmore. This union produced three known children:

William Herschel: born 11 October 1905 Gold Hill (Boulder) Colorado and died 24 March 1906 Gold Hill (Boulder) Colorado; buried Gold Hill Cemetery, Gold Hill (Boulder) Colorado; see CROSS, William Herschel

Clarence Vern: born 28 November 1903 Mondamin (Harrison) Iowa and died May 1976 Ironton (Crow Wing) Minnesota; burial unknown; married Faye Smothers

Isabel Jane (adopted daughter): born 18 February 1918 Denver (Denver) Colorado and died 26 September 1982 Houston (Harris) Texas; cremation; married Charles Bleiler

By 1910 they were living in Boulder (Boulder) Colorado with his occupation being a miner. By 1918 Curtis was an oil driller, living with his family in Thermopolis (Hot Springs) Wyoming.

Interesting to note that on Curtis' 1918 registration card for WW1 noted "first finger on right hand gone."

In 1925 Curtis with his family lived in Mondamin (Harrison) Iowa.

By 1930 they were living in Logan (Harrison) Iowa where Curtis was the County Sheriff at the age of 58.

Bessie died on 27 March 1940 and is buried in the Little Sioux Cemetery in Harrison (Harrison) Iowa. Curtis then was living with his niece in Jefferson (Harrison) Iowa where he was a salesman. He died 12 May 1951 and is buried also in the Little Sioux Cemetery.

Digging Up Dirt

Logan Herald Observer 17 May 1951:

"C.F. Cross, Former Sheriff Dies Suddenly Saturday...

Curtis Frazer Cross, of Logan, Harrison county sheriff from 1927 until 1939 collapsed and died Saturday evening while assisting in dynamiting a ditch to release flood waters near Blencoe, Iowa.

Mr. Cross had been wading in deep mud on the John Walker farm. Monona County Coroner E.E. Jingles said Mr. Cross, shortly before collapsing, declared: "I've had about all of this I want for today."

Death was due to a heart attack, apparently brought on by over-exertion.

Mr. Cross was born January 6, 1872 at Slayton, Minn. He was the son of Cyrus E. and Sible Cross.

At the time of his death his age was 79 years, four months and six days.

In early life he attended school in Minnesota and Pennsylvania.

From 1896 to 1897 he was employed in blacksmith shops in Cambry, Wyo. From 1898 to 1912 he engaged in mining in Wyoming and Colorado. Mr. Cross was a contractor in Wyoming oil fields from 1912 to 1920. From 1920 to 1926 he was engaged in the walnut log and trucking business in western Iowa. By his friends he was known as "Curt."

Mr. Cross was a former resident of Mondamin, Iowa.

A Democrat, Mr. Cross was elected Harrison county sheriff in 1926, defeating the late Walter Milliman, the incumbent, who was a Republican. Mr. Cross served as sheriff for 12 years until January 1, 1939. He was defeated for re-election in 1938 by Cass A. Bullis, Republican.

As sheriff, Mr. Cross became widely known among law enforcement officers in western Iowa and over the state.

After leaving the sheriff's office, he was engaged as a salesman for the Stark Nurseries for a number of years. He also did carpentry work and blasting at various periods of time.

Mr. Cross was a member of I.O.O.F. lodges No. 355 of Logan and was very active in the works of that order for a number of years. He was also a member of the Rebekahs, A.F. & A.M. No. 544, and of the Scottish Rite.

Surviving are his wife, Mary, of Logan; son, Clarence, of Aitkin, Minn.; daughter, Isabel Cross of Carcas [Caracas], Venezuela; brother, Walter of Mann, Florida; sister, Mrs. Lottie Morrow of Mondamin; two half-brothers, Anthony Cross of Mondamin, and Leo of Kansas City, Mo.; and three half-sisters, Mrs. Tillie Remington of Penelope, Colo., Mrs. Irene Chambers of Junction City, Oregon; and Mrs. Victor Norris of Mondamin.

The body is at the Bolton-Cranston Funeral home in Logan.

Services were held in the Bolton Cranston Funeral home at 2 p.m. Wednesday with Bishop W.R. Adams of the R.L.D.S. church officiating. Interment will be in the Little Sioux cemetery. Pallbearers: J.C. Hammitt, Ansel Thomas, Ralph Hartsock, Stanley Sprinkle, Everett Logan and R.M. Morgan. Masonic services were conducted in the funeral home of Acmode lodge of Modale."

Logan Herald Observer 04 April 1940:

"MRS. C.F. CROSS...

Mrs. Bessie Cross departed this life at her home in Logan Wednesday night, March 27, 1940. She had been in poor health for more than a year, following a serious operation. Her condition had been critical all of this time, but her immediate family helped to keep up her good spirits by the hope that better health was just ahead. She took to her bed only six days previous to her passing, and all of the attention, kindness and devotion of her family and friends helped to keep her comfortable to the end.

Bessie Florence Cross was born April 23, 1880, on a farm south of Little Sioux. She was the second oldest child of Charles and Isabell Gilmore. She had three brothers and one sister. Her oldest brother Lester preceded her in death by a number of years. Her third brother Max resides in Omaha and her sister Lottie in Mondamin with the aged mother.

On January 1, 1903, she was united in marriage to Curt Cross who lived in Wyoming at that time. There she made her home for many years. There were three children, two boys and one girl, Clarence Cross, now living in Davenport, Hershel, who died in infancy, and Isabel of Ames.

She united with the Christian church in Boulder, Colo., many years ago. Her life was a busy one, but she always was kind and considerate to others, and did not give up to her own feelings even when her suffering was greatest.

Funeral services in charge of the Bolton Funeral Home, Logan, were held at the Christian church, Mondamin, Saturday afternoon at 2 o'clock conducted by Rev. E.O. Sweany of the Logan Christian church. Two favorite songs "Sweet Rose of Sharon" and "The Old Rugged Cross" were sung by Mrs. Mitchell Graham, accompanied by Frances Duty Yager of Missouri Valley. Pallbearers were A.J. Griffith, Jake Griffith, Marion Griffith, Leo Cross, Roy Durell and W.T. Morrow. Burial was in Little Sioux cemetery."

D

D'AMBROSIO, Jeannette Therese (*Nussbaum*)

> Birth: 01/23/1943
> Death: 07/12/2017
> Cemetery Location: I3

Father: John Joseph Nussbaum; Mother: Rose Ann (*Donohue*); born in Manhattan (New York) New York and died in Longmont (Boulder) Colorado at the age of 74 years, 5 months, 19 days; spouse might have been Matthew D'Ambrosio; no obituary published

DEWING, Edward Eugene

> Birth: 09/25/1932
> Death: 04/10/1967
> Cemetery Location: E2

Father: John Harry Dewing; Mother: Lillian Margaret (*Gould*); Wife: Ruth (*maiden name unknown*); born in Missoula (Missoula) Montana and died in Boulder (Boulder) Colorado at age 34 years, 6 months, 16 days-head injury; SSgt USMC-Korean War; Montana Birth Index states Anaconda (Deer Lodge) Montana as place of birth

Boulder Daily Camera 10 April 1967:

"CU Student Dies After Fall On Road

A University graduate student died today of a head injury he received when he fell from an automobile Saturday night. The victim was Edward Eugene Dewing, 34, of Gold Hill, mountain community west of Boulder.

The accident happened just before midnight near the Gold Hill residence where Dewing lived with his wife and their ten-year-old son. He died at 7:25 a.m. today at Community Hospital.

Dewing left the Gold Hill Inn with an unidentified friend to walk to his home about a block away, according to Frank Finn, proprietor of the tavern. In front of the Inn, Dewing jumped onto the hood of a passing car, apparently intending to ride the short distance to his home.

Dewing fell to the ground and struck his head. He was taken back into the tavern and, believed not to be seriously injured, was taken home. Dewing began showing effects of the injury later, and Edward Howard, of Boulder, took him to Community Hospital, arriving at 2 a.m. Sunday.

Dewing underwent head surgery.

Finn did not know the name of the driver of the car on which Dewing jumped, but said the driver was a friend or acquaintance of Dewing.

The State Patrol had no information this morning about the accident. If investigation confirms the reports that Dewing's death was a traffic fatality, it would be the fourth in Boulder County this year, compared with eight a year ago.

Edward Dewing was born Sept. 25, 1932, at Missoula, Mont. He was a Marine, having served in Korea. Mr. Dewing was a graduate of the University of Pittsburg, where he won Phi Beta Kappa scholastic honors in the social science field.

He was working at CU on a graduate degree in anthropology. He was employed at the University library on a research project, the Colorado Academic Library's Book Processing Center.

Mr. Dewing is survived by his wife Ruth; their son, Michael; his mother, Mrs. Lillian Dewing of Tucson, Ariz; one sister, Alice McDonald, and a brother, Bill Dewing.

The Geddes-Hibbard Mortuary is in charge of funeral arrangements, which will be announced Tuesday."

Boulder Daily Camera 11 April 1967:
"Edward E. Dewing—Graveside services will be held in the Gold Hill Cemetery Wednesday at 11:30 a.m., with

Rev. Donald L. Snavely of Nederland officiating. The Geddes-Hibbard Mortuary is in charge."

Boulder Daily Camera 12 April 1967:

"Graveside services were at 11:30 this morning in the Gold Hill Cemetery, with Rev. Donald Snavely officiating. The Geddes-Hibbard Mortuary was in charge."

DUDLEY, Infant

Birth: Unknown
Death: 02/03/1898
Cemetery Location: Unknown

Father: Joseph Lobb Dudley; Mother: Rosena/Rosina (*Barnett*) Edwards; born and died in Gold Hill (Boulder) Colorado-cause of death unknown; no tombstone; see **About the Joseph Lobb Dudley Family**

Boulder Daily Camera 03 February 1898:

"The death of the infant child of Joseph Dudley occurred this morning at Gold Hill. Mr. Trezise will conduct the funeral tomorrow at that place."

DUDLEY, Infant

Birth: 01/1899
Death: 04/20/1899
Cemetery Location: Unknown

Father: Joseph Lobb Dudley; Mother: Rosena/Rosina (*Barnett*) Edwards; born and died in Gold Hill (Boulder) Colorado at age 3 months (approximately)-cause of death unknown; no tombstone; see **About the Joseph Lobb Dudley Family**

Boulder Daily Camera 21 April 1899:

"Mr. Trezise this morning sent a casket to Gold Hill for the remains of the three month old child of Mr. and Mrs. J.L. Dudley whose death occurred there last night."

Boulder County Herald Weekly 26 April 1899:

"The three month old boy of Joseph L. Dudley of Gold Hill died Thursday. Trezise sent up a coffin Friday morning. The funeral took place that afternoon."

About the Joseph Lobb Dudley Family

Joseph Lobb Dudley was born in 1861 (some sources states 1862) in Ludgvan (Cornwall) England; the son of Francis and Jane (*Lobb*) Dudley. He immigrated to the United States (a passenger on the ship "Germanic"), arriving in New York on 02 April 1887.

About 1893 he married Rosena (*Barnett*) Edwards, born 13 October 1867 Michigan; the daughter of William and Mary Ann (*Williams*) Barnett. Rosena's first husband, William Edwards (whom she married on 02 January 1886 in Gold Hill (Boulder) Colorado) died in 1891

from pneumonia and is buried in the Gold Hill Cemetery; see EDWARDS, William "Billy."

When Rosena married Joseph she brought to this union a daughter:

Mary "Mamie/Mayme" Edwards: born 03 November 1888 Caribou (Boulder) Colorado and died 06 September 1985 Boulder (Boulder) Colorado; buried Columbia Cemetery, Boulder (Boulder) Colorado; married James Lyons McLellan; see EDWARDS, William "Billy"

Joseph and Rosena were blessed with children of their own:

William Harvey: born 05 January 1894 Aspen (Pitkin) Colorado and died 20 September 1972 (Marion) Oregon; buried Highland Cemetery, Casper (Natrona) Wyoming; married Susan Bradley

Infant: died 03 February 1898 Gold Hill (Boulder) Colorado; buried Gold Hill Cemetery, Gold Hill (Boulder) Colorado; see DUDLEY, Infant

Infant: died 20 April 1899 Gold Hill (Boulder) Colorado; buried Gold Hill Cemetery, Gold Hill (Boulder) Colorado; see DUDLEY, Infant

Three more infants: according to Mary Ellen "Mamie" (Edwards) McLellan; all died from spinal meningitis—no further information

Ruby Maxine: born 14 January 1896 Gold Hill (Boulder) Colorado and died 10 November 1989 Casper (Natrona) Wyoming; buried Highland Cemetery, Casper (Natrona) Wyoming; married John Wesley Carlisle

The family moved to Boulder (Boulder) Colorado by 1918 and then to Nederland (Boulder) Colorado by 1920 where Joseph was a miner. In 1923 they were living in Denver (Denver) Colorado where Joseph was a janitor. In 1930 the family lived in Casper (Natrona) Wyoming where Joseph died on 10 October 1933. His body was brought to Boulder (Boulder) Colorado and buried in the Columbia Cemetery there. Rosena continued to live with her daughter, Ruby, in Casper (Natrona) Wyoming where she, too, died there on 31 May 1942. Her body was brought to Boulder (Boulder) Colorado and is buried beside her husband in the Columbia Cemetery.

Interview with Mary Ellen "Mamie" (*Edwards*) McLellan (Courtesy of Anne McLellan and Carol (*McLellan*) McConica):

"This here William McCloud or McAlister, he wanted to marry Mama. He was a fella that was boarding at Grandma's. And I think Mama [Rosena] didn't want to get married to him like that. He told her lets run off and your mother can take care of the two children. So she married Joe Dudley. He was seven years older than Mama. Never been married and owned nineteen debts when he married. And Mama didn't like that when she found it out. She didn't know that he'd done that, so every month some money had to be taken out to pay off the debts.

[Then Ruby was their first child?]

No, Willy. Willy and then they had five after that and they died right away, spinal meningitis. They wouldn't live to be very old and the doctors didn't know what they was doing back then. Mama had eight [children]. They're ahead of us now; with the Lord's help. They all died in Gold Hill. Willie was born in Aspen. Ruby was born in Gold Hill."

(However the count of eight children born to Rosina doesn't add up: Earl, Mary Ellen, Pearl, William Harvey, two infants buried in Gold Hill Cemetery, three more infants and Ruby Maxine equal ten children—in the 1900 census Rosina claims she had only three children with three children living: Mary Ellen "Mamie," William and Ruby.)

Boulder Daily Camera 10 October 1933:

"Joseph Dudley Old-Time Miner Dies At Casper... Joseph Dudley, miner in Boulder county [sic] for many years, died in Casper, Wyo., during the night and his body is to be brought to Boulder for burial.

The message was received by Mrs. Mary J. Harris of 21st and Marine. Her husband, the late W. Z. Harris, was a cousin of Mr. Dudley [sic].

Mrs. Dudley was formerly Rose Barnett. She and two daughters and a son survive."

Boulder Daily Camera 13 October 1933:

"Funeral Services for Joseph L. Dudley, who died at Casper Oct., 10, were held from the Howe mortuary this afternoon. Rev. C.O. Beckman officiated. Mrs. Adam Weber and Wendell Solem sang.

Pallbearers were Ed Payne, Frank Marshall, Tom Keeley, Ed Demmon, Oscar Walton and Alex McLellan. Interment was in Columbia cemetery."

Boulder Daily Camera 01 June 1942:

"Mrs. Jos. Dudley, Pioneer, Dies, Funeral Here... Mrs. Rosena Dudley-widow of Jos. Dudley, died Sunday at Casper, Wyo., and her body is being brought to Boulder for interment [sic] in the family lot in Columbia cemetery.

Mrs. Dudley was the daughter of Mr. and Mrs. William Barnett, pioneers of Gold Hill, and was brought there as a very young child. She was born Oct. 13, 1867, but the information as to place of birth was not available today.

She lived at times at Caribou, Nederland and Gold Hill. She was married twice—her first husband being the late Billy Edwards. She married Mr. Dudley some 37 years ago.

The Dudleys moved to Casper to be near their children, Mrs. Wesley Carlisle and Wm. Dudley. Mr. Dudley died there about eight years ago. Besides the two another daughter, Mrs. Mamie McLellan, of 1430 Pine, Boulder, survives. There are also 11 grandchildren and four great-grandchildren.

Funeral services will be at the Howe mortuary at 4 o'clock Tuesday afternoon. Rev. C.S. Linkletter, pastor of the First Christian church, will officiate. Interment will be in the family lot in Columbia cemetery. Mrs. Dudley was a cousin of Mrs. Mary Harris, 2102 Marine and frequently visited at their home."

Boulder Daily Camera 02 June 1942:

"Mrs. Rosina Dudley—Services were held from the Howe mortuary this afternoon at 4. Rev. C.S. Linkletter, pastor of the Christian church, officiated. Miss Alliene Hardy sang. Interment was in Columbia cemetery. Pallbearers were Ed Demon, Alex McLellan, Wm. Mator, John Pughe, Albert Walter and Ralph Tiles. Mrs. Dudley died at Casper, Wyo., May 31, and the body arrived this morning."

E

ECKLUND/EKLUND, Erik/Eric

Birth: 12/19/1858
Death: 12/27/1902
Cemetery Location: Removed

Father: Johan Jakobsson Peth; Mother: Kajsa Greta Johansdotter (*Jakobs*); Wife: Ida Sophia (*Peterson*); born in Hirvlax, (Lansi-Suomen Laani-now Western Finland Province) Munsala Finland and died in Gold Hill (Boulder) Colorado at age 44 years (approximately)-lingering illness; other sources state Sweden as birth place; brother to Johan Jakob "John" Ecklund/Eklund; body removed to Green Mountain Cemetery, Boulder (Boulder) Colorado; see ECKLUND/EKLUND, Johan Jakob "John"

Boulder Daily Camera 27 December 1902:
"Eric Ecklund, a prominent Gold Hill miner, is dead."

Boulder County Miner 03 January 1903:
"Mr. E. Eukland [sic], one of the best known engineers and miners in the county, died at his home in Gold Hill on Saturday last, after a lingering illness of several months duration. For over two years previous to his last fatal illness, Mr. Eukland had been employed as head engineer at the Lucky Star mine and for a period of several months occupied the position of foreman. He has been a citizen of this county for more than 20 years and was noted for his honesty and integrity of character. Besides a brother and two sisters living in this state, he leaves a wife and four children, fortunately well provided for. Mr. Eukland will be missed in this community in which he has so long lived as one of its best and most honored citizens. The funeral was one of the largest ever held in Gold Hill, all of the principal mines closing down for the day, in honor of Mr. Eukland. The Rev. of Jamestown conducted services at the residence, after which the Odd Fellows order took charge of the funeral. He was about 44 years of age and up to the time of the last illness was an active, sober and industrious worker."

About Erik/Eric Ecklund/Eklund

Erik/Eric Eklund was born 19 December 1858 in Hirvlax (Lansi-Suomen Laani-now Western Finland Province) Munsala Finland however other sources state Sweden; the son of Johan Jakobsson and Kajsa Greta Johansdotter (*Jakobs*) Pet and brother to Johan Jakob "John" Ecklund/Eklund; see ECKLUND/EKLUND, Johan Jakob "John."

According to family member, Bendt Granefelt from Sweden he noted that "Pet is the name of the farm in Finland, and they seemed to use the farm name in their full name as a middle name. Pet farm is located among other similar farms (like "neighbor farms"). All farms together will be a small village and the place is called Hirvlax. Jakobs is probably a "farm name" and used as a middle name. Hirvlax belongs to Munsala parish."

He immigrated to the United States where arrival date is recorded as 09 June 1887 from Russia and was naturalized on 2 October 1894 with witnesses T.J. Johnson and Joseph Luxon.

Eric married Ida Sophia Peterson on 09 October 1892 at the Ryssby Church in Longmont (Boulder) Colorado. Ida was born 12 January 1873 Vislanda (Kronoberg) Sweden; the daughter of (August?) Peter and Anna Sara (*Karlsdotter/Peterson*) Magnusson. Their union produced five known children:

Esther G.: born 24 June 1893 Gold Hill (Boulder) Colorado and died 02 January 1965 Englewood (Arapahoe) Colorado; buried Green Mountain Cemetery, Boulder (Boulder) Colorado; married Mark Loser; some records state place of birth for Esther as Vislanda (Kronoberg) Sweden

Anna Jean: born 28 September 1895 Gold Hill (Boulder) Colorado and died 27 July 1984 Arlington (Arlington) Virginia; cremated; married Burton Owen Young; some records state place of birth for Anna as Vislanda (Kronoberg) Sweden

"Lilly" Edith Elvira: born 06 November 1898 Vislanda (Kronoberg) Sweden and died 09 December 1989 Littleton (Arapahoe) Colorado; burial unknown; married Earl George Loser

Olga Ruth Louise: born 27 August 1900 Gold Hill (Boulder) Colorado and died December 1977 Manitou Springs (El Paso) Colorado; buried Crystal Valley Cemetery, Manitou Springs (El Paso) Colorado; married Lyle Lee Rutherford

Carl Erik Wilmer: born 03 March 1903 Gold Hill (Boulder) Colorado and died 18 December 1940 San Angelo (Tom Green) Texas; buried Green Mountain Cemetery, Boulder (Boulder) Colorado; married Estelle (maiden name unknown)

Erik "Eric" Ecklund/Eklund died on 03 January 1903 in Gold Hill (Boulder) Colorado. First buried in the Gold Hill Cemetery, Gold Hill (Boulder) Colorado, his body was removed in December of 1905 and reburied in the Green Mountain Cemetery, Boulder (Boulder) Colorado.

File 480 EKLUND, ERIK Estate
"Fred White app't gdn 15 Dec 1903 of Karl Erik Wilmer Eklund born 3 Mar 1903. Gdn ad litum: Elbert B. Greenman. Mother: Ida Eklund. 1/10th int in father's estate. Karl, one of five ch of Erik, lived with Ida. Because she had other minor ch to support, she needed financial aid. Abt $300 in Gold Hill mining claims, notes, accts."

His widow (Ida) lived about 54 years longer until her death on 26 February 1956. She is buried beside her husband, Erik, their son Carl and Erik's brother, Johan "John."

Boulder Daily Camera 27 February 1956:

"Ida S. Eklund...
A resident of Boulder County since 1889, Ida S. Eklund, died at the home of a daughter, Mrs. Esther (Mark) Loser, 3839 East Seventh Ave. in Denver, Sunday morning. Her death was sudden.

Born in Sweden to August and Sarah Peterson, she came to Boulder County with them and was married at the historic Ryssby church, northeast of Boulder, to Eric Eklund, who was killed in a mine accident at Gold Hill in 1902.

She and her children resided at 618 University Avenue for many years. Mrs. Eklund was active in the First Lutheran church of Boulder until moving to Denver in 1951.

Besides the daughter, Mrs. Esther Loser, she is survived by three other daughters, Mrs. Edith (Earl) Loser, Mrs. Olga Ruth (Lysle [sic] Lee) Rutherford and Mrs. Anna Jean (Burton O.) Young. A son, Carl E. Eklund, died in San Angelo, Texas, in December 1940.

Two brothers of Mrs. Eklund and a sister reside in Sweden and one sister, Mrs. Gerda Johnson, in Altadena, Calif. There are four grandchildren, two great-grandchildren.

Funeral services are to be held at 11 Wednesday at the Howe Mortuary with Rev. Arnold Ostlund, pastor of the Mount Calvary Church, formerly the First Lutheran, officiating. Interment will be held in Green Mountain."

According to family member Bendt Granefelt:
"I think the newspaper or someone else has mixed up the names in the obituary. In the Swedish church records it clearly says that Ida' father is called Peter Magnusson. I also checked the records of birth and there he is listed as Peter.

In the obituary it says Sara Peterson. Sara is correct. Her full name was Anna Sara, but she might have been just called Sara by Ida's family. But they mixed up Anna Sara's last name. But I can understand the sea-
son why. Ida S. last name was Peterson when she immigrated to US. In Sweden (before circa 1900) used to have patronymic. That means that a son took over his father first name like "son of." Example: father name is Peter, then his son's last name will be Petersson, same with daughters—Petersdotter. But in the end of 1800s the girls seem to drop –dotter and starts using –son, just same as their brothers are called. So in the obituary Sara is listed with the same last name as her daughter Ida was called before marriage to Erik Eklund. From circa 1900 the family name, last name, was kept and not changed anymore. If it was Petersson, a son and his son etc., will have the Peterson as their last name; same with the girls but their last name often changes to their husband's last name when they marry."

ECKLUND/EKLUND, Johan Jakob "John"
Birth: 06/08/1846
Death: 01/16/1896
Cemetery Location: Removed

Father: Johan Jakobsson Peth; Mother: Kajsa Greta Johansdotter (*Jakobs*); Wife: Maria Lovisa (*Martensdotter*); born in Hirvlax (Lansi-Suomen Laani-now Western Finland Province) Munsala Finland and died in Calumet (Huerfano) Colorado at age 52 years (approximately)-cause of death unknown; other sources state Sweden as birth place; brother to Erik/Eric Ecklund/Eklund; body removed to Green Mountain Cemetery, Boulder (Boulder) Colorado; wrong death date (19 January 1896) on tombstone; see ECKLUND/EKLUND, Erik/Eric

About Johan Jakob "John" Ecklund/Eklund
Johan Jakob "John" Ecklund/Eklund was born 08 June 1846; the son of Johan Jakobsson and Kajsa Greta Johansdotter (*Jakobs*) Peth/Pet in Hirvlax (Lansi-Suomen Laani-now Western Finland Province) Munsala Finland-other sources state Sweden. He was the brother to Erik/Eric Ecklund/Eklund; see ECKLUND/EKLUND, Erik/Eric.

Johan, a carpenter by trade, married Maria Lovisa Martensdotter on 28 August 1875. She was born in Finland on 23 August 1855 and died on 12 December 1897 in Hirvlax Munsala Finland. To their union four known children were born:

Johan Bernhard: born 08 April 1877 St. Petersburg, Russia and died 25 July 1897 Pet Hirvlax, Munsala Finland

Maria Emilia: born 17 December 1879 St. Petersburg, Russia-death unknown; married Estonia (last name unknown)

Erik Alexander: born 23 September 1882 Sardavala, Russia and died 14 November 1900 Jakobstad (Ostrobothnia) Finland

Edla Johanna: born 09 April 1887 Sardavala, Russia; married N.N. Bogonoff

Johan immigrated to the United States leaving his wife and family in Sweden. He met up with his brother, Erik, in Gold Hill (Boulder) Colorado. He then traveled to Calumet (Huerfano) Colorado (now a ghost town) where he died 16 January 1896 of tuberculosis. In the Munsala Parish records there is a notation "does not write to wife." Apparently they lived separate but not divorced.

His body was transported to Boulder (Boulder) Colorado and then buried in the Gold Hill Cemetery, Gold Hill (Boulder) Colorado in an unknown grave.

After the death of Erik/Eric (John's brother) apparently it was decided in December of 1905 to remove both bodies (John and Erik) from the Gold Hill Cemetery and to rebury them in Green Mountain Cemetery, Boulder (Boulder) Colorado.

When Erik's wife, Ida Sophia (*Peterson*) Eklund died on 26 February 1956 she was buried also in the Green Mountain Cemetery (Location D114) beside her husband, their son Carl and Eric's brother, Johan Jakob "John."

Early Days In Gold Hill by George Cowell (courtesy of Carnegie Library For Local History):

"Used to be a guy at the end of town (Gold Hill) named Eckley, lives in this house over here. He was a Norwegian. He had a little black horse with just a harness and lines on it, real long lines, and that horse would pull him all over town on a pair of skis. He was an expert skier."

(This could be in reference to either Eric or John.)

EDWARDS, Mary Josephine "Jessie"

Birth: 03/30/1891
Death: 04/06/1897
Cemetery Location: E3

Father: Morgan Edwards; Mother: Martha "Mattie" Ellen "Ella" (*Wilson*); born and died in Gold Hill (Boulder) Colorado at age 6 years, 7 days-cause of death unknown; see **About the Morgan Edwards Family**; see PUGHE, Eleanor/Elinor "Ellen" (*Edwards*); see EDWARDS, William "Billy"

About the Morgan Edwards Family
Morgan Edwards was born in Wales 08 September 1863; the son of Stephen and Mary Ellen (*Morgan*) Pugh Edwards. He immigrated to the United States in 1883 and naturalized in 1888.

On 10 March of 1888 he married Martha "Mattie" Ellen "Ella" Wilson. Martha was born 15 September 1868 at Coal Creek Ranch (Boulder) Colorado (Coal Creek Ranch was located between Boulder, Longmont and Superior, Colorado); the daughter of Langford Robert and Hannah

Josephine (*Dwyer*) Wilson. To this union three known children were born:

George Lankford: born 09 November 1888 Gold Hill (Boulder) Colorado and died 16 August 1953 Colorado; buried Fairmount Cemetery, Denver (Denver) Colorado; married Ada/Ida M. Jones

Mary Josephine "Jessie": born 30 March 1891 Gold Hill (Boulder) Colorado and died 06 April 1897 Gold Hill (Boulder) Colorado; buried Gold Hill Cemetery, Gold Hill (Boulder) Colorado; see EDWARDS, Mary Josephine "Jessie"

Wilbur Charles: born 22 June 1895 Gold Hill (Boulder) Colorado –died 17 March 1922 Boulder (Boulder) Colorado; buried Green Mountain Cemetery, Boul-

"MARY JOSEPHINE
DAU OF M. & M.E. EDWARDS
MAR 30, 1891-APR 6, 1897"

Lower inscription hard to read but might be:
"Beautiful lovely Jessie was given
__?__ bud to earth to bloom in heaven
Forever."

der (Boulder) Colorado; married Mildred Emma Mc-Naught/McNaughton

Morgan and Martha divorced in 1900. On 12 January 1903 Martha married Claus J. Peterson who was born 1870 in Sweden. This union produced two known sons:

Robert Nelson/Neils.: born 12 March 1904 (Boulder) Colorado and died February 1985 Wheatridge (Jefferson) Colorado; buried Fairmount Cemetery, Denver (Denver) Colorado; married Hilda S. Jessen

Louis Radar: born 12 April 1908 (Boulder) Colorado and died 05 October 1955 Los Angeles (Los Angeles) California; buried Anaheim Cemetery, Anaheim (Orange) California; married Edna (maiden name believed to be McGauren)

Martha died at the age of 79 and was buried on 04 February 1948 in the Fairmount Cemetery, Denver (Denver) Colorado. Claus died in 1946 in Denver (Arapahoe) Colorado and is buried beside his wife.

Morgan was a brother to Eleanor (*Edwards*) Pughe and William "Billy" Edwards; see PUGHE, Eleanor/Elinor "Ellen" (*Edwards*); see EDWARDS, Mary Josephine "Jessie;" see EDWARDS, William "Billy."

By 1936 Morgan Edwards was living in the County Home in Boulder (Boulder) Colorado. He died from an automobile accident on 21 December 1937 in Boulder (Boulder) Colorado and is buried in the city's Columbia Cemetery.

Boulder Daily Camera 22 December 1937:

"Boulder Man is Fatally Hurt By Hit-And-Run Car... Morgan Edwards, 74, Is Victim; Officers Have Door Handle As Clew [sic]

Authorities worked with a single clew [sic] today to find the hit-and-run driver who killed Morgan Edwards, 74, pioneer resident of Boulder County, on the North 12th highway just north of the city limits Tuesday night.

Sheriff's officers this morning found an automobile which for a moment they believed was the car they are seeking—a 1937 Plymouth with a right door handle broken off—but it proved to be the wrong machine, as did several other auto of different makes found with broken handles.

'HOT' CLEW [sic] TRACED...Sheriff's officers this afternoon started tracing a clew [sic], which they said "looks hot," to the identity of the hit-and-run driver. Details were not divulged pending further investigation.

Sheriff George Richart and Coroner George Howe said they believed Edward's death was the first hit-and-run fatality in Boulder County. It raised the county's traffic toll for this year to 17.

Walking At Top Of Hill...He died at the county hospital at 8:10 p.m., about a half hour after he was struck while walking along the road just at the top of Maxwell hill, a few yards north of the chamber of commerce sign suspended above the North 12th highway.

He suffered a deep gash in the back of his head which fractured the skull and injured the brain. His right leg was broken.

Was At Side Of Road...Deputy Sheriff Arthur Everson, who made the original investigation, said the man was walking north on the west side of the road-the side on which pedestrians are supposed to walk-and probably was off the oil-paved section when he was struck by the automobile travelling south into Boulder.

About fifty yards south of the point where Edward's body lay, Everson found the man's hat, teeth, and a door handle which had broken off the car by the impact.

Mr. and Mrs. Bruce Cole, of Lee Hill, were driving north and had just passed the point of impact when they heard the "thud." If the Coles had been about 15 seconds later, they doubtless could have obtained the license number of the hit-and-run machine and probably some description of its occupants.

Car Sped Out Of Sight...As it was, the death car sped out of sight before Cole could stop and look back. The accident occurred almost directly in front of the home of J.K. Edmondson, who notified the sheriff's office and called an ambulance.

Richard Everson and State Highway Patrolmen William Robinson and Roy Calhoun quickly made an investigation which disclosed that the door handle found at the scene came from a 1937 Plymouth automobile. An alarm was sent immediately to Denver police and broadcast throughout the state.

The first of several clews [sic] which proved ineffective came a few hours after the accident when a Boulder garage, which already had been contacted, reported a car had been brought in with a broken door handle and headlight. It was discovered, however, that the handle found at the accident scene did not match those of the car in the garage.

Strange Coincidence Found...This morning Deputy Sheriff Everson noticed on a downtown street a 1937 Plymouth sedan with the handle of the right front door broken off—and he felt certain he had found the hit-and-run driver. The woman who owned this car, however, had the broken handle in her possession. It was knocked off when she struck a piece of county road equipment in Boulder canon [sic] about ten days ago.

Edwards was born in Wales on Sept. 8, 1863, came to the United States in 1883 and was naturalized in Boulder in 1885. When he came to Boulder he was employed by his half-brother, John Pughe, now of 1324 Pine street, who was a pioneer gold mine operator.

Mr. and Mrs. Edwards were divorced in 1900. He is survived by a son, George Edwards, of Denver, and by a sister, Mrs. Ellen Pughe, wife of Charles Pughe of Gold Hill.

John Pughe is a half-brother of Mrs. Ellen Pughe and a cousin of Charles Pughe.

Funeral arrangements have not been completed. The body is at Howe mortuary."

Boulder Daily Camera 23 December 1937:

"HIT-AND-RUN AUTO DRIVER IS ARRESTED... Denver Liquor Salesman Denies Knowing He Struck And Killed Boulder Man But Admits He 'Felt Bump' Which Damaged Car

Arrested in Denver late Wednesday afternoon as the hit-and-run driver who killed Morgan Edwards, 74, north of Boulder. Gerald Gurley, 26, of Denver, was being held in jail here today, facing possible charges of manslaughter, or of failing to stop and give aid to an injured person, or both.

Gurley, a liquor salesman, denies knowing the struck Edwards, a pioneer of Boulder County, as the man was walking along the North 12th highway Tuesday night.

Sheriff George A. Richart said Gurley, arrested on a tip received here, at first denied he had been in an accident. After lengthy questioning by Denver police the man admitted, according to Richart, that he discovered a door handle had been knocked off his automobile and that he had the repairs made at a Denver garage. He declared he did not know how the handle was broken.

'Felt a Bump'...The sheriff said as he and Deputy Arthur Everson were bringing Gurley to Boulder Wednesday night, the salesman admitted for the first time he had "felt a bump" as he neared the top of the North 12th hill but insisted he did not know he had hit a person.

Richart asserted Gurley admitted he had tasted liquor from a sample bottle a short time before the accident, but declared he was not intoxicated.

Mr. and Mrs. Bruce Cole, of Lee Hill, who were passing the scene of the accident, going the opposite direction, just as the impact occurred, said they heard the thud of the other car striking the pedestrian and stopped immediately, although they did not see the accident.

Tip is Not Divulged...Sheriff Richart declined to reveal the nature of the tip which led to Gurley's arrest. It was learned that Richart's earlier investigation had disclosed the fact that a car which might have been at a liquor store near the scene of the accident a short time before it happened.

The broken door handle found at the scene was checked and found to have come from a 1937 Plymouth. Gurley's car is of that model.

Sheriff Richart and Deputy District Attorney James D. Lewis said today they plan to take Gurley into district court next Monday, but the charge to be filed against him will not be determined until further investigation is made.

Maximum of One Year...Lewis said there is a specific law against "hit-and-run" drivers, providing a maximum penalty of one year in jail, or a maximum fine of $5,000, or both, for any driver involved in an accident who fails to stop and to render aid to any injured person.

The maximum penalty for involuntary manslaughter is one year in jail, and no fine is provided. Lewis said it does not appear from the facts at hand that Gurley could be guilty of voluntary manslaughter, which carries a penalty of one to eight years in the penitentiary."

EDWARDS, Pearl

Birth: 1891
Death: 1891
Cemetery Location: D3

Father: William "Billy" Edwards; Mother: Rosena/Rosina (*Barnett*); born in Gold Hill (Boulder) Colorado and died in Aspen (Pitkin) Colorado at age 6 months-something wrong with neck; believed actually buried in (Pitkin) Colorado but a memorial on the tombstone of William "Billy" Edwards; see EDWARDS, William "Billy;" see **About William "Billy" Edwards**

EDWARDS, William "Billy"

Birth: 03/1859
Death: 07/20/1891
Cemetery Location: D3

Father: Stephen Edwards; Mother: Mary Ellen (*Morgan*) Pugh(e); Wife: Rosena/Rosina (*Barnett*); born in Wales and died in Gold Hill (Boulder) Colorado at age 32 years (approximately)-pneumonia; see EDWARDS, Mary Josephine "Jessie;" see **About the Morgan Edwards Family**; see **About William "Billy" Edwards**; see DUDLEY, Joseph Lobb

Boulder News 23 July 1891:

"Wm. Edwards, a well-known miner of Gold Hill, died of pneumonia on Monday and was buried on Wednesday. Rev. Davis of this city conducting the ceremonies. He leaves a wife and three small children."

Boulder News 30 July 1891:

"Wm. Barnett and wife, the parents of Mrs. Wm. Edwards, were here to attend the funeral of Mr. Edwards and returned home to Aspen Friday taking their daughter and three children with them."

About William "Billy" Edwards

Mary Ellen Morgan was born about 1821 in (Cardiganshire) Wales; the daughter of Thomas and Mary (maiden name unknown) Morgan. She had an "unofficial" marriage with Tudor Pugh(e). He was born about 1819 in Trefeurig, Llanbadarn Fawr (Cardiganshire) Wales; the son of Griffith and Jane (*Owen*) Pugh(e). This union produced five known children:

Charles Edward: born 14 February 1844 Penygraig, Penybont, Trefeurig (Cardiganshire) Wales and died 1927 Longmont (Boulder) Colorado); buried Mountain View Cemetery, Longmont (Boulder) Colorado; married Mary Dorothy Davis

Mary: born March 1846 Llanbadam Fawr (Cardiganshire) Wales; no further information

Tudor: born 18 February 1848 Penygraig, Trefeurig (Cardiganshire) Wales; no further information

John "Silvertip": born 06 August 1850 Penybont, Trefeurig (Cardiganshire) Wales and died 26 March 1939 Boulder (Boulder) Colorado; buried Columbia Cemetery, Boulder (Boulder) Colorado; married Mary Ellen Teal

Isaac: born 1853 Trefeurig (Cardiganshire) Wales and died 05 March 1864 Penygraig, Trefeurig (Cardiganshire) Wales; no further information

Apparently, after the birth of Isaac Tudor and Mary separated. In the 1861 census Tudor is a servant in the household of James Watkins in Llanbadarn Fawr (Cardiganshire) Wales. Twenty years later in the 1881 census he is living in the same area with his sisters Mary and "Ellenor" along with nephews Evan Pugh and Hugh Jones. Tudor died 26 August 1898 at 'Tyn Cefn Brith' Trefeurig (Cardiganshire) Wales.

"OUR BABY"

Mary married Stephen Edwards on 23 May 1853 in Wales. (It is interesting to note that on the marriage entry Mary is listed as a spinster with her maiden name of Morgans.) Stephen was born 1826 in Wales; the son of Thomas and Eleanor (*Jones*) Edwards. This union brought forth three known children:

Eleanor/Elinor "Ellen": born 04 June 1856 Llanbadarn Fawr, Aberystwyth (Cardiganshire) Wales and died 21 November 1941 Gold Hill (Boulder) Colorado; buried Gold Hill Cemetery, Gold Hill (Boulder) Colorado; married Charles Pughe; see PUGHE, Charles "Charley" (no middle initial E); see PUGHE, Eleanor/Elinor "Ellen" (*Edwards*)

William "Billy": born March 1859 Wales and died 20 July 1891 Gold Hill (Boulder) Colorado; buried Gold Hill Cemetery, Gold Hill (Boulder) Colorado; see EDWARDS, William "Billy"

Morgan: born 08 September 1863 Wales and died 21 December 1937 Boulder (Boulder) Colorado; buried Columbia Cemetery, Boulder (Boulder) Colorado; married Martha "Mattie" Ellen "Ella" Wilson; see EDWARDS, Mary Josephine "Jessie"

Mary died on 24 July 1882 in Cwmsymlog, Trefeurig (Cardiganshire) Wales and Stephen died 14 March 1883 also in Cwmsymlog, Trefeurig (Cardiganshire) Wales. According to the Probate of the Will of Stephen Edwards (dated 09 February 1883) the estate was divided between Eleanor (Ellen) and Morgan with Eleanor receiving one third and Morgan two thirds. Perhaps William was not included as by that time he had left his home in Wales, living in Gold Hill (Boulder) Colorado by 1880 where he met and married Rosena/Rosina/Rosa Barnett 02 January 1886. She was born in October of 1867 in Michigan; the daughter of England natives William Sr., and Mary Ann (*Williams*) Barnett. This union produced three known children:

The Edwards Plot in September 2006
Fence was burned in the 2010 Four Mile Canyon fire

Earl: born about 1886 Caribou (Boulder) Colorado and died Colorado; burial unknown; died young

Mary Ellen "Mamie/Mayme": born 03 Nov 1888 Caribou (Boulder) Colorado and died 06 September 1985 Boulder (Boulder) Colorado; buried Columbia Cemetery, Boulder (Boulder) Colorado; married James Lyons McLellan

Pearl: born 1891 (Boulder) Colorado and died 1891 Aspen (Pitkin) Colorado at 6 months of age; buried (Pitkin) Colorado; memorial reference on William "Billy" Edwards' tombstone; see EDWARDS, Pearl

William "Billy" died shortly after the birth of his daughter, Pearl, from pneumonia and was buried in the Gold Hill Cemetery in Gold Hill (Boulder) Colorado. A few years later on 15 December 1892 Rosena (*Barnett*) Edwards married Joseph Lobb Dudley in Aspen (Pitkin) Colorado; see DUDLEY, Joseph Lobb.

"Earth has one pure spirit less Heaven one inmate more."

Interview with Mary Ellen "Mamie" (*Edwards*) McLellan (Courtesy of Anne McLellan and Carol (*McLellan*) McConica):

"Mama wasn't too old; she was about your age Marge (daughter-in-law). I loved my mother. When she was twenty one and she had three little babies and the oldest one was Earl, he was two years older than me and I was the next, just a little older than the baby (Pearl) and she was six months and she lived just a little while after my father (William "Billy" Edwards) died. She was only six months old when she died. My father died with pneumonia and then she—Mama went to Aspen—living at grandmom's to help take care of the boarders. She didn't have any money but what people had given her. But she had a few things like that—and the baby was six months old and she died: she had something the matter with her neck.

My mother was left with three small children: the oldest was four years old, that was Earl, and then she went to grandma to help work to raise the children. And while she was working there she met this man. Like she said I didn't want to get married but she said what could I do? She said he was a good man and she said there were three children and then the baby died—six months old and she (Rosena) was married in Aspen.

She (Rosena) went up to Leadville when Earl was a baby. And they (William "Billy" and Rosena Edwards) rented, my father rented a very cheap apartment, ah, a room in the Denver Hotel, a couple of rooms, and she lived there and water was kinda scarce and they had to buy it you know and she went out and was shoveling up some snow and she looked up and this man was there and she looked scared and he said don't be scared—he said I was just looking at your baby. I'd like to steal him. And she was scared then. So my father (William) got a little pistol and I wonder what ever become of tat little pistol, it was a little white one—and he said if ever he bothers you, you just shoot him. She'd have shot herself!

[When was that, Mamie?]

1880"

(Interesting as William and Rosena weren't married until 1886—must have been the late 1880s)

By 1900 Joseph and Rosina were living in Gold Hill (Boulder) Colorado along with their children Mamie Edwards, Willie and Ruby; for more information see **About the Joseph Lobb Dudley Family**

EISELE, John Jacob

Birth: 1854
Death: 05/28/1887
Cemetery Location: Unknown

Father: unknown; Mother: unknown; never married; born in Germany and died near Gold Hill (Boulder) Colorado at age 33 years (approximately)-internal injuries due to explosion

Boulder County Herald Weekly 01 June 1887:

"Killed Near Gold Hill... Jacob Eisele, unmarried, aged about 30, member of the A.O.U.W. [Ancient Order of United Workmen] picked out a delayed blast in the Corning tunnel Friday morning, causing its explosion and such internal injuries to the man as to cause his death that night. He leaves a brother and two sisters, one in Denver, the other in San Francisco. The latter is the beneficiary of the insurance."

Boulder County Herald Weekly 01 June 1887:

"Resolutions of Respect.
   Gold Hill Lodge No. 20, A.O.U.W.
   Valley Legion, No. 2, Boulder, Colo.
   Gold Hill, Col., May 30, 1887.
   Whereas, Death has removed from our midst, Bro. J. Eisele, a member of thus Lodge and citizen of Gold Hill, therefore be it
   Resolved, That we deplore the loss of a worthy brother, a good citizen and a faithful friend, that his cheerfulness, charitable disposition and friendly spirit in addition to his many other manly and pleasing qualities are worthy of emulation.
   Resolved, That we extend our sympathy to his immediate relatives and friends.
   Resolved, That these resolutions be spread upon the records of the Lodge, that a copy of thereof be published in the Boulder papers.
   O.C. HANSBROUGH,
   J.J. HARRIS,
   D.H. BURLINGAME,
      Com. Valley Legion, No. 2.
   G. KIRKBRIDE,
   R. WILSON,
   J. MUGEUS,
      Com, Gold Hill Lodge No. 20"

Boulder County Estate Files, Compiled by Lois Wescott & Indexed by Ruth Ratliff (page 23; file 459):

"EISELE, JOHN J. died Gold Hill 28 May 1887. Admr, creditors: T.J. Thompson appt 12 Sept 1887. 3 sisters, 2 brothers, names unknown. House on Left Hand Cr., note $400 ins., kraut cutter, coffee mill, leather punch, tools, picture of Pres Garfield and family."

About John Jacob Eisele

It appears that John Jacob Eisele (Eissele/Eiszele) immigrated to the United States from Germany and was naturalized on 07 December 1880. In December of 1882 he purchased parcel #1: SEC T R TR BIG TUNNEL LODE from Nicholas J. Mayer.

In the 1885 Colorado State Census he was living in the Gold Hill (Boulder) Colorado region and it was recorded in (Boulder) Colorado on 18 February 1887 that "Jacaob" J. Eisele purchased a house on Left Hand Creek from David M. Reedy.

ELSON, Mark

   Birth: 10/23/1942
   Death: 10/15/1974
   Cemetery Location: B1

Father: Ralph Elson; Mother: Ruby Almeda (*Kennedy*); Wife: Rosalie (*Scimeca*); born in Dallas (Dallas) Texas and died in Boulder (Boulder) Colorado at age 31 years, 11 months, 22 days-heart attack

Boulder Daily Camera 16 October 1974:

"Mark Elson, 31, of 1910 Athens Court, died Tuesday in Community Hospital following a brief illness.

Mr. Elson was a student was a student at the University Of Colorado School Of Law.

He was born in Dallas, Tex., Oct. 23, 1942, and had been a Boulder resident for seven years, coming here from New York City, N.Y. He was married in Boulder, Dec. 26, 1972, to Rosalie Scimeca.

Mr. Elson received a bachelor's degree in mathematics from Rice University and did post-graduate work at Stanford University. He was also a noted author in computer science.

Besides his wife, survivors include his parents, Mr. and Mrs. Ralph Elson, Oak Ridge, Tenn., and two sisters, Martha Elson, Va., and Mary Bloom, Tennessee.

There will be no funeral services. Crist Mortuary is in charge of arrangements."

Digging Up Dirt

Chicago Tribune "My Brother, Too, Died A Young Man" by Mary Elson, Tribune (deputy metropolitan editor) 25 July 1999:

"On a lamp table in what was my brother Mark's bedroom at my parents' home in Tennessee is a photo cube filled with images of him: Mark rappelling down a mountain cliff, skiing in Colorado, bicycling in a funny hat, sitting at his piano bench, playing his guitar.

That was Mark the athlete, the musician, a person who took risks and challenged himself at any skill that appealed to him. Then there was Mark the intellect. The student who scored 800 on his math SAT, who was voted most likely to succeed, who was the top-finishing boy in the National Spelling Bee, who went to Rice and Stanford Universities, who became one of the bright lights among a young, irreverent group of math whizzes at buttoned-down IBM when the personal computer revolution was just beginning.

More than 20 years ago, just days before his 32nd birthday, Mark was walking his bicycle across campus at Denver University, where he was a professor of computer science, when he had a heart attack and died. I was 22. I had been working late at a newspaper job in Nashville when I got a call from my husband, asking in what seemed a slightly odd time when I would be home. When I arrived, he asked me to sit down and then delivered the news. Mark? Dead? The most vibrant, funny brilliant, accomplished person I had ever known? An only brother who traveled the world and brought back gifts from Switzerland, German, Italy—from wherever he happened to be on business or pleasure? Who brought my sister and me guitars and taught us to play Bob Dylan? Who faithfully corresponded in a loopy script, whose latest chatty letter was open even then on my bureau? A champion at bridge, billiards, Ping-Pong and golf? Dead?

Although even new memories of Mark drift in and out of my thoughts almost daily, the death of John F. Kennedy Jr. has made those reflections particularly intense. From my completely unobjective perspective, my brother was the same sort of figure as JFK Jr. Though he was never in the public spotlight Mark made an impression on nearly everyone who knew him. His startling mélange of talents always seemed to make others look like laggards, though Mark never succumbed to any inflated view of himself. But even more important, in the days since Kennedy and his fie and sister-in-law plunged into the ocean in a private plane, I also have thought about his sister, Caroline, how she must feel about losing her only brother, one who embodied such a dashing mixture of looks, brains, charm and wit.

Losing a sibling at any age is devastating. I can still feel the jolt of disbelief when I heard what had happened, a moment that remains in a discrete realm of emotion. In that instant, an entire dimension of my future simply vanished. I had expected to make many visits to his home in the mountains outside Boulder, but I have never returned there. Nothing can replace the role he would have played in my life. There is no good side to having a brother die so young, at the height of his abilities. Yet over the years, I have come to be grateful in a strange way for that very fact.

When I think about Mark's life and look at his pictures, I know that I will never see Mark lose his remarkable keenness of fail physically; he will always be tall and lanky, with a boyish smile and a quiet, backdoor sentimentality. He will always be the near-perfect older brother who set standards that still influence my life today.

In Mark's case, the story has an added dimension. The robust, almost reckless way he lived belied an inescapable fact: he was born with a heart murmur and knew that his whole life was circumscribed by that defect. At some point, we believed, he would have to have an operation to replace a heart valve, and I can only assume that he thought anything that smacked of infirmity was antithetical to his existence. As he grew up, my parents had taken him to various doctors at special medical centers, where he was tested and evaluated. In Boulder, he had a doctor we thought he saw regularly. But maybe he didn't. His wife once told me that he knew of a friend in New York who had had a similar operation and never quite recovered, who became a semi-invalid. That was a fate that Mark never could have accepted and that no one who knew him would have wanted to witness.

It appears that his answer was to avoid the operation, instead to plunge even more single-mindedly into his regimen of athletics and physical endurance, perhaps ignoring or dismissing symptoms that something was seriously wrong.

In the meantime, in his 20s—a time when many young adults are struggling to find a career or just getting started in one—he was busy inventing a computer language that was considered a significant advance in the field. In college, he had worked as a computer programmer for one of the government laboratories in my hometown of Oak Ridge, Tenn., holing up in his bedroom with stacks of computer printouts, scouring the programs until he found the bug that had sent one awry.

Such perseverance also allowed him to write two textbooks—"Data Structures" and "Concepts of Programming Languages"—that, to someone who had trouble grasping FORTRAN in a high school computer class, are at once mind-bogglingly complex and deftly readable. His mind was equally comfortable with math and language, the rare person in which the right brain and left brain were in perfect balance.

I've always been convinced that Mark would have been part of Bill Gates' idiosyncratically brilliant monarchy at Microsoft had he lived. And that, of course, is one of the hardest things to accept in losing a sibling so young; the sense of lost potential. Certainly, that has been an abiding question surrounding JFK Jr.'s death, whether he might someday have held high office or risen in another field.

Still, the dedication by a friend to Mark's second book, published after his death, offers another view: "On October 15, 1974, Mark Elson died of a heart attack on his way to class in Boulder, Colorado. He was thirty-one years old. A great loss has been suffered by Mark's family and friends; another loss is to the many readers of his books who will never have the opportunity of knowing him. Mark was a computer science teacher, a law student, a musician, an IBM language designer, a singer, a scratch golfer, a skier, a champion billiard player, an author, and a warm and generous human being. Roughly a year before his death, his close friend Jim remarked to me, "What amazes all of Mark's friends is that he has accomplished more in his 30 years than most of us will in a lifetime."

If Mark ever felt any symptoms, he disguised it. I never saw him when he wasn't energetic. I remember as a college student roaring through the mountains outside Boulder in his unpredictable van—he was one of the first to adopt the post-Woodstock style-listening to "American Pie" on his radio and eating cold pizza. He took me skiing twice, at Aspen and Breckenridge, patiently coaching—and fixing errant ski boots—until I could go down an intermediate slope. One exhilarating moment was flying down a trail trimmed with evergreens, in perfect snow, perfect weather, and stopping at a stand for blueberry crepes and cider. On the weekends, he often traveled to a little town in Colorado called Gold Hill, where Stephen Stills and Judy Collins and other folk singers gathered. He knew them all and made sure we knew their music. In my living room today is Mark's Martin guitar, propped up against the wall, along with a 15th Century Austrian lute he picked up on one of his travels and never quite got around to restringing. He once had a pet anteater that had been on "The Tonight Show." But those are just a few memories. I have hundreds more, images that never get stale, that reveal him—and fix him forever—as the inimitable person he was. My biggest regret is that my children never got to meet him. But they know their Uncle Mark through my recollections. We talk of him often.

As Caroline Kennedy Schlossberg begins to face her brother's death—a process that will take the rest of her life—I hope she can take comfort in knowing that she and the rest of the world remember John at his very best. That's how I remember Mark. And that, like my brother himself, will never change."

EVANS, David

Birth: 03/1840
Death: 09/07/1911
Cemetery Location: Unknown

Father: unknown; Mother: unknown; Wife: Nellie L. (*Beckwith*); born in Wales and died Summerville (Boulder) Colorado at age 71 years (approximately)-Bright's disease (kidney disease accompanied by hypertension and evidence of heart disease); see NICHOLLS, Nellie L. (*Beckwith*) Evans

Boulder Daily Camera 07 September 1911:

"DEATH OF DAVID EVANS A WELL KNOWN MINER—David Evans, who has lived in Summerville for the past forty years, died there this morning of Bright's disease [a type of kidney disease]at the age of 67 years. The remains are at Howe & Ewry's undertaking parlors and will be taken to Gold Hill Friday afternoon for interment. He leaves a wife, but no children. He had been a miner all of his life and had many friends who will regret his death."

Boulder Daily Herald 07 September 1911:

"SUMMERVILLE PIONEER DIES OF HEART DISEASE

David Evans Aged 71, Passes Away at Mountain Home—Funeral Tomorrow at Gold Hill

David Evans, for more than forty years a resident of Summerville, died of heart disease at his home in that town this morning. He had been in poor health for a year and had been confined to his bed for the past six weeks.

Mr. Evans was seventy-one years of age. A native of Wales, he came to this country and lived for a while in Ohio. He immigrated to Colorado in the sixties and finally located at Somerville (sic). He was the owner of several mining claims and town property at Summerville.

He is survived only by his wife, Mrs. Nellie Evans, who is about thirty years his junior. So far as is known in this county there are no other living relatives.

The funeral will take place at Gold Hill tomorrow afternoon, at 2:30 o'clock. George Kirkbride will conduct the services. Interment will be made at the Gold Hill cemetery under the direction of Howe & Ewry."

Boulder Daily Camera 07 September 1911:

"David F. Evans, another prominent pioneer, died in September 1911. Evans was a miner, as well as "the largest real estate owner in Summerville," and had worked in his mines from 1873 until the winter before his death, at age seventy-two."

About David Evans

David was born in Wales March of 1840; parents unknown. He immigrated to the United States in 1860. Coming from Ohio and eventually to Colorado, he married Nellie L. Beckwith when he was in his mid-forties (first marriage) and she was a mere seventeen years old. This union took place on 08 March 1887 in Boulder (Boulder) Colorado. Nellie was born February 1869 in Burlington (Boulder) Colorado; the daughter of Oscar Fenton and Hattie Elvira (*Ward*) Beckwith.

David, a Civil War veteran, was the discoverer of six mines in the Summerville/Gold Hill area 1873-1881. He still worked in his mines when he was almost 70 years old.

Upon his death in 1911 Nellie inherited all of his property and remarried five years later to Henry G. Nicholls, the brother of Benjamin Allen and Richard John Nicholls; see NICHOLLS, Benjamin Allen; see NICHOLLS, Richard John. Nellie died 14 November 1937 and is buried near David Evans in the Gold Hill Cemetery, Gold Hill (Boulder) Colorado; see NICHOLLS, Nellie L. (*Beckwith*) Evans.

F

FEATHER, Daniel Wayne

> Birth: 08/16/1956
> Death: 08/20/1956
> Cemetery Location: B2

Father: Gilbert Lee Feather; Mother: Gwendolyn Lois (*Sewell*); born in Sterling (Logan) Colorado and died in Denver (Denver) Colorado at age 4 days-cause of death unknown; tombstone has incorrect death year of 1957; 2nd great nephew of Mary Parker (Kirkbride) Boyd; see BOYD, Mary Parker (*Kirkbride*); see FEATHER, Gilbert Lee; see FEATHER, Gwendolyn Lois (*Sewell*)

Boulder Daily Camera 22 August 1956:
> "David Wayne Feather—Five day old son of Mr. and Mrs. Gilbert Feather who died at Children's Hospital will be held Monday, Howe Mortuary is in charge of arrangements."

Boulder Daily Camera 23 August 1956:
> "Graveside services will be held Monday morning at 11 at Gold Hill. Rev. Marvin Adams, pastor of the first Methodist church, will officiate. Howe Mortuary in charge."

FEATHER, Gilbert Lee

> Birth: 04/22/1932
> Death: 02/12/2014
> Cemetery Location: B2

Father: Ralph Lee Feather; Mother: Dorothy Elizabeth (*Gilbert*); Wife: Gwendolyn Lois (*Sewell*); 2nd Wife: Jessie (*Ghere*); born in Houston (Harris) Texas and died in Tulsa (Tulsa) Oklahoma at age 81 years, 9 months, 21 days-natural causes; see FEATHER, Gwendolyn Lois (*Sewell*); see FEATHER, Daniel Wayne

Tulsa Word 14 February 2014:
> "Gilbert Lee Feather of Jenks, Oklahoma passed away in his home surrounded by his family on Wednesday, February 12th. Gilbert was born on April 22nd 1932 in Houston, Texas to Ralph and Dorothy Feather.

> He graduated high school in Biloxi, Mississippi and went on to attend college at the University of Wyoming where he earned his degree in Mechanical Engineering. Gilbert went on to be a corporal in the Army where he served as an instructor. He married his first wife, Gwendolyn Sewell in June 1953 in Biloxi, Mississippi and they had 4 children: Lee, Scott, Rob and Chris Feather. Gilbert spent his entire professional career as a petroleum engineer and had a lifelong love of science. He was an avid nature lover and spent many years as a campground host in Rocky Mountain National Park Colorado upon his retirement from engineering. He loved camping and hiking and took pride in climbing Longs Peak Mountain. When Gwendolyn passed away in 1997, Gilbert moved back to Tulsa, Oklahoma where he later married Jessie Ghere in the year 2000.

> Gilbert was preceded in death by his parents Ralph and Dorothy Feather, his sister Gaynor Johnson, and his wife Gwendolyn Feather. He is survived by his wife Jessie Feather, his brother Kenneth Wayne Feather, brother-in-law Bill Johnson, his children; Lee, Scott, Rob and Chris and their spouses, five step-children; Teresa Shelly, Michael, Scott, Amanda and their spouses, sixteen grandchildren, and five great-grandchildren.

> A memorial service will be held at Southern Hills United Methodist Church in Tulsa, Oklahoma where he was a long time member on Monday, February 17th at 11am. Anyone wishing to donate to a memorial fund in his honor may do so through the church."

FEATHER, Gwendolyn Lois (*Sewell*)

Birth: 03/30/1933
Death: 09/23/1997
Cemetery Location: B2

Father: Reginald H. Sewell; Mother: Olga Leab Beatrice (*Swetman*); Husband: Gilbert Lee Feather; born in Biloxi (Harrison) Mississippi and died in Loveland (Larimer) Colorado at age 64 years, 5 months, 24 days-cancer; see FEATHER, Daniel Wayne; see FEATHER, Gilbert Lee

Loveland Reporter Herald 24 September 1997:
"Gwendolyn Lois Feather, 64, of Loveland, died Sept. 23, 1997, at home.

She was born March 30, 1933, in Biloxi, Miss., to Reginald H. and Olga Sewell. She married Gilbert L. Feather on June 14, 1953, in Biloxi.

She and her family lived in many cities around the country because of her husband's work in the petroleum industry. She came to Loveland in 1993.

She was active in Meals on Wheels and was a member of the Loveland United Methodist Church and a board member of the United Methodist Women. She was a volunteer at Rocky Mountain National Park, working as a campground host and interpretive program assistant.

She enjoyed reading, baking, traveling, and square-dancing and was an artist in cross-stitching.

She is survived by her husband, Gilbert L. Feather, Loveland; sons Lee and wife Diane of Sheridan, Wyo., Scott and wife Sue of Casper, Wyo., Robert and wife Janece of Austin, Texas, and Christopher and wife Lucy of Tulsa, Okla; and eight grandchildren.

She was preceded in death by an infant son, David.

Cremation has been conducted.

A memorial service is 10:30 a.m. Friday at First United Methodist Church of Loveland.

Memorial contributions may be made to the American Cancer Society, Hospice of Larimer County, First United Methodist Church of Loveland, or First United Methodist Church of Tulsa, Okla."

Fort Collins Coloradoan 25 September 1997:
"Gwendolyn L. Feather—Gwendolyn Lois Feather, 64, of Loveland died Tuesday, Sept. 23, 1997, at home.

A memorial service will be held at 10:30 a.m. Friday at First United Methodist Church in Loveland. Cremation has been conducted.

Gwendolyn Sewell was born March 30, 1933, in Biloxi, Miss., to Reginald H. and Olga Sewell.

She married Gilbert L. Feather on June 14, 1953, in Biloxi.

Mrs. Feather was a member of First United Methodist Church, serving on the board of the United Methodist Women. She also was active and Meals on Wheels and Volunteers in the Park at Rocky Mountain National Park, serving as campground host and interpretive program assistant. She enjoyed reading, baking, traveling, cross-stitch and square-dancing.

She lived in Loveland since 1993.

Survivors include her husband; four sons, Lee Feather of Sheridan, Wyo., Scott Feather of Casper, Wyo., Robert Feather of Austin, Texas, and Christopher Feather of Tulsa, Okla.; and eight grandchildren.

She was preceded in death by one infant son, David Feather.

Memorial contributions may be [made] to the American Cancer Society, Hospice of Larimer County, the First United Methodist Church of Loveland or the First United Methodist Church of Tulsa in case of Warren-Bohlender Funeral Chapel."

FINN, Barbara (*MacFetridge*)

Birth: 05/29/1929
Death: 06/19/2006
Cemetery Location: B4

Father: Clyde Kemmerer MacFetridge; Mother: Olive Caroline (*Wheeler*); Husband: Luke Francis Finn; born in Syracuse (Onondaga) New York and died in Longmont (Boulder) Colorado at age 77 years, 19 days-illness

Boulder Daily Camera 21 June 2006:
"Barbara Finn May 29, 1929-June 17, 2006 [error]— Barbara Finn, the co-founder of the Gold Hill Inn, midwife to a host of worthy causes, and a great good heart, died Saturday being stricken at her home in Longmont. She was 77.

Barbara leaves behind her husband, Frank, two sisters, Mary Jean McMorran of Boulder and Anne McCracken of Anacortes, Washington, four children, Deborah Millennor of Broomfield, Christopher, Matthew and Brian Finn of Gold Hill, and four grandchildren, Shivaun C. Finn, Luke Casey Finn, Katie Marie Finn, and Amy Kay Millennor—and thousands of friends.

Barbara MacFetridge Finn was born May 29, 1929, in Syracuse, New York, the daughter of Clyde and Olive MacFetridge. She attended Elmira College, graduating in 1950 with a degree in Chemistry.

She went to work for American Cyanamid in Stanford, Connecticut. At a company Christmas party in 1950, held at the Greenwich, Connecticut YMCA, she met her future husband. He was the lifeguard. The couple was married on January, 26, 1952 in Syracuse.

The Finns moved to boulder in 1955, where Frank worked for the YMCA for two years before taking a job in Salina, Kansas, in 1957. They returned to Boulder County permanently in 1959. Frank worked for the Post Office and as caretaker for the Trojan Ranch west of Gold Hill.

In 1962, Barbara and Frank purchased the old Bluebird Lodge in Gold Hill, ten miles west of Boulder and opened the Gold Hill Inn in the lodge's former dining hall, a unique restaurant that has become a Boulder County institution and achieved international fame.

The restaurant opened on June 15, 1962, but not before its opening had been twice delayed by spring storms.

Barbara was responsible for the Inn's menu, personally creating some of its more memorable dishes, including Lamb Venison, a lamb roast marinated in buttermilk, and Glasgow Roast Beef, a sirloin tip stuffed with liver pate.

Special offerings included roast suckling pig and clam bakes. The Inn also featured unique entertainment, like a volunteer jug band made up largely of CU and National Bureau of Standards physicists.

Barbara took great pride in the fact that the kitchen kept waste to a minimum. And she was particularly insistent on putting fresh-cut mountain flowers on the tables.

The Inn broke all the rules of business—except the ones that mattered: those concerning customer service and product integrity.

At first the Finns attempted to keep the Inn open year round, although the drafty building was at the time heating only by fireplaces and pot-belly stoves and the guests who braved the ten-mile drive over unpaved roads in the winter often had to keep their gloves on while they ate. Eventually Barbara and Frank settled on the May-October schedule.

In the most recent edition of the Inn's cookbook, Barbara recalled one particularly memorable evening when a busload of scientists attending an international conference in Boulder, was stranded in a storm on the way to the Inn and they had to hike up Lick Skillet Road in a blizzard to get there. The staff plied the guests with brandy and massaged their feet in front of the fireplaces. The featured speaker that evening was then Gov. John Love-who had arrived by a different road-and the moment he began to talk the power failed. The guests found the banquet so memorable that they returned the following year.

Word slowly spread about the unique restaurant ten miles west of Boulder, accessible only by a harrowing drive over unpaved roads, and after several years it turned into a success and eventually an institution.

"On them days on Red Hoss Mountain,
when the skies wuz fair 'nd blue.
When the money flowed like likker,
'nd the folks was brave 'nd true!
—Eugene Field"

Barbara and Frank drew inspiration from the poet Eugene Field, who had visited Gold Hill while working as a Denver newspaper man and who wrote five poems about the camp and the lodge, including one called Casey's Table d-Hote.

"We loved the poem. It's a bit long winded, but amazingly prophetic for us," she later wrote. "We didn't design the Inn after the poem, but the similarities are pretty stunning."

"Every time I enter the Inn, I feel the same affection for the golden tones of the old log and helter-skelter struts of the roof," she said. "It is a feeling of belonging. I'm always thankful that I have been allowed to be the caretaker of this place for a period in its life."

"The Inn was Barbara's baby, it was really her fifth child," said Deborah.

It was not, however, her only interest.

She never lost interest in the social work that had originally brought her and Frank to Boulder County. For many years they took in troubled teens and foster children, leasing the Broken Arrow Ranch for a year, in the 1970s as a summer camp for them. In some respects Barbara considered the restaurant as the means of allowing her to pursue her work with them. A number went to distinguished careers, including one who became a neurosurgeon.

The Finns also hosted dozens of benefits for political candidates, mostly Democrats, and worthy causes, including the victims of the black Tiger Fire, a benefit that Barbara organized in five days and which raised $11,000.

In later years, Barbara helped organize the drive to turn an abandoned Catholic church in Gold Hill into the town museum. She spearheaded the fund-raising to buy the building and the campaign to acquire artifacts.

Barbara and Frank gave their four children an upbringing as unique as their restaurant. One reason they chose to live in Gold Hill was the town's one-room school house, the oldest continually operating school in Colorado, which all four Finn children attended.

The kids had a burro, named Twinkles, who for years wandered the streets of Gold Hill, charming guests at the Inn, including the late Senator William Fulbright.

All four Finn children worked in the Inn, which today is run as a family owned and operated business.

Barbara was always attracted by two things. One was water. She loved to take her repose by it, whether it was an ocean, a lake, or a pond.

The other was new things and ideas.

At Barbara's insistence, the Finns regularly vacationed in Mexico, driving south in an old school bus and camping on the beach, years before Mexico became a popular destination.

At the time of the first energy crisis in 1973, they built a large solar-heated greenhouse onto their home.

When Toyota brought out the hybrid-electric Prius, Barbara became an early adopter.

She never stopped thinking and learning. She was always on the cutting edge.

Janos Wilder, a cook at the Gold Hill Inn who went on to open a restaurant in Tucson and win a James Bear award, dedicated his book to Barbara. The dedication read "At the Gold Hill Inn Barbara Finn taught me that anything was possible."

A memorial service and Fest of Barbara will be held at 4 p.m. Sunday, June 25, at the Gold Hill Inn to celebrate Barbara's life. The family requests that in lieu of flowers, contributions be made to Historic Gold Hill Inc., c/o Howe Mortuary, 439 Coffman St., Longmont, CO 80501.

Please share your thoughts and memories with the family at www.howemortuary.com."

Rocky Mountain News 24 June 2006 (excerpts-article by Lisa Bornstein)

"Barbara MacFetridge Finn was born May 29, 1929, in Syracuse, N.Y. She graduated from Elmira College in 1950 with a degree in chemistry and went to work for American Cyanamid. During a Christmas party that year at the YMCA in Greenwich, Conn., she met Frank Finn, a lifeguard there. The couple was married on January 26, 1952, in Syracuse.

In 1955 the couple moved to Boulder. They left briefly for Kansas; then settled in the Boulder area in 1959. Three years later, they bought the ramshackle Bluebird Lodge and opened the Gold Hill Inn in the dining area. "It was an old building up in the mountains in the middle of nowhere, and she decided she wanted to do a restaurant that served a six-course meal. And the way she put it together, with her Scotch blood, there was just nothing wasted. How it became a success was being creative with everything," says her son Brian Finn, who runs the restaurant with his brother Chris.

Social justice was important to the Finns, so they began opening their home to wayward children. Before more stringent programs were put in place, they would find juvenile delinquents in the courts and offer them homes; one summer the Finns ran a camp for them.

A celebration of life will be at 4 p.m. Sunday at the Gold Hill Inn. The family requests that, in lieu of flowers, contributions be made to Historic Gold Hill, Inc.

In addition to her husband, she is survived by a daughter, Deborah Millennor, of Broomfield, sons Christopher, Matthew and Brian Finn of Gold Hill, sisters Mary Jean McMorran of Boulder, and Anne McCracken, of Anacortes, Wash., and grandchildren Shivaun C. Finn, Luke Casey Finn, Katie Marie Finn, and Amy Kay Millennor"

FINN, Luke Francis

Birth: 05/16/1927
Death: 09/26/2009
Cemetery Location: B4

Father: William Finn; Mother: Josephine (*Cotter*); Wife: Barbara (*MacFetridge*); born in Greenwich (Fairfield) Connecticut and died in Louisville (Boulder) Colorado at age 82 years, 4 months, 10 days-illness

Boulder Daily Camera 02 October 2009:

"Frank Finn May 16, 1927-September 26, 2009—Luke Francis Finn of Gold Hill and Longmont Colorado and Key West, Florida, died on Saturday, September 26, surrounded by his family in the tranquil comfort and care of Boulder County Hospice at Balfour in Louisville, Colorado, after a brief illness. He was 82.

Frank was born in Greenwich, Connecticut, on May 16, 1927, the son of William Finn and Josephine Cotter Finn; he was the first of six children. As a teenager, he worked as caddy master and lifeguard before entering New York University, where he majored in Physical Education.

In 1950 he met Barbara MacFetridge in Greenwich at a Christmas party held by American Cyanamid, where she worked. They were married on January 26, 1952, in

Syracuse, New York. In 1955, Frank and Barbara moved with their two-year-old daughter, Deborah, to Boulder, where sons Christopher and Matthew were born. Franks was cofounder of the Boulder YMCA, and worked there until 1957, when the family moved to Salina, Kansas. Two years later, after the birth of their third son, Brian, they returned to the Boulder area permanently.

In the fall of 1959, Frank and his family moved to the Trojan Ranch west of Gold Hill. The following spring they moved into a home attached to the Red Store on Main Street in Gold Hill. It was while living there and selling groceries that Frank and Barbara bought the 3-story hotel in town, and its adjacent dining hall, from the Bluebird organization [Holiday House Association]. The Finns settled in the hotel, known as the Bluebird Lodge, and in June, 1962, they welcomed their first customers to the Gold Hill Inn, a gourmet dinner restaurant in the spacious dining hall.

The Gold Hill Inn is a seasonal business, closed during the winter months, and for years Frank and Barbara would gather their four kids, with school assignments, into a school bus and rive to their winter destination in Playa Los Cocos, Mexico. Back at Gold Hill for the Summer and Fall, Barbara created the elaborate, imaginative six-course dinners for which the restaurant has become known to visitors from around the world, and Frank became the beloved irreverent friend of countless men and women, young and old, from his station behind a bar where beverage offerings were top-shelf rather than common, and where his Irish wit and charm filled the air between the massive fireplaces.

At various times, Frank Finn served as mayor of Gold Hill; he was Gold Hill Fire Chief and helped establish the Sunshine Fire Department; he and Barbara were instrumental in the Gold Hill elementary school becoming part of Boulder Valley Schools; they were active in establishing

historic zoning for Gold Hill and its eventual inclusion in the national Register of Historic Places. Frank also found tine to help establish Little League baseball in Boulder.

Perhaps nothing besides their family was more important to frank and Barbara than offering alternatives to troubled youth. They opened their home to boys in trouble around Boulder County, and in 1970 they established Uncle Charlie's, a youth camp west of Gold Hill for juvenile delinquents. It was their growing business that funded these endeavors, and the Gold Hill Inn sponsored many fundraising events over the years for the People's Clinic, the Community Free School of Boulder, YMCA, and other projects. Many special events benefitted local, regional, and national Democratic candidacies.

By the early 1980s Frank and Barbara had a second home in Key West, Florida, and were able to travel, leaving the operation of the Gold Hill Inn to their children, primarily Chris and Brian. The Gold Hill Inn has continued to flourish unchanged since its opening in 1962. The American poet Eugene Field spent time at the hotel in Gold Hill, and the first poem in his A Little Book of Western Verse (1889) recounts his visit there. "Casey's Table d'Hote" conveys Field's deep affection for the proprietor of the In and restaurant—it's a poem that Frank memorized and loved to recite, and many who knew Frank characterized him with Casey.

"Oh them days on Red Hoss Mountain, when the skies wuz fair 'nd blue, when the money flowed like likker, 'nd the folks wuz brave 'nd true? When the nights wuz crisp 'nd balmy, 'nd the camp wuz all astir, With the joints all throwed wide open 'nd no sheriff to demur!

And you, O cherished brother, a sleepin' 'way out West, With Red Hoss Mountain huggin' you close to its lovin' breast.—Oh, do you dream in your last sleep of how we used to do, Of how we worked our little claims together, me 'nd you? Why, when I saw you last a smile wuz restin' on your face, Like you wuz glad to sleep forever in that lonely place; And so you wuz, *'nd I'd be, too, if I was sleepin' so, But, bein' how a brother's love ain't for the world to know; Whenever I've this heartache 'nd this chokin' in my throat, I lay it all to thinkin' of Casey's table dote."*

Barbara Finn died in June, 2006. Frank is survived by twin sisters Mary and Margaret; brothers William Jr., Patrick, and Daniel; four children and spouses Deborah and Gary Millennoor, Christopher and Leslie Finn, Matthew Finn and Nana Will, Brian and Marilyn Finn; four grandchildren Shivaun, Amy, Katie, Luke; cousin Jerry Starratt.

Cremation has been entrusted to Howe Mortuary and Crematory, Longmont, Colorado.

Friends are invited to a traditional Irish wake for Frank on Sunday, October 18th, 2:00 p.m. at the Gold Hill Inn. In lieu of flowers, contributions may be made in Frank's name to Attention Homes, 3080 Broadway, Boulder, 80304.

Please share your thought, memories and condolences with the family at www.howemortuary.com."

FOLSOM, James King

Birth: 08/09/1933
Death: 05/03/1988
Cemetery Location: G2

Father: Frederick K. Folsom; Mother: Elizabeth Edna (*Yost*); Wife: Margaret "Kaye" (*Frolhingham*) Page; born in Cleveland (Cuyahoga) Ohio and died in Boulder (Boulder) Colorado at age 54 years, 8 months, 24 days-CVA (cerebrovascular accident or commonly known as a stroke)

Boulder Daily Camera 05 May 1988:

"JAMES KING FOLSOM—Former University of Colorado English Professor James King Folsom of 1447

"SERVE THE LORD WITH GLADNESS"

S. Foothills Parkway, Boulder, died Tuesday, May 3, at Boulder Community Hospital. He was 54.

Mr. Folsom was born in Cleveland, Ohio, on August 9, 1933, the son of Frederick K. Folsom and Elizabeth Edna Yost Folsom. He moved to Boulder in 1968 from New Haven, Conn., and married Kay Fox in Boulder on Nov. 27, 1977.

He graduated Phi Beta Kappa from Northwestern University in 1955 and went on to earn a Ph. D. from Princeton University in 1959. He then taught English at Yale University and worked as a Bruern fellow in American literature at Leeds University in England. In 1969 he joined the University of Colorado, where he was a professor until 1985.

At CU he was, among other things, chairman of the department of English (1981-82), director of graduate studies (1973-75) and director of creative writing (1978-79). He was the author of many books including "The American Western Novel," which was translated into Japanese.

He also was a visiting professor of English at the American College of Greece in Athens from 1970-1980.

He was a member of the Modern Language Association of America, the Rocky Mountain Modern Language Association and the Western Literature Association.

Mr. Folsom is survived by his wife of Boulder, a son, Christopher Folsom, of New York; a daughter, Elisabeth Folsom of Boston; five stepsons, Ed Mores of Boulder, Joseph Mores of Colorado Springs, Peter Mores of Juneau, Alaska, Franklin Mores of Sun City, Calif., and Paul Mores of San Francisco; two stepdaughters, Peggy Mores of Golden and Adele Mores of Grand Junction; and one grandchild.

Memorial services will be Friday at 10 a.m. at St. Aidan's Episcopal Church, 2425 Colorado Ave., in Boulder, with the Rev. David L. Mustian of the church, officiating."

FRASER, Mary

Birth: 1905
Death 05/11/1908
Cemetery Location: Unknown

Father: George William Fraser; Mother: Anna May (*Sabin*); born and died in Ward (Boulder) Colorado at age 3 years (approximately)-heart disease; no tombstone; see **About the George William Fraser Family**

Boulder Daily Camera 12 May 1908:
"Mary, the three-year-old daughter of Mr. and Mrs. George Fraser of Ward, died Monday noon. Interment will be in Gold Hill."

Boulder Daily Herald 12 May 1908:
"Mary, the three year old daughter of Mr. and Mrs. George Fraser of Ward, died yesterday morning of heart disease. The funeral will be held tomorrow afternoon from the residence in Ward and the interment will be in the Gold Hill cemetery."

About the George William Fraser Family

George William Fraser was born 18 March 1868 in (Nova Scotia) Canada; the son of Abraham and Susannah (*McIntosh*) Fraser. George came to the United States about 1891.

In Lincoln [now Breckenridge] (Summit) Colorado on 24 March 1894 he married Anna May Sabin. She was born 14 September 1870 Iowa; the daughter of New York natives William Jerome and Mary Ann "Mercy" (*Clark*) Sabin.

To the union of George and Anna eight known children were born:

Margaret Ann: born 14 February 1895 Ward (Boulder) Colorado and died 07 February 1965 Boulder (Boulder) Colorado; buried Mountain View Memorial Park, Boulder (Boulder) Colorado; married Joseph M. Walters

Bertha Christina: born 26 June 1898 Ward (Boulder) Colorado and died 18 February 1968 Los Angeles (Los Angeles) California; buried Forest Lawn Memorial Park (Hollywood Hills), Los Angeles (Los Angeles) California; married Herbert L. Platt and Joseph Peter LaLonde

William Donald: born 16 April 1899 Ward (Boulder) Colorado and died 01 March 1962 Kearney (Buffalo) Nebraska; buried Ridge Cemetery, Fremont (Dodge) Nebraska; married Gertrude Weaver and Clara Marie Louise Ibsen

George Elwood: born 04 February 1902 Ward (Boulder) Colorado and died 03 June 1960 Sacramento (Sacramento) California; buried East Lawn Memorial Park, Sacramento (Sacramento) California; married Pearl E. (maiden name unknown)

Mary: born 1905 Ward (Boulder) Colorado and died 11 May 1908 Ward (Boulder) Colorado; buried Gold Hill Cemetery, Gold Hill (Boulder) Colorado; see FRASER, Mary

Anna May: born 13 April 1908 Ward (Boulder) Colorado and died 02 September 1988 San Bernardino (San Bernardino) California; burial unknown; married John H. Dexter and Fred D. Rollins

Milton F.: born 05 March 1910 Boulder (Boulder) Colorado and died 06 October 1969 Pueblo (Pueblo) Colorado; buried Green Mountain Cemetery, Boulder (Boulder) Colorado; married Ada Louise Hall

Mary E.: born 17 December 1916 Boulder (Boulder) Colorado and died 25 January 1989 (Stanislaus) California; buried Lakewood Memorial Park, Hughson (Stanis-laus) California); married Clifford Ray Moss

George and Anna lived in Breckenridge (Summit) Colorado in 1892 and then in Ward (Boulder) Colorado in 1894. By the U.S. 1920 census they were living south of the University of Colorado in Boulder (Boulder) Colorado.

Anna died 05 March 1937 from pneumonia and was buried in the Columbia Cemetery, Boulder (Boulder) Colorado. George died 09 November 1941 from chronic myocarditis and was buried beside his wife.

Boulder Daily Camera 10 November 1941:

"George W. Fraser...

George William Fraser, 73, who followed stone mason work in Boulder for many years following a career of mining in Boulder county, died at 2 o'clock this morning at the home of a daughter, Mrs. Joe M. Walters, 1425 Pine street. He had been ill two weeks.

Mr. Fraser was born in Nova Scotia, Canada, and came to Colorado 47 years ago. He mined at Ward and other districts of Boulder County then came to Boulder. He constructed homes, garages, walls and other structures of stone and was employed on many contracts.

Seven children survive him. They are Mrs. Walters, Milton F. Fraser, a clerk in the college grocery, and Mrs.

Mary E. Moss, all of Boulder; Mrs. H.L. Platts, of Pomona, Calif., whose husband died a week ago Sunday, William D. Fraser, Fort Collins; George E. Fraser, Pomona, Calif., and Mrs. Anna M. Dexter, Los Angeles, Calif. A sister of Mr. Fraser lives in Nova Scotia. He is also survived by seventeen grandchildren.

The body is at the Hall-Kelso Home mortuary."

Boulder Daily Camera 05 March 1937:

"Mrs. Geo. W. Fraser Dies of Pneumonia...

Mrs. Anna M. Fraser, wife of George W. Fraser, stone mason, died at the Community hospital early this morning of pneumonia. She was 65 years of age.

Mrs. Fraser had been a resident of Boulder 43 years and was widely known. Her home was at 605 Baseline. Besides her husband, survivors are four daughters, Mrs. J.M. Walter, Boulder; Mrs. J.H. Dexter, Longmont; Mrs. Clifford R. Moss, Longmont, and Mrs. H.T. Platt, Pomona; and three sons, George E. Fraser, Ward; William D. and Milton F. Fraser, Boulder; and 14 grandchildren.

Mrs. Fraser was a member of the Security Benefit association. She had lived in Breckenridge and Ward as well as Boulder.

Funeral services will be held on Monday afternoon at 2 at Howe mortuary. Rev. J.H. Sanders of the Presbyterian Church will officiate. Burial will be in Columbia cemetery."

G

GALLAGHER, Bertha "Katie"

Birth: 03/18/1885
Death: 11/27/1896
Cemetery Location: Unknown

Father: John Gallagher; Mother: Margaret Ann (*Williams*) Carlisle; born in Missouri and died in Ward (Boulder) Colorado at age 12 years, 8 months, 9 days-overexertion from jumping rope; previous records have death date as 11/28/1896; other sources state date of birth as 03/31/1884; no tombstone; see **About the John Gallagher Family**

Boulder Daily Camera 28 November 1896:

"Bertha Gallagher of Ward, aged 12, and a bright and healthy young miss but three or four days ago, died last night and will be buried at Gold Hill tomorrow. Her death is reported to have been due to jumping rope. She is accredited with having jumped 170 times without stopping and one of the vital organs was so affected that she was shortly taken to her bed from which she never rose again."

Boulder News 03 December 1896:

"Bertha Gallagher, aged twelve years, died at Ward last Friday. Her death was said to be caused by over-exertion in jumping the rope."

About the John Gallagher Family

John Gallagher was born 30 June 1860 in Irondale (Washington) Missouri; the son of Michael and Anna (*McCarron*) Gallagher. John married Margaret "Margret" Ann (*Williams*) Carlisle on 13 February 1883 in (Iron) Missouri. She was born May of 1858 in Ohio; the daughter of Pennsylvania natives William C. and Eleanor "Ellen" (maiden name unknown) Williams. This was Margaret's second marriage as her first marriage was on 16 December 1874 in (St. Francois) Missouri to George Alonzo Carlisle, born 1856 and the son of Alex M. and Sarah M. (*Holman*) Carlisle. To the union of Margaret and George two known children were born:

Lulu Blanche: born 19 March 1877 Missouri and died 07 March 1909 (Jackson) Illinois; buried Central Cemetery, De Soto (Jackson) Illinois; married John Henry Crews; some sources have death place as Kentucky

George Alonzo Jr.: born May 1880 Missouri-death unknown; burial unknown; 1880 census lists George's name as "Bird H.;" There is a George Carlisle (born 1880 Missouri; married Jane (*Smith*) McGuire) who died 17

July 1906 in Illinois and was buried in the Tower Grove Cemetery, Murphysboro (Jackson) Illinois

George Alonzo and Margaret were only married about six years as he died on 17 May 1880. Margaret then apparently met John Gallagher in (Iron) Missouri and they were married there on 13 February 1883. Their marriage produced six known children:

Bertha "Katie": born 18 March 1884 Missouri and died 27 November 1896 Ward (Boulder) Colorado; buried Gold Hill Cemetery, Gold Hill (Boulder) Colorado; see GALLAGHER, Bertha "Katie"

John "Jack": born 19 April 1886 Missouri and died July 1957 Espanola (Rio Arriba) New Mexico; buried E.U.B. Cemetery, Alcalde (Rio Arriba) New Mexico; married Margert Nina Irene Williams

Charles: born 09 October 1888 (Teller) Colorado; no further information

William: born 12 May 1894 Ward (Boulder) Colorado and died 26 September 1918 Ardennes (Champagne-Ardenne) France; buried Meuse-Argonne American Cemetery and Memorial, Romagne-sous-Montfaucon, Departmente de la Meuse, Lorraine, France-World War I casualty; believed never married

Lawrence: born 05 September 1896 Ward (Boulder) Colorado and died 03 March 1977 Bonne Terre (St. Francois) Missouri; buried Woodlawn Cemetery, Leadington (St. Francois) Missouri; married Mary Adeline Swaringim

Arthur: born 17 October 1901 (Boulder) Colorado and died 10 March 1928 Flat River (St. Francois) Missouri; buried Flat River (St. Francois) Missouri; married Stella Pritchett

By 1888 John and his family were living in (Teller) Colorado where John was a miner. The family then traveled to Ward (Boulder) Colorado where John is listed in the 1892 Boulder County Directory as a miner. It is not clear if John went back to (Teller) to mine, leaving his family in Ward (Boulder) Colorado or if the entire family moved back there. However the death of daughter Bertha "Katie" in 1896 might have prompted the move to ease their grief.

John Gallagher died on 04 August 1908 in Elkton (Teller) Colorado. By 1910 Margaret had returned to (St. Francois) Missouri with her sons, William, Lawrence and Arthur. In the 1920 census Margaret was still living there along with sons John, Lawrence and Arthur (her son,

William, died in 1918).

In the 1930 census Margaret was living with her son, John, and his wife, Margert Nina. They moved to Cliff (Grant) New Mexico where soon afterward Margert Nina passed away, leaving John with two young daughters.

On 10 January 1936 John's mother, Margaret Ann (*Williams*) Carlisle Gallagher died in Cliff (Grant) New Mexico and was buried at Mesa Cemetery, Gila (Grant) New Mexico; her tombstone has birth year as 1863.

GARNETT, David Roger

Birth: 08/21/1932
Death: 12/16/2016
Cemetery Location: C4

Father: John Garnett; Mother: Lulu Maude (*Roberts*); Wife: Carol (*Ridyard*); born on the family ranch near Syracuse in the southwest corner of the state and died in Bisbee (Cochise) Arizona-congestive heart failure

Bisbee Observer 22 December 2016:

"Roger Garnett of Gold Hill, Colo., and Bisbee passed away at home on the morning of Dec. 16, 2016. He was born on Aug. 21, 1932, at the family ranch on the Colorado/Kansas border. He grew up in Holly, Colo., and received a Bachelor's degree in Music Education and Mast of Music degree from the University of Colorado. He was a kind man who enjoyed travel, cooking, wine and music. He worked as a ranch hand, butcher, Porsche mechanic, middle school music teacher, voice teacher, choir director, restaurant manager and in the wine business. A man of many skills.

Roger was preceded in death by his parents and his sister and brother.

He leaves three children, Dana Garnett of Colorado, Diane Barry and DeLynn Cleveland of Connecticut, his grandchildren and many friends. Carol, his wife and best friend of 43 years, will miss him every day.

Services and celebration of Roger's life will be held in Gold Hill, Colo., in the summer of 2017.

May he rest in peace."

GIBSON, Robert Wallace

Birth: 11/30/1928
Death: 12/08/2004
Cemetery Location: B5

Father: Edwin Wallace Gibson; Mother: Martha (*Clayton*); Wife: Shirlee (*Rowan*); born in Aurora (Kane/DuPage) Illinois and died in Boulder (Boulder) Colorado at age 76 years, 0 months, 8 days-natural causes; see GIBSON, Shirlee C. (*Rowan*); see CARPENTER, Michael Glen

Boulder Daily Camera 11 December 2004:

"ROBERT W. GIBSON—Robert W. Gibson of Boulder died of natural causes Wednesday, Dec. 8, 2004, in Boulder at his son's home. He was 76.

The son of Edwin W. Gibson and Martha Clayton Gibson, he was born Nov. 30, 1928, in Aurora, Ill. He married Shirlee Rowan on Aug. 28, 1948, in Aurora. She died in 1991. He married Valerie McKimmy on April 27, 1999, in Hawaii. They divorced.

Mr. Gibson moved to Boulder County in 1950, living in Gold Hill and Boulder.

He earned a Bachelor of Arts degree from the University of Colorado in history and education in 1954. He attended CU on the GI Bill.

He served in the Army's 82nd Airborne Division as a paratrooper from 1946 to 1948.

Mr. Gibson worked for the Colorado Department of Employment as a senior employment counselor from 1955 to 1960. He worked for Flatiron Companies of Boulder from 1960 to 1981 as an asphalt plant superintendent for Flatiron Paving Co., and a vice president and general manager for Flatiron Sand and Gravel Co. and as president and general manager Flatiron Pre-Mix Concrete until his retirement.

He was a past president and board member of the Colorado Sand and Gravel Association, regional chairman for the National Ready Mixed Concrete Association's concrete promotional committee, and a board member for the association.

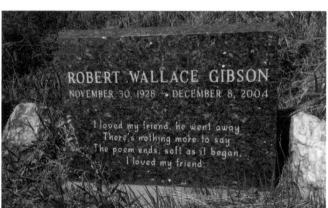

After retiring he went into partnership with his son Bret Gibson, owning and operating Boulder Mountain Lodge.

Mr. Gibson was a past president and board member of the Boulder Valley School District, the YMCA of Boulder Valley, Junior Achievement of Boulder, the Boulder Pow Wow, and the Boulder Chamber of Commerce; a past president of the Boulder Historical Society; and a past board member of Eco-Cycle of Boulder.

He was a supporter of the University of Colorado Golden Buffalo Scholarship Fund. "Bob was a man of words, he led by example. He was dedicated to his family, his friends and to his community," his family said.

Survivors include his sister, Mary M. Runninger of Rome, Ga.; three daughters, Kerry Gibson of Silverthorne, Kathy Gibson of Sunset and Kris Gibson of Gold Hill; and two sons, Clay Gibson of Loxahatchee, Fla., and Bret Gibson of Boulder.

A memorial service will be at 1 p.m. Wednesday at the Chautauqua Community House, 900 Baseline Road, Boulder. Chaplain Todd Theilmann of Hospice Care of Boulder and Broomfield Counties will officiate. A reception follows. Intimate graveside services will be at 10:30 a.m. Wednesday at Gold Hill Cemetery.

Contributions may be made to Junior Achievement Programs, in care of Kristi Shaffer, 2455 Market St., Suite 200, Denver, CO 80202. Allstate Cremation handled arrangements."

GIBSON, Shirlee Corinne (*Rowan*)

Birth: 07/30/1928
Death: 05/31/1990
Cemetery Location: B5

Father: Vernon Charles "Chuck" Rowan; Mother: Cora Dorothy "Doll" (*Walden*); born in Earlville (LaSalle) Illinois and died in Longmont (Boulder) Colorado at age 61 years, 10 months, 1 day-airplane crash; see GIBSON, Robert Wallace; see CARPENTER, Michael Glen

Boulder Daily Camera 02 June 1990:
"Shirlee R. Gibson —Shirlee Rowan Gibson died May 31 in Longmont United Hospital as a result of injuries suffered in an airplane crash near Longmont Municipal Airport. She was 61.

She was born July 30, 1928 in Earlville, Ill., the daughter of Vernon "Chuck" Rowan and Cora Dorothy Rowan.

She married Robert Gibson on Aug. 28, 1948, in Aurora, Ill. The Gibsons moved to Boulder in 1950, and she was active in the marketing and advertising professions. Most recently, Mrs. Gibson was owner and operator of the Boulder Mountain Lodge in Four Mile Canyon.

Survivors include her husband of Boulder; three daughters, Kerry Gibson, Kathleen Gibson Carpenter and Kristen Gibson, all of Boulder; two sons, Robert "Bret" Gibson of Boulder and Clayton Gibson of West Palm Beach, Fla.; and two grandchildren. Also surviving are her mother of Boulder, and two sisters, Shari Balsley Van Alsburg of Boulder and Virginia McDuffee of San Diego.

A memorial service will be held at 11 a.m. Monday at Howe Mortuary. Burial will follow in the Gold Hill Cemetery. Friends will be received after 2 p.m. Monday at the Boulder Mountain Lodge.

In lieu of flowers, contributions may be made to Judson Flying School, 1083 North 85th Str. Longmont 80503."

GOUDGE, Alfred Charles

Birth: 12/17/1858
Death: 07/28/1902
Cemetery Location: Unknown

Father: John Alfred Goudge; Mother: Harriett "Hattie/Attie" Elizabeth "Libby" (*Wicks*); Wife: Annie Clara (*Harrison*); born in Michigan and died in Gold Hill (Boulder) Colorado at age 43 years, 7 months, 11 days-traumatic pneumonia; great grand uncle of author; brother to Edwin David "Ned" Goudge; no tombstone; see GOUDGE, Edwin David "Ned"

Boulder Daily Camera 29 July 1902:
"Alfred Goudge, who has made his home in Gold Hill the past twenty-eight years, died at that place on Monday and was buried there this afternoon. He was 43 years of age and a native of England."

(Death certificate and family genealogy states he was born in Michigan)

"EVEN ANGELS FLY TOO CLOSE
TO THE GROUND
WE LOVE YOU"

About Alfred Charles Goudge

Alfred Charles Goudge was born 17 December 1858 Michigan; the son of John Alfred and Harriett "Hattie/Attie" Elizabeth "Libby" (*Wicks*) Goudge.

In 1870 the Goudge family was living in Reading (Berks) Pennsylvania. In 1880 Alfred was single and working as a miner at Caribou (Boulder) Colorado. He married Annie Clara Harrison on 21 November 1885 in Mahanoy City (Schuylkill) Pennsylvania. She was born 04 July 1866 (family Bible states 03 July 1965) in England; the daughter of Peter and Elizabeth (*Moffat*) Harrison. Their union produced five known children:

Nathan "Ned": born 1887 Mahanoy City (Schuylkill) Pennsylvania and died 13 February 1888 Negaunee (Marquette) Michigan; buried Negaunee (Marquette) Michigan

Harrison: born 04 February 1888 Negaunee (Marquette) Michigan –died 11 August 1960 Los Angeles (Los Angeles) California; buried Forest Lawn Memorial Park, Glendale (Los Angeles) California; married Iva (Ivey) Keturah MacFarlane; Interesting to note that Harrison owned part of the land that became Disneyland in Anaheim (Orange) California.

Alfred Charles: born 27 August 1889 Negaunee (Marquette) Michigan and died 22 November 1920 Cedar City (Iron) Utah; buried Cedar City Cemetery, Cedar City (Iron) Utah; married Jennie Urie Hunter

Leonard D.: born 21 March 1893 Negaunee (Marquette) Michigan and died 23 January 1944 Seal Beach (Orange) California; buried Inglewood Park Cemetery, Inglewood (Los Angeles) California; married Eva Rebecca Houchen

Norman: born 06 January 1894 Negaunee (Marquette) Michigan and died 20 March 1958 Salinas (Monterey) California; buried Garden of Memories, Monterey (Monterey) California; married Louisa M. Adams; Norman changed his last name from Goudge to Green due to the remarriage of his mother however some legal documents are still in the name of Goudge

Raymond: born 04 March 1897 Gold Hill (Boulder) Colorado and died 19 October 1942 Los Angeles (Los Angeles) California; buried Forest Lawn Memorial Park, Glendale (Los Angeles) California; married Mary Emma Gower; Raymond changed his last name from Goudge to Green due to the remarriage of his mother however some legal documents are still in the name of Goudge

Alfred, like his father, was a miner and worked many of the Gold Hill area mines along with his brother, Edwin David "Ned" Goudge.

Alfred died 28 July 1902 in Gold Hill (Boulder) Colorado at the age of 43 years from "foreign matter in lungs" and is buried in an unmarked grave in the Gold Hill Cemetery, Gold Hill (Boulder) Colorado. His widow, Anna, married Dr. Ernest Flint Green who was the attending physician when Alfred died. They were married on 28 June 1904 in Salt Lake City (Salt Lake) Utah. This union produced three known children:

Ruth Dacre: born 20 June 1906 Cedar City (Iron) Utah and died 13 October 1933 Los Angeles (Los Angeles) California; buried Forest Lawn Memorial Park Cemetery, Glendale (Los Angeles) California; married Herman "Henry" H. Franklin and a Mr. Wilcox

Ernest John Moffat: born 19 September 1908 Cedar City (Iron) Utah and died 22 August 1985 Hayward (Alameda) California); burial unknown; married Norma Leone Barraclough

Grace Fowler: born 14 December 1909 Cedar City (Iron) Utah and died 16 May 1993 (Orange) California); burial unknown; married Everett M. Koontz

Dr. Ernest Flint Green died 31 December 1945 and his wife, Annie Clara (*Harrison*) Goudge Green, died 30 March 1949. Both are buried together in the Forest Lawn Cemetery in Glendale (Los Angeles) California.

GOUDGE, Annie Elizabeth (*Bennett(s)*)

Birth: 04/06/1856
Death: 09/09/1930
Cemetery Location: D4

Father: John Thomas Bennett(s); Mother: Amelia Anne (*Johns*); Husband: Edwin David "Ned" Goudge; born in St. Blazey (Cornwall) England and died in Gold Hill (Boulder) Colorado at age 73 years, 5 months, 3 days-apoplexy (stroke); great grandmother of author; family Bible, marriage certificate and tombstone state birth year as 1856; see GOUDGE, Edwin David "Ned;" see **About Edwin David "Ned" and Annie Elizabeth (*Bennett(s)*) Goudge**

Boulder Daily Camera 09 September 1930:

"Mrs. Annie Goudge Pioneer, Found Dead In Bed— Mrs. Annie Goudge, widow of the late Edwin Goudge, was found dead in her bed at Gold Hill today when her daughter, Mrs. Nell Humphrey, went to awaken her for breakfast. She died of apoplexy sometime during the night. There was no evidence of a struggle and relatives and friends believe she died while in her sleep.

Mrs. Goudge was to come to Boulder today to make her home with her son, Wilbur Goudge, at 625 Maxwell, after a summer in Gold Hill. He moved to Boulder from the mountains a few days ago.

Mrs. Goudge was born in England, April 6, 1858 [error] and was married at Dover, N.J. 59 years ago. She and her husband came to Colorado on their honeymoon and liked this state so well that they located in the mountains.

Most of their residence was at Gold Hill. Six children survive. They are Mrs. Martha Liebee of Boulder, Mrs.

Nell Humphrey of Gold Hill, Mrs. Esther [Ethel] Nichols of Boulder, Wilbur D. Goudge, Walter Goudge of Boulder and Arthur Goudge of Crisman, and fourteen grandchildren and two great grandchildren. The men of the family, like their father, are miners. The remains are at the Howe mortuary awaiting funeral arrangements."

Boulder Daily Camera 09 September 1930:

"Mrs. Annie Goudge, Gold Hill Pioneer, Dies At 73 Years—Mrs. Annie Goudge, 73 years old, who has lived in and near Gold Hill for 59 years, died at her home in Gold Hill this morning following a stroke of apoplexy.

Mrs. Goudge was the widow of Edwin Goudge, who died seven years ago.

Mrs. Goudge and her husband came to Colorado immediately following their marriage 59 years ago in Dover, N.J., and settled in the mountains west of Boulder. Most of the time, they resided at Gold Hill where their children were born.

The six children who survive are: Mrs. Martha Libee of Boulder, Mrs. Nell Humphrey of Gold Hill, Mrs. Ethel Nichols of Boulder, Wilber [sic] D. Goudge and Walter Goudge of Boulder, and Arthur Goudge of Crisman. There are fourteen grandchildren and two great-grandchildren.

Mrs. Goudge was one of the best known pioneers of the Gold Hill section, and had many friends in Boulder also, having often visited here with her children.

She was born in England April 6, 1857.

Her body has been taken to the Howe mortuary and funeral announcements will be made from there later."

Boulder Daily Camera 11 September 1930:

"MRS. ANNIE GOUDGE—Funeral for Mrs. Annie

Goudge, who died at Gold Hill, Sept. 9, will be held at the Howe Mortuary Sunday afternoon at 2 o'clock. Rev. A.L. Hipple of the Nazarene church will officiate. Interment will be in the Gold Hill cemetery."

Boulder Daily Camera 15 September 1930:

"Funeral Services for Mrs. Annie Goudge—Funeral services for Mrs. Annie Goudge were held at the Howe mortuary yesterday afternoon at two o'clock. Mrs. Goudge died September 9 at Gold Hill, where she had lived for a number of years.

The services were in charge of Rev. A.L. Hipple, Mrs. Barnett Grams, Denver, sung beautifully during the services.

The mortuary was crowded for the services with her many friends and relatives. There were a large number of floral offerings. Pallbearers were: Frank Richards, Loren Harris, Richard Mitchell, Chas. Humphrey, Phillip Godge [Goudge] and William Mitchell, all grandsons of the deceased.

Burial was in Gold Hill cemetery beside the body of her husband."

GOUDGE, Edwin David "Ned"

Birth: 01/09/1853
Death: 08/04/1923
Cemetery Location: D4

Father: John Alfred Goudge; Mother: Harriett "Hattie/Attie" Elizabeth "Libby" (*Wicks*); Wife: Annie Elizabeth (*Bennett(s)*); born in Galena (Jo Davies) Illinois and died in Boulder (Boulder) Colorado at age 70 years, 6 months, 26 days-miners' consumption; great grandfather of author; sometimes his first name is incorrectly referred to as "Edward;" brother of Alfred Charles Goudge; see GOUDGE, Alfred Charles; see GOUDGE, Annie Elizabeth (*Bennett(s)*); see **About Edwin David "Ned" and Annie Elizabeth (*Bennett(s)*) Goudge**

Boulder Daily Camera 06 August 1923:

"E.D.GOUDGE, AGED 70, DIED AT HIS HOME HERE—E.D. Goudge, 70 years old, a resident of Boulder county for 49 years, died at his home, 1740 Spruce street, Saturday night at 9:30 o'clock. Death was caused by miners' consumption. He had been in poor health eleven years.

Mr. Goudge came to Colorado from his home at Dover, N.J., in 1874, two years before the state of Colorado was admitted to the union. Shortly before leaving New Jersey he was married, and the journey was in the nature of a honeymoon trip. Mr. and Mrs. Goudge located first at Caribou, and later moved to Gold Hill, where they lived until eleven years ago, when they moved to Boulder.

Besides his wife, Mrs. Annie Goudge, deceased is survived by six children, all of whom were at his bed-

Digging Up Dirt

side when he died. They are: Arthur, Wilbur and Walter Goudge, Mrs. Martha Liebee, Mrs. Nellie Humphrey and Mrs. Ethel Nichols, all of Boulder. Mr. Goudge is also survived by two brothers, John and William Goudge of Negaunee, Mich., and two sisters of Philadelphia. He had thirteen grandchildren.

Funeral services will be held Tuesday afternoon at 2 o'clock, at Howe's mortuary. The Rev. Frank Ashba of the Friends' church will be in charge of the services. Burial will be in the Gold Hill cemetery."

Boulder Daily Camera 07 August 1923:

"Edwin Goudge—The funeral of Edwin Daniel [David] Goudge, who died August 4, took place at 2 o'clock this afternoon from Howe's mortuary. Rev. Ashby, of the Nazarene church, conducted the service. A quartette of the church sang. The pallbearers were Richard Brown, Thomas Daley, Oscar Walton, Benj. Walton, Peter Burger, and Homer Pennock. Interment was in Goldhill."

Boulder Daily Camera 08 August 1923:

"Funeral Car Turned Over While On Road To Gold Hill...Car bearing Remains of E.D. Goudge from Boulder Saved from Disaster to Party by Swift Action of Norman Howe—Casket Was Not Shunted From the Funeral Car as Rumored—

Norman Howe, son a A.E. Howe undertaker, suffered a bruised leg and a hearse containing the body of Edwin D. Goudge, which was being taken to Goldhill for burial, turned over on its side, when the gears on the hearse motor were stripped at the Reese pitch, near Sommerville Tuesday afternoon at 3 o'clock.

Contrary to rumors on the street this morning the body was not thrown from the casket. The casket was not injured in the accident. It was taken from the wrecked hearse, placed in a private motor car, and conveyed to the Goldhill cemetery where services were held as planned.

Wilbur Goudge, a son of the late E.D. Goudge today praised Norman Howe, who was driving the hearse, for his head-work. Goudge declared that had not Howe

Original Burial Photo 04 August 1923

turned the hearse into the bank, it would have continued down the hill, struck the car containing members of the Goudge family, and probably would have caused one or more deaths and serious injuries. The hill upon which the accident happened is a 25 per cent grade.

Motor Wouldn't Pull Car Up the Hill—Just before the hearse started up the hill, Howe noticed something was wrong with the motor. He put the car in low gear and by having it pushed by several men in the funeral procession, nearly reached the summit of the hill. The motor then refused to pull, and Howe slipped the gears into reverse, intending to back down the hill on compression. He stripped the low and intermediate gears, and the brakes were unable to hold the heavy hearse on the steep hill. The hearse started downhill. Wilbur Goudge, who was assisting to push the hearse, tossed a large rock against one of the rear wheels. In doing so, his thumb became caught. Today it was necessary for physicians to amputate part of the thumb.

Howe then backed the hearse into the bank. It tipped over on one side. The casket slipped from the hearse but was not damaged. Damage to the hearse will amount to $250."

About Edwin David "Ned" and Annie Elizabeth (*Bennett(s)*) Goudge

Edwin David "Ned" Goudge was born on 09 January 1853 in Galena (Jo Davies) Illinois; the son of Cornish parents John Alfred and Harriett "Hattie/Attie" Elizabeth "Libby" (*Wicks*) Goudge. He married Annie Elizabeth Bennett(s) on 01 August 1874 in Randolf Township (Morris) New Jersey. Annie was born on 06 April 1856 in St. Blazey (Cornwall) England; the daughter of John Thomas and Amelia Ann (*Johns*) Bennett(s). Eleven known children were born to this union; three died in infancy (one of the three infants died before 1877 and was buried in the Caribou Cemetery, Caribou (Boulder) Colorado) and eight surviving into adulthood:

Martha: born 13 November 1877 Summerville (Boulder) Colorado and died 15 August 1952 Boulder (Boulder) Colorado; buried Mountain View Cemetery, Boulder (Boulder) Colorado; married Wilbur C. "Billy" Abbott, John Vivian Richards, John Franklin Leibee and James Adair King

Nell Gladys: born 08 September 1879 Gold Hill (Boulder) Colorado and died 20 September 1966 San Diego (San Diego) California; cremated-ashes at Cypress View Mausoleum, San Diego (San Diego) California; married Charles Stanley Humphrey

Arthur "Art" Garfield: born 15 October 1881 Summerville (Boulder) Colorado and died 16 December 1948 Denver (Denver) Colorado; buried Golden Cemetery, Golden (Jefferson) Colorado; married Mae (May) Victoria Ardourel

James D.: born 15 December 1885 Summerville (Boulder) Colorado and died 10 October 1918 Boulder (Boulder) Colorado; buried Gold Hill Cemetery, Gold Hill (Boulder) Colorado; married Gladys Holman; see GOUDGE, JAMES D.

Mabel L.: born 26 February 1888 Gold Hill (Boulder) Colorado and died 14 June 1916 Boulder (Boulder) Colorado; buried Green Mountain Cemetery, Boulder (Boulder) Colorado; married John L. "Jack" Walsh

Ethel: born 15 October 1892 Gold Hill (Boulder) Colorado and died 14 July 1981 Boulder (Boulder) Colorado; cremated-ashes at Mountain View Cemetery, Boulder (Boulder) Colorado; married Richard John Nicholls; Ethel changed the spelling of her married name to "Nichols;" see NICHOLLS, Richard John; see **About the Bradford Family**

Wilbur Dewey: born 17 February 1898 Gold Hill (Boulder) Colorado and died 02 January 1969 Boulder (Boulder) Colorado; buried Mountain View Cemetery, Boulder (Boulder) Colorado; married Carrie Leona Livingston; grandfather of author

Walter S.: born 30 April 1900 Gold Hill (Boulder) Colorado and died 06 June 1976 Boulder (Boulder) Colorado; buried Mountain View Cemetery, Boulder (Boulder) Colorado; married Dorothy Mary "Dode" Pancost

It was said that all the male children had middle names of past United States presidents. Unfortunately not all middle names were known or written down.

Annie worked as a housekeeper in the Kinney House (aka Gold Hotel Hotel) in Gold Hill (Boulder) Colorado and in 1900 she bought the place while Edwin was mining in Cripple Creek (Teller) Colorado. This building became known as the "Goudge Hotel." In 1920 papers were signed to sell the property to the Holiday House Association (aka Bluebirds) and in 1922 it was official. The Goudge Hotel became the Bluebird Lodge.

Due to his failing health Edwin knew he was dying so he began to dig his own grave in the Gold Hill Cemetery in Gold Hill (Boulder) Colorado. Family story says he came upon an unmarked grave while digging so he had to adjust his burial site.

By 1913 Edwin and Annie had moved to Boulder (Boulder) Colorado where Edwin died in 1923 from "fibroid phthisis" (tuberculosis). Annie then lived in the Wee Comfort cabin on Main Street in Gold Hill (Boulder) Colorado for about seven more years and then in 1930 decided to move to Boulder and live with her son, Wilbur, and family. Unfortunately she died in her sleep from "apoplexy" (venerable term for stroke) in the cabin the night before she was to make this journey. Edwin and Annie are buried beside each other in the Gold Hill Cemetery.

GOUDGE, Edwin Gerald "Bud"

Birth: 12/12/1920
Death: 10/13/1990
Cemetery Location: D4

Father: Wilbur Dewey Goudge; Mother: Carrie Leona (*Livingston*); Wife: Ruth Catherine Awilda (*Eastman*); born in Boulder (Boulder) Colorado and died in Portland (Multnomah) Oregon at age 69 years, 10 months, 1 day-heart failure; uncle of author; grandson of Edwin David "Ned" and Annie (*Bennett(s)*) Goudge; see GOUDGE, Edwin David "Ned;" see GOUDGE, Annie Elizabeth (*Bennett(s)*); see **About Edwin David "Ned" and Annie Elizabeth (*Bennett(s)*) Goudge**

Boulder Daily Camera 18 October 1990:

"Edwin G. "Bud" Goudge—Edwin G. "Bud" Goudge, a former Boulder resident, died Saturday, Oct. 13, of heart failure in Portland, Ore. He was 69.

He was born December 12, 1920, in Boulder, the son of Wilbur D. Goudge and Leona Goudge. He married Ruth Eastman on Nov. 11, 1949, in Portland. He attended the University of Colorado where he was a Sigma Chi.

He enlisted in the U.S. Marine Corps in 1942 and saw action in Okinawa, earning two Bronze Stars and a presidential citation for bravery.

He also served in the South Pacific at Midway Island until 1946 and returned to the United States where he was a captain in the USMC reserves until 1956.

He moved to Portland in 1947 and worked for the steamship division of Pope and Talbot and then managed lumber sales at the Oakridge sawmill in Oregon until he retired in 1983.

Mr. Goudge was a member of the Portland Golf Club, the Multonomah Athletic Club and the Elks Club. He also contributed time to the Good Neighbors and the Boy Scouts of America.

Survivors include his wife of Portland, two sons, William G. Goudge and Charles Goudge, both of Portland; three daughters, Sheila Goudge of Seattle, Wash., Brenda Daggett and Carrie Goudge, both of Portland; his mother in Boulder; one sister, Maxine Bush of Boulder; and five grandchildren.

Funeral services will be held today at 1:30 p.m. at St. Barnabas Episcopal Church in Portland.

Contributions can be sent to the charity of the donor's choice."

About Edwin Gerald Goudge

Edwin Gerald Goudge was the grandson of Edwin David "Ned" Goudge; see GOUDGE, Edwin David "Ned" and see GOUDGE, Annie Elizabeth (*Bennett(s)*). He was born 12 December 1920 in Boulder (Boulder) Colorado; the son of Wilbur Dewey and Carrie Leona (*Livingston*) Goudge. Edwin had two siblings: Mable Maxine (mother of author) and Donna Lee.

Edwin went to the Gold Hill School in Gold Hill (Boulder) Colorado and worked at the Double M Ranch west of town where he was a favorite of Mrs. MacCleay and Mrs. Malloy (owners).

He enlisted in the United States Marine Corp and was a veteran of World War II.

He married Ruth Catherine Awilda Eastman on 09 November 1949 in Portland (Multnomah) Oregon. She was born 21 October 1927 in Victoria (British Columbia) Canada, the daughter of William Watson and Adelaine Francis (*Price*) Eastman. To their union five known children were born:

Brenda Jo: born 1950-still living
William "Bill" Gerald: born 1951-still living
Sheila Cay: born 1954-still living
Charles Brian: born 1958-still living
Carrie Lorraine: born 1960-still living

Edwin Gerald "Bud" Goudge was cremated;

"...whenever the wrath comes it might be a little difficult for your Uncle Bud to get "all together." The rest of his ashes are at Riverview Mausoleum in Portland along with Ruth. Of course there was a slight spillage in the suitcase on the air flight from PDx-Denver...we did the best we could to collect them all for the Gold Hill spot but a few landed under the tree out in the backyard from the suitcase! Oh yeah and Bill at the time thought it was a good idea to throw a few from the continental divide plaque. That should cover it!!"

—Sheila Goudge, daughter of Edwin Gerald "Bud" and Ruth Catherine (*Eastman*) Goudge

His widow, Ruth, died on 19 January 1995 in Portland (Multnomah) Oregon and was laid to rest in the Riverview Abby Cemetery in Portland (Multnomah) Oregon.

GOUDGE, James D.

Birth: 12/15/1885
Death: 10/10/1918
Cemetery Location: D4

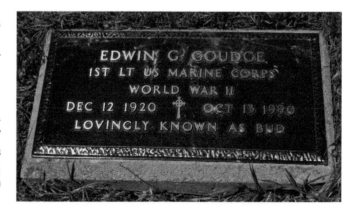

Father: Edwin David "Ned" Goudge; Mother: Annie Elizabeth (*Bennett(s)*); Wife: Gladys Mary (*Holman*); born in Summerville (Boulder) Colorado and died in Boulder (Boulder) Colorado at age 32 years, 9 months, 25 days-pneumonia/flu; grand uncle of author; see GOUDGE, Edwin David "Ned;" see GOUDGE, Annie Elizabeth (*Bennett(s)*); see **About Edwin David "Ned" and Annie Elizabeth (*Bennett(s)*) Goudge**

Boulder Daily Camera 10 October 1918:
"JAMES GOUDGE OF GOLD HILL IS DEAD OF PNEUMONIA—James Goudge died at a local institute [Colorado Sanitarium in Boulder, CO] this morning of pneumonia, age 32 years and 9 month. He was brought from Gold Hill Sunday ill with pneumonia. He was born in Summerville, the son of Mr. and Mrs. Edwin Goudge and had been a very popular merchant of Gold Hill for many years. Besides his parents he leaves a wife, brothers; Arthur, Walter and Wilbur Goudge, the latter in service in France and three sisters, Mrs. Martha Richards, Mrs. Nellie Humphrey and Mrs. Ethel Nichols. The remains are at the Boulder Undertaking Co., waiting funeral arrangements."

Boulder Daily Camera 11 October 1918:
"JAMES GOUDGE WILL SLEEP NEAR GOLD HILL NIEGHBORS—The body of James Goudge, who died yes-

terday in this city, will leave tomorrow at 10 a.m. for Gold Hill where he had been engaged in business. The funeral will be held at 2:30. The pallbearers will be chosen from among his Gold Hill friends."

About James D. Goudge

James Goudge was born 15 December 1885 in Summerville (Boulder) Colorado; the son of Edwin David "Ned" and Annie Elizabeth (*Bennett(s)*) Goudge; see GOUDGE, Edwin David "Ned" and see GOUDGE, Annie Elizabeth (*Bennett(s)*).

A miner before becoming a merchant of Gold Hill he married Gladys Mary Holman on 20 May 1912 in Boulder (Boulder) Colorado. Gladys was born 29 October 1894 in Gold Hill (Boulder) Colorado; the daughter of England natives John and Mary Ellen (*Williams*) Holman. No children blessed this marriage as James died a short six years later on 10 October 1918 from pneumonia and flu. After his death, Gladys became a postmaster in 1919 for the Gold Hill area.

Less than two years later Gladys married her second husband, John Bill Miller on 27 May 1920 in (Boulder) Colorado. He was born 18 April 1890 in Romania; parents unknown (Tombstone has 16 April 1890). This union produced one son:

John Herbert "Herb" Miller: born 07 October 1927 Colorado Springs (El Paso) Colorado and died 19 June 2001 Mesa (Maricopa) Arizona; cremated; never married but had a partner, Verna Anderson

John and Gladys operated a store and café and supervised rentals of cottages at Gold Hill (Boulder) Colorado for eight years before moving to Boulder.

John B. Miller died 13 November 1953 in Boulder (Boulder) Colorado and is buried at the Fort Logan Military Cemetery, Denver (Denver) Colorado (veteran of World War I). Gladys died at Rapid City (Pennington) South Dakota on 10 July 1960 while on vacation and is buried in the Green Mountain Cemetery, Boulder (Boulder) Colorado.

GROVER, Lafayette L.

> Birth: 10/30/1864
> Death: 06/18/1912
> Cemetery Location: Unknown

Father: Levi Grover; Mother: Elisabeth/Elizabeth (*Walter/Walters*); Wife: Dorthea (Dorothy) "Dorris/Dora" (*Christian*) Walsted; born in Liberty (Jackson) Ohio and died in Ward (Boulder) Colorado at age 48 years, 7 months, 19 days-miners' consumption; no tombstone; see SMITH, Dorthea (Dorothy) "Dorris/Dora" (*Christian*) Walsted Grover

Digging Up Dirt

Boulder Daily Herald 18 June 1912:

"Lafayette L. Grover, for 24 years a resident of Ward, died at that town last night. He leaves his wife, Mrs. Dora Grover. The deceased was a member of the K.O.T.M. and of the Fraternal Aid. The funeral will take place Friday at Ward. Interment will be made in the Gold Hill cemetery."

Boulder Daily Camera 18 June 1912:

"Deputy Coroner Leslie P. Kelso went to Ward this morning to take charge of the funeral arrangements of L. L. Grover, who died there last night."

Boulder Tribune 21 June 1912:

"LAFAYETTE GROVER DIES AT HOME IN WARD...

Lafayette L. Grover, for twenty-four years a miner in the Ward district, died at his home Monday night. The deceased was 52 years of age and was a member of the K.O.T.M., and Fraternal Aid orders. His wife, Mrs. Dorah [sic] Grover, survives him. Grover was injured in a mine by falling timber six years ago and has been in poor health ever since. The funeral services will be conducted at Ward this afternoon. Interment will be made at Gold Hill."

Boulder Daily Camera 21 June 1912:

"The funeral services over the remains of the late Lafe Grover, the well-known Boulder county mining

man, were held at Ward today. It was a largely attended funeral. Interment was made at Gold Hill. F.E. Eckel, an old friend of the deceased and a former resident of Ward officiated."

About Lafayette L. Grover

Lafayette L. Grover was born on 30 October 1864 in Liberty (Jackson) Ohio; the son of Ohio natives Levi and Elizabeth (*Walter/Walters*) Grover. He was one of nine known living children:

James Alexander: born 06 September 1849 Morgan (Gallia) Ohio and died 07 March 1937 Stanwood (Mecosta) Michigan; burial unknown; married Emma J. Griffin

Madison George: born 31 May 1851 (Gallia) Ohio and died 21 April 1922 Richmondale (Pike) Ohio; buried Allen Chapel Cemetery, Beaver (Pike) Ohio; married Hester Athey

Elesa: born 11 April 1853 Liberty (Jackson) Ohio and died 21 June 1871 Liberty (Jackson) Ohio; burial unknown; spouse unknown

Eunice E.: born about 1855 Ohio and died 1931 Jackson (Jackson) Ohio; burial unknown; married Augustus R.P. Otto or John Stather (possibilities)

Luther B.: born 09 October 1857 (Gallia) Ohio and died 10 November 1935 Jackson (Jackson) Ohio; burial unknown; married Charlotte Dewitt

Caroline: born 12 June 1860 Jackson (Jackson) Ohio and died 1911 Athens (Athens) Ohio; burial unknown; married Harvey Rice; other sources state death in 1918

Francis Sophia: born 19 April 1862 and died 24 December 1887; burial unknown; spouse unknown

Lafayette L.: born 30 October 1864 Liberty (Jackson) Ohio and died 18 June 1912 Ward (Boulder) Colorado; buried Gold Hill Cemetery, Gold Hill (Boulder) Colorado; married Dorthea (Dorothy) "Dorris/Dora" (*Christian*) Walsted; see SMITH, Dorthea (Dorothy) "Dorris/Dora" (*Christian*) Walsted Grover

John Sherman: born 03 May 1867 Liberty (Jackson) Ohio and died 20 January 1941 Liberty (Jackson) Ohio; buried Bethel Ridge Cemetery, Liberty (Jackson) Ohio; married Almira Glassburn

Lafayette came to Ward (Boulder) Colorado in the early 1890s where he met and married Dorthea (Dorothy) "Dorris/Dora" (*Christian*) Walsted on 12 January 1893 in Boulder (Boulder) Colorado. She was born 25 May 1856; the daughter of Norwegian parents. Dorthea was the widow of Nels/Nils Jacobsen Walsted; see WALSTED, Nels/Nils Jacobsen. This marriage of Lafayette and Dorthea produced no children.

Lafayette and Dorthea moved from Ward (Boulder) Colorado to a homestead near Gold Hill that was destroyed in the 1894 fire and was never rebuilt. They then moved back to Ward where in the 1900 census Lafayette was listed as "Leney L. Graver" and that he was a veteran. The middle initial L. could stand for Levi (his father's name).

After the death of Lafayette, Dorthea married William Henry Smith in August of 1919 in Boulder (Boulder) Colorado; see SMITH, Dorthea (Dorothy) "Dorris/Dora" (*Christian*) Walsted Grover.

GUSTAFSON/PETERSON/PETERSEN, Infant

Birth: 12/1892
Death: 12/21/1892
Cemetery Location: F3 (possibly)

Father: Augustus Gustof Louis "Gus" Gustafson/Peterson/ Petersen; Mother: Ida Matilda (*Burke*); born and died in Gold Hill (Boulder) Colorado at age less than 4 days-possibly tonsillitis; no tombstone; see PETERSON/ PETERSEN/ GUSTAFSON, Augustus Gustof Louis "Gus" and see PETERSON/PETERSEN/GUSTAFSON, Ida Matilda (*Burke*)

Boulder Daily Camera 21 December 1892:
"GOLD HILL ITEMS...Shortly after August Gustison [sic] buried his little baby."

Peterson/Petersen/Gustafson Plot in the Gold Hill Cemetery

Only marker in the plot is that of William Bernard Peterson/Petersen/Gustafson

Formations of graves in the plot are very difficult to visualize.

H

HALTMAN, Allen John

See **HULTMAN**, Allen John

> Birth: 1841
> Death: 08/21/1904
> Cemetery Location: Unknown

HASENJAEGER, Ella Anna Katherine

> Birth: 06/12/1892
> Death: 07/13/1973
> Cemetery Location: E3

Father: Karl August Friedrich Hasenjaeger; Mother: Augusta Louisa (*Mueller*); never married; born in Chicago (Cook) Illinois and died in Denver (Denver) Colorado at age 81 years, 1 month, 1 day-cerebral arteriosclerosis

Boulder Daily Camera 13 July 1973:

"Ella Hasenjaeger—Ella Hasenjaeger, 81, died early today in Valley Manor Nursing Home. Funeral arrangements by Howe Mortuary are pending. Born in Chicago, Ill., June 12, 1892, she was a retired nurse who was employed in Bellville, N.J. for many years before moving to Gold Hill in 1961. Miss Hasenjaeger was a member of Trinity Lutheran Church. Survivors include two brothers, Charles W. Hasenjaeger of Memphis, Tenn., and Richard Hasenjaeger of Miami, Fla."

[error as Richard died in 1970]

Boulder Daily Camera 14 July 1973:

"Ella Hasenjaeger—Graveside services will be held Thursday at 1:30 p.m. with Pastor Donald Knudson of

Trinity Lutheran Church officiating. Interment will be at Gold Hill Cemetery. Howe Mortuary is in charge of arrangements."

Boulder Daily Camera Focus (article by Laura Sickenberger) 01 November 1981:

"Another interesting Gold Hill summer resident was Ella Hasenjaeger a registered nurse who had grown up on the North Side of Chicago. After nurse's training at the Cook County Hospital in Chicago, she spent six years in Sao Paulo, Brazil, working for the Rockefeller foundation. She was an authority on nursing people having contagious diseases...She was always full of fun and frolic, often entertaining large groups of her mountain neighbors. One of her favorite offerings at these parties was a light cocktail she called the Hilty-Bilty, composed of apricot brandy, grenadine and orange juice."

About Ella Anna Katherine Hasenjaeger

Ella Hasenjaeger was born 12 June 1892 in Chicago (Cook) Illinois; the daughter of German descendants Carl August and Augusta Louisa (*Mueller*) Hasenjaeger. Immigrating to the United States in 1882, this family consisted of six known children:

Rudolph Emil Otto: born 21 October 1876 Stettin, Germany and died 18 February 1963 Chicago (Cook) Illinois; buried Beverly Cemetery, Blue Island (Cook) Illinois; married Bertha Baader

Richard Hugo John: (born 03 March 1879 Germany and died 19 September 1970 Miami (Dade) Florida; burial unknown; married Hattie Kruse

Arthur Gustav: born 02 March 1883 Chicago (Cook) Illinois and died 10 October 1913 Chicago (Cook) Illinois; buried Oak Woods Cemetery, Chicago (Cook) Illinois; married Elsa Wahl

Hattie Anna Dorothy: born March 1886 Illinois-possible death October 1964 (Dade) Florida; burial unknown; married Charles Gustaf Swanson

Charles W.: born 11 July 1888 Chicago (Cook) Illinois and died April 1978 Memphis (Shelby) Tennessee; buried Memorial Park Cemetery, Memphis (Shelby) Tennessee; married Margarete A. Biegler

Ella: born 12 June 1892 Chicago (Cook) Illinois and died 13 July 1973 Denver (Denver) Colorado; buried Gold Hill Cemetery, Gold Hill (Boulder) Colorado; never married

Ella was a long-time active Gold Hill summer resident as well as a Bluebird. Her name was spelled "Haesenjaeger" in the 1964 Bluebird active member list with address being Essex County Hospital, Belleville, New Jersey.

HASTINGS, Alice Marion "Allie"

Birth: 05/03/1880
Death: 09/10/1896
Cemetery Location: C/D 4 & 5

Father: Henry Hiram Hastings; Mother: Emily Lorinda (*McAllister*); born in Lebanon (Grafton) New Hampshire and died in Gold Hill (Boulder) Colorado at age 16 years, 4 months, 7 days-complications induced by diphtheria; 1880 census lists name as "Delia;" see **About the Henry Hiram Hastings Family**

Boulder County Herald Weekly 16 September 1896:
"Allie Hastings, aged 17, daughter of H.H. Hastings and wife, of Gold Hill, died last Wednesday of a complication of diseases super induced by diphtheria. She had recovered from the diphtheria when the other troubles set in. They were too much for her exhausted condition. The funeral took place yesterday, a large number of friends of the family attending the services. The family desires the Herald to extend kindest thanks to the many friends who assisted them during the illness and the trying ordeal following the death. Their consideration will ever be held in grateful remembrance."

Boulder News 17 September 1896:
"Miss Allie Hastings, the 17 years old daughter of H.H. Hastings and wife, of Gold Hill, died last week and was buried Sunday."

Funeral Card (courtesy of Leah Mckin, relative)
"To The Memory Of

Allie Hastings

Died Sept. 10, 1896

Aged 17 Years

One precious to our heart has gone,

The voice we loved is stilled,

The place made vacant in our home

Can never more be filled

Our father in his wisdom called

The boon his love had given,

And though on earth the body lies,

The soul is safe in heaven."

("Someone apparently got her age wrong. The dates indicate that she was 16 years 4 months and 7 days. This funeral card is in a scrapbook that an aunt of mine has." Leah Mckin)

HASTINGS, Emily Lorinda (*McAllister*)

Birth: 02/14/1848
Death: 03/16/1930
Cemetery Location: C/D 4 & 5

Father: Isaac Edson McAllister; Mother: Mary Millington (*Gray*); Husband: Henry Hiram Hastings; born in Lebanon (Grafton) New Hampshire and died in Casper (Natrona) Wyoming at 82 years, 1 month, 2 days-acute bronchitis; see **About the Henry Hiram Hastings Family**

Boulder Daily Camera 17 March 1930:
"MRS. EMILY HASTINGS OLD TIME RESIDENT DIES IN CASPER, WYO. Mrs. Emily Hastings, an aunt of D.E. McAllister of the Lashley-Persons Investment Company, of Milo McAllister and W.W. McAllister, owner and manager of the McAllister Hardware store, died Sunday morning at the home of her daughter, Mrs. Curtis Swallow, in Casper, Wyo.

The body is to leave Casper tomorrow night and arrive in Boulder Wednesday morning. It will be removed to the Howe mortuary where funeral services will be held at 1 o'clock on Thursday. Later the body will be taken to Gold Hill to be buried beside the remains of her husband, Henry H. Hastings, who died May 10, 1922.

Mrs. Hastings was a sister of the late I.T. McAllister, pioneer Boulder lumberman. Her marriage to Mr. Hastings occurred Nov. 14, 1866, in New Hampshire. She was born in Lebanon and of a family of three brothers and four sisters only two sisters survive—Mrs. Julia Cole, residing in Winchendon, Mass., and Mrs. Mary Kenniston at the old home in Lebanon.

Mr. Hasting Early Day Freighter in the Mountains—Mr. Hastings was a veteran of the Civil war, serving with Co. H, 7th Vermont Volunteer Infantry. He enlisted Dec. 20, 1861 and served to March 14, 1866. He became an active member of Nathaniel Lyon Post, G.A.R., of this city.

The Hastings came to Colorado Jan. 21, 1881. He engaged in the freighting business in the mountains, starting the first regular route from Gold Hill to Salina. I the early nineties he drove a stage coach between Boulder and Caribou.

In 1908 the family moved to Boulder and made their home at 1713 Fifteenth Street. The family was active in the Friends church.

Surviving children are Mrs. Swallow of Casper; Mrs. Dan Coughlin of Midwest, Wyo., and Mrs. Jim Pittman of Denver. The latter's husband was killed at Silver Lake last summer. There are 20 grandchildren and 17 great grandchildren."

Boulder Daily Camera 20 March 1930:
"FUNERAL OF MRS. HASTINGS HELD AT HOWE'S TODAY—Funeral service for Mrs. Emily L. Hastings, who died at Casper, March 16, was held at the Howe mortuary this afternoon at 1 o'clock. Rev. Alfred Young, of Denver, officiated. Mr. Ray Collins sang 'The City Four Square,' 'Some Time We'll Understand,' and 'Rock of Ages.'

Pallbearers were Messrs. John Coughlin, John Romig, John Holman, Milton Dalton, Charles Gustafson and William Dixon. Burial was in Gold Hill cemetery."

HASTINGS, Florence Elizabeth "Lizzie"

Birth: 09/15/1877
Death: 12/07/1890
Cemetery Location: C/D 4 & 5

Father: Henry Hiram Hastings; Mother: Emily Lorinda (*McAllister*); born in Lebanon (Grafton) New Hampshire and died in Gold Hill (Boulder) Colorado at age 13 years, 2 months, 22 days-cause of death unknown; see **About the Henry Hiram Hastings Family**

Boulder County Herald Weekly 17 December 1890:
"Died...Dec. 7th, 1890, Florence L., daughter of Henry H. and Emily L. Hastings, aged 13 yrs. 20 mos., and 22 days. Jesus calls his own."

HASTINGS, Henry Hiram

Birth: 12/21/1844
Death: 05/10/1922
Cemetery Location: C/D 4 & 5

Father: Simeon S. Hastings; Mother: Mary A. (*Penniman*); Wife: Emily Lorinda (*McAllister*); born in Windsor (Hillsborough) Vermont and died in Boulder (Boulder) Colorado at age 77 years, 4 months, 19 days-cerebral hemorrhage; see **About the Henry Hiram Hastings Family**

Boulder Daily Camera 10 May 1922:

"H.H. Hastings, Veteran Of the Great Civil War-An Early Day Freighter Died Here This Morning—Henry H. Hastings, who was stricken with paralysis last Friday near the Central school, died at his home, 1713 Fifteenth street at 12:30 this morning. Mr. Hastings was born December 21st, 1844 in Vermont and was united in marriage November 14th, 1866, to Emily L. McAllister. He enlisted in the Civil war in the U.S. service in Co. H. 7th Vermont Volunteer Infantry on December 20th, 1861, and was mustered out on March 14th, 1866. He was a member of Nathaniel Post No. 5, G.A.R. and enjoyed being with the veterans and talking of their days in service. He was a member of the Friends' church where he was much loved and has a wide circle of friends to mourn his death. The deceased and family came to Colorado January 21, 1881, when he engaged in the freighting business in the mountains, starting the first regular stage route from Gold Hill to Salina, and in the early nineties drove a stage from Boulder to Caribou moving from the mountains to Boulder in 1908. Eight children were born to Mr. and Mrs. Hastings. The widow and the following children survive: Mrs. James Pittman of 2204 Mapleton, Mrs. Dan Coughlin of Mills, Wyo., Mrs. Curtis Swallow of Casper Wyo., also a sister Mrs. Julia Grey of Lebanon, N.H., Mrs. Abbie Wheeler of Oxford, N.H., twenty grandchildren and five great grandchildren. Funeral arrangements are not yet made."

Boulder Daily Camera 11 May 1922:

"The funeral of Henry H. Hastings will be held Sunday at the Friends church at 11 o'clock. Interment will be in Goldhill."

The American Friend (Philadelphia, Pennsylvania) 16 June 1922:

"HASTINGS—At his home in Boulder, Colorado, May 10, 1922, Henry H. Hastings, in his 77th year. He was a member of the Boulder Friends Church. Interment in Gold Hill cemetery."

History of Gold Hill, Colorado by Elmer Curtis Swallow 1961 (courtesy of Tolliver Swallow, grandson of Elmer Curtis & Blanche Hastings Swallow):

"Henry H. Hastings operated one of the larger freight outfits at Gold Hill, at one time running four outfits of two and four horse teams and employing four or five extra men. Mr. Hastings and family came to Boulder from New Hampshire in 1881, locating at Gold Hill in 1883. He built their house and barn just east of the school house in 1883-83. In the early spring of 1894 they moved to the ranchy west of town, were burned out by the forest fire that November, rebuilt their home on the ranch and lived there for several years. Mr. Henry Hastings started the first stage line between Salina and Gold Hill in 1884."

Boulder County Herald Weekly 12 August 1885:

"H.H. Hastings, of Gold Hill, called to-day [sic]. Mr. Hastings is running the stage line between Gold Hill and the railroad station at Salina. He says business is very good in his line."

HASTINGS, Maude Luella

Birth: 05/26/1886
Death: 07/30/1902
Cemetery Location: C/D 4 & 5

Digging Up Dirt

Father: Henry Hiram Hastings; Mother: Emily Lorinda (*McAllister*); born and died in Gold Hill (Boulder) Colorado at age 16 years, 2 months, 4 days-endocarditis due to rheumatism; tombstone has 29 July 1902 as death date but death certificate states 30 July 1902; father stated birth date as 25 May 1886; see **About the Henry Hiram Hastings Family**

Boulder Daily Camera 30 July 1902:
"MISS HASTINGS DEAD—Maude, daughter of Hugh [Henry] Hastings; of Gold Hill, and a niece of O.T. McAllister, died at her home this morning of heart disease. She was but 16 years of age and a general favorite of the camp."

Boulder County News 31 July 1902:
"Miss Maude Hastings, of Gold Hill, aged 16, died of heart disease yesterday morning. She was a niece of I.T. McAllister of this city."

Funeral Card (courtesy Leah Mckin, relative)
"In Loving Remembrance
Of
Maud Hastings,

Died Aug. 6, 1902.

Age 15 years.

Gone but not forgotten

'Tis hard to break the tender cord

When love has bound the heart.

'Tis hard, so hard, to speak the words.

"We must forever part."

Dearest loved one, we must lay thee

In the peaceful grave's embrace.

But thy memory will be cherished

'Til we see thy heavenly face."

(Copyright 1898 by H.F. Wendell, Leipsic, O.)

("The funeral card is in a scrapbook in the possession of my aunt."—Leah McKin)

About the Henry Hiram Hastings Family

Henry Hiram Hastings was born 21 December 1844 in Windsor (Hillsborough) Vermont; son of Simeon S. and Mary A. "Polly" (*Penniman*) Hastings.

Henry spent the formative years of his life in Vermont and then moved to New Hampshire where he met Emily Lorinda McAllister and married her on 14 November 1866 in Lebanon (Grafton) New Hampshire. Emily was born 14 February 1848 in Lebanon (Grafton) New Hampshire; the daughter of Isaac Edson and Mary Millington (*Gray*) McAllister.

To this union eight known children were born with information on seven:

Mary Emily: born 28 October 1869 Lebanon (Grafton) New Hampshire and died 27 January 1939 Denver (Denver) Colorado; buried Columbia Cemetery, Boulder (Boulder) Colorado; married James Eli Pittman

Eva Julia: born 21 May 1873 Lebanon (Grafton) New Hampshire and died 07 February 1920 Denver (Denver) Colorado; buried Columbia Cemetery, Boulder (Boulder) Colorado; married Charles C. Fliniau

Jessie Elva: born 17 August 1875 Lebanon (Grafton) New Hampshire and died 15 August 1963 Casper (Natrona) Wyoming; buried Highland Cemetery, Casper (Natrona) Wyoming; married Daniel Coughlin

Florence Elizabeth "Lizzie": born 15 September 1877 Lebanon (Grafton) New Hampshire and died 07 December 1890 Gold Hill (Boulder) Colorado; buried Gold Hill Cemetery, Gold Hill (Boulder) Colorado; never married; see HASTINGS, Florence Elizabeth "Lizzie"

Alice Marion "Allie": born 03 May 1880 Lebanon (Grafton) New Hampshire and died 10 September 1896 Gold Hill (Boulder) Colorado; buried Gold Hill Cemetery, Gold Hill (Boulder) Colorado; never married; see HASTINGS, Alice Marion "Allie"

Blanche Edna: born 17 August 1884 Gold Hill (Boulder) Colorado and died 09 October 1969 Casper (Natrona) Wyoming; buried Natrona Memorial Gardens, Casper (Natrona) Wyoming; married Elmer Curtis Swallow

Maude Luella: born 26 May 1886 Gold Hill (Boulder) Colorado and died 30 July 1902 Gold Hill (Boulder) Colorado; buried Gold Hill Cemetery, Gold Hill (Boulder) Colorado; never married; see HASTINGS, Maude Luella

Gold Hill, Colorado-Our Home Town by Elmer Curtis Swallow (Courtesy Tolliver G. Swallow & Leah McKin):

"The first stage line between Gold Hill and Salina was opened in 1884 by Henry H. Hastings, to make connection with the railroad. He operated this stage run for about four years, when he bought a stage line from Boulder to Nederland and Caribou.

Henry H. Hastings operated one of the larger freight outfits at Gold Hill, at one time running four outfits of two and four horse teams and employing four or five extra men. Mr. Hastings and family came to Boulder from New Hampshire in 1881, locating at Gold Hill in 1883. In the early spring of 1894 they moved to the ranch west of town, were burned out by the forest fire that November, rebuilt their home on the ranch and lived there for several years."

Interesting to note that Henry owned the land which is now referred to as Mount Alto, located off County Road 52, about two miles west of Gold Hill (Boulder) Colorado.

HAYDEN, Virginia Lee

Birth: 07/16/1936
Death: 07/16/1936
Cemetery Location: B5

Father: Joseph Delaney Hayden; Mother: Elfried Lillian (*Kaufmann*); born and died in Boulder (Boulder) Colorado-stillborn

Boulder Daily Camera 17 July 1936:
"VIRGINIA LEE HAYDEN, infant daughter of Mr. and Mrs. Joseph D. Hayden, died early this morning. Funeral services were held at the Howe mortuary. Burial was in Gold Hill."

About the Joseph Delaney Hayden Family

Joseph Delaney Hayden was born 01 December 1910 Anamosa (Jones) Iowa; the son of Joseph Delaney and Nina Mae (*Hart*) Hayden. He married Elfried Lillian Kaufmann on 28 December 1928 in Monticello (Jones) Iowa. She was born 30 May 1910 (Delaware) Iowa; the daughter of Rudolf and Bertha (*Sulzner*) Kaufmann. This union produced two known children:

Virginia Lee: born 16 July 1936 Boulder (Boulder) Colorado and died 16 July 1936 Boulder (Boulder) Colorado; buried Gold Hill Cemetery, Gold Hill (Boulder) Colorado; see HAYDEN, Virginia Lee

Jo Anne: born 03 July 1937 Boulder (Boulder) Colorado and died 10 January 2017 Cedar Rapids Iowa; buried Wilcox Cemetery, Anamosa (Jones) Iowa; married a Mr. Martin

Joseph was employed at the Slide Mine in the Gold Hill area (Boulder) Colorado. In 1940 the family was living in Nederland (Boulder) Colorado but by 1946 they were living in Boulder (Boulder) Colorado.

Joseph Delaney Hayden died 02 March 1990 at Cedar Rapids (Linn) Iowa and Elfried died 07 January 1997 at Marion (Linn) Iowa. Both are buried at the Wilcox Cemetery, Anamosa (Jones) Iowa.

Newspaper Unknown (Ancestry.com Family Tree):
"Joseph D. Hayden, 79, of Viola, died Friday in St. Luke's Hospital, Cedar Rapids, after a short illness.

Born Dec. 1, 1910, at Anamosa, he married Elfried Kaufmann Dec. 28, 1932, at Monticello. Mr. Hayden was a custodian and school bus driver for Viola schools for 24 years. He was a member of Viola Methodist Church.

Surviving are his wife; a daughter, Jo Anne Martin of Cedar Rapids; and a grandson.

Services: 2pm Monday, Viola Methodist Church, by the Rev. Brown Garlock. Burial: Wilcox Cemetery, rural Viola. Friends may call from 1 to 9 p.m. Sunday at Goettsch Funeral Home, Anamosa. Memorial donations may be made to the church."

(died 02 March 1990)

The Gazette (Cedar Rapid-Iowa City, IA) 09 January 1997:
"Elfried Hayden, 86, died Tuesday evening, Jan. 7, 1997, in Willow Gardens Care Center, Marion, after a lengthy illness. Services: 10 a.m. Friday, Viola Methodist Church, by the Rev. Joan Erbe. Burial: Wilcox Cemetery near Viola. Friends may greet the family after 9 a.m. Fri-

day at the church. Arrangements are with Goettsch Funeral Home, Anamosa.

Survivors include a daughter, Jo Anne Martin of Cedar Rapids; two brothers, Allen Kaufman of Monticello and Elmer Kaufman of Royal Oak, Mich.; and a sister; Clara McGuire of Bloomfield Hills, Mich.

Also surviving is a grandson, Dennis Martin of Cedar Rapids.

She was preceded in death by her parents; her husband, Joseph in 1990; and a grandson Duane Martin.

Born May 30, 1910, in Hazel Green Township, Delaware County, Iowa, Elfried Lillian was the daughter of Rudolf and Bertha Sulzner Kaufman. She received her education in Delhi, graduating from Delhi High School. On Dec. 28, 1932, she married Joseph Hayden in Monticello. After their marriage the couple farmed near Viola on Joseph's parents' farm. In 1935, they moved to Boulder, Colo., where they lived for 12 years. In 1947, they moved back to Viola. Elfried was a cook at Viola School for 25 years. In addition to being a member of Viola Methodist Church, she was a member of Viola Civic League and United Methodist Women's Society.

Memorials may be given in Elfried's name to Viola Methodist Church."

(Interesting to note that her deceased daughter, Virginia Lee, wasn't mentioned in the obituary)

HEMINGWAY, Charles Arthur
(Previously listed as HEMMINGWAY)

> Birth: 06/14/1912
> Death: 09/18/1916
> Cemetery Location: Unknown

Father: Henry Gleason Hemingway; Mother: Josephine Elizabeth (*Renkes/Rinkes*); born and died in Boulder (Boulder) Colorado at age 4 years, 5 months, 4 days-dysentery; no tombstone; see HEMINGWAY, Nancy (*Griffin/Griffen*)

Boulder Daily Camera 18 Sept 1916:

"LITTLE CHARLES HEMINGWAY TAKEN FROM FOND PARENTS—The death this morning of Charles Arthur, the bright and loving son of Mr. and Mrs. Henry Hemingway, came as a great shock to the parents and their host of friends of the mountain districts and in Boulder. The deceased was but four and one-half years old, being born June 14, 1912, and was the only son of Mr. and Mrs. Hemingway who reside at Glendale, a short distance east from Rowena. He was taken ill about ten days ago and on Tuesday of last week was brought to University hospital for treatment for dysentery. He had alternate sinking and improving spells and hopes were held out for his recovery until a few minutes before his death. The funeral services will be from the home of Mrs.

Hemingway's aunt, Mrs. C.A. Butsch, and will be private. Interment will be in the Gold Hill cemetery, where Mr. Hemingway's mother is buried. Mrs. Hemingway is a teacher of the Rowena School which was closed today in sympathy for the bereaved parents.

The mother has been ill since Wednesday of last week with the same disease at the home of Mr. and Mrs. C.A. Butsch. She was formerly Miss Josephine Renkes and is a sister of Mrs. Lee R. Evans of this city and Mrs. Della Tarbel of Los Angeles, Calif. The heartfelt sympathy of a wide circle of friends is with Mr. and Mrs. Hemingway."

About the Henry Gleason Hemingway Family

Henry Gleason Hemingway was born on 04 May 1878 in New York State; the son of Isaac Dwight and Nancy (*Griffin/Griffen*) Hemingway; see HEMMINGWAY, Nancy (*Griffin/Griffen*).

At the age of 33 years he married Josephine Elizabeth Renkes/Rinkes on 12 June 1911 in Boulder (Boulder) Colorado. She was 27 years of age at the time. Josephine was born 28 October 1883 in Boulder (Boulder) Colorado; the daughter of Charles Westly and Ellen Harriet (*Smith*) Renkes. Josephine taught school at Sunshine (Boulder) Colorado in 1909 then after marriage taught at the Rowena School at Rowena (Boulder) Colorado. The marriage produced two known children:

Charles Arthur: born 14 June 1912 Boulder (Boulder) Colorado and died 18 September 1916 Boulder (Boulder) Colorado; buried Gold Hill Cemetery, Gold Hill (Boulder) Colorado; see HEMMINGWAY, Charles Arthur

Nancy Adele: born 18 July 1920 Boulder (Boulder) Colorado and died 09 August 2010 Missoula (Missoula) Montana; buried Sunset Memorial Gardens, Missoula (Missoula) Montana; married Frederick W. "Fritz" Krieger

Henry Gleason Hemingway, a pipefitter for an oil company, died on 14 October 1953 in (Silver Bow) Montana at the age of 75 years from silicosis myocarditis. The remains of Henry were forwarded to Great Falls (Cascade) Montana for cremation.

Josephine died from pneumonia on 10 June 1969 in Warm Springs (Deer Lodge) Montana. Her ashes are in the Mountain View Cemetery, Butte (Silver Bow) Montana.

HEMINGWAY, Nancy (*Griffen/Griffin*)
(Previously listed as HEMMENWAY)

> Birth: 09/29/1836
> Death: 12/20/1907
> Cemetery Location: Unknown

Father: Simeon Richard Griffen/Griffin; Mother: Sarah "Ruth" (*Stedman*); Husband: Isaac Dwight Hemingway;

born in New York and died in Rowena (Boulder) Colorado at age 71 years, 2 months, 21 days-pneumonia; other sources state birth as February 1839; no tombstone; grandmother of Charles Arthur Hemingway; see HEMINGWAY, Charles Arthur; see **About the Henry Gleason Hemingway Family**

Boulder County Miner & Farmer 26 December 1907:

"Mrs. Nancy G. Hemminway [sic] died on Friday, Dec. 20, at Glendale on Left Hand Creek, after a month's illness, the immediate cause of death being pneumonia. Mrs. Henninway [sic] was born in New York State 71 years ago, and has resided in Boulder County, principally at Glendale during the past 18 years. Her surviving descendants are Richard, Henry and De Witt Hemminway [sic], and Mrs. Harry Forsythe, all of whom were present at the time of their mother's death excepting De Witt, who is confined to his bed with sickness at Cripple Creek. The deceased lady was noted for her zeal in all charitable work and her active interest church matters, but more than all she was beloved by all who knew her for her sweet womanly qualities, which were emphasized by a cultured mind and gentle and refined manners, which made her a power for good in the community. The funeral services was [sic] held at her late home in Glendale on Monday, Dec. 23, after which the remains were taken to Gold Hill for burial."

About Nancy (*Griffin/Griffen*) Hemingway

Familysearch.org 26 January 2014:

"Isaac Dwight Hemingway (1831-1893)

Isaac Dwight Hemingway was born 4 January 1831 in Harford, Cortland County, New York to Jacob and Lydia (*Smith*) Hemingway. He had 4 brothers and 1 sister, and 5 half-sisters. He spent most of his early years in Harford, Cortland County, New York.

Isaac married Nancy Griffin the daughter of Simeon and Sarah (*Stedman*) Griffin about 1862. She was born on February 1839 in Tioga County, New York (mortuary record states incorrect names of parents).

Isaac and Nancy had five known children:

Richard Griffin "Dick": born 27 April 1866 (Cortland) New York and died 10 October 1910 Colorado; buried Mountain View Cemetery, Nunn (Weld) Colorado; married Isabelle "Belle" Marshall

Sarah Lydia: born 17 September 1867 Harford (Cortland) New York and died 01 November 1935 Cheyenne (Laramie) Wyoming; buried Mountain View Cemetery, Nunn (Weld) Colorado; married Henry "Harry" Gordon Forsythe

Isaac Dwight Jr.: born 06 August 1870 Harford (Cortland) New York and died 14 June 1897; burial unknown

Abraham Dewitt: born 1873 Harford (Cortland) New York and died after 26 December 1907; burial unknown; last location was Cripple Creek (Teller) Colorado; might have married Rose L. Bernhardt

Henry Gleason: born 04 May 1875 Harford (Cortland) New York and died 04 October 1953 Butte (Silver Bow) Montana; cremated at Great Falls (Cascade) Montana; death certificate lists birth as 04 May 1878; married Josephine E. Renkes

(There is a John Hemingway in the 1880 census at age six but not verified as he is not listed in the New York State census of 1875; perhaps incorrectly listed as a son and perhaps another family member such as nephew)

On the Cortland County, New York County Clerk's office records, Isaac is listed in the land records with 24 separate recordings on the grantor index and 13 separate recordings on the grantee index.

On the 1865 state census Isaac and Nancy were living in Harford (Cortland) New York in a frame house valued at $800.

On the 1870 census Isaac was listed in Harford as a farmer with $3000 worth of real estate and $5000 of personal property.

In 1880, Isaac and his son Isaac D. Jr. were living with his brother, Jacob, in Sterling (Cayuga) New York. Isaac was farming while his brother was a speculator.

In 1885, Isaac and Nancy and their family were living in Clark Precinct (Dixon) Nebraska. On that census was the following information: he owned 70 tilled acres, 30 acres of permanent meadows and pasture and 60 acres of unimproved. The value of the farm was $2000, $100 for the farming implements and machinery, $1131 for the livestock and $450 of farm productions sold in 1884. He had 5 horses, 4 milch [sic] cows, 3 other cows, 2 calves dropped in 1884, 9 swine, 48 poultry. He produced 39 dozen eggs in 1884, 12 acres of Indian corn producing 450 bushels, 14 acres of oats producing 450 bushels, 5 acres of wheat producing 58 bushels.

Isaac died September 12, 1893 at 62 years old and is buried in Oak Grove Cemetery, LeRoy (McLean) Illinois. His sister, Lydia Hemingway Morehouse Burt was also buried in this cemetery in 1915.

A book about the Morris family says: "Isaac Dwight Hemingway possessed a strong sense of truth and justice, with great fortitude. Became largely engaged in gold mining, was a president of a mining and milling company where his health failed."

His widow, Nancy moved to (Boulder) Colorado where in the 1900 census she is living in Sunshine (Boulder) Colorado with her son, Henry. According to the mortuary record Nancy was living in Rowena (Boulder) Colorado at the time of her death on 20 December 1907

(Rowena is about three miles from Glendale (Boulder) Colorado.)

Nancy is buried in an unmarked grave in the Gold Hill Cemetery, Gold Hill (Boulder) Colorado however it is likely to assume she and her grandson, Charles Arthur, are buried in close proximity there; see HEMINGWAY, Charles Arthur; see **About the Henry Gleason Hemingway Family**.

HEYN, Effie (*Newcomb*)

> Birth: 10/08/1865
> Death: 12/13/1892
> Cemetery Location: E5

Father: George W. Newcomb; Mother: Sarah Ellen (*maiden name unknown*); Husband: Edmund D. Heyn; born in Minnesota and died in Gold Hill (Boulder) Colorado at age 27 years, 2 months, 5 days-tonsillitis; 1892 calendar puts death date as 13 December 1892; see HEYN, Norbert; see **About the Edmund D. Heyn Family**

Boulder Daily Camera 15 December 1892:
"Mrs. Effie Heyn, wife of Ed Heyn, died at Gold Hill at 2 p.m. yesterday of tonsillitis. It is reported that her three children are down with the same disease. Mrs. Heyn is well known in Boulder and counted many friends here."

Boulder News 15 December 1892:
"Mrs. Ed Heyne, well-known and highly esteemed in this city, died at Gold Hill Tuesday afternoon of tonsillitis. She leaves a husband and three small children."

Boulder Daily Camera 16 December 1892:
"Mrs. Heyn's Funeral...The death of Mrs. Heyn at Gold Hill was a sad event, but one rendered much sadder by the fact that the funeral yesterday was over her remains and those of a child. Interment of the two occurred at the same time and two more are reported dangerously ill with tonsillitis. The many friends of the family in this place extend their heartiest sympathy through these columns."

Boulder Daily Camera 17 December 1892:
"...the two surviving children of Ed Heyn are mending rapidly, being in charge of their aunt, Mrs. Frank Newcomb."

Boulder Daily Camera 21 December 1892:
"Probably the saddest point being the death of Mrs. Effie Heyn, which was followed by the death of her youngest child, only two years old. They were buried in the same coffin and presented one of the saddest scenes Gold Hill has ever witnessed. None but the immediate relatives of the family attended the funeral on account of the nature of the disease from which they died."

Boulder News 22 December 1892:
"Mr. Al Heyn and wife of Rawlins, Wy., were here last week to attend the funeral of Mrs. Ed Heyn."

About Effie (*Newcomb*) Heyn

George W. Newcomb was born 16 April 1833 in Massachusetts; parents unknown. He married Sarah Ellen (maiden name unknown). She was born 31 March 1838 in either Massachusetts or New York; parents unknown. To their union five unknown children were born:

Frank: born 18 March 1862 Minnesota and died 30 November 1912 (Larimer) Colorado; buried Grandview Cemetery, Fort Collins (Larimer) Colorado; married Lena Heyn

Ella: born about 1864 Minnesota and died 25 August 1889 Boulder (Boulder) Colorado; buried Columbia Cemetery, Boulder (Boulder) Colorado; married John P. Vaughn

Effie: born 08 October 1865 Minnesota and died 13 December 1892 Gold Hill (Boulder) Colorado; bur-

ied Gold Hill Cemetery, Gold Hill (Boulder) Colorado; married Edmund D. Heyn; see HEYN, Effie (*Newcomb*); see HEYN, Norbert; see **About the Edmund D. Heyn Family**

Bell: born 31 October 1867 Minnesota and died 25 March 1965 Fort Collins (Larimer) Colorado; buried Grandview Cemetery, Fort Collins (Larimer) Colorado; married William Donavon

Sarah Bessie: born about 1869 Minnesota-death unknown; burial unknown; married J.P. Vaughn

Sarah E. Newcomb died on 17 January 1918 (Larimer) Colorado and was buried in the Grandview Cemetery, Fort Collins (Larimer) Colorado alongside her husband, George W. Newcomb who died on 29 March 1919

Fort Collins Courier 29 March 1919:

"GEO. NEWCOMB DEAD...Death again struck the Donovan home north of this city today when it claimed George Newcomb, father of Mrs. Donovan, mother of two boys who gave their lives in the world war. The deceased was 86 years old and made his home with Mr. and Mrs. Donovan. Funeral arrangements have not been completed."

HEYN, Norbert

Birth: 08/19/1890
Death: 12/15/1892
Cemetery Location: E5

Father: Edmund D. Heyn; Mother: Effie (*Newcomb*); died at age 2 years, 3 months, 26 days- tonsillitis; buried with his mother, Effie (see above Boulder Camera newspaper article dated 21 December 1892); see HEYN, Effie (*Newcomb*)

About the Edmund D. Heyn Family

Edmund D. Heyn was born 04 March 1858 in Glen Beulah (Sheboygan) Wisconsin; the son of Eduard and Bertha (*Schleigelilch*) Heyn. Edmund made his way to Colorado where he married Effie Newcomb on 05 November 1884 in Boulder (Boulder) Colorado. She was born 08 October 1865 in Minnesota; the daughter of George W. and Sarah E. (maiden name unknown) Newcomb.

To their union three known children were born:

Alma E.: born 28 October 1885 Gold Hill (Boulder) Colorado and died 22 November 1944 Sheboygan (Sheboygan) Wisconsin; buried Grandview Cemetery, Fort Collins (Larimer) Colorado; married George H. Remele

Chester Arthur: born 25 October 1887 Gold Hill (Boulder) Colorado and died 18 July 1942 Boulder (Boulder) Colorado; buried Grandview Cemetery, Fort Collins (Larimer) Colorado; believed never married

Norbert: born 19 August 1890 Gold Hill (Boulder) Colorado –died 15 December 1892 Gold Hill (Boulder) Colorado; buried Gold Hill Cemetery, Gold Hill (Boulder) Colorado; see HEYN, Norbert

The 1885 Colorado State Census has Edward Hine (bartender) and wife, Effie, living in Boulder (Boulder) Colorado. In the 1889 edition he is listed as running a saloon in Gold Hill along with John Luxon.

The 1900 United States census has E.D. Heyne living with his brother, Albert C. Heyne, in Eldora (Boulder) Colorado. He is listed as a widower with his two children, Chester and Alma.

Soon afterward Edmund moved to Sheboygan (Sheboygan) Wisconsin where he married Flora Janssen on 31 December 1907. She was born 20 October 1853 in Belgium (Ozaukee) Wisconsin, daughter of Luebbe Tammen and Agatha Catherine (*Ross*) Janssen. This marriage produced no known children nor did her previous marriage in 1887 to Henry Edward Wiehn.

Edmund died 28 April 1929 and is buried in Wildwood Cemetery in Sheboygan (Sheboygan) Wisconsin. Flora died 02 November 1936 and is buried in the Janssen Family plot at the Wildwood Cemetery in Sheboygan (Sheboygan) Wisconsin.

HITCHINGS, John A.

Birth: 01/01/1821
Death: 08/18/1912
Cemetery Location: Unknown

Father: William Hitchings; Mother: Lucretia (*Bond*); Wife: Elizabeth (*Stretch*); born in Saint Stephens (New Brunswick) Canada and died in Boulder (Boulder) Colorado at age 91 years, 7 months, 17 days-senility; no tombstone

Boulder Daily Camera 19 August 1912:

"PIONEER MAN OF '59 DIES OF OLD AGE—JOHN J. HITCHINGS, AGED 92, A RESIDENT OF GOLD HILL SINCE THE GREAT GOLD EXCITEMENT, DIES OF OLD AGE—John J. Hitchings, one of the most interesting and picturesque pioneers of Boulder county, having been a resident of the county since the famous Gold Run strike at Gold Hill in 1859, died early Sunday morning at the University hospital of senility, aged 92 years.

Mr. Hitchings, who was known by everyone who has resided in the county any length of years, was a globe-trotter and there are few places in all of America that he has not visited, having been one of the first of the band that rushed to California during the gold excitement of '48 and one of the first to come to Colorado following the discovery of gold.

He was born in South Maine, 92 years ago, and while residing there learned the printing trade. He was not yet of age when he got the "wanderlust" and drifted from town to town, finally landing in New Orleans in the early '40s. He spent several years there working at his trade, later going to Panama for a year and in '48 joined the gold rushers who crossed the isthmus by the thousands enroute to the Pacific coast.

He struck it rich in a placer claim in California and after making his stake crossed overland to Cincinnati, O., where he was married. After a few years at Cleveland he again acquired the gold fever and came west arriving at Gold Hill shortly after the discovery by Charles Clouser and party of the famous Gold Run placer claim. He was joined here by his wife and daughter, Miss Fannie, in about 1864. Mrs. Hitchings died about 15 years ago. The daughter still survives, her home being at Denver, but at present she is at the home of Boulder friends.

Mr. Hitchings was one of the first printers in Colorado and worked for a number of years on Denver, Greeley and other papers in the states. He was a charter member of the Denver local of the International Typographical union and of the Colorado Pioneer society. He was the inventor of several processes and devices for the treatments of ores, none of which he ever was able to find a market for.

He was recently removed from his cabin in Gold Hill to the University hospital where he was given the best of care during the last days of his life. Of late months he had been assisting Prof. James F. Willard, of the University of Colorado, in writing a history of Boulder County.

His remains will be shipped to Gold Hill for interment. Funeral services will be held there tomorrow."

Gold Hill, Colorado-Our Home Town by Elmer Curtis Swallow (courtesy of Tolliver Swallow & Leah McKin):

"We [Elmer and wife, Blanche] enjoyed very much visiting with Mr. Hitchings in his little cabin by the side of the Horsfal road. He once told us of how he had carried the little cook-stove that he had in the cabin, all the way from Central City to Gold Hill on his back and how long it took for the trip. One day when we called on him he was frying up a batch of flapjacks and we were curious to know how many of them he could eat at one time, but he told us he always made up enough at one time to last for a week.

Mr. and Mrs. John Hitchings and their daughter, Fannie, were among the outstanding religious families in the new town. Everyone who knew Mrs. Hitchings always spoke of her as a remarkably fine woman, so kind and thoughtful of others.

Reverend John R. Wood in mentioning the women at Gold Hill in 1872 says, "Yes; of course there was one more, last, but by no means least—Mrs. John Hitchings. Mrs. Hitchings mothered the whole camp. I remember the first time I saw her. I was walking across the top of the hill when I saw a lady coming. As we met, she had her hands out-stretched and said, "This is Johnnie" and shook hands as from the heart. It went straight to the heart of a sixteen year old boy never to be forgotten." Mrs. Hitchings lived her later years in Denver where she supported herself and daughter by nursing. Mr. Hitchings, a very religious gentleman lived his last years alone in his little cabin, spending much time in reading and study. In his declining years he had to have help from friends in order to live. He died in August, 1912 at the age of ninety-one and a half years."

About John A. Hitchings

John A. Hitchings was born on 01 January 1821 in St. Stephens (New Brunswick) Canada; the son of William and Lucretia (*Bond*) Hitchings.

John was a mere five years old when his father, William, died on 21 July 1826 which perhaps this was a factor in John's traveling lust as seven years later John was sent to Brooklyn (Kings) New York, to reside with his uncle. From there he went to Cincinnati (Hamilton) Ohio where his printing experience began and for the next few decades with his travels there was no place he really called home.

March of 1858 found John in Springfield (Clark) Ohio where he married Elizabeth Stretch on 31 March 1858 (obituary states Cincinnati, Ohio). Elizabeth was born about 1834 in (New Brunswick) Canada; parents unknown.

I Was Homesteading-Autobiography of John A. Hitchings of Gold Hill, Colorado; pages 47-48:

"On the last day of the previous March, Saturday, (1858) there came to the hotel a young woman I had known from a boy,—from Lawrence, Mass., where she had been a factory girl and dressmaker. She was a second cousin of mine, her father being a cousin of my father's. She came at my request and expense, and expected me to make a life-partnership with her, which we entered into that evening at the Columbia street M.E. parsonage, his wife and daughter for witnesses. This is the last time I will marry on a Saturday night, for every business venture has gone wrong with me since.

So when I left Springfield Mrs. H. remained until the following March, when I sent for her to come to St. Louis, en route to Colorado."

To this union only one known child was born:
Fannie L.: born 31 March 1860 Kansas and died 03 December 1912 Denver (Denver) Colorado); buried Riverside Cemetery, Denver (Denver) Colorado; never married

Apparently John made his tracks to the Gold Hill area in Boulder County as early as 22 June 1870 and traveled back and forth throughout the country whereas his wife and daughter had gone to his uncle's house in Cleveland (Cuyahoga) Ohio and remained there until October of 1871 before Elizabeth finally came to Colorado as she mortally dreaded the western Indians.

For the next seventeen years John, Elizabeth, and their daughter, Fannie, lived as a family in the Gold Hill area until about 1889 when Elizabeth and Fannie moved to Boulder and then to Denver, earning their own living.

Theirs was a very religious family as John even in his eighties was involved in teaching Sunday school in the Gold Hill school house each week. John served many years as Justice of the Peace in Gold Hill (Boulder) Colorado.

Well into his eighties John still mined and worked various lodes such as the Greenflint lode and the Barnum lode (among other mining ventures) at age 82.

By the end of 1903 John developed kidney troubles but 1908 was a decent health year for him and gave his predictions of the future to come:

I Was Homesteading-Autobiography of John A. Hitchings of Gold Hill, Colorado; page 107:

"I think it is in preparation in part for a war to come upon this country in a few years to punish the people for their selfish criminal wickedness. What excuse will start it is just now quite blind, but the rich will not permit the poor to share their special income; sooner than do so they will bring on a war to kill off the poor who must do the fighting, for these will keep away if possible. The years 1916 to 1919 are likely to be one long fight between the people and their rulers in civilized nations, similar to 1848, about homesteads, and money, incomes, rent, and usury.

As a prophet gesser of the future, this June day of 1909, I would expect Mr. Roosevelt to be reelected President in 1912, and in 1916 to be clothed by the U.S. Senate with dictatorship as was Mr. McKinley for the Spanish War, and term prolonged to meet the foreign war of Washington's vision, printed in Philadelphia Press of July 5, 1860, and in Rev. Hoag's vision of 1808-16. If the Jews are restored to Palestine in 1912-13, they will rebuild Ezekiel's temple directly, and the Russians and Germans will make war on them in 1919, other nations put in also."

The last record found for Elizabeth Stretch Hitchings was the 1898 Denver (Denver) Colorado Directory where she was living at 1960 Park Avenue. Ancestry.com Family Trees have her death as "before 1900" however not able to locate any burial in Denver (Denver) Colorado.

John A. Hitchings died in Boulder (Boulder) Colorado at the University Hospital on 18 August 1912 from senility. He is buried in an unmarked grave in the Gold Hill Cemetery, Gold Hill (Boulder) Colorado.

HOLMAN, Jonathan

Birth: 01/26/1866
Death: 11/24/1918
Cemetery Location: E1

Father: John Holman; Mother: Ann (*Oatey*); Wife: Mary Ellen (*Williams*); born in Crowan (Cornwall) England and died in Gold Hill (Boulder) Colorado at age 52 years, 9 months, 29 days-miners' consumption; see HOLMAN, Mary Ellen (*Williams*); see **About the Holman Family**

Boulder Daily Camera 25 November 1918:
"JONATHAN HOLMAN'S DEATH DUE TO MINERS' CONSUMPTION—Jonathan Holman died at Gold Hill at three o'clock Sunday afternoon of miners' consumption, aged 52 years. He had been failing very fast for six months. For thirty years he had made his home there and was known by everyone far and near who regret his death. The funeral will take place at 2 o'clock Wednesday from the Methodist church and interment will also be in Gold Hill. Besides his wife, he leaves one daughter, Mrs.

Digging Up Dirt

James Goudge, a son Charles Holman, of Gold Hill, and a son, John Holman, who is in the service at Fort McArthur."

Boulder News-Herald 25 November 1918:

"GOLD HILL MINER DIES...

Jonathan Holman, 52, a resident of Gold Hill for a number of years, died at his home there at 3:00 o'clock yesterday afternoon of miner's consumption. He is survived by a widow, one daughter, Mrs. James Goudge, and two sons, Charles and John Holman. Funeral services will be held at the Methodist church at Gold Hill Wednesday afternoon at 2 o'clock, with Dr. C.A. Rowand, pastor of the local Methodist church in charge. Interment will be made in the Gold Hill cemetery."

HOLMAN, Mary Ellen (*Williams*)

Birth: 07/11/1855
Death: 11/13/1941
Cemetery Location: E1

Father: Thomas Henry Williams; Mother: Catherine (*Griller*); Husband: Jonathan Holman; born in (Cornwall) England and died in Gold Hill (Boulder) Colorado at age 86 years, 4 months, 2 days-natural causes; see HOLMAN, Jonathan; see **About the Holman Family**

Boulder Daily Camera 13 November 1941:

"Mrs. Mary Holman, Long-Time Gold Hill Resident Dies—Mrs. Mary Ellen Holman, widow of John Holman, died at her home in Gold Hill this morning at 6 o'clock. She was 86 years of age. Mrs. Holman came to Gold Hill in 1889 from Cornwall, England, where she was born July 11, 1855. Mr. Holman died in 1918. Three children survive—they are Mrs. John Miller, Charles and John

In Loving memory
JONATHAN HOLMAN
JAN 26 1866 NOV 24 1918
At rest
He was a kind husband & father

Holman, all of Gold Hill, and a grandson, Herbert Miller. Funeral services are to be held from Howe mortuary Saturday at 2. Interment will be in Gold Hill cemetery."

Boulder Daily Camera 14 November 1941:

"Mrs. Mary Ellen Holman—Late of Gold Hill—Services are to be held from the Howe mortuary Saturday at 2 o'clock. Rev. Rufus C."

Boulder Daily Camera 15 November 1941:

"Mrs. Mary Ellen Holman—Services were held from the Howe mortuary this afternoon at 2. Rev. Rufus C. Baker officiated. Mrs. Marylee Fritschle and Mrs. T.E. Howe sang, accompanied by F.J. Barnett. Interment was in Gold Hill cemetery. Pall bearers were: William B. Peterson, George Corey, John Pughe, John Miller, Alex McLellan and Albert Walter."

"MOTHER"

About the Holman Family

John William Holman (believed father of Jonathan) was born 1821 in Crowan (Cornwall) England and died before the 1881 census of England. He married Ann Oatey on 29 October 1842 in Crowan. Ann was baptized 24 June 1821 in Crowan (Cornwall) England); believed daughter of Samuel and Alice Oatey or Richard and Catherine (*Chapple*) Oatey.

Their union produced twelve known children with Jonathan being the last born on 26 January 1866 in Crowan (Cornwall) England.

Jonathan married Mary Ellen Williams in the fourth quarter of the year 1889 in Redruth (Cornwall) England. She was born on 11 July 1855 in (Cornwall) England; the daughter of Thomas Henry and Kathryn (*Griller*) Holman.

They immigrated to the United States in 1888 (according to the 1900 census) and settled in Gold Hill (Boulder) Colorado in 1889 where they had three known children:

Charles Henry: born 06 November 1890 Gold Hill (Boulder) Colorado and died 05 February 1958 Denver (Denver) Colorado; buried Green Mountain Cemetery, Boulder (Boulder) Colorado; married Almetta A. Kivett

John "Jonathan": born 23 March 1892 Gold Hill (Boulder) Colorado and died 22 October 1975 Boulder (Boulder) Colorado; buried Green Mountain Cemetery, Boulder (Boulder) Colorado; never married

Gladys Mary: born 29 October 1894 Gold Hill (Boulder) Colorado and died 10 July 1960 Rapid City (Pennington) South Dakota; buried Green Mountain Cemetery, Boulder (Boulder) Colorado; married James D. Goudge and John B. Miller; see GOUDGE, James D.

After years of mining Jonathan died at his home in Gold Hill (Boulder) Colorado from miners' consumption on 24 November 1918. He is buried in the Gold Hill Cemetery in Gold Hill (Boulder) Colorado. His widow, Mary Ellen (*Williams*) Holman, lived many years after the death of her husband in her beloved Gold Hill home. She passed away there on 13 November 1941 from old age and is buried alongside her husband.

HOLT, Gus "Gussie"

Birth: 12/16/1884
Death: 08/16/1886
Cemetery Location: E5

Father: Matthew "Mack" John Holt; Mother: Ella "Ellen" Everdina (*Morgan*); died at age 1 year, 8 months-cause of death unknown; Little Gussie was named after his maternal grandfather, Gus Morgan, who died in a wagon accident; see newspaper article below (*Boulder Daily Camera* 06 December 1918)

About the Matthew "Mack" John Holt Family

Matthew "Mack" John Holt was born December of 1858 in (New Brunswick) Canada; the son of James Thomas and Hanora (*McCann*) Holt. By 1860 the family had immigrated to the United States.

In the 1870 census James Thomas Holt, widower, was living in Golden (Jefferson) Colorado by himself, working as a miner. In the 1900 census James Thomas, age 81, was living with his son, Matthew, in (Pitkin) Colorado.

Matthew "Mack" John Holt married Ella "Ellen" Everdina Morgan on 04 May 1880 in Gold Hill (Boulder) Colorado by the town's Justice of the Peace, John A. Hitchings; see HITCHINGS, John A.

Ella was born 16 March 1861 in Eddyville (mainly Wapello but extends into Mahaska and Monroe) Iowa; the daughter of Augustus "Gus" and Sophronia/Sophrona Belle (*Trowbridge*) Morgan. To this union three known children were born:

Mamie "Marie" E.: born 19 February 1881 Gold Hill (Boulder) Colorado and died 24 July 1937 Boulder (Boulder) Colorado; buried Green Mountain Cemetery, Boulder (Boulder) Colorado; married Robert J. Hill, M.G. Conley and Louis H. Cochran

Bartholomew Warren: born 16 December 1882 Gold Hill (Boulder) Colorado and died 21 September 1972 Red Lodge (Carbon) Montana; buried Red Lodge Cemetery, Red Lodge (Carbon) Montana; married Florence M. (maiden name unknown) and Mary Alice "Mollie" (*Crockett*) Davis Parker

Gus "Gussie": born 16 December 1884 Gold Hill (Boulder) Colorado and died 16 August 1886 Gold Hill (Boulder) Colorado; buried Gold Hill Cemetery, Gold Hill (Boulder) Colorado; see HOLT, Gus "Gussie"

By 1900 Ella and her children were living in Fort Collins (Larimer) Colorado while husband Matthew was mining in Thomasville (Pitkin) Colorado with his father, James. Ten years later in the 1910 census Ella (listed as married) was living with her daughter, Mamie Hill, in (Garfield) Colorado.

By 1918 Ella was living in Boulder (Boulder) Colorado; listed as widow of Matthew in the city's directory. By 1930 Ella moved to Denver (Denver) Colorado along with her daughter, Mamie, and Mamie's third husband, Louis H. Cochran.

However ten years later Ella was back in Boulder living out her remaining years. She died on 29 March 1945 at the Sanitarium Hospital in Boulder from arteria sclero-

Inscription unreadable

sis and is buried in the Green Mountain Cemetery, Boulder (Boulder) Colorado.

Matthew's father, James Thomas, died in 1902 and is buried in the Red Butte Cemetery in Aspen (Pitkin) Colorado however Matthew is not buried there. He might have died in either (Garfield) or (Pitkin) Colorado between 1910 and 1918 even though in Ella's obituary (below) states he died in 1935. No additional records have been located to verify when Matthew John Holt actually died and where he is buried.

Boulder Daily Camera 29 March 1945:

"Mrs. Ella Holt, Pioneer, Dies At Sanitarium

Mrs. Ella Holt, wife of Mart [sic] Holt, died at the Sanitarium this morning. She had been in failing health for some time and entered the Sanitarium March 1 for treatment.

Born March 16, 1861, at Eddyville, Ia., she came to Gold Hill, in Boulder County, at the age of two with her parents, Mr. and Mrs. Gus Morgan. She was married at Gold Hill in 1879 to Mr. Holt, who died in 1935.

Surviving are a brother, James Morgan of Gold Hill; a sister, Mrs. D.B. Bier, Greeley, and a granddaughter, Capt. Berniece M. Hill, army nurse corps at Fort Sam Houston, Tex.

Body at Kelso-Allardice mortuary."

Boulder Daily Camera 02 April 1945:

"Mrs. Ella Holt, late of 745 Walnut, services this afternoon at 1 at the Kelso-Allardice mortuary. Rev. Sherman B. Moore, pastor of the First Christian church, officiated. Ben Walker sang, accompanied by Mrs. F.P. Cattermole. Pallbearers were John Andrews, Willard Phillips, Marshall Long, and Loring Pickering. Interment, Green Mountain." (daughter of Gus Morgan, wife of Matthew "Mack" John Holt)

Boulder Daily Camera 06 December 1918:

"GUS MORGAN KILLED BY HIS HORSES AS THEY FELL INTO BOULDER CREEK...

Gus Morgan, veteran teamster, of 1917 Seventh Street, Boulder, was almost instantly killed at 3 o'clock this afternoon and died when being taken by Dr. F.H. Farrington to University hospital.

Mr. Morgan had driven up to the Luckie 2 mill of the Tungsten Products Company and unloaded ore. In backing away his team became unmanageable and the wagon went over the embankment into Boulder creek, pulling the team after it. The horses and wagon all fell on the aged driver and he was terribly bruised and broken. Mr. Morgan was over 80 years old, and he had kept at freighting all his life.

His sons Ernest and Harry both died within the past year. Ernest was care-taker at Silver Lake for the city of Boulder.

Mr. Morgan is survived by his wife and daughter, Mrs. Marshall Long [Eunice Augusta], of Fourth and Pearl streets, and by a son James, a rancher who lives near Ward."

(Interesting to note that his other surviving daughter, Ella Morgan Holt, was not mentioned)

HOVEN, Catherine "Kay"(*Owen*)

Birth: 01/11/1916
Death: 09/05/1971
Cemetery Location: F4

Father: Willard Clinton Owen; Mother: Alice (*Raham*); Husband: Harold Arthur Hoven; born in Chicago (Cook) Illinois and died in Salina Star Route area (Boulder) Colorado at age 55 years, 7 months, 25 days-fatal gunshot; no obituary published

Boulder Daily Camera 06 September 1971:

"Bullet Takes Life Of Area Woman—A Boulder County woman was shot and killed Sunday night in what is being listed as an accident, pending further investigation. She was Mrs. Catherine Hoven, 55, of Salina Star Route.

The Boulder Sheriff's Department reports Mrs. Hoven, who lives with her daughter in Four-Mile Canyon west of Boulder, went to a neighbor's residence about 11 p.m. Sunday, and when the occupant opened the door to her a gun he was carrying discharged.

Mrs. Hoven was shot in the head. The neighbor, taken into custody for investigation, was identified as Charles Henry Manney, 31, of Logan Mill Road, Four-Mile Canyon.

Sheriff Brad Leach, Under-sheriff David Voorhis, Detective Sgt. Walt Young and Officer John Williams went to the mountain residence following the shooting. However, no further details were available today."

Boulder Daily Camera 07 September 1971:

"Inquest Set In Shooting Of Woman—District Attorney Stanley Johnson said today that an inquest into the shooting death of Mrs. Catherine Hoven has been scheduled for 9 a.m. Friday.

The inquest to be held in the County Commissioners hearing room on the fifth floor of the county courthouse building, will determine if Mrs. Hoven's death was accidental or not.

Mrs. Hoven, 55, who lives in Four-Mile Canyon, was shot and killed Sunday when she went to a neighbor's residence.

According to the sheriff's department, when the occupant of the house opened the door, he had a gun that discharged, hitting Mrs. Hoven in the head.

Digging Up Dirt

Charles H. Manny, 31, who also lives in Four-Mile Canyon, was arrested and is still being held in the county jail for investigation of homicide."

Boulder Daily Camera 10 September 1971:

"Inquest Held In Shooting—A coroner's inquest, into the shooting death of 55-year-old Catherine Hoven last Sunday, was held this morning.

Testimony was completed by noon, but no decision has been reached by the jury by press time.

The coroner's jury is to determine the facts surrounding the shooting and if her death was accidental or if there was felonious intent involved.

Mrs. Hoven was shot just outside the door of a cabin just off Four-Mile Canyon, according to testimony. The resident of the cabin was 31-year-old Charles H.

Manney, an electronics engineer employed by the National Bureau of Standards. Manney was arrested and jailed for investigation of homicide.

The witnesses this morning included a pathologist, three sheriff's officers, an ambulance driver and the district attorney's chief investigator.

Manney also testified, as did Mrs. Hoven's daughter.

Dr. John J. Rower, a Boulder pathologist, said that Mrs. Hoven died of a gunshot wound that severed the up-per portion of her spinal cord. Dr. Rowe testified that the bullet entered her left cheek, in a nearly level trajectory, and exited at the back of the neck.

Dr. Rowe added that there were powder burns on her face indicating the shot was fired from short range.

Deputy John Williams and Sgt Walt Young were the first two officers on the scene Sunday night, arriving around 11 p.m.

Williams said Mrs. Hoven, who had been pulled inside the cabin, appeared to be dead when he arrived.

Det. Richard Watts testified that he did the investigation at the scene and said he found a .41 caliber magnum revolver in a drawer of a chest in the bedroom and a belt and holster on top of another chest in the bedroom.

Manney said that Sunday night he was reading in the living room when he heard a noise at the front door. He said he didn't hear a knock or anyone call out. Since he wasn't expecting anyone, he said, it "scared me."

Manney testified that he got the gun which he had bought primarily for camping trips. He explained that he and Mrs. Hoven had been to Montana on such a trip about three weeks earlier.

He said he went to the door, cocked the gun and opened the door quickly. Manney said he thought it might be a dog or maybe a prowler since, he explained, he has

*"KAY HOVEN
COME LIGHT SHINE ON ME"*

*"Catherine Owen Hoven
"Kay"
January 11, 1916-September 5, 1971
Reborn the day I came to Colorado"
(May 1966)*

had problems in the past. He added that the day before he had opened the door and found a man standing there.

He said that when he saw someone standing outside, it "startled me and the gun went off." It was then, he said, that he noticed it was Mrs. Hoven.

"I couldn't believe what had happened," Manney stated.

He said he examined her and then called the sheriff's office and later tried to revive her without any results.

When asked what his relationship with Mrs. Hoven was, Manney replied, "She's my best and dearest friend, is what she is."

Manney added that they had considered marriage and had discussed it.

In reply to other questions, Manney said he doesn't recall pointing the gun and didn't see any headlights and didn't hear a car drive up.

Manney also said that he didn't know why Mrs. Hoven had come to his house and he couldn't understand why she didn't knock.

Mrs. Hoven's daughter, 23-year-old Kathy Hoven, volunteered to testify to answer some of the jury's questions about where Mrs. Hoven had been before arriving at Manney's cabin.

Manney testified that Mrs. Hoven and her daughter were going to Denver that day and she had said the night before that she would call him when they returned. However, he added, he had had problems with his telephone earlier that evening and didn't know if she had tried to call or not."

Boulder Daily Camera 11 September 1971:

"Coroner's Jury Clears Man In Woman's Gunshot Death
    Charles H. Manny, Jr., 31, was cleared of any crimi-

nal intent in the shooting death of a 55-year-old woman by a six member coroner's jury Friday.

After hearing about three hours of testimony, the jury determined that Mrs. Catherine Hoven died of a gunshot wound inflicted by Manney and that the shooting was non-felonious.

Manney, who was arrested shortly after the shooting last Sunday told the jury that Mrs. Hoven was a good friend and they had considered marriage. He described her as his "best and dearest friend."

According to Manney, he was sitting in his living room Sunday night when he heard a noise at the front door. Since his cabin is isolated Manney said he was frightened by the noise.

Not knowing who or what was outside, he continued, he got a revolver, went to the door and cocked the weapon before opening the door.

Thinking it might be a dog making noise, Manney said he was startled when he saw a person standing there. He explained that he stepped back and the gun went off accidentally.

Manney, who is an electronics engineer with the National Bureau of Standards, said his cabin has been burglarized in the past and the day before he had opened the door and found a man standing just outside.

Pursuing that subject further, one of the jurors asked him; "Do you have much trouble with those pigs that run loose in the mountains?"

Manney didn't understand what the juror was talking about.

"You know, those pigs—hippies or pigs, whatever you wanna call 'em."

Manney replied that there weren't many people in the area where he lives. He added that the nearest neighbor is about a quarter of a mile away. Manney said he had considered moving because of the isolated location."

HOWARD, Mary (*Murphy*)

> Birth: 07/18/1915
> Death: 07/09/1995
> Cemetery Location: F3

Father: Frank J. Murphy; Mother: Maude (*Tanner*); Husband: Roswell C. Howard; born in Chicago (Cook) Illinois and died in Boulder (Boulder) Colorado at age 79 years, 11 months, 21 days-natural causes

Boulder Daily Camera 12 July 1995:
    "MARY M. HOWARD—Mary M. Howard, 79, passed away July 9, 1995 of natural causes in Boulder, CO. She was born July 18, 1915 in Chicago, IL.

She married Roswell C. Howard on January 3, 1935, he preceded her in death in 1972 in Boulder, CO. Beginning in 1939 she lived on a ranch north of Boulder. In

1950, the ranch was sold and she returned to Illinois and became officer of the State Bank of Geneva, where she remained until her retirement in 1982. She then returned to Boulder and remained here.

She attended school at St. Clare Academy in Sinsinawa, WI and Clark College in Dubuque, IA. During World War II she opened and operated the Boulder Ration Board, under the supervision of the Price Administration, with the City Manager McClintock and City Attorney Frank Moorhead. Her history of the *Boulder Ration Board During Its Operation In Boulder* was chosen by Chester Bowles, Administrator, of the Price Administration, to be included in the National Archives. She was later transferred to District VII, which was composed of six states. This position required frequent travel between District VII states. She remained with the office of Price Administration until the end of WWII.

She is survived by her son-in-law, Robert Porath and two grandchildren, Mariah M. Howard-Porath and Thomas N. Howard-Porath of Boulder. She is preceded in death by her husband, Roswell C. Howard in 1972 and by her daughter, Terry Swan Howard-Porath in 1992.

Memorial services will be held Friday July 14, 1995 at 2:00 P.M. at the Community United Church of Christ, 2650 Table Mesa Drive, Boulder, CO with the Reverend Kayrene Pearson officiating. Private interment will be held at Gold Hill Cemetery, Gold Hill, CO.

Contributions may be made in lieu of flowers to: the Boulder County Humane Society, 2323 55th Street, Boulder, CO 80301.

Howe Mortuary is handling arrangements."

HOWARD-PORATH, Swan Terry

Birth: 02/11/1949
Death: 01/14/1992
Cemetery Location: F3

Father: Roswell C. Howard; Mother: Mary (*Murphy*); Husband: Robert Porath; born and died in Boulder (Boulder) Colorado at age 42 years, 11months, 3 days-injuries suffered in a snowmobile accident

Boulder Daily Camera 17 January 1992:
"Swan Terry Howard—Swan Terry Howard of 1633 Gold Run Road, Boulder, died Tuesday, Jan. 14, in Boulder Community Hospital from injuries suffered in a snowmobile accident. She was 42.

She was born on Feb. 11, 1949, in Boulder, the daughter of Roswell Howard and Mary Murphy Howard.

She moved to Boulder 11 years ago from Bellingham, Wash.

She attended high school at Boulder High and Elgin Academy in Elgin, Ill. She also attended Augustana College, the University of Colorado and Western Washington University.

She was active in the Democratic Party and volunteered at the Boulder Historical Society. She was interested in childhood education and was involved with Flatirons Elementary School, serving as PTO treasurer and other volunteer positions at the school.

She held a variety of jobs, including Longmont Head Start, the Boulder County Jail, the Boulder Valley School District and cooking at Longmont United Hospital. Most recently, she was in rental property management.

Survivors include her mother of Boulder; her husband, Robert Porath of Boulder; one son, Thomas Neal Howard-Porath of Boulder; and one daughter, Mariah Murphy Howard-Porath of Boulder.

Memorial services will be held at 3:30 p.m. Tuesday at the Community United Church of Christ, 2650 Table Mesa Drive, Boulder, with Kayrene Pearson officiating, and at 7 p.m. Thursday at Flatirons Elementary School, 1150 Seventh St., Boulder.

In lieu of flowers, contributions may be made to Friends of Terry Howard, Affiliated National Bank, P.O. Box 7, Boulder, Colo. 80306 or to the Rocky Mountain Rescue Group, University Campus, Boulder, Colo. 80301.

Howe Mortuary of Boulder is handling arrangements."

HULL, Angus Clifton Jr. Reverend

Birth: 04/06/1909
Death: 01/15/1974
Cemetery Location: I3

Father: Angus Clifton Hull; Mother: Ethel Walker (*Henrich*); Wife: Eleanor (*Means*); born in Buenos Aires, Argentina and died in New York City (New York) New York at age 64 years, 9 months, 9 days-possible heart attack; see HULL, Eleanor (*Means*); see HULL, Stephen Carlton

Boulder Daily Camera 16 January 1974:

"Dr. Angus Hull...News has been received by Florence Crannell Means that her son-in-law, Dr. Angus Hull, former pastor of the First Baptist Church of Boulder, died suddenly Tuesday in New York City as he was on his way to attend a Martin Luther King service.

Further details will be available later."

Boulder Daily Camera 17 January 1974:

"Dr. Angus Hull...Dr. Angus Hull, son-in-law of Florence Crannell Means of 596 Baseline Rd., died suddenly Tuesday in New York City where he was attending a Martin Luther King memorial service. He was 64.

Dr. Hull was born in Buenos Aires and after coming to this country spent his childhood summers in Estes Park with his parents and later with his own family.

He was the former pastor of the First Baptist Church of Boulder, serving from 1939 to 1944. He and his wife had planned to return to Colorado and take up residence in their Gold Hill home upon his retirement in the fall of 1974.

Dr. Hull was educated at the University of Redlands in California and at Colgate-Rochester Divinity School. He received a Doctor of Theology degree from Iliff School of Theology in Denver.

He held pastorates Oakmont, Pa., and Peoria, Ill., as well as Boulder. Following these ministries he went into organizational work in Cleveland, Ohio were he headed the Baptist organization. From there, in 1963, he went to New York City where for the past ten years he was executive secretary of the American Baptist Churches of Metropolitan New York, working with 150 churches.

He is survived by his widow, Eleanor, an author of several books, five children, two sisters, Mrs. John Griffith of Denver and Mrs. Marydel McNamara, Maryland, and two brothers, Henrich Hull and Robert Hull, both of California.

Services will be Friday from Judson Memorial Church in New York City. Contributions may be made to the Heart Disease Research Foundation, 963 Essex, Brooklyn, N.Y."

HULL, Eleanor (*Means*)

Birth: 08/19/1913
Death: 11/05/2013
Cemetery Location: I3

Father: Carlton Bell Means; Mother: Florence (*Crannell*); Husband: Rev. Angus Clifton Hull, Jr.; born in Denver (Denver) Colorado and died Boulder (Boulder) Colorado at age 100 years, 2 months, 17 days- natural causes; see HULL, Angus Clifton Jr. Reverend; see HULL, Stephen Carlton

Boulder Daily Camera 12 November 2013:

"Eleanor Means Hull was born into a religious and literary family in Denver, Colorado on August 19, 1913, the only child of Florence Crannell Means, a noted author, and Carlton Bell Means, a lawyer. Eleanor advanced quickly through the school system, finishing college by the age of 18. She was educated at Colorado Women's College, the University of Redlands and the University of Denver.

In 1938 she married Angus Hull, a Baptist minister, and over the next 35 years they moved several times as Angus became the pastor of churches in Boulder and Peoria, and then a church executive in Cleveland and New York City.

Following his death in 1974 she moved to the house they had planned to retire to in Gold Hill, Colorado. She lived in Gold Hill for 10 years before moving to Boulder.

Eleanor authored 16 books for children and young adults between 1949 and 1984, focusing on minorities, religious and social justice issues. Her books include The Sling and the Swallow (1963), a retelling of Bible stories from a child's viewpoint, The Second Heart (1973), a story about a Mexican maid pursuing an education, and Alice with Gold Hair (1981) about a mentally handicapped girl working in a nursing home. She also worked as a social worker in the New York area in the 1960s. She remained passionate about social justice throughout her life.

Eleanor joined the Boulder Meeting of Friends (Quakers) in 1981 and worshipped there for over 30 years.

She moved to the Frasier Meadows retirement community in Boulder in 2003.

On Aug. 19 this year Eleanor achieved a milestone, celebrating her 100th birthday with family, friends and members of the Frasier Meadows community.

She passed away peacefully in bed at Frasier Meadows Health Center on Nov. 5. She is survived by four children: Mary Margaret of New York City, Angus (Lydia) of Mill Valley, CA, Peter (Linda) of Hinckley, OH, and Jeremy (Linda) of Winnipeg, Canada, as well as eight grandchildren and 13 great grandchildren. She was predeceased by her husband, Angus, and her son Stephen. A memorial service will take place at the Frasier Meadows Manor chapel on Wednesday, Nov. 13 at 2:00 pm."

HULL, Stephen Carlton

Birth: 05/08/1942
Death: 08/08/2007
Cemetery Location: I3

Father: Rev. Angus Clifton Hull, Jr.; Mother: Eleanor (*Means*); died in Lafayette (Boulder) Colorado at age 65 years, 3 months-cause of death unknown; see HULL, Angus Clifton Jr. Reverend; see HULL, Eleanor (*Means*)

Boulder Daily Camera 13 August 2007:

"Beloved son of Eleanor and the late Angus Hull; brother of Mei Mei, Buzz, Peter, and Jeremy; father of Stacey and grandfather to three; companion of Jean.

Help us celebrate Steve's life: 4:30 p.m., August 14, 2007, Frasier Meadows Manor, Mountain Vista Room."

HULTMAN, Allen John
(Previously listed as HALTMAN)

Birth: 1841
Death: 08/21/1904
Cemetery Location: Unknown

Father: Charles Hultman; Mother: unknown; born in Sweden and died in Boulder (Boulder) Colorado at age 63 years (approximately)-rheumatism; 1900 census lists birth date as March 1843; no tombstone

Boulder Daily Herald 22 August 1904:

"John Hultman, aged 63 years, who died at the county farm yesterday of rheumatism, was taken to Gold Hill today by coroner Buchheit for interment."

About Allen John Hultman

Allen (John) Hultman was born in Sweden about 1841; the son of Charles Hultman.

A miner, Allen (John) immigrated to the United States in 1863 (according to the 1900 census where his last name is listed as "Aultman"). Believed never married he lived with Johanna Johnson and her sister, Anna, south of the Gold Hill Cemetery on Dixon Road as it bends to the east to connect to Four Mile Canyon.

The Boulder County Farm in 1904 where Allen John died was located at what was originally the Chambers homestead on 63rd Street, north of Valmont. The doctor in charge at the time of Allen (John) Hultman's death was Dr. George H. Cattermole. Gold Hill's physician Dr. E.B. Trovillion was appointed county physician in 1908 for $45/month.

HUMPHREY, Charles Stanley

Birth: 08/07/1872
Death: 10/06/1930
Cemetery Location: C4

Father: Charles Samuel Humphrey; Mother: Letitia M. "Lettie" (*Smiley*); Wife: Nell "Nellie" Gladys (*Goudge*); born in Winfield (Lake) Indiana and died in Erie (Boulder) Colorado at age 58 years, 1 month, 29 days-aortic sclerosis; grand uncle of author; see GOUDGE, Annie Elizabeth (*Bennett(s)*); see GOUDGE, Edwin David "Ned;" see **About Edwin David "Ned" and Annie Elizabeth (*Bennett(s)*) Goudge**

Boulder Daily Camera 07 October 1930:

"C. HUMPHREY DROPPED DEAD AT STATE MINE—WELL KNOWN MINER OF BOULDER COUNTY-He had quite the Mines in the Mountains and His Grocery Store at Gold Hill to Work As Coal Miner Near Erie—Charles Humphrey, 58 years old, one of Boulder County' early day mining men, dropped dead while working at the State Mine at Erie, yesterday afternoon about 3 o'clock. He had apparently been enjoying the best of health. His death comes a great shock to his many friends.

Mr. Humphrey had been identified with mining in Boulder County for almost forty years having leased and worked mining properties at Salina, Gold Hill, Nederland and Tungsten.

During the past two years Mr. and Mrs. Humphrey operated a small grocery store at Gold Hill and a week ago moved to Erie to be close to his new work.

Besides his wife he is survived by a son Charlie, Jr., and two daughters, Mrs. Bertha Harris and Mrs. Mildred Ackers. Mrs. Harris is a resident of Boulder; Mrs. Ackers is living in California.

No funeral arrangements have been made awaiting word from relatives. The body is at the Howe Mortuary."

Boulder Daily Camera funeral 13 October 1930:

"Mortuary Filled With Friends Of Chas. Humphrey—The Howe mortuary was filled with relatives and friends of Charles S. Humphrey yesterday for the funeral which was held at 2. Rev. M.M. McGorrill of the Baptist church officiated.

Mrs. Myrtle Barnett Grams of Denver sang. Alex McLellan, John Romig, George Corey, Benj. Walton, Charles Gustafson and John Kirkbride were the pallbearers. Interment was in Gold Hill cemetery."

HUMPHREY, Edwin

Birth: 03/09/1907
Death: 03/13/1907
Cemetery Location: D4

Father: Charles Stanley Humphrey; Mother: Nell "Nellie" Gladys (*Goudge*); born and died in Gold Hill (Boulder) Colorado at age 4 days; cause of death unknown; no tombstone; family members state Edwin's grave is close to that of his grandmother Annie Goudge; see GOUDGE, Annie Elizabeth (*Bennett(s)*); see GOUDGE, Edwin David "Ned;" see **About Edwin David "Ned" and Annie Elizabeth (*Bennett(s)*) Goudge**; see **About Charles Stanley Humphrey**

Boulder Daily Camera 13 March 1907:

"The infant child of Mr. and Mrs. Charles Humphrey of Gold Hill died this morning at 9 o'clock. The funeral will occur Thursday. Interment at Gold Hill."

About Charles Stanley Humphrey

Charles Stanley's father, Charles Samuel Humphrey, was born 18 October 1840 in Winfield (Lake) Indiana; the son of Augustin and Harriet Augusta (*Woodbridge*) Humphrey. By the 1850 census and into the 1860 census he was living with his parents in Winfield (Lake) Indiana along with his three brothers (Henry, George and Theron).

According to Ancestry Family Trees, Charles Samuel Humphrey was first married on 05 November 1862 to Phebe Ellen Lee. She was born 29 November 1829 in Shreve (Wayne) Ohio (some sources state Kentucky); the daughter of Abel and Elizabeth (*Hough*) Lee. This union produced one known child:

Rose Ann: born 21 October 1867 Indiana and died 22 August 1962 (Perry) Indiana; buried Paradise Cemetery (also known as White Church Cemetery), Duquoin (Perry) Indiana; married Richard H. Ragland

Charles then married Letitia M. "Lettie" M. Smiley on 29 January 1868 in (Lake) Indiana. She was the daughter of Andrew J. and Jane (*Nealy*) Smiley. To this union two known children were born:

Bertha M.: born 1869 Winfield (Lake) Indiana and died 24 July 1953 Seattle (King) Washington; burial unknown; married Oliver J. Kelly; was a teacher at the Gold Hill school in Gold Hill (Boulder) Colorado 1896-1898

Charles Stanley: born 07 August 1872 Winfield (Lake) Indiana and died 06 October 1930 Erie (Boulder) Colorado; buried Gold Hill Cemetery, Gold Hill (Boulder) Colorado; married Nellie Gladys Goudge

The 1870 United States census has Charles Samuel living in Winfield (Lake) Indiana with his family (wife Letitia and daughters Rose A. and Bertha M. along with his father, Augustin at age 71 years).

From this point it is believed that Charles Samuel died prior to the death of his father, Augustine.

Encyclopedia of Genealogy and Biography of Lake County, Indiana: with a compendium of history, 1834-1904: a record of the ach: 1904: Ancestry.com:

"He (Augustine Humphrey) died many years ago (some sources state 1874), the last of his household except the daughter-in-law's family (Letitia) who moved to Colorado, and the burial of his body (Augustine) was one of the most lonely burials ever in this county."

The 1880 United States census has Lettie living in Gold Hill (Boulder) Colorado, a widow, keeping house with her children Bertha and Charles Stanley.

Lettie then met and married John Manson Morey in Boulder (Boulder) Colorado 24 February 1881; see MOREY, John Manson. This union produced one known child:

Iris Mary: born 1884 (Boulder) Colorado and died 20 July 1956 Seattle (King) Washington; burial unknown; married Louis Julius Markert, Ellis Perry Knowlton and Ulysses S. Attix

The next census record (1900) Leticia was living in Denver (Arapahoe) Colorado with her daughters, Bertha Humphrey and Iris M. Morey while Leticia's husband, John Manson Morey, was living in Gold Hill (Boulder) Colorado making a living as a farmer.

At this time Lettie's son, Charles Stanley Humphrey was living in the household of Henry Jensen along with several other fellow ore miners in Gold Hill (Boulder) Colorado.

While in Gold Hill (Boulder) Colorado Charles Stanley met the "girl of his dream," Nellie Gladys Goudge whose parents (Edwin and Annie (*Bennett(s)*) Goudge) owned and operated the Gold Hill Hotel at that time.

Charles and Nellie were married 29 September 1901 in Gold Hill (Boulder) Colorado in the presence of Charles' sister, Bertha and Bertha's future husband, Oliver J. Kelly. Their union produced four known children:

Charles E. "Chuck": born 1902 Gold Hill (Boulder) Colorado-death unknown; burial unknown; married Margaret Graham and Ida May Wiggett; there is a Charles E. Humphrey born 1902 and died 25 October 1939 (Alameda) California with burial unknown

Bertha Lenore "Birdie": born 08 July 1904 Gold Hill (Boulder) Colorado and died 15 January 1993 Santee (San Diego) California; entombment at Cypress View Mausoleum, San Diego (San Diego) California; married Loren Leroy Harris

Edwin: born 09 March 1907 Gold Hill (Boulder) Colorado and died 13 March 1907 Gold Hill (Boulder) Colorado; buried Gold Hill Cemetery, Gold Hill (Boulder) Colorado; see HUMPHREY, Edwin

Mildred Gladys: born 06 November 1908 Gold Hill (Boulder) Colorado and died 10 May 1975 San Diego (San Diego) California; entombment at Cypress View Mausoleum, San Diego (San Diego) California; married Donald J. Geiger and Virgil Akers

Charles Stanley Humphrey died on 06 October 1930 while working at the State Mine in Erie (Boulder) Colorado from an apparent heart attack and is buried in the Gold Hill Cemetery, Gold Hill (Boulder) Colorado. His widow, Nellie Gladys (*Goudge*) Humphrey moved to the sunny weather of San Diego (San Diego) California where she was found dead on 20 September 1966 and her body was entombed at the Cypress View Mausoleum in San Diego (San Diego) California.

HUNT, Ernest Virgil

Birth: 07/11/1868
Death: 05/11/1941
Cemetery Location: Unknown

Father Henry Harrison Hunt; Mother: Elsie "Effie" Isadora "Dora" (*Verplank/VerPlanck*); Wife: Jennie Baker (*Magner*) Hall; born in Albion (Calhoun) Michigan and died in Boulder (Boulder) Colorado at age 72 years, 10 months-heart failure; no tombstone; see HUNT, Ida J. "Jennie" Baker (*Magner*) Hall; see **About Ida J. "Jennie/Jenny" Baker (*Magner*) Hall Hunt**

Boulder Daily Camera 12 May 1941:

"Ernest V. Hunt...Ernest V. Hunt, 72, widely known resident of Summerville, died suddenly of a heart attack early Sunday morning at the home of James A. Garrison, 712 Spruce Street. He had been visiting there for the last five days coming to Boulder to receive medical care, as he had been in ill health.

Mr. Hunt was born July 11, 1868, in Albion, Michigan. He located at Summerville, which is a mining town between Salina and Gold Hill, 23 years ago, and engaged in mining. Ill health caused him to retire in 1935.

Mrs. Jennie Hunt, his wife, died Aug. 22, 1938. Surviving them are Everett Hunt, a son, living at Summerville; F.L. Hunt, a brother, living in Temple City, Calif.; two sisters, Mrs. Earl Hemperly of Denver and Mrs. B.E. Hart of Central City, Neb."

Boulder Daily Camera 14 May 1941:

"Ernest V. Hunt—Services were held from the Howe mortuary this afternoon at 1:30. Rev. J.H. Sanders, pastor of the Presbyterian, officiated. Mrs. Wm. Morris sang accompanied by Mrs. A.R. Peebles.

Pallbearers were George Parks, L.W. Telinde, Ernest Meyring, George Pomeroy, Henry Trask and Everett Brown. Interment Gold Hill cemetery."

About Ernest Virgil Hunt

Ernest Virgil Hunt was born in Clarence (Calhoun) Michigan on 11 July 1868; the son of Henry Harrison and Elise "Effie" Isadora "Dora" (*Verplank/VerPlanck*) Hunt.

His father, Henry Harrison Hunt (a Civil War veteran) was born 24 November 1840 in New City (Rockland) New York; the son of Charles and Sarah (maiden name unknown) Hunt. He married Elsie "Effie" Isadora "Dora" Verplank on 02 July 1867 in (Calhoun) Michigan. She was born October 1851 in Michigan; the daughter of David Henry and Abigail (*Tichenor*) Verplank.

According to the 1900 and the 1910 United States Census six known children were born to the union of Henry Harrison and Elsie with only five records found:

Ernest Virgil: born 11 July 1868 Clarence (Calhoun) Michigan and died 11 May 1941 Boulder (Boulder) Colorado; buried Gold Hill Cemetery, Gold Hill (Boulder) Colorado; married Jennie Baker (*Magner*) Hall

Myrtle Augusta: born 24 July 1870 Albion (Calhoun) Michigan and died 28 September 1956 Central City (Merrick) Nebraska; buried Central City Cemetery, Central City (Merrick) Nebraska; married Harry Shipley Meredith and Bertrand E. Hart

Mary Jeanette/Janet "Jennie": born March 1878 (York) Nebraska and died 1933; buried Fairmount Cemetery, Denver (Denver) Colorado; married George A. Cheramy

Nellie I: born 1880 (York) Nebraska and died 22 September 1881 (York) Nebraska; buried Lincoln Creek Cemetery, Bradshaw (York) Nebraska

Frederick Leroy 'Roy": born 15 September 1882 (York) Nebraska and died 21 April 1950 Los Angeles (Los Angeles) California; buried Forest Lawn Memorial Park, Glendale (Los Angeles) California; married Gertrude Alma Sexton

In the 1870 census Henry Harrison Hunt and wife, Elsie Isadora, were living with Elsie's parents, David Henry and Abigail (*Tichenor*) Verplank/VerPlanck in Clarence

(Calhoun) Michigan. Ten years later Henry Harrison and Elsie Isadora were living in Morton (York) Nebraska with their children Earnest V., Myrtle A., Mary J., and Nellie I.

In 1885 the family was still living there however by the 1900 census the household split up as only Henry Harrison and Elsie Isadora were living in Clarksville (Merrick) Nebraska whereas Ernest was living in Ward (Boulder) Colorado along with his sister, Mary Jeanette and his brother, Frederick Leroy.

On 05 December 1900 Ernest married Jennie Baker (*Magner*) Hall in (Arapahoe) Colorado. She was the daughter of Azariah and Susanna Catherine "Susan" (*Baker*) Magner; see HUNT, Ida J. "Jennie" Baker (*Magner*) Hall

To this union four known children were born with records on two:

Wilmer F.: born 23 January 1910 Noland (Boulder) Colorado and died after 23 April 1910; buried Lyons Cemetery, Lyons (Boulder) Colorado

Everett Vernon: born 06 January 1917 (Boulder) Colorado and died 12 November 1975 San Bernardino (San Bernardino) California; buried Lancaster Cemetery, Lancaster (Los Angeles) California; married Marvell Pauline (*Cothern*) Clark; Everett was a private in the United States Army, World War II

The United States 1910 census has Ernest and his wife Jennie living in Lyons (Boulder) Colorado with their son, Wilmer F. while Ernest's parents (Henry Harrison and Elsie Isadora) were living in Hygiene (Boulder) Colorado where Henry was a carpenter. Henry Harrison Hunt died about one year later on 02 December 1911 and is buried in the Hygiene Cemetery in Hygiene (Boulder) Colorado.

By 1912 Ernest and Jennie, along with their son Everett, were living in Summerville (Boulder) Colorado where Ernest was a "stationary Engineer" in a quartz mine. Five years later on 05 September 1925 Ernest's mother, Elsie "Effie" Isadora, died at the Denver home of her daughter, Mary Jeanette/Janet "Jennie" (*Magner*) Cheramy, and was buried in the Hygiene Cemetery alongside her husband, Henry Harrison Hunt. Her tombstone has the name "Dora E. Hunt."

Boulder Daily Camera 08 September 1925:

"MRS. EFFIE HUNT...The funeral of Mrs. Effie Isadore Hunt, wife of the late H.H. Hunt, was held this afternoon at the Home [Howe] Mortuary followed by interment beside the remains of her husband at Hygiene. Mrs. Hunt died in Denver Saturday after an illness of a number of years, being removed to the home of her daughter, Mrs. Jennie Cheramy, a week ago Monday from her own home at 2342 Twentieth Street.

Mrs. Hunt was the mother of Ernest Hunt, a miner at Salina, of Roy Hunt, residing in Pasadena, Calif., of Mrs. Myrtle Hart, residing at Central City, Neb., and Mrs. Cheramy of Denver. She was born Oct. 29, 1851 in Calhoun County, Michigan, and was married to Mr. Hunt who was a civil war veteran, on July 2, 1867. They lived at Hygiene for years. Mr. Hunt died in 1911 and soon after that Mrs. Hunt moved to Boulder."

On 22 August 1938 Jennie died at her Summerville (Boulder) Colorado home. Her cause of death was not listed in the mortuary record or in the newspapers. She is buried in the Gold Hill Cemetery in Gold Hill (Boulder) Colorado in an unknown location; see HUNT, Ida J. "Jennie/Jenny Baker (*Magner*) Hall

After the death of Jennie it appears that Ernest and his son, Everett, lived together in Salina (Boulder) Colorado. Apparently after the 1940 census Ernest moved to 712 Spruce Street Boulder (Boulder) Colorado where he passed away on 11 May 1941 at the age of 72 years from heart failure. He, too, was buried in an unknown location (no tombstone) in the Gold Hill Cemetery in Gold Hill (Boulder) Colorado alongside his wife, Jennie.

The Mining Camps: Salina & Summerville by M.M. Anderson, ISBN 0-9772230-0-0; pgs. 277-278:

"Ernest was a carpenter, a miner, and a photographer. In 1904, he and his wife ran the Studio Grand, at 14th and Pearl Street in Boulder. Four years later in 1908, Ernest was the Superintendent of the West Point mine on Modoc Hill near Ward. The Hunts lived in Lyons in 1910, and the first mention of Ernest being in Summerville was in February 1912. He was descending Belle's Pitch between Summerville and Salina when the wagon tongue broke and his horses became frightened. Ernest was thrown to the ground and run over by the wagon wheels. Ernest went to work in the Summerville mines and continued to take photographs, but instead of portraits, they were primarily images of Boulder County scenery. Jennie was an officer of the Salina Sunday School in the 1920s."

HUNT, Ida J. "Jennie/Jenny" Baker (*Magner*) Hall

> Birth: 09/13/1870
> Death: 08/22/1938
> Cemetery Location: Unknown

Father: Azariah "Elias" Magner; Mother: Susanna Catherine "Susan" (*Baker*); Husband: Ernest Virgil Hunt; born in Iowa and died in Summerville (Boulder) Colorado at age 67 years, 11 months, 9 days-cause of death unknown; no tombstone; see HUNT, Ernest Virgil

Boulder Daily Camera 22 August 1938:

"MRS. JENNIE HUNT OF SUMMERVILLE DIES—Mrs. Jennie V. Hunt of Summerville, died this morning. Funeral services will be held at Howe's at 2:30 Thursday afternoon and burial will be at Gold Hill. Mrs. Hunt was born in Iowa and has lived in Summerville 16 years. Besides her husband, a son, Everette Lee Hunt survives. She was a member of the Presbyterian church."

Boulder Daily Camera 25 August 1938:

"MRS. JENNIE V. HUNT...Services were held at Howe's at 2:30 o'clock this afternoon with Rev. J.H. Sanders officiating. Mrs. Mary Sanders sang. Pallbearers were George Pomroy, Tom Trask, Fred Musse, Homer Bird, Gene Wilson, Henry Trask. Interment in Gold Hill cemetery."

Boulder Daily Camera 27 August 1938:

"Relatives who came to attend funeral services held for Mrs. Ernest V. Hunt of Summerville Thursday were Mr. and Mrs. John Wagner, Mr. and Mrs. Oliver Magner and James and Leona Magner, all of Hastings, Nebr., and Mr. and Mrs. Earl Hemperley and his mother, all of Denver."

About Ida J. "Jennie/Jenny" Baker (*Magner*) Hall Hunt

Ida's father, Azariah "Elias" Magner, was born 13 April 1822 in Ohio; the son of John and Nancy (*Woods*) Magner. He married Susanna Catherine Baker on 09 March 1841 in (Van Wert) Ohio. She was born 1823 in Tully (Van Wert) Ohio; the daughter of John and Catherine (*Miller*) Baker. To their union thirteen known children were born:

Elias "Eli": born 15 May 1841 Monroeville (Allen) Indiana and died 01 December 1862 Monroeville (Allen) Indiana; buried Old Methodist Cemetery, Monroeville (Allen) Indiana; never married; served in the Civil War (Union) and died of dysentery while at home on furlough

Amelia: born 26 July 1845 Monroeville (Allen) Indiana and died 20 February 1922 Walla Walla (Walla Walla) Washington; buried Mountain View Cemetery, Walla Walla (Walla Walla) Washington; married Thomas James Stewart

John: born 19 July 1848 Monroeville (Allen) Indiana and died 1878 Guide Rock (Webster) Nebraska; buried Guide Rock Cemetery, Guide Rock (Webster) Nebraska; married Mary Jane Motter; John was a twin to Nancy Agnes

Nancy Agnes: born 19 July 1848 Monroeville (Allen) Indiana and died 28 January 1917 Riverton (Franklin) Nebraska; burial unknown; married Richard Granderson Parker; Nancy Agnes was a twin to John

Sarah A.: born 12 June 1850 Monroeville (Allen) Indiana and died 1930 Beaver (Beaver) Oklahoma; buried Fairview Cemetery, Clear Lake (Beaver) Oklahoma; married Elias Parker and James Herkles Landon

Sylvanus F.: born 1852 Monroeville (Allen) Indiana (some sources state Fort Wayne (Allen) Indiana and died 25 November 1937 Omaha (Douglas) Nebraska; buried Juniata Cemetery, Juniata (Adams) Nebraska; married Angeline E. Doughman

Henry B.: born 09 August 1854 (Van Wert) Ohio and died 29 November 1923 Waterloo (Black Hawk) Iowa; buried Oak Hill Cemetery, Tama (Tama) Iowa; married Sarah C. Schaffer

Harvey: born 1856 Monroeville (Allen) Indiana-death unknown; burial unknown

William Nelson: born 01 September 1859 Monroeville (Allen) Indiana and died 25 March 1938 Hastings (Adams) Nebraska; buried Blue Hill Cemetery, Blue Hill (Webster) Nebraska; married Cora M. Gannon and Harriet Emma Falley

Susannah "Annie": born 16 June 1861 Monroeville (Allen) Indiana and died 04 July 1955 Norton (Norton) Kansas; buried Norton Cemetery, Norton (Norton) Kansas; married Frederick William Moody

Samantha "Mattie": born 1863 Monroeville (Allen) Indiana and died 03 March 1896 Fairfield (Clay) Nebraska; buried Fairfield Cemetery, Fairfield (Clay) Nebraska; married James S. Casada

Levi Harlan: born 14 November 1865 Fort Wayne (Allen) Indiana and died 22 February 1923 Hastings (Adams) Nebraska; buried Blue Hill Cemetery, Blue Hill (Webster) Nebraska; married Mary L. Taylor

Ida Jennie/Jenny: born 13 September 1870 Iowa and died 22 August 1938 Summerville (Boulder) Colorado; buried Gold Hill Cemetery, Gold Hill (Boulder) Colorado; married Philip H. Hall and Ernest Virgil Hunt; see HUNT, Ernest Virgil

It seems the family was en route from Indiana to Nebraska as their last child, Ida Jennie, was born in Iowa. About a year and a half later her mother, Susanna Catherine (*Baker*) Magner, died on 16 March 1872 near Guide Rock (Nuckolls) Nebraska and was buried in the Guide Rock Cemetery, Guide Rock (Webster) Nebraska (no tombstone).

By the 1880 census widower Azariah "Elias" Magner married Emily Jane "Emma" (*Taylor*) Lafountain on 08 October 1874 in (Webster) Nebraska. Emily (24 years) was quite younger than Azariah (52 years), being born on 02 April 1850 in Austerlitz (Columbia) New York; the daughter of Eli and Cynthia E. (*Winters*) Taylor. Previously married, she brought no children into this union.

In 1880 the family was living in Stillwater (Webster) Nebraska where Azariah and Emily had two children to add to the family:

Frank E.: born 1878 Nebraska-not listed in the 1885 Nebraska State census; burial unknown

Alfred: born 09 May 1880 Nebraska and died 29 December 1926 Omaha (Douglas) Nebraska; buried

Graceland Park Cemetery, Omaha (Douglas) Nebraska; never married

Azariah died 17 December 1907 and was buried at the Blue Hill Cemetery in Blue Hill (Webster) Nebraska. Emily died 11 February 1909 Blue Hill (Webster) Nebraska and was buried alongside her husband, Azariah in unmarked graves.

On 04 May 1890 their daughter, Ida Jennie, married Phillip H. Hall in Central City (Merrick) Nebraska. Phillip was born about 1865 in Pennsylvania to New York native Thomas L. and Canadian native Elizabeth (maiden name unknown) Hall. No known children blessed this marriage. There is a Philip Hall who died in 1890 and buried in an unmarked grave in Greenwood Cemetery, York (York) Nebraska.

In the June 1900 United States census Jennie, widowed, was living in York (York) Nebraska with her niece Viola Casada. A short six months later she made her way to Colorado and on 05 December 1900 she married Ernest Virgil Hunt in (Arapahoe) Colorado making their home in Ward (Boulder) Colorado; see HUNT, Ernest Virgil.

By 1910 Jennie and Ernest were living in Lyons (Boulder) Colorado. The census record of that year states she was the mother of three children with one living (Wilmer F.).

In the 1920 Jennie was living in Salina (Boulder) Colorado and was an officer in the Salina Sunday School.

On 22 August 1938 Jennie died at her Summerville (Boulder) Colorado home. Her cause of death was not listed in the mortuary record or in the newspapers. She is buried in the Gold Hill Cemetery in Gold Hill (Boulder) Colorado in an unknown location (no tombstone).

Family Notes by Edith (Ancestry.com):
"Magner tribe came by covered wagon to Guide Rock in 1871. Azariah married twice-second wife Emma Taylor had Alfred.

Indian visitors came to see white baby (Mike-Nan's son). Another time they traded a pile of buffalo meat for a dead skunk.

Once the family visited an Indian camp. The squaws were making moccasins. When they were done they that had moccasins wore them, those that did not went barefoot in the snow.

Azariah had a saddle horse when he courted and won his wife, Susannah Baker. She jumped up and rode away behind him."

HUTH, Anne Hollis "Holly" (*Young*) Hirsch

Birth: 02/07/1944
Death: 01/18/2018
Cemetery Location: C5

Father: Chester Robinson Young; Mother: Florence "Tossie" (*Hollis*); 1st Husband: Gerald Strasser Hirsch; 2nd Husband: Thomas Richard Huth; born in Bronxville (Westchester) New York and died in Santa Barbara (Santa Barbara) California at age 73 years, 11 months, 11 days-Parkinson's disease

Courtesy of Thomas Huth:
"Holly was 31 years old when she landed in Gold Hill in 1975 with her boyfriend Tom and sons Scott and Robb. She'd grown up in New York as a child of privilege. But she was a rebel. So Gold Hill was the perfect fit.

The mountains brought out her inner Sherpa. She loved to hike, to backpack, to camp, to ski, to mountain-bike, to swim, to run rivers, to glory in her romance with nature.

Gold Hill brought out her passion for teaching and community service. She started a preschool which endeared her to children and parents alike.

She knew how to party. But she also cultivated a spiritual side, which helped her to endure the Parkinson's disease which shadowed the last twenty years of her life."

I

ISAAC, Hodeahnohtah Tokala

> Birth: 07/11/1982
> Death: 06/07/2003
> Cemetery Location: F1

Father: Clyde; Mother: Kathy; died at age 20 years, 10 months, 27 days; was an artist
> No further information is available

IVEY, Infant

> Birth: 07/16/1888
> Death: 08/12/1888
> Cemetery Location: B3

Father: John Henry Ivey; Mother: Nettie Bertha (*Grigg*); male child born and died in Gold Hill (Boulder) Colorado at age 27 days-cause of death unknown

Boulder News 14 August 1888:
> "Mr. Trezise sent a coffin up to Gold Hill Monday for a little child of Jas. Ivey which died Sunday night."

Hodeahnohtah Tokala Isaac has a natural tombstone of rock

About the Ivey Family

John Henry Ivey was born 24 October of 1857 in Beer Alston (Devon) England; the son of John Ivey and Louisa (*Robinson*) Ivey.

John Henry came to the United States with his brother, James Ivey and their uncle Joseph Luxon who was married to Louisa's sister, Lydia (*Robinson*) Luxon.

They boarded the ship "Arizona," leaving from Liverpool, England and arriving at the Port of New York on 11 July 1882.

The 1900 United States census record states that John' mother, Louisa, arrived in 1871. The Colorado State census of 1885 shows Louisa (a widow) living in Gold Hill (Boulder) Colorado with her two sons, John H. and James. It appears that John Henry's father (John) died in England.

In the 1885 Colorado State census John Henry Ivey is living in Gold Hill (Boulder) Colorado where he might have meet Nettie Bertha Grigg as she, too, was living there with her father, Robert Grigg.

About two years later on 28 September 1887 John Henry Ivey married Nettie Bertha Grigg in Boulder (Boulder) Colorado. She was born 24 July 1859 and baptized 11 October 1859 at St. Dennis (Cornwall) England; the daughter of Robert and Victoria (*Grigg*) Grigg.To their union four known children were born:

Infant: born 16 July 1888 Gold Hill (Boulder) Colorado and died 12 August 1888 Gold Hill (Boulder) Colorado; buried Gold Hill Cemetery, Gold Hill (Boulder) Colorado; see IVEY, Infant

Mabel Bertha: born 28 August 1889 Gold Hill (Boulder) Colorado and died 20 February 1972 (Orange) California; burial unknown; married Earl Wilbur Thomas and a Mr. Phillips

Kathleen/Eliza: born 1894 Gold Hill (Boulder) Colorado and died 12 April 1897 Gold Hill (Boulder) Colorado; buried Columbia Cemetery, Boulder (Boulder) Colorado (died from falling into a tub full of hot water-*Boulder News* 15 April 1897)

Robert John: born 31 December 1898 Gold Hill (Boulder) Colorado and died 07 November 1965 (Santa Clara) California; burial unknown; never married

By 1900 Bertha and John were living in Boulder (Boulder) Colorado with their two surviving children, Mabel and Robert. John's mother, Louise, was living in the household of his uncle, Joseph Luxon, in Boulder.

Later that year John left for Victor (Teller) Colorado.

Denver Rocky Mountain News 21 August 1900:

"BOULDER, Colo., Aug. 20—Joseph R. Luxon of Boulder left for Victor Sunday evening. Mr. Luxon has been appointed superintendent of Stratton's Independence mine. He is one of the best known miners of this county and, as a boy, worked in the mines of England. He has had charge of such well known Boulder county properties as the Slide Richmond, Boulder County and Grand Central. Mr. Luxon was given authority to select some good Boulder county miners as foremen on the Independence and to-day [sic] Hon. J.A. Jester, former sheriff of Boulder county, and John H. Ivey, one of Boulder's police force, left for Victor to assume positions of that kind under his management. They are experienced miners."

John's mother, Louise, died 23 December 1909 and is buried in the Ivey family plot in Columbia Cemetery in Boulder (Boulder) Colorado.

Boulder Daily Camera 24 December 1909:

"MRS. LOUISE IVEY DIES ATER PARALYTIC STROKE...

Serenely and painlessly Mrs. Louise Ivey passed to the beyond at the home of her son, former City Marshal John H. Ivey, this city, at 10 o'clock last night. The lady had lived in Boulder County since 1880, when as a widow she arrived at Gold Hill from the Black Hills, with her sons, James and John. The former died 14 years ago at Gold Hill. He was a Knight Templar at Mt. Sinai commandery, and a well-known citizen. Her son, John, came down from Cardinal immediately he learned of his mother's illness and was with her at the last moment. The lady was born in Devonshire, England, March 4, 1834. The funeral will be from Trezise's undertaking parlors at 2 p.m. Sunday."

Boulder Herald 24 December 1909:

"DEATH OF MRS. IVEY...

Mrs. Louisa Ivey died at the home of her son, John Ivey, 2233 Fifteenth Street, at 10 o'clock last night. She had been sick but a week and death was due to paralysis. Mrs. Ivey was seventy-six years old, and is survived only by her son. The funeral will take place from Trezise's parlors Sunday afternoon at 2 o'clock. Interment will be made in the old cemetery, Rev. Canon Sibbald officiating."

After 1910 John and Bertha, with son Robert, moved to California in hopes that the lower climate would help Bertha's heart condition. Unfortunately she died from "fatty degeneration of the heart" on 07

September 1913 in Oakland (Alameda) California. Her body was shipped to Boulder and buried in the Ivey family plot in Columbia (Pioneer) Cemetery there."

A short four years later (07 September 1913) John's wife, Nettie Bertha (*Grigg*) Ivey, died from "fatty degeneration of the heart" in Oakland (Alameda) California. She is buried in the Columbia Cemetery, Boulder (Boulder) Colorado.

Boulder Daily Camera 10 September 1913:

"Word was received this morning by Miss Mabel Ivey, shortly after going to her school near Erie, that her mother was dead. Further particulars are lacking but the supposition is that heart trouble was the cause, as she and her husband recently went to California for the lower altitude. The remains are now enroute to Boulder from Oakland, accompanied by the bereaved husband. It is expected they will reach here Friday."

Boulder Daily Camera 13 September 1913:

"John Ivey and son (Robert) came with the remains of the wife and mother from California this morning. They are at the home of Guy A. Adams."

Boulder Daily Camera 13 September 1913:

"The funeral of Mrs. John N. [error, should be the initial H] Ivey, who died suddenly in Oakland, California Tuesday, was conducted at 3 o'clock this afternoon from the J.G. Trezise chapel, Rev. R.H. Forrester officiating. A quartet composed of Mesdames Roy True and O.B. Yarger and Messrs. George F. Fonda and L.B. Kelso, sang. Interment was made in Columbia Cemetery. A large number of friends from Primos and other mining camps were in attendance at the services."

Widower John Henry and his son, Robert, decided not to return to California after the funeral of his wife, Bertha:

Boulder Daily Camera 15 September 1913:

"John Ivey and son Robert will again make their home in Boulder. They are at present stopping at the home of Guy A. Adams."

Unfortunately John only lived about five more years until he died from "bronchial pneumonia following influenza" on 29 October 1918 at the St. Joseph Hospital in Denver (Denver) Colorado. He had been mining and living in Lakewood (Boulder) Colorado with his son, Robert.

He, too, is buried in the Ivey family plot in the Columbia Cemetery in Boulder (Boulder) Colorado. His son, Robert John, eventually returned to California where he was a conduit man in Palo Alto (Santa Clara).

Boulder Daily Camera 29 October 1918:

"JOHN H. IVEY IS DEAD...ONCE BOULDER MARSHAL...

"John H. Ivey died at St. Joseph's hospital, Denver at 2 o'clock this morning of pneumonia following influenza. At 9 o'clock last night a nurse at St. Joseph's telephoned William Loach in Boulder that Mr. Ivey was getting along finely. Monday afternoon his children, who had been with him in the hospital returned to Lakewood because their father was so much better.

For several days Mr. Ivey was missed by the workers for the Red Cross who took charge of the epidemic in the mountains. He had been nursing a patient at Lakewood. It seems that he took the patient t St. Joseph's and that his long vigils and generous sacrifice cost him his own life.

The first Mr. Loach ad T.A. McHarg, attorney for the Wolf Tongue Company heard from him was thru [sic] a nurse last Friday who asked that Mr. McHarg meet him at the hospital. This r. McHarg did. He was called to write Ivey's will.

Ivey was superintendent of one of the mines of the Wolf Tongue Company and lived at Lakewood with his two children. His wife died in this city some years ago.

John H. Ivey was for years a miner in the hills about Boulder and moved here from Gold Hill. For several years he was either a member of the police force or city marshal of Boulder. He was highly esteemed by the entire community.

Mr. Ivey leaves one son and one daughter. The son's name is Robert. The daughter is Mrs. Mabel Thomas. Both live at Lakewood where Robert and Mr. Thomas work in the mines."

J

JACKSON, Susan Elizabeth

Birth: 06/18/1961
Death: 12/30/1999
Cemetery Location: D5

Father: Richard O. Jackson; Mother: Dorothy (*Moore*); born in Chapel Hill (Orange) North Carolina and died in Boulder (Boulder) Colorado at age 38 years, 6 months, 12 days-flu and strep throat symptoms

Boulder Daily Camera 05 January 2000:

"Susan E. Jackson of Gold Hill died Thursday, Dec. 30, 1999, at Boulder Community Hospital. She was 38.

She was born on June 18, 1961, in Chapel Hill, N.C., to Richard and Dorothy Jackson.

She was employed by Atkinson-Noland & Associates and the Gold Hill Store.

She lived in Princeton, N.J., Greensboro, N.C., Vero Beach, Fla., and moved to Gold Hill in 1993.

She graduated from the University of North Carolina at Greensboro in 1984 and attended the New York School of Interior Design.

Survivors include her mother of Princeton Junction, N.J.; her father of Greensboro; a sister, Catherine Newman of Hamilton, N.J.; her grandmother, Dorothy Moore of Princeton Junction; and her companion, Matthew Finn of Gold Hill.

A memorial service will be at 4 p.m. Sunday at the Gold Hill Inn in Gold Hill. A second service will be held for family and friends at a later date.

Contributions may be made to the Gold Hill Fire Protection District, 1011 Main-Gold Hill, Boulder, CO 80302. Howe Mortuary is handling arrangements."

Mountain Ear (Nederland, CO) 06 January 2000:

"Susan E. Jackson—At noon on Friday a group of Gold Hill residents gathered on Main Street in front of Susan Jackson's house. They held each other and cried, mourning the death of a friend and, as many say, a light that brightened this small mountain town.

She had died the preceding evening, Dec. 30, after weeks of fighting flu and strep throat symptoms.

Members of the Gold Hill Fire Department, Boulder County Sheriff's Department and Pridemark Ambulance responded to the 911 call and found Jackson unconscious and not breathing. Emergency and medical personnel performed CPR, and Jackson was transported by ambulance to Boulder Community Hospital. She was pronounced dead a few hours later.

Susan was born in Chapel Hill, North Carolina, on June 18, 1961. She graduated from the University of North Carolina at Greensboro in 1984 and attended the New York School of Interior Design. She lived in Princeton, N.J.; Greensboro, N.C.; Vero Beach, Florida, and moved to Gold Hill in 1993. She was employed by Atkinson-Noland & Associates, Inc. and more recently worked at the Gold Hill General Store.

One friend describes Susan as the kind of person who always smiled, even if she was having a bad day. She cooked and waited on people at the general store which caters to locals and tourists. She was especially kind to the children who would burst into the store after school looking to buy their afternoon candy.

Susan had just purchased a house in Gold Hill, in the middle of town. She liked to photograph scenery, recently illustrated a book for a friend, enjoyed her cat Sadle, Fleetwood Mac and growing plants.

Another friend says Susan was charming and lovely, always dressed well, even in her mountain setting. "She had a contagious laugh and could always make you laugh, even if you didn't know what was so funny."

She came from the East, but opted to stay in a place where she had to lug five-gallon jugs of water. She saw things in rocks, liked to paint them changing them into turtles or fish, and giving them to friends. She also had the gift of finding arrowheads.

"She was a bright comet that came through town."

Susan is survived by her mother Dorothy M. Jackson, of Princeton Junction, N.J., father and stepmother, Richard O. Jackson and Sheryl Jackson of Greensboro, N.C.; a sister and brother-in-law, Catherine J. and Ronald C. Newman of Hamilton, N.J.; grandmother, Dorothy D. Moore of Princeton Junction; two aunts, several cousins; and her special friend, Matthew Finn of Gold Hill.

There will be a memorial service on Sunday, Jan. 9, at 4 p.m. at the Gold Hill Inn for her Gold Hill friends. A second service will be held for a wider circle of family and friends in June 2000 as a celebration of Susan's life. Howe Mortuary is handling arrangements.

In lieu of flowers, memorial contributions may be made to the Gold Hill Fire Protection District, 1011 Main, Gold Hill, Boulder, CO 80302."

JAMES, James Rowe

Birth: 05/31/1883
Death: 07/02/1914
Cemetery Location: E2

Father: William Thomas "Tommy" James; Mother: Elizabeth "Lizzie" (*Brown*); Wife: Ida Mae (*Pughe*); born and died in Gold Hill (Boulder) Colorado at age 31 years, 1 month, 2 days-pneumonia; see JAMES, William Thomas "Tommy;" see **About the William Thomas "Tommy" James Family;** see SMITH, Elizabeth (*Brown*) James; see PUGHE, Charles (no middle initial E) "Charley;" see PUGHE, Eleanor/Elinor "Ellen" (*Edwards*); see **About the Pughe Family**

Boulder Daily Camera 02 July 1914:

"The entire camp of Gold Hill is in mourning owing to the death of James Rowe James which occurred at three o'clock this morning of pneumonia, aged 31 years, after an illness of nine days. He contracted a cold at that time and thought he would get rid of it and continued with his work mining until a few days ago. The deceased was a typical Boulder boy, was born and lived all his live in Gold Hill. Besides his bereaved wife and two children, his mother, Mrs. Elizabeth James and sister-in-law, Mrs. Albert Walters, a large circle of friends, mourn his death.

The funeral will take place from the church at Gold Hill Sunday afternoon at 2:30. Mr. Tippetts will be in charge."

Boulder Daily Herald 02 July 1914:

"PNEUMONIA CLAIMS LIFE OF ROWE JAMES

Rowe James, 31, a native of Gold Hill died at his home in that town early this morning of pneumonia. He had been ill scarcely more than a week, and his death came as a great shock to the residents of the town. The deceased was popular and held in high esteem by all who knew him.

He was born in Gold Hill, May 31, 1883 and had lived here for the greater part of his life. Eight years ago he was married to Miss Ida Pughe who with two children, Lawrence aged 7 and Eleanor aged 5, survives to mourn his loss. He is also survived by his mother, Mrs. Elizabeth James.

The deceased was a member of the Foresters of America and of the Odd Fellows. The funeral will take place Sunday afternoon at Gold Hill. Practically all his life, the deceased had been engaged in mining. At the time he became ill, he was employed by the Gold Hill Mining Company."

Boulder Daily Herald 06 July 1914:

"The funeral of the late James Rowe James at Gold Hill yesterday was one of the largest ever held in that place. The Odd Fellows and Foresters of America turned out in a body. The casket was completely covered with flowers, and every one of the twenty-two Odd Fellows and Foresters who acted as an escort carried a large bouquet to the Gold Hill cemetery, where interment was made. Rev. Stevens of Denver conducted the services."

Boulder Daily Camera 07 July 1914:

"ALL GOLD HILL MOURNED AT ROWE JAMES' FUNERAL

The largest funeral ever held in Gold Hill Sunday was that of Rowe James Sunday afternoon at 2:30 at the church. Three of the pall bearers were I.O.O.F. and three Forresters of America, the deceased being a member of both lodges. The pall bearers carried the casket from the house to the church and after the service by Rev. Stevens the remains were carried to the cemetery for interment. Every citizen of the camp was in attendance with the exception of two old ladies too feeble to walk. The casket was covered with flowers. The church was decorated with a large stacking of evergreens and columbines. Emblematic floral pieces were carried by the respective lodges and placed on the grave."

JAMES, William Thomas "Tommy"

Birth: 1848
Death: 03/26/1891
Cemetery Location: E3

Father: unknown; Mother: unknown; Wife: Elizabeth "Lizzie" (*Brown*); born in England and died in Gold Hill (Boulder) Colorado at age 43 years (approximately)-pneumonia; see JAMES, James Rowe; see SMITH, Elizabeth (*Brown*) James

Boulder News 26 March 1891:

"News comes of the death of Thos. James one of the best known miners of the county, at Gold Hill last night. His disease was pneumonia."

Boulder County Herald 01 April 1891:

"W.T. James, of Gold Hill, who has had the management of E.W. Bald's mines at Gold Hill died early Thursday morning, of pneumonia."

About the William Thomas "Tommy" James Family

William Thomas "Tommy" James was born in England about 1848; parents unknown. It appears that by 1870 he was possibly living in Georgetown (Clear Creek) Territory of Colorado as a miner. About nine years later he married Elizabeth "Lizzie" Brown in Denver (Arapahoe) Colorado on 31 March 1879. She was born 19 June 1852 in Pennsylvania; the daughter of Ireland native James Brown and Pennsylvania native Margaret (maiden name unknown). (Mortuary record states birth year incorrectly as 1856)

To the union of William Thomas James and Elizabeth "Lizzie" Brown one known child was born:

James Rowe: born 31 May 1883 Gold Hill (Boulder) Colorado and died 02 July 1914 Gold Hill (Boulder) Colorado); buried Gold Hill Cemetery, Gold Hill (Boulder) Colorado; married Ida Mae Pughe; see JAMES, James Rowe

By 1880 William Thomas James was living in Gold Hill (Boulder) Colorado along with his wife, Elizabeth "Lizzie" where he was a miner. Some of the mines he located in the Gold Hill Mining District were:

Arlington Mine on 27 April 1885 (Locater)

Poor Man's Friend 19 Dec 1885 (Locater with Joseph Stoppler Jr. [Steppler])

Good Credit 20 April 1886 (Locater)

Gold Ring 01 May 1886 (Locater)

Deserted Star 18 June 1886 (Locater)

Make Shift 01 Nov 1886 (Locater)

Hogback 05 Nov 1886 (Locater)

My Queen Mine 20 July 1887

Gay Deceiver 23 October 1889

Unfortunately William Thomas James didn't live to a grand old age as he died from pneumonia on 26 March 1891 in Gold Hill (Boulder) Colorado and is buried in the town's cemetery. It has been said that William Thomas was a veteran, having served in the Civil War.

His widow, Elizabeth, continued living in Gold Hill (Boulder) Colorado along with her son, James, until he married Ida May/Mae Pughe on 31 May 1905 in Gold Hill (Boulder) Colorado. Ida was born on 10 May 1886 Gold Hill (Boulder) Colorado; the daughter of Charles and El-

eanor "Ellen (*Edwards*) Pughe; see PUGHE, Charles (no middle initial E) "Charley"; see PUGHE, Eleanor "Ellen" (*Edwards*). To their union two known children were born:

Lawrence Roah: born 21 October 1906 Gold Hill (Boulder) Colorado and died 09 January 1992 Vallejo (Solano) California; burial unknown; married Hazel Fall

Eleanor Elizabeth: born 21 May 1909 Gold Hill (Boulder) Colorado and died 02 May 1992 Citrus Heights (Sacramento) California; buried Sylvan Cemetery, Citrus Heights (Sacramento) California; married Sterling Price Brownlee

Elizabeth's household in Gold Hill was quite full with her son and family. All was well until her son, James Rowe, became ill which resulted in a fatal case of pneumonia. He died 02 July 1914 just three days before he was to be best man at the wedding of his good friend, Albert Charles "Tim" Walter and Pearl Pughe, sister of Ida.

By 1920 Elizabeth was living in Denver (Denver) Colorado with her nephew, Milton P. Givens, and family until her death; see SMITH, Elizabeth "Lizzie" (*Brown*) James.

Her daughter-in-law Ida (*Pughe*) James moved to Louisville (Boulder) Colorado by 1920 where she was a nurse to the household of Herman F. Lutzke and also working as a nurse in the Boulder Community Hospital in Boulder (Boulder) Colorado. Ten years later she was married to Earl E. Belding and living in Tonopah (Nye) Nevada. To this union one known child was born:

Barbara M: born about 1929 Nevada-death unknown; burial unknown; married Rev. Miles W. Renear

In 1940 the family was living in Grass Valley (Nevada) California. Ten years later on 30 June 1950 Ida May/Mae (*Pughe*) James Belding died in (Nevada) California and is buried in Cypress Lawn Memorial Park, Colma (San Mateo) California. A short couple of months later Earl E. Belding, a Colorado native, died 04 August 1950 in (Nevada) California and is buried beside his wife, Ida.

JOHNSON, Charles Moneys

Birth: 03/09/1843
Death: 12/03/1916
Cemetery Location: F3

Father: Moneys Johnson; Wife: Ingried Gustava (*Burke*); born in Sweden and died in Rowena (Boulder) Colorado at the age of 74 years, 8 months, 24 days-pneumonia; mortuary record states birth year as 1842 but all other records as well as tombstone have 1843; veteran; see JOHNSON, Ingried Gustava (*Burke*)

Boulder Daily Camera 04 December 1916:

"Rowena Miner Is Dead—Charles Moneys Johnson after a week's illness died at his home in Rowena at 4:30 o'clock this morning of pneumonia, aged 74 years and 8 months. The deceased was an old-timer in the Rowena section, having made his home there for forty years, being engaged in farming and mining. He was of a reserved disposition and did not mix much with those in the vicinity but was a good, upright citizen and had many true friends. Besides his wife he leaves a son, Arthur Johnson, who is mining at Gold Hill where interment will take place at 2 o'clock Tuesday afternoon."

Boulder News Herald 04 December 1916:

"DEATH OVERTAKES THREE IN 2 DAYS...Mrs. W.H. Jameson, Charles M. Johnson and Bert Elmet Babb All Succumb in Last 48 Hours; Two Had Lived in County for Long Time...

OLD SETTLER DEAD AT ROWENA

Charles M. Johnson, one of the old settlers in Boulder County, has lived near Rowena for 40 years and was widely known. Pneumonia was the cause of his death, altho the old man had been in poor health for several months. Mr. Johnson was a native of Sweden, and came to this country when he was still a young man. Mrs. C.M. Johnson and their son, Arthur, a miner at Goldhill, survive him. The funeral will be held at 2 o'clock tomorrow afternoon at the Goldhill church and interment will be made in the Goldhill cemetery."

Boulder Daily Camera 05 December 1916:
"A.E. Howe went to Gold Hill this morning to conduct the funeral of Charles Johnson, a pioneer miner and rancher of the Rowena district, who died of pneumonia Monday morning."

JOHNSON, Infant

Birth: About 1875
Death 02/15/1876
Cemetery Location: F3 (possibly)

Father: Thomas Cunningham Johnson; Mother: Sophia Margaret (*Bowers*); born and died in Gold Hill (Boulder) Colorado at age of under 1 year old-cause of death unknown; infant's name might have been named James; no tombstone; see JOHNSON, Sophia Margaret (*Bowers*)

Boulder County News 18 February 1876:
"DIED...At Gold Hill, February 15th, infant child of Thomas Johnson."

JOHNSON, Infant

Birth: 05/12/1884
Death: Prior 06/1885
Cemetery Location: F3 (possibly)

Father: Thomas Cunningham Johnson; Mother: Sophia Margaret (*Bowers*); born and died in Gold Hill (Boulder) Colorado-cause of death unknown; no tombstone; see JOHNSON, Sophia Margaret (*Bowers*)

In the 1885 Colorado State census only three children were listed in the Gold Hill (Boulder) Colorado household of Thomas C. Johnson: Carrie, William and Annie along with his niece Annie Johnson (20 years old, born in Canada).

JOHNSON, Infant

Birth: About 1887
Death: Prior 1900
Cemetery Location: F3 (possibly)

Father: Charles Moneys Johnson; Mother: Ingried Gustava (*Burke*); born and died in Gold Hill (Boulder) Colorado; no tombstone-assumed buried in the Gold Hill Cemetery, Gold Hill (Boulder) Colorado; see JOHNSON, Charles Moneys; see JOHNSON, Ingried Gustava (*Burke*); see **About Charles Moneys & Ingried Gustava (*Burke*) Johnson**

JOHNSON, Ingried Gustava (*Burke*)

Birth: 12/09/1849
Death: 01/26/1927
Cemetery Location: F3

Father: Johannas Burke; Mother: Christina "Stina" (*Kissa/Kessa*); Husband: Charles Moneys Johnson; born in Sweden and died in Tungsten (Boulder) Colorado at age 77 years, 1 month, 17 days-cancer of the stomach; Ingried was a sister to Ida Matilda (*Burke*) Gustafson/Peterson); see PETERSON, Ida Matilda (*Burke*) Gustafson; see JOHNSON, Charles Moneys; see **About Charles Moneys & Ingried Gustava (*Burke*) Johnson**

Boulder Daily Camera 27 January 1927:
"MRS. CHARLES M. JOHNSON—Mrs. Charles M. Johnson died at ten minutes passed eleven last night of cancer of the stomach at her home at Tungsten, a mining town in Boulder canon. Mrs. Johnson had been seriously ill for three months and confined to her bed for a month. The deceased was born in Sweden in 1849 and came to the United States and directly to Boulder County when but twenty-four years of age. She was a resident of Gold Hill until ten years ago, following the death of her husband, when she moved to Tungsten to be with her only son, Arthur, who is superintendent of the Vasco Mine. Survivors in addition to the son are a sister, Mrs. Ida Peterson, a nephew William Peterson, both of Tungsten, and a niece, Mrs. H.A. Holloway, of Arapahoe, Neb. The deceased was also the aunt of Frank, Carl, Arthur and Elmer, all of this city, tho Frank is now visiting in California, and of Mrs. Emma Hall and Mabel Burke of San Diego, also of Lucy Burke of Boulder. Funeral arrangements will be announced later."

Boulder Daily Camera 31 January 1927:
"MRS. JOHNSON BURIED AT GOLD HILL SUNDAY
The funeral of Mrs. Ingred Johnson who died Jan. 26 at Tungsten, took place Sunday at 1 o'clock from the Howe mortuary. Rev. J.H. Skeen was in charge. Miss Bernice Smercheck, J.A. Paro, and L.S. Farnsworth sang. The body was taken to Gold Hill where the grave service was held at the rink rather than the grave as snow had blocked the road for a half mile to the cemetery. The pallbearers were E.F. Green, Arnold Hughes, J.W. Conklin, Albert Scogland, Reuben Olson, and Edward Smith."

About Charles Moneys & Ingried Gustava (*Burke*) Johnson

Charles Moneys was born 09 September 1843 in Sweden; the son of Moneys Johnson, mother unknown. He immigrated to the United States in 1868 according to the 1910 United States census records.

In the 1870 census there is a Charles Johnson, born about 1841 Sweden, who was a miner located near Oro City (Lake) Colorado but not verified if this is Charles Moneys Johnson.

The first verified record is of his marriage to Ingried Gustava Burke on 25 December 1886 in Boulder (Boulder) Colorado when he was 43 years of age and Ingried was 30. She was born on 09 December 1849 in Sweden; the daughter of Swedish natives Johannas and Christina "Stina" (*Kissa/Kessa*) Burke.

According to the 1920 census she immigrated to America in 1867 however the obituary calculates the immigration year as 1873. She probably met Charles in Gold Hill as the marriage certificate states they both were living there. Their union produced two known children:

Infant: born about 1887 Gold Hill (Boulder) Colorado and died Gold Hill (Boulder) Colorado; burial is unknown but possibly Gold Hill Cemetery, Gold Hill (Boulder) Colorado

Arthur: born 18 September 1891 Gold Hill (Boulder) Colorado and died 13 November 1953 Boulder (Boulder) Colorado; buried Green Mountain Cemetery, Boulder (Boulder) Colorado; married Edna Mae Reinhart

According to Charles' obituary he lived in the Rowena (Boulder) Colorado area for forty years as a miner and farmer however he isn't listed in any census record prior to 1900 for that region. He was a man who basically kept to himself. He died at his home in Rowena (Boulder) Colorado on 03 December 1916 from pneumonia and is buried in the Gold Hill Cemetery in Gold Hill (Boulder) Colorado. His widow, Ingried, and son, Arthur, moved to Tungsten (Boulder) Colorado where on 26 January 1927 she died from stomach cancer and is buried beside her husband.

JOHNSON, Sophia Margaret (*Bowers*)

Birth: About 1854
Death: 05/12/1884
Cemetery Location: F3

Father: unknown; Mother: unknown; Husband: Thomas Cunningham Johnson; born in Ohio and died in Gold Hill (Boulder) Colorado at age 30 years (approximately)-childbirth complication; no tombstone; see JOHNSON, Infant born 1875; see JOHNSON, Infant born 12 May 1884

Boulder County Herald 14 May 1884:

"Mrs. T.C. Johnson of Gold Hill died Monday afternoon. The friends of Mr. Johnson extend to him the deepest sympathy. The little babe is the unconscious cause of the mother's death and survives her." (baby died prior to the 1885 Colorado State Census)

Boulder County Herald 21 May 1884:

"The funeral of Mrs. T.C. Johnson took place at Gold Hill Wednesday, May 14. The husband and four children have with the death of the loving wife and tender doting mother suffered an irreparable loss. The funeral was attended largely by the citizens of Gold Hill as well as Boul-

der. The heart-felt sympathy of all is extended to the bereaved family."

About Sophia Margaret (*Bowers*) Johnson

Sophia M. (possibly Margaret) Bowers was born in Ohio about 1854; the daughter of Ohio natives. She apparently made her way to Colorado where she married Thomas Cunningham Johnson on 08 November 1874 in (Jefferson) Colorado. He was born about 1847 in Canada; the son of William Johnson and (wife's first name unknown) (*Cunningham*) Johnson.

The union of Thomas Cunningham and Sophia M. (*Bowers*) Johnson produced five known children; three surviving into adulthood:

Infant: born 1875 Gold Hill (Boulder) Colorado and died 15 February 1876 Gold Hill (Boulder) Colorado; buried Gold Hill Cemetery, Gold Hill (Boulder) Colorado; baby's name might have been James; see JOHNSON, Infant, born 1875

Caroline "Carrie": born 25 March 1876 Gold Hill (Boulder) Colorado and died 07 September 1957 Boulder (Boulder) Colorado; buried Green Mountain Cemetery, Boulder (Boulder) Colorado; married Evart B. Copeland and Carl C. Butts

William Andrew: born 18 February 1879 Gold Hill (Boulder) Colorado and died 11 February 1948 Boulder (Boulder) Colorado; buried Green Mountain Cemetery, Boulder (Boulder) Colorado; married Mary Daisy B. Allen; served with Company H of Boulder in the Spanish-American War

Anna "Annie": born 09 September 1880 Gold Hill (Boulder) Colorado and died 21 November 1943 Boulder (Boulder) Colorado; cremated; married Frank Henry Whitman

Infant: born 12 May 1884 Gold Hill (Boulder) Colorado and died before June 1885 Gold Hill (Boulder) Colorado; buried Gold Hill Cemetery, Gold Hill (Boulder) Colorado; see JOHNSON, Infant, born 12 May 1884

Sophia did not survive this fifth childbirth. She died 12 May 1884 and is buried in an unmarked grave in the Gold Hill Cemetery in Gold Hill (Boulder) Colorado. The little infant did survive for a while however died before the June 1885 Colorado State Census in which Thomas is listed living in Gold Hill (Boulder) Colorado with his three children: Carrie, William and Annie along with his niece Annie Johnson (20 years old, born in Canada).

Thomas Cunningham Johnson didn't remain a widower for long as on 05 December 1885 he married a widow Susan (*Thompson*) Barker Luther in Boulder (Boulder) Colorado. She was born about 1835 in Vermont; the daughter of David Thompson, mother unknown. She was married first to Andrew J. Baker and then to Amos Origin Luther.

Thomas Cunningham Johnson lived the remaining years of his life with Susan in Boulder (Boulder) Colorado when on 26 January 1909 he passed away at the age of 68 years from an apparent heart attack. He is buried in the Green Mountain Cemetery in Boulder (Boulder) Colorado alongside his wife, Susan, who died on 19 March 1921 in Boulder (Boulder) Colorado.

Boulder Daily Camera 26 January 1909:

"THOMAS C. JOHNSON GETS SUDDEN CALL...WELL KNOWN BOULDER CITIZEN STRICKEN AS HE SAT IN A CHAIR AND DIES IN THE FLUSH OF APPARENT HEALTH...

Thomas C. Johnson died as he sat in a chair in the dry goods store conducted by himself and son between noon and one o'clock this afternoon. Mrs. William Martin and Mr. Miller were in the store at the time—employees of the firm. There had been no complaint of ill-health on Mr. Johnson's part. Suddenly he leaned back in his chair in apparent pain. Mrs. Martin went to him and asked if she could assist. "I'm dying," he muttered. There was a gasp or two after this and all was over. Dr. E.B. Trovillion had been summoned but there was nothing for him to do—it was all over.

Mr. Johnson moved to Boulder from Gold Hill 26 years ago, after having been a successful miner and a county commissioner of Boulder County for a term or two. He was engaged in mercantile business at various times with J.G. Rutter, James C. Hankins and D.R. McNaughton and was an honorable man in all callings. "For twenty-six years we were neighbors." said Mel Copeland today. "One couldn't hope for a better neighbor."

Mr. Johnson leaves a widow and three children to mourn an indulgent father—Mrs. Whitman of Pueblo, Will Johnson, his business partner, and Miss Carrie, who resides at home. He was 64 years old [mortuary record states 68 years, 5 months, 4 days] and one of Boulder's substantial citizens respected by all.

Though having generally spoken of good health and the absence of aches and pains, Mr. Johnson had suffered recently from indigestion, which may have involved a heart weakness. He was in excellent health when he walked from the store to his home on Water Street at the noon hour today.

Deceased was a member of Columbia lodge No. 14, A.F. & A.M., which body will conduct the funeral Thursday afternoon."

Boulder Daily Camera 28 January 1909:

"The funeral of the late T.C. Johnson was very largely attended this afternoon, the Masons, Eastern Star, and friends being there to pay their last respects. By request, ex-Grand Master J.A. Davis had charge of the services, and Mesdames Theo. L. Strawn and George McCutcheon

and the Messrs. Charles Ingram and George Fonda sang a number of selections."

JONATHAN
(Previously listed as such)
See **REESE**, Jonathan

> Birth: abt 07/1976
> Death: 04/08/1977
> Cemetery Location: B1

JONES, Ernest L.

> Birth: About 1877
> Death: 02/09/1933
> Cemetery Location: Unknown

Father: unknown; Mother: unknown; Wife: Mamie (*Hebert*); born in Kentucky and died in Gold Hill (Boulder) Colorado at age approximately 56 years-heart attack; other sources states birth year as 1873 and death age about 60; no tombstone

Boulder Daily Camera 10 February 1933:

"E.L. Jones of Gold Hill Dies Of Heart Attack—Ernest L. Jones of Gold Hill died suddenly of a heart attack yesterday afternoon in a cabin where he had stopped to rest after telling Paul Romig, with whom he had been working, storing wood, that he was not feeling well. Romig was urged by Jones to continue work and when Romig returned shortly afterwards with another load of wood, he found Jones dying. He summoned John Romig and Chas. B. McGowen, but Jones was dead before they arrived. Jones lived at Gold Hill for five years. He had been engaged in farming with John Romig. His former home was in Garden City, Kan. Funeral arrangements will be announced by the Howe mortuary later."

Boulder Daily Camera 11 February 1933:

"Funeral services for Ernest L. Jones, who died Thursday afternoon, will be held Tuesday afternoon from Howe mortuary. Burial will be at Gold Hill."

Diary of Ellen Romig Regnier, courtesy Richard D. Regnier:

"February 9th—Mr. Jones died very suddenly of a heart attack: A great shock to all of us, especially Dad [John W. Romig]. He'll miss him."

"February 13th—Mr. Jones was buried up here in Gold Hill today. No relatives could be located."

About Ernest L. Jones

Ernest L. Jones was born about 1877 in Kentucky; the son of unknown Kentucky natives.

The earliest known record of Ernest was a marriage license issued on 20 October 1906 in Newton (Harvey)

Kansas to marry Mamie Hebert. It is interesting to note that Ernest returned this license on 21 November 1906 to the county office unused however the 1910 United States census states that Ernest was living in Newton (Harvey) Kansas along with his wife, Mamie, of three years with their daughter, Irene (born about 1909).

By 1915 the family was living in Garden City (Finney) Kansas and remained there until about 1925 when their location was Deerfield (Kearny) Kansas in the state census.

According to the obituary of Ernest L. Jones it was about that time Ernest made his way to Gold Hill (Boulder) Colorado where in the 1930 census he is listed as living there and divorced. No further records have been located on Mamie or the daughter, Irene.

The following newspaper articles are a bit confusing especially since Ernest listed himself as never married prior to his marriage in 1906 to Mamie Hebert.

Boulder Daily Camera 22 November 1894:
"Ernest Jones and Miss Nellie May Wright were united in marriage at 2:30 this afternoon at the home of the bride, 1890 12th street, Rev. R.A. Chase officiating."

Boulder Daily Camera 13 November 1895:
"Mr. and Mrs. Ernest Jones mourn the loss of their little three week old child and have the sympathy of many friends."

Boulder Daily Camera 02 March 1897:
"Ernest Jones, headman at the Allen's mill at Salina, came down to spend Sunday with his wife and recently arrived seven pound daughter. Mrs. S. Wright, mother of Mrs. Jones, is here from Rocky Ford to spend a few weeks with her daughter."

JONES, Gertrude M. "Trudy"

> Birth: 05/17/1909
> Death: 10/20/1991
> Cemetery Location: E3

Father: James W. Jones; Mother: Estella (*Thompson*); born in Zanesville (Muskingum) Ohio and died in Boulder (Boulder) Colorado at age 82 years, 5 months, 3 days-massive subarachnoid hemorrhage and chronic arteriosclerosis

Boulder Daily Camera 22 October 1991:
"Gertrude "Trudy" M. Jones—Gertrude "Trudy" M. Jones of 516 Valley View Drive, Boulder, died Sunday, Oct. 20, at Boulder Community Hospital. She was 82. She was born May 17, 1909, in Zanesville, Ohio, the daughter of James W. Jones and Estella Thompson Jones. She earned bachelor's degrees and a master's degree. She attended East Central College in Ada, Okla., the

University of California at Berkley, Peabody College in Nashville, Tenn., Vanderbilt University in Nashville and the University of Southern California. She taught in the Oklahoma City, Okla., and Kansas City, Mo., school systems. In 1969, she moved to Boulder from Kansas City, Mo. She belonged to the American Association of Retired Persons, Rocky Mountain Climbers Club, Boulder Senior Center, First Christian Church and the Upsilon chapter of Sigma Sigma Sigma. She also worked with the Meals on Wheels program, delivering meals and helping with garage sales and bazaars. She liked fishing, bridge and hand clay building. Three sisters and a brother preceded her in death. Surviving are four nephews and a niece. A memorial service will be Wednesday at 3 p.m. at Howe Mortuary Chapel, 2121 11th St., Boulder. The Rev. Clarence Doss and Barbara Wilkins of the First Christian Church of Boulder will officiate. Burial will be at Gold Hill Cemetery after the service. Contributions may be made to Meals on Wheels of Boulder or the First Christian Church of Boulder."

Boulder Daily Camera Focus 01 November 1981:
"Gertrude Jones is 72. She has been coming to Gold Hill since 1952 when she bought a cabin over the phone from someone in New York.

"Problem was," Gertrude says, "The only thing good as the logs outside." The former physical education teacher from Kansas City quickly learned how to handle power tools, resheathing [sic] the house inside and out. She lives in the cabin in the summer months with her long-time friend Mary Gonnerman, another teacher whom she met at a girls' camp in Arkansas when she was a teenager.

Gertrude notes, "When I first came to Gold Hill I was tired all the time. I have low blood pressure, and the higher I go in altitude, the higher my pressure goes. I'm energetic in the mountains."

Back in the 1950s, the town was restful and quiet, 'quite primitive,'" Gertrude says. "The atmosphere was one of trustfulness. Then the hippies came. They may not have been trashy people, but they sure lived trashy.

Now there's a better feeling in the town than in the '60s. Life has changed. We older people realize that. I

have a moped and a Bronco now. The young are here, I think, not so much for the quiet and isolation as for the freedom. They can do what they want."

"One thing I love is, when you get up in the morning, you never know what's going to happen. You may be in Podunk by sundown. You may have drunk 10 cups of coffee before you get up Main Street."

"In the summertime it's a different story. We only stayed up here one winter. It was so desolate. Between 4 and 9 in the afternoon seemed to last forever. There are no street lights and nobody was ever out on the street. Not even a dog. And it was so terribly cold. That winter it got to 30 below zero."

Gertrude and Mary are like an old married couple: They've divided the chores of their mountain living; Gertrude does all of the repairs on the house and Mary is the firewood gatherer and "the brains," Gertrude says. Their place is cozy and cared for; their presence in the town is comforting to the younger single women making a go of it in the mountains."

(article by Vicki Groninger)

JONES, Leonard Ralph Jr. "Chip"

Birth: 10/07/1959
Death: 06/30/2006
Cemetery Location: B1

Father: Leonard Ralph Jones; Mother: Lee (*Richardson*); born in Boulder (Boulder) Colorado and died in La Veta (Huerfano) Colorado-cause of death unknown

Boulder Daily Camera 13 July 2006:
"Leonard R. "Chip" Jones, of La Veta, formerly of Boulder, died Friday, June 30, 2006, in La Veta. The cause of death has yet to be determined. He was 46.

The son of Leonard R. Jones and Lee Richardson Jones, he was born Oct. 7, 1959, in Boulder.

Mr. Jones lived in Boulder until 1990.

He was a Boulder High School graduate and a glassblower.

He enjoyed cats, skiing, bicycling and the Colorado mountains.

"Chip was a world-class glassblower and one of the nicest men you will ever meet," his family said. "He had a wonderful gift for telling stories, and his family and friends will his sweet silly, sense of humor."

Survivors include his mother, of Colorado City; three sisters, Lenda Jackson, of Franktown, Lynn Lemmon-Oliver, of Penrose, and Leslie Finn, of Gold Hill; and one brother, Loren Jones, of Portland, Ore.

He was preceded in death by his father.

A celebration of life will be at 1 p.m. Sunday in the Blue Bird Lodge at Gold Hill Inn, 401 Main St., Gold Hill.

Contributions in memory of Mr. Jones may be sent to the Boulder Shelter for the Homeless, 4869 N. Broadway, Boulder, CO 80304.

Spartan Funeral and Cremation Services, in Colorado Springs, handled arrangements."

JOY, Michael

Birth: 1844
Death: 09/20/1884
Cemetery Location: F3

Father: unknown; Mother: unknown; Wife: unknown; born in Ireland and died in Gold Hill (Boulder) Colorado at age about 40 years old-fatal gunshot wound; John Luxon's wife, Mary (*Joy*) Luxon, was also born in Ireland-might be related

Boulder County Herald 24 September 1884:
"Bullet Struck Innocent Target—Homicide At Gold Hill! John Paul Intends to Shoot J.L. Herzinger, But Kills Mike Joy, a Miner. Gold Hill was the scene of a homicide last Saturday evening, in which the intended victim escaped unhurt. Ed Heyn's saloon had been the scene of a good-natured scuffle between a few Cornishmen and John Paul. Finally John L. Herzinger, the constable, took a hand in the matter. It is said that he grabbed Paul by the shirt collar without any provocation and almost choked him. Paul Is represented as saying, 'Let's not fight, John, but talk the matter over,' or words to that effect, but Herzinger struck him on the forehead with metal knuckles. This so incensed Paul that he rushed behind the bar and took a revolver from a drawer. Herzinger told him to draw it and Paul did so. Then Herzinger made for the door. He had just dodged out when a ball came after him and missing his head struck the partially closed door, went through it and over the heads of two men standing on the outside.

Digging Up Dirt

Herzinger cut around the north-east corner of the building and Paul rushing out with drawn revolver fired as he supposed at Herzinger. The latter had gotten beyond range of the ball, but Mike Joy stood near the door and in line of the shot. The ball, fired from a .38-caliber revolver, cut through the fleshy part of the arm about four inches below the shoulder, passed through the right lung, cut the aorta near the heart and lodged in the left lung, near the outside. He fell dead on the spot, not knowing what hurt him. Paul was arrested soon afterwards by John Lester, and with the assistance of Jim Wycoff brought to Boulder Sunday morning at 3 o'clock and lodged in the jail. The coroner's jury investigated the matter Sunday and found the facts to be substantially as related above.

Dead Man Was Popular Citizen The Dead Man Mike Joy had been in Gold Hill for some time and had a good reputation, save that once in a while he would allow liquor to get the best of him. He was in Boulder a few days ago and had his shoulder dislocated by falling on it. He had nothing whatever to do with the scuffle and was an entirely innocent man. He was about 40 years old and leaves a wife and family in the east. They were preparing to come to Colorado in a few days. Joy had many warm friends in Gold Hill, who deeply deplore his death.

The Murderer John Paul has had a bad reputation, being often under liquor, and when in that condition very quarrelsome and wanting to fight everybody. In an encounter at Gold Hill some time ago he had part of his lip bitten off. He once tried to shoot John Luxon, and has threatened when drunk to kill various persons. He is about 35 years old and as far as is known is unmarried. Although often drunk, it is said that at the time of the quarrel Saturday night that he was not drunk and that Herzinger was to blame for the occurrence. When he shot Joy he is said to have remarked, 'I thought it was Herzinger,' showing he intended to kill Herzinger, but in the dark it being between 9 and 10 o'clock at night, and in the excitement of passion under which he labored, he fired without knowing who was to receive the bullet.

The Blame of the affair is laid mainly on Herzinger, who was the attacking person. The people of Gold Hill are more incensed at him than at Paul, and many of them say if Herzinger had been the victim instead of Joy there would have been little disposition to trouble Paul.

Gold Hill was our first mining camp, established in 1859, and it is doubtful if more than a handful of people went down in gun fights, but we do have evidence of this one. We think it a story to stir the imagination: the arrogant, bullying constable, the man who wouldn't take anything off anybody, the innocent well-liked bystander, the good people of Gold Hill who had at once spotted the aggressor and laid the blame squarely on him. And not the least is the frontier journalism, not afraid to set her down."

(reprinted 30 December 1957 *Boulder Daily Camera*-People I Meet by Forest Crossen)

Boulder County Herald Weekly 15 October 1884:

"John Paul's Trial......

The case of The People vs. John Paul, accused of murdering Michael Joy, was taken up in the District Court yesterday. The following are the jury: John Hunter, W.B. Neeley, George Walker,

Wm. Stimson, Albert Baker, George Clark, Gerald Denlo, John Johnson, J.M. Jones, J.W. Smith, B.F. Pine, John Mitchell."

Boulder County Herald Weekly 22 October 1884:

"Paul's Trial...

The case of The People vs. Paul was resumed on the part of the prosecution Wednesday afternoon.

David Vessels testified that he was in the hotel looking out of the window in the second story across the street from the saloon, heard both shots fired, came downstairs and found Joy's dead body on the ground.

Cross-ex. by Whiteley developed the same testimony as above.

Mr. Herzinger was next called upon the witness stand and after being sworn said: I have lived in Gold Hill 2 years, known Joy 5 or six years. He was killed on the 20th

of Sept. I walked into the saloon about half past 9, saw Mr. Paul. He called me G-d d-m s-n of a b—h. I told him if he did not stop that kind of talk I would arrest him. I caught him by the throat and struck him with his piece of ore (a long slim stone 4 inches long). We parted and I went to the door. Paul shot, the ball passing over my head about three inches. I ran, he came out and shot again. I did not know he hit anyone.

Cross-ex. by Whiteley—Where were you when the first shot was fired? Right by the door, N.E. part of the door. Where when the second? At the N.W. corner of the saloon. Are you a constable? That's what they call me. Did you enter in that capacity? Yes. Did you say you came in to make peace? I don't know. Myers told me to take hold of Paul and arrest him. I was at the end of the bar. Mr. Paul and Myers were standing 2 ½ feet away from me. Don't know where Heyn was at the time. Did you go out of the saloon without being told to by Mr. Heyn? Yes. I did not put my hand on Paul at this time. I was out some fifteen minutes. Where was Paul when you returned? At the card table with Joy. When I came in I heard Paul call Joy you G-d d-m s-n of a b—h. Didn't you catch him by the neck tie and jerk him over to the other end of the room? That is a lie, I did not. Did you cuss him? I did not. Did Ed. Heyn come up to you and tell you to go home? He did not. Didn't he turn you out? He did not. I was not drunk, only took one drink. I said to Ed. the son of a gun is taking your pistol. Did you strike Paul when you took him in the corner? I say it is a lie. I struck him when he tore my shirt. I was 10 feet from the door when I struck him with the ore. Did you go out after you struck Paul? I tell you it is pretty hard to testify. When I went out he was washing his face. Didn't you see the blood streaming down his face? I don't know, he was washing his face. Heyn asked me to let the thing drop and I would not. Was there a fight there? Yes. Who was fighting? Paul. Who besides? I don't know. Did you tell two men not to go away as there would be fun here to-night? I did not. Did you show them some knuckles and say you were about to polish someone off with them? That is a lie, the whole thing is a lie. When Paul first came to the Hill I took him to my house. I liked him very much. Did you like him on the night in question? I don't know. Was Paul angry when you entered? I judge so (in a whisper). Were they talking loudly? Don't make fun of me. I heard some men much better than others. Paul's voice is sharp and I can hear very well. Did you have any knuckles with you that evening? I did not.

Dr. King testified to being sent for at a quarter to 10 p.m. and examining the wound, which was a most fatal one.

Fleming Herzinger testified to seeing Paul strike his father; take a pistol from the drawer and fire. Several persons tried to hold him, but he got away and fired a second shot.

Cross-examined by Whiteley—I was about 9 o'clock when I went in. Paul was standing up and Joy was sitting down in front of him. Paul and Joy were talking loudly. They did not talk long together. Paul called joy a s-n of a b—h and he was himself the best s-n of a b—h in Gold Hill. Paul said when Joy got well he would have a tussle with him. Father took Paul by the neck tie and pulled him away. Father struck him. We put father out. How long after he struck Paul before you and Heyn took him out? A few minutes. The next I saw the firing. Where was you your father [sic] when he fired the first shot? Don't know, outside with the door shut. I went out when Paul went out to fire the second shot. Did not see him shoot, saw the flash, that was all. Just bobbed my head out and back again and shut the door. I took a specimen out of father's hand after he struck Paul. Saw the blood upon his face.

This closed the prosecution.

Major Whiteley examined witnesses for the defense. The testimony for the defense was opened by John Jester, who said he was in the saloon. Mr. Herzinger came in, had some words with Paul and said, "I can whip any son of a b—h in Boulder County." He took Paul by the shirt collar and jerked him across the room. They were parted and Herzinger was put out. Herzinger soon returned and threatened to kill Paul. He took a piece of iron from his pocket and struck Paul. They were separated and Ed. Heyn put Herzinger out of the saloon, and I followed him. He said he would go back and whip Paul, but immediately the first shot was fired.

George Bennett testified that he was in the saloon. Paul was trying to get Herzinger to dance with him when they got into the fight. Heyn put Herzinger out, but he returned with the knuckles on and hit Paul 2 or 3 times. Paul struck him. Ed. Heyn and I put Herzinger out again, while Paul went to the counter to wash the blood off his face. Herzinger said he would kill Paul yet. I went out with Herzinger and did not see Paul fire the first shot, as the door was shut. Herzinger then went north in the dark. Mike Joy was standing in the street when the first shot was fired. Paul came to the saloon door and fired the second time, saying, "Skin, you son of a b—h, Herzinger."

Cross=ex. by Livelsay.

James Burnett testified that he was in the saloon at the time of trouble between Paul and Joy. Herzinger took hold of Paul and Paul said he did not want any trouble with him. After some quarreling Heyn put Herzinger out. In about five minutes he came in with knuckles on and threatened to kill Paul. He was in the room when Paul first shot and tried to get out; don't know where he went when he got out.

Was not cross-ex.

Tom Johnson testified that he came out of store, heard the noise at the saloon, went across the street, saw

Joy going north, met Jester and was talking with him when the first shot was fired; saw flash of the second shot.

Robert Ray, Mr. Short, Mr. McMastere testified in substance that Herzinger had threatened to whip Paul, that he used metal knuckles when he struck him, that Herzinger was the aggressor and called Paul vile names. The case closed before dinner, the defendant not taking the stand.

The jury in the Paul case returned a verdict Thursday night of voluntary manslaughter."

Interesting to note that prior to this unfortunately incident the *Boulder County Herald Weekly* published this short article on 22 August 1883:

"John Paul of Gold Hill a good fellow when sober but the very incarnation of the devil when in drink, attacked two men at different times in Gold Hill last Saturday and was justly thumped John should let drink alone and be a man."

About Michael Joy

Little is verified about Michael except that he was born in Ireland; unknown Ireland native parents.

One family tree on Ancestry states Michael's wife was Eliza Jane Lancaster who was born in 1852 in (Lake) Illinois; the daughter of Dennis and Elizabeth (*Curran*) Lancaster. Michael married her on 03 August 1874 in (Cook) Illinois (no primary evidence to support this yet). Eliza Jane died on 17 November 1884; just a few months after Michael was killed. She is buried in the St. Patrick Cemetery in Lake Forest (Lake) Illinois. This family tree also states there were two known children born to Michael and Eliza: a daughter born 16 August 1875 and a son born 28 September 1882; both born in (Cook) Illinois.

The first real verified record of Michael Joy is in the United States Federal Mortality Census 1850-1885 listing Michael Joy: male, white, married, birth about 1844, Birth Place Ireland, Age 40, Death Date September 1884, Cause of Death Pistol Shot, Father's Birth Place Ireland, Mother's Birth Place Ireland. For some reason he is also listed in the Colorado State Census of 1885 (married and a miner) even though at that time he was quite dead.

K

KEIL, Rosemary (*Brummet*)

> Birth: 03/11/1936
> Death: 09/01/1986
> Cemetery Location: C4

Father: Roscoe Brummet; Mother: Edna (*Psadt*); Husband: Jamshid Drakhti; born in Toledo (Lukas) Ohio and died in Boulder (Boulder) Colorado at age 50 years, 5 months, 21 days-natural causes

Boulder Daily Camera 05 September 1986:
> "Rosemary Ann Keil—Rosemary Ann Keil, a Gold Hill retailer, died Monday, September 1, at Boulder Community Hospital. She was 50. Mrs. Keil was born in Toledo, Ohio, on March 11, 1936. She was the daughter of Roscoe and Edna Psadt Brummet. She married Jamshid Drakhti in Denver on April 2, 1986. She was the owner/operator of Rosey Reflections in Gold Hill. She moved to Gold Hill in 1974; from Fort Lauderdale, Fla. Survivors include her husband of Gold Hill, her mother of Toledo, Ohio, and one sister, Nancy Cummings of Toledo. A service will be held at 10 a.m. Sunday at Gold Hill Cemetery. In lieu of flowers, contributions may be made to Boulder Humane Society, 2323 55th St., Boulder 80301."

"Rosie's Bench" by her tombstone

KINGSBURY, Joseph

> Birth: About 1836
> Death: 08/07/1911
> Cemetery Location: C5

Father: unknown; Mother: unknown; born in England and died in Rowena (Boulder) Colorado at the age of about 75 years-acute dilation of the heart and myocarditis

Boulder Daily Camera 08 August 1911:
> "Jos. Kingsbury, a civil war veteran and Colorado pioneer, died at his cabin 2 miles from Gold Hill on Left Hand last night of heart trouble. His funeral will be held tomorrow afternoon at Gold Hill at 2 o'clock."

Boulder County Herald 08 August 1911:
> "Joseph Kingsbury, 75 years old, an old soldier and pioneer, died of old age at Rowena yesterday afternoon. The funeral arrangements are in charge of the Trezise Undertaking establishment. Kingsbury had no relatives surviving so far as is known. He had lived in Colorado 46 years, devoting the most of that time to mining. Although he had been a resident of Gold Hill for the past twelve years, little is known about him there. He was a veteran of the Civil war and was on the pension list."

U.S. Civil War Soldier Records and Profiles, 1861-1865; Illinois-Roster of Officers and Enlisted Men:
> "Enlisted in Company Band, Illinois 51st Infantry Regiment on 15 Oct 1861; mustered out on 30 June 1862"
> (http://civilwar.illinoisgenweb.org/fs/051-fs.html#band states Joseph's enlistment date as 05 October 1861; Rank of 1st Class).

Digging Up Dirt

About Joseph Kingsbury

Joseph was born in England; parents unknown. He apparently never married and died at age 70 years (approximately)-acute dilation of the heart and myocarditis. The 1900 census has birth date November of 1846; 1910 census has Joseph at 73 years old (making birth year as 1838).

He came to the Gold Hill (Boulder) Colorado area in 1899. There is a Joseph Kingsbury, born about 1848 in England with parents born in Wales, single, living at Lawson (Clear Creek) Colorado in the 1880 United States census.

On 17 June 1902 Joseph filed for a Civil War pension; listing himself as an invalid. He died 07 August 1911 at his cabin in Rowena (Boulder) Colorado and is buried in the Gold Hill Cemetery in Gold Hill (Boulder) Colorado.

KINSEY, Infant

> Birth: After 06/18/1900
> Death: 11/06/1905
> Cemetery Location: Unknown

Father: Theodore T. Kinsey; Mother: Matilda "Tilley" B. (*Porter*); born in Gold Hill (Boulder) Colorado and died in Ward (Boulder) Colorado at age of less than 5 years-cause of death unknown; no tombstone

About the Kinsey Family

Theodore T. "Pete" Kinsey was born on 27 March 1871 in Union Township (Miami) Ohio; the son of Joseph and Lorena "Lovenia/Lavinia" (*Bowlen*) Kinsey. He married Matilda B. "Tillie" Porter in 1891 in Ohio. She was born on 28 March 1873 in Covington (Miami) Ohio; the daughter of Richard Newton and Emma (*Reynolds*) Porter. To this marriage three known children were born:

Helen Imogene: born September 1892 Ohio and died between 1920 and 1959; burial unknown

Lenore "Jennie": born 24 January 1897 Ohio and died 03 January 1979 Shasta Lake (Shasta) California; burial unknown; married Edward Bellmer Humphrey

Infant: born Gold Hill (Boulder) Colorado and died 06 November 1905 Ward (Boulder) Colorado; buried Gold Hill Cemetery, Gold Hill (Boulder) Colorado; see KINSEY, Infant

By 1900 the family was living in Ward (Boulder) Colorado where Theodore was a farmer. His parents (Joseph and Lavinia) were living in the household with Joseph working as a druggist.

In the 1910 United States census the household was smaller with only Theodore, Tillie and their daughter, Lenore, making up the family as Theodore's parents moved back to Ohio where Joseph died in 1918 and Lovenia in

1926; both buried in the Shiloh Park Cemetery in Shiloh (Montgomery) Ohio.

Theodore suddenly died 20 June 1914 and is buried in the Green Mountain Cemetery in Boulder (Boulder) Colorado.

Boulder Daily Camera 20 June 1914:

"DEATH OF "PETE" KINSEY SADDENS HOSTS OF FRIENDS...

Theodore T. Kinsey, known in every mining district of Boulder County as "Pete" died at University hospital from an entanglement of the intestines resulting from ptomaine poisoning caused by eating canned goods. He became suddenly ill yesterday afternoon at the mine which he is leasing near Nederland and was rushed to the University hospital in one of the Hickox and Fields automobiles.

Mr. Kinsey had been sick but twelve hours, dying at the hospital this morning at 4:30. He was one of the most popular mining men in this county and his death will be mourned by all the Boulder Elks, of which he had been a very prominent member, as well as by his host of friends. He was a resident of Ward for a good many years and at one time was forest ranger.

His wife and two daughters, Miss Helen, a student at the University and Miss Lenore, a student at the Prep school came from Ward last night where they went for the summer after the closing of the schools here. During the school year they made their home at 1217 Spruce Street.

Funeral arrangements are awaiting word from parents and sisters of Mr. Kinsey in Iowa."

Boulder Daily Camera 22 June 1914:

"PETE KINSEY BURIED BY THE BOULDER ELKS...

In the presence of a large company of friends the Elks this afternoon conducted their impressive ritualistic services over the remains of Theodore T. Kinsey, better known as "Pete," who died Saturday morning after less than a day's illness of acute indigestion and ptomaine poisoning. Charles O'Connor delivered the eulogy and George F. Fonda sang "Nearer My God To Thee" and "The Vacant Chair." The casket was covered with floral offerings. The pall bearers were William Carter, Kenneth McDonald, George Metz, Nels Norsted, John Pughe and Ross Johnson.

Mrs. O.C. Oyler, a sister of the deceased, her husband and daughter were here from Denver for the funeral. Mr. Kinsey's parents, who reside in Dayton, Ohio, were unable to make the trip to Boulder. Interment was in the Green Mountain Cemetery."

After Theodore's death his widow, Matilda "Tillie", married Willis "William" Valentine Gilbreth on 06 October 1915 in Denver (Denver) Colorado. He was born 13

February 1885, son of Willis and Orpha B. (maiden name unknown) Gilbreth.

By 1920 both daughters (Helen and Lenore) were living in Los Angeles (Los Angeles) California however by 1930 Lenore was living in Hueneme (Ventura) California with her husband of eight years, Edward B. Humphrey, and their 5 year old daughter, Margery. Living next door to them was Lenore's mother, Matilda, and her second husband, William Valentine Gilbreth. There are no records found for the oldest daughter, Helen Imogene.

About three years later William died on 14 March 1933 in (Inyo) California; burial unknown. His widow, Matilda, moved in with her daughter, Lenore, and daughter, Margery, in Rural (Inyo) California.

By 1940 they were living in Shasta (Shasta) California where Matilda "Tillie" died on 27 August 1959; burial at Inglewood Cemetery, Inglewood (Los Angeles) California. (California Death Index has 29 August 1959)

Sacramento Bee (Sacramento, California) 29 August 1959:

"In Central Valley, Shasta County, August 27, 1959; Matilda B. Gilbreth, mother of Lenore Humphrey of Central Valley, sister of Minnie Boley of Golden, Colo.; a native of Ohio, aged 86 years. Funeral services will be conducted at 2pm tomorrow with interment in the Inglewood Park Cemetery."

KITTO, Elizabeth Harriet Jane "Emma" (*Ellis*)

Birth: 01/09/1878
Death: 04/14/1955
Cemetery Location: B2

Father: Richard Ellis; Mother: Harriet (*Tonkin*-possibility); Husband: James William Kitto; born in Penzance

Digging Up Dirt

(Cornwall) England and died in Boulder (Boulder) Colorado at age 77 years, 3 months, 5 days-illness; naturalization papers for her mother Harriet Bennetts state Jane was born on 09 January 1884 and obituary (see below) states 09 January 1878; see KITTO, James William; see **About James William Kitto and Harriett Janes (*Ellis*) Kitto;** see KITTO, Laura; see KITTO, William James

Boulder Daily Camera 15 April 1955:

"Mrs. Harriett Kitto, Early-Day Resident of Colorado Dies—Mrs. Harriett Kitto, who came to Colorado from Cornwall, Mich., when she was six years of age, died at the Boulder General Hospital Thursday afternoon at the age of 77. She had been ill but a short time. Her parents were Richard and Harriet Ellis and the date of her birth Jan. 9, 1878. Her husband, James Kitto, also an early resident of Boulder, died at their home in Gold Hill Dec. 19, 1925. Survivors are two daughters, Mrs. Edith L. Shayewitz of 912 Marine and Mrs. Lela M. (Fred C.) Walter of 1120 Marine. Melvin Walter and Mrs. Leona Goff, both of Boulder, are grandchildren. There are two great grandchildren. Mrs. Kitto was a member of the Gold Hill Club. Funeral services are to be at 2 Monday from Howe Mortuary. Interment will be beside her husband in Gold Hill."

Boulder Daily Camera 16 April 1955:

"Mrs. Harriet Kitto, mother of Mrs. Lila Walter and Mrs. Edith Shayewitz of Boulder. Services to be held at 2 o'clock Monday from the Howe Mortuary chapel with Dr. Warren S. Bainbridge, pastor of the First Methodist church, officiating. Interment is to be in the Gold Hill Cemetery beside her husband James Kitto, who died Dec. 19, 1925."

KITTO, James William

Birth: 1869
Death: 12/19/1925
Cemetery Location: B2

Father: William Kitto; Mother: possibly Elizabeth (*Williams*); Wife: Elizabeth Harriett Jane "Emma" (*Ellis*); born in (Cornwall) England and died in Gold Hill (Boulder) Colorado at the age of about 53 years old-miner's consumption; naturalization records state birth year 1868; see KITTO, Elizabeth Harriet Jane "Emma" (*Ellis*); see KITTO, William James; see **About James William Kitto and Elizabeth Harriet Jane "Emma" (*Ellis*) Kitto;** see KITTO, Laura

Boulder Daily Camera 21 December 1925:

"JAMES KITTO—James Kitto, an old-time resident of Gold Hill, died quite suddenly at his home there Saturday, after a serious illness for some time with miner's consumption. He was in Boulder Friday and appeared to be better at that time tho his condition was such that it was not expected that he would be able to live thru the winter. Mr. Kitto was 53 years of age and was born in Cornwall, England. He came to the United States when he was 19 and went directly to Gold Hill where he engaged in mining. He is survived by a wife, two daughters, Mrs. Shayewitz of 505 University Avenue, Boulder; Lelia, who lives at home and Wm. Kitto, who also lives at Gold Hill. His brother [Charles] was associated with the German House in Boulder for a great many years and the latter's widow, Mrs. Emma Kitto, is coming from Denver tomorrow. The funeral is to be held tomorrow at Gold Hill in charge of Rev. J.H. Skeen. The body is at the Tippett-Powell mortuary."

About James William and Elizabeth Harriet Jane "Emma" (*Ellis*) Kitto

James William Kitto was born in July of 1869 in (Cornwall) England, the son of James Kitto and possibly Elizabeth "Harriet" Williams.

According to the 1910 United States Census James William immigrated in 1889 but other census records state 1890 and 1891; date of naturalization 26 October 1904 with John Pughe (Gold Hill resident) as a witness.

James married Elizabeth Harriett Jane Ellis on 24 August 1895 in Gold Hill (Boulder) Colorado. She was born 09 January 1878 in Penzance (Cornwall) England, daughter of Richard and Harriett (*Bennetts*) Ellis; see BENNETTS, Harriet (*Tonkins*-possibility).

James William and Harriett Jane had four known children:

Laura: born about 1896 Gold Hill (Boulder) Colorado-1898 Gold Hill (Boulder) Colorado; buried Gold Hill Cemetery, Gold Hill (Boulder) Colorado; see KITTO, Laura

William James: born 01 February 1898 Gold Hill (Boulder) Colorado and died 06 May 1943 Boulder (Boulder) Colorado; buried Gold Hill Cemetery, Gold Hill (Boulder) Colorado; married Ruth Evelyn Poole; see KITTO, William James

Lela M.: born 01 March 1901 Gold Hill (Boulder) Colorado and died 01 November 1974 Boulder (Boulder) Colorado; buried Mountain View Memorial Park, Boulder (Boulder) Colorado; married Fred C. Walter

Edythe Leona: born 19 August 1903 Gold Hill (Boulder) Colorado and died 30 March 1989 Boulder (Boulder) Colorado; buried Mountain View Memorial Park, Boulder (Boulder) Colorado; married Morris Shayewitz

James and Harriet lived their married life in Gold Hill (Boulder) Colorado and at one time Harriett ran a boarding house there.

KITTO, Laura

> Birth: About 1896
> Death: About 1898
> Cemetery Location: B2

Father: James William Kitto; Mother: Elizabeth Jane Harriet "Emma" (*Ellis*); born in Gold Hill (Boulder) Colorado and died in Gold Hill (Boulder) Colorado at the age of 2 years-cause of death unknown; no tombstone; see KITTO, Elizabeth Jane Harriet "Emma" (*Ellis*); see KITTO, James William; see **About James William Kitto and Elizabeth Harriet Jane "Emma" (*Ellis*) Kitto;** see KITTO, William James

KITTO, William James

> Birth: 02/01/1898
> Death: 05/06/1943
> Cemetery Location: B2

Father: James William Kitto; Mother: Elizabeth Jane Harriet "Emma" (*Ellis*); Wife: Ruth Evelyn (*Poole*); born in Gold Hill (Boulder) Colorado and died in Boulder (Boulder) Colorado at the age of 45 years, 3 months, 5 days- miners' consumption; see KITTO, Elizabeth Jane Harriet "Emma" (*Ellis*); see KITTO, James William; see **About James William and Elizabeth Harriet Jane "Emma" (*Ellis*) Kitto;** see KITTO, Laura

Boulder Daily Camera 06 May 1943:

"William J. Kitto—William James Kitto, who was born at Gold Hill In this county Feb. 1, 1898, died at the hospital this morning at 9:30 after a short illness. He was taken to the hospital last night from 513 University Avenue where he had been living. Though his death was sudden he had been in failing health for years with miner's consumption. Mr. Kitto was a son of a Gold Hill pioneer family. His parents came from England in the early days of Gold Hill. The father died many years ago but his mother, Mrs. Jane Kitto of Gold Hill survives. Other survivors are two sisters, Mrs. Edythe Shayewitz of 912 Marine and Mrs. Lela Walters of 1228 Mapleton. Mrs. Leona Goff of 912 Marine is a niece and Melvin Walters of 1228 Mapleton a nephew. Body is at Howe mortuary."

Boulder Daily Camera 07 May 1943:

"William James Kitto—Services at Howe mortuary Monday afternoon at 2. Interment, Gold Hill cemetery."

Boulder Daily Camera 10 May 1943:

"William James Kitto—Services at Howe mortuary this afternoon at 2. Rev. Angus C. Hull Jr., pastor of the First Baptist church, officiating. Mrs. A.B. Owens sang, accompanied by Mrs. A.R. Mason at the organ. Pallbearers were William Peterson, Randall Goff, Albert Walters, Lloyd Snively, Harvey Pool, and W.J. McDonald. Interment, Gold Hill cemetery."

About William James Kitto

William James Kitto was born 01 February 1898 in Gold Hill (Boulder) Colorado; the son of James and Elizabeth Jane Harriet "Emma" (*Ellis*) Kitto; see KITTO, Elizabeth Harriett Jane "Emma" (*Ellis*) Kitto and see KITTO, James William.

William lived with parents and siblings (Lela and Edythe) in Gold Hill (Boulder) Colorado for over three decades, being a miner, when on 17 September 1927 he married Ruth Evelyn Pool (spelled Poole on the marriage record) in Boulder (Boulder) Colorado. Ruth, daughter of Harvey Edward and Florence Ethel (*Barron*) Pool, was born on 22 December 1908 in Boulder (Boulder) Colorado. To this union no children were born. It is interesting

to note that Ruth always called William by the name of "Terry."

In April of 1930 William and Ruth were living in Los Angeles (Los Angeles) California in the household of Ruth's mother while Harvey (Ruth's father) was living as a lodger, owner of an auto repair shop in Boulder (Boulder) Colorado.

By the 1940 census Harvey and Florence Pool (Ruth's parents) were living on University Avenue in Boulder while William and Ruth Kitto were living on 7th Street.

William and Ruth divorced right after the 1940 census. Ruth then met Esker Otus Lewellen at a barn dance in Longmont (Boulder) Colorado and they were married in Sidney (Cheyenne) Nebraska 05 April 1942 (Easter Sunday); eventually moving to Oklahoma. Esker already had three grown children of his own and in 1949 Ruth and Esker were blessed with the birth of their only child together, a daughter.

Esker died 27 January 1969 Phoenix (Maricopa) Arizona; buried Glendale Memorial Park Glendale (Maricopa) Arizona. Ruth died 17 July 1982 San Diego (San Diego) California; private cremation by Featheringill Mortuary.

After the divorce William James was living with his in-laws (Harvey and Florence Pool) at 513 University Avenue in Boulder (Boulder) Colorado when, in 1943, he was taken to Community Hospital, dying there on 06 May from miners' consumption. There is no mention of Ruth in William's obituary or in his mortuary records however Harvey Pool (Ruth's father) was listed as a pallbearer.

Harvey Pool died five months later on 05 October; buried in the Columbia Cemetery Boulder (Boulder) Colorado. Ruth's mother (Florence) died 24 July 1979; buried also in the Columbia Cemetery.

FYI: In previous generations the spelling was Pool however somehow an "e" was added to become Poole. Ruth used the later spelling.

KNAPP, Dorothy Grace (*Perry*)

> Birth: 01/24/1917
> Death: 09/19/2004
> Cemetery Location: E3

Father: Eugene D. Perry; Mother: Blanche Kies (*Burnam*); Husband: Robert George Knapp; born in Des Moines (Polk) Iowa and died in Louisville (Boulder) Colorado at the age of 87 years, 7 months, 21 days-Alzheimer's disease; see KNAPP, Robert George Knapp

Boulder Daily Camera 26 September 2004:

"DOROTHY PERRY KNAPP—Dorothy Perry Knapp of Louisville died of Alzheimer's disease Sunday, Sept. 19, 2004, in Louisville. She was 87. The daughter of Eugene D. Perry and Blanche Kies Burnam Perry, she was born

Jan. 24, 1917, in Des Moines, Iowa. She married Robert G. Knapp on Jan. 24, 1948, in Des Moines. Mrs. Knapp worked for many years with the National Council of Camp Fire Girls. She graduated from Iowa State University and volunteered with the Red Cross in World War II in Louisiana. She spent summers in Gold Hill from 1951 to 2001 and moved to Louisville in 2001. She was a member of Pi Beta Phi sorority at Iowa State; an active member of St. Michael's and All Angels Episcopal Church in Mission, Kan.; a past-president and active member of the Shawnee Mission Kansas La Sertoma Club; and a member of the Rocky Mountain Climbers Club, Boulder. "She had a wonderful sense of humor and embraced life. She was warm-hearted with a twinkle in her eye, "the family said. "She loved people and animals and they loved her." Survivors include a son, Tom Knapp of Ashland Ore.; a daughter, Martha Knapp of Boulder; and a sister, Mary Crosten of Orcas Island, Wash. She was preceded in death by her husband, two brothers and a sister. An informal gathering and interment will be at 5 p.m. today at the Gold Hill Cemetery. Contributions may be made to the Alzheimer's Association, Colorado Chapter, 455 Sherman St., Suite 500, Denver, CO 80203. Crist Mortuary of Boulder is in charge of arrangements."

The Mountain-Ear 30 September 2004:

"Gold Hill rodeo queen dies

Summer didn't arrive in Gold Hill until Dorothy arrived to brighten the social life. Every summer, from May to September, Dorothy Perry Knapp leaned on the gate in front of her cabin and greeted people as they walked

down the dirt streets of Gold Hill. Sometimes she invited them into her house, treating them to a glimpse of the past, regaling them with stories of her youth, of the town, and most of all, listening intently to what they had to say. She loved people and cared about who they were and where they came from. Her sister Martha says Dorothy was a party girl and loved the people in her life.

Dorothy died of Alzheimer's Sunday, Sept 19 in Louisville at the age of 87. She was buried in the Gold Hill Cemetery last Sunday.

Dorothy was born Jan. 24, 1917 in Des Moines, Iowa and married Robert G. Knapp on Jan. 24, 1948, in Des Moines. She worked for many years with the National Council of Camp Fire girls. She graduated from Iowa State University and volunteered with the Red Cross in World War II in Louisiana.

Dorothy was a member of Pi Beta Phi sorority at Iowa State; an active member of St. Michael's and All Angels Episcopal Church in Mission, Kansas; a past president and active member of the Shawnee Mission Kansas La Sertoma Club; and a member of the Rocky Mountain Climbers Club of Boulder. In 1960 Dorothy and her two children hopped into their station wagon, pulling a trailer full of used furniture to spend the summer in their Gold Hill cabin, located right across from the Gold Hill School, a perfect location for a people-loving person. The car over-heated in the canyon and a foot long section of the bed had to be cut off. The bed remains in the cabin to this day. "Mom always had a knack for telling stories and she always had a story to tell. She also kept a plate of chocolate cookies, just in case someone walked by," remembers her daughter Martha. The cabin came with an outhouse and an outdoor shower and as Dorothy bathed she would wave at the planes flying over her. She never minded making fun of herself.

Dorothy started the Women's Pot Club in Gold Hill which meant no men, no dogs and no kids. No men, that is, until she decided it would be a hoot to invite two men, dressed as women, to the Pot Luck, just to see what would happen. According to an old account of the incident, there was much laughter and even a date arranged from the tomfoolery.

This summer, Dorothy came to celebrate the Fourth of July in Gold Hill. In 1985, she had been crowned the Gold Hill Rodeo Queen and ever since then, the Fourth was her favorite holiday. Although she had had trouble communicating this past year, she found her voice for a while and evidently enjoyed watching the parade as it circled the town twice, going right past her cabin. "She was so happy to have found the ability to communicate for the day," says her daughter.

"She had a wonderful sense of humor and embraced life. She was warm-hearted with a twinkle in her eye and she loved people and animals and they loved her."

Survivors include a son, Tom Knapp of Ashland, Ore; a daughter, Martha Knapp of Boulder; and a sister Mary Crosten of Orcas Island, Washington. She was preceded in death by her husband, two brothers and a sister. Contributions may be made to the Alzheimer's Association, Colorado Chapter, 455 Sherman St., Suite 500, Denver, CO 80203. Crist Mortuary of Boulder handled the arrangements."

(article by Barbara Lawlor)

KNAPP, Robert George

Birth: 05/17/1913
Death: 08/07/1975
Cemetery Location: E3

Father: George Joshua Knapp; Mother: Clara Louise (*Thielen*); Wife: Dorothy Grace (*Perry*); born in Dubuque (Dubuque) Iowa and died in Boulder (Boulder) Colorado at the age of 62 years, 2 months, 21 days-illness; see KNAPP, Dorothy Grace (*Perry*)

Boulder Daily Camera 08 August 1975:

"Robert G. Knapp, 62, of Overland Park, Kansas, died at 9:15 a.m. Thursday in Boulder Community Hospital. He was a summer resident of Gold Hill for 18 years, and had been attending Estes Planning Seminar at University of Colorado when he became ill.

Born May 17, 1913 in Dubuque, Iowa, to George and Clara Knapp, he married Dorothy Grace Perry in Des Moines, Iowa on Jan. 24, 1948.

Mr. Knapp was a practicing attorney in Mission, Kansas, and had practiced law for 25 years in the Kansas City area. He was a member and officer of numerous civic and professional associations including park boards, polio association, Sertoma Club, mental health board, Boy Scott committee, Masonic Lodge, bar associations, Kansas Supreme Court, American Trial Lawyers Assoc., and was a government appeal agent in this county.

Survivors are his wife, Dorothy Grace Knapp of Overland Park, Kansas; one son and one daughter, Thomas A. and Martha P. Knapp of Overland; a brother, John A. Knapp, Denver; two sisters; Mrs. Ralph Kimes, Fresno, Calif., and Mrs. Harriet Stroh, Phoenix, Ariz.

Memorial services will be Monday at 10:30 a.m. in How Chapel, Boulder, with Seventy Myron F. LaPointe officiating. In Mission Kansas, memorial service will be 10 a.m. Friday, Aug. 15, at St. Michael and All Angels Episcopal Church, where Mr. Knapp was a member. Interment will be in Mission, Kansas. Friends wishing to do so may donate to Memorial Fund, St. Michaels Shawnee Mission Sertoma Fund."

L

LARNER, Burnyce Anne (*Brady*)

> Birth: 10/10/1925
> Death: 04/19/2006
> Cemetery Location: B1

Father: John Brady; Mother: Emma Lou (*Hesmer*); Husband: Ray Larner; born in Bethesda (Montgomery) Maryland and died in Austin (Travis) Texas at the age of 80 years, 6 months, 9 days-chronic obstructive pulmonary disease; see LARNER, Jeffrey Max; see LARNER, Ray Albert

Boulder Daily Camera 23 April 2006:

"Burnyce Anne Larner, of Austin Texas, formerly of Boulder, died of chronic obstructive pulmonary disease Wednesday, April 19, 2006 in Austin. She was 80.

The daughter of John F. Brady and Emma Lou Hessmer Brady, she was born on October 10, 1925 in Bethesda, Maryland.

Mrs. Larner lived in Boulder from 1965 to 1970 and from 1974 to 1978. She lived in Gold Hill from 1981 to 1996.

She attended the University of Maryland and worked at IBM.

She enjoyed poetry, reading "The New Yorker," scotch, good friends and spending time in Boulder.

"Burnyce was one of a kind: not sweet, but always sophisticated, witty, and loving," her family said.

Survivors include her husband, two daughters, Amy Adams, and Annabelle Larner; and two grandchildren.

She was preceded in death by a son, Jeffrey Max Larner, in 1981.

Services will be held later in Boulder.

Contributions in Mrs. Larner's name may be made to Hospice Austin, 4107 Spicewood Springs Road, Suite 100, Austin, Texas 78759.

Superior Mortuary in Austin is handling arrangements."

Boulder Daily Camera 28 May 2006:

"Burnyce Larner October 10, 1925-April 19, 2006—Burnyce Anne Brady Larner, known for her charm and acerbic wit, died peacefully on Wednesday, April 19th, at the Christopher House Hospice in Austin Texas. Born to Emma Lou and John Brady in Washington, D.C. on October 10th, 1925, Burnyce grew up in Baltimore and then spent time in The Philippines, San Francisco, and New York City, where she met her husband, Ray. They married in 1959, and had three children: Amy, Max, and Annabelle. Burnyce was a full-time homemaker, an occupation that she accepted with gusto. The family lived in many places: England, Colorado, New York, Japan, and Texas. She charmed all who met her with her dead-on wit, hilarity and unique Burnyce-ness. She adored good scotch, good food and literature, and was an avid reader of The New Yorker. Sometimes she pleasantly stunned her friends by quoting a wicked limerick-the best of which we simply cannot publish here. She is survived by her husband, Ray, daughters Amy Adams and Annabelle Larner; their husbands Mike Adams and David Todd; two grandchildren, Violet and Fiona Adams. She will be buried in Gold Hill, Colorado, where she will join her beloved son, Max, and her mother. Burnyce was one-of-a-kind; not sweet, but always sophisticated, witty, and loving. Thank you to the wonderful people at The Christopher House and to all of her doctors and caretakers. A celebration in

her honor will be held at the Gold Hill Inn on Sunday, June 4th from 12-3pm. In lieu of flowers, please consider a donation to Hospice Austin, 512-322-0747."

LARNER, Jeffrey Max

Birth: 11/03/1962
Death: 02/14/1981
Cemetery Location: B1

Father: Ray Albert Larner; Mother: Burnyce Anne (*Brady*); born in New York City (Bronx) New York and died in Georgetown (Williamson) Texas at the age of 18 years, 3 months, 11 days-head and internal injuries; see LARNER, Burnyce Anne (*Brady*); see LARNER, Ray Albert

V.W. Hiker (Ancestry.com)
"Max smiled at his Aunt Marilyn as she was leaving his home the week before he was struck and killed by a drunk driver as he left the high school Valentine Day dance. He would have graduated from high school the following May."

LARNER, Ray Albert

Birth: 06/17/1931
Death: 04/15/2009
Cemetery Location: B1

Father: Ray Albert Larner; Mother: Jeanne (*Steele*); Wife: Burnyce Anne (*Brady*); born in Fort Worth (multiple counties) Texas and died in Austin (Travis) Texas at the age of 77 years, 9 months, 29 days-natural causes; Ray was one of three people who compiled the indexes (December 1993 and June 1994) of the Gold Hill Cemetery; see LARNER, Burnyce Anne (*Brady*); see LARNER, Jeffrey Max

Austin American-Statesman 26 April 2009:
"Ray Larner June 17, 1931-April 15, 2009 Ray Albert Larner, Jr, a gentle, quiet-spoken man, died peacefully

on Wednesday, April 15th in Austin, Texas. Born June 17, 1931, to Ray Albert Larner and Jeanne Steele Larner of Fort Worth, Texas, Ray grew up in Fort Worth and Eastland, Texas. He earned his degree in mathematics at Rice University and then served as an officer in the US Navy, where he traveled throughout the Mediterranean and Bermuda. In the 1950s, Ray moved to New York City to work for IBM. There he met his beloved, Burnyce Anne Brady. The couple married in 1959 and had three children. At IBM, Ray was a pioneer in computer languages, working on the definition and implementation of FORTRAN, and the creation and implementation of the new PL/I language for the IBM System/360 computers. The PL/I work took Ray and family to Hursley, England, and then to Boulder, Colorado, where the family put down deep roots. Later, he worked on text-processing software for the IBM DisplayWriter in Austin, and holds two patents from that work. Ray had a quick, mathematical mind, finished the Times crosswords in pen, competed semi-professionally in Scrabble, and was a wicked card player whom was seldom beat. He had a great passion for piano music and jazz, amongst his favorites were Thelonious Monk and Glenn Gould. He was loved and admired by all who met him. Throughout his life he was devoted to his beloved Burnyce, who preceded him in death in 2006. He is survived by his daughters, Amy Adams and Annabelle Larner; their husbands, Mike Adams and David Todd; grandchildren, Violet and Fiona Adams; sisters Marilyn Lu Hicks and Lois Jeanne Conte. He will be buried in Gold Hill, Colorado where he will join Burnyce and his beloved son, Max. Thank you to all the wonderful doctors, nurses, and caretakers at Buckner Villas in Austin, Texas. A celebration in his honor will be held in Austin at Amy Adams' residence on Saturday, May 2nd from 2:00 p.m. – 5:00 p.m."

LISLE/LEISLE, Henrietta/Elizabeth "Etta" (*Bell*)

Birth: About 1859
Death: 11/1892
Cemetery Location: B2 (possibly)

Father: John Bell; Mother: Sarah (*maiden name unknown*); Husband: John R. Lisle; born in Illinois and died in Gold Hill (Boulder) Colorado at the age of 33 years (approximately) and died in child birth; see LISLE/LEISLE, Sadie; see **About the Lisle/Leisle Family**

Herald Weekly 23 November 1892:
"Lisle, Mrs. John died a short time ago. John of Gold Hill works in a mine all day and there is no one to look after the children. Their two sons, Leon age 9 and George age 4, were sent by train to their uncle, E.A. Willis, in North Manchester, IN. Cards were sewn on their clothes with their destination."

LISLE/LEISLE, Sadie

> Birth: 07/28/1881
> Death: 07/04/1887
> Cemetery Location: B2

Father: John R. Lisle; Mother: Henrietta/Elizabeth "Etta" (*Bell*); born in Illinois and died in Gold Hill (Boulder) Colorado at age 5 years, 11 months, 6 days-cause of death unknown; see LISLE/Leisle, Henrietta "Etta" (*Bell*); see **About the Lisle/Leisle Family**

About the Lisle/Leisle Family

John R. Lisle was born June 1855 in (Daviess) Indiana; the son of Basil and Adaline (*Winfield*-possibility) Lisle (Liles/Lyle/Leisle).

He married Henrietta/Elizabeth "Etta" Bell on 22 March 1881 in White Oak Springs (Lafayette) Wisconsin. (It appears that Henrietta's brother, John, and wife Mary were living in White Oak Springs and perhaps that is why Henrietta was there; not known if she meet John Lisle there or not.)

Henrietta was born in 1859 Illinois (other sources state England); the daughter of English natives John and Sarah (maiden name unknown) Bell.

After the marriage of John and Henrietta they traveled to Illinois where their first child, Sadie, was born on 28 July 1881. By 1883 they were living in Colorado where their remaining four known children were born:

John Leon: born 28 September 1883 Gold Hill (Boulder) Colorado and died 24 December 1937 San Diego (San Diego) California; cremated-ashes in the Greenwood Memorial Park Cemetery, San Diego (San Diego) California; married Maud Rosetta Greek

George Basil: born 02 July 1888 Gold Hill (Boulder) Colorado and died 08 March 1926 Detroit (Wayne) Michigan; buried Woodmere Cemetery, Detroit (Wayne) Michigan; married Nellie Smith Tooley

Daughter: no information is known except she was adopted by Mr. and Mrs. Brennan in 1892

Infant: born November 1892 Gold Hill (Boulder) Colorado; no further information is known except the baby was adopted by Mr. and Mrs. Kessler in 1892

Boulder Daily Camera 18 November 1892:

"At Gold Hill, a woman died, after having given birth to a child. Three other tributes of motherly love remained. The wife of John R. Lisle was dead and four helpless children remained to a father whose day light or night time employment is down deep in the mines. What to do with the "childer" has often been asked by parents bereit [sic] as he. The baby was quickly adopted by Mr. and Mrs. Kessler while the eldest girl was taken as a child by Mr. and Mrs. Brennan. A sister wrote from North Manchester, Indiana, that she would take them all and so the two boys, one seven and the other nine years old, were "shipped" to the kind aunt and sister yesterday. Kind hearted Conduc-

tor D.R. McGaffey affixed the tags, directing the children as first class freight and then he sat down and wrote a letter to all conductors to see that they were passed from hand to hand in as good form as when delivered. The father remained behind to toil for his "bairns" and provide for their wants. Supt. Hammond of the Cash-Burkin tells us this story:

"I saw them on the train—these two boys. They looked disconsolately, one at the other. They were being shipped away from the grave of their mother they hardly knew how far. When the conductor came around and read McGaffy's letter, he passed on, but I noticed a portly man was attracted to the victims. He looked wistfully at me and then I went over to his seat and explained the situation to him. Great tears welled up into his eyes and he said: I have four boys at home whom I have not seen for a long time. Suppose my boys had lost their mother and I was compelled to tag them to some address thousands of mils away?" I said nothing, but later I saw this stranger pilot the conductor to the rear of the coach, and later the conductor returned and told the boys they would have a place in a palace sleeping car, with a colored porter and a friend to see them safely landed at North Manchester. I looked up in surprise, but the stranger was nowhere to be seen. I finally found him and begged to know his name. "No sir," said he, "my name is my own. I have children and I am away from home."

I awaited my chance, however, and from his grips and trunks gathered the information that his name is H.B. Eldridge, No. 1, Broadway, New York. Don't tell me again that the commercial traveler is hard of heart. I found in that man's tremendous tones, in his modesty defying recognition and acknowledgement, that there are noble men on the road and far from home. The children left on that night's train and I know that they were accompanied by a friend who accorded them fully as much care and attention as could the fondest parent."

Herald Weekly 23 November 1892:
"Lisle, Mrs. John died a short time ago. John of Gold Hill works in a mine all day and there is no one to look after the children. Their two sons, Leon age 9 and George age 4, were sent by train to their uncle, E.A. Willis, in North Manchester, IN. Cards were sewn on their clothes with their destination."

Though Henrietta died in Gold Hill (Boulder) Colorado it is not certain she was indeed buried in the Gold Hill Cemetery however there is an unmarked grave next to that of her beloved daughter, Sarah. It is presumed she was buried next to her.

After the death of his wife, Henrietta, John continued his work as a miner at the American Star mine in the Central District near Jamestown (Boulder) Colorado.

Boulder Daily Camera 14 December 1893:
"John R. Lisle has attached a car lead of American Star ore. What is the matter with this company? The mine looks as though it ought to pay."

By 09 June 1896 John had left Colorado for the Prescott (Yavapai) Arizona area. In the 1900 census he is listed as a widowed miner, living as a boarder there. On 18 September 1905 John allocated three mines in the Agua Fria District in (Yavapai) Arizona. From there the trail grows cold.

It is interesting to note that his son, John Leon, and wife lived in Tucson (Pima) Arizona in the 1930 census. However in 1937 John Leon and family were living in San Diego (San Diego) California where he died there on Christmas Eve, taking his own life.

LIVELY, Infant

Birth: 1883
Death: 1883
Cemetery Location: Unknown

Father: Henry Turner Lively; Mother: Mary Elizabeth (*McLaughlin*); born and died in Gold Hill (Boulder) Colorado at age 4 days; no tombstone; see LIVELY, Mary Elizabeth (*McLaughlin*); see **About Mary Elizabeth (*McLaughlin*) Lively**

LIVELY, Mary Elizabeth (*McLaughlin*)

Birth: 08/07/1854
Death: 02/07/1884
Cemetery Location: Unknown

Father: unknown; Mother: unknown; Husband: Henry Turner Lively; born in Ireland and died in Gold Hill (Boulder) Colorado at the age of 29 years, 6 months-childbirth; no tombstone

About Mary Elizabeth (*McLaughlin*) Lively

Mary Elizabeth McLaughlin was born 07 August 1854 in Ireland; parents unknown.

In the 1870 United States census Mary was living in (Perry) Illinois with her two sisters, Margaret and Acordin, in the household of Samuel and Mary E. Shaw.

On 26 September 1878 she married Henry Turner Lively in Marissa (St. Clair) Illinois and within two years later they were living in Gold Hill (Boulder) Colorado. Their union was blessed with three known children:

Mary Lucinda "Lucy": born 14 March 1881 Gold Hill (Boulder) Colorado and died June 1966 (Brown) South Dakota; buried Riverside Memorial Park, Aberdeen (Brown) South Dakota; married Robert Telford Montgomery

Infant: born 1883 Gold Hill (Boulder) Colorado and died 1883 Gold Hill (Boulder) Colorado; buried Gold Hill

Cemetery, Gold Hill (Boulder) Colorado; see LIVELY, Infant

Cynthia Augusta "Gussie": born 07 February 1884 Gold Hill (Boulder) Colorado and died 24 February 1949 Americus (Lyons) Kansas; buried Americus Cemetery, Americus (Lyons) Kansas; married Arthur Francis Edmiston

According to a Lively family history book Mary Elizabeth (*McLaughlin*) Lively died while giving birth to her daughter, Cynthia Augusta "Gussie" and was buried in the Gold Hill Cemetery. Her widowed husband, Henry, apparently moved to his homeland in (Randolph) Illinois where he died on 05 April 1885 and was buried in the Lively Cemetery in Sparta (Randolph) Illinois.

It appears the orphaned children (Mary Lucinda "Lucy" and Cynthia Augusta "Gussie") went to live with their aunt, Lucinda (*Lively*) Mathews in Lively Grove (Washington) Illinois.

LIVELY, William Sidney

Birth: About 1854
Death: 11/26/1892
Cemetery Location: Unknown

Father: William Jasper Lively; Mother: Emily Augusta (*Sturges*); Wife: Lucy Belle (*Marion*); born in (Randolph) Illinois and died in Gold Hill (Boulder) Colorado at the age of 38 years (approximately)-possibly tonsillitis; no tombstone

Boulder Daily Camera 21 December 1892:
"This place has recently seen a great deal of sickness and death. Inside of four weeks five have been taken from among us. The first was Mrs. John Lyle who left four children. Shortly after August Gustison [sic] buried his little baby. Sidney Lively, after a short illness, was the next to be taken."

Boulder News 29 December 1892:
"26, Death of W.S. Lively, Gold Hill"

About William Sidney Lively

William Sidney Lively was born about 1854 in (Randolph) Illinois; the son of Illinois natives William Jasper and Emily Augusta (*Sturges*) Lively. He was blessed with three known siblings:

John Augustus: born 17 December 1849 Sparta (Randolph) Illinois and died 31 August 1936 Peoria (Maricopa) Arizona; buried Glendale Memorial Park, Glendale (Maricopa) Arizona; married Mary Elizabeth Long

Samuel Newton: born 26 February 1857 Indiana and died 26 January 1904 Prescott (Yavapai) Arizona; buried Citizens Cemetery, Prescott (Yavapai) Arizona; married Rosetta "Etta" Runyan

Albert James: born June 1865 Sparta (Randolph) Illinois and died 01 August 1919 Jamestown (Boulder) Colorado; Jamestown Cemetery, Jamestown (Boulder) Colorado; married Florence "Floss" Evans

In the 1860 census the family was living in Wilson (Audrain) Missouri. By 1880 William Sidney was living in Gold Hill (Boulder) Colorado in the household of H.T. Lively (Henry Turner Lively, brother to Sidney's father, William Jasper Lively).

The 1885 Colorado State census lists William Sidney (teamster) living in his parents' household along with his wife, Lucy Belle Marion whom he married on 11 December 1883 (Boulder) Colorado. She was born about 1850 in Illinois; parents unknown. It appears no children were born to this union. William Sidney's brother, Albert James, was also living in this household.

The family soon went their separate ways. William Jasper Lively and his wife, Emily Augusta moved to Peoria (Maricopa) Arizona where their oldest son, John Augustus, was living.

William Jasper died 28 June 1910 and Emily Augusta died 30 July 1898; both are buried in Glendale Memorial Park, Glendale (Maricopa) Arizona. Their other sons, William Sidney and Albert James, remained in the Gold Hill (Boulder) Colorado area however by 1919 Albert lived in Jamestown (Boulder) Colorado where he ran a grocery store.

During a tonsillitis epidemic William Sidney passed away on 26 November 1892 in Gold Hill (Boulder) Colorado and is buried in the cemetery there.

His widow, Lucy, moved to Denver (Denver) Colorado where she was a housekeeper for a boarding house in 1910. In 1925 she passed away and was buried in the Evergreen Cemetery, Colorado Springs (El Paso) Colorado on 05 August 1925.

Colorado Springs Gazette 05 August 1925:
"The funeral of Mrs. Lucy Belle Lively, who passed away at the Myron Stratton home, will be held at the Law Chapel Thursday morning at 10 o'clock. Rev. George W. McDonald will officiate. Interment in Evergreen cemetery."

LONGAN, Infant

(Previously listed as LOGAN)

Birth: 04/03/1908
Death: 05/19/1908
Cemetery Location: Unknown

Father: Jesse B. Longan; Mother: Mary Etta/Marietta (*Billings*) Burns; born and died in Rowena (Boulder) Colorado at age 1 month, 16 days-cause of death unknown; no tombstone; see **About the Longan Family**

LONGAN, Oscar Dale
(Previously listed as LOGAN)

Birth: 05/27/1909
Death: 05/15/1910
Cemetery Location: Unknown

Father: Jesse B. Longan; Mother: Mary Etta/Marietta (*Billings*) Burns; born and died in Rowena (Boulder) Colorado at age 11 months, 18 days-cause of death unknown; no tombstone; see **About the Longan Family**

About the Longan Family

Jesse B. Longan was born 21 May 1871 (other sources state 01 May 1871) in Arvada (Jefferson) Colorado; the son of John Bowles and Sarah E. (*Matthews*) Longan.

In the 1880 census the family was living in Ralston (Jefferson) Colorado. Twenty years later in the 1900 census John and Sarah Longan (parents of Jesse) were living in Jamestown (Boulder) Colorado but there was no listing for Jesse Longan.

It appears Mary Etta/Marietta was previously married to a Mr. Burns. That union produced two known children:

Phillip Nathaniel: born 23 July 1897 Montana (obituary states Boulder (Boulder) Colorado) and died 11 May 1965 Denver (Denver) Colorado; buried Mountain View Cemetery, Longmont (Boulder) Colorado; married Martha Louise Timken

Amelia M: born 12 November 1899 Colorado and died 10 October 1975 Denver (Denver) Colorado; buried Fort Logan National Cemetery, Denver (Denver) Colorado; married John Williams

About 1903 Jesse B. Longan married Mary Etta/Marietta (*Billings*) Burns. This union produced four known children:

Kay L: born 18 July 1904 Colorado and died 03 July 1964 Sacramento (Sacramento) California; burial unknown

Bessie Bell: born 01 May 1907 Rowena (Boulder) Colorado and died 19 April 1957 south of Lafayette (Boulder) Colorado; buried Columbia Cemetery, Boulder (Boulder) Colorado; married Bradley W. Billings and Elmer A. Dean

Infant: born 03 April 1908 Rowena (Boulder) Colorado and died 19 May 1908 Rowena (Boulder) Colorado-buried Gold Hill Cemetery, Gold Hill (Boulder) Colorado; see LONGAN, Infant

Oscar Dale: 27 May 1909 Rowena (Boulder) Colorado-15 May 1910 Rowena (Boulder) Colorado-buried Gold Hill Cemetery, Gold Hill (Boulder) Colorado; see LONGAN, Oscar Dale

By the 1910 census Jesse and Marietta were living in Boulder (Boulder) Colorado with the five children (Philip, Amelia, Kay, Bessie and Oscar) where Jesse was a wagon driver.

In the 1930 census Jesse is living with his sister, Sarah, in Boulder (Boulder) Colorado. Interesting to note that Jesse listed himself as "widowed" in this census however his mortuary records state he was divorced. Jesse died about three years later at the Boulder County Hospital in Boulder (Boulder) Colorado.

Boulder Daily Camera 27 May 1933:
"Jesse B. Longan, resident of the city for the last 40 years, residing at 1939 Water Street, died at 10:30 this morning.

He had been engaged in mining. He leaves a son, Kay Longan, of Leadville, Colo., and a daughter, Mrs. Bessie Billings of Lincoln, Neb., besides sisters and brothers here."

Boulder Daily Camera 29 May 1933:
"Funeral services for Jesse B. Longan, who died Saturday morning, will be held at the Howe mortuary Tuesday afternoon at 2 o'clock. Rev. C.T. Dwiggins of the Free Methodist church will officiate. Burial will be in Columbia cemetery."

Boulder Daily Camera 30 May 1933:
"Funeral services for Jesse B. Longan, who died May 27, were held at the Howe mortuary this afternoon at 2 o'clock. Rev. C.T. Dwing officiated. Mrs. Dwing sang. Pallbearers were Messrs. Phillip Stringham, Wm. Stringham, Walter Stringham, Hugh McCammon, Charles Longan and Wm. Longan. Burial was in Columbia cemetery."

LUXON, John Rosewarn "Captain Jack"

Birth: 05/1841
Death: 01/31/1906
Cemetery Location: E3

Father: John Luxon; Mother: Mary (*Rosewarn*); Wife: Mary E. (*Joy*); born in Saint Blazey (Cornwall) England and died in Boulder (Boulder) Colorado at age approximately 64 years, 8 months-heart trouble; see LUXON, Thomas Henry; wife Mary E. (*Joy*) might be related to Michael Joy; see JOY, Michael; see **About John Rosewarn "Captain Jack" Family**; might be related to Thomas Mugford; see **About the Mugford Family**

Boulder Daily Camera 31 January 1906:
"JACK LUXON DEAD-WELL KNOWN MINER COLLAPSES FROM HEART TROUBLE AND DIES SHORTLY AFTER TEMPORARY EXCITEMENT—John R. Luxon, one of the best known characters about town, died suddenly of heart trouble at the Metropolitan room last

night. Sometime before "Captain Jack," as he was familiarly called, had a little altercation with a friend in Borger's saloon. There was no fight though "Jack" struck at a man with whom he had been drinking. The blow failed to tell and he fell over on the floor in collapse. He was carried to the Metropolitan and Dr. F.H. Farrington was summoned. He expired a short time after, death being pronounced due to heart failure. Jack Luxon was nearly sixty years old and had been a miner in this county for thirty years. For some of this time he was foreman of the Slide mine under the ownership of Colonel William Campbell and others. He was known as a jovial good fellow. Of recent years he was not working owing to a heart trouble. He bought a little place east of Boulder and has lived there for several years. Morgan Edwards, a Gold Hill friend of his, says that Mr. Luxon complained of his heart Tuesday morning and told him he did not expect to live 24 hours. His son, John Luxon, is one of the most highly esteemed young mining men of the county, being foreman for the Cash mine under the superintendency of Lou R. Johnston. He, also, leaves a daughter. His brother, Joseph Luxon, is a well-known mining man of Scaryblight, Nevada."

Denver Rocky Mountain News 01 February 1906:

"HEART FAILS DURING ROW AND AGED MINER DIES

BOULDER, Colo., Jan. 31.—Last night a well-known character about town and a former miner, Captain Jack Luxon, was attacked with heart trouble while warding off a blow aimed at him by a fellow citizen during a heated controversy. He was removed to an apartment house nearby and died. No blow had been struck. He was 66 years old and father of John Luxon, foreman of the Cash mine at Gold Hill. At one time Luxon was foreman of the Sloyd [sic] mine. He was generally known throughout northern Colorado, and in earlier years frequently participated in sparring matches."

Boulder Daily Camera 02 February 1906:

"JOHN LUXON SLEEPS. The funeral of the late John R. Luxon at Trezise's parlors this morning was largely attended. The great hearted "Captain Jack" as he was familiarly known, had many friends and a large delegation followed the casket to Gold Hill where he was buried beside his dead son. His son and daughter were chief mourners but there were many others. The employees of the Cash mine, of which the son is foreman, attended the interment ceremony of the body."

LUXON, Thomas Henry

> Birth: 04/01/1872
> Death: 11/02/1879
> Cemetery Location: E3

Father: John Rosewarn Luxon; Mother: Mary E. (*Joy*); born in Missouri and died in Sunshine (Boulder) Colorado at age 7 years, 7 months, 1 day-cause of death diphtheria; might have been named after his uncle (brother of John Rosewarn Luxon); see LUXON, John Rosewarn "Captain Jack;" might be related to Thomas Mugford; see **MUGFORD**, Jane Ann (*Wills*)

About John Rosewarn "Captain Jack" Luxon Family

John Rosewarn "Captain Jack" Luxon was born May 1841 (some sources state 1842) in Saint Blazey (Cornwall) England; the son of Cornish natives John and Mary (*Rosewarn*) Luxon.

His father, John Luxon, was born 18 March 1808 in Saint Enoder (Cornwall) England; the son of Charles and Ann (maiden name unknown) Luxen [sic]. He married Mary (*Rosewarn*) Richards on 21 January 1833 in Saint Blazey (Cornwall) England. She was born June 1810 in Gwinear (Cornwall) England; the daughter of Thomas and Ann (*Bottrell*) Rosewarn/Rosewarne. To their union several known children were born:

John: born about 1834 Saint Blazey (Cornwall) England and died prior to the 1851 England census

Mary Ann: born about 1836 Saint Blazey (Cornwall) England; married John Rundell

Charles: born about 1839 Saint Blazey (Cornwall) England and died 1903 (Cornwall) England; married Elizabeth Thomas

William: born about 1840 Saint Blazey (Cornwall) England and died 29 March 1925 London, England; buried West Norwood Cemetery and Crematorium, West Norwood, London Borough of Lambeth, Greater London, England; married Selina Nettle

John Rosewarn: born May 1841 (baptized 08 June 1842) Saint Blazey (Cornwall) England and died 31 January 1906 Boulder (Boulder) Colorado; buried Gold Hill Cemetery, Gold Hill (Boulder) Colorado; married Mary E. (maiden name unknown); see LUXON, John Rosewarn "Captain Jack;" see LUXON, Thomas Henry

George: born about 1844 Saint Blazey (Cornwall) England; married Anne Bunny

Eliza Jane: born about 1848 Saint Blazey (Cornwall) England and died 01 February 1909 (Devon) England; never married

Thomas Henry: born about 1850 (baptized 20 October 1850) Saint Blazey (Cornwall) England; married Evelina Farr

Joseph: born May 1853 (baptized 26 June 1853) Saint Blazey (Cornwall) England and died 12 July 1926 San Diego (San Diego) California; burial unknown; married Lydia Robins

John Luxon died in 1861 and his wife, Mary, died ten years later in September of 1871; the location of their burials in Cornwall is unknown.

The 1900 United States census states John Rosewarn Luxon came to the United States in 1859 however that is incorrect as he was living in the household of Ann Gundry in Tywardreath (Cornwall) England in 1861.

John Rosewarn Luxon first married Catherine Hill on 20 February 1862 at the Parish of Tywardreath in Cornwall. She was the daughter of James Hill (mother unknown). No known children blessed this marriage. Apparently she died prior to John coming to America.

He married Mary E. Joy who was born about 1848 Ireland; parents unknown. (There is a possibility that she was the sister of Michael Joy; see JOY, Michael.) To this union of John Rosewarn and Mary E. (*Joy*) Luxon three known children were born:

Thomas Henry: born 01 April 1872 Missouri and died 02 November 1879 Sunshine (Boulder) Colorado; buried Gold Hill Cemetery, Gold Hill (Boulder) Colorado (cause of death-diphtheria); see LUXON, Thomas Henry

Viola Victoria: born 10 June 1874 Granby (Newton) Missouri and died 14 August 1942 Billings (Yellowstone) Montana; buried Highland Cemetery, Casper (Natrona) Wyoming; married John William Houseworth

John Richard Jr.: born 10 September 1877 Summerville (Boulder) Colorado and died 04 June 1960 Casper (Natrona) Wyoming; buried Highland Cemetery, Casper (Natrona) Wyoming; married Crola "Rola/Lola" Cunningham

By February 1879 John leased the Ingram lode in the Silver Plume Gulch (Gold Hill Mining District) area.

Boulder News & Courier 28 February 1879:

"Silver Plume Gulch, which contains a number of well known, reliable mines, among which the grat [great] importance is the Ingram Lode, owned by Buckingham and others, now being worked under a lease by John Luxson [sic] and others. The development consists of a 92-foot shaft and a tunnel 100 feet. The mine has been idle for some time, and work having only lately commenced, no great amount of ore has been taken out, but it was looking well."

The 1880 United States census has the family living in Gold Hill (Boulder) Colorado where in July of 1883

Digging Up Dirt

"Captain Jack" was the manager of the Slide Mine (Gold Hill Mining District).

Apparently the marriage of John and Mary was falling apart and divorce proceedings were filed 19 April 1886 (Divorce Action # 1654).

By December of 1887 he also ran a liquor store.

Boulder News & Banner 13 December 1887:
"John Luxon is now engaged in the liquor business at Gold Hill. With John's experience, age and qualifications, he should make a success of the undertaking."

Less than two years later it seemed the liquor business wasn't quite the success as first thought.

Boulder County Herald (Weekly) 19 June 1889:
"Jack Luxon reports the saloon business very dull indeed. There are only 3 saloons in town and these are not patronized as they used to be some time ago. Miners are looking after number 1 instead of spending their time away from home."

Unfortunately his marriage fell apart and John sued for divorce in 1888 which was finalized in 1889. Perhaps the cause of this divorce was due to the erratic behavior of Mary.

Boulder County Herald (Weekly) 19 June 1889:
"A Life Sentence

Mrs. Mary L. Luxon's condition as prisoner in the jail is a peculiar one. She was tried at Gold Hill May 22nd before Justice Romig on a charge of assault with a deadly weapon, the charge having been brought by Mrs. H. Drummond. A jury in the case found her guilty. Instead of imposing a fine the justice after reciting the verdict held her in $1,000 bail to await the actions of the grand jury. Inasmuch as a grand jury cannot consider cases where verdicts have been found the sentence of Mrs. Luxon virtually one for life, unless sooner released on a habeas corpus proceeding."

Then three months later she had another confrontation but this time with the Marshall.

Boulder County Herald (Weekly) 18 September 1889:
"Mrs. Mary Luxon was jailed Sunday by Marshall Madera. She was boiling drunk and fought like a cat when Shep arrested her. She was tried Monday and fined $3 and costs."

Just a week later Mary was arrested again.

Boulder County Herald (Weekly) 25 September 1889:
"Mrs. Luxon was jailed Wednesday again on account of being drunk."

To end 1889 in splendor John was selling liquor without a license.

Boulder County Herald 25 December 1889:
"Jack Luxon of Gold Hill was bound over to the grand jury, by Justice Borden Monday, with bail fixed at $100, to await the action of that body on the charge of his having sold liquor to minors."

Boulder County Herald (Weekly) 25 December 1889:
"Jack Luxon of Gold Hill pleaded guilty today to the charge of selling liquor without a license. He was charged $50 and costs."

In less than two months' time John "Jack" was caught again.

Boulder County Herald (Weekly) 12 February 1890:
"Jack Luxon was tried for selling liquor without a license. Luxon was fined $25 and costs this afternoon"

Life began to look up for John as in April of 1898 he gave his daughter, Viola Victoria, away in marriage. A glorious wedding event however there was no mention of Viola's mother, Mary.

Boulder Daily Camera 27 April 1898:
"Capt. Luxon came down from Gold Hill to exhibit the generosity of his soul in giving his daughter away in marriage."

Boulder Daily Camera 28 April 1898:
"Houseworth-Luxon...

Rev. Dr. Notman as presiding officer, the bride's father, Capt. Jack Luxon of Gold Hill, as donor of the bride to the groom, young and energetic J.W. (Billy) Houseworth as recipient and groom, about 1 o'clock Wednesday, April 27, and the groom's father's house near the fairgrounds as time and place, and you have the story of how Billy Houseworth wedded Victoria Luxon, Captain Jack's "baby girl." A fine wedding breakfast followed the event, and the couple, after a day or two in Boulder, will leave for their Gold Hill home. A popular couple they and a happy twain, who are being showered with congratulations."

The trail grows cold for Mary E. (*Joy*) Luxon. No primary records have been located to figure out what happened to her.

In the 1900 census John and his son (John Richard) were living in Gold Hill (Boulder) Colorado where he listed as divorced and employed as an ore miner. Four years later John was naturalized on 14 October 1904 in the District Court of Boulder (Boulder) Colorado.

John lived a few more years until he died from heart failure on 31 January 1906 in Boulder (Boulder) Colorado. He is buried in the Gold Hill Cemetery beside his son, Thomas Henry.

M

MACK, Henry William

Birth: 11/28/1843
Death: 10/22/1885
Cemetery Location: E3

Father: Henry Mack; Mother: "Mary" Catharine/Katherine (*maiden name unknown*); Wife: Mary Anna "Annie" M. (*Huberty*); born in Pennsylvania and died in (Boulder) Colorado at age of 41 years, 10 months, 24 days-broken neck and internal injuries; see MACK, Infant; see **About the Henry William Mack Family**

Boulder County Herald Weekly 28 October 1885:

"Death of Henry Mack

Henry Mack, formerly of Gold Hill, and of late of Allen's Park, left Boulder for his home Thursday morning. He left Jamestown Thursday afternoon in a two-wheeled cart. During the night some time two men travelling along the road came upon the cart, which was upset, at what is known as Miller's rock at the Middle Fork of the St. Vrain creek. Underneath the cart lay Henry Mack, dead. Judging by appearances the pin which held the cart-bed down, got loose, and the bed turned up, as the team was going up an incline, throwing Mack out in such a way to break his neck."

MACK, Infant

Birth: 09/22/1878
Death: 09/22/1878
Cemetery Location: E3

Father: Henry Mack; Mother: Anna "Annie" M. (*Huberty*); born and died in Gold Hill (Boulder) Colorado at age 0-stillborn; see MACK, Henry Mack; see **About the Henry William Mack Family**

About the Henry William Mack Family

Henry Mack Sr., was born 04 September 1813 in Berwaugne (Baden) Germany. He married Catherine (maiden name might be *Goehringer*) in Germany. She was born there in 1818; parents unknown. Five known children were born to their union:

Henry William: born 28 November 1843 Pennsylvania and died 22 October 1885 (Boulder) Colorado; buried Gold Hill Cemetery, Gold Hill (Boulder) Colorado; married Mary Anna "Annie" M. Huberty; see MACK, Henry William

Catherine/Katherine "Kate": born 10 July 1846 Ohio and died 10 October 1898 (Dane) Wisconsin; buried Arlington Park Cemetery, Greenfield (Milwaukee) Wisconsin; married Charles Hedler; not completely verified as cemetery records has Katherine *Von Mack* Hedler but marriage record has maiden name of Mack

Inscription at top:

"We miss you at home"

Inscription above hands:

"OUR DEAR BELOVED HUSBAND & FATHER"

John: born about 1849 Ohio-wasn't listed in the 1860 census

Elizabeth: born about 1854 Iowa-death unknown; burial unknown; there is an Elizabeth Mack in the 1870 census living in the household of Michael McCraith in Clear Creek (Johnson) Iowa; might have married a "Leo." W. Smith

George Albert: born March 1859 Fairfield (Jefferson) Iowa and died 25 August 1947 Everett (Snohomish) Washington; burial unknown; married Margaret Elizabeth Thompson

In the 1850 census the family was living in Cincinnati (Hamilton) Ohio where Henry was a baker.

The obituary of Henry William's brother, George, tells some history about the family:

Boulder Daily Camera 16 September 1947:
"Mr. Mack (George) came with his family from Iowa in 1862 locating at Central City, the trip across the prairies being made by wagon. Mr. Marshall (family friend) says Mr. Mack (George) was at Caribou in the early days of that once prosperous silver camp. Later worked at Ward, Gold Hill, Jamestown and Magnolia...

Mr. Mack's father (Henry) at one time homesteaded in Allenspark."

Henry William, a Civil war veteran, married Anna "Annie" M. Huberty in August of 1876. She was born 25 October 1859 (Dubuque) Iowa; daughter of Nicholas and Mary (*Keller*) Huberty. To this union four known children were born:

Henry William: born 16 May 1877 Gold Hill (Boulder) Colorado and died 09 August 1961 Nashville (Davidson) Tennessee; buried Mountain View Memorial Park, Boulder (Boulder) Colorado; married Catherine Sophia Bach and Stella McCall

Infant: born 22 September 1878 and died 22 September 1878; buried Gold Hill Cemetery, Gold Hill (Boulder) Colorado; see MACK, Infant

Alice Rosetta: born 09 August 1879 Gold Hill (Boulder) Colorado and died 23 February 1959 Boulder (Boulder) Colorado; buried Columbia Cemetery, Boulder (Boulder) Colorado; married Ernest J. Chambers

Fred Jerome: born 05 August 1881 Allenspark (Boulder) Colorado and died 16 August 1942 Santa Barbara (Santa Barbara) California; buried Santa Barbara Cemetery, Santa Barbara (Santa Barbara) California; married Nell/Nellye Fremont Clark

Henry and his family lived in Gold Hill (Boulder) Colorado in 1878 where in the Colorado Business Directory of that year he ran a saloon however by 1881 the saloon was operated by his brother, George Mack.

In the 1880 census the parents of Henry William (Henry, Sr. and Catherine Mack) were living in Gold Hill (Boulder) Colorado where Henry, Sr. was a road operator at the age of 67 years.

In 1880 their son, Henry William, and his wife, Anna "Annie," were living in Ward (Boulder) Colorado where Henry was working as a stockman. About five years later he died 22 October 1885 coming home from work in a two-wheeled cart accident which broke his neck; see above newspaper article *Boulder Daily Camera* 28 October 1885.

His widow, Annie, married William Henry Arnold on 04 June 1892 in Boulder (Boulder) Colorado.

Together they had two known children:

Reference to Baby on tombstone however large white quartz rock to the left front of the tombstone which is assumed to be the original grave marking

Edna M: born 20 February 1893 (Boulder) Colorado and died 12 January 1896 (Boulder) Colorado; buried Columbia Cemetery, Boulder (Boulder) Colorado

Esther: born 14 November 1897 (Boulder) Colorado and died 08 September 1911 Valmont (Boulder) Colorado; buried Columbia Cemetery, Boulder (Boulder) Colorado

Tremendous grief hit William and Annie as on 08 September 1911 when their only living child, Esther, committed suicide.

Boulder Daily Camera 08 September 1911:

"13-YEAR-OLD GIRL COMMITS SUICIDE! ESTHER ARNOLD, PIQUED AT INTERFERENCE OF PARENTS IN LOVE AFFAIR WITH BOY, DIES BY TAKING POISON...

Esther, daughter of Mr. and Mrs. William H. Arnold, who live north of Boulder in the oil belt, died at 9:00 o'clock this morning from poison self-administered. She was but 13 years old and had been reprimanded by her parents for keeping company with a young man of the neighborhood, objection to clandestine meetings having been based on her extreme youth. Last night there was a scene with her parents and this morning early she took five bichloride [sic] of mercury tablets, which her mother had in the house for an infected hand. Dr. O.M. Gilbert was notified between 5 and 6 o'clock and arrived as soon as possible, but the young girl's system was full of the poison and he could do nothing. She was conscious and a great sufferer until 9 o'clock, when she died. The parents are heart-broken. She was their only child at home."

William Henry Arnold died 07 February 1928 and is buried in the Columbia Cemetery, Boulder (Boulder) Colorado. Annie Mack Arnold lived in Boulder (Boulder) Colorado until her death on 30 March 1941 and is also buried in the Columbia Cemetery in Boulder (Boulder) Colorado alongside her husband, William.

MAGOR, Frederick/Fredrick "Fred"

> Birth: 05/03/1863
> Death: 11/03/1887
> Cemetery Location: C2

Father John Samuel Magor/Meagor; Mother: Susannah (*Broad*); born in Golant (Cornwall) England and died in Gold Hill (Boulder) Colorado at age 24 years, 6 months-pneumonia; brother to William John Magor; see MAGOR, William John; see **About the William John Magor Family**; see MAGOR, Mary Elizabeth "Polly" (*Lee*); see **About the Magor Family**

Boulder News 08 November 1887:
  "Fred Magor died at Gold Hill last Thursday of pneu-

monia, at the age of 24 years. Rev. Abams officiated at the funeral."

About the Magor Family

John Samuel Magor (spelled many ways) was born about 1829 in Lanliberg (Cornwall) England; the son of John Magor (mother unknown). He married Susannah Broad on 03 March 1855 in St. Sampson (Cornwall) England. She was born about 1928 in Golant (Cornwall) England; the daughter of John and Jenefer (maiden name unknown) Broad. To their union four known children were born:

William John: born 06 February 1859 Golant (Cornwall) England and died 04 September 1907 Boulder (Boulder) Colorado; buried Gold Hill Cemetery, Gold Hill

(Boulder) Colorado; married Mary Elizabeth "Polly" Lee; see MAGOR, William John; see **About the William John Magor Family**; see **About the Magor Family**

Mary Jane: born about 1860 Golant (Cornwall) England-death unknown; burial unknown; spouse unknown

Frederick "Fred": born 03 May 1863 Golant (Cornwall) England and died 03 November 1887 Gold Hill (Boulder) Colorado; buried Gold Hill Cemetery, Gold Hill (Boulder) Colorado; never married; see MAGOR, Frederick "Fred"

Charles Albert: born about 1871 Golant (Cornwall) England-death unknown; burial unknown; married Ada Alice Wells and possibly Irene M. Sloggett

Little is known about Frederick "Fred" Magor. Raised in St. Sampson (Cornwall) England he was a laborer (perhaps for the railways like his father, John Samuel). There is no listing for Fred in the 1885 Colorado State census records and two years later he died in his Gold Hill home on 03 November 1887 from pneumonia. Unmarried, he was buried in the Gold Hill Cemetery, Gold Hill (Boulder) Colorado.

MAGOR, George H.

> Birth: 05/02/1889
> Death: 04/06/1890
> Cemetery Location: C2

Father: William John Magor; Mary Elizabeth "Polly" (*Lee*); born and died in Gold Hill (Boulder) Colorado at age 11 months; 4 days-cause of death unknown; see MAGOR, William John; see **About the William John Magor Family**; see MAGOR, Mary Elizabeth "Polly" (*Lee*); see MAGOR, Frederick "Fred;" see **About the Magor Family**

MAGOR, Mary Elizabeth "Polly" (*Lee*)

> Birth: 07/04/1863
> Death: 10/18/1902
> Cemetery Location: C2

Father: Frederick John Lee; Mother: Sarah (*Hambly*); Husband: William John Magor; born in England and died in Gold Hill (Boulder) Colorado at 39 years, 3 month, 13 days-typhoid pneumonia; tombstone has incorrect death year 1903; see MAGOR, William John; see **About the William John Magor Family**; see MAGOR, Frederick "Fred;" see **About the Magor Family**

Boulder Daily Camera 18 October 1902:

"MRS W. J. MEAGER DEAD. Mrs. W. J. Meager, wife of the prominent Gold Hill mining man, died this morning at that place of typhoid pneumonia. She leaves, besides her husband, four small children and a son of seventeen. The funeral will take place from the Meager home

tomorrow at 2 p.m., under the direction of Undertaker Buchheit. This is the second death occurring in the Harrison Burial association."

MAGOR, Pearl

Birth: 11/01/1897
Death: 06/01/1898
Cemetery Location: C2

Father: William John Magor; Mother: Mary Elizabeth "Polly" (*Lee*); born and died in Gold Hill (Boulder) Colorado at age 7 months-cause of death unknown; no tombstone; see MAGOR, William John; see **About the William John Magor Family**; see MAGOR, Mary Elizabeth "Polly" (*Lee*); see MAGOR, Frederick "Fred;" see **About the Magor Family**

MAGOR, Samuel C.

Birth: 06/12/1887
Death: 08/17/1887
Cemetery Location: C2

Father: William John Magor; Mother: Mary Elizabeth "Polly" (*Lee*); born and died in Gold Hill (Boulder) Colorado at age 2 months, 5 days-cause of death unknown; tombstone states died at aged 8 weeks and 3 days; see

MAGOR, William John; see **About the William John Magor Family**; see MAGOR, Mary Elizabeth "Polly" (*Lee*); see MAGOR, Frederick "Fred;" see **About the Magor Family**

MAGOR, William John

Birth: 02/06/1859
Death: 09/04/1907
Cemetery Location: C2

Father: John Samuel Magor; Mother: Susannah (*Broad*); Wife: Mary Elizabeth "Polly" (*Lee*); born in England and died in Boulder (Boulder) Colorado at age 48 years, 6 months, 29 days-miners' consumption; brother to Frederick Magor; see MAGOR, Frederick "Fred;" see **About the Magor Family**; see MAGOR, Mary Elizabeth "Polly" (*Lee*); see **About the William John Magor Family**

Boulder Daily Camera 04 September 1907:

"Death of Veteran Miner...William John Magor died this morning at 6 o'clock at 365 Arapahoe street of miner's consumption. Mr. Magor leaves two boys at Nederland and one daughter here. The body will be shipped to Gold Hill for interment."

Magor Family Plot

Boulder County Herald 04 September 1907:

"DEATH OF WILLIAM J. MAGOR

William John Magor, of Gold Hill, died this morning at six o'clock at the home of Richard Stoneman, 365 Arapahoe Avenue, of miners' consumption. Funeral arrangements have not yet been made, pending the arrival of his children. Mr. Magor has been a prominent mining engineer for a number of years in and around Gold Hill, Boulder and other mining towns. The body is lying at the Boulder undertaking parlors and will be shipped to Gold Hill for interment."

About the William John Magor Family

William John Magor was born 06 February 1859 in (Cornwall) England; the son of John Samuel and Susannah (*Broad*) Magor/Meagor.

He married Mary Elizabeth "Polly" Lee on 27 October 1883 in Par (Cornwall) England. She was born 04 July 1863 in (Cornwall) England; the daughter of Frederick John and Sarah (*Hambly*) Lee. To this union seven known children were born:

Frederick John: born 01 October 1885 (Cornwall) England and died 16 October 1960 Boulder (Boulder) Colorado; buried Green Mountain Cemetery, Boulder (Boulder) Colorado; married Myrtle Colvin

Samuel C.: born 12 June 1887 Gold Hill (Boulder) Colorado and died 17 August 1887 Gold Hill (Boulder) Colorado; buried Gold Hill Cemetery, Gold Hill (Boulder) Colorado; see MAGOR, Samuel C.

George H.: born 02 May 1889 Gold Hill (Boulder) Colorado and died 06 April 1890 Gold Hill (Boulder) Colorado; buried Gold Hill Cemetery, Gold Hill (Boulder) Colorado; see MAGOR, George H.

William Arthur: born 01 March 1890 Gold Hill (Boulder) Colorado and died 02 July 1949 San Francisco (San Francisco) California; buried Golden Gate National Cemetery, San Bruno (San Mateo) California; married Laura B. (maiden name unknown)

Charles Albert: born 29 June 1893 Gold Hill (Boulder) Colorado and died 31 May 1951; buried Highland Cemetery, Casper (Natrona) Wyoming; married Vivian Viola Humiston

Pearl: born 01 November 1897 Gold Hill (Boulder) Colorado and died 01 June 1898 Gold Hill (Boulder) Col-

orado; buried Gold Hill Cemetery, Gold Hill (Boulder) Colorado; see MAGOR, Pearl

Myrtle Leona: born 17 May 1899 Gold Hill (Boulder) Colorado and died 13 April 1991; buried Mountain View Memorial Cemetery, Boulder (Boulder) Colorado; married Hale Moody Tenhaeff

Rubye V.: born 23 April 1902 and died August 1982 Denver (Arapahoe) Colorado; buried Fairmont Cemetery, Denver (Denver) Colorado; married Harold D. Brady

According to information recorded in the 1900 United States census it appears that William John and Mary Elizabeth "Polly" were only married about a year when he immigrated to the United States in 1884. The timing is such that perhaps William didn't know his wife was pregnant with Frederick when he left. About two years later wife and son joined William, locating in Gold Hill (Boulder) Colorado where the rest of their children were born.

On 18 October 1894 William John Magor was naturalized in the District Court of Boulder (Boulder) Colorado with the witnesses of James Cowie and John W. Nicholson.

According to the mortuary record on 17 October 1902 Mary Elizabeth "Polly" (*Lee*) Magor died at the age of 39 years, 3 months, 13 days in her Gold Hill home from typhoid pneumonia leaving her husband and their five children. She is buried in the Gold Hill Cemetery (Boulder) Colorado) with her tombstone being installed many years later however the tombstone death date of 1903 is incorrect; see MAGOR, Mary Elizabeth "Polly" (*Lee*).

After years of mining William John Magor moved to 365 Arapahoe Street in Boulder (Boulder) Colorado where he died on 04 September 1907 from tuberculosis pulmonary at the young age of 46 years, 6 months and 26 days (according to the mortuary record). His tombstone in the Gold Hill Cemetery also was installed several years after his death with the incorrect death date of 1905.

By 1910 their living children were scattered about. The oldest, Frederick John, was married to Myrtle Colvin and living in Boulder (Boulder) Colorado with his occupation listed as engineer. William Arthur (19 and single) had joined the United States Navy; stationed on the USS Yorktown, Mare Island, California. Charles (16 and single) was a boarder in the household of T.D. Rockery, living in Huge (Lincoln) Colorado. Myrtle Leona (10) was living in Gold Hill (Boulder) Colorado with a family relative, Margaret (*Arbuthnot*) Colvin Turner (mother-in-law of William John's son, Frederick John (Myrtle *Colvin* Magor)). There wasn't a 1910 census listing for the youngest child, Rubye, however in 1918 she was living at 2028 Marine Street in Boulder (Boulder) Colorado and in 1920 at the age of 17 years old she was a servant in the Boulder (Boulder) Colorado household of Joe Mills.

MAYER, Caroline "Carrie" Elizabeth Dorothy (*Hertwig*)

Birth: 10/07/1847
Death: 04/15/1929
Cemetery Location: C2

Father: Hertwig; Mother: unknown; Husband: Nicholas Jacob Mayer; born in Saxony, Germany and died in Denver (Denver) Colorado at age 82 years, 6 months, 8 days-senility; tombstone states birth year as 1847 but mortuary records state 09 October 1846; see MAYER, Nicholas Jacob; see **About the Nicholas Jacob Mayer Family**

Boulder Daily Camera 15 April 1929:
"MRS. CAROLINE E. MAYER—Mrs. Caroline E. Mayer, 82, a pioneer resident of Gold Hill, died at the home of a daughter, Mrs. M. Barnett, Denver, at 5:45 a.m. today. The body was brought here. The funeral will be held at the Howe mortuary at 1:30 o'clock Wednesday afternoon with the Rev. C.S. Linkletter officiating. Burial in Gold Hill cemetery. She came to Gold Hill from Elizabeth N.J., forty-seven years ago. She was born in Saxony, Germany. Her husband died here in 1901. Aside from her daughter she is survived by two grandchildren, Myrtle Barnett Grams, Denver, and Oscar Walton, Boulder."

[Error: Mrs. M. Barnett was the granddaughter of Caroline E. Mayer]

Boulder Daily Camera 16 April 1929:
"MRS. CARRIE MAYER...Funeral services for Mrs. Carrie Mayer of Gold Hill, who died at the residence of her granddaughter, Mrs. Myrtle Barnett Grams of Denver, April 15, will be held at the Howe mortuary Wednesday at 1:30 o'clock. Rev. C.S. Linkletter will officiate and interment will be in the Gold Hill cemetery."

Boulder Daily Camera 17 April 1929:

"FUNERAL OF MRS. MAYER WAS HELD TODAY
The funeral of Mrs. Caroline Mayer, who died in Den-

ver April 15th, was held at the Howe mortuary this afternoon at 1:30 o'clock. Rev. C.S. Linkletter officiated, being assisted by Rev. A. Young of Denver. Mrs. Adam Weber sang "Love Divine," "Beautiful Isle of Somewhere" and "Abide With Me."

The pallbearers were Messrs. John White, John Ingold, Oscar Lagerlund, James A. Francis, H. Berkley and Edward Demmon. Interment was in the Gold Hill cemetery."

Gold Hill, Colorado-*Our Home Town* by Elmer Curtis Swallow (courtesy of Tolliver Swallow & Leah McKin):

"Mrs. Nick Meyers [sic], who came to Gold Hill about 1878, also a religious lady, was superintendent of the Sunday School and leader of the religious education program, such as it was in the early days of a mining camp, and a member of the Methodist denomination. She was called "Auntie" by all who knew her."

MAYER, Frances "Fannie" Maude "Minnie" (*Foster*)

> Birth: 03/1871
> Death: 11/01/1937
> Cemetery Location: C2 (possibly)

Father: Josiah J. Foster; Mother: Victoria (*Dailey*); Husband: Frederick Mayer; born St. Marys Township (Adams) Indiana and died in Denver (Denver) Colorado at age 66 years (approximately)-arterial sclerosis; no tombstone; see MAYER, Frederick; see **About the Nicholas Jacob Mayer Family**

Boulder Daily Camera 01 November 1937:
"Gold Hill Woman Dies In Denver...Mrs. Maud Mayer of Gold Hill died in a Denver hospital this morning. She had been there two weeks.

Word of her death was received by Mrs. Margaret D. Smith, of the Gold Hill store. It is thought the body will be brought to Gold Hill for burial beside her husband, Fred Mayer, who was killed in a fall in Cash mine in 1911 or 1912.

Mrs. Mayer came to Boulder County from the east and taught at Gold Hill before her marriage to Mr. Mayer, whom she met there. Her maiden name was Foster.

They had no children. The Misses McCormick, formally on the University administrative staff, are nieces of the deceased and live in Denver."

Boulder Daily Camera 04 November 1937:
"MRS. MAUDE MAYER—Funeral services will be held Friday morning, 10 o'clock at the Howe mortuary. Rev. Marcus Baker will officiate. Burial will be in the Gold Hill cemetery."

Boulder Daily Camera 05 November 1937:
"MRS. MAUDE MAYER—Widow of Fred Mayer. Services were held at Howe mortuary at 10 o'clock this morning. Rev. Rufus C. Baker of the Methodist church officiated. Ben Walker sang. Burial was at Gold Hill, where Mrs. Mayer had lived for years. Pallbearers were Frank Burnett, Jas. Smith, John Holman, Charles Holman, John Kirkbride and Loren Bremmer."

About Frances "Fannie" Maude "Minnie" (*Foster*) Mayer

Frances "Fannie" Maude "Minnie" Foster was born March of 1871 in St. Marys Township (Adams) Indiana; the daughter of Ohio native Josiah Joseph and Indiana native Victoria (*Dailey*) Foster. She had four known siblings:

Viola May: born March 1864 Indiana and died 24 November 1935 West Newton (Middlesex) Massachusetts; buried Crown Hill Cemetery, Indianapolis (Marion) Indiana; married Rufus King Allison

Davis J.: born 01 November 1866 (Adams) Indiana and died 12 October 1950 Indianapolis (Marion) Indiana; buried Crown Hill Cemetery, Indianapolis (Marion) Indiana; never married

Lola: born about 1868 (Adams) Indiana and died before the 1880 census; buried possibly in (Adams) Indiana

Carrie Helen: born 17 February 1874 St. Marys (Adams) Indiana and died 15 December 1931; buried Green Mountain Cemetery, Boulder (Boulder) Colorado; married Edward J. McCormack; mortuary record states birth year as 1870

Frances "Fannie" Maude "Minnie" Foster came to Gold Hill (Boulder) Colorado where she was the school teacher. She met and married Frederick Mayer on 03 September 1905 in Denver (Denver) Colorado at the age of 31 years. No children blessed this marriage; see MAYER, Frederick; MAYER, Nicholas Jacob; MAYER, Caroline Elizabeth Dorothy (*Hertwig*).

After the death of her husband (Frederick) in 1912 she moved to Boulder (Boulder) Colorado where she was a cashier in a restaurant.

By 1930 she was living in Indianapolis (Marion) Indiana making a living as a matron at a women's prison. She made her way back to Denver (Denver) Colorado living there until she died from anterior sclerosis in a psychopathic hospital 01 November 1937 at the age of 66 years (mortuary record states 63 years).

MAYER, Frederick

> Birth: 06/23/1878
> Death: 10/16/1912
> Cemetery Location: C2 (possibly)

Father: Nicholas Jacob Mayer; Mother: Caroline "Carrie" (*Hertwig*); Wife: Frances "Fannie" Maude "Minnie" (*Foster*); born in Salina (Boulder) Colorado and died in Gold Hill (Boulder) Colorado at age 34 years, 3 months, 23 days-fracture of skull; no tombstone; see MAYER, Nicholas Jacob; see MAYER, Caroline "Carrie" (*Hertwig*); see MAYER, Frances "Fannie" Maude "Minnie" (*Foster*); see **About the Nicholas Jacob Mayer Family**

Boulder Daily Camera 17 October 1912:

"GOLD HILL MINER FALLS DOWN SHAFT—FRED MAYER, PROMINENT MINER, FALLS 300 FEET DOWN SHAFT OF THE CASH MINE—DEATH OCCURRED INSTANTLY.

Frederick Mayer, one of the best known metaliferous miners in this county, was instantly killed yesterday afternoon by a fall of over 300 feet down the shaft of the famous Cash mine at Gold Hill, which he and his brother-in-law, John Barnett, had been leasing. His body was crushed to a pulp, the badly smashed condition of his head indicating that he had struck upon it at the bottom of the shaft.

The body remained in the slump of the mine for three hours after the accident, efforts to recover it proving futile until the water standing in that portion of the shaft had been drawn off.

The accident was due to Mayer's attempt to alight from the mine bucket as he and John Barnett were being hoisted to the surface shortly after 4 o'clock in the afternoon. When the bucket reached the 400 foot level on its assent, Mayer swung over its side in an effort to make a landing. Finding that the platform was not in place he did not release his hold, but made an effort to get back into the bucket. His struggles caused it to swing in under the roof of the level and a moment later his hold was loosened.

The accident was due to carelessness on the part of Mayer, according to Mr. Barnett and to Arthur Johnson,

Mayer Family Plot

Digging Up Dirt

Fred Biscoff, John Holmes, Sr., John Holmes, Jr., and Fred Walters who were standing at the 400-foot level but were powerless to do anything to save him. This theory is taken by Deputy Coroner Kelso, who removed the remains to this city after conducting an investigation.

Mr. Mayer was one of the most popular mining men of the county, O.J. Miller, the Salina merchant, and others, declaring him to have been 'all wool and a yard wide.' He was born at Salina June 23, 1878 and had resided in this county all his life, for 31 years at Gold Hill. For the past few years he had been leasing on the Cash mine. He is survived by a wife and a mother, Mrs. Mayer of Gold Hill, and a sister, Mrs. John Barnett. Funeral arrangements have not been made."

Boulder Daily Camera 18 October 1912:
"The funeral of Fred Mayer, who was killed in the Cash mine Wednesday, will take place Sunday afternoon at 2 o'clock from his late residence at Gold Hill. Rev. A.L. Chase, presiding elder of the district, will conduct the services."

At age Frederick 16 he drove the stage from Gold Hill down through Salina to the railroad station and back.

MAYER, Louisa H. "Lulu"

Birth: 12/19/1880
Death: 08/11/1885
Cemetery Location: C2

Father: Nicholas Jacob Mayer; Mother: Caroline "Carrie" (*Hertwig*); born in Salina (Boulder) Colorado and died in Gold Hill (Boulder) Colorado at age 4 years, 7 months, 23 days-cause of death unknown; *Boulder County Pioneers* (compiled & edited by Jennie E. Stewart), page 149 states birth date as July of 1882; see MAYER, Nicholas Jacob; see MAYER, Caroline "Carrie" (*Hertwig*); see **About the Nicholas Jacob Mayer Family**

MAYER, Nicholas Jacob

Birth: 01/08/1846
Death: 09/05/1901
Cemetery Location: C2

Father: Johann Jakob Maier; Mother: Christina Katharina (*Danner*); Wife: Caroline "Carrie" Elizabeth Dorothy (*Hertwig*); born in Breitenholz, Wurttemberg, Germany and died in Gold Hill (Boulder) Colorado at age 55 years, 7 months, 28 days-pneumonia; see MAYER, Caroline "Carrie" Elizabeth Dorothy (*Hertwig*); see **About the Nicholas Jacob Mayer Family**

Boulder Daily Camera 05 September 1901:
"NICK MEYER DEAD—-Nick Meyer died at 1 o'clock this afternoon at his home in Gold Hill. His illness was a short one. He did not complain until last Sunday and only consented to have a doctor when his friends insisted upon it. He was found to have a serious case of pneumonia. He expected to recover and hoped to go to work on Thursday, but he will never work again. At the time of his death he was an employee at the Slide mine and had several good claims of his own. He was 59 years old and leaves a son age 23 and a daughter, Mrs. James Barnett, both at Gold Hill. A brother lives in Pueblo. Undertaker Trezise was summoned from Boulder and the funeral will probably be held Saturday. The G.A.R., of which organization Mr. Meyer was a member, will conduct the services."

Boulder Daily Camera 07 September 1901:
"G A R Attention—Comrades of Nathaniel Lyon Post No. 5 are requested to attend the funeral of our comrade, Nick J. Meyer, at Gold Hill on Saturday at 2 o'clock. D.W. King, Commander L.W. Kimball, Adjutant"

"He that walketh with wise men shall be wise."

About the Nicholas Jacob Mayer Family

"Nikolaus" Jakob Maier/Mayer was born 08 January 1846 in Breitenholz, Wurttemberg, Germany (baptized 11 January 1846); believed to be the son of Johann Jakob and Christina Katharina (*Danner*) Maier (spelling of Mayer in the early records).

According to the 1900 census he immigrated to the United States in 1859. He made his way to New Jersey where he enlisted in Company Batty C, New Jersey 3rd Light Artillery Battery on 27 September 1864 and was mustered out 19 June 1865 at Trenton (Mercer) New Jersey with the rank of private.

He married Caroline "Carrie" Elizabeth Dorothy Hertwig on 12 July 1868 at Elizabeth City (Union) New Jersey. She was born 09 October 1846 in Breitenbach (a Jewish community) in Germany; parents unknown. According to the 1910 census she immigrated to the United States in 1862; see MAYER, Caroline "Carrie" Elizabeth Dorothy (*Hertwig*).

The first three children of Nicholas and Caroline were born in New Jersey:

Wilmina "Minnie": born 07 March 1869 Elizabeth City (Union) New Jersey and died 03 August 1940 Denver (Denver) Colorado; buried Gold Hill Cemetery, Gold Hill (Boulder) Colorado; married James Barnett;; see

3.N.J.L.A.
(3rd New Jersey Light Artillery)

BARNETT, Wilmina "Minnie" (*Mayer*); see BARNETT, James; see **About the James Barnett Family**

Magdalena: born: 1873 Newark (Essex) New Jersey and died 20 February 1873 Newark (Essex) New Jersey; buried Newark (Essex) New Jersey

Catherine: born 08 July 1874 Newark (Essex) New Jersey and died 05 December 1875 Newark (Essex) New Jersey; buried Newark (Essex) New Jersey

Between 1874 and 1878 the family moved to (Boulder) Colorado settling in the little mining town of Salina where their next child was born:

Frederick: born 23 June 1878 Salina (Boulder) Colorado and died 16 October 1912 Gold Hill (Boulder) Colorado; buried Gold Hill Cemetery, Gold Hill (Boulder) Colorado; married Maude "Minnie" Foster; see MAYER, Frederick; see MAYER, Maude "Minnie" (*Foster*)

Nicholas dabbled between being a miner and butcher (ran the local meat market in Salina) until about 1882 when he then became a full-time miner and moved the family to Gold Hill (Boulder) Colorado where his daughter was born:

Lulu H.: born 19 December 1880 Gold Hill (Boulder) Colorado and died 11 August 1885 Gold Hill (Boulder) Colorado; buried Gold Hill Cemetery, Gold Hill (Boulder) Colorado; see Mayer, Lulu H.

Due to a mining accident in 1878 Nicholas was never quite the same physically. On 23 August 1890 "Invalid" pension was filed however the physical limitations were not listed.

Sunshine Courier 8 June 1878:

"Nicholas Myers [sic], one of the hands employed on the Melvina, discovered a large scale just as it was becoming detached from the wall in the 70-foot level. His partner was working above and he thought to protect him from injury by supporting the lower end of the scale from below. Accordingly, he braced himself against it, but having become fairly started, it continued to crumble all around him until he was buried in a mass of rock weighing at least two tons. It gave him a pretty bad squeezing, but Dr. Bowker, who was called; say the patient is doing well, and that there is no evidence of serious internal injury. Mr. Myers' arms were very lame for several days, so much so that he could hardly raise them. In such a trying emergency he must have exerted almost superhuman strength in trying to force back the rocky avalanche."

Their only living daughter, Wilmina "Minnie" married James Barnett 11 August 1886 in Boulder (Boulder) Colorado with James' brother George as a witness; see BARNETT, Wilmina "Minnie" (*Mayer*).

Nicholas was working at the Slide Mine in Gold Hill at the time of his death in 1901. His widow, Caroline, continued to live in Gold Hill (Boulder) Colorado where she was a proprietress of a restaurant.

Tragedy struck again when her only son, Frederick, was accidently killed (fracture of the skull) by falling down a mining shaft in the Cash Mine in the Gold Hill Mining District on 16 October 1912 at the tender age of 34 years, 3 months and 23 days, leaving a wife, Maude; see MAYER, Frederick; see MAYER, Maude "Minnie" (*Foster*).

The winters in Gold Hill proved difficult for Caroline living alone. In December of 1923 she weathered the cold in the Denver home of Mr. and Mr. W.H. Lloyd on Sixteenth Street.

She developed senility which caused her death at the age of 82 years, 6 month, 8 days on 15 April 1929 at the Denver home of her granddaughter, Myrtle (*Barnett*) Grams. Her remains were taken to the Gold Hill Cemetery where she is buried beside her husband, Nicholas.

McFALL, John B.

Birth: 11/26/1841
Death: 09/22/1904
Cemetery Location: Unknown

Father: William McFall; Mother: Elizabeth (*Hardin*); Wife: Mary (*maiden name unknown*); born in Kentucky and died in Gold Hill (Boulder) Colorado at age 62 years, 9 months, 27 days-internal injuries from fall; no tombstone

Boulder Daily Camera 23 September 1904:
"The funeral of John B. McFall, who died yesterday at Gold Hill, occurred at that place this afternoon."

Boulder Daily Herald Weekly 23 September 1904:
"The funeral of J.B. McFall was had at Gold Hill today. Mr. McFall fell off a ladder in the Maxon mine at Gold Hill on Wednesday, a distance of forty feet and received internal injuries from the effects of which he died yesterday morning soon after midnight. He was conscious long enough to realize that he was about to die and gave instructions as to his funeral. He was 62 years old, a veteran of the civil war, and has lived at Gold Hill for upwards of thirty years."

McFALL, Mary J. (*maiden name unknown*)

Birth: 02/02/1833
Death: 03/12/1914
Cemetery Location: Unknown

Father: unknown; Mother: unknown; Husband: John B. McFall; died at age 81 years; 1 months; 10 days; born in Cairo (Alexander) Illinois and died in Boulder (Boulder) Colorado at age 81 years, 1 month, 10 days-illness and old age; no tombstone

Boulder Daily Camera 12 March 1914 & *Boulder County Tribune* 13 March 1914:
"Mrs. Mary McFall, who was brought from Crisman Sunday and taken to the University hospital, died at 10 o'clock this morning, aged 81 years. The remains will be taken to Gold Hill Friday morning by Undertaker Trezise and the funeral will take place at 2 o'clock, interment to be by the side of her husband, who died seven years ago. The deceased has made her home in and around Boulder for the past 11 years, coming here from Cairo, Illinois."

About John B. and Mary J. McFall

John B. McFall was born 26 November 1841 in Kentucky; believed to have been the son of Kentucky natives William and Elizabeth (*Hardin*) McFall. (Some sources state William was born in Virginia and Scotland and some sources state Elizabeth was born in Maryland and Scotland.)

John B. McFall had six known siblings:
Caroline: born about 1823 Kentucky; no further information

Cyrenius W.: born about 1829 Kentucky; no further information

Louisa Y.: born about 1832 Kentucky and died 1863-possibly in childbirth (Pulaski) Kentucky; married Henry Alexander Vaughan

James: born about 1835 Kentucky; no further information

William: born about 1836 (Pulaski) Kentucky-15 January 1861-drowning (Pulaski) Kentucky; buried possibly at White Oak Cemetery, Nancy (Pulaski) Kentucky; never married

Elizabeth: born 12 July 1838 Kentucky and died 08 June 1904 Nancy (Pulaski) Kentucky; buried White Oak Cemetery, Nancy (Pulaski) Kentucky; married Charles Silas Pitman

Being a civil war veteran records were found for a John McFall who enlisted in the Patterson's Engineer Company on 01 October 1861 at Cumberland Gap, Kentucky and mustered out 12 August 1863 at Vicksburg (Warren) Mississippi with the rank of private.

By 1870 John was living in the household of James M Lewis, living at Pawnee (Sangamon) Illinois where it appears he then met Mary J. (maiden name unknown). She was born 02 February 1833 in Cairo (Alexander) Illinois; parents unknown (father born in Germany, mother born in South Carolina). John and Mary were married in 1872. No known children blessed this marriage.

A few years later they made their way to Colorado, locating at Gold Hill (Boulder) Colorado where in 1874 John, along with David J. Rollin, were the proprietors of the Clarence Mine located in the Gold Hill Mining District in Gold Hill (Boulder) Colorado.

There are no 1880 census records for either John or Mary however Mary is listed in the 1885 Colorado State Census living in Gold Hill (Boulder) Colorado as married but with no husband in the household.

In March of 1903 John became the foreman of the Clarence Mine.

Boulder County News 10 March 1903:
"Capt. J.B. McFall has succeeded Dick Stoneman as foreman on the Clarence Mine. A good force has been recently put on the mine and work is being continued rapidly."

John and Mary continued living in Gold Hill (Boulder) Colorado until John died from injuries sustained when he fell off a ladder while mining in the Maxon Mine (Gold Hill Mining District) on 22 September 1904. His widow continued to live in Gold Hill until her death when she was brought down from Crisman (Boulder) Colorado to the University Hospital in Boulder (Boulder) Colorado where she died from Parenchymatous (possibly related to stomach swelling).

Interview with Pearl Walter (Courtesy of Lynne Walter):
"There was [sic] more bachelors than there were married people, by a lot, in those days. They never brought them with them, but they would send for them as soon as they got their little cabins fixed up. These Mac Fall [sic] people, they lived there just east of the Hedley house. You see quite a lot of stone foundations and walls just east of there. Well, that was the Mac Fall people, and he was killed in a mine over there. He fell a couple of hundred

"His loving heart and laughter
will be missed by many."

feet. In them days they used candles and the old time candle sticks. When he fell he landed on his candle stick and it punctured and killed him, but he was a big man, immense. I don't know anybody around here that's anywhere near his size. They used to say of Old Mac, if you see a tree coming down the road, why Mac Fall was under it. He dragged his own wood. He would go out and cut down a tree, a dry tree, and he'd just crawl under it and bring it home—limbs, tree, and the whole business."

Gold Hill Colorado-Our Home Town by Elmer Curtis Swallow:
"I, Elmer Curtis Swallow, remember the first time I saw Mrs. McFall. Some of us boys were playing around Horsfal Hill, our favorite playground, when I saw a lady coming up the road carrying two pails of water. We found out that it was Mrs. McFall, and she was toting water from the Cold Spring well to her home on top of the hill for laundry water. She was doing laundry for some of the miners."

MILLER, Wyatt Cole

Birth: 08/01/1980
Death: 06/09/2018
Cemetery Location: B5

Father: Thomas Raymond Miller; Mother: Kristen Kee (*Gibson*); born in Boulder (Boulder) Colorado and died on a camping trip at the age of 37 years, 10 months, 8 days-heart failure

Boulder Daily Camera 19 June 2018:
"With wounded hearts we announce the passing of Wyatt Cole Miller, Father, Son, Brother, Husband and a soul of boundless love, kindness and knowledge. Born at home August 1, 1980, Wyatt attended Whitter Elementary, Casey Middle and Boulder High Schools, and enlisted in the Marines, gathering lifelong friends at every stop. On June 9th, while on a family camping trip, he passed suddenly yet peacefully in his sleep due to heart failure. He is survived by hundreds who loved him. From the cradle to his new home in the stars, Wyatt graced us all with humility in spirit and a wit in mind that brushed against us too briefly. We take solace, hope and joy to witness his genius for tenderness live on in his astonishing children, Aliyah and Colton, guarded by their unstoppable mother, Julia. Wyatt reveled in his family and friends and us in him. We adored his uncanny memory for the details of moments decades past, down to the day, the hue of clothing, the lines on our faces and the tenor of the joke. We were riveted by his faculties as a father, gentle and firm, encouraging and engaged in every interaction with his beautiful children, cousins, nieces and nephews. Wyatt was a creature of care, sacrifice for others his talent and

gift. The safety and joy of those he loved were his paramount goals. We will hold Wyatt in our memory as he was; as gentle and imperfect, as brave and questioning, as complex and lovely a man as The Lord ever made. Today we ask that you hug and kiss, that you cuddle and cradle, that you communicate with, and care for those you love ad those you barely know. And if the means are available we ask that you donate to The Wounded Warriors Project, and think of Wyatt and his family. A service and celebration will be held, and hugs will be plenty at Salberg Park at 3045 19th St. in Boulder on Sunday, June 24th from 11:00-2:00."

MOREY/MOWREY/MOWRY, Elizabeth Ann (*Rhodes*)

Birth: 09/01/1847
Death: 10/09/1925
Cemetery Location: B4 (possibly)

Father: Reuben Perkins/Perkl Rhodes; Mother: Phebe Jane (*Chute*); Husband: Justus Winchester Morey/Mowrey/Mowry; born in (Nova Scotia) Canada and died in Gold Hill (Boulder) Colorado at age 78 years, 1 month, 8 days-acute bronchitis; no tombstone but believed buried beside her husband (Justus Winchester Morey/Mowrey/Mowry) and her son (Frederick Herbert "Ted" Morey/Mowrey/Mowry); see MOREY/MOWREY/MOWRY Justus Winchester; see MOREY/MOWREY/MOWRY, Frederick Herbert "Ted"; see **About Justus Winchester Morey/Mowrey/Mowry**

Boulder Daily Camera 10 October 1925:
"MRS. ELIZABETH MOREY—Mrs. Elizabeth Mowry died last night, at 7 o'clock, at the home of her son, Fred Mowry, at Gold Hill, aged 78 years. For 45 years she had made her home in Gold Hill. Her husband, the late J. Winchester Mowry, passed away in 1907. The funeral

will be held from the residence at 1 o'clock Sunday. Rev. Frank R. Hollenback will conduct the service."

(J. Winchester Mowry died in 1906-newspapaer error; see MOREY/MOWREY/MOWRY, Justus Winchester)

MOREY/MOWREY/MOWRY, Frederick Herbert "Ted"

Birth: 09/06/1872
Death: 08/26/1938
Cemetery Location: B4

Father: Justus Winchester Morey/Mowrey/Mowry; Mother: Elizabeth Ann (*Rhodes*); wife: never married; born in Granville, Annapolis (Nova Scotia) Canada and died in Soap Lake (Grant) Washington at age 65 years, 11 months, 20 days-cardio vascular disease; spelling on birth records is "Mowrey;" tombstone states birth year as 1871; mortuary record states died at age 70 years; naturalized on 03 April 1905; see MOREY/MOWREY/MOWRY, Elizabeth Ann (*Rhodes*); see MOREY/MOWREY/MOWRY, Justus Winchester; see **About Justus Winchester Morey/Mowrey/Mowry**

Boulder Daily Camera 28 April 1938:

"Howe mortuary received a telegraph this afternoon announcing the death of Ted Mowry and stating the body was being shipped to Boulder. The message was from Ephrapa [sic] Wash., and gave no particulars."

MOREY/MOWREY/MOWRY, John Manson

Birth: 10/08/1831
Death: 02/22/1920
Cemetery Location: B4 (possibly)

Father: Uriah Morey; Mother: Elizabeth Francis (*Giggey*); Wife: Letitia "Lettie" "Lottie" M. (*Smiley*) Humphrey; born in Westfield Parish, Kings (New Brunswick) Canada and died in Denver (Denver) Colorado at age 87 years (approximately)-old age; brother to Susan "Matilda" (*Morey/Mowrey/Mowry*) Buckler and Justus "Winchester" "Ted" Morey/Mowrey/Mowry; no tombstone; see MOREY/MOWREY/MOWRY, Justus Winchester; see **About John Manson Morey/Mowrey/Mowry**; see **About Justus Winchester Morey/Mowrey/Mowry**

Boulder County Herald 23 February 1920:

"John M. Morey, Well-Known Miner Is Dead

John M. Morey, 87, for 40 years a resident of Boulder County, died at the home of his daughter, Mrs. Marquette, in Denver yesterday of old age. Mr. Morey has been residing at Gold Hill the greater part of his life until about five years ago when he moved to Denver. While at Gold Hill he had a large mountain farm and did considerable mining. He was well known in the hills. The body was brought to Boulder today by the Rose Undertaking parlors.

He requested about six years ago that at his final services Dr. John R. Furlong be in charge. Services will be held tomorrow afternoon at 2 o'clock at the Rose mortuary parlors. Interment will be in Gold Hill."

Boulder Daily Camera 24 February 1920:

"DEATH OF JOHN MOREY CITIZEN OF GOLD HILL—John Morey of Gold Hill died at the home of his daughter, Mrs. Marquette at Denver Sunday morning, aged 87 years. The funeral will be held from Rose and Tippett undertaking parlors at 2 o'clock Wednesday. S.R. Furlong will conduct the services. Dr. Furlong was an old time friend of the deceased. He was a miner and ranch man at Gold Hill for 40 years and where interment will take place."

Possible location of the Morey/Mowrey/Mowry family.

Digging Up Dirt

Boulder Daily Camera 25 February 1920:

"The funeral service of John Morey was conducted at the Rose and Tippett chapel this afternoon. S.R. Furlong, an old time friend of the deceased, gave the obituary. The remains will be taken to Gold Hill Thursday morning to be interred, as was Mr. Morey's request."

Gold Hill, Colorado-*Our Home Town* by Elmer Curtis Swallow (Courtesy Tolliver G. Swallow & Leah McKin):

"I remember Mr. John Mowery [sic] and his yoke of oxen pulling a big cumbersome cart coming to town with a load of vegetables from his ranch south of town. He walked beside the cart with a gee and a haw to keep the oxen going."

About John Manson Morey/Mowrey/Mowry

According to the 1900 census John Manson Morey was born in October 1831 in Westfield Parish, Kings (New Brunswick) Canada (Ancestry records state 08 October 1831); first known child born to Canadian natives Uriah and Elizabeth Frances (*Giggey*) Morey. Uriah was a widower when he married Elizabeth Francis Giggey on 23 December 1830 Westfield, Kings (New Brunswick) Canada. According to Ancestry.com she was born about 1809 in (New Brunswick) Canada; parents unknown.

To the union of Uriah and Elizabeth Francis (*Giggey*) Morey three known children were born:

John Manson: born 08 October 1831 Westfield Parish, Kings (New Brunswick) Canada and died 22 February 1920 Denver (Denver) Colorado; buried Gold Hill Cemetery, Gold Hill (Boulder) Colorado; married Letitia "Lettie" "Lottie" M. (*Smiley*) Humphrey; see MOREY/MOWREY/MOWRY, John Manson

Justus Winchester: born November 1837 (New Brunswick) Canada and died 23 April 1906 Gold Hill (Boulder) Colorado; buried Gold Hill Cemetery, Gold Hill (Boulder) Colorado; married Susan E. Schofield and Elizabeth Ann Rhodes; see MOREY/MOWREY/MOWRY, Justus Winchester

Susan Matilda: born 06 April 1849 (New Brunswick) Canada and died 03 April 1924 Boulder (Boulder) Colorado; buried Columbia Cemetery, Boulder (Boulder) Colorado; married Joseph Buckler

John Manson Morey immigrated to the United States about 1875 and his brother, Justus Winchester Morey immigrated about 1880. A few years later both were living in the Sugar Loaf (Boulder) Colorado area making their fortune as miners; see MOREY/MOWREY/MOWRY, Justus Winchester.

On 24 February 1887 John married Letitia M. (*Smiley*) Humphrey in Boulder (Boulder) Colorado. She was born about 1845 in Pennsylvania; the daughter of Scottish descendants Andrew J. and Jane (*Nealy*) Smiley. She was the widow of Charles Samuel Humphrey whom she married 29 January 1868 in (Lake) Indiana. Letitia and Charles were the parents of Charles Stanley Humphrey; see HUMPHREY, Charles Stanley.

To the union of John Manson and Letitia M. (*Smiley*) Humphrey Morey one child was born:

Iris Mary: born August 1884 (Boulder) Colorado and died 20 July 1956 Seattle (King) Washington; burial unknown; married Louis Julius Markert, Ellis Sperry Knowlton and Ulysses S. Attix

In 1885 the family was living in Gold Hill (Boulder) Colorado where John was a miner. In 1900 John was still living in Gold Hill however in this census record he is listed as a farmer, living near the homestead of Charles Pughe (south of Gold Hill near the cemetery). His wife, Letitia (along with daughters Bertha and Iris) was living in Denver (Arapahoe) Colorado.

It appears John remained in Gold Hill (Boulder) Colorado whereas his wife, Letitia, remained in Denver (Arapahoe) Colorado until about 1920 where they are both listed in that year's census living with their daughter, Iris Mary, and husband Louis Julius Markert in Denver.

On 23 February 1920 John Manson Morey died at his daughter's (Iris Mary) Denver home. His remains were taken to the Gold Hill Cemetery in Gold Hill (Boulder) Colorado for burial however there is no tombstone for his grave and the grave location is unknown.

Letitia then moved to Spokane (Spokane) Washington where on 15 April 1923 she died and is buried in the Riverside Memorial Park Cemetery there.

MOREY/ MOWREY/MOWRY, Justus Winchester

Birth: 11/1837
Death: 04/23/1906
Cemetery Location: B4

Father: Uriah Mowry; Mother: Elizabeth Frances (*Giggey*); 1st Wife: Susan E. (*Schofield*); 2nd Wife: Elizabeth Ann (*Rhodes*); born in (New Brunswick) Canada and died in Gold Hill (Boulder) Colorado at age 68 years, 5 months (approximately)-cause of death unknown; no tombstone but believed buried beside his wife (Elizabeth Ann (*Rhodes*) Morey/Mowrey/Mowry) and his son (Frederick Herbert "Ted" Morey/Mowrey/Mowry); brother to Susan "Matilda" (*Morey/Mowrey/Mowry*) Buckler and John Manson Mowry; see MOREY/MOWREY/MOWRY, Elizabeth Ann (*Rhodes*); see MOREY/MOWREY/MOWRY, Frederick Herbert "Ted"; see MOREY/MOWREY/MOWRY, John Manson; see **About John Manson Morey/Mowrey/Mowry**; see **About Justus Winchester Morey/Mowrey/Mowry**

Boulder Daily Camera 23 April 1906:

"WINCHESTER MOREY DEAD. Mr. Winchester Morey, who has resided in Gold Hill for the past eighteen years died at his home Sunday evening at 8 o'clock. Mr. Morey was past 68 years old. The funeral will take place at Gold Hill Tuesday at 2 p.m."

About Justus Winchester Morey/Mowrey/Mowry

Justus Winchester was born November of 1837 in (New Brunswick) Canada; the son of Uriah and Elizabeth Frances (*Giggey*) Morey/Mowrey/Mowry and was the younger brother to John Manson; see MOREY/MOWREY/MOWRY, John Manson. For more information on Uriah and Elizabeth Frances (Giggey) Morey/Mowrey/Mowry see **About John Manson Morey/Mowrey/Mowry.**

Justus Winchester Morey/Mowry first married Susan E. Schofield on 29 (or 25th) May 1867 in Granville, Annapolis (Nov Scotia) Canada. Susan was born about 1843 Annapolis (Nova Scotia) Canada; the daughter of John and Charlotte (possibly *Ward*) Schofield. She died only about a year after their marriage on 27 August 1868 Bridgetown, Annapolis (Nova Scotia) Canada. Justus then married Elizabeth Ann Rhodes 17 October 1871 Granville, Annapolis (Nova Scotia) Canada. She was born 01 September 1847 in Granville, Annapolis (Nova Scotia) Canada; the daughter of Reuben Perkins/Perkl and Phebe Jane (*Chute*) Rhodes. To this marriage only one known child was born:

Frederick Herbert "Ted": born 06 September 1872 Granville, Annapolis (Nova Scotia) Canada and died 26 August 1938 Soap Lake (Grant) Washington; buried Gold Hill Cemetery, Gold Hill (Boulder) Colorado; never married; see MOREY/MOWREY/MOWRY, Frederick Herbert "Ted"

According to the 1900 United States census the family immigrated to the United States in 1880. By 1885 they were living in (Boulder) Colorado where Justus was a miner. According to Justus' obituary the family was living in Gold Hill (Boulder) Colorado by 1888.

Justus died at his Gold Hill home on 23 April 1906 and was buried in the Gold Hill Cemetery, Gold Hill (Boulder) Colorado with no tombstone and location unknown.

His widow, Elizabeth, continued to live in Gold Hill (Boulder) Colorado along with her son, Frederick, until she died there on 09 October 1925 at the age of just over 78 years from acute bronchitis. She was buried in the Gold Hill Cemetery, Gold Hill (Boulder) Colorado without a tombstone but location is known as when her son, Frederick, died on 26 August 1936 from cardio vascular disease he was buried in the same location in the Gold Hill Cemetery with a tombstone. Apparently the tombstone was ordered by Mrs. Romig through Frederick's estate. Mrs. Zulu Romig was the wife of John W. Romig who was the son of Gold Hill pioneers John Felix and Athalia (*Neville*) Romig; see ROMIG, John Felix and see ROMIG, Athalia (*Neville*). Also see MOREY/MOWREY/MOWRY, Elizabeth Ann (*Rhodes*) and see ROMIG, John W.

MUGFORD, Jane Ann (*Wills*)

> Birth: 11/13/1831
> Death: 01/21/1890
> Cemetery Location: B3

Father: Thomas Wills; Mother: Maria (*maiden name unknown*); Husband: Thomas Mugford; born in Stoke Climsland (Cornwall) England and died in Gold Hill (Boulder) Colorado at age 58 years, 2 months, 8 days-cause of death unknown; 1851 census has Thomas Wallis; see **About the Mugford Family**

Boulder County Herald 22 January 1890:

"Mrs. Mugford of Gold Hill died yesterday."

Boulder News & Banner 23 January 1890:

"Mrs. John Mugfur [sic] of Gold Hill died Tuesday and was buried to-day [sic]."

In the original cemetery records it is listed that Jane's husband, Thomas, was buried in the Gold Hill Cemetery but not correct; see **About the Mugford Family**

About the Mugford Family

Thomas was born on 18 February 1829 in Kenwyn (Cornwall) England, the son of John and Jane (*Rosewarn*) Mugford. He married Jane Ann Wills in 1853 in Liskeard (Cornwall) England. Jane was born 13 November 1831 in Stoke Climsland (Cornwall) England; the daughter of Thomas and Maria (maiden name unknown) Wills; see MUGFORD, Jane Ann (*Wills*).

Their union produced no children of their own however it appears that Jane brought a daughter into the marriage:

Mary Ann: born 1849 Stoke Climsland (Cornwall) England and died 13 November 1906 Boise (Ada) Idaho; buried Morris Hill Cemetery, Boise (Ada) Idaho; married James Bennett (not the James Bennett who was married to Mary Ann Shea and buried in the Gold Hill Cemetery)

A short few years later the 1861 (Cornwall) England census has Thomas and Jane living in Kenwyn (Cornwall) England and in the household: Mary A. Wills (stepdaughter to Thomas), George Wills (brother-in-law to Thomas) and "Thamson" Wills (sister-in-law to Thomas).

By 1870 Thomas and Jane along with Mary Ann (*Wills*) Bennett and husband James Bennett were living in Washington (Lehigh) Pennsylvania.

Digging Up Dirt

The 1880 census is quite interesting as it lists Thomas and Jane living in Walker (Ellis) Kansas along with their 10 year old granddaughter, Jane Bennett. Five years later (1885) they were living in Gold Hill (Boulder) Colorado again with their granddaughter, Jane. From this point the trail grows cold for the granddaughter, Jane, however not for Thomas' wife, Jane Ann (*Wills*) Mugford. She died 21 January 1891 in Gold Hill (Boulder) Colorado and is buried in the cemetery there.

After the death of his wife Thomas continued to live in Gold Hill (Boulder) Colorado for a while, living with John A. Hitchings; see HITCHINGS, John A.

In 1906 his stepdaughter, Mary Ann Bennett died so Thomas decided to move to Boise (Ada) Idaho to live with the widowed husband, James, and his daughter, Lillie. About four years later Thomas died on 02 October 1910 there and is buried in the Morris Hill Cemetery, Boise (Ada) Idaho where his stepdaughter and husband (Mary Ann and James Bennett) are also buried.

Interesting to note that Thomas might be related to John Rosewarn "Captain Jack" Luxon; see LUXON, John Rosewarn "Captain Jack"

"Farewell dear wife, again farewell,
'Till I arise to three.
And when we meet no tongue can tell
How great our joys may be."

The tombstone plot of Jane Ann (*Wills*) Mugford/Mugfur
prior the Four Mile Canyon Fire of September 2010
Photo by Dina C. Carson

N

NEAL, Barbara Ruth (*Holly*)

 Birth: 04/11/1921
 Death: 10/17/2007
 Cemetery Location: B1

Father: Benjamin J. Holly; Mother: Edith Gertrude (*Noyes*); Husband: Bruce William Neal; born in Iowa and died in Minneapolis (Hennepin) Minnesota at age 86 years, 6 months, 6 days-natural causes

StarTribune (Minneapolis, MN) 03 November 2007:
 "Neal, Barbara Ruth Holly age 86, of Gold Hill, CO, died Oct. 17, in Minneapolis. Survived by her sister, Doris Holly Peters of Rockford, IL, and children, Douglas Neal, Robert Neal, Holly Neal Griffin, and Mary Elizabeth (Marybeth) Neal, their spouses, and 9 grandchildren. A memorial meeting for worship will be held 11am on Nov. 17 at Twin Cities Friends Meeting, 1725 Grand, St. Paul. Memorials to Friends School of Minnesota or Friends School of Detroit."

NEAL, Bruce William

 Birth: 09/09/1919
 Death: 04/01/1995
 Cemetery Location: B1

Father: William James Neal; Mother: Mabel (*Brookbank*); Wife: Barbara Ruth (*Holly*); born in Iowa and died in Gold Hill (Boulder) Colorado at age 75 years, 6 months, 23 days-natural causes; tombstone has Bruce William Neal but obituary has Bruce Robert Neal

Boulder Daily Camera 07 April 1995:
 "Bruce Robert Neal of Gold Hill died at his home Saturday, April 1, 1995. He was 75.
 He was born on Sept. 9, 1919, to William James Neal and Mabel Brookbank Neal in Arthur, Iowa. He married Barbara Holly on Dec. 27, 1942, in Des Moines, Iowa.
 He and his wife lived in Iowa, Louisiana, Colorado, New Jersey and Michigan. In 1937, he studied engineering at Iowa State, completing his degree at the University of Denver. He earned his master's degree in international relations and completed his thesis on the newly formed United Nations Educational, Scientific, and Cultural Organization.
 He was a conscientious objector during World War II, but later enlisted in the Army, serving as a typing teacher and editor of a base newspaper. In 1957, the family moved to New Jersey, and Mr. Neal worked for advertising firms in Manhattan. He later was an executive in the advertising and sales promotion research division of Ford Motor Co.
 He ran for the Democratic nomination for a congressional seat in 1970, but lost in the primary. He retired in 1974, then started his own firm, Neal and Associates Research, which specialized in computer-assisted telephone interview surveys. After 23 years in Ann Arbor, Mich., he moved to Gold Hill in 1987.
 Survivors include his wife of Gold Hill; two sons, Douglas Neal of McLean, Va., and Robert Neal of Lee's Summit, Mo.; two daughters, Holly Neal Giffen of Gold Hill and Marybeth Neal of Minneapolis, Minn.; and nine grandchildren.
 Services will be at 2 p.m. Saturday at the Boulder Friends Meeting House, 1825 Upland Ave., Boulder. Interment will be in Gold Hill Cemetery."

NELSON, Charles Hansen

 Birth: 03/15/1876
 Death: 05/07/1897
 Cemetery Location: Unknown

Digging Up Dirt

Father: Hans Christian "Chris" Nelson/Nielsen; Mother: Caroline Sophia (*Jeffers/Joffers/Jossers*); born in Caribou (Boulder) Colorado and died in Ward (Boulder) Colorado-injuries from a mining accident; no tombstone

Boulder Daily Camera 07 May 1897:

"KILLED AT WARD...CHARLES NELSON KILL-ED. Struck on the Head by a Falling Roller in the Shaft of the Gold King...Ward, May 7—At 3 o'clock this afternoon Charles Nelson, who had a contract sinking the shaft in the Gold King, was struck on the head by a roller falling down the shaft and was instantly killed. Nelson would have completed his contract within fifteen minutes had the accident not occurred. Deceased was unmarried. The nearest relative is a brother.

Coroner Trezise has been summoned."

Boulder Daily Camera 08 May 1897:

"Will be Buried at Gold Hill...Coroner Trezise was summoned to Ward last night to attend the remains of Charles Nelson, the man that was killed there yesterday. Upon arriving there, however, he found that the case was the result of an accident and did not deem it necessary to hold an inquest.

The accident, which resulted in Nelson's death, occurred in the Gold King mine. The unfortunate man was one of a trio of miners who had been engaged in sinking a shaft and had just finished up their contract. Mr. Nelson had dropped a hammer into the bottom of the shaft and was engaged in bailing the water out from the sump into the water bucket to enable him to recover the lost tool, when a heavy iron roller fell from a point 250 feet above him and struck him, on the top of the head. On the end of the roller was an iron pin about four inches in length and a half inch in diameter. This pin entered the miner's head the full length. Death was instantaneous.

The deceased was 21 years of age and has lived in Boulder county all his life, having been born in Caribou. He leaves a father, Chris Nelson, a leaser on the John Jay mine, and five brothers and one sister. He was a man of good moral habits and was highly respected by all who knew him.

The funeral will occur tomorrow at Gold Hill."

Boulder News 13 May 1897:

"KILLED AT WARD—Struck on the Head by a Falling Roller

While working in the shaft of the Gold King at Ward last Friday afternoon, Chas. Nelson was struck on the head by a roller placed in the shaft to keep the rope from the sides and instantly killed. The roller was thirty feet from the surface and 245 feet from the bottom of the shaft. Mr. Nelson would have completed his contract that

Gravesite of Barbara Ruth (*Holly*) and Bruce William Neal

day, and when the bucket was lowered for the last time the fastenings at one end were loosened and allowed the roller to drop. Coroner Trezise went up and after investigating decided that it was clearly an accident and that no inquest was necessary. He brought the body to Gold Hill where it was interred Sunday.

The deceased was twenty-one years of age and leaves a father, five brothers and a sister. He had lived in Boulder County all his life and leaves many friends to mourn his untimely end."

About Charles Hansen Nelson

Charles Hansen Nelson was born 15 March 1876 in Caribou (Boulder) Colorado; the son of Denmark natives Hans Christian "Chris" and Caroline/Carolyn Sophia (*Jeffers/Joffers/Jossers*) Nelson/Nielsen.

Some family trees on Ancestry state that Hans Christian Nelson was born 16 January 1845 in Copenhagen, Denmark and that his first wife was Louise Loel Zanner who he married about 1869 in Copenhagen. She is listed as deceased about 1870.

No verified marriage records have been located for Hans Christian "Chris" Nelson and Caroline/Carolyn Sophia (*Jeffers/Joffers/Jossers*), however, she was born about 1852 in Copenhagen, Denmark; parents unknown. To their union ten known children were born:

Alexander "Alfred" Carl: born 19 September 1872 Central City (Gilpin) Colorado and died 01 October 1941 Reno (Washoe) Nevada; buried Mountain View Cemetery, Reno (Washoe) Nevada; married Christine A. Hildebrand; family source states born in Cripple Creek (Teller) Colorado

Harry Conrad: born 05 October 1874 Caribou (Boulder) Colorado and died 01 May 1949 Ogden (Weber) Utah; entombed Aultorest Mausoleum, Ogden (Weber) Utah; married Laura Bell Pinkerton and Minnie Munson

Charles Hansen: born 15 March 1876 Caribou (Boulder) Colorado and died 07 May 1897 Ward (Boulder) Colorado; buried Gold Hill Cemetery, Gold Hill (Boulder) Colorado; never married; see NELSON, Charles Hansen

Christine: born September 1877 (Boulder) Colorado and died 15 September 1878 eight miles north of Boulder (Boulder) Colorado; buried Columbia Cemetery, Boulder (Boulder) Colorado

Odin Carl: born 28 October 1879 Fort Collins (Larimer) Colorado and died 16 October 1923 Bingham (Salt Lake) Utah; burial unknown; married Florence Bartle; body sent to Denver (Denver) Colorado

Estella Marie: born 30 October 1882 (Boulder) Colorado and died 07 September 1944 Los Angeles (Los Angeles) California, burial unknown; married Thomas Wasley and Clarence J. Holley

John A.: born about 1883 Colorado-death unknown; burial unknown; spouse unknown; 1910 census living in Tokna School District (Dawson) Montana; divorced

Louisa: born 1885 (Larimer) Colorado-death unknown; burial unknown; not in the 1900 census records

Louie Julius: born 10 November 1886 Loveland (Larimer) Colorado and died 01 September 1949 Martinez (Contra Costa) California; buried Memory Gardens Cemetery, Concord (Contra Costa) California; married Clara Eva Hill

Benjamin Sophis: born 05 January 1888 Altona (Boulder) Colorado and died May 1958 Denver (Denver) Colorado; buried Mount Olivet, Wheat Ridge (Jefferson) Colorado; married Mary Elizabeth Cavanaugh

The family immigrated to the United States in the early 1870s as Charles' oldest brother, Alexander, was born in Central City (Gilpin) Colorado in September 1872. By 1880 they were living in Left Hand (Boulder) Colorado where Hans was listed as a farmer.

Five years later the family moved to District One (Larimer) Colorado where Hans was a farmer. (District One encompasses Arkins Area and Thompson Valley, Berthoud, Loveland and Estes Park)

Apparently Charles' mother, Caroline Sophia, died after the 1885 Colorado State census (some sources state June 1893) as Hans Christian "Chris" married Martha Louisa (maiden name unknown) about 1894 and by 1900 the family was living in Gold Hill (Boulder) Colorado. Martha was born July 1850 in Ohio; daughter of German parents. According to the 1900 census record Martha had been married before; mother of two children with none living.

First Presbyterian Church records state Martha Louisa Nelson died 01 January 1908 and was buried in Nunn (Weld) Colorado:

Denver Post 04 January 1908:

"MELSON [sic]—Louisa V. Melson died Jan. 2. Remains will be shipped from McGovern's parlors tomorrow morning to Munn [sic], Colo., for burial."

Interesting to note the same source (and also the Colorado State Marriage Records) state H.C. Nelson (age 62) married Mrs. Anna E. Mann (age 57) in Greeley (Weld) Colorado on 20 August 1908, a mere eight months after the death of Martha Louisa.

Records are confusing as it seems Hans Christian Nelson was somewhat of a common name thus to verify exact death records have been quite challenging. According to Ancestry family trees he died on 17 July 1916 in Denver (Denver) Colorado; burial unknown but a family member states he died 24 July 1916 Denver (Denver) Colorado. A burial permit however was located for Hans:

Denver Post 25 July 1916:
"Hans C. Nelson, 70, 4661 Decatur"

NELSON, Child

Birth: Unknown
Death: 09/05/1897
Cemetery Location: Unknown

Father: Chris Nelson; Mother: unverified; born in Colorado and died in Gold Hill (Boulder) Colorado; not enough primary evidence has been located to definitely determine relationship to Hans Christian "Chris" Nelson; no tombstone

Boulder Daily Camera 06 September 1897:
"Undertaker Sullivan sent a casket to Gold Hill yesterday for the child of Chris Nelson who died there yesterday morning."

NEWLAND, Matilda "Tillie" (*Peterson/Petersen/ Gustafson*) Bowman Holloway Brickman

Birth: 08/1896
Death: 04/30/1952
Cemetery Location: F3

Father: Gustof L. "Gus" Peterson/Petersen/Gustafson; Mother: Ida Matilda (*Burke*); 1st Husband: George Fern Bowman; 2nd Husband: Mr. Holloway; 3rd Husband: Henry E. Brickman; 4th Husband: Alert Lo Newland; born in Gold Hill (Boulder) Colorado and died in Pueblo (Pueblo) Colorado at age 55 years, 8 months (approximately)-illness of many years; some sources state birth year as 1898; no tombstone but buried in the Petersen/ Peterson/Gustafson family plot; see PETERSON/PETERSEN/GUSTAFSON, Gustof Louis "Gus;" see PETERSON/PETERSEN/ GUSTAFSON, William Bernard; see **About the Peterson/Petersen/Gustafson Family**; see BOWMAN, George Fern

Boulder Daily Camera 30 April 1952:
"Mrs. Tillie Newlin Dies In Pueblo—Mrs. Matilda (Tillie) Newlin died in Pueblo last night after an illness of many years. She was a long-time resident of Boulder and worked here in many restaurants. Funeral arrangements have not been completed. The Camera was informed that her husband, Al Newlin [sic], now resides in Denver. A son Gilbert Bowman is in Winston Salem, North Carolina. Art Johnson, widely known Nederland miner, is a cousin as are Carl, Art and Elmer Burke of Boulder."

Boulder Daily Camera 01 May 1952:
"Mrs. Al (Mathilda) Newland—Private funeral services Saturday at Howe mortuary. Rev. Warren S. Bainbridge, pastor of the First Methodist church, will officiate. Interment in Gold Hill cemetery beside her parents, Mr. and Mrs. Gus Peterson. She is survived by her husband,

Peterson/Petersen/Gustafson Family Plot

Al Newland of 1776 Williams, Denver and two sons, Gilbert, West Salem, S.C., and Wilbert of Denver. There are four grandchildren."

Boulder Daily Camera 02 May 1952:

"Mrs. Al Newland—Private service Saturday afternoon at Howe mortuary with Rev. Warren S. Bainbridge, pastor of the First Methodist church, officiating. Interment, Gold Hill cemetery."

About Matilda "Tillie" (Peterson/Petersen/Gustafson) Bowman Holloway Brickman Newland

Matilda was born in August of 1896 in Gold Hill (Boulder) Colorado; the daughter of Swedish natives Gustof L. "Gus" and Ida (*Burke*) Peterson/Petersen/Gustafson; see PETERSON /PETERSEN /GUSTAFSON, Gustof Louis "Gus," see PETERSON/PETERSEN/GUSTAFSON, Ida Matilda (*Burke*) and see **About the Peterson/Petersen/Gustafson Family**

Matilda married George Fern Bowman 14 January 1915 in Boulder (Boulder) Colorado. This union produced one child:

Gilbert William: born 09 January 1917 Boulder (Boulder) Colorado and died 13 December 1969 Longmont (Boulder) Colorado; buried Fort Logan National Cemetery, Denver (Denver) Colorado; married Helen Frand

After the death of her first husband, George T. Bowman in 1920, Matilda married a Mr. Holloway. This union produced one child:

Wilbert Henry: born 30 April 1922 (Boulder) Colorado and died 24 June 1960 Los Angeles (Los Angeles) California; buried Los Angeles National Cemetery, Los Angeles (Los Angeles) California; married Evelyn Faye Lull; was a seaman in the United States Navy

Interesting to note that in the 1930 United States census Matilda (Mitelda) is living with her sons, Gilbert and Wilbert; both sons have the last name of Holloway (Gilbert's last name should have been listed as Bowman). Matilda's mother, Ida (*Burke*) Peterson is living with them on Water Street (now Canyon Boulevard) in Boulder (Boulder) Colorado.

On 22 November 1931 Matilda then married Henry E. Brickman in (Gilpin) Colorado. For some reason Matilda's son, Wilbert Henry, then used the last name of Brickman from then on instead of Holloway.

Unfortunately Matilda and Henry divorced on 30 March 1938 in Boulder (Boulder) Colorado. The same day her divorce was final Matilda and Alert Lo Newland applied for a marriage license and on 03 April 1938 they were married in Boulder (Boulder) Colorado. They continued living in Boulder however by 1952 Matilda was living in Pueblo, Colorado and Alert living in Denver, Colorado.

Eventually Alert Lo Newland moved to Phoenix (Maricopa) Arizona where he died in February 1976.

NEWMANN, Benjamin "Bennie"

Birth: 07/27/1902
Death: 03/02/1979
Cemetery Location: G2

Father: Michael Novak; Mother: Antonia (*Schwanine/Schwamine*); never married; born in Szamocin (Chodziez) Poland and died in Boulder (Boulder) Colorado at age 76 years, 7 months, 3 days-respiratory failure, pulmonary fibrosis (scarring of the lung issue), coronary pulmonale (condition that causes the right side of the heart to fail); death certificate states place of birth as Germany

Boulder Daily Camera 06 March 1979:

"Bennie Newmann—Bennie Newmann, 311 Maxwell, died March 2 in his home. He was 76. Born July 27, 1902, in Germany, Mr. Newmann was a civil service employee until retiring in 1968. He also was a miner in the Snow Bound Mine in Sunshine Canyon. Mr. Newmann, who never married, is survived by his sister, Margaret Rienol of Buffalo Grove, Ill., three nieces, Irma Betlinski of Harvard, Ill., Margaret Kender of Fort Atkinson, Ill., and Geraldine Rienol of Buffalo Grove, Ill.; and three nephews, Leo Neuman of Franklin Park, Ill., Paul Neuman of Harvard, Ill., and Raymond Newman of LeGrange, Ill. Funeral services will be held this afternoon at 2:30 at Howe Mortuary Chapel with the Rev. Warren Heidgen of Sacred Heart of Jesus church officiating. Services will conclude at the chapel."

Digging Up Dirt

About Benjamin "Bennie" Newmann

Bennie Newman was born in Szamocin Poland (Germany) on 27 July 1902; son of Michael and Antonia (*Schwanine/Schwamine*) Novak.

Several children blessed the marriage of Michael and Antonia with records on four:

Regina: born January 1885 "Federal Republic of Germany" and died 08 August 1949 Chicago (Cook) Illinois; burial unknown; never married

Margareta (Margaret): born 27 July 1902 Szamocin (Chodziez) Poland (Germany) and died 06 January 1982 Arlington Heights (Cook) Illinois; buried Acacia Park Cemetery, Norwood Park (Cook) Illinois; married Martin Reinel; twin to Benjamin

Benjamin "Bennie": born 27 July 1902 Szamocin (Chodziez) Poland (Germany) and died 02 March 1979 Boulder (Boulder) Colorado; buried Gold Hill Cemetery, Gold Hill (Boulder) Colorado; never married; twin to Margareta (Margaret)

Leo: born 23 June 1905 Germany; died 07 July 1960 Barrington (Cook) Illinois; buried Eden Memorial park, Schillar Park (Cook) Illinois; married Bernadine Hachmeister

The family arrived in the Port of New York on 02 December 1913 (according to the nationalization record of Margareta). From there no other verified records have been located until Bennie's World War One registration card of 1942 where he is living up the Nederland Star Route (about 9 miles from Boulder (Boulder) Colorado) and working the Eureka Mine about 9 miles up Boulder Canyon (close to Boulder Falls).

In February of 1945 he and Nicholas Bode purchased the Snowbound Mine located up Four Mile Canyon Road, a few miles east of Gold Hill (Boulder) Colorado. However the last known year of operation for the Snowbound was 1947.

There are stories of how "Bennie Newmann Memorial Highway" came into existence. This short stretch of paved road is actually a very small part of County Road 52 that runs by the property of the Snowbound site (between the mining towns of Gold Hill and Sunshine (Boulder) Colorado). To this day locals always remember Bennie when driving on this brief section of non-dirt road.

Bennie died in his Boulder (Boulder) Colorado apartment on Maxwell Street from respiratory failure, pulmonary fibrosis (scarring of the lung issue) and coronary pulmonale (condition that causes the right side of the heart to fail). He is buried in the Gold Hill Cemetery, Gold Hill (Boulder) Colorado and his twin sister, Margareta/Margaret, (who died in 1982) is buried in the Acacia Park Cemetery and Mausoleum in Chicago (Cook) Illinois.

Newman Info for Cemetery Records 03 October 2008 Courtesy of Karen Simmons

"Benny was a World War I veteran. He came to the US through Canada and lived in Chicago with his twin sister for a number of years, before 1951. He was a professional baker by training and worked for the bakery that made buns for "Cub Park!" [Chicago Cubs baseball team]

A physician told him he had to get out of the baking business or lose his eyesight so he came to Colorado to "dem golden mountains' he'd heard about in Germany. He arrived in Boulder sometime before March of 1940. He worked the Eureka and Midway tungsten mines in Boulder Canyon during World War II until the government dropped the subsidy for tungsten.

He went into partnership with Nick Bode in the Snowbound (gold) Mine (who had purchased it from Charlie Guhse in January of 1944) in February of 1945. They worked the Snowbound, with Guhse helping, until the Korean War forced gold mines to close. He also dabbled with uranium mining on the western slope for a winter sometime in there.

Benny then went to work in the US government Civil Service. He worked as a steamfitter at Pearl Harbor and later in Bishop, California before retiring in 1868. He returned to the Snowbound after retiring. He moved to the Boulder Sanitarium when his miners' lung disease caused him to have trouble breathing at the Snowbound altitude."

Personal Letter 06 October 2008 to Karen Simmons from Paul E. and Mary Ann Neuman (nephew and niece of Bennie Newman):

"Dear Karen Simmons,

Will try to answer some of your questions. Looks like you already have most of what I know.

As to where he was born-only know Germany and he came to this country in "31."

The bakery in Chicago was Eagle Bakery that made buns for the Cubs.

He left Chicago in "33" and no one knew where he was until "35" when he bought into Snowbound Mine.' He was working for the government in Nebraska in "45" until he bought Eureka. He lived in Barstow, Cali., working for the Marines until he retired.

The Snowbound wasn't worked after he went to Nebraska in "45"-no money in it.

As far as we know, he never worked a mine before Eureka.

The food pkgs sent-were to cousins.

When Uncle Bennie and Paul's dad [Leo] came to U.S. they changed their last name to Neuman and Newmann. They couldn't agree on spelling so each took their own.

Uncle Bennie left Germany after his brother Leo-Paul's dad,-but there were still sisters that stayed there.

Sorry we don't have more to add-Hope this fills in some of the blanks.

Sincerely,
Paul Neuman (MaryAnn)"

NICHOLLS, Benjamin Allen

Birth: 03/31/1885
Death: 09/22/1951
Cemetery Location: C3

Father: Henry "Harry" Grenful (some records have Granville) Nicholls; Mother: Elizabeth Jane (*Allen*); never

married; born in Ophir (Tooele) Utah and died in Boulder (Boulder) Colorado at age 66 years, 5 months, 22 days-old age-failing health; grand uncle of author; brother to Henry W. Nicholls and Richard John Nicholls; see NICHOLLS, Nellie (*Beckwith*) Evans; see NICHOLLS, Richard John; see **About the Henry Grenful/Granville Nicholls Family**

Boulder Daily Camera 24 September 1951:

"Benj A. Nichols, Retired Metal Miner, Is Dead... Benjamin A. Nichols of 603 Dewey, a retired metal miner, died at the Boulder General hospital Saturday night at 10. He had been in failing health for some time. Born in Ophir, Utah, March 31, 1885, he came to Colorado 59 years ago and worked in many of its mining communities, including Gold Hill, from which community he moved to Boulder eight years ago. He is survived by two nieces, Mrs. H.E. Bradford of Boulder and Mrs. Stanley Goff of Long Beach, Calif. Richard Mitchell of Denver is a nephew. Funeral services will be held at Howe's Mortuary, Wednesday morning at 10:30. Interment will be in Gold Hill cemetery."

Boulder Daily Camera 25 September 1951:

"Benjamin A. Nicholls—retired miner, late of 603 Dewey.—Services to be held at Howe's Mortuary Wednesday at 10 o'clock with Rev. Paul O. Madsen, pastor of the First Baptist church, officiating. Interment family lot in the Gold Hill Cemetery."

Boulder Daily Camera 26 September 1951:

"Benjamin A. Nicholls-late of 603 Dewey—Services were held at 10:30 o'clock today from Howe Mortuary with Rev. Paul O. Madsen, pastor of the First Baptist Church, officiating. Dorothy Rosenberg and Ben Walker sang accompanied by Margaret Hascall. Pallbearers were Fred Magor, Everett Brown, Emil Enenlame and Leonard Kirby. Interment Gold Hill cemetery."

Interview with Albert C. "Bud" Walter by Lynne Walter (no date):

"There were three bachelors in Gold Hill, There was my dad [Albert James "Tim" Walter], Jimmy McLellan and Ben Nickols [sic]. They'd meet over at Dad's house and play cards or make wine or beer. They made wine out of just about anything that was available. Primarily, raisins, dried apricots, dried peaches, prunes or any type of dried fruit that was available. Dad had a great big crock. It must have been a fifty gallon crock. Jimmy McLellan and Ben would own these mines and Dad would build as much as there was work to do. He didn't particularly care about mining. Jim and Ben —they had gold fever and between making wine and beer, the men would play cards or listen to the radio."

NICHOLLS, Edwin Grenful

> Birth: About 09/1910
> Death: 12/08/1910
> Cemetery Location: D4

Father: Richard John Nicholls; Mother: Ethel (*Goudge*); born and died in Gold Hill (Boulder) Colorado at 3 months of age; no tombstone but buried in the Goudge family plot; cousin of author; see NICHOLLS, Richard John; see **About the Henry Grenful/Granville Nicholls Family**; see **About Edwin David "Ned" and Annie Elizabeth (*Bennett(s)*) Goudge**

Boulder County Miner 15 December 1910:
> "We extend our most heartfelt sympathy to Mr. and Mrs. Dick Nichols in the loss of their baby boy. The little fellow passed away the night of December 7, after a short illness. Mrs. Nichols, who is having trouble with her stomach, is still unable to be out of bed."

NICHOLLS, Nellie L. (*Beckwith*) Evans

> Birth: 02/08/1870
> Death: 11/14/1937
> Cemetery Location: Unknown

Father: Oscar Beckwith; Mother: Hattie E. (might be Emma) (*Ward*); 1st Husband: David Evans; 2nd Husband: Henry W. Nicholls; born in Burlington, near Longmont (Boulder) Colorado and died in Summerville (Boulder) Colorado at age 67 years, 9 months, 6 days-cause of death unknown but might have been natural causes; Henry W. Nicholls was the brother to Benjamin Allen Nicholls and to Richard John Nicholls; no tombstone; see NICH-OLLS, Benjamin Allen; see NICHOLLS, Richard John; see **About the Henry Grenful/Granville Nicholls Family**

Boulder Daily Camera 15 November 1937:
> "Mrs. Nellie Nichols, who was born at the old town of Burlington, near Longmont, on Feb. 8, 1870, died at her home at Summerville Sunday morning at 8:30.
>
> She was the widow of Henry W. Nichols, who was a mining man. She had resided at Summerville for 47 years and owned most of the houses in that mining camp located between Salina and Gold Hill.
>
> Funeral services will be held Tuesday at 1 o'clock at Howe's mortuary. Rev. John H. Sanders of the Presbyterian Church will officiate. Burial will be in Gold Hill cemetery."

Boulder Daily Camera 16 November 1937:
> "MRS. NELLIE NICHOLS—Funeral services were held from Howe's mortuary this afternoon. Rev. J.H. Sanders, pastor of the Presbyterian church, officiated. Miss Marylee Copeland sang. Pallbearers were George H. Pomeroy, Fred Guhse [sic], William Cowdrey, John Holman, Paul Maurer, Henry Trask. Burial in Gold Hill cemetery, beside the grave of her first husband, David Evans. Mrs. Nichols lived at Summerville, a mining town in this county, 47 years."

About Nellie (*Beckwith*) Evans Nicholls

Nellie L. Beckwith was born 08 February 1870 Burlington (Boulder) Colorado; the daughter of Oscar Fenton and Hattie E. (might be Emma) (*Ward*) Beckwith. Another child was born into this marriage:

Edwin Grenful Nicholls plot

Walter E: born about 1875 (Boulder) Colorado and died 23 July 1899 (Boulder) Colorado; buried Columbia Cemetery, Boulder (Boulder) Colorado; never married

Oscar Fenton married his first wife Elvira Emerson on 10 April 1832 in Alsted (Cheshire) New Hampshire however he left her for a much younger woman by the name of Keturie (according to a family member). A divorce was granted to Elvira in December of 1868 on the grounds of adultery.

No marriage records have been located for any marriage in any state for Oscar Fenton Beckwith and a "Keturie." Family story goes that this "Keturie" was actually Hattie however no marriage records for any Beckwith have been located for that name either.

On 22 October 1880 Hattie divorced Oscar Fenton and married Harmon Bunn 19 October 1881. Apparently that marriage didn't last long (divorced in 1886) as on 28 December 1886 (Boulder) Colorado she married Jacob Stombaugh, divorced and then remarried on 16 June 1888. But on 17 August 1891 (Arapahoe) Colorado Elvira married her last husband, William R. Chapman. No children blessed any of those marriages.

During Elvira's "trading of husbands" Nellie L. Beckwith married David Evans on 08 March 1887 in Boulder (Boulder) Colorado when she was a mere seventeen years old and he was in his mid-forties.

By 1885 Oscar Fenton Beckwith ended up in the County Hospital in Boulder (Boulder) Colorado listed as divorced and an "inmate." About a decade later on 21 February 1897 Oscar passed away and was buried in the city's Columbia Cemetery with no headstone:

Boulder Daily Camera 22 February 1897:
"Mr. Trezise was called to take charge of the remains of old man Beckwith, an inmate of the poor farm, who died yesterday morning. Mr. Beckwith was 88 years old, and had been inmate of the home for 18 years."

About a year later Nellie's mother, Hattie Elvira Chapman, passed away:

Boulder Daily Camera 29 June 1898:
"Mrs. H.E. Chapman died this morning at her residence on Walnut Street from a tumor on the stomach. Mrs. Chapman was the mother of Mrs. Dave Evans of Summerville and Walter Beckwith of Niwot. The funeral will be held from Sullivan's undertaking rooms. The date has not yet been set."

And if that wasn't enough about a year after that death Nellie's brother, Walter, committed suicide:

Boulder Daily Camera 24 July 1899:

"DOSE OF DEAD—Walter Beckwith Committed Suicide at Summerville...

Summerville yesterday was the scene of a tragedy. Walter Beckwith, a young man, 22 years of age and a brother of Mrs. Dave Evans, put a pistol to his head and blew his brains out as the result of a jilt from a girl visiting in Gold Hill. He went to Gold Hill Saturday night to attend a dance and while there, made a proposal of marriage to the girl, whom it seems he had known but a short time. She replied with a profession of friendship, but flatly refused to marry him. After the dance he proceeded to get full [drunk] and early yesterday morning in a fit of despondency ended his life.

Coroner Trezise was summoned and went up yesterday. He decided that the case was too conclusive to necessitate an inquest.

The funeral will be held tomorrow morning at 10 o'clock from Trezise's undertaking parlors."

All three of them (Oscar, Hattie and Walter) are buried in the Columbia Cemetery in Boulder (Boulder) Colorado in unknown graves in an unknown location.

Nellie and David enjoyed about 24 years of marriage until David died 07 September 1911 from Bright's disease in his Summerville (Boulder) Colorado home. He is buried in the Gold Hill Cemetery, Gold Hill (Boulder) Colorado in an unknown location; see EVANS, David

Upon his death, Nellie inherited all of his Summerville (Boulder) Colorado property and on 05 July 1916 she married Henry W. Nicholls who had only been divorced a year from his first wife, Minnie Viola (*Croul*). Henry was the son of Henry "Harry" Grenful and Elizabeth Jane (*Allen*) Nicholls; brother to Benjamin Allen Nicholls and Richard John Nicholls; see NICHOLLS, Benjamin Allen; see NICHOLLS, Richard John.

Theirs was a short marriage with no children produced as on 29 November 1925 Henry took his own life.

Boulder Daily Camera 30 November 1925:

"HENRY W. NICHOLS, 55, RESIDENT OF SALINA WELL KNOWN MINER OF BOULDER COUNTY ENDED ILLNESS BY TAKING HIS OWN LIFE...

Henry W. Nichols, 55, a resident of Boulder county [sic] for thirty years, killed himself at his home at Somerville [sic] near Salina, ten miles west of Boulder at 10:50 o'clock Sunday morning by shooting himself thru the head.

While chopping wood August 9 Nichols was stuck in the eye by a splinter, infection developed and the eye had to be removed. He had suffered considerable pain from the injury and the note left to his wife would indicate the pain suffered from the loss of the eye had driven him to suicide. It read: "Nellie, Dear Wife: It's best I put a stop to this suffering. So here goes. Goodby. Henry."

Nichols killed himself by placing the gun to his right temple, near the ear, and pulling the trigger. The gun was a .38 revolver that Nichols had owned several years. The bullet lodged in the brain.

Nichols and his wife arose at the usual hour Sunday and ate breakfast. Suffering pain, Nichols stayed in the dining room of their home, after breakfast had been finished, while Mrs. Nichols went outside to feed the chickens.

During her absence Nichols wrote the note to his wife on a cardboard with pencil, and took his life. Mrs. Nichols heard the shot, and returning to the house found her husband dead.

She called her brother-in-law, Richard J. Nichols, 1014 Portland avenue [sic], Boulder, who notified Coroner A.E. Howe. Howe brought the body to Boulder at 2 o'clock Sunday afternoon. He said today no inquest would be held.

Nichols is survived by his wife and brother. There are no children.

Nichols at one time had been a janitor of the Elks lodge here. He was born in England March 27, 1870. He had mined in the hills near Salina nearly thirty years and at one time had made considerable money as a tungsten producer.

Funeral services will be held at the Howe mortuary at 2 o'clock Wednesday afternoon. The Rev. J.H. Skeen of the First Baptist church will officiate and burial will be in Columbia cemetery."

Nellie continued to live in Summerville (Boulder) Colorado until her death in 1937. All of her seven Summerville homes were inherited by Henry and Elsie Trask. She is buried beside her first husband, David Evans, in unmarked graves with the location unknown in the Gold Hill Cemetery, Gold Hill (Boulder) Colorado.

NICHOLLS, Richard John

Birth: 12/04/1887
Death: 09/24/1941
Cemetery Location: C3

Father: Henry Grenful (some records have Granville) Nicholls; Mother: Elizabeth Jane (*Allen*); Wife: Ethel (*Goudge*); born in Ophir (Tooele) Utah and died in Boulder (Boulder) Colorado at age 53 years, 9 months, 20 days-silicosis; wrong birth year (1888) on tombstone; grand uncle of author; brother to Henry W. Nicholls and Benjamin Allen Nicholls; see NICHOLLS, Benjamin Allen; see NICHOLLS, Edwin Grenful; see NICHOLLS, Nellie (*Beckwith*) Evans; see **About the Henry Grenful/Granville Nicholls Family**; see **About Edwin David "Ned" and Annie Elizabeth (*Bennett(s)*) Goudge**

Boulder Daily Camera 24 September 1941:
"Richard J. Nichols—Richard John Nichols, who was a blacksmith at the Slide mine for five years preceding a long illness, died this morning at his home, 2033 Pine. Mr. Nichols was born Dec. 4, 1887, in Ophir, Utah, Dec. 4, 1887. He came to Boulder forty-nine years ago. Much of his life was spent in working in the mines of Boulder County. Mr. Nichols is survived by his wife, Ethel Goudge Nichols, two daughters, Mrs. Anna Bradford, Casper, Wyo., and Jean Nichols, who graduated from Boulder high school last year. Other survivors are a brother, Benj. Nichols of Boulder, three grandsons, Richard, Wilber and Buckie Bradford. Body at Howe mortuary. Funeral arrangements later."

Boulder Daily Camera 26 September 1941:
"Richard J. Nichols.—Services from Howe mortuary Saturday at 1:30. Rev. Rufus C. Baker, pastor of the Methodist church will officiate. Interment will be in Gold Hill cemetery. Mrs. Anna Bradford, daughter, arrived from Casper today for funeral services and to be with her mother."

About the Henry Grenful/Granville Nicholls Family

Henry Grenful/Granville Nicholls was born about 1850 in (Cornwall) England. It is believed that Henry's middle name was actually Grenful, not Granville as on his tombstone. Richard John (Henry's son) named his first born child, Edwin Grenful, in honor of his wife's father (Edwin David "Ned" Goudge) and his own father (Henry Grenful Nicholls); see **About the Bradford Family**

From Henry's first marriage in (Cornwall) England (wife unknown) one known child was born:

Henry W.: born 27 March 1870 (Cornwall) England and died 29 November 1925 Salina (Boulder) Colorado; buried Columbia Cemetery, Boulder (Boulder) Colorado; married Minnie Viola Croul and Nellie L. (*Beckwith*) Evans; see NICHOLLS, Nellie L. (*Beckwith*) Evans

Henry Grenful/Granville Nicholls then married Elizabeth Jane Allen before 1879 (Cornwall) England. To this union four known children were born:

Janice (Jennie): born April 1879 (Cornwall) England and died December 1914 Breckenridge (Summit) Colorado; burial unknown; married William Shellhammer and Thomas Setten

Henrietta: born 25 October 1883 Utah and died 01 December 1918 Boulder (Boulder) Colorado; buried Green Mountain Cemetery, Boulder (Boulder) Colorado; married Thomas Henry Mitchell

Benjamin Allen: born 31 March 1885 Ophir (Tooele) Utah and died 22 September 1951 Boulder (Boulder) Colorado; buried Gold Hill Cemetery, Gold Hill (Boulder) Colorado; never married; see NICHOLLS, Benjamin Allen

Richard John: born 04 December 1887 Ophir (Tooele) Utah and died 24 September 1941 Boulder (Boulder) Colorado; buried Gold Hill Cemetery, Gold Hill (Boulder) Colorado; married Ethel Goudge; see NICHOLLS, Richard John

The family arrived in Salina (Boulder) Colorado in the early 1890s as Charles F. Cobb (Salina teamster) moved the Nicholls' furniture there. Henry Grenful/Granville Nicholls worked as a miner and also a liquor supplier.

When Henry Grenful/Granville Nicholls died in his Salina home on 15 January 1899 it was first reported in the newspaper that he died from consumption and then a day later the cause of death was changed that he committed suicide however a few days later the cause of death was back to consumption.

Boulder County Herald 18 January 1899:
"W.H. Nichols died at Salina early Sunday morning of consumption."

Boulder News 19 January 1899:
"Suicide...W.N. [wrong initials] Nichols, a Salina miner, committed suicide last Sunday morning, by cutting his throat with a razor. He was a victim of miner's consumption, and it is supposed that he did the deed while despondent. The body was brought here and buried from Trezise's rooms, Rev. E.G. Lane conduction the ceremony, which was attended by a large number of Salina people. He leaves a wife and four children."

Boulder County Herald 25 January 1899:
"W.H. [wrong initials] Nichols, who died at Salina

Sunday, Jan. 156, did not commit suicide as was erroneously reported. He did cut his neck some but he died from the effects of consumption."

On the 9th day of April 1910 Richard John Nicholls married Ethel Goudge in Boulder (Boulder) Colorado in the presence of Mrs. Charles Humphrey (Nellie Goudge, sister of Ethel) and Arthur Goudge (brother of Ethel).
Ethel was born 15 October 1892 in Gold Hill (Boulder) Colorado; the daughter of Edwin David "Ned" and Annie Elizabeth (*Bennett(s)*) Goudge; see GOUDGE, Edwin David "Ned"; see GOUDGE, Annie Elizabeth (*Bennett(s)*).
To this union three known children were born:

Edwin Grenful: born about September 1910 Gold Hill (Boulder) Colorado and died 08 December 1910 Gold Hill (Boulder) Colorado; buried Gold Hill Cemetery, Gold Hill (Boulder) Colorado; see NICHOLLS, Edwin Grenful

Elizabeth Ann "Annie": born 17 December 1912 Gold Hill (Boulder Colorado and died 01 March 1994 Louisville (Boulder) Colorado; buried Mountain View Memorial Park Cemetery, Boulder (Boulder) Colorado; married Harlie Elmer Bradford; see **About the Bradford Family**

Margaret Jean: born 11 March 1924 in Boulder (Boulder) Colorado and died 17 June 1996 Longmont (Boulder) Colorado; buried Mountain View Memorial Park Cemetery, Boulder (Boulder) Colorado; married Ernest Loyd Rapier, Stanley Allen Goff and again to Ernest Loyd Rapier; see **About the Bradford Family**

Henry Grenful/Granville Nicholls' widow, Elizabeth Jane, continued to live in Salina (Boulder) Colorado where she ran a boarding house for many years until her death on 07 March 1921 at University Hospital in Boulder (Boulder) Colorado. She died from cancer of both breasts.

Boulder Daily Camera 08 March 1921:
"Mrs. Elizabeth Jane Nicholls, died at a local institution Monday night at 11:30, at the age of 66 years. She was taken to the institution Sunday in hopes that something could be done to prolong her life. She had been ill with a cancer for a year and a half and this trouble was the cause of her death.
Mrs. Nicholls is the widow of the late H.D. Nicholls, who died 20 years ago at Salina, where he was engaged as a miner. Mrs. Nicholls kept roomers and boarders at Salina since his death, coming to Boulder ten days ago. She leaves two sons, Richard Nicholls and Benjamin Nicholls, and a stepson H.W. Nicholls. Her daughter Mrs. Henrietta Mitchell died two years ago of influenza. Seven grandchildren survive. Mrs. Nicholls was born in Cornwall, Eng.
The body is at the Howe mortuary awaiting funeral arrangements."

Boulder News Herald 08 March 1921:

"Mrs. Elizabeth Jane Nicholls, well known Salina resident, died last night at 11:30 o'clock at the University hospital, where she was taken several days ago. Death was due to cancer, from which she had suffered for eighteen months. Mrs. Nicholls came to Boulder county 27 years ago and during most of the time since had conducted a boarding house at Salina. Through her work she became known to every resident of that district. She was 66 years old.

Surviving relatives are two sons, Richard and Ben, one step-son, H.W. Nicholls and seven grandchildren, all of whom reside in the county. A daughter, Mrs. Henrietta Mitchell of Boulder, died a year ago during the influenza epidemic.

The body is at the Howe mortuary awaiting funeral arrangements."

Henry Grenful/Granville Nicholls, his wife, Elizabeth Jane (*Allen*) Nicholls and Henry's son, Henry W. Nicholls are all buried in the Columbia Cemetery in Boulder (Boulder) Colorado, sharing the same tombstone.

Richard John spent his life mining (blacksmith) in (Boulder) Colorado until his death on 24 September 1941 from silicosis (lung disease from breathing in small particles of silica, a mineral that is part of sand, rock and mineral ores such as quartz). He is buried in the Gold Hill Cemetery in Gold Hill (Boulder) Colorado.

His widow, Ethel, lived about another forty years until her death on 14 July 1881 at Boulder Manor Health Care in Boulder (Boulder) Colorado. Cremated, her ashes are at Mountain View Memorial Park Cemetery, Boulder (Boulder) Colorado.

Boulder Daily Camera 15 July 1981:

"Ethel Goudge Nichols, 4685 Baseline Road, died Tuesday at Boulder Manor Nursing Home. She was 88.

She was born Oct. 15, 1892, at Gold Hill, the daughter of Edwin and Ann Goudge. She married Richard John Nichols in Boulder in April 1909.

She attended Gold Hill elementary and high schools and worked at the University of Colorado for 15 years, retiring in June 1961.

Survivors include two daughters, Ann Bradford and Margaret Jean Rapier, both of Boulder; seven grandchildren, 17 great-grandchildren, and five great-great-grandchildren.

Funeral services will be at 10 a.m. Thursday at Howe Mortuary Chapel. Visitation will be Wednesday evening. A private cremation follows the service."

Author was told by her great Aunt (Ethel (*Goudge*) Nichols), that she was the one who changed the spelling of Nicholls to Nichols, saying "one L was enough."

NILES, William James

Birth: Unknown
Death: 12/22/1888
Cemetery Location: Unknown

Father: unknown; Mother: unknown; Wife: unknown; birth unknown and died in the Spring Gulch area about three miles from Gold Hill (Boulder) Colorado—boiler explosion; Coroner's Inquest Book has 12/24/1888 for date of death; no tombstone; see NOBLE, Henry

Boulder County Herald Weekly 26 December 1888:

"Four Men Killed by a Boiler Explosion...

The boiler at the Hastings saw mill exploded last Saturday afternoon at 3:30 o'clock killing four men. This saw mill was situated about three miles from Gold Hill and about one mile and a half from Left Hand creek, on the way to Gold Lake. The employees were anxious to do a big day's work and bad up a booming fire with low water. The gauge showed 115 pounds of steam. Hastings, the owner, had left the place about 3:15. The water got too low and cold water was run in and this did the damage. Ed. Battles, who saw what was coming yelled "Run boys for your lives, she's going to bust." Either those who were injured did not hear him or did not heed the warning. Battles ran for his life, James Vaughn and "Doc" Barnard got to a place of safety. It was not long before a terrific noise shook the surroundings. The air was full of flying pieces of iron, wood etc., while hot water was running where the boiler had stood. When the smoke had cleared away those who were not injured turned in to hunt for their comrades.

"Lack" Barnard was soon picked up badly scalded. He was taken to the house and there with good care it is hoped he will recover.

James Niles was also picked up badly battered and dead. He leaves a wife and five children, the oldest one 12 years old in Kansas.

Noblet, the sawyer, who was married a year ago, was also found dead. He leaves a wife and a child three weeks old.

Andy Barnard, single, aged about 24 years was also found dead. He was hurt about the head.

Andy McDonald lately from North Carolina was found headless. His body was picked up soon after the accident but his head was nowhere to be seen. Sunday, when the rubbish was cleared away, the head was found in the pit under the fly wheel. McDonald bears no other wound, and the head was cut off so smoothly that it is supposed to have been done by the belt.

It is said that the boiler was blown into so many small pieces that a man could carry the largest piece that was left.

176

Undertaker Trezise went up to the scene of the accident Sunday with four coffins and put the mangled corpses into recognizable shape. The accident has cast a gloom over the entire surroundings and Christmas will not be as happily passed in that vicinity as it was hoped."

Boulder County Herald Weekly 26 December 1888:
"James Niles, one of the men killed at the saw mill explosion, was buried yesterday."

Boulder News 27 December 1888:
"The Christmas tree Tuesday evening at the Gold Hill school house was a grand success. The tree was loaded to its utmost with valuable presents. At the close of the entertainment a collection was taken up for the benefit of the widow and five children in Kansas, left by the death of Wm. Niles, who was killed last Saturday, to be sent to them as a Christmas present."

NOBLET, Henry

Birth: About 1863
Death: 12/22/1888
Cemetery Location: Unknown

Father: Samuel Thompson Noblet; Mother: Rhoda Ann (*Thomas*); Wife: unknown; born about 1863 Kansas and died in the Spring Gulch area three miles from Gold Hill (Boulder) Colorado at age about 38 years-boiler explosion; no tombstone; see NILES, William James

About Henry Noblet

Henry Noblet was born about 1863 in Kansas; the son of Pennsylvania natives Samuel Thompson and Rhoda Ann (*Thomas*) Noblet. They were married in 1841 (Adams) Illinois. To their union seven known children were born:

Elizabeth: born 1846 Missouri-no further information

Samuel Stroul: born 13 January 1848 Lebanon (Collin) Texas (tombstone has 1844) and died 09 April 1916 Rock Springs (Sweetwater) Wyoming; buried Rock Springs Cemetery, Rock Springs (Sweetwater) Wyoming; married Jane Elizabeth Woolstenhulme and Jemima Adeline McCormick

John: born 1850 Texas-no further information

Rhoda Ann: born 15 June 1854 Kansas and died 11 November 1932 Oak Grove (Pawnee) Oklahoma; buried Sinnett Memorial Cemetery, Oak Grove (Pawnee) Oklahoma; married Joseph Staley

Emily "Emma" I.: born 01 March 1860 Kansas and died 11 September 1949 Renton (King) Washington; cremated-ashes at Wright Crematory and Columbarium, Seattle (King) Washington; married John A. King

Henry: born about 1863 Kansas and died 22 December 1888 Hastings Saw Mill near Gold Hill (Boulder) Colorado; buried Gold Hill Cemetery, Gold Hill (Boulder) Colorado; wife's name unknown; see NOBLET, Henry

Bertha Viola: born June 1866 (some records state June 1864) Colorado and died 1906 Denver (Denver) Colorado; buried Fairmount Cemetery, Denver (Denver) Colorado; married A.Z. Hutto and Joseph W. Eads

After traveling through numerous states (Missouri, Texas and Kansas) the family settled in Colorado in the late 1860s and by 1870 they were living in the St. Vrain area (Boulder) Colorado Territory.

Ten years later Rhoda was still living there along with her daughter, Bertha, however Rhoda's husband, Samuel, was living by himself in Left Hand (Boulder) Colorado at that time, working as a ranchman. Henry must have left with his father, Samuel, at the same time as he too ended up in Left Hand (Boulder) Colorado, living in the household of George Batchelder where he was a laborer at the age of 18 years old.

It is believed Rhoda and Samuel parted ways as she was living in the St. Vrain area (Boulder) Colorado with her son, Henry, in the 1885 census. Interesting as she listed herself as widowed.

Samuel married Fannie M. Suthphen in Denver (Denver) Colorado on 12 September 1884 and in the 1885 Colorado census the couple was living in District 2 Gold Hill area (Boulder) Colorado where Samuel was listed at 66 years of age and Fannie at 70 years of age.

According to one family tree on Ancestry.com Samuel died in 1890 Colorado. Rhoda Ann (*Thomas*) Noblet died 24 May 1888 in Spring Gulch near Gold Hill (Boulder) Colorado. No burial records have been located for either Samuel or Rhoda.

According to the newspaper articles Henry was just married (about 1887) but no marriage records have been found in Colorado. It is unknown what happened to his wife or his 3-week old baby.

NOEHRN, Johannes "John" Peter

Birth: 05/13/1861
Death: 09/28/1897
Cemetery Location: Unknown

Father: August Noehrn; Mother: Christine (*Jorgenson/ Juergensen*); Wife: Emma Wilhelmia Francesca (*Klingenberg/Klingenberger*); born in Schleswig-Holstein, Germany and died in Gold Hill (Boulder) Colorado at age 36 years, 4 months, 15 days-heart disease; possible burial; no tombstone

Boulder Daily Camera 28 September 1897:
"John Noehrn, a former resident of Boulder, died at Gold Hill this morning from heart failure. Noehrn was engaged in the drug store business at Gold Hill and

Digging Up Dirt

Harrison Safety Boiler

Engineering and Mining Journal Volume XXXIX
(January to June 1885)

With a passion for safety Joseph Harrison Jr founded the Harrison Safety Boiler Works where he invented the Harrison Safety Boiler that won the First Medal and Diploma for safety, economy of space, and economy of fuel at the American Institute Fair in New York 1869. In May 1871 he received the great gold and silver Rumford medals by the American Academy of Arts & Science "for the mode of constructing steam boilers invented and perfected by [Mr. Harrison] which secures great safety in the use of high-pressure steam, ad is, therefore, an important improvement in the application of heat." (Proceeding of the American Philosophical Society Vol. 14 No. 94 (January to June 1885)

Perhaps if the Hastings Mill had this boiler the tragedy might have been avoided.

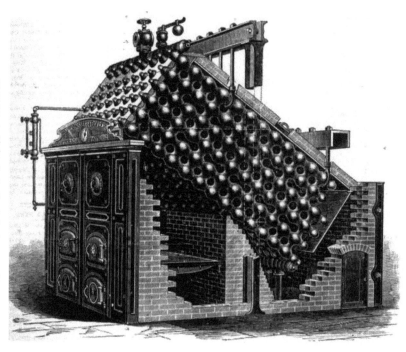

Old mining boiler and hoist at the Fourth of July mine (on the way up to Arapahoe Pass)
Pettem-Raines Collection

formerly worked in Boeck's and Geyler's drug stores in this place. He leaves a wife and five children. Undertaker Trezise sent up to Gold Hill this morning for the remains and they will be held in Boulder until word is received from relatives in Nebraska."

Boulder County Herald (Weekly) 29 September 1897:

"John Noern [sic] died at Gold Hill yesterday of heart trouble. He was in bed chatting with his wife who was up, when he suddenly gasped and was dead. Noern was about 38 years old and leaves a wife and five children. He was conducting a drug store in Gold Hill. He was for a long time connected with the Parlor Drug Store of this place, being night clerk. His remains were brought to Boulder that afternoon by embalmer Trezise."

Boulder News 30 September 1897:

"John Noren [sic] died very suddenly of heart disease Tuesday morning. He was a druggist formerly employed at the Parlor drug store in this city but conducting a store of his own at the time of his death at Gold Hill. The remains were brought to Boulder for burial. He leaves a wife and five children."

Boulder County Herald (Weekly) 06 October 1897:

"J. Noehrn, the druggist who died in Gold Hill of heart disease was buried in Boulder Thursday. His father-in-law H. Klingerber of Chapman, Neb., arrived in time to attend the funeral and provide for his daughter and her children."

About Johannes "John" Peter Noehrn

Johannes "John" Peter Noehrn was born 13 May 1861 in Schleswig-Holstein, Germany; the son of Germany natives August and Christine (*Jorgenson/Juergensen*) Noehrn.

August was born 1832 in Kiel, Schleswig-Holstein, Germany; parents unknown. He married Christine Jorgenson/Juergensen in Germany around 1855. This union produced two known children:

Ann Marie "Mary": born February 1857 Germany and died 07 December 1945 (Clatsop) Oregon; buried Ocean View Cemetery, Warrenton (Clatsop) Oregon; married Asmus Marxen

John (Johannes) Peter: born 13 May 1861 Schleswig-Holstein, Germany and died 28 September 1897 Gold Hill (Boulder) Colorado; buried Gold Hill Cemetery, Gold Hill (Boulder) Colorado or Columbia Cemetery, Boulder (Boulder) Colorado; see NOEHRN, Johannes "John" Peter

The family immigrated to the United States in 1880 (according to the 1900 census records). Ann Marie "Mary" was already married to Asmus Marxen (assuming in Germany) and living in Alda (Hall) Nebraska along with brother, John (Johannes) Peter working as a farmer.

Four years later John (Johannes) Peter Noehrn married Emma Wilhelmia Francesca Klingenberg/Klingenberger on 02 August 1884 in Grand Island (Hall) Nebraska. She was born 29 February 1860 in Davenport (Scott)

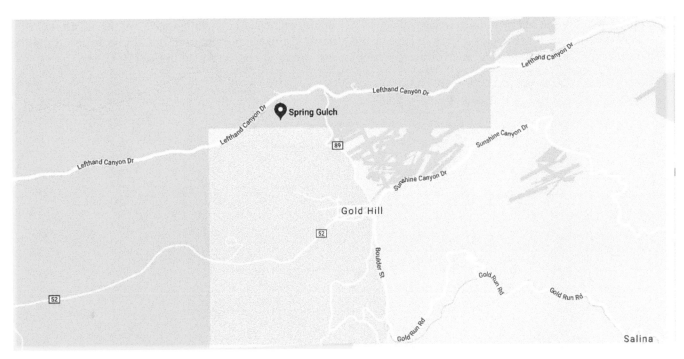

Hastings Mill was located in the Spring Gulch area, located about three miles from Gold Hill and about one mile and a half from Left Hand creek, on the way to Gold Lake (in the upper left corner)

Iowa; the daughter of Hans Asson and Helena Augusta (*Untiedt*) Klingenberg/Klingenberger. To their marriage five known children were born:

Johannes August: born 29 August 1885 Grand Island (Hall) Nebraska and died 20 February 1942 Grand Island (Hall) Nebraska; buried Grand Island Cemetery, Grand Island (Hall) Nebraska; married Lois E. Walker

Adela H.: born 29 October 1888 Grand Island (Hall) Nebraska and died 22 October 1976 Grand Island (Hall) Nebraska; buried Grand Island Cemetery, Grand Island (Hall) Nebraska; married Adolph D. Boehm

Marie Antoinette: born 17 July 1891 Grand Island (Hall) Nebraska and died 18 April 1979 Lutcher (St. James) Louisiana; burial unknown; married Col. Loren Read Brooks

Florence Agnes: born 04 May 1893 Grand Island (Hall) Nebraska and died 07 June 1965 Grand Island (Hall) Nebraska; buried Westlawn Memorial Cemetery, Grand Island (Hall) Nebraska; married Albert Fred Schmidt

Augusta C.: born 22 July 1897 Gold Hill (Boulder) Colorado and died 05 January 1975 Kearney (Buffalo) Nebraska; buried Kearney Cemetery, Kearney (Buffalo) Nebraska; married Gerhardt A. Schmidt and Emmett M. Register

After the death of John (Johannes) Peter Noehrn his widow, Emma married Claus Dammann on 18 October 1906 in Worms (Merrick) Nebraska. He was born 25 July 1850 in Hannover, Stadt Hannover, Niedersachsen, Germany; the son of Johann Hinrich and Metta (*Bosselman*) Dammann. No children blessed this marriage.

Claus died on 26 March 1930 and is buried in the Zion Lutheran Church Cemetery in Worms (Merrick) Nebraska. Emma died on 31 May 1940 in Grand Island (Hall) Nebraska and is buried in the Grand Island Cemetery, Grand Island (Hall) Nebraska.

Kim Dryer-Church (relative):

"The story of my 2nd time Great-Grandfather [John/Johannes Peter Noehrn] has been hotly contested since my Grandmother was a little girl. The Noehrn's moved to Gold Hill from Grand Island, Nebraska after my Great Grandfather (also Johannes) was born in 1885. They lived and ran the pharmacy/general store. Johannes (Peter) died suddenly at the young age of 36, leaving behind a wife and 5 children, one of whom (Great Aunt Augusta or 'Gussy' to her family) was only 2 months old.

His widow [Emma] struggled to make ends meet and eventually had to move back to Nebraska to be near family. The contested part of the story surrounds the fact that he was buried in the dirt floor basement of the shop temporarily, as he died in late Sept and the cemetery ground was already frozen over for the winter. My Grandmother left pages and pages of notes and dozens of phone numbers and names of people that she talked to in her quest to find out whether or not he (John) actually made it to Columbia Cemetery the next spring. In her opinion, he was undoubtedly removed from the cellar of the shop, but back in the 50's, the cemetery manager/keeper couldn't confirm that he was actually in a plot at Columbia. According to my Grandmother (who is now passed), there is a record of his registration but he was not assigned a plot, which happened once the body arrived. This drove my Grandmother crazy, and she made multiple trips to Boulder and Gold Hill, talking to all of the old-timers. She never got to the bottom of it, but always believed that he was put in the potter's field in Gold Hill."

O

OLIVIERI, Frances Rosemary (*Wojcik*)

Birth: 05/20/1931
Death: 11/19/2006
Cemetery Location: G2

Father: Joseph S. Wojcik; Mother: Mary Ellen (*Hagerman*); Husband: Michael Lill Olivieri; born in Mansfield (Richland) Ohio and died in Brighton (Adams) Colorado at age 75 years, 5 months, 30 days-natural causes

Brighton Standard Blade 22 November 2006:

"Francis Olivieri, 75, of Brighton passed away on November 19, 2006 at her home. Her husband, Michael Sr., daughter Katherine, and parents Mary and Joseph Wojcik predeceased her. She is survived by her daughter Margaret Carleton (Randy), son Joseph (Bonnie), and son Michael Jr. (Janet). Five grandchildren, one step-grandchild, five great-grandchildren, three sisters, one brother and numerous nieces and nephews also survive her. Frances loved music, reading, the mountains, flowers, and all forms of nature. Most of all she loved her husband, her family and her friends."

Personal letter from Frances Rosemary (Wojcik) Olivieri 02 July 1997:

"My husband, Mike, and I bought the Horseshoe claim 37 years ago. (We moved to Colorado from our home in Ohio in 1959) We spent every weekend and most summers there. Our three children and so far, five grandchildren have been able to enjoy it.

Mike started the first Vocational Auto Mechanics Program at Brighton High School in 1964, then advanced to counselor, and retired as Assistant Principal in 1985. He was very active in community affairs in Brighton, including serving as City Councilman for two terms. In Brighton he belonged to the community and his job. At the cabin, he belonged to the family. Thus, the bench—the Good Times.

We did not socialize a lot with the people of Gold Hill, as the cabin was our "get away from it all" haven. However, we did know some of the citizens—the Finns, the Masons, Kip Carpenter, etc. We did not intend to be standoffish, just needed some quiet time after the hectic lifestyle in Brighton.

Mike passed away Jan. 31, 1993. (DOB 1-4-30). He was cremated. His ashes have not been scattered or buried, as the plan is for me to be cremated when the time comes, our ashes mixed, then disposed of as our children see fit. The bench is just a tangible symbol of what the mountains meant to us, and still means to me and our children. A memorial to Mike and the Good Times."

OLIVIERI, Michael Lill

Birth: 01/04/1930
Death: 01/31/1993
Cemetery Location: G2

Father: Camillo Olivieri; Mother: Ester (*Travalengia/ Travaglino/Travaine*); Wife: Frances Rosemary (*Wojcik*); died at age 63 years, 0 months, 27 days-cause of death unknown

Personal letter from Mike Olivieri (date unknown):

"Mike and Fran moved to Brighton, Colorado from Mansfield, Ohio in 1959. They had come to Colorado a year earlier on vacation and fell in love with it. A few years later, they bought the Willie W Claim near Gold Hill. Weekends were spent working on the cabin and exploring the mine tunnel into the side of the mountain. A few more years went by until they found out that the cabin at the Willie W they had been working on actually sat on the Horseshoe claim owned by Mr. Moore. Mr. Moore finally agreed to sell the Horseshoe Claim to Mike and

Fran. The deal was done on January 27, 1967, the same night as the Apollo 1 fire that took the life of three astronauts. Weekends, summers, falls, anytime possible was spent at the Horseshoe fixing it up. Mike and Fran enjoyed the Gold Hill area, the Gold Hill Inn, fishing in Left Hand Canyon, and sending the grandkids to the Trojan Ranch during the summer. After their children had left home and married, many family reunions were held at the Horseshoe. Fire, rains, snow, and animals were just a few of the stories that were able to be told about the area and our visits.

After Mike passed in 1993, Fran did her best with the help of the children to keep the property up. Fran would spend nights on her own at the Horseshoe watching the stars and taking time to read. After 13 years, Fran was no longer able physically to get to the property. After her passing, it was the decision of all three children to sell the property to Boulder County for open space so the area would not be developed into a "Mountain Mansion." Two of the children still check on the Horseshoe and Willie W to this day.

It was the wish of Mike and Fran to be buried together in the Gold Hill Cemetery. Fran had a red stone bench placed in the cemetery at the spot where they wanted to be buried after Mike died. On July 1, 2007, family, friends, and relatives met at the Gold Hill Cemetery to fulfill the last wish of Mike and Fran.

I cannot find the obituary for Dad. I don't know where it went. I can tell you that his parents moved to America from Italy and that dad [Michael] was the first generation American born in 1930. He married Fran in 1950 in Mansfield, Ohio while in the Marines. After the service, he worked as an auto mechanic for Ford. When he moved to Colorado, he worked for Ling Ford (now Brighton Ford). He went into business with a partner and had his own auto service shop before becoming an auto mechanics teacher at Brighton High School. He worked his way up to Assistant Principal at the school before retiring in 1988. During the summers and after retiring from the school, Mike worked with Bob Sakata at Sakata Farms in Brighton. Mike really liked to work with his hands. Auto mechanics, farm equipment, and doing wood work on both the Willie W and the Horseshoe dwellings was [sic] a passion."

About Michael L. and Frances Rosemary (*Wojcik*) Olivieri

Frances Rosemary was born 20 May 1931 in Mansfield (Richland) Ohio; the daughter of Joseph S. and Mary E. (*Hagerman*) Wojcik. Frances married Michael Lill Olivieri on 06 February 1950 in (Richland) Ohio at the young age of 18 years.

Michael Lill Olivieri was born 04 January 1930 in Mansfield (Richland) Ohio; the son of Camillo and Ester (*Travalengia/Travaglino/Travaine*) Olivieri. To their union four children were born: Michael Jr., Joseph, Margaret and Katherine who died a few days after being born.

After the death of Frances, the ashes of Michael and Frances were mixed and interred in the area of their beloved bench in the Gold Hill Cemetery, Gold Hill (Boulder) Colorado.

ORR, Elizabeth A. (*McWilliams*)

Birth: 02/1831
Death: 01/18/1907
Cemetery Location: D1

Father: John M. McWilliams; Mother: Sarah (*maiden name unknown*); Husband: James Washington Orr; born in Pennsylvania and died in Gold Hill (Boulder) Colorado at age (approximately) 76 years-old age

About Elizabeth A. (*McWilliams*) Orr

Elizabeth A. McWilliams was born in Pennsylvania on February 1831; the daughter of Pennsylvania natives John/James M. and Sarah (maiden name unknown) McWilliams.

In the 1850 census Elizabeth was 19 years old, living in Pulaski (Lawrence) Pennsylvania with her parents and siblings:

George: born about 1830 Kittanning (Armstrong) Pennsylvania-death unknown; burial unknown; married Nancy Jane Thompson

Samuel R.: born about 1833 Pulaski (Mercer) Pennsylvania and died 08 November 1892 Leavenworth (Leavenworth) Kansas; buried Leavenworth National Cemetery, Leavenworth (Leavenworth) Kansas; never married

Jane C.: born about 1836 Pennsylvania-no further information

James M.: born April 1838 New Castle (Lawrence) Pennsylvania and died 1929 (Rock Island) Illinois; buried Coal Valley Cemetery, Coal Valley (Rock Island) Illinois; married Nancy Griffin

In the early 1850s Elizabeth A. McWilliams married James Washington Orr. Born in 1827 in Maryland, he was the son of Maryland natives James and Sarah (maiden name unknown) Orr. To this union four known children were born:

Nellie: born 13 September 1853 Illinois and died 19 July 1924 Riverton (Franklin) Nebraska; buried Riverton Valley View Cemetery, Grant (Franklin) Nebraska; married Charles A. Holden; 1860 census and 1870 census has Nellie's name as Sarah

Anna M.: born 19 August 1858 Illinois and died 29 August 1920 Chico (Butte) California; buried Chico Cemetery, Chico (Butte) California; married Benjamin Thomas Fuller

Emma Jane "Jenny": born September 1863 (Marshall) Illinois and died 30 July 1923 (Highlands) Florida; buried Pinecrest Cemetery, Sebring (Highlands) Florida; married Ira Munsell/Munselle

Hattie J.: born about 1867 Lima (Adams) Illinois; 1885 living in Grant (Franklin) Nebraska

By 1860 the family was living in Richland (Marshall) Illinois where James Washington Orr was a farmer. His real estate was valued at $5,000 and his personal estate valued at $1,443.

Sometime between the 1860 census and the 1870 census James died leaving Elizabeth a widow at the young age of 39 years. It is believed he died in (Marshall) Illinois.

In the 1870 census Elizabeth Orr and her children (Nellie (Sarah), Anna, Emma (Jenny) and Hattie) along with her parents (John and Sarah McWilliams) were living in Steuben (Marshall) Illinois where Elizabeth was keeping house.

Sometime between 1870 and 1880 Elizabeth's mother, Sarah McWilliams, died as in 1880 her father, John McWilliams, is listed as a widow. Interesting to note that in the 1880 census John McWilliams is listed as Elizabeth's brother which is incorrect. It states Elizabeth's parents were born in Pennsylvania and John's parents were born in Ireland. Also, there is a 34 year difference in age between John and Elizabeth. Obviously the census taker didn't write down the correct relationship between John McWilliams and Elizabeth (*McWilliams*) Orr.

Five years later Elizabeth (age 54 years) moved to Grant (Franklin) Nebraska with her daughter, Hattie, (age 18 years) and her father, John McWilliams, (age 88 years). In this census record John is listed as Elizabeth's father. He died sometime between 1885 and 1900 however there are no burial records for a John McWilliams in (Franklin) Nebraska.

Elizabeth made her way to Gold Hill (Boulder) Colorado to live with her daughter, Anna (*Orr*) Fuller, son-in-law, Benjamin Thomas Fuller and granddaughter, Hazel.

Digging Up Dirt

Elizabeth enjoyed the Gold Hill area for seven years until her death on 18 January 1907 where she died at approximately 76 years old (probably from old age). Her daughter, Anna, and son-in-law, Benjamin, erected a most beautiful tombstone in her memory in the Gold Hill Cemetery.

P

PATTON, Allie R. (*Walton*)

> Birth: 04/28/1868
> Death: 09/05/1888
> Cemetery Location: C3

Father: Leonard R. Walton; Mother: Elizabeth Ellen H. (*Rule*); Husband: William Howard Patton; born in Shullsburg (Lafayette) Wisconsin and died in Gold Hill (Boulder) Colorado at age 20 years, 4 months, 8 days-rupture of a blood vessel; see WALTON, Leonard R.; see WALTON, Elizabeth "Lizzie" Ellen H. (*Rule*); see **About Leonard R. and Elizabeth "Lizzie" Ellen H. (*Rule*) Walton**; see PATTON, William Howard; see **About William Howard Patton**

Boulder News 11 September 1888:

> "Mrs. Patton, of Gold Hill, died last Tuesday night caused, by the rupture of a blood vessel. Her sudden

death was a great shock to the community, where she was known and loved by all. The funeral was at the church on Thursday afternoon, preached by Rev. Kirkbride and was largely attended by the sorrowing friends of the deceased. Her death is a great loss."

About Allie R. (*Walton*) Patton

Allie R. Walton was born 28 April 1868 in Shullsburg (Lafayette) Wisconsin to Leonard R. and Elizabeth Ellen (*Rule*) Walton; see WALTON, Leonard R.; see WALTON, Elizabeth "Lizzie" Ellen (*Rule*).

On 28 September 1887 Allie married William Howard Patton in Boulder (Boulder) Colorado. Unfortunately Allie died before any children blessed this marriage.

History of the Oscar Walton and Minnie Pearl Barnette Family (as of June 1999) sent to Jim Cox by Kathleen Kautzman 31 May 1999:

> "A story of Allie Walton Patton is that she was pregnant and went to the outhouse one day. Her mother had seen her go, while she was hanging out clothes. She meant to check on Allie but forgot and when William came home and couldn't find Allie, her mother remembered the outhouse. When they checked it they found that Allie had miscarried and bled to death."

PATTON, Harriet "Hattie" May (*Hedges*)

> Birth: 11/13/1866
> Death: 11/18/1957
> Cemetery Location: E1

Father: David Jones Hedges; Mother: Elizabeth (*Ward*); Husband: William Howard Patton (his first wife was Allie R. Walton; see PATTON, Allie R. (*Walton*)); 2ⁿᵈ Husband: Jacob N. Dillenburg; born in Eureka (Woodford) Illinois and died in Denver (Denver) Colorado at age 91 years, 0 months, 5 day-natural causes; other sources state born in Panola (Woodford) Illinois; see PATTON, William Howard; see **About Harriet "Hattie" May (*Hedges*) Patton**; see **About William Howard Patton**

Boulder Daily Camera 20 November 1957:

"Mrs. Hattie Dillenburg

Interment in the Gold Hill Cemetery will follow funeral services Friday at 11 for Mrs. Hattie M. Dillenburg, 2400 S. Lincoln, Denver, who died Monday. The services are to be held from the Howard Mortuary, East 17ᵗʰ and Marion at Park Avenue in Denver.

Mrs. Dillenburg, better remembered in Boulder as the widow of W.H. Patton, suffered a fractured hip in a fall last summer. She was 91 and a former teacher at Jamestown and Gold Hill, coming to Boulder county [sic] in 1888 from Eureka, Ill., where she was born Nov. 13, 1866.

She was married to Mr. Patton, who was a miner and rancher at Gold Hill, in 1890. Years after his death she married Joseph Dillenburg who preceded her in death.

Surviving are three children by her first marriage, Howard Patton, Denver; Alva J. Patton, Watkins, Colo.; and Mrs. Rosamond Westover, Yreka, Calif., who was at her mother's bedside. There are ten grand and fourteen great grandchildren."

About Harriet "Hattie" May (*Hedges*) Patton

Hattie "Hattie" May Hedges was born in Panola or Eureka (Woodford) Illinois on 13 November 1866, the daughter of West Virginia natives David Jones and Elizabeth B. (*Ward*) Hedges.

Her father, David Jones Hedges, was a farmer in Greene (Woodford) Illinois who died about two years after Hattie/Harriet May was born, leaving his widowed wife, Elizabeth, with five children to care for. She died on 29 March 1873 in Eureka (Woodford) Illinois and was buried in the Old Methodist Cemetery, Eureka (Woodford) Illinois alongside her husband, David, who died 14 May 1868.

In 1880 Harriet "Hattie" May was living with her grandmother, Harriett Ward, along with sisters Nancy Edora and Mary Ellen in Bloomington (McLean) Illinois.

Oldest sister, Nancy Edora, ventured to Colorado where on 16 September 1884 she married Cyrus W. Montgomery and lived in Jamestown (Boulder) Colorado. The 1885 Colorado State Census lists her as a school teacher. In 1888 Harriet "Hattie" May followed her sister to Colorado where she, too, was a school teacher in Jamestown and Gold Hill (Boulder) Colorado.

She met and married widower William Howard Patton on 02 September 1890 at the Trinity Methodist Church in Denver (Denver) Colorado. To this union five known children were born:

Rosamond Edith: born 17 May 1891 Gold Hill (Boulder) Colorado-17 April died 1965 San Bernardino (San Bernardino) California; buried Green Acres Memorial Park & Mortuary, Bloomington (San Bernardino) California; married Albert Edward McClellen and Nester A. Westover

Howard: born 02 March 1893 Gold Hill (Boulder) Colorado and died 01 July 1962 Denver (Denver) Colorado; buried Fort Logan National Cemetery, Denver (Denver) Colorado; never married

Rosalia: born 13 March 1895 Gold Hill (Boulder) Colorado and died 13 April 1911 Gold Hill (Boulder) Colorado; buried Gold Hill Cemetery, Gold Hill (Boulder) Colorado; never married; see PATTON, Rosalia

Marian: born 23 November 1898 Gold Hill (Boulder) Colorado and died 24 February 1955 Abilene (Taylor) Texas; buried Casper (Natrona) Wyoming; married Richard Oscar Langworthy

Alva John: born 01 July 1900 Gold Hill (Boulder) Colorado and died 17 June 1972 Watkins (Adams) Colorado; buried Ft. Logan National Cemetery, Denver (Denver) Colorado; married Russella P. Pelton

The family lived west of Gold Hill (Boulder) Colorado on a ranch which was located on the property now known as Colorado Mountain Ranch (County Road 52). William Howard Patton bought this property from Frank Johnson in the late 1890s.

William and Hattie enjoyed over 14 years of marriage until his death on 27 March 1915 in his Gold Hill home from myocarditis (an inflammation of the middle layer of the heart wall which could lead to a stroke or heart attack). He was buried in the Gold Hill Cemetery, Gold Hill (Boulder) Colorado.

About two years later his widow remarried.

Boulder Daily Camera 23 April 1917:

"MRS. HATTIE PAATON [sic] MARRIED.

Friends of Mrs. Hattie M. Patton of Gold Hill will be surprised to hear of her marriage, which took place in Denver on Saturday to Jacob M. Dillenburg of Fleming, Colo., where she has been teaching the past year. The bride and groom returned to Gold Hill last evening to make their home on the fine ranch, which their sons, Alvan and Howard, have been in charge of. She has a daughter in Wellington, who teaches school there and one in the telephone office."

By 1920 Harriet "Hattie" May and her second husband, Jacob M. Dillenburg, moved from Gold Hill (Boulder) Colorado to Barr (Adams) Colorado along with Hattie's children Howard, Marian and Alva John.

Apparently the marriage didn't work out as on 28 April 1928 in Boulder (Boulder) Colorado a divorce was granted and Hattie ended up as a matron at the Denver Orphans Home in 1930.

She died in Denver (Denver) Colorado on 18 November 1957 at the age of 91 years and is buried in the Gold Hill Cemetery, Gold Hill (Boulder) Colorado. Interesting to note she dropped "Dillenburg" from her name.

PATTON, Jennifer Sue

Birth: 06/17/1959
Death: 02/05/2003
Cemetery Location: B1

Father: Hager Patton; Mother: Elinor Ruth "Elli" (*Emerick*); born in Boulder (Boulder) Colorado and died in Blythe (Riverside) California at age 43 years, 7 months, 19 days and died in her sleep; sister to Sharrel "Shari" Lea Patton; see PATTON, Sharrel "Shari" Lea; see COX, Elinor Ruth "Elli" (*Emerick*) Patton

Boulder Daily Camera 08 February 2003:
"Jennifer Sue Patton—Jennifer Sue Patton of Blythe, Calif., formerly of Boulder, died in her sleep on Wednesday, February 5, 2003, in Blythe. She was 43. The cause of death is pending coroner's investigation. Born June 17, 1959, in Boulder, she was the daughter of Hager Patton and Elinor Emerick Patton. Ms. Patton worked in accounting. She attended Gold Hill Elementary, Ecole Thonex in Geneva, Switzerland, and Boulder High School, and graduated from Barnes Business College in Denver. Survivors include her father of Texas; her mother, Elinor Cox of Boulder; a stepbrother, Andy Cox of Denver; and two stepsisters, Cindy Cox Dyer of Maryland and Patricia Cox Shellhaas of Georgia. She was preceded in death by a sister, Shari Patton, in 1990, and her stepfather, Jim Cox. A private family burial will be at Gold Hill. Contributions

may be made to the Gold Hill Cemetery Fund, in care of the Gold Hill Town Meeting, 1011 Main St., Boulder, CO 80302. Frye Chapel and Mortuary in California is in charge of arrangements."

PATTON, Rosalia

Birth: 03/13/1895
Death: 04/13/1911
Cemetery Location: E1

Father: William Howard Patton; Mother: Harriet "Hattie" May (*Hedges*); born and died in Gold Hill (Boulder) Colorado at age 16 years, 1 month-typhoid fever; see PATTON, William Howard; see **About William Howard Patton**; see PATTON, Harriet "Hattie" May (*Hedges*); see **About Harriet "Hattie" May (*Hedges*) Patton**

Boulder County Miner 06 April 1911:
"Miss Rosalia Patton has been sick and it will be some time before she will be able to return to Boulder, where she is attending school."

Boulder County Miner 13 April 1911:
"Rosalie Patton, the sixteen-year-old daughter of Mr. and Mrs. W.H. Patton of Gold Hill, died at her home in Gold Hill this morning at 10 o'clock. Miss Patton was well known in Boulder where, up to the spring vacation, she had been attending the Prep. School."

Boulder Daily Camera 13 April 1911:
"DEATH OF ROSALIE PATTON POPULAR GOLD HILL GIRL...
The death of Miss Rosalie Paton at Gold Hill comes as a great shock to her many Boulder friends, especially her schoolmates at Prep school, of which she had been a student and had gone home for her spring vacation when taken ill with typhoid fever. She died this morning at the age of sixteen years. While in Boulder she made her home with Mr. and Mrs. Norman Mills and was an active worker in the Epworth League and a member of the M.E. Sunday school. Mr. and Mrs. W.H. Patton, of Gold Hill, her

parents, are heartbroken over her death. She was their oldest child and loved by all who knew her."

PATTON, Sharrel "Shari" Lea

Birth: 12/30/1960
Death: 01/30/1990
Cemetery Location: B1

Father: Hager Patton; Mother: Elinor Ruth "Elli" (*Emerick*); born in Boulder (Boulder) Colorado and died in Fort Collins (Larimer) Colorado at age 29 years, 1 month-sudden illness; sister to Jennifer Sue Patton; see PATTON, Jennifer Sue; see COX, Elinor Ruth "Elli" (*Emerick*) Patton

Boulder Daily Camera 01 February 1990:

"Shari Patton—Shari Patton, a former Boulder resident, died Tuesday, Jan. 30th, of a sudden illness at the Poudre Valley Memorial Hospital in Fort Collins. She was 29. She was born Dec. 30, 1960, in Boulder, the daughter of Hager Patton and Elinor Emerick Patton. She grew up in Gold Hill and graduated from Boulder High School in 1978. She moved to Fort Collins in 1987 and was a child care worker. She is survived by her father of Fort Worth, Texas; her mother, Elinor Cox of Boulder; her fiancé, Clifford Stevens of Fort Collins; a sister, Jennifer Shepard of Gold Hill; a half-brother, John Cox of Boulder; and a maternal grandfather, Ralph D. Emerick of Parkersburg, W. Va. Graveside services will be held at 2 p.m. Saturday at the Gold Hill Cemetery, with the Rev. L. Gerald Burrus officiating. Contributions can be sent to the Shari Patton Memorial Fund, in care of the Gold Hill Town Hall, Salina Star Route, Boulder 80302. Howe Mortuary is handling arrangements."

PATTON, William Howard

Birth: 03/30/1858
Death: 03/27/1915
Cemetery Location: E1

Father: John Anderson Patton; Mother: Virginia E (*Carter*); 1st Wife: Allie R. (*Walton*); 2nd Wife: Harriet "Hattie" May (*Hedges*); born in Tiskilwa (Bureau) Illinois and died in Gold Hill (Boulder) Colorado at age 56 years, 11 months, 27 days-myocarditis; tombstone states birth 04/06/1858; see **About William Howard Patton**; see PATTON, Allie R. (*Walton*); see PATTON, Harriet "Hattie" May (*Hedges*); see **About Harriet "Hattie" May (*Hedges*) Patton**; see PATTON, Rosalia

Boulder Daily Camera 29 March 1915:

"W.H. PATTON IS DEAD AT GOLD HILL HOME

After a brief illness William H. Patton died at Gold Hill this morning. He would have been 57 had he lived until March 30, having been born in Michigan in 1858. For 36 years he was a resident of Boulder county, most of the time at Gold Hill. His widow, Hattie M. Patton, two sons and two daughters survive. Three of the children live at Gold Hill and one, "Miss Rosamund," is teaching on the Western Slope. She started for home on receipt of notice of her father's probable demise.

Mr. Patton was a fine type of man, as a miner and mountain ranchman successfully coping with such obstacles as presented. He is best known as a former esteemed commissioner of Boulder county, having been selected as a Democrat in the 90s. Later years he devoted his time to farming and wrote much of value regarding ranching in the mountains. He grew some of the best potatoes on his little place near Gold Hill that were ever brought to Boulder and was paid an extra price for them. He contended that in the foothills of Colorado agriculture is to develop conditions akin to those in Switzerland, where millions of people live by the culture of root, grain and grapes. He was known to his friends as Howard and esteemed by all who knew him. The funeral will be at Gold Hill Wednesday at 1 p.m."

Boulder Daily Camera 31 March 1915:

"The funeral of W.H. Patton, who died Monday at his home in Gold Hill, took place at 1:30 this afternoon at the Methodist church, Rev. R.H. Forrester of the M.E. church of Boulder, was in charge of the services. He with Mrs. Montgomery, sister of Mrs. Patton, drove to Gold Hill this morning. The church was crowded with the many friends of the family and many mines were closed so the employees could attend the services. The school was closed as Mrs. Patton for many years was a member of the board, refusing nomination last year on account of ill health. Mrs. J. Goudge presided at the organ and Mesdames Oscar Walton, John Copps and Mesara Scott, Brown and John Romig sang several selections."

About William Howard Patton

William Howard Patton was born 30 March 1858 in (Bureau) Illinois; the son of Pennsylvania native John Anderson and Maryland native Virginia E. (*Carter*) Patton.

In the 1860 census the family was living in Indiantown (Bureau) Illinois where John was a tailor. Years later the family increased with six known siblings for William:

Charles A.: born 1861 (Bureau) Illinois and died 15 August 1862 (Bureau) Illinois; buried Mount Bloom Cemetery, Tiskilwa (Bureau) Illinois

Virginia Jennie "Virgie": born 1864 Indiantown or Tiskilwa (Bureau) Illinois and died 1886 Tiskilwa (Bureau) Illinois; buried Mount Bloom Cemetery, Tiskilwa (Bureau) Illinois; never married

George R.: born 1867 Indiantown or Tiskilwa (Bureau) Illinois and died after 1880 Tiskilwa (Bureau) Illinois; buried Mount Bloom Cemetery, Tiskilwa (Bureau) Illinois; He is listed in the Early Burials with no death date

Susie: born Tiskilwa (Bureau) Illinois and died Tiskilwa (Bureau) Illinois; no dates given but in the Early Burials at age 2 (not in the 1870 or the 1880 census records)

Infant "Sweaney": born 1874 Tiskilwa (Bureau) Illinois and died 1874 Tiskilwa (Bureau) Illinois; buried Mount Bloom Cemetery, Tiskilwa (Bureau) Illinois

Mary Isabelle: born 25 June 1875 (Bureau) Illinois and died 21 June 1958 Tiskilwa (Bureau) Illinois; buried Mount Bloom Cemetery, Tiskilwa (Bureau) Illinois; married Joseph Kaufmann Jr.

Peterson Plot in the Gold Hill Cemetery
The only marker in the plot is that of William Bernard Peterson/Petersen/Gustafson
Formations of graves in the plot are very difficult to visualize

Digging Up Dirt

In the 1880 census William Howard Patton had left the household and ventured to Black Hawk (Gilpin) Colorado to pursue his dreams of mining. He first married Allie R. Walton on 28 Sept 1887, however this marriage was a short one as she miscarried and died on 5 Sept 1888; see PATTON, Allie R. (*Walton*). On 2 September 1890 he married Harriet "Hattie" May Hedges on 02 September 1890 in Denver (Denver) Colorado and moved to Gold Hill (Boulder) Colorado. The family lived west of town on a ranch which was located on the property now known as Colorado Mountain Ranch (County Road 52). William Howard Patton bought this property from Frank Johnson in the late 1890s. On 09 November 1898 a fire occurred at the Patton home:

Boulder County Herald 16 November 1898:

"FIRE AT GOLD HILL...

County commissioner Patton left for his home at Gold Hill last Thursday on information that his house had been visited by a fire last Wednesday. Nick Meyer, the Gold Hill detective, was in the city Thursday and says the damage done may amount to two hundred dollars.

That evening while Mrs. Patton was at work in one room the children were playing in another. The little boy in running around the table accidentally had his clothes caught in the table cloth. In running he pulled it off and down came the lamp on the floor. Mrs. Patton rushed in, grabbed the blazing lamp and wanted to throw it out of the door. The children had locked the door, so she ran into the other room to throw it out of the front door. Before she got there the blaze became too hot and she was obliged to drop the lamp and the house caught fire. Neighbors rushed in and saved the house from utter destruction."

Boulder County Herald 17 November 1898:

"County commissioner Patton was in his chair in the commissioners' office last Monday. He says the damage by fire, at his home at Gold Hill last week, was about two hundred dollars. He shudders when he talks of the narrow escape his wife and children had from being burned to death."

Along with his mining he was quite known for his ability to grow potatoes.

Boulder County Miner & Farmer 23 February 1911:

"AGRICULTURAL POSSIBILITIES

Farmer Patton of Gold Hill, who has made good in

Peterson Plot in the Gold Hill Cemetery
The only marker in the plot is that of William Bernard Peterson/Petersen/Gustafson
Formations of graves in the plot are very difficult to visualize

potato growing at an altitude of over 8,000 feet, truly said in his address before the Mountain and Plain Institute, "I fully realize that I am about 25 years ahead of my time—It may be that long before the faming possibilities of the mountains will be appreciated."

William and Hattie enjoyed over 14 years of marriage until his death on 27 March 1915 in his Gold Hill home from myocarditis (an inflammation of the middle layer of the heart wall which could lead to a stroke or heart attack). He was buried in the Gold Hill Cemetery, Gold Hill (Boulder) Colorado.

PETERSON/PETERSEN/GUSTAFSON, Billie Bernard

> Birth: 02/02/1931
> Death: 02/04/1931
> Cemetery Location: F3

Father: William Bernard Peterson/Petersen/Gustafson; Mother: Bertha (*Schleiger/Schleigher*); born and died in Gold Hill (Boulder) Colorado at age 2 days-cause of death unknown; no tombstone; see PETERSON/ PETERSEN/ GUSTAFSON, Gustof Louis "Gus;" see PETERSON/ PETERSEN/ GUSTAFSON, Ida Matilda (*Burke*); see PETERSON/PETERSEN/GUSTAFSON, William Bernard; see **About the Peterson/Petersen/Gustafson Family**

Boulder Daily Camera 06 February 1931:

"BILLIE B. PETERSON
    Funeral services for Billie Bernard Peterson, infant son of Mr. and Mrs. William B. Peterson, who died Wednesday, Feb. 4th, was held at the Howe mortuary at 11 o'clock this morning. Rev. C.O. Beckman of the Methodist church officiated. Interment was in the Gold Hill cemetery."

PETERSON/PETERSEN/GUSTAFSON, Gustof Louis "Gus"
(Previously listed as PETERSON, Gustof Adolph)

> Birth: 01/10/1859
> Death: 01/24/1921
> Cemetery Location: F3

Father: unknown; Mother: unknown; Wife: Ida Matilda (*Burke*); born in Sweden and died in Boulder (Boulder) Colorado at age 62 years, 0 months, 14 days-fibrosis phthisis (tuberculosis); mortuary record is under the name of Gustof L. Gustofson; 1910 census lists his name as "Augustus;" Gustof was previously listed in the Gold Hill Cemetery Record (Second Edition June, 1994) as Gustof Adolph which is incorrect. There is a Gustof Adolph Gustafson (born 16 June 1872 and died 18

October 1913) who lived in the Boulder County area. He was married to Hadda Mathilda Latt and both are buried in the Mountain View Cemetery in Longmont (Boulder) Colorado; no tombstone; see PETERSON/ PETERSEN/ GUSTAFSON, Ida Matilda (*Burke*); see **About the Peterson/Petersen/Gustafson Family**

Boulder Daily Camera 25 January 1921:

"GUS PETERSEN, PIONEER MINER IS DEAD FROM PNEUMONIA
    "Gus" Petersen, an early pioneer and miner in Boulder County died at his home at Twenty-third and Walnut streets last night. Death was due to pneumonia. Mr. Petersen came to Boulder county thirty years ago, and was one of the early settlers of Gold Hill. He is survived by a son, William Petersen [sic], and a daughter Mrs. Matilda Boman [sic]. The funeral arrangements have not been perfected. Burial will take place in Gold Hill. The body will remain at the Boulder Undertaking company until the cemetery at Gold Hill is opened up."
    (Mortuary record states cause of death was fibrosis phthisis.)

Boulder Daily Camera 26 January 1921:

"FUNERAL OF GUS PETERSEN
    The funeral of "Gus" Petersen will be held at the funeral parlors of the Boulder Undertaking company at 10 o'clock Thursday morning. Rev. Lou Harris will be the pastor in charge. Pallbearers will be selected from the friends of the deceased who live at Gold Hill. Burial will be made at Gold Hill."

PETERSON/PETERSEN/GUSTAFSON, Ida Matilda (*Burke*)

> Birth: 12/06/1866
> Death: 05/28/1933
> Cemetery Location: F3

Father: Johannas Burke; Mother: Stenia (*Kissa*); Husband: Gustof Louis "Gus" Peterson/Petersen/Gustafson; born in Sweden; died in Boulder (Boulder) Colorado at age 66 years, 5 months, 22 days-heart trouble; mortuary record has birth date 12/09/1866; Bernard Dale "Biffy" Peterson (grandson) states that Ida's maiden name was originally *"Bjork;"* Ida was a sister to Ingried Gustava (*Burke*) Johnson; some sources state Christina Youngsberg as Johannas Burke's wife however she was the wife of John Augusta "Gus" Burke who was a brother to Ida Matilda; no tombstone; see PETERSON/PETERSEN/GUSTAFSON, Gustof Louis "Gus;" see **About the Peterson/Petersen/Gustafson Family**

Diary of Ellen Romig Regnier, courtesy Richard D. Regnier:

"May 28th—Mrs. Peterson died today."

Boulder Daily Camera 29 May 1933:

"MRS. IDA PETERSON

Mrs. Ida Burke Peterson died at her home, 711 Walnut street, Sunday afternoon at 4:15 of heart trouble. She had been a resident of Boulder for 24 years. Mrs. Peterson was born in Ryssby, Sweden, Dec. 6, 1866, and came to the United States 45 years ago. Surviving are her son, William Peterson, and a daughter, Mrs. Matilda Barnham, both of this city, and three grandchildren. Funeral services will be held at the Howe mortuary Wednesday at 1:30. Rev. C. O. Beckman will officiate. Burial will be in the Gold Hill cemetery."

Boulder Daily Camera 30 May 1933:

"IDA PETERSON

Funeral services for Mrs. Ida Peterson, who died May 28th, will be held at the Howe mortuary on Wednesday afternoon at 1:30. Rev. O.C. Beckman will officiate. Burial will be at Gold Hill."

PETERSON, Jennie "Jimmie" (*Kinsman*) Murray (Incorrectly listed as being buried in the Gold Hill Cemetery)

Birth: 03/24/1895
Death: 09/27/1939
Cemetery Location: N/A

Father: James J. Kinsman; Mother: Daisy Jannett (*Curtis*); Husband: Chester D Peterson; name seems to be Jimmie, not Jennie; she is not buried in the Gold Hill Cemetery as previously listed; she is buried at Eldorado Springs Cemetery. Eldorado Springs (Boulder) Colorado

Boulder Daily Camera 28 September 1939:

"Mrs. C.D. Peterson of Eldorado Springs Died Wednesday—Mrs. Jimmie Peterson, wife of Chester D. Peterson, of Eldorado Springs, died Wednesday morning at 11:50. She was born in Canon City March 24, 1895, and was 44 years of age. Funeral services will be held Saturday morning at 10 at Howe mortuary. Interment in Eldorado Springs cemetery. Besides Mr. Peterson she is survived by a daughter, Mrs. Jane Conda."

Boulder Daily Camera 29 September 1939:

"Mrs. Jimie Peterson—wife of C.D. Peterson of Eldorado Springs. Services at Howe mortuary Saturday morning at 10. Christian Science service, in charge of A.W. Fitzgerald of Boulder. Interment, Eldorado Springs."

PETERSON/PETERSEN/GUSTAFSON, William Bernard

Birth: 10/27/1893
Death: 09/28/1948
Cemetery Location: F3

Father: Gustof Louis "Gus" Peterson/Petersen/Gustafson; Mother: Ida Matilda (*Burke*); Wife: Bertha (*Schleiger/Schleigher*); born in Gold Hill (Boulder) Colorado and died in Boulder (Boulder) Colorado at age 52 years, 11 months, 7 days-illness; mortuary record states date of birth 22 October 1894 and date of death 28 September 1949; obituary states date of birth 22 October 1895; see PETERSON/PETERSEN/GUSTAFSON, Gustof Louis "Gus;" see PETERSON/PETERSEN/GUSTAFSON, Ida Matilda (*Burke*); see **About the Peterson/Petersen/Gustafson Family**; sister to Matilda "Tillie" (*Peterson/Petersen/Gustafson*) Bowman Newland; see NEWLAND, "Tillie" (*Peterson/Petersen/Gustafson*) Bowman Holloway Brickman

Boulder Daily Camera 30 September 1948:

"William B. Peterson, Native of Gold Hill, Dies Early Today...

William Bernard Peterson, native of Gold Hill and a resident of Boulder county all his life, died this morning at Community hospital. He followed metal mining and was a millman for the Boulder Tungsten Mills, at one time.

He was the son of the late Mr. and Mrs. Guy [sic] Peterson and was born at Gold Hill, Oct. 11, 1895. He was married to Bertha Schleiger, Sept. 15, 1927, and she and three children survive. The children are Darlene, Biffy, and Ida Lou. A sister, Mrs. Alfred Newland lives in Denver.

Funeral services are to be Saturday at 1:30 at Howe Mortuary. Interment will be at Gold Hill."

[wrong birth date-should be 27 October 1893]

Boulder Daily Camera 01 October 1948:

"Relatives Arrive For Funeral Of William B. Peterson...

Mrs. Freida Hethering and daughter, Jane of Lincoln, Neb., sister and niece of Mrs. William Bernard Peterson of 902 Spruce are here to be with Mrs. Peterson and family until after the funeral of the husband and father, at 1:30 Saturday at Howe mortuary. Will Schleiger, of Lincoln, Neb., a brother of Mrs. Peterson; her nephew, Martin and Mrs. Shaw of Lincoln, Neb., a brother, John Schleiger, Mrs. Schleiger and sons of Fort Collins and a sister Mrs. Kathryn Shaw, of Lincoln are here or coming.

Mr. Peterson, the son of the late Mr. and Mrs. Gus Peterson, pioneers of Gold Hill, was born at Gold Hill Oct. 22, 1895. He followed mining the greater part of his life in Boulder county and in the San Juan region. Among the mines in which he worked in Boulder county were the Yellowpine at Crisman, while leased by Charles Wahlstrom; Slide mine at Gold Hill, as foreman, under Supt. McDonald.

Worked For County Seven Years...

For seven years he was blasting and powder man for Boulder county when Elmer Hetzer was commissioner for the mountain district. The last two years Mr. Peterson was employed by Platt Rogers, Inc., in its construction work at the University.

Ill health this spring forced him to retire and with his family he moved back to Gold Hill. This summer, however, the family moved to 902 Spruce. He was thought to be making a good recovery when he suffered a sudden relapse. His death occurred at 5:50 Wednesday afternoon.

Survivors are Mrs. Peterson and three children—Darlene, Biffy, and Ida Lou. A sister, Mrs. Alfred Newland lives in Denver.

Rev. Warren S. Bainbridge will officiate at the services. Interment will be in Gold Hill."

Boulder Daily Camera 02 October 1948:

"William Bernard Peterson...Services were held today at 1:30 at Howe mortuary. Rev. Warren S. Bainbridge of Methodist church officiated. Ben Walker sang, accompanied by Margaret Haascall. Pallbearers were Elmer Hetzer, W.J. McDonald, Kenneth McKenzie, Tim Walter, Wilbur Goudge and Fred Magor. Interment, Gold Hill."

About William Bernard Peterson/Petersen/ Gustafson

William Bernard Peterson/Petersen/Gustafson was born 27 October 1893 (according to his World War II draft card in his own handwriting) in Gold Hill (Boulder) Colorado, the son of Gustof Louis "Gus" and Ida Matilda (*Burke*) Peterson/Petersen/Gustafson. He married Bertha Schleiger/Schleigher on 15 September 1928 in Boulder (Boulder) Colorado.

Bertha was born about 1910 in (Lancaster) Nebraska; the daughter of German parents John and Katharine (maiden name unknown) Schleiger/Schleigher. By the 1920 census both her parents (John and Katharine) were deceased and their children (Freida, John, William "Will," Jacob "Joel," Martha and Bertha) were placed in numerous homes; Freida, Martha and Bertha ended up in the Tabitha Home in Lincoln (Lancaster) Nebraska. The oldest child, Katherine, was a maid in a private household. She married Martin L. Shaw and younger sister, Freida, married a Mr. Hethering. Both sisters are mentioned in William Bernard's obituary as well as Bertha's brothers; Will and John (see above newspaper article *Boulder Daily Camera* 01 October 1948).

To the union of William Bernard and Bertha (*Schleiger/Schleigher*) Peterson/Petersen/Gustafson four known child was born:

Darlene Mae: born 07 June 1929 Boulder (Boulder) Colorado-still living; married Dwight Lee Williams

Billie Bernard: born 02 February 1931 Gold Hill (Boulder) Colorado and died 04 February 1931 Gold Hill (Boulder) Colorado; buried Gold Hill Cemetery, Gold Hill (Boulder) Colorado; see PETERSON/PETERSEN/GUSTAFSON, Billie Bernard

Bernard Dale "Biffy": born 23 December 1937 Boulder (Boulder) Colorado-still living; married Lynn Myers

Ida Lou: born 19 October 1942 (Boulder) Colorado-still living; never married

By 1935 the family was rented a house at 840 Maxwell Street, Boulder (Boulder) Colorado where they lived there for over five years while William worked as a laborer.

After a brief move to Gold Hill the family returned to Boulder living at 902 Spruce Street. William and Bertha enjoyed their time together with their three children (Darleen/Darlene, Bernard Dale "Biffy" and Ida Lou) until he was taken to the Community Hospital in Boulder

Peterson Plot in the Gold Hill Cemetery

(Boulder) Colorado where he died 28 September 1948 from ill health. Burial was in the Gold Hill Cemetery, Gold Hill (Boulder) Colorado; the only marked grave in the Petersen/Peterson/Gustafson plot.

Bertha continued living in Boulder and made her living as a cook for various sororities and fraternities. She died 07 May 1972 in Boulder (Boulder) Colorado. Cremated, her ashes were scattered on Horsfal Hill (Boulder) Colorado.

Boulder Daily Camera 08 May 1972:

"Bertha (Pete) Peterson 1536 Pearl St., the cook for the Alpha Phi sorority, died Sunday at her home. She was 62.

She was born in Lincoln, Neb., on Oct. 12, 1909, and came to Boulder when she was 17. She was married to William B. Peterson in Boulder on Sept. 15, 1927. Her husband died in 1948.

Mrs. Peterson had also been the cook for the Kappa Kappa Gamma sorority and the Sigma Phi Epsilon fraternity. She was a member of the Protestant Church.

She is survived by one son, Bernard Dale (Biff) Peterson, 2045 Glenwood Dr.; two daughters, Mrs. Dwight (Darlene) Williams, 2980 17th St.; and Ida Lou Peterson 1210 Lindon Ave.; one brother, John Schleigher, Fort Collins; two sisters, Katherine Shaw, Lincoln, and Fredida Heatherington of Germany, and three grandchildren.

Funeral services will be announced in Tuesday's Camera. Howe Mortuary is in charge of arrangements."

About the Peterson/Petersen/Gustafson Family

Gustof Louis "Gus" Peterson/Petersen/Gustafson was born in Sweden in December of 1858; parents unknown.

According to the 1900 United States census he left Sweden and sailed for America, arriving in 1890 in Colorado. Immigration records have Augustus Gustafson arriving in 1890 at the Port of New York at the age of 26 years.

At the age of 32 years, Gustof of Gold Hill married Ida Burke (aged 23 years) of Boulder on 09 April 1892 in Boulder (Boulder) Colorado. Ida was born in Ryssby, Sweden, 06 December 1866 and immigrated to the United States about 1888.

This union brought forth three known children:

Infant: born 1892 Gold Hill (Boulder) Colorado and died 1892 Gold Hill (Boulder) Colorado; buried Gold Hill Cemetery, Gold Hill (Boulder) Colorado; see GUSTAFSON/PETERSON/PETERSEN, Infant

William Bernard: (27 October 1893 Gold Hill (Boulder) Colorado and died 29 September 1948 Boulder (Boulder) Colorado; buried Gold Hill Cemetery, Gold Hill (Boulder) Colorado; see PETERSON/PETERSEN/GUSTAFSON, William Bernard

Matilda "Tillie": born August 1896 Gold Hill (Boulder) Colorado and died 30 April 1952 Pueblo (Pueblo) Colorado; buried Gold Hill Cemetery, Gold Hill (Boulder) Colorado; married George Fern Bowman, Mr. Holloway, Henry E. Brickman and Alert Lo Newland; see BOWMAN, George Fern; see NEWLAND, Matilda "Tillie" (*Peterson/Petersen/Gustafson*) Bowman Holloway Brickman

On 08 July 1905 in Boulder (Boulder) Colorado Gustof L. and Ida divorced, both citing cruelty. It seems they overcame their differences as on 19 September 1905 they were remarried in Boulder by Justice of the Peace, Vinton Garrett Holliday.

It is interesting to note that in the 1900 and 1910 U.S. census Gustof L. and family are listed as "Gustafson." In his newspaper obituary of 1921 he is listed as "Gus Peterson" however the mortuary record has "Gustof L. Gustafson." The 1930 census has "Ida Peterson" as well as her newspaper obituary however the mortuary record has "Ida Burke Peterson Gustafson." The children (William Bernard and Matilda) were first known as Gustafson but later as Peterson/Petersen. Ida never remarried after "Gus" passed away so it remains a mystery why this family originally known as Gustafson was later known as Peterson/Petersen as early as 1916.

Early Days in Gold Hill-Interview #1 by George Cowell (as told to Chuck & Doll Rowan and Bob & Shirley Gibson; transcribed by Lynne Walter) no date:

"This Gus Peterson, he used to get home late at night. He had a son [William Bernard] who was about fourteen years old. Seemed to me like he'd get mad at him every night and he'd start out, maybe ten or eleven o'clock at night, chasing his 'Wooley.' His son, Wooley, would get scared and he'd run. Gus would chase him all over town all night long trying to catch him. I don't know. As far as I know he never did catch him. Of course, there were no lights in town which helped 'Wooley' find a place to hide.

We lived on Main Street and he'd just bust right in our house. Doors wasn't locked. We never had locks up here on any of the doors. Nobody locked their doors. Wolley'd run right into our house and holler, "My Dad's after me Mrs. Cowell." He'd run and get in one of the back bedrooms. Well, Mother got tired of it. She'd meet Gus at the door and argue with him; Wooley wasn't in there. So, finally, one night Mother was disgusted with it. Wooley came running in and Mother stood in the door and told Gus he wasn't in there. He said, "I know he came in here." Mother said, "Get off the porch," and she took a shot at him. She put two bullets right between his legs and he turned around and left."

Well, when Wooley'd run in our house from then on, Gus wouldn't stop and he'd go right on home and he wouldn't come in."

PFARR, Sylvester Lawrence

Birth: 08/08/1918
Death: 04/24/1965
Cemetery Location: E3

Father: William Robert Pfarr; Mother: Anna Mathilda (*Volkmann*); Wife: Alberta Belle (*Reed*) Hamilton Stanisbery/Sailsbery (spelling on marriage certificate to Sylvester); born in Balsam Lake (Polk) Wisconsin and died west of Gold Hill (Boulder) Colorado on County Road 52 at age 46 years, 8 months, 16 days-broken neck, crushed chest & internal injuries from auto accident

Boulder Daily Camera 25 April 1965:

"Gold Hill Man, 46, Dies As Car Rolls Into Canyon

A Gold Hill resident, Sylvester L. Pfarr, 46, was killed Saturday afternoon when his car flipped into a canyon between Gold Hill and Nederland.

His brother, Albert Pfarr, 26, a passenger in the car, escaped with minor cuts. Investigating officers reported the younger Pfarr managed to climb back up to the road and walked for about an hour before he reached a house where he called to report the accident.

The accident occurred about 2:45 p.m. and the sheriff's officer received word of it at 3:45 p.m. A state patrol car, sheriff's car and an ambulance were sent to the scene but the man was dead when the officers arrived.

Pfarr was crushed to death when he was thrown out and the car rolled over him, officers said. County Coroner Norman Howe reported Pfarr died of a broken neck and a crushed chest. Howe said the brothers were returning home from Nederland with a supply of groceries.

The crash occurred about three miles west of Gold Hill along the canyon road which connects with the Nederland-Ward Highway.

Sylvester Pfarr survived an almost identical crash in January, 1953. The report of that accident said Pfarr's automobile overturned on the Sunshine Canyon Road. Pfarr was unhurt and was walking down the road for aid when officers found him. He was driving down the canyon road when the car rolled over on a curve about three and a half miles west of Boulder and landed on its top in the road.

Pfarr, an employee of the City of Boulder, was born on Aug. 8, 1918, in Minnesota [error]. He had been a resident of Boulder County for about 25 years. He is also survived by six other brothers and four sisters. Further obituary information and further arrangements will be announced by Howe Mortuary."

Boulder Daily Camera 26 April 1965:

"Funeral services will be conducted Wednesday at 10 a.m. at the Howe Mortuary for Sylvester Lawrence Pfarr of Gold Hill, who was killed in an automobile accident Saturday afternoon on the canyon road between Gold Hill and Nederland.

Mr. Pfarr was born in Balsam Lake, Wis., Aug. 18, 1918, and came to Boulder 25 years ago from Minnesota. He served for a short time in the Army in World War II and was given a medical discharge. He was employed on the street and road crew of the City of Boulder.

Surviving are his widow, Alberta B. Pfarr of Sacramento, Calif., five stepchildren; seven brothers, Albert G. of Gold Hill, Roy of Hotchkiss, Orville of Denver, Glenn, William, Merlin and Floyd, all living in Minnesota.

There are four sisters, Mrs. Leona Conte of Denver, Mrs. Lucille Hart of Longmont, Mrs. Lois Stensrud of Cottonwood, Minn., and Mrs. Eileen Hausman of Montevideo, Minn.

Interment is to be in Gold Hill."

Boulder Daily Camera 27 April 1965:

"Sylvester L. Pfarr—Services will be Wednesday at 10 a.m. at the Howe Mortuary. Interment will be in Gold Hill."

Boulder Daily Camera Focus 01 November 1981:

"Gertrude [Jones] speaks fondly of a fellow who looked after the cabins for those who spent the winters away: She remarked, "Sylvester was the most honest man I ever knew. But he went over the mountain...Yeap, over the mountain. Broke his neck when his car skidded over the side of the mountain one winter."

(article by Vicki Groninger)

PITTMAN, Grace Estella

> Birth: 10/27/1896
> Death: 11/09/1909
> Cemetery Location: C/D 4 & 5

Father: James Eli Pittman; Mother: Mary Emily (*Hastings*); born and died in Gold Hill (Boulder) Colorado at age 13 years, 0 months, 13 days-cause of death unknown; see **About the Pittman Family**

Boulder Daily Camera 09 November 1909:

"GRACE PITTMAN'S GRAVE WILL BE AT GOLD HILL...Grace Estella Pittman, the twelve-year-old daughter of Mr. and Mrs. James E. Pittman of 529 University Avenue, died yesterday afternoon at 1 o'clock. Her remains will be shipped to Gold Hill for burial Thursday. Mr. Pittman, father of the deceased, is a well-known Boulder county miner and winner of several rock-breaking contests."

PITTMAN, Irvin Robert

> Birth: 11/22/1898
> Death: 06/27/1899
> Cemetery Location: C/D 4 & 5

Father: James Eli Pittman; Mother: Mary Emily (*Hastings*); born and died in Gold Hill (Boulder) Colorado at age 7 months, 5 days-cause of death unknown; other sources state name as Robert Irvin Pittman with a birth date of 11/23/1898; see **About the Pittman Family**

Boulder County Herald Weekly 28 June 1899:

"A casket was sent by Trezise up to Gold Hill today for the remains of a 7-months old *girl* of James Pitman." (clerical error)

Boulder News 29 June 1899:

"The little *daughter* of James Pittman died at Gold Hill Tuesday night." (clerical error)

PITTMAN, Oliver James

> Birth: 01/29/1893
> Death: 11/27/1896
> Cemetery Location: C/D 4 & 5

Father: James Eli Pittman; Mother: Mary Emily (*Hastings*); born and died in Gold Hill (Boulder) Colorado at age 3 years, 9 months, 29 days-cause of death unknown; see **About the Pittman Family**

About the Pittman Family

James Eli Pittman was born 18 December 1867 in Darlington (Montgomery) Indiana; one of nine known children born to Joseph M. and Rebecca (*Garrison*) Pittman.

James married Mary Emily Hastings on 15 September 1892 in Boulder (Boulder) Colorado. Mary was born 28 October 1869 in Lebanon (Grafton) New Hampshire; the daughter of Henry Hiram and Emily Lorinda (*McAllister*) Hastings; see HASTINGS, Henry Hiram and HASTINGS, Emily Lorinda (*McAllister*). The union of James and Mary brought forth nine known children:

Oliver James: born 29 January 1893 Gold Hill (Boulder) Colorado and died 27 November 1896 Gold Hill (Boulder) Colorado; buried Gold Hill Cemetery, Gold Hill (Boulder) Colorado; see PITTMAN, Oliver J.

Ethel Margaret: born 25 December 1894 Gold Hill (Boulder) Colorado-08 April 1974 Clackamas-suburb of Portland (Multnomah) Oregon; burial unknown; married Charles C. Fliniau

Grace Estella: born 27 October 1896 Gold Hill (Boulder) Colorado and died 09 November 1909 Gold Hill (Boulder) Colorado; buried Gold Hill Cemetery, Gold Hill (Boulder) Colorado; see PITTMAN, Grace Estella

Irvin Robert: born 22 November 1898 Gold Hill (Boulder) Colorado and died 27 June 1899 Gold Hill (Boulder) Colorado; buried Gold Hill Cemetery, Gold Hill (Boulder) Colorado; some sources state Robert Irvin Pittman, born 23 November 1898; see PITTMAN, Irvin Robert

Edna Luella: born 11 June 1900 Gold Hill (Boulder) Colorado and died 31 August 1960 Cheyenne (Laramie) Wyoming; buried Beth El Cemetery, Cheyenne (Laramie) Wyoming; married Charles Everett Schneider

Irma Emily: born 27 December 1902 Gold Hill (Boulder) Colorado and died 24 September 1998 Los Alamos (Santa Barbara) California; buried Los Alamos Cemetery, Los Alamos (Santa Barbara) California; married Lloyd Anthony Epperson

Alice Mary: born 27 July 1905 Gold Hill (Boulder) Colorado and died 11 October 1997 (Orange) California; burial unknown; married Charles Everett Schneider-widower of her sister Edna Luella (*Hastings*) Schneider

Albert Earl: born 21 July 1907 Boulder (Boulder) Colorado and died 03 August 1986 Denver (Jefferson) Colorado; burial unknown; married May Isabel Boyd

Genevieve Ellen: born 06 September 1909 Boulder (Boulder) Colorado and died 12 November 1994 Fullerton (Orange) California; buried Loma Vista Memorial Park, Fullerton (Orange) California; married William E. Rosen

It appears that James was interested in photography as he took a few photos in and around the Gold Hill (Boulder) Colorado area in the late 1890s (photos are on file at Carnegie Library For Local History).

By 1907 the family moved to Boulder (Boulder) Colorado and in 1910 was living on Marine Street. Even though living in Boulder James was still very active in his drilling contests.

Early Days In Gold Hill by George Cowell (courtesy Carnegie Library For Local History):

"Pittman lived in Gold Hill, and Smith and Pittman were a team of what we called double-jacking...drilling. A single-jack, a man turned his own drill and did his own drilling. On the Fourth of July and holidays we would have drilling contests and races and baseball games...But the drilling contest—-it's held in solid granite and the single-jack man had to turn his own bit and change his own drill and hammer at the same time. At that time the record was 11 inches. Double-jack—a man drills one minute then he drops to his knees and turns the drill while the other man hammers and then they holler "time" he drops his drill and the other man hammers and they go just as hard as they can to do it. I was with Jim Pittman in 1928 when Pittman lost the championship to somebody in Idaho Springs and Old Man Pittman sat down on a rock and cried. And he said that he would challenge any man in the United States for a drilling contest at his age and he says I'm 70 years old. He was 70 when he lost the championship."

(Interesting to note that about one year later Jim died and his age was listed as 61 years old.)

OLIVER J. PITTMAN
JAN. 29, 1893
NOV. 27, 1896

Digging Up Dirt

Boulder Daily Camera 06 April 1929:

"JIM PITTMAN, PIONEER MINER, SAYS THERES GOLD IN HILLS...

Grubstake a Few Honest Prospectors and Get Results, Pleads Man Who Holds World's Championship in Corn Husking and Hard Rock Drilling...

James E. Pittman is 62 years ago and he may not have the ability to dash off the 100-yard dash in 9.3 seconds, but he still is full enough of sap and vinegar to declare there still are millions to be found in the mines of Colorado.

Pittman, world's champion hard rock driller, and the world's champion corn husker, now an employee of Jack Clark, is 62 years old, and according to his own statement, has never been arrested or in jail, believes that capitol properly invested in Boulder county mines would bring back the mining prosperity in the county enjoyed years ago when thousands of miners worked in hundreds of mines west of Boulder.

Pittman has worked in and around the quartz mines the last forty years.

"I'm still digging for the various metals," he told City Manager George Teal recently. "There are untold millions of undiscovered metals that could be found and opened up if only sufficient money was put up to put old reliable prospectors in the field and keep them there."

The confidence of Ponce de Leon belongs to Pittman and the other old timers in Boulder County say that "Jim is usually right." One of these days, it is predicted, someone will grubstake Jim for a few thousand dollars and he will make himself and his associates wealthy in a very few years.

Few men, not excluding Jack Bowen, kindly old bell-ringer at the University of Colorado, who was a musician, prospector, inventor, stage driver and scholar, who died here last year, have had the experiences of Pittman.

A Pretty Good Mix

Pittman's father was born in Montgomery County, Indiana, Dec. 18, 1867. He missed being a civil war baby by two years.

A farm boy at home until his mother died in March, 1883, Pittman was more or less "put on his own" when his father broke up their home. He drifted to Iowa for seven winters, then to Gage County, Nebr., in the spring of 1884. In Nebraska he made the highest wages paid a hired man—$26 per month. On his birthday in 1886 he was challenged for a 25-bushel cornhusking for a $25 side bet and he accepted the bet. The money was given to stake holders and the game started. The proposition was to husk twenty-five bushels of corn off the stock and shovel it into the bin, time going to and from the field not counted.

Champion Husker

Pittman put his twenty-five bushels of clean husked corn into the bin in 56 ¾ minutes, beating his man 16 ½ minutes and, establishing a world's record that has never been broken. (He got the $25.)

From Nebraska he "drifted" to Colorado and started following the "drifts." Another eventful day in his life was on the Fourth of July, 1890—thirty-eight years ago, plus. He was at Ward and the "champions" of the state in rock drilling were present to win first prize in the miners' drilling contest. Prizes were from $75 to $150 to the team drilling the deepest hole in hard granite in fifteen minutes. Pittman and his partner won second money.

"From that day on," says Pittman, "I took part in all the contests that came up in this part of the state, both double and single handed, in which I drilled from one to four times a year, and my partner and I won seventeen first prizes, six second prizes, seven third prizes, and seven fourth prizes, a total of 35 prizes. The holes drilled double-handed were from 34 to 39 9/16 inches and "all depended on the hardness of the rock and good luck," he says. In the single-handed drilling contests, he drilled from 21 ½ to 25 ½ inches in fifteen minutes.

George Teal says that Pittman is "a durned good man," and he is."

Unfortunately James Eli Pittman was killed in a freak act of nature.

Boulder Daily Camera 17 July 1929:

"Jim Pittman Killed Today When Struck By Lightning...Miner Dies From Bolt That Hit 80 Feet Off...Prof. Fred Dungan Knocked Down, But Was Unhurt; Jim Rode On Miners' Float In July 4 Parade...

James (Jim) E. Pittman, 61, who claimed the title of world's champion hard rock driller and world's champion cornhusker, was instantly killed when struck by lightning today at Silver Lake, where he was employed as a blacksmith by the city now engaged in increasing the storage capacity of the lake.

Pittman was repairing the roof of the blacksmith shop. Lightning struck a tree eighty feet away. It knocked Pittman off the roof. Prof. Fred Dungan, assistant professor of city engineering at the University of Colorado, employed as an engineer at the project this summer, saw the accident. Dungan was knocked down, but he saw Pittman tumble from the roof into a pile of rock and scrap iron. Had not the lightning killed him the fall undoubtedly would have caused his death, City Engineer Earle W. Devalon said.

Dr. H.H. Heuston and a Public Service company employee, hurried by auto to Silver Lake. Heuston said Pittman probably was instantly killed. Efforts to revive him by means of pulmotor and inhalator failed. Coroner A.E. Howe brought the body to Boulder.

Pittman has no relatives. He had worked in and around the quartz mines of Boulder county for forty years. He rode on the old mining methods exhibit in the July 4 parade.

Recently City Manager George Teal asked Pittman to write his life's history. Teal read it, thought it good and a Camera reporter asked to publish it. In the statement Pittman said he had "never been arrested or put in jail." The Camera April 6 said: "I am still digging for the various metals," he told City Manager George Teal recently. "There are untold millions of undiscovered metals that could be found and opened up if only sufficient money was put up to put old reliable prospectors in the field and keep them there."

The confidence of Ponce de Leon belongs to Pittman, and the other old miners in Boulder county say that "Jim is usually right." One of these days, it is predicted, someone will grubstake Jim for a few thousand dollars and he will make himself and his associates wealthy in a very few years.

Few Men, not excluding Jack Bowen, kindly old bell ringer at the University of Colorado, who was a musician, prospector, inventor, stage drive and scholar, who died here last year, have had the experiences of Pittman.

A Pretty Good Mix...Pittman's father was born in New Jersey of Scotch-Irish parents. His mother was born in Pennsylvania of Dutch parents. "This makes me a bad mix, but O.K. if you please," he has commented.

Pittman was born in Montgomery county, Indiana, Dec. 18, 1867. He missed being a Civil War hero by two years.

A farm boy at home until his mother died in March, 1883, Pittman was more or less "out on his own" when his father broke up their home. He drifted to Iowa for seven winters, then to Gage county, Nebraska, in the spring of 1884. In Nebraska he made the highest wages paid a hired man—$26 a month. On his birthday in 1886 he was challenged for a 25-bushel corn husking for a $25 side bet and he accepted the bet. The money was given to stakeholders and the game started. The proposition was to husk 25 bushels of corn off the stock and shovel it into the bin, time going to and from the field not counted.

World Champion Husker...Pittman put his 25 bushels of clean husked corn into the bin in 56 ¾ minutes, beating his man 16 ½ minutes, and establishing a world's record that has never been broken.

From Nebraska he 'drifted' to Colorado and started following the 'drifts." Another eventful day in his life was on the Fourth of July, 1890—thirty-eight years ago, plus. He was at Ward and the 'champions' of the state in rock drilling were present to win first prize in the miners' drilling contest. Prizes were from $75 to $150 to the team

drilling the deepest hole in hard granite in 15 minutes. Pittman and his partner won second money.

"From that day on," says Pittman, "I took part in all the contests that came up in this part of the state, both double and single-handed, in which I drilled from one to four times a year, and my partner and I won seventeen first prizes, eight second prizes and two fourth prizes making a total of twenty seven prizes and were defeated only twice."

Single-handed Pittman won fifteen first prizes, six second prizes, seven third prizes, and seven fourth prizes, a total of 35 prizes. The holes drilled double-handed were from 31 to 39 9/16 inches, and "all depended on the hardness of the rock and good luck," he says. In the single handed drilling contests he drilled from 31 ½ to 25 ½ inches in fifteen minutes."

Boulder Daily Camera 18 July 1929:

"Pittman Killed In Fall And Not By Lightning, Howe Says... Pioneer Miner Survived By Widow and Six Children; Prof. Dungan Unhrt; Mrs. Pittman Here; No Inquest, According To Coroner A.E. Howe...

Whether Jim Pittman, 61, pioneer Boulder county mining man, was killed by lightning or suffered a fractured skull when the lightning struck a tree eight [sic] feet from the place he was working and knocked him into a pile of rock and scrap iron, probably will not be determined until the Colorado Industrial commission makes an investigation, it was stated today.

Pittman was working on the roof of the black smith shop at Silver Lake yesterday when lightning struck the tree. He toppled from the roof into the rocks and iron. He died instantly, according to the attending physician.

It also was developed today that Prof. Fred R. Dungan, engineer in charge of the work of enlarging the storage capacity of Silver Lake, was not knocked down by lightning, but was jarred, lost his breath because of the vacuum created by the lightning, and fell. As he fell he saw Pittman fall from the roof. Prof. Dungan, who is an assistant professor of civil engineering at the University of Colorado, continued his work today. Pittman's body is at Howe's mortuary.

Pittman's Family...Pittman was married forty years ago. His widow, Mrs. Mary Pittman, resides at 3128 Gilpin street, Denver.

Pittman is survived, aside from the widow, by five daughters and a son. There are: Mrs. Charles (Ethel) Fliniau, Portland, Ore.; Mrs. Enda [sic] Schneider, Cheyenne, Wyo.; Mrs. Lloyd Epperson, Sugar Loaf; Misses Genevieve and Alice Pittman, who live with their mother; Albert Pittman, Denver, employe [sic] of the Morey Mercantile company, formerly employed by the Foster Honey company, Boulder. Albert also lives with his mother.

Digging Up Dirt

Miss Grace Pittman, oldest daughter of Mr. and Mrs. Pittman, died at Gold Hill about 1909.

A nephew of Jim Pittman, Elmer Coughlin, now lives at Sugar Loaf. Genevieve Pittman was visiting in Casper, Wyo., when she heard of her father's death. She is en route to Boulder. Pittman's son-in-law, Lloyd Epperson, also now is employed at Silver Lake. He went to Denver last night and brought Mrs. Pittman here today.

The accident, according to city officials, happened about a quarter of a mile from the cabin of Caretaker George Pederson. Prof. Dungan gave the first aid to Pittman, then ran to Pederson's house to telephone city hall and ask for medical care. He was unaware that Pittman was instantly killed.

City Engineer Earle W. Devalon said that Dungan and Pittman were the only workmen near the place the lightning struck.

Coroner A.E. Howe said today that a fall from the roof of the building that resulted in a broken neck was the cause of Pittman's death rather than the first report that Pittman was directly killed by lightning.

Howe said that no inquest would be held.

Funeral services will be held at the Howe Mortuary at 2:30 o'clock Saturday afternoon.

Rev. Alfred Jones, former Friends' pastor here, now of Denver, will officiate. Burial will be in Green Mountain cemetery."

(Burial was actually in Columbia Cemetery, Boulder (Boulder) Colorado.)

After the death of her husband, James, Mary moved to Denver (Denver) Colorado with her three children (Alice, Albert and Genevieve). About a decade later Mary died on 27 January 1939 and is buried beside her husband in Columbia Cemetery, Boulder (Boulder) Colorado.

Boulder Daily Camera 28 January 1939:

"Mrs. Mary Pittman, Pioneer, Dies in Denver Friday...

Mrs. Mary E. Pittman, wife of the late James E. Pittman, early day miner of Boulder county, died Friday at her home in Denver of complications of a heart nature. She had been in poor health for three years and seriously ill for the last two weeks.

She was the former Mary E. Hastings and was married in 1892 to Mr. Pittman. He was struck by lightning and killed at Silver Lake while working for the city, July 17, 1929.

Nine children were born to them, six of whom survive. They are a son, Albert Earl Pittman, of Edgewater;

Pitman/Coughlin/Hastings Plot in the Gold Hill Cemetery

Mrs. Ethel Pliniau, of North Bend, Wash., Mrs. Erma Epperson, of Chitwood, Ore., Mrs. Edna Schneider, of Cheyenne; Mrs. Genevieve Rosen, of Cheyenne; Miss Alice Pittman, of 952 Osceola street, Denver, with whom the mother lived. There are twelve surviving grandchildren and two sisters, Mrs. Dan Coughlin and Mrs. Curtis Swallow, of Casper, Wyo.

The body was brought to the Howe mortuary in Boulder, where funeral services will be held at 2 p.m. Tuesday."

Boulder Daily Camera 31 January 1939:

"Mrs. Mary E. Pittman—Services at Howe's this afternoon at 2 o'clock. Rev. Norman Young of Denver, son of the late Rev. Alfred Young, officiated. Eugene Hilligoss sang. Pallbearers were Alfred and Roy Perkins, Raymond and Elmer Coughlin, John Dolton [Dalton] and Paul Teets. Interment, Columbia cemetery."

POPE, Dudley Bennett

Birth: 07/12/1914
Death: 09/16/1990
Cemetery Location: C1

Father: Dudley Benjamin Pope; Mother: Margaret (*Stewart*); Wife: Mildred Lucille (*Coffin*); born in Newburgh (Orange) New York and died in (Fulton) Georgia at age 76 years, 2 months, 4 days-cancer

The (GA) Atlanta Journal-Constitution 18 September 1990:

"Mr. Dudley B. Pope of Atlanta, a retired vice president of Rich's who had a role in the annual Christmas tree lighting event at the store died of cancer Sunday at St. Joseph's Hospital. He was 76.

A memorial service will be at 2 p.m. Wednesday at Oglethorpe Presbyterian Church. The body was cremated.

Mr. Pope worked for Rich's from 1951 until his retirement in 1979.

As vice president of visual merchandising, he was responsible for a public ceremony surrounding the lighting of the Great Tree, a Christmas tree on Rich's roof for 25 years.

Mr. Pope was also responsible for store design and special events including "Hail Britannia," a small English village set up on the roof of the downtown Rich's, and "Italia Magnifica," an exhibit with an Italian theme.

Dudley Bennett Pope was born July 12, 1914, in Newburgh, N.Y., the son of Dudley Benjamin Pope and Margaret Stewart Pope. He graduated from the Pratt Institute of Art.

During World War II, he was a captain in the Army Corps of Engineers in the Pacific.

He was an elder at Oglethorpe Presbyterian Church.

Surviving are his wife, Lucille Coffin Pope, a daughter, Elizabeth P. Vanek of Gold Hill, Colo.; and a grandchild.

In lieu of flowers, the family requested that contributions be made to Oglethorpe Presbyterian Church."

POPE, Mildred Lucille (*Coffin*)

Birth: 05/18/1914
Death: 08/27/2005
Cemetery Location: C1

Father: Russell E. Coffin; Mother: Elizabeth A. (*Somerville*); Husband: Dudley Bennett Pope; born in Kingston (Ulster) New York and died in Lafayette (Boulder) Colorado at age 91 years, 3 months, nine days-old age

Boulder Daily Camera 30 August 2005:

"Lucille C. Pope passed away August 27th 2005 at Hospice of Boulder County. Lucille was born in Kingston N.Y. May 18th 1914. She graduated from Pratt Institute with a degree in Interior Design. Lucille was married to Dudley Pope; they lived in Atlanta, Georgia. They adopt-

Photo by Dina C. Carson

ed a daughter, Elizabeth in 1952. Seven years later they adopted a son, Christopher. Christopher and Dudley preceded her in death.

Lucille was an active member of the Oglethorpe Presbyterian Church. She also participated in her children's school activities at Pace Academy. Lucille moved to Boulder, Colorado in 1994 to be near her daughter and son-in-law, Steven and her one and only grandson, Christopher Snowhawk Vanek. Lucille started taking art classes in 2004. Everyone was very impressed by her work in acrylics and pen & ink.

She will be missed by many. Lucille was soft spoken, very generous, loving and honest in all she did. Her final resting place will be in Atlanta with Dudley and Christopher. A memorial will be held in her honor Thursday, September 1st at 4:00 pm at the Good Samaritan Retirement Home; then in Gold Hill on Sunday, September 4th at noon at the Vanek's residence. The final Memorial will be held in Atlanta, Georgia at the Oglethorpe Presbyterian Church Wednesday, September 21st at 3:00 pm. In lieu of flowers, donations can be made to Hospice of Boulder County, Boulder Good Samaritan or Meals on Wheels of Longmont."

The (GA) Atlanta Journal-Constitution 07 September 2005:

"Lucille C. Pope, 91, of Boulder Colo., formerly of Atlanta, died Aug. 27. Memorial service, 3 p.m. Sept.21, Oglethorpe Presbyterian Church, Atlanta; Boulder Mortuary."

PUGHE, Charles (no middle initial E) "Charley"

Birth: 04/13/1854
Death: 09/15/1943
Cemetery Location: D3

Father: Charles Pughe; Mother: Rebecca L. (*Thomas*); Wife: Eleanor "Ellen" (*Edwards*); born in Llanbadarn Fawr, Aberystwyth (Cardiganshire) Wales and died in Boulder (Boulder) Colorado at age 89 years, 5 months, 2 days-illness and old age; see PUGHE, Eleanor "Ellen" (*Edwards*); see PUGHE, Frederick; see PUGHE, Mary Ellen; see PUGHE, William Charles; see **About the Pughe Family**

Boulder Daily Camera 16 September 1943:

"Charles Pughe, Pioneer of Gold Hill, Dies Today

Charles Pughe, 89, resident of Gold Hill and Boulder since 1883, died at a convalescent home this morning. He had been in failing health for some time.

Mr. Pughe was born in Wales, British Isles, April 13, 1854, and was married there on Oct. 16, 1876, to Miss Eleanor Edwards who preceded him in death Nov. 21, 1941.

He came to Colorado in 1880 and then returned to Wales and brought his wife and son, John S. Pughe, back with him. They lived in Left Hand canon [sic] for two years, then moved to Gold Hill and it was there that Mrs. Pughe died.

Mr. Pughe followed mining and ranching and was one of the most widely known of the early day miners of Boulder County. Following the death of his wife he moved to Boulder. Last June he entered the Sanitarium and from there was later taken to the convalescent home at 952 Marine.

He is survived by two daughters, Mrs. Earl Belding of Grass Valley, Calif., and Mrs. A.J. Walter, 874 University Avenue, and John S. Pughe, who moved two years ago from Gold Hill to a farm in the Pleasant View district northeast of Boulder. Four other children preceded their parents in death. Eleven grandchildren and seven great-grandchildren also survive.

Funeral services will be held at Howe mortuary, date to be announced later. Interment will be in the family plot at Gold Hill."

Boulder Daily Camera 17 September 1943:

"Charles Pughe—Services at the Howe mortuary, Saturday at 2. Rev. Angus C. Jull [error should be Hull] Jr., pastor of the First Baptist church will officiate. Interment, family lot in Gold Hill cemetery."

Boulder Daily Camera 18 September 1943:

"Charles Pughe—Funeral services were held from Howe mortuary this afternoon at 2. Rev. Angus C. Jull [error should be Hull], Jr., pastor of the First Baptist church, officiated. Ben Walker and Mrs. Marylee Fritschle sang, accompanied by Mrs. H.A. Searcy at the organ. Pallbear-

ers were William Peterson, George Cory, Rufus Watson, Charles Gustafson, John Ingold and Alex McLellan. Burial was in the family lot in Gold Hill cemetery. Mrs. Ida Belding, daughter of the deceased, arrived in Boulder and will remain a short time with her brother, John Pughe and her sister, Mrs. A.J. Walter."

Bluebird Bulletin (no date):

"DEATH OF MR. PUGHE...

Friends who visit Blue Bird Lodge at Gold Hill will be grieved to learn of the death of Mr. Pughe, which occurred in September. We will always miss Mr. and Mrs. Pughe, who from the very first days of the Lodge, welcomed us at their beautiful ranch home. On our rambles to Sherwood Point, the Pughe meadow, where flowers grow in profusion, always we stopped for a glass of cold spring water, and often were given fresh from the churn buttermilk. These were the material welcomes; the friendly handshake from these two lovable souls will live in our memories. For more than sixty years Mr. and Mrs. Pughe lived in this beautiful farm home, which was always one of the rare spots for the Blue Birds."

Boulder Daily Camera 04 May 1944:

"CHARLES PUGHE ESTATE VALUED AT $4, 087.83

Hearing of a petition for settlement of the estate of the late Charles Pughe, who died Sept. 15, 1943, has been set for June 5 by the county court.

Estate is valued at $4,087.83. There are three heirs; Pearl A. Walter, 874 University, of Boulder, who was appointed administratrix by the court, Ida J. Belding and

John S. Pughe, the latter two of California. All are children of the deceased, who died without leaving a will."

PUGHE, Eleanor "Ellen" (*Edwards*)

Birth: 06/04/1856
Death: 11/21/1941
Cemetery Location: D3

Father: Stephen Edwards; Mother: Mary (*Morgan*) Pughe; Husband: Charles (no middle initial E) "Charley" Pughe; born in Llanbadarn Fawr, Aberystwyth (Cardiganshire) Wales and died in Gold Hill (Boulder) Colorado at age 85 years, 5 months, 17 days-coronary thrombosis (heart attack due to the formation of a blood clot inside a blood vessel of the heart); see PUGHE, Charles (no middle initial E) "Charley; see PUGHE, Frederick; see PUGHE, Mary Ellen; see PUGHE, William Charles; see **About the Pughe Family**

Boulder Daily Camera 21 November 1941:

"Mrs. John Pughe [Charles-newspaper error]

Mrs. John Pughe, resident of Gold Hill since 1885, died at her home in Gold Hill this morning at 9:15.

Her death ended one of the longest marriages existing in Boulder county—65 years—and she died in a home that she and her husband built in 1883 on a ranch a short distance from the town of Gold Hill, in the development of which community they had played a prominent part.

Mrs. Pughe, who was 84, is survived by her husband, by two daughters, Mrs. Albert Walter of 874 University and Mrs. Earl Helding of Grass Valley, Calif., and by a son, John S. Pughe, of Gold Hill. Born in Aberystwyth, Wales, on June 3, 1857, she married there Oct. 15, 1876—the year Colorado was admitted to statehood, to John Pughe. In 1883 they left Wales for Boulder County, being attracted by letters from John Pughe, a cousin, who was engaged in mining at Gold Hill. The Pughes located in Left Hand canon, near Rowena, and two years later moved to Gold Hill. They built a log cabin on a ranch that they secured and it was in this house—many times enlarged and improved in the 56 years of residence at Gold Hill, that, Mrs. Pughe died. Their wedding anniversary was quitely celebrated last October. Besides the two daughters and son, 11 grandchildren and 6 great grandchildren survive. Body is at Howe mortuary. Funeral arrangements later."

Boulder Daily Camera 22 November 1941:

"Mrs. Elinor [error should be Eleanor] Pughe—wife of Chas. Pughe, of Gold Hill. Services from Howe Mortuary Tuesday at 2. Rev. Angus C. Hull, pastor of the Baptist church will officiate. Interment will be in Gold Hill."

Boulder Daily Camera 25 November 1941:

"Mrs. Elinor [error should be Eleanor] Pughe—Wife

of Chas. Pughe—service from Howe Mortuary this afternoon at 2. Rev. Angus C. Hull, pastor of the Baptist church officiated. Mrs. Marylee Fritschle and Ben Walker sang. F.J. Barlett played the accompaniment. Pallbearers were Rufus Watson, Charles Gustafson, John Ingold, Alex McLellan, George Corey, and William Peterson. Interment in Gold Hill cemetery."

PUGHE, Frederick

> Birth: 01/05/1889
> Death: 09/27/1918
> Cemetery Location: D3

Father: Charles (no middle initial E) "Charley" Pughe; Mother: Eleanor "Ellen" (*Edwards*); born in Gold Hill (Boulder) Colorado and died in Camp Dix (Burlington) New Jersey at age 29 years, 7 months, 22 days-influenza; see PUGHE, Charles (no middle initial E) "Charley; see PUGHE, Eleanor "Ellen" (*Edwards*); see **About the Pughe Family**

Boulder Daily Camera 23 September 1918:

"FRED PUGH HAS INFLUENZA...

Mr. and Mrs. Charles Pugh of Gold Hill received a telegram today stating their son, Fred Pugh, was seriously ill in New York with Spanish influenza which has developed pneumonia. He left here in June for some place in Mexico, and with his troop was awaiting embarkation to go overseas."

Boulder Daily Camera 28 September 1918:

"PRIVATE FRED PUGH IS DEAD AT CAMP DIX FROM PNEUMONIA...

Fred Pugh, of Gold Hill, whose serious illness at Camp Dix had been reported to his parents by wire a few days ago, died yesterday afternoon. Mr. and Mrs. John Pugh received a telegram to that effect last night which added that the body was being shipped to this city. The funeral date will be announced later. Interment will take place at the Gold Hill cemetery."

Boulder Daily Camera 03 October 1918:

"FUNERAL OF FRED PUGH...

W.H. Rose, of the Boulder Undertaking Co., took the remains of Fred Pugh to Gold Hill this morning where the funeral services will be conducted Friday afternoon from the church by Rev. E.R. Curry. Interment will be in the Gold Hill cemetery."

Boulder Daily Camera 04 October 1918:

"Several people went to Gold Hill this morning to attend the funeral of Fred Pugh, who died at Camp Dix of Spanish influenza. Miss Myrtle Barnett, 1418 Walnut street, sang a solo and several selections were sung by Miss Ivy Blosser, 717 Grant street, Miss Barnett and Wm. Tippett."

[All newspaper articles incorrectly spelled the last name of Pughe.]

PUGHE, Mary Ellen

> Birth: 02/17/1896
> Death: 12/22/1896
> Cemetery Location: D3

Father: Charles (no middle initial E) "Charley" Pughe; Mother: Eleanor "Ellen" (*Edwards*); born and died in Gold Hill (Boulder) Colorado at age 10 months, 5 days-cause of death unknown; Mary Ellen was added to the tombstone of her brother, William Charles; see PUGHE, Charles (no middle initial E) "Charley; see PUGHE, Eleanor "Ellen" (*Edwards*); see **About the Pughe Family**

PUGHE, Rebecca L. (*Thomas*)

    Birth: 04/02/1828
    Death: 12/19/1907
    Cemetery Location: D2

Father: Morgan Thomas; Mother: Mary (*Griffiths*); Husband: Charles Pughe; born in Daren Fawr, Cwmsymlog, Llanbadarn (Cardiganshire) Wales and died in Ro-

wena (Boulder) Colorado at age 80 years, 7 months, 19 days-gastritis; see **About the Pughe Family**

Boulder Daily Herald 20 December 1907:

"A PIONEER PASSES AWAY…

    Mrs. Rebecca Pugh [error should be Pughe], who, for about thirty years has lived in Gold Hill and vicinity, died last evening at her home in Rowena where she was living with her son John G. Pugh. She is survived by two sons, John G. and Charles, of Gold Hill, and a daughter who lives in Wales. The funeral arrangements have not

"In loving remembrance"

yet been completed but will occur in Gold Hill Sunday afternoon."

Boulder Daily Camera 21 December 1907:

"The funeral of Mrs. Rebecca Pugh [error should be Pughe], who died at the home of her son, John G. Pugh, at Rowena, Thursday evening, will take place at Gold Hill Sunday afternoon. The deceased had been a resident of Boulder county for thirty years and has hosts of friends besides her son John, of Rowena, and Charles, of Gold Hill, and a daughter in Wales, to mourn her death."

PUGHE, William Charles

Birth: 10/28/1892
Death: 08/10/1893
Cemetery Location: D3

Father: Charles (no middle initial E) "Charley" Pughe; Mother: Eleanor "Ellen" (*Edwards*); born and died in Gold Hill (Boulder) Colorado at age 9 months; 13 days-bowel issues; William's sister, Mary Ellen Pughe, was buried alongside him when she died; see PUGHE, Charles (no middle initial E) "Charley; see PUGHE, Eleanor "Ellen" (*Edwards*); see **About the Pughe Family**

Boulder Daily Camera 11 August 1893:

"The infant child of Charles Pugh of Gold Hill died yesterday morning from bowel complaint. The funeral will take place tomorrow morning from the home."

About the Pughe Family

(Note: records were located with both spellings of Pugh and Pughe)

Charles Pugh/Pughe was born about 1821 in Cwm Canol, Trefeurig, Llanbadarn Fawr, Cardiganshire, Wales; the son of Griffith and Jane (*Owen*) Pugh.

He married Rebecca L. Thomas in July of 1854 in Aberystwyth (Cardiganshire) Wales. She was born 02 April 1828 in Daren Fawr, Cwmsymlog, Llanbadarn (Cardiganshire) Wales; the daughter of Morgan and Mary (*Griffiths*) Thomas; see PUGHE, Rebecca L. (*Thomas*). Five known children were born to Charles and Rebecca:

Maria: born 1852 Llanbadarn Fawr, Aberystwyth (Cardiganshire) Wales and died October 1910 Aberystwyth (Cardiganshire) Wales; married Charles Lloyd

Charles: born 13 April 1854 Llanbadarn Fawr, Aberystwyth (Cardiganshire) Wales and died 15 September 1943 Boulder (Boulder) Colorado; buried Gold Hill Cemetery, Gold Hill (Boulder) Colorado; married Eleanor "Ellen" Edwards; see PUGHE, Charles (no middle initial E) "Charley" and PUGHE, Eleanor "Ellen" (*Edwards*)

John Griffith: born June 1855 Llanbadarn Fawr, Aberystwyth (Cardiganshire) Wales and died 1928 Australia; burial unknown; believed never married

Jane: born May 1857 Trefeurig (Cardiganshire) Wales and died 02 August 1857 Daren Bach, Trefeurig (Cardiganshire) Wales

Edward: 31 July 1862 Daren, Parcel Canol (Cardiganshire) Wales and died 16 April 1874 Salem, Coedgruffydd (Cardiganshire) Wales

Charles Pugh/Pughe died 26 June 1891 in Trefeurig (Cardiganshire) Wales and about five years later his widow, Rebecca L. (*Thomas*), immigrated to the United States; her son, John Griffith, accompanying her. They sailed on the ship Alaska and arrived at the Port of New York on 20 October 1894. Rebecca's other son, Charles, had already made the voyage to the United States around 1880 but later returned to Wales about 1883 to bring his wife, Eleanor/Elinor "Ellen" and their infant son, John Stephen, back to Colorado. Rebecca's only living daughter, Maria, was married and remained in Wales with her family.

By 1900 Rebecca, age 72 years, lived in Gold Hill (Boulder) Colorado with her son, John Griffith where he was a miner. Her other son, Charles (no middle initial E) and wife, Eleanor "Ellen" (*Edwards*) Pughe also settled in the Gold Hill area, raising their family on a homestead which he built in the mid-1880s (about a mile south of Gold Hill (Boulder) Colorado). They had six known children:

John Stephen: born 10 January 1880 Aberystwyth (Cardiganshire) Wales and died 23 October 1959 Bellflower (Los Angeles) California; buried Rose Hill Memorial Park, Whittier (Los Angeles) California; married Florence Sanders Bennett

Ida May: born 10 May 1886 Gold Hill (Boulder) Colorado and died 30 June 1950 (Nevada) California; buried Cypress Lawn Memorial Park, Colma (San Mateo) California; married James Rowe James and Earl Elbert Belding; see JAMES, James Rowe

Frederick: born 05 January 1889 Gold Hill (Boulder) Colorado and died 27 September 1918 Camp Dix (Burlington) New Jersey; buried Gold Hill Cemetery, Gold Hill (Boulder) Colorado; never married; see PUGHE, Frederick

William Charles: born 28 October 1892 Gold Hill (Boulder) Colorado and died 10 August 1893 Gold Hill (Boulder) Colorado; buried Gold Hill Cemetery, Gold Hill (Boulder) Colorado; see PUGHE, William Charles

Pearl Annabell: born 27 January 1894 Boulder (Boulder) Colorado and died 01 April 1981 Boulder (Boulder) Colorado; buried Mountain View Memorial Park, Boulder (Boulder) Colorado; married Albert James "Tim" Walter

Mary Ellen: born 17 February 1896 Gold Hill (Boulder) Colorado and died 22 December 1896 Gold Hill

(Boulder) Colorado; buried Gold Hill Cemetery, Gold Hill (Boulder) Colorado; see PUGHE, Mary Ellen

It was a most pleasant life in Gold Hill but not without incidences:

Boulder Daily Camera 27 July 1903:
"Fred Pugh [error should be Pughe], 14, and Albert Walters, 10, were sitting on the porch of Albert's home at Gold Hill this morning playing with a 22 caliber rifle, which was unloaded, of course. When young Walters pulled the trigger the bullet went through Fred's foot at the top. Boulder surgeons was summoned by the wife of Dr. Trovillion, whose husband was absent from the camp."

Charles and Eleanor Pughe celebrated numerous wedding anniversaries:

Boulder Daily Camera 18 October 1926:
"The Golden Wedding Of Mr. and Mrs. Chas. Pughe...

Mr. and Mrs. Charles Pughe gave a family dinner at their home in Gold Hill Sunday in celebration of their fiftieth wedding anniversary. The day was ideal and permitted the attendance at the reunion of relatives from Boulder and Denver.

The home was beautifully decorated with roses and chrysanthemums as was a long table at which guests were seated. The center piece was a huge wedding cake which was cut as the last course by Mrs. Pughe.

The dinner was followed by a merry time singing old-time songs, Mrs. George Edwards of Denver playing the accompaniment. She also played familiar selections on the piano.

Mr. and Mrs. Pughe were married October 17, 1876, at Aberesthwith [Aberystwyth] Wales, in Aberesthwith [Aberystwyth] Castle. They came to Colorado in 1883. After two years on Left Hand they moved to Goldhill [sic] where they homesteaded and have lived ever since.

Six children were born to this union. Two died in infancy and one son, Fred, a fine young man, died at Camp Dix, Sept. 27, 1918, while in World War service. The living children are John S. Pughe, Ida Mae Pughe, now Mrs. Balding, and Pearl Anabell Pughe, now Mrs. A.J. Walter of Gold Hill.

At the dinner were Mr. and Mrs. John S. Pughe and six children, Elizabeth Orville, Violet, Ernest, Glen and Edward of Boulder; Mr. and Mrs. A.J. Walters, children, Gertrude and Albert of Gold Hill; John Pughe of this city, a brother of the host, Mrs. John Pughe, Mr. and Mrs. Clinton S. Banks of Boulder, Mr. and Mrs. George Edwards, Mr. and Mrs. James McLellan and son Russell, Miss Alma Crocker, Miss Sarah McKenzie and George Foxhoven of Denver.

It was impossible for Mr. and Mrs. Earl Balding and daughter, Elinore James of Tonopah, Nev., to be present, but their son, Lawrence James of Denver, was present to represent the family."

Boulder Daily Camera 16 October 1933:
"Gold Hill Couple Celebrate 57th Anniversary Today

Mr. and Mrs. Charles Pughe, residents of Gold Hill for fifty years, celebrated their fifty-seventh wedding anniversary today.

The day was spent quietly with two grandchildren present—Mrs. Verde Andrus of Boulder and two daughters, Shirley Jean and Allene, and Mrs. Lee Albright of Benkleman, Neb., and daughter, Patsy Lee. A number of friends also called to offer congratulations to the couple whose marriage occurred in Wales.

Mr. and Mrs. Pughe have three children, none of whom could be present. They are Mrs. Earl Nelding of Jackson, Calif.; John Pughe of Alamosa; Mrs. Albert Walters, Gold Hill.

The Pughes are well known in the vicinity of Gold Hill, where they have farmed and had mining interests for many years. There was an elaborate celebration when the couple observed their golden wedding anniversary"

Boulder Daily Camera 16 October 1936:
"Gold Hill Couple Celebrate 60th Wedding Anniversary There Today...

At their comfortable mountain home at Gold Hill, Mr. and Mrs. Charles Pughe, today quietly celebrated their 60th wedding anniversary.

There was no party or family reunion. Friends from Boulder, other mountain towns and throughout the nation united in sending them letters, cards and other forms of congratulations. Many friends called on them at their home.

Members of the family were present and are arranging a dinner for Sunday.

Mr. and Mrs. Pughe were married on Oct. 16, 1876 at Aberesthwyth [Aberystwyth] England [Wales], where both were born. They became interested in Colorado through letters from his brothers John Pughe, now of 1324 Pine Street and the late Charles Pughe, who were pioneers of Colorado. The latter became a pioneer from England to Gold Hill in 1883 and have lived there ever since.

Mr. Pughe mined at Gold Hill for many years and took up a homestead there. They became widely known throughout all of the mountain district and in Boulder.

They became parents of John S. Pughe, who resides at 1428 Spruce; of Mrs. Pearl Walters, wife of A.J. Walters, of Boulder and Gold Hill; of Mrs. Ida Belding of Sonora, Calif., and of Charles [Frederick] Pughe. The latter died at Camp Dix, N.J., during the World War. He was stationed there only a short time while waiting for shipping orders to go overseas. He belonged to Co. 157 Infantry of Boulder.

They are grandparents of eleven and great-grandparents of three. The grandchildren are the following children of Mr. and Mrs. John S. Pughe; Elizabeth Andrus, wife of A.V. Andrus, living on a farm near Valmont; Orville, Ernest and Glenn Pughe who are employed at Alamosa; Violet, wife of Lee Albright, living at Scotts Bluff, Neb., and Edward Pughe, living at home; the following children of Mr. and Mrs. Walters—Gertrude, University student, and Albert, attending junior high school; and the following children of Mrs. Belding, Lawrence Jones residing at Oakland, Calif., and Barbara Belding living at Sonora with her parents."

Eleanor "Ellen" (*Edwards*) Pughe lived over 85 years in her beloved home in Gold Hill. After 65 years of marriage to Charles she died 21 November 1941 from basically a heart attack and was buried in the town's cemetery. Her husband, Charles (no middle initial E) "Charley" Pughe lived about two years longer when he, too, passed away on 15 September 1943 at a convalescent home in Boulder (Boulder) Colorado and buried beside his wife, Eleanor, in the Gold Hill Cemetery, Gold Hill (Boulder) Colorado.

Q

There are no Qs.

Photograph by Dina C. Carson

R

RALPHS, Delbert Lloyd

> Birth: 05/05/1919
> Death: 09/07/2006
> Cemetery Location: H3

Father: Lloyd Noble Ralphs; Mother: Rose Ethel (*Higley*); Wife: Audrey Ann (*Bennett*); born in Brigham City (Box Elder) Utah and died in Louisville (Boulder) Colorado at age 87 years, 4 months, 2 days-pneumonia; Social Security states death date as 09/08/2006

Boulder Daily Camera 14 September 2006:

"Delbert L. Ralphs, of Louisville, died of pneumonia Thursday, Sept. 7, 2006, in Louisville. He was 87.

The son of Lloyds Ralphs and Rose Higley Ralphs, he was born May 5, 1919, in Brigham City, Utah.

Mr. Ralphs lived in Boulder from 1955 until 1987, when he moved to Louisville.

He earned a master's degree in chemistry from Oregon State University and did doctoral work at the University of Colorado.

He was a member of the U.S. Coast Guard and the U.S. Navy from 1939 until 1942 and worked for Dow/Rockwell at Rocky Flats from 1955 until 1981.

Mr. Ralphs was involved with Rocky Mountain Rescue Group and taught Junior Achievement in Boulder.

He enjoyed hiking, hunting, fishing, mountain climbing and gardening.

Survivors include two daughters, Megan Stewart, of Loveland, and Ann Tomsic, of Parker; one son, Randall Ralphs, of Pinecliff; nine grandchildren; and one great-grandchild.

He was preceded in death by a sister, Beth Ralphs; a brother, Honorus Ralphs; and a son, Delbert Ralphs Jr.

Gravesides services will be at 11 a.m. Friday at the Gold Hill Cemetery.

Darrell Howe Mortuary in Lafayette handled arrangements."

RAMSAY, David Robert Bevington III

> Birth: 09/30/1947
> Death: 09/18/1986
> Cemetery Location: B1

Father: David Robert Bevington Ramsay II: Mother: Evelyn (*Haines*); Wife: Debra S. (*Long*) Reich; born in Detroit (Wayne) Michigan and died in Boulder (Boulder) Colorado at age 38 years, 11 months, 19 days-coronary thrombosis, severe coronary atherosclerosis

Boulder Daily Camera 19 September 1986:

"David R. Ramsay

David R. Ramsay of 856-B Walnut St., Boulder, died at his home Thursday, September 18. He was 38.

Mr. Ramsay was born on Sept. 30, 1947, in Detroit, Mich. He was the son of David R. and Evelyn Haines Ramsay.

He married Debra S. Reich on April 4, 1981, in Ann Arbor, Mich.

He grew up In Redford, Mich., and moved to Ann Arbor in 1980. He moved to the Boulder area in 1983.

Mr. Ramsay was the owner of Ramsay Heating and Cooling in Boulder.

Survivors include his wife of Boulder; two daughters, Michelle Taritas of Ann Arbor and Heather Ramsay of Pinckney, Mich.; one brother, Alan Ramsay of Fort Myers, Fla.; one sister, Vickie Mackay of Redford, Mich.; and one grandson.

Visitation will be from 10 a.m. to 4 p.m. Saturday at Howe Mortuary, Boulder. Private services will be at 11 a.m. Monday at the Howe Mortuary Chapel.

Contributions in Mr. Ramsay's memory may be made to the Boulder County Humane Society, 2323 55th St., Boulder 80301."

REA, Marilyn T. (*Hein*)

> Birth: 11/28/1947
> Death: 01/10/2011
> Cemetery Location: C4

Father: Anthony J. Hein; Mother: Marie M. "Peg" (*maiden name unknown*); Husband: Timothy Rea; 2nd Husband: Tom Morris; born in Hastings (Barry) Michigan and died in Boulder (Boulder) Colorado at age 63 years, 1 month, 13 days-cancer

Las Cruces Sun-News (Las Cruces, New Mexico) 19 January 2011:

"Marilyn Rea 63 passed away Jan. 10th at her home surrounded by family and friends. She was born on Nov. 28, 1947 in Hastings, MI to Peg (Marie) and Tony Hein. Marilyn graduated from Hastings High School, received her bachelor's degree from Western Michigan University, and her teaching degree from Rudolph Steiner College. In 1976 she and her husband moved to Colorado where they lived in Gold Hill and Boulder. In 1998 she and her current husband moved to Silver City, NM for 44 years where they adopted their son, Dagan Pierce, before returning to Boulder.

Marilyn was a Waldorf Kindergarten teacher for 30 years where she cherished and nurtured generations of children. She was a much-loved part of the community for her warmth, her love of truth and integrity, and her enduring devotion to her family. Survivors include her daughter, Jamel (Raleigh Renfree) Rea; Husband Tom Morris; Son Dagan Pierce; Sister, Debra (John) Scott; previous Husband, Timothy Rea; Grandchildren, Rowan and Kyla Renfree.

A memorial service will be held at 1:00 p.m., Sat., Jan. 22nd, Unity Church of Boulder, 2855 Folsom St., Boulder. A reception will follow at the church. Donations may be sent to the family to help cover medical expenses. M.P. Murphy & Associates Funeral Directors is in charge of arrangements."

REEDY, Edward "Eddie"

> Birth: About 1875
> Death: About 1875
> Cemetery Location: Unknown

Father: Robert Hamill Reedy; Mother: Sylvia (*maiden name unknown*); born and died in Gold Hill (Boulder) Colorado at age infancy-cause of death unknown; according to NSDAR records the baby was one year old; no tombstone; see REEDY, Mary Kerr (*Rankin*)

Digging Up Dirt

About Edward "Eddie" Reedy

Edward's father, Robert Hamill Reedy, was born 08 December 1849 in Pennsylvania; the son of William Mickel (Michael) and Mary Kerr (*Rankin*) Reedy; see REEDY, Mary Kerr (*Rankin*).

On 24 February 1850 Robert was baptized at the Sinking Creek Presbyterian Church in Rebersburg (Centre) Pennsylvania.

In 1857 the family was living in Marengo (McHenry) Illinois where William Mickel Reedy died on 27 July 1857; buried at Marengo City Cemetery. His widow, Mary Kerr (*Rankin*) Reedy, married James Akervyd (Akroyd) Carpenter on 21 August 1867 in (Winnebago) Illinois.

The 1870 census shows Mary and her two sons, James and Edward, living with her new husband, James A. Carpenter in Jefferson (Greene) Iowa. Mary's other son, Robert Hamel, was out of the household.

According to the family letter below Mary and her four sons were living in (Boulder) Colorado.

Family letter 26 February 1959—written by Oliver T. Reedy to his brother, Edward Hagar Reedy (courtesy Robin Aslin, granddaughter of Edward Hagar Reedy):

"Dear Ed,

I want to make a start on telling you what I know about Father's [Oliver Kerr Reedy] three older brothers—as you requested some time ago—and will begin with Robert, next older than Father. I know least about him and the data I can put my finger on doesn't furnish much more. You may have some details that I don't know.

As you probably know Father was born in Curwensville, Clearfield Co., Penn. (I used to think it was Altoona.). Father spelled the place with a K, which made it a little difficult to identify. Since Robert H. (don't know what the "H" is for) was less than two years older than Father (Robert was born Dec. 8, 1849) I have been thinking that probably he also was born at Curwensville,—have no definite information.

Now to catch up with Robert again we'll have to skip to Melrose, Harlan Co., Nebr., where Mary [daughter of Oliver Kerr Reedy] was born Oct. 2, 1874. (Some years ago I learned from the Nebraska Historical Society that Melrose was the only town in Harlan Co., and was quite important as a trading center about 1870-1875.) Dr. Hoyt was Mother's physician. A family from Iowa consisting of the doctor's mother, about 60, and a grown brother and sister, on their way to her husband (presumably her second), a prospector for many years living near Nederland, Colo., (something like 23 miles from Gold Hill) had been living off Dr. Hoyt's family for several months. So in the summer of 1875 the doctor hired Father for the sum of $40.00 and all expenses to take the family to their destination in a light lumber wagon. Then Father went on

up to Gold Hill to visit his mother and three brothers, Robert, David and Edward. Four miles before reaching Gold Hill he passed thru a little place called Salina, where John had an assay office and small stock of merchandise. He also had a residence and his family with him. Father stayed there one night.

Apparently Robert's wife Sylvia was with him in Gold Hill. At one time I had a picture of her but have not been able to find it for several years. Their baby [Edward] is buried in the cemetery at Gold Hill. Father built a little picket fence around the grave, presumably on this trip. About 1925 during one of Father's early visits in Denver, we motored up to Gold Hill and out to the cemetery. The little fence, Father said, was in as good condition as when it was built, a half-century earlier. About four or five years ago we again visited the cemetery, and I can report the same.

Father started back to Harlan County in August. At Greeley, Colo., on Sept. 3, 1875, he wrote me a postal card asking me to "be a good boy and help Mama." (On Sept. 3, 1925 I replied, apologized for delaying so long in answering, and assured him that I had "helped Mama.") When Father reached his home, lo and behold there wasn't any Melrose. It had been amalgamated with the new town on the railroad several rods [sic] and was now a part of Orleans.

I don't know when Robert and Sylvia left Gold Hill—and each other, nor how much Father heard from or about Robert until almost exactly 79 years ago today. We had moved from the homestead to Orleans the summer before. Father received a wire from the Omaha Police that Robert had been killed in the railroad yards Feb. 22, 1880. Father went to Omaha right away and took care of the matter, and I suppose burial was in Omaha. At the time Robert was doing barbering, as evidenced by things in his baggage that Father brought home—a pair of scissors which we always called "barber scissors" because of a little curl outside the ring of the handle, for another finger. Perhaps you remember that pair of scissors. Also a couple of razors. I don't remember anything else.

Love from us both to both of you,

P.S.—I have, as you will of course note, mentioned many things not directly relating to Robert, but which I think will interest you as family history. Matters connected with Father's trip to Gold Hill were gleaned from Eva's notes as related to her by him on one of his visits to Denver. During that visit we tried to re-travel his route in general from Greeley toward Julesburg, but there were so many new paved roads, new buildings and fields distinct from the old trail and prairie that he could not identify much. He did feel sure he had one location identified from the terrain, but it was a different house,—entirely explainable."

Family Letter to Ed and Edna Reedy 27th February (year unknown) (courtesy Robin Aslin, relative):

Dear Ed and Edna,

I'm haunted by the idea that I've seen Robert. If so, the only time it could have been was on the homestead before we went to Orleans.—Off the record, as I remember, Robert was sorta the black sheep of the family—and Sylvia (?) was attractive but not the type to help him much. It seems to me that after the separation none of the Reedys ever heard of her again...

Love from us both you both [sic]

Oliver"

REEDY, Edward A. Hagar

Birth: 11/06/1856
Death: 02/20/1930
Cemetery Location: C1

Father: William Mickel (Michael) Reedy; Mother: Mary Kerr (*Rankin*); Wife: Martha Ann (*Wallick*); born in Marengo (McHenry) Illinois and died in Boulder (Boulder) Colorado at age 73 years, 3 months, 14 days-miners' consumption; wrong death year on tombstone; see REEDY, Mary Kerr (*Rankin*); see REEDY, Martha Ann (*Wallick*)

Boulder Daily Camera: 20 February 1930:

"EDWARD H. REEDY—Edward H. Reedy, a resident of Boulder for 58 years, died at his home at 1743 Walnut Street at 11 o'clock this morning of miner's consumption. He was engaged in mining at Gold Hill and vicinity for many years. He leaves the widow and four sons, Paul and Clyde Reedy, Doral of Denver and Edward of Rawlins, Wyo.; also two daughters, Mrs. Rachel Utterbeck of Denver and Mrs. Sarah Jacobson of Boulder. The remains are at Howe mortuary awaiting funeral arrangements."

Boulder Daily Camera 22 February 1930:

"EDWARD H. REEDY—Funeral services for Edward H. Reedy, who died Feb. 20, will be held at the Howe mortuary Sunday at one o'clock. Rev. M.M. McGorrill will officiate and burial will be in the Gold Hill cemetery."

About Edward Hagar Reedy

Edward Hagar Reedy was born 06 November 1856 in Marengo (McHenry) Illinois; the son of William Mickel (Michael) and Mary Kerr (*Rankin*) Reedy; see REEDY, Mary Kerr (*Rankin*).

He married Martha Ann Wallick on 25 March 1894 in Gold Hill (Boulder) Colorado; see REEDY, Martha Ann (*Wallick*). She was born 21 October 1872 in Victor (Poweshiek/Iowa) Iowa; the daughter of Ohio natives Henry Albion and Rachael (*Neville*) Wallick; see WALLICK, Rachel (*Neville*).

To this union six known children were born:

Rachael R.: born 14 January 1895 Gold Hill (Boulder) Colorado and died June 1975 Denver (Denver) Colorado; buried Fairmount Cemetery, Denver (Denver) Colorado; married Charles B. Utterback

Edward Phillip: born 10 January 1898 Gold Hill (Boulder) Colorado and died 31 October 1956 Denver (Denver) Colorado; buried Gold Hill Cemetery, Gold Hill (Boulder) Colorado; married Ella May Vallett; see REEDY, Edward Phillip

Lora L.: born 26 June 1900 Colorado and died 23 July 1982 Boulder (Boulder) Colorado; buried Green Mountain Cemetery, Boulder (Boulder) Colorado; married Clarence F. Jacobson; listed as Sarah in the obituary of Edward Hagar Reedy

Paul Wallick: born 16 July 1906 Boulder (Boulder) Colorado and died 14 September 1989 Mesa (Maricopa) Arizona; burial unknown; married Edith Mae Waldridge and Virginia Willamson (according to Ancestry)

Clyde R.: born 02 July 1915 Grand Junction (Mesa) Colorado and died 17 January 1997 Boulder (Boulder) Colorado; burial unknown; married Margaret Price

Doral E.: born 02 November 1908 Rural Colorado and died 12 September 1996 Arvada (Jefferson) Colorado; burial unknown; married Grace Estelle Pense

Prior to their marriage, Edward Hagar Reedy discovered the First National Bank lode in 1875 in Summerville (Boulder) Colorado along with Samuel Lindsey and Thomas Carlton. About five years later he was living in Gothic (Mesa) Colorado where he was a miner. His future bride, Martha Ann Wallick, was living in Solomon (Norton) Kansas in 1880 at the tender age of seven with her family. Five years later Martha was still there but soon her family was on their way to Colorado.

In 1900 Edward and Martha were living in Gold Hill (Boulder) Colorado where Edward was a mine foreman however ten years later the family was living in Pomona (Mesa) Colorado where Edward was working on a farm.

Apparently this line of work didn't suit him as by 1920 he was back living in Boulder (Boulder) Colorado where once again he worked in the mines. He remained in Boulder, living at 1743 Walnut Street until his death on 20 February 1930 from a heart attack. He is buried in the Gold Hill Cemetery in Gold Hill (Boulder) Colorado.

His widow, Martha, continued living in the same house in Boulder (Boulder) Colorado until about 1944 when she moved to Denver (Denver) Colorado. She died in St. Anthony's Hospital in Denver (Denver) Colorado after a long illness. She is also buried in the family plot in the Gold Hill Cemetery.

It is interesting to note that in the previous Gold Hill Cemetery records Edward Hagar Reedy was listed as serving in Company F 45th Iowa Infantry however no records for Edward have been located for either Iowa or Illinois (Union or Confederate) and Edward would have only been no more than 9 years old at the time of the Civil War.

REEDY, Edward Phillip

Birth: 01/10/1898
Death: 10/31/1956
Cemetery Location: C1

Father: Edward Hagar Reedy; Mother: Martha Ann (*Wallick*); Wife: Ella May (*Vallett*); born in Gold Hill (Boulder) Colorado and died in Denver (Denver) Colorado at age 58 years, 9 months, 21 days-heart attack; see REEDY, Edward Hagar; see REEDY, Martha Ann (*Wallick*); see

About Edward Hagar Reedy

Boulder Daily Camera 31 October 1956:

"Edward P. Reedy Dies Suddenly Of Heart Attack...A heart attack suffered in Denver Tuesday night by Edward P. Reedy resulted in his death in St. Joseph's Hospital this morning at 10 o'clock. He was in Denver for the winter from Craig, where he was in the sheep business, to be with a sister, Mrs. Rachel Utterback.

Mr. Reedy was a brother of Clyde R. Reedy, cashier of the National State Bank. He was born at Gold Hill, west of

Boulder Jan. 10th, 1898 to Edward H. Reedy and Martha W. Reedy who preceded him in death. Besides Mrs. Utterback he is survived by another sister, Mrs. Lora Jacobson of Estes Park, and besides Clyde two other brothers, Paul of Glenwood Springs and Doral of Mt. Morrison.

Funeral services are to be held in charge of Howe Mortuary."

Boulder Daily Camera 01 November 1956:

"Edward P. Reedy, who died in St. Joseph's Hospital Wednesday morning of a heart attack suffered the previous night in Denver—Private services Friday at Howe Mortuary Chapel. Family requests flowers not be sent. Interment is to be in the family plot in the Gold Hill Cemetery."

Boulder Daily Camera 02 November 1956:

"Edward P. Reedy—Private services today from Howe Mortuary chapel, with Rev. Marvin Adams, pastor of the First Methodist church, officiating. Mrs. Margaret Hascall, organist. Interment Gold Hill cemetery."

About Edward Phillip Reedy

Edward Phillip Reedy was born 10 January 1898 in Gold Hill (Boulder) Colorado; the son of Edward Hagar and Martha Ann (*Wallick*) Reedy; see REEDY, Edward Hagar; see REEDY, Martha Ann (*Wallick*).

In the 1910 census the family was living in Pomona (Mesa) Colorado where it is suspected Edward met Ella May Vallett and married her on 30 November 1917 there. She was born 18 February 1895 in Elmdale (Morrison) Minnesota; the daughter of Gilbert Rensellaer and Mary Ann (*Lovell*) Vallett. To their union four known children were born:

Forrest Vallett: born 16 September 1918 Colorado and died 29 September 1971 (Kern) California; buried Forest Lawn Memorial Park, Glendale (Los Angeles) California; married Elaine Finch

Martha Lovell: born 11 January 1921 Thompson (Grand) Utah and died 21 January 2013 Denver (Lancaster) Pennsylvania; burial unknown; married Albert Danzel Sebastian

Glen Farrington: born 18 December 1922 Boulder (Boulder) Colorado and died 30 October 1978 United States; burial Norton Cemetery, Norton (Norton) Kansas; married Audrey Luvina McFarland; U.S. Marine Corps

Betty Jane: born 24 February 1927 Oak Creek (Routt) Colorado and died 10 September 1995 Wichita (Sedgwick) Kansas; buried Resthaven Gardens of Memory, Wichita (Sedgwick) Kansas; married Sidwell Vance Phipps

Three years later in 1920 Edward and Ella were living in Glade Park (Mesa) Colorado with their infant son, Forest.

The 1930 census is interesting as it lists Ella as a widow with four young children: Forrest (11 years), Martha (9 years), Glen (7 years) and Betty Jane (3 years). She was working as a laundress in her home on Carbon Avenue in Oak Creek (Routt) Colorado.

There isn't a 1930 Colorado census record for Edward however his World War II registration card (1940-1947) indicates he was living in Rawlins (Carbon) Wyoming with his mother, Martha, as contact person. It seems likely to conclude that Edward and Ella were separated and possibly divorced and it was common that the woman would list herself as a widow than a divorcee.

Ella lived only two years after the 1930 census, dying on 15 December 1932 in Denver (Denver) Colorado. She was buried in the Fairmount Cemetery there. Her children went to various households. In the 1940 census Forrest was living in Fort Collins (Larimer) Colorado with his wife, Katherine. His sister, Martha, was living with her Aunt Rachael Utterbeck (Edward Phillip's sister) in Denver (Denver) Colorado. Glen, at 17 years of age, was a ward in the household of Thomas B. Zaughlin, living in Oak Creek (Routt) Colorado. The youngest, Betty Jane, was a mere 3 years old when her mother died and ended up in the household of Robert B. Anglin where she is listed as his "daughter." Social Security Index for her has both Reedy and Anglin as her maiden names.

Edward lived more than two decades longer, dying on 31 October 1956 in St. Joseph's Hospital in Denver (Denver) Colorado from an apparent heart attack. He was buried in the family plot in Gold Hill (Boulder) Colorado.

REEDY, Eva Marie (*McCune*)

Birth: 10/30/1877
Death: 02/13/1963
Cemetery Location: C1

Father: Calmer McCune; Mother: Julia (*Bell*); Husband: Oliver Thomas Reedy; born in David City (Butler) Nebraska; incorrect birth year on tombstone; remembrance tombstone; see REEDY, Oliver Thomas; see **About Oliver Thomas Reedy**

Rocky Mountain News 13 February 1963:

"Memorial services for Mrs. Eva M. Reedy, longtime Denver resident will be at 3 p.m. Wednesday in Moore Mortuary. Private cremation will follow.

Mrs. Reedy died Sunday in Presbyterian Hospital. She lived at 2340 Dahlia st. She was 85.

Born Oct. 30, 1877, in David, City, Nebr., she came to Denver in 1918 from Torrington, Wyo.

Mrs. Reedy was a member of First Plymouth Congregational Church and the Wednesday Morning Study Club.

Surviving is a son, William, of 780 Field st., Lakewood.

Persons who wish may make memorial donations to CARE.

Officiating at the Memorial Service will be the Rev. William Spence, pastor of the First Plymouth Congregational Church."

REEDY, Lois Jean (*Hammond*)

Birth: 02/12/1919
Death: 11/05/2000
Cemetery Location: C1

Father: James M. Hammond; Mother: Elizabeth (*Hemler*); Husband: William Wesley Reedy; born in Lincoln (Lancaster) Nebraska and died Lakewood (Jefferson) Colorado; see REEDY, William Wesley

Rocky Mountain News 28 November 2000:

"Lois Hammond Reedy, 81, of Lakewood died Nov. 5. Services will be at 4 p.m. Thursday, Nov. 30, at First Presbyterian Church of Lakewood, 8210 W. 10th Ave. Mrs. Reedy was born in Lincoln, Neb., on Feb. 12, 1919. She married William Reedy, 1941. She was a homemaker and artist. Survivors include her husband, daughters Gail Iskiyan of Highlands Ranch, Anna Rain of Maryland, son Bruce of Washington D.C; seven grandchildren, a great grandchild."

REEDY, Martha Ann (*Wallick*)

> Birth: 10/21/1872
> Death: 01/18/1952
> Cemetery Location: C1

Father: Henry Wallick; Mother: Rachael K. (*Neville*); Husband: Edward Hagar Reedy; born in Victor (Poweshiek/Iowa) Iowa and died in Denver (Denver) Colorado at age 79 years, 3 months, 28 days-long illness; see REEDY, Edward Hagar; see WALLICK, Rachael K. (*Neville*)

Boulder Daily Camera 18 January 1952:

"Mrs. Martha Reedy, Mother of Boulder Bank Officer, Dies…A long illness resulted in the death this afternoon Of Mrs. Martha W. Reedy, mother of Clyde R. Reedy, assistant cashier of the National State bank of Boulder. Her death occurred in St. Anthony's hospital Denver. The body is being brought to Howe Mortuary. Further particulars were not available at press time today."

Boulder Daily Camera 19 January 1952:

"Mrs. Martha W. Reedy—Funeral services will be held at How mortuary Tuesday morning at 10 for Mrs. Martha W. Reedy, who died in St. Anthony's hospital in Denver Friday, after a long illness. She was the mother of Ed H. Reedy and the mother of Clyde Reedy, assistant cashier of the National State bank.

Mrs. Ready was born in Victor, Iowa, October 21, 1872 and came to Colorado from Norton, Kansas, 61 years ago. Besides the son, Clyde, there are three other sons, Paul of Basalt, Colorado; Ed of Rawlins, Wyo.; and Doral of Mt. Morrison, Colorado. There are also two daughters, Mrs. Rachel Utterback of Denver and Mrs. Lora Jacobson of Colorado Springs. There are eleven grandchildren and seven great grandchildren.

Rev. Earl Williams, pastor of the Nazarene church, will officiate. Interment will be in Gold Hill."

REEDY, Mary Kerr (*Rankin*)

> Birth: 08/14/1824
> Death: 09/14/1902
> Cemetery Location: C1

Father: John McGinley Rankin; Mother: Catherine (*Kerr*); Husband: William Mickel Reedy; born in Pennsylvania and died in Boulder (Boulder) Colorado at age 78 years, 1 month-dropsy (heart failure)

Boulder Daily Camera 15 September 1902:

"BURIAL AT GOLD HILL—Mrs. M.R. Reedy, who died at the home of her son, D.M. Reedy, Sunday morning at 3 o'clock of dropsy, was buried from the Presbyterian church this morning and the remains taken to Gold Hill for interment."

About Mary Kerr (*Rankin*) Reedy

Mary Kerr (*Rankin*) Reedy was born 14 August 1824 in Pennsylvania; the daughter of John McGinley and Catherine (*Kerr*) Rankin. She married William Mickel Reedy 30 December 1845 in Pennsylvania. William was born 06 July 1821 in Pennsylvania; the son of Henry Edward and Margaret (*Mickel*) Reedy. Their union produced seven known children:

John Rankin: born 06 October 1846 Pennsylvania and died 28 September 1914 Steamboat Springs (Routt) Colorado; buried Steamboat Springs Cemetery, Steamboat Springs (Routt) Colorado; married Mary Jane Alley

William Henry: born 15 February 1848 Pennsylvania and died 21 August 1917 Bloomington (McLean) Illi-

nois; buried Chicago (Cook) Illinois; married Sarah Jane Slemmons and Helen Nellie Fincham; he was a physician

Robert Hamill: born 08 December 1849 Pennsylvania and died 22 February 1880 Omaha (Douglas) Nebraska; burial unknown; married Silvia (maiden name unknown)

Oliver Kerr: born 16 October 1851 Curwensville (Clearfield) Pennsylvania and died 10 February 1945 Pomona (Los Angeles) California; buried in Pomona (Los Angeles) California; married Elizabeth Catherine "Kate" B. Sherrill

James Jay/Jackson Hamilton: born 03 May 1853 Pennsylvania and died 06 February 1941 Tulsa (Tulsa) Oklahoma; buried Memorial Park Cemetery, Tulsa (Tulsa) Oklahoma; married Candace "Carrie" E. MacDougal

David M.: born 01 January 1855 Illinois and died 18 February 1935 (San Diego) California; buried Green Mountain Cemetery, Boulder (Boulder) Colorado; married Mary E. Wright and Ida Elizabeth Hunter

Edward Hagar: born 06 November 1856 Marengo (McHenry) Illinois and died 20 February 1930 Boulder (Boulder) Colorado; buried Gold Hill Cemetery, Gold Hill (Boulder) Colorado; married Martha Ann Wallick; see REEDY, Edward Hagar; see REEDY, Martha Ann (*Wallick*)

The early married life of William Mickel and Mary Kerr (*Rankin*) Reedy was spent at Curwensville (Clearfield) Pennsylvania. By 1855 they had moved to Freeport (Stephenson) Illinois. A few years later they moved again to Marengo (McHenry) Illinois where there was a Presbyterian Academy, founded in 1852 however burned down in 1854. A historian in McHenry County states that the town of Marengo still might have been a center of importance to Presbyterian ministers for some reason. Since William was a Presbyterian missionary this might had been a reason for moving there.

At the young age of 36 years old, William died 27 July 1857 in Marengo (McHenry) Illinois. The reason for his death is not known but he is buried in Marengo City Cemetery there.

His widow, Mary, was left with seven young sons-one not yet a year old and the oldest not yet 11 at the time of William's death. Three years later (1860) Mary is living still in Marengo with her three sons, Robert, David and Edmund where she is a dressmaker.

About seven years later she married James Akervyd (Akroyd) Carpenter on 21 August 1867 in (Winnebago) Illinois. Born about 1810 in England, he was a cabinetmaker.

By 1870 they were living in Jefferson (Greene) Iowa with Mary's sons, James H. and Edward H. It appears that James A. Carpenter either left the family or died between 1870 and 1875 as Mary and her sons, John, David,

Robert and Edward were all living in Gold Hill (Boulder) Colorado (John in Salina (Boulder) Colorado) by 1875.

It is said that Mary acquired a teaching certificate on 19 March 1898 at the age of 74 years however no records of her actually teaching have been located.

Two years later in the 1900 census Mary Kerr (*Rankin*) Reedy was living alone in Boulder (Boulder) Colorado, renting a house on 17th Street at listed age of 75 years old and a widow. It is interesting to note that Mary did not use her second marriage name of Carpenter. A short two years later she passed away at the home of her son (David M. Reedy) at 1828 Bluff Street in Boulder (Boulder) Colorado from dropsy (heart failure). She is buried in the family plot in Gold Hill (Boulder) Colorado.

REEDY, Oliver Thomas

> Birth: 03/10/1873
> Death: 05/24/1965
> Cemetery Location: C1

Father: Oliver Kerr Reedy; Mother: Elizabeth Catherine "Kate" B. (*Sherrill*); Wife: Eva Marie (*McCune*); born in Nebraska City (Otoe) Nebraska and died in unknown; remembrance tombstone; see REEDY, Eve Marie (*McCune*)

Denver Post 30 May 1965:

"Services for Oliver T. Reedy, 92, of 780 Field St., Lakewood, retired former senior assistant Colorado state highway engineer, will be at the First Presbyterian Church of Lakewood, 8210 W. 10th Ave. at 2 p.m. Tuesday. Burial will be in Fairmount.

He died Monday at Beth Israel Hospital after a brief illness.

Reedy was born March 10, 1873, at Nebraska City, Neb. He was a graduate of the University of Nebraska. Most of his professional career was with the U.S. Reclamation Bureau and the Colorado State Highway Department. Prior to his retirement in 1950, he had been senior assistant state highway engineer for 29 years.

He married Eva M. McCune in Stromsburg, Neb., in 1904. She died in 1963.

Reedy was past president of the Colorado Society of Engineers and Colorado Section, American Society of Engineers. He was a life member of both societies and of the Colorado Engineering Council. He was a member of the First Plymouth Congregational Church and Park Hill Lodge 148, AF&AM.

Survivors include two sons, William W. Reedy of Lakewood and Oliver C. Reedy of Billings, Mont., and a daughter, Mrs. Victor R. Seymour of Lincoln, Neb., and nine grandchildren."

Rocky Mountain News 30 May 1965:

"Funeral services for Oliver T. Reedy, retired senior

assistant state highway engineer, will be at 2 p.m. Tuesday in First Presbyterian Church of Lakewood. Cremation will be at Fairmount.

Mr. Reedy, who lived at 780 Field st., Lakewood, died Monday at Beth Israel Hospital. He was 92.

Born in Nebraska City, Nebr., on March 10, 1873, he was a graduate of the University of Nebraska. Most of his professional career was with the U.S. Reclamation Service and the Colorado Highway Department. Before his retirement he had been senior assistant state highway engineer 29 years.

He married Eva M. McCune in Stromsburg, Nebr. on September 20, 1904. Mrs. Reedy died in 1963.

Mr. Reedy was past president of the Colorado Society of Engineers and the Colorado Section American Society of Engineers. He was a life member of both societies and of the Colorado Engineering Council. He was a member of First Plymouth Congregational Church and Park Hill Masonic Lodge.

Friends may contribute to the memorial scholarship fund of the Colorado Section of Civil Engineers in care of David Day, Engineering Society Bldg., 1380 S. Santa Fe dr.

Surviving are two sons, William W. of Lakewood and Oliver C. of Billings, Mont., a daughter, Mrs. Victor R. Seymour of Lincoln, Nebr., two brothers, J. Albert Reedy of Santa Susana, Calif., and Ray R. Reedy of Santa Cruz, Calif.; two sisters, Miss Effie Reedy of San Francisco and Miss Katherine Reedy of Paradise, Calif., and nine grandchildren."

About Oliver Thomas Reedy

Oliver Thomas Reedy was born 10 March 1873 in Nebraska City (Otoe) Nebraska; the son of Oliver Kerr and Elizabeth Catherine "Kate" Blodgett (*Sherrill*) Reedy. His father, Oliver Kerr Reedy, was an older brother to Edward Hagar Reedy; see REEDY, Edward Hagar. His mother, Elizabeth Catherine "Kate" Blodgett Sherrill, was born 26 September 1849 in (Moniteau) Missouri; the daughter of Thomas and Mary Anslis (*Blodgett*) Sherrill.

Oliver Thomas married Eva Marie McCune 20 September 1904 in Stromsburg (Polk) Nebraska. Eva Marie McCune was born 30 October 1877; the daughter of Calmar and Julia (*Bell*) McCune; see REEDY, Eva Marie (*McCune*). To this union three known children were born:

Oliver Calmar: born 13 November 1909 Orman Dan, 8 miles east of Belle Fourche (Butte) South Dakota and died 21 March 2005 Sykesville (Carroll) Maryland; married Lucie Margaret Starr

Margaret Maribel: born 01 October 1911 Orman Dam, 8 miles east of Belle Fourche (Butte) South Dakota and died 01 December 2001 Lincoln (Lancaster) Nebraska; married Victor R. Seymour

William Wesley: born 22 December 1916 Wheatland (Platte) Wyoming and died 12 October 2007 Colorado; buried Gold Hill Cemetery, Gold Hill (Boulder) Colorado; married Lois Jean Hammond; see REEDY, William Wesley; see REEDY, Lois Jean (*Hammond*)

The last known address for Oliver Thomas and Eva Marie (*McCune*) Reedy was Denver (Denver) Colorado.

REEDY, William Wesley

Birth: 12/22/1916
Death: 10/12/2007
Cemetery Location: C1

Father: Oliver Thomas Reedy; Mother: Eva Marie (*McCune*); Wife: Lois Jean (*Hammond*); born in Wheatland (Platte) Wyoming and died in Englewood (Arapahoe) Colorado at age 90 years 9 months, 20 days-old age; see REEDY, Oliver Thomas; see REEDY, Eva Marie (*McCune*); see REEDY, Lois Jean (*Hammond*)

Rocky Mountain News 26 October 2007:

"William Wesley Reedy was born on December 22, 1916 in Wheatland, Wyoming, while his father was working for the Bureau of Reclamation in Ft. Laramie. He joined an older brother, Calmar, and an older sister, Margaret. Will spent his childhood in the Park Hill neighborhood of Denver, and the family attended Montview Presbyterian Church for many years.

After graduating from East High in 1935 he attended Denver University for one year before transferring to the University of Nebraska. He graduated with distinction, receiving a degree in civil engineering 1939. There, he met Lois Jean Hammond, whom he married in May, 1941. The two were unfailing Nebraska supporters, attending uncountable football games, often in unspeakable weather. Up until the last week of his life, whenever Nebraska was mentioned, Will would burst into song with "There is no place like Nebraska."

Will and Lois lived in Boise, Idaho, in the first year of their marriage, while Will worked for the Bureau of Reclamation. There, their daughter Gail Elizabeth was born in 1945 and son Bruce William, was born in 1946.

Will and Lois were adventurers, and did not hesitate to take a job in Juneau, Alaska, in 1947, when the area was still a territory.

In both Boise and Juneau, they were active in church and square dance communities. Will was an accomplished and popular square dance caller, and Lois accompanied him on the piano.

The family relocated to the Denver area in 1952, eventually settling in Lakewood.

They spent a year in Boston, in 1957-8, while Will completed a Master's in Public Administration at the Litthauer School of Harvard University. Their third child, Anna Caroline, was born in 1961.

Will's extensive community service centered around the First Presbyterian Church of Lakewood, where he served several terms as an elder, and sang in the church choir along with Lois. He also played cello in the Jefferson Symphony Orchestra for 36 years. Both Will and Lois sang in the Colorado Chorale in the early 1980s, and Lois continued with the group for many more years. Music—informal, spontaneous, and joyful—was always present in the Reedy home.

Will's talents also included that of an athlete: he played tennis most of his life, starting at East High. Over the years, the basement of the Reedy house was filled with trophies from his tennis escapades.

Will retired from the Bureau of Reclamation in 1979 (?) His father and brother also worked for the Bureau, with nearly 100 years of service among the three of them.

While with the government, Will was awarded both the silver medal of meritorious service and the gold medal of distinguished service. After retirement, Will continued to work as a consultant on water source issues with Texaco.

Will was a kind, gentle, moral man, whose quiet strength and deep humility were an example to all who knew him. He was a life-long Christian who lived each day by the precept, "What would Jesus have done?" long before this phrase was made popular. His heart-felt Christian beliefs led him to become a conscientious objector during WWII.

He lived the last four years at the Meridian Retirement Community in Englewood, where his cheerful demeanor made him a favorite of the staff. He was grateful for small kindnesses, and never failed to make his love and appreciation known.

He leaves his three children, two sons-in-law (Tom Iskiyan; David Rain), and seven grandchildren (Brad Iskiyan; Malinda Grommet; Lauren Reedy; Avery Rain; Lydia Rain; Callen Rain; Jasper Rain), as well as two great-grandchildren (Emily Iskiyan; Davis Iskiyan). His family and friends will dearly miss him. Services will be held on Friday, November 9, 2007, at 4 pm at the First Presbyterian Church of Lakewood, at 8210 W. 10th Ave., Lakewood. Donations in Will's name are welcome to the Music Program at the First Presbyterian Church."

REESE, Jonathan

Birth: About 07/1976
Death: 04/08/1977
Cemetery Location: B1

Father: Ron Reese; Mother: Bonnie (*maiden name unknown*); died at 9 months from what was believed to have been an unusual flash reaction to a pneumonia germ

Washington Post (article in part by Tom Huth) 29 May 1977:

"He was Jonathan Reese, 9 month old, son and only child of Ron and Bonnie. And it was every parent's secret horror come to pass. Ron woke up in the morning and, when he went to see if his son was awake, he was dead. There was no reason, no apparent struggle, no warning; Jonathan was dead. The doctors tried to explain later that it was some unusual flash reaction to a pneumonia germ, but that was no explanation at all. It was no one's fault, the coroner said, but Jonathan was dead...

...out here [Gold Hill Cemetery at Jonathan's burial] in the dusky coming-of-evening he [Chuck Ogsbury] was

quoting a Blackfoot Indian chief, named Crowfoot. Crowfoot said:

What is life?

It is the breath of a buffalo in wintertime.

It is the little shadow

Which runs across the grass

And loses itself in the sunset."

REGNIER, Ellen Rosellia (*Romig*)

Birth: 09/30/1907
Death: 01/01/1982
Cemetery Location: C1

Father: John W. Romig; Mother: Zula M. (*Reedy*); Husband: James Dussart Regnier; born in Gold Hill (Boulder) Colorado and died in Boulder (Boulder) Colorado at age 74 years, 3 months, 2 days; great granddaughter of Mary Kerr (*Rankin*) Reedy; see REEDY, Mary Kerr (*Rankin*); see REGNIER, James Dussart; see REGNIER, Richard James Dussart; see **About the Regnier Family**

Boulder Daily Camera 06 January 1982:

"Ellen R. Regnier—Ellen Rosellia Regnier, 1050 Arapahoe Ave., died Jan. 1 at her home. She was 74. She was born September 30, 1907, in Gold Hill, the daughter of John and Zula Romig. She married James D. Regnier in Boulder on Sept. 29, 1950. A school teacher with the Weld County Public Schools, she attended Colorado State Teachers College in Greeley. She taught in Gold Hill and Erie schools and for the Department of Continuing Education of the University of Colorado. She was a lifelong resident of the Boulder area. She is survived by a stepson, Richard Regnier of Malibu, Calif.; two stepdaughters, Verna Williams of Lafayette and Celia Green of Berthoud; 13 step-grandchildren and six step-great-grandchildren. Her husband died in December 1972. Memorial services will be Friday at 2 p.m. at Trinity Lutheran Church; the Rev. Donald P. Knudsen will officiate. Contributions may be made to the Heart Fund, in care of Diana Kahn, 760 Flagstaff Road, Boulder 80302. Crist Mortuary is handling arrangements."

REGNIER, James Dussart

Birth: 06/30/1899
Death: 12/12/1972
Cemetery Location: C1

Father: Modestus/Modeste/Modest "Mike" Dussart; Mother: Celia (*Phiefer/Phifer*); Wives: Daisy (*Dryer*), Iris Diane Ruby (*Stogsdill*), Ellen Rosellia (*Romig*); born in Aguilar (Las Animas) Colorado and died in Longmont (Boulder) Colorado-silicosis (black lung); see REGNIER, Ellen Rosellia (*Romig*); see REGNIER, Richard James Dussart; see **About the Regnier Family**

Boulder Daily Camera 14 December 1972:

"James Regnier—James D. Regnier, 73, of Erie, died at Longmont United Hospital Tuesday. He was born on June 30, 1899, in Aguilar, and was married in Boulder on Sept. 29, 1950 [Ellen Romig]. He was a coal miner in Erie for 30 years. Survivors include his wife, Ellen of Longmont; one son, Richard, Odessa, Tex.; two daughters, Mrs. Verna Williams, Brownsville, and Mrs. Celia Green, Berthoud; four brothers, one sister and 14 grandchildren. Funeral services will be Friday at 10:30 a.m. at Erie Methodist Church with Rev. Milton Berg officiating. Interment will be in Gold Hill Cemetery. Howe Mortuary, Longmont, is in charge of arrangements."

REGNIER, Kathleen Doris (*Grannis*)

Birth: 10/14/1957
Death: 02/16/1995
Location: C1

Father: Ellsworth Barnes Grannis; Mother: Doris Sophia (*Lockyer*); Husband: Richard J. Regnier Jr.; born and died in Phoenix (Maricopa) Arizona at age 37 years, 4 months, 2 days; see **About the Regnier Family**

The Arizona Republic 23 February 1995:

"Kathleen Doris Regnier, 37, of Phoenix, died Feb. 16th, 1995. She was born in Phoenix. Survivors include her husband, Richard; daughter, Christina; sons, Richard and Robert; mother, Doris Grannis; sisters, Betty Renshaw, Ann Hensley and Edith Clark; brother, David Grannis. Services: noon to 6pm. Saturday, Covenant of Grace Christian Fellowship, 906 W. Peoria Ave. Contributions: Katy Regnier Memorial Fund, 1720 N. 36th Lane, Phoenix, AZ 85308. Best Funeral Services."

REGNIER, Richard James Dussart

    Birth: 08/17/1928
    Death: 10/28/2015
    Cemetery Location: C1

Father: James Dussart Regnier; Mother: Iris Diane Ruby (*Stogsdill*); Wives: Elsie May (*McCaghren*), Gwendolyn (*Mercer*) Hunter, Helen Swanson; born in Erie (Boulder/Weld) Colorado and died in Westminster (Broomfield) Colorado at age 87 years, 2 months, 11 days-natural causes; see REGNIER, James Dussart; see REGNIER Ellen Rosellia (*Romig*); see **About the Regnier Family**

Denver Post 01 November 2015:

"RICHARD JAMES DUSSART REGNIER...Richard, 87, of Westminster, passed away October 28, 2015. Visitation, Sun., Nov. 1, 2-4 PM, Horan & McConaty, 80th Ave. & Wadsworth, Arvada. Graveside Service, Tues., Nov. 3, 12 PM, Gold Hill Cemetery. Memorial Service, Wed., Nov. 4, 1 pm, Covenant Village of Colorado—Smith Hall, 9221 Wadsworth. View life story and guestbook at HoranCares.com."

Online Obituary (www.horancares.com):

"Richard is known in Covenant Village for his detailed pencil drawings. He was not only an accomplished art-

ist but also a prolific writer—one who prided himself on writing good, clean Christian books. He did a series of 10 books for children called the "Feather books." Four are presently on Amazon.com under the name Richard James Dussart Regnier and the other six are being read for publication. Richard gave his life to God when he was stationed in Greenland. It was then that his talents started to blossom. He also wrote numerous history books about Gold Hill, CO, having interviewed many of the old timers there. He drew all 88 of their original cabins. The history books can be found in the Gold Hill Museum-Library and in Boulder's Carnegie library where he also gave presentations of the history of Gold Hill.

He has written over 1,000 poems that he considered his songs. Everyone knew his love of music for in a church service or musical, he would be "directing the choir." And that is what he did in Midland, Texas, he directed the choir in the Baptist church.

He has been recognized by many groups in which he was active such as the Veterans of Foreign Wars, Lions Club, and his work as a probation officer in Lamesa, TX. He is a life member of The Disabled Americans and has a lifetime membership in the Gideons which he supported generously.

Richard taught school in Texas and is a retired teacher. He also is a retired U.S. Air Force Staff Sergeant. Rich-

"ARTIST; POET; AUTHOR; SONGWRITER;
21-YEAR VETERAN, U.S.A.F.; GIDEON;
TEACHER; MASTER OF INDUSTRIAL ARTS;
GOLD HILL HISTORIAN"

ard was talented in many ways. He had owned a TV repair shop which prepared him to work in Texas for a Christian TV station interviewing guest missionaries. He had a huge workshop. From there he built a free-standing art studio for himself and was a locksmith. While stationed in Mississippi Richard flagged for car races and was a member of the Sons of the American Revolution and Spearfishing & Skindiving Clubs. His interests were numerous and varied, from the arts to the practical every day events as working for the railroad and summer jobs on the farm.

Survived by his wife, Helen Swanson; siblings Celia, Carol and Mike; sons, Rick Jr., Russell, and Ronald; grandchildren, Rick, III, Robert, Christina, Rusty, Pascal Schrix, Ronald, Scott Ross, Kelly Ross, and Ryan Valder; and 17 great grandchildren. Proceeded in death by his daughter, Renee.

Richard has been known at CVC to be generous with his artwork and has given prints of some of his drawings to people in appreciation of their efforts and attention. He said that God gave him the talent and he wanted to share it with others. Helen chose her favorite which is a pencil drawing of a Texas windmill shrunk to half a page and a poem also done by Richard on the other half. Please accept it as his gift to you. One per family please. He wants to be known as "one who pulled a few weeds and planted some flowers as I pass this way."

Visitation, Sunday, November 1, 2-4 PM, Horan & McConaty Family Chapel, 7577 West 80th Avenue, Arvada. Graveside Service, Tuesday, November 3, 12 PM, Gold Hill Cemetery, Boulder, CO 80302. Memorial Service, Wednesday, 1PM, Covenant Village of Colorado—Smith Hall, 9221 Wadsworth Parkway, Westminster.

In lieu of flowers, memorials may be made in his name to Covenant Village of Colorado, 9153 Yarrow Street, Westminster, CO 80021 or The Gideons International, Denver Northwest Camp, PO Box 839, Westminster, CO 80036."

About the Regnier Family

James Dussart (Regnier) was born 30 June 1899 in Aguilar (Las Animas) Colorado; the son of Modestus/Modeste/Modest "Mike" and Celia (*Phiefer/Phifer*) Dussart.

Modestus was one of five known children born to Louis Frederick and Catherine (*Rinchon*) Dussart on 18 January 1876 in Belgium. (Social Security Applications and Claims Index lists date of birth 18 February 1870 with birth place Trinidad (Las Animas) Colorado which is incorrect.) His siblings were:

Louis Frederick Jr.: born 04 May 1874 Brussels (Brabant) Belgium and died 31 March 1919 Aguilar (Las Animas) Colorado; buried Knights of Pythias Cemetery, Aguilar (Las Animas) Colorado; married Agnes "Aggie" Seppi/Seppie

Arthur G.: born 04 September 1877 Belgium and died November 1962 Colorado; burial unknown; married Clara Tasso

Julia Ghislaine: born 01 April 1886 (Hainaut) Belgium and died 25 March 1982 Henryetta (Okmulgee) Oklahoma; buried Okmulgee Cemetery, Okmulgee (Okmulgee) Oklahoma; married Benjamin Joseph Thirionet/Olhirionet; Social Security Applications and Claims Index has Julia D. Grayson (Julia D. Dussart)

Edith L.: born 12 September 1892 Colorado and died 29 May 1981 (Napa) California; burial unknown; married George E. Yaminsky and Elmer Frank George

It appears Louis Frederick Dussart immigrated to the United States a few years earlier than the rest of his family. He located in Aguilar (Las Animas) Colorado where he was a coal miner. His wife, Catherine, and five children (Louis, Mary, Modestus, Arthur and Julia) left Antwerp, Belgium on the ship Noordland, arriving at the Port of New York on 14 May 1891 with their final destination listed as Trinidad (Las Animas) Colorado.

After settling in Colorado Louis Frederick and Catherine had one more child, a daughter Edith.

Gold Hill Men 1859 to 1850 by Richard J. D. Regnier 2005:

"My great-grandpa, Louis Dussart, came from Belgium to Aguilar, Colorado where he found work as a coal miner. I believe he had been a coal miner in Belgium. My grandpa (Modestus/Modeste/Modest "Mike" Dussart) and my dad (James Dussart Regnier) were both coal miners."

Louis Frederick Dussart died at the age of 44 years on 04 July 1896 and is buried in St. Anthony's Cemetery in Aguilar (Las Animas) Colorado. His widow, Catherine, lived quite a number of years longer until 1929.

Boulder Daily Camera 23 December 1929:

"Louisville Woman Dies Here Of Burns Received When Stove In Her Home Exploded Sunday...

An explosion of an unknown source caused the death of Ms. Katherine Dussart, 77, aged Louisville widow last night. Mrs. Dussart was alone in her little cottage near the Acme mine when about 9:15 an explosion was heard by neighbors. As soon as they could ascertain the location of the explosion they rushed to the house to find Mrs. Dussart badly burnt.

Dr. Walter E. Reed was called to the Community Hospital where Mrs. Dussart was brought shortly after the accident. She was treated for her severe burns. She died at the Community Hospital at 7:20 this morning.

Coroner A. E. Howe went to Louisville this afternoon to determine the cause of the explosion. It is thought that

Mrs. Dussart was trying to build a fire, and that she used something which she thought to be kerosene. She was severely burned from her head to her feet, and hospital attaches were surprised that she lived as long as she did.

Mrs. Dussart was born in Belgium and came to this country 39 years ago. She leaves a large family, who will have to be notified. Her husband passed away several years ago. Two years ago she came to Louisville where she had lived up until the time of her death. Funeral arrangements await word from relatives, and Coroner Howe's investigation.

Mrs. Dussart is survived by three daughters, Mrs. J. Regnier of Boulder, Mrs. Ben Thirlonet of Oklahoma, Mrs. Edith George of Los Angeles, Calif., and two sons, Modeste Dussart of Oklahoma and Arthur Dussart of Trinidad. In addition she leaves 34 grandchildren and 15 great grandchildren."

Boulder Daily Camera 24 December 1929:

"COAL OIL POURED ON FIRE WAS CAUSE OF DEATH OF A LOUISVILLE WOMAN HERE

An attempt to cause a fire to burn better by pouring coal oil on it caused the death of Mrs. Catherine Dussart aged Louisville widow who died here yesterday at the Community hospital from burns which she received in the explosion that followed.

Coroner A.E. Howe visited the home of Mrs. Dussart and discovered the cause of the explosion.

Evidently Mrs. Dussart had just put some coal in the stove and when it did not burn as she thought it should she took some coal oil and poured it onto the coal. An explosion followed which set her clothing on fire. As she fell she dropped the oil can onto the stove and a second explosion followed.

Little damage was done to the house by the fire, and only a few things were burned.

A neighbor, Nestor Soupely, heard the first explosion and rushed over to Mrs. Dussart's home. He was forced to break into the house. As he entered he saw Mrs. Dussart standing all in flames and trying to move towards the door. He through rungs over her and put out the flames, after which he called for help. A grandson was the second to reach her home.

Mrs. Dussart was brought to the hospital where she was treated by Dr. Walter K. Reed. She passed away shortly after seven the next morning. Funeral arrangements await the arrival of relatives."

Catherine Dussart was buried in the Green Mountain Cemetery, Boulder (Boulder) Colorado with an incorrect death year of 1930 on her tombstone.

Her son, Modestus Modeste "Mike," first married Celia Phiefer/Phifer on 24 July 1898 in Aguilar (Las Animas) Colorado. Celia was born September 1883 in Colorado, the daughter of John and Maria Dolores (*Montoya*) Phifer/Fifer. Family story says that this John Phifer actually changed his name from Henry Knerr (from Pennsylvania) when he moved to Colorado and according to an oral history by Richard James Dussart Regnier Celia was a "half-breed."

The union of Modestus Modeste "Mike" and Celia (*Phiefer/Phifer/Fifer*) Dussart was blessed with one child:

James: born 30 June 1899 Aguilar (Las Animas) Colorado and died 02 December 1972 Longmont (Boulder) Colorado; buried Gold Hill Cemetery, Gold Hill (Boulder) Colorado; married Daisy Dryer, Iris Diane Ruby Stogsdill and Ellen Rosellia Romig; see REGNIER, James Dussart

Being quite young at the time of her marriage (14 years old) and attractive Celia was the victim of a very unfortunate death and (according to grandson Richard James Dussart Regnier) his father, James Dussart, (son of Modestus and Celia) was present at the time of this incident:

Rocky Mountain News 24 July 1903:

"SHOT WOMAN AND FLED TO HILLS...Army Posse and Deputy Sheriffs Are Now on Murderer's Trail and Lynching May Follow His Capture. Victim Had Spurned His Attentions and, Angered by Her Actions, the Mexican Killed Her in Her Own Home.

TRINIDAD, Colo., July 23,—David Arguillo, a Mexican miner working for the Union Coal and Coke company at Bowen, shot and killed Celia Dussart his morning in her house in that camp. Arguillo, a married man, had fallen in love with the woman and had been forcing his attentions on her. This morning he went to her house and she sent for Mrs. Arguillo. In a few minutes Mrs. Arguillo put in an appearance with a heavy crockery sugar bowl in her hand, with which she beat her faithless husband over the head. Then she marched him home. Arguillo then put a revolver in his pocket and went back to Mrs. Dussart's house. Three shots were heard and Arguillo calmly went out the front door and proceeded in a leisurely manner to climb the hill back of the town.

Shot Through Heart...

People rushed into the house and found Mrs. Dussart lying on her face in the door between two rooms dead, shot through the heart. Arguillo had fired three shots and but one had hit his victim, who had attempted to run from him. A brother of the dead woman soon loaded a shotgun and ran after the murderer. Arguillo, who was taking his time climbing the hill, saw him coming and turned to meet him. The brother halted and the murderer pulled up his revolver, firing it several times and chasing the man down into town.

Thereupon the miners, to whom word of the killing had been sent, left the mines and formed a posse about twenty-five strong, all armed, and set out after Arguillo. Meanwhile word had been sent to Trinidad and three deputy sheriffs took out after the murderer, who disappeared. At a late hour he had not been captured and it is feared that when he is found there will be bloodshed for the friends of the dead woman are determined to have a lynching, and the three deputies are men who will not allow anything alive to intimidate them. The husband of the dead woman, when he was told of the killing went to his house and sat down on a chair as if stunned, saying nothing the entire morning nor taking any part in the endeavor to capture the murderer. Mrs. Dussart had been married five years and was 19 years old. She was a very pretty woman. Her husband is a Frenchman."

On 20 October 1905 Dave Arguillo was finally captured: *Denver Post* 20 October 1905:
"ALLEGED COLORADO MURDERER SHOOTS DEPUTY THROUGH HEART WHILE RESISTING ARREST...

Raton, N.M., Oct. 20—Dave Arguello, a Mexican, wanted for the murder of Mrs. Celia Dussart, at Bowen, Las Animas county, Colorado, July 23, 1903, was captured on Johnson's mesa, fifteen miles east of Raton, yesterday afternoon, after a desperate resistance, during which he shot Deputy Sheriff Francisco Garcia of Las Animas county, who was trailing him..."

On 06 April 1906 jury returned a death verdict and on 25 May 1906 in Raton (Colfax) New Mexico Dave Arguello was hanged, neck broken.

Burial for Celia Phifer/Phiefer Dussart has not been located and the town of Bowen (Huerfano) Colorado is extinct with precise location unknown.

Modeste then married Sara Lopes/Lopez on 28 February 1904 in Aguilar (Las Animas) Colorado. Sara was born 11 August 1883; daughter of New Mexico native Antonio Lopez and Colorado native Marie Delaluz "Louisa" Armijo.

According to grandson Richard James Dussart Regnier, Sara was from another Indian tribe and had "issues" with her step son (James Dussart) being part Taos Indian. She didn't like him living in the house which resulted in James living under the porches until his father's sister, Mary Louise (*Dussart*) and her husband, Jules Regnier, rescued him at around 14 years of age.

James' new family lived on a farm in Valmont (Boulder) Colorado where he worked. Eventually he was adopted by Jules and Mary Regnier. Thus James Dussart became a Regnier.

While James Dussart Regnier lived in Valmont (Boulder) Colorado with his new adopted family his father Modeste and step mother, Sarah, lived in Somerset

(Gunnison) Colorado in the early 1900s where they raised their seven known children (eight were born):

George: born 18 February 1905 Eaton (Weld) Colorado and died 01 November 1990 Colorado; buried Mount Olivet Cemetery, Wheat Ridge (Jefferson) Colorado; spouse unknown; obituary states death 06 November 1990

Arthur Loyid/Lloyd: born 22 August 1908 Eaton (Weld) Colorado and died 22 November 1996; buried Fort Logan National Cemetery, Denver (Denver) Colorado; married Valda Lorene Young

Mary F.: born 04 October 1910 Colorado and died 08 December 1987 Westminster (Adams) Colorado; burial unknown; spouse unknown

Esther Ruth: born 13 October 1912 Delta (Delta) Colorado and died 27 May 1995 Broomfield (Boulder, now Broomfield) Colorado; buried Mount Olivet Cemetery, Wheat Ridge (Jefferson) Colorado; married Alfonso Fajardo

Ralph Joseph: born 02 May 1915 Somerset (Gunnison) Colorado and died 15 March 1995 Denver (Denver) Colorado; buried Mount Olivet Cemetery, Wheat Ridge (Jefferson) Colorado; married Josephine M. Lunares and Moadelyn C. Looney

Jacob J. "Jake": born 27 July 1916 Colorado and died 29 October 1984 Denver (Denver) Colorado; buried Mount Olivet Cemetery, Wheat Ridge (Jefferson) Colorado; believed never married

Lucille "Lucy": born 10 October 1919 Colorado and died 14 February 2010 Colorado; buried Mount Olivet Cemetery, Wheat Ridge (Jefferson) Colorado; married Avel Joseph Lucero

Modeste and Sarah moved to Denver (Denver) Colorado by 1928 but a year later Modeste lived in Oklahoma and in 1930 Sarah and her children were living in (Weld) Colorado where she is listed as a widow in the census record. Then by 1937 Modeste was living in Denver (Denver) Colorado with an Evangeline Dussart who was listed as his wife.

Modestus/Modeste/Modest "Mike" died in 1957 and is buried in Fairmount Cemetery, Denver (Denver) Colorado. Interesting to note than the Social Security Index lists his birthdate as 18 February 1870 and that he was born in Trinidad (Las Animas) Colorado (which is incorrect).

On 06 March 1930 Sarah (*Lopez*) Dussart married Walter E. Smith in Golden (Jefferson) Colorado however in the 1940 census she is listed as divorced. She died on 15 December 1968 in Denver (Denver) Colorado; burial unknown.

It appears that James Dussart Regnier (son of Modestus Modeste "Mike" and Celia (*Phiefer/Phifer*) Dussart) married Daisy Dryer as an application for marriage was filed in (Boulder) Colorado 13 December 1923. Later a divorce was granted there on 31 August 1925.

He then married Iris Diane Ruby Stogsdill about 1926 in Kansas. They moved to Erie (Boulder) Colorado where their first child was born, Richard James, on 17 August 1928; see REGNIER, Richard James Dussart. Two more children were born to this union:

Verna Mae: born 09 May 1934 Erie (Boulder/ Weld) Colorado and died 15 September 1992 Longmont (Boulder) Colorado; buried Gold Hill Cemetery, Gold Hill (Boulder) Colorado; married Richard Williams Jr.; obituary and tombstone state 09 November 1934 as birth; see WILLIAMS, Verna Mae (*Regnier*)

Celia Marie: born 25 November 1938 Erie (Boulder/Weld) Colorado; married Robert D. Green

According to Richard James Dussart Regnier's book, "*A Long U Turn*," the family moved to California August 1941 and remained there for about two years when James and Iris (Richard's parents) decided on a divorce. Richard was to move back to Colorado with his dad, James Dussart Regnier, and the two sisters (Verna Mae and Celia Marie) were to remain with their mother, Iris. A year later they came to Colorado however Iris returned to California alone while the two sisters lived with their dad (James Dussart Regnier) and their brother, Richard.

Iris Diane Ruby did remarry, had two more children (Michael J. Adiano and Carol (*Adiano*) Frazier) and lived in Texas until her death on 10 September 2000. She is buried in the Cook-Walden Capital Parks Cemetery and Mausoleum, Pflugerville (Travis) Texas.

On 29 September 1950 James Dussart Regnier married Ellen Rosellia Romig in Boulder (Boulder) Colorado. She was born 30 September 1907 in Gold Hill (Boulder) Colorado; the daughter of early Gold Hill pioneers, John W. and Ersula "Zula" M. (*Reedy*) Romig and the granddaughter of John Felix and Athalia (*Neville*) Romig who had a homestead on a large section of land west of Gold Hill in the 1870s (now part of Colorado Mountain Ranch on County Road 52); see REGNIER, Ellen Rosellia (*Romig*); see ROMIG, John Felix; see ROMIG, Athalia (*Neville*); see ROMIG, John W.

In that same year Richard James Dussart Regnier married Elsie May McCaghren on 30 September 1950 in Texas. She was born 15 July 1933 in Oklahoma; the daughter of William Henry and Edith "Elsie" Mae (*Callison*) McCaghren. Four children blessed this marriage:

Renee Jacqueline "Jackie": born 30 May 1953 Travis Texas and died 30 May 2005 Durango (La Plata) Texas; buried Greenmount Cemetery, Durango (La Plata) Colorado; married Robert John Howsey

Richard Jr.: Private Information
Russell: Private Information
Ronald: Private Information

Unfortunately Richard and Elsie divorced 31 October 1984 Dawson (Navarro) Texas. Elsie died on 15 April 2001 (some sources state 30 April 2001) in Pryor (Mayes) Oklahoma; buried in the Bryan Chapel Cemetery, Boatman (Mayes) Oklahoma.

The black lung disease from his early mining days finally caught up with James Dussart Regnier, father of Richard James Dussart Regnier:

Gold Hill Men by Richard James Dussart Regnier:
"Dad [James Dussart Regnier] had black lung from breathing coal dust all of those early years of his life. Then two heart attacks had weakened him. On the 12th of Dec., 1972 he was at the post office when a neighbor slipped and fell and broke his arm. Dad drove his car home for him while he waited for the ambulance to come from Longmont, Colorado, twelve miles away. The air was icy cold that day and my dad ran back downtown after parking his neighbor's car at his house. When he arrived at the post office he collapsed and died...It had been ten years since I'd seen Gold Hill, but this time it was different. My dad and Ellen had built a house in Gold Hill and after he retired they spent their summers there. They both loved it and it was where my dad wanted to be buried. The whole town took on a new meaning for me after I had helped carry my dad's coffin up the steep hill to the Romig plot, lowered the coffin into the grave and placed the cover over it. Part of me was now part of Gold Hill."

Ellen sold their house in Erie (Boulder/Weld) Colorado, living the winters in Boulder (Boulder) Colorado and summers in Gold Hill (Boulder) Colorado. When Ellen passed away on 01 January 1982 Richard James inherited the cabin that his dad and Ellen built. Richard spent many summers with his wife, Gwen, enjoying Gold Hill where he wrote numerous books (novels, histories, poetry) and drew etchings of the Gold Hill cabins. Most of his many works can be viewed in the Gold Hill Museum in Gold Hill (Boulder) Colorado.

It was a sad day when Richard's second wife passed away. Richard James Dussart Regnier and Gwendolyn (*Mercer*) Hunter were married 11 May 1985 in Lamesa (Dawson) Texas. She was born 25 August 1935; believed to have been the daughter of Thomas J. and Nora Bell (*Anthony*) Mercer. She died 27 December 2008 in Midland (Midland) Texas and was buried in the Resthaven Memorial Park beside her first husband, John L. Hunter.

Richard then married his high school sweetheart, Helen Swanson, who survived him when he passed away 28 October 2015 in Westminster (Broomfield) Colorado. He was buried in the Regnier/Romig family plot in the Gold Hill Cemetery, Gold Hill (Boulder) Colorado.

Digging Up Dirt

RICHARDS, John Vivian

>Birth: 06/05/1866
>Death: 01/28/1939
>Cemetery Location: E5

Father: William Richards; Mother: Mary (*Adams*); Wife: Martha (*Goudge*); born in Camborne Parish (Cornwall) England and died in Boulder (Boulder) Colorado at age 72 years, 7 months, 23 days-mitral regurgitation (disorder of the heart); grand uncle of author; see RICHARDS, William; see RICHARDS, Mary (*Adams*); see GOUDGE, Edwin David "Ned;" see GOUDGE, Annie Elizabeth (*Bennett(s)*); see **About the Richards Family**

Boulder Daily Camera 30 January 1939:

"John Richards, Pioneer Of This County, Dies—Came to Caribou In 1876; Worked In Many Boulder County Mines—John Richards, whose boyhood was spent at Caribou, once a famous mining camp of Boulder county, died late Saturday afternoon. He had been ill for several weeks. He was 72 years of age. Mr. Richards was born in Camborne Parish, Cornwall, England, June 5, 1866. He came to the United States with his parents, Mr. and Mrs. William Richards, and an older brother, William, when he was seven.

They came to Colorado, locating at Central City in 1875. A year later they went to Caribou. There he attended the one-room grade school and witnessed the fire that swept Caribou in 1879. He went in work in the mines directly after his parents moved to Gold Hill from Caribou in the early eighties. He was familiar with Boulder county gold, silver and tungsten mines—working in all of them.

Unlike his father, who had been a wanderer, John Richards remained in Boulder County, not leaving it for any length of time since he moved into it the year Colorado was admitted to statehood.

He had a very keen memory for events that occurred in Caribou a half century ago—some of which have been reported in The Camera by Forest Crossen. He was one of the last of the old-timers who came to Caribou from Cornwall.

Mr. Richards lived at 2232 12th street. He is survived by two sons, William Richards, Frank Richards and a daughter, Mrs. Martha Hockett, all of Boulder. The brother, William, lives in Oakland, Calif.

Funeral services will be held at the Howe mortuary at 10 o'clock Tuesday morning. Rev. W.F. Keimel, pastor of the Church of the Nazarene, will officiate. Burial will be in Gold Hill."

Unmarked graves (believed to be those of John Vivian Richards and Mary (*Adams*) Richards by the tombstone of William Richards

Boulder Daily Camera 31 January 1939:

"JOHN RICHARDS—Services this morning at 10 o'clock at Howe mortuary. Rev. W.F. Kiemel of the Nazarene church officiated, Mrs. And Mrs. George Snyder and Mr. and Mrs. Robert Schneider sang. Pallbearers were P.A. Stromberg, Lou Patton, Benj. Moon, Milton Dalton, George Watkins and Frank Marshall. Interment, Gold Hill."

RICHARDS, Mary (*Adams*)

Birth: 05/13/1837
Death: 05/22/1918
Cemetery Location: E5

Father: William Adams; Mother: Maude (*Vivian*); Husband: William Richards; born in (Cornwall) England and died in Nederland (Boulder) Colorado at age 81 years, 0 months, 9 days-mitral regurgitation (disorder of the heart); see RICHARDS, William; see RICHARDS, John Vivian; see **About the Richards Family**

Boulder Daily Camera 24 May 1918:

"GEORGE KIRKBRIDE TO CONDUCT FUNERAL OF MRS. RICHARDS—Mrs. Mary Richards who died at her home in Nederland at midnight Wednesday, of heart trouble, age 81 years, will have funeral services in her memory at Howe's undertaking parlors Sunday morning at 10 o'clock. Mr. George Kirkbride, an old time friend, will have charge of the services. The deceased had lived in Gold Hill, Caribou and Nederland for forty years. Her husband died twenty years ago. She is survived by two sons, John D. Richards of Nederland and William Richards of [Balperita], California. Interment will be in Gold Hill cemetery beside her husband."

Boulder Daily Camera 27 May 1918:

"The funeral of Mrs. Mary Richards who died at Nederland last Thursday was held at Gold Hill Sunday at 2 p.m. Mr. George Kirkbride officiated. A short service was held at Howe's undertaking parlors at 10 a.m. before leaving for Gold Hill."

Unmarked graves (believed to be those of John Vivian Richards and Mary (Adams) Richards by the tombstone of William Richards

RICHARDS, William

Birth: 03/01/1837
Death: 09/01/1898
Cemetery Location: E5

Father: possibly Henry Richards; Mother: possibly Elizabeth (*maiden name unknown*); Wife: Mary (*Adams*); born in Camborne (Cornwall) England and died in Ward (Boulder) Colorado at age 61 years, 6 months, 0 days-dropsy (abnormal accumulation of fluid); other sources have birth as 05/01/1837; see RICHARDS, Mary (*Adams*); see RICHARDS, John Vivian; see **About the Richards Family**

Boulder Daily Camera 01 September 1898:
"A telephone message was received at Trezise's today announcing the death of William Richards at Ward. Richards was about 65 years old and was the father of William Richards, who is well known as an engineer in Boulder County. His death resulted from dropsy."

Boulder County Herald Weekly 07 September 1898:
"Wm. Richard aged 65 years, died at Ward Thursday of dropsy. He was buried at Gold Hill Friday, a casket having been sent up from Trezise's establishment."

RICHARDS, William Edwin

Birth: 12/14/1910
Death: 05/14/1986
Cemetery Location: D4

Father: John Vivian Richards; Mother: Martha (*Goudge*); Wife: Iris (*Henwood*); born in Gold Hill (Boulder) Colorado and died in Boulder (Boulder) Colorado at age 75 years, 5 months- pneumonia; U.S. Post Officer-mail carrier; no obituary published; no tombstone; see RICHARDS, John Vivian; see RICHARDS, Mary (*Adams*); see

"No pain, no grief, no anxious fear,
Can reach the peaceful sleeper here"

GOUDGE, Edwin David "Ned;" see GOUDGE, Annie Elizabeth (*Bennett(s)*); see **About the Richards Family**

About the Richards Family

William Richards was born 01 March 1837 in Camborne (Cornwall) England. In the 1851 England census there is a William Richards, son of Henry and Elizabeth, born in Camborne and Ancestry connects the record to other records that do correlate to this William Richards.

William married Mary Adams in (Cornwall) England about 1859. She was born about 1838 in Camborne (Cornwall) England; the daughter of William and Maria (*Vivian*) Adams.

To this union two sons were born:

William Vivian: born 18 September 1861 Camborne (Cornwall) England and died 06 April 1943 (Butte) California; buried Chico Cemetery, Chico (Butte) California; married Anna C." Katie" Lloyd

John Vivian: born 05 June 1866 Camborne (Cornwall) England and died 05 June 1939 Boulder (Boulder) Colorado; buried Gold Hill Cemetery, Gold Hill (Boulder) Colorado; married Martha Goudge; see RICHARDS, John Vivian

In 1872 William immigrated to the United States and according to his son, John Vivian, William came to Colorado from Nevada (possibly Nevada City (Nevada) California.

William returned to (Cornwall) England to bring his wife, Mary, and their two sons, William Vivian and John Vivian to the United States; leaving from Bristol (Bristol) England. Sailing on the ship *Somerset* they arrived at the Port of New York on 10 April 1876.

By 1880 the family was living in Caribou (Boulder) Colorado. A few years later they moved to Gold Hill (Boulder) Colorado where William was a miner along with his son, John.

In 1894 the family moved again but this time to Ward (Boulder) Colorado where William died four years later on 01 September 1898 from dropsy (abnormal accumulation of fluid); being buried in the Gold Hill Cemetery.

William's widow, Mary, moved to Sunshine (Boulder) Colorado where she lived with her son, John Vivian. The oldest son, William Vivian, made his reputation as a well-known engineer of Boulder County, living in Ward (Boulder) Colorado along with his wife, Anna C. "Katie" Lloyd, whom he married 03 November 1884 in (Boulder) Colorado.

John Vivian Richards was naturalized on 13 June 1892 in Boulder (Boulder) Colorado. About six years later he married Martha (*Goudge*) Abbott on 11 September 1907 in Cheyenne (Larimer) Wyoming. She was born 13 November 1877 in Summerville (Boulder) Colorado; the daughter of Gold Hill pioneers Edwin David "Ned" Goudge and Annie Elizabeth (*Bennett(s)*) Goudge; see GOUDGE, Edwin David "Ned;" see GOUDGE, Annie Elizabeth (*Bennett(s)*).

To their union four children were born:

John Edwin: born and died possibly in Cripple Creek (Teller) Colorado-stillborn; no further information (as told by Martha Mae "Little Mart" (*Richards*) Hockett)

Francis "Frank" John: born 22 October 1908 Summerville (Boulder) Colorado and died 06 November 1960 Denver (Denver) Colorado; buried Fort Logan National Cemetery, Denver (Denver) Colorado; never married

William Edwin: born 14 December 1910 Gold Hill (Boulder) Colorado and died 14 May 1986 Boulder (Boulder) Colorado; buried Gold Hill Cemetery, Gold Hill (Boulder) Colorado; married Iris Henwood; see RICHARDS, William Edwin

Martha Mae "Little Mart": born 29 July 1913 Boulder (Boulder) Colorado and died 08 NOV 1998 Portland (Multnomah) Oregon; buried River View Cemetery, Portland (Multnomah) Oregon; married Glen Albert Hockett

In the 1910 census John Vivian Richards was living in Gold Hill (Boulder) Colorado along with his wife, Martha, their son Francis J., and John's mother, Mary. Later

William Edwin Richards was cremated and his ashes were interred close
to the tombstone of Annie Elizabeth (*Bennett(s)*) and Edwin David "Ned" Goudge

Mary moved to Nederland (Boulder) Colorado where she died on 22 May 1918; see RICHARDS, Mary (*Adams*).

Two years later, in 1920, John Vivian and family were living on Pearl Street in Boulder (Boulder) Colorado next door to Martha's brother, Arthur Garfield Goudge, and family.

Unfortunately Martha (*Goudge*) Abbott Richards filed for divorce and the summons was issued and served to the defendant (John Vivian Richards) on 21 July 1920. The cause was listed as desertion and non-support. The plaintiff (Martha) was entitled to a Decree of Divorce in February 1921. The children were divided between Martha and John: the boys (Francis J. and William E.) were awarded to their father and Martha Mae was awarded to her mother.

Interesting to note that in the 1930 census William Edwin was living with his mother, Martha on Pine Street in Boulder (Boulder) Colorado and Francis John was off living on his own. Their father, John Vivian, was living at 2537 5th Street in Boulder (Boulder) Colorado in June of 1933.

John Vivian Richards moved to 2232 12th Street (now Broadway) in Boulder (Boulder) Colorado and then to 1309 Walnut Street when he was taken to Boulder Community Hospital in Boulder (Boulder) Colorado where he died on 28 January 1939 from mitral regurgitation. He is buried in the Gold Hill Cemetery in Gold Hill (Boulder) Colorado.

His ex-wife, Martha, was married two more times (John Franklin Liebee and James Adair King) before her death on 15 August 1952 at the age of 74 years and 9 months from an inoperable tumor of the pancreas. She died at her home on 3048 9th Street in Boulder (Boulder) Colorado and is buried in the city's Mountain View Cemetery alongside her 4th husband, James Adair King.

Boulder Daily Camera 30 June 1933:
"JOHN RICHARDS...

"I saw the corner stone laid, coming from Caribou for the ceremony and I saw the courthouse destroyed by fire in February 1932," said John Richards today.

Richards, who lives at 2537 Fifth Street, is a son of Mr. and Mrs. William Richards. His father came to Colorado in '72 from Nevada and his wife in '76 from Pennsylvania, accompanied by their two sons, John and William, the latter now living in Oakland, California.

The Richards lived in Central City for two years and then went to Caribou. In 1882 they went to Gold Hill; in 88 returned to Caribou; in 91 went to Sunshine and in 94 went to Ward. The father died there in 98. The family then moved to Gold Hill.

John Richards was married at Gold Hill [incorrect-Cheyenne (Laramie) Wyoming] to Martha Goudge, daughter of a pioneer. They have three children, Frances

J., William Edwin and Martha May.

Mr. Richards has mined at Cripple Creek and in nearly every mining town in Boulder County. He was at Nederland from 1915 to 1919, then at Salina and at present is working at Caribou."

RIEMENSCHNEIDER, Karl Heinrich Ferdinand "Fred"

Birth: 03/21/1847
Death: 05/24/1904
Cemetery Location: Unknown

Father: August Ludwig "Louis" Riemenschneider; Mother: Friederike Ernestine (*Momeier*); 1st Wife: Salvina/Sonora M. (*Buehner*); 2nd Wife: Gestina (*Cordes*); born in Brunswick/Braunschweig (Lower Saxony) Germany and died at University Hospital, Boulder (Boulder) Colorado at age 57 years 2 months 3 days-old injuries due to an old mining accident injury; no tombstone

Boulder Daily Camera 25 May 1904:
"FRED RUMSCHNEIDER DEAD—Fred Rumschneider who died here Tuesday morning from the effects of a mine accident which happened several years ago, and who has made his home in this county for the past fifteen years, was buried at Gold Hill this afternoon. He was 58 years old and leaves a wife, a daughter and two sons."

Boulder News 26 May 1904:
"Fred Rumschneider, an old miner, died here Tuesday of an old injury received several years ago and was buried at Gold Hill yesterday afternoon."

RIEMENSCHNEIDER, Salvina/Sonora M. (*Buehner/Beevin/Bevin*)

Birth: About 1850
Death: 05/09/1878
Cemetery Location: Unknown

Father: Behner/Buehner; Mother: unknown; Husband: Karl Heinrich Ferdinand "Fred" Riemenschneider; born about 1850 Iowa and died (Boulder) Colorado at age approximately 28 years; no tombstone

About the Riemenschneider Family

Karl Heinrich Ferdinand "Fred" Riemenschneider was born 21 March 1847 in Braunschweig (also known as Brunswick) (Lower Saxony) Germany; the son of German parents August Ludwig "Louis" and Friederike Ernestine (*Momeier*) Riemenschneider. He was one of seven known children born to their union:

Heinrich Wilhelm Ludwig "Henry": born 10 December 1844 Brunswick (Lower Saxony) Germany and died 26 April 1913 State Center (Marshall) Iowa; buried

Hillside Cemetery, State Center (Marshall) Iowa; married Caroline "Lena" Soelter

Karl Heinrich Ferdinand "Fred": born 21 March 1847 Brunswick/Braunschweig (Lower Saxony) Germany and died 24 May 1904 Boulder (Boulder) Colorado; buried Gold Hill Cemetery, Gold Hill (Boulder) Colorado; married Sonora Salvina Buehner M. and Gesina Cordis/Cardis; see RIEMENSCHNEIDER, Karl Heinrich Ferdinand "Fred"

Heinrich Carpatius Wilhelm "William": born 04 June 1850 Wenzen (Niedersachsen) Germany and died 10 June 1911 State Center (Marshall) Iowa; buried Hillside Cemetery, State Center (Marshall) Iowa; married Mary Ann Wantz

August Heinrich Christian: born 01 December 1854 Brunswick (Lower Saxony) Germany and died 27 June 1916 State Center (Marshall) Iowa; buried Hillside Cemetery, State Center (Marshall) Iowa; married Josephine Wantz

Hermann Christian Ernest: born 05 June 1857 Wenzen (Niedersachsen) Germany and died 25 August 1927 State Center (Marshall) Iowa; buried Hillside Cemetery, State Center (Marshall) Iowa; married Dorathea "Dorette" Ziesness

Ernestine Adolphine (Caroline) "Lena": born 10 February 1860 Brunswick (Lower Saxony) Germany and died 09 December 1934 Marshalltown (Marshall) Iowa; buried Riverside Cemetery, Marshalltown (Marshall) Iowa; married Frederick A. Ahrens

Albert Gustav Adolph: born 22 July 1864 Brunswick (Lower Saxony) Germany and died 01 September 1929 Cody (Cherry) Nebraska; buried Prairie Lawn Cemetery, Cody (Cherry) Nebraska; married Martha Ellen (Wilson) Herron

The family traveled from Wenzen, Germany to Bremen, Germany and then on to Southampton, England where they boarded the ship *Union* sailing to the United States. They arrived at the Port of New York on 20 June 1868.

According to the obituary of Ernestine Adolphine "Caroline" (*Riemenschneider*) Ahrens the family came directly to State Center (Marshall) Iowa where the parents (August Ludwig and Friederike Ernestine (*Momeier*) Riemenschneider are buried in the French Grove Cemetery (now Saint John's Lutheran Cemetery) in the State Center/Minerva (Marshall) Iowa area.

Karl Heinrich Ferdinand "Fred" married Salvina/Sonora M. Buehner/Beevin/Bevin on 24 July 1873 (Marshall) Iowa; parents unknown. They left Iowa for Colorado where lived in Brainard's Camp near Ward (Boulder) Colorado. To their union one known child was born:

Maria Anna Josephina "Mary Ann": born 02 August 1875 Brainard's Camp (Boulder) Colorado and died 17 July 1952 Ogden (Weber) Utah; buried Ogden City Cemetery, Ogden (Weber) Utah; married William H. Stimson; maiden last name changed to "Schneider"

Salvina died 09 May 1878 and was buried Gold Hill Cemetery. Unfortunately there are no records as to the grave's location.

Apparently Fred returned to his home area as the 1880 census shows him farming in Minerva (Marshall) Iowa, single and age 33 years old. His daughter, Maria Anna, wasn't listed as living with him.

Fred then married Gestina (Lucila as per the 1885 census record) Cordes on 16 May 1881 in Marshalltown (Marshall) Iowa. She was born 24 March 1859 in Germany; the daughter of German parents Frederick Cordes and mother unknown. To this union seven known children were born:

August Edward O.: born 14 May 1882 (Marshall) Iowa and died after 1904; lived in Ward (Boulder) Colorado) but before 1952 according to the obituary for Maria Anna Josephina "Mary Ann" Riemenschneider (*Schneider*) Stimson

Friedrich Carl Herman: born 02 August 1883 (Marshall) Iowa and died before 1952 according to the obituary for Maria Anna Josephina "Mary Ann" Riemenschneider (*Schneider*) Stimson); last name changed to "Schneider"

Katherine/Kathryn Gestine "Kate": born 07 January 1886 Iowa and died September 1969 Hasbrouck Heights (Bergen) New Jersey; burial unknown; married Rudolph Waagner and William Koether

Lillian Mata: born May 1889 Nebraska and died 07 October 1918 Utah; married Leonard Ancell

Gracey F.: born July 1893 Colorado and died before 1952 according to the obituary for Maria Anna Josephina "Mary Ann" Riemenschneider (*Schneider*) Stimson; 1910 living with her sister, Lillian, in Utah

Frederick H.: born April 1896 Colorado and died after 1952 according to the obituary for Maria Anna Josephina "Mary Ann" Riemenschneider (*Schneider*) Stimson

Louis L.: born 27 March 1901 Colorado and died 21 March 1974 Las Vegas (Clark) Nevada; buried Salt Lake City Cemetery, Salt Lake City (Salt Lake) Utah; married Ruth Celestine Lamoin; last name changed to Schneider

By 1885 Fred and his wife, Gestina "Lucila" were living in Des Moines (Boone) Iowa long with their two sons, August Edward and Friedrich Carl Herman as well as Fred's daughter, Kathryn.

The family traveled to Nebraska where their daughter, Lillian Mata, was born in 1889. By 1894 the family was living in Ward (Boulder) Colorado where Fred, at the listed age of 53 years, was a miner.

Fred died on 24 May 1904 at the University Hospital in Boulder (Boulder) Colorado from old injuries due to a mining accident. His death notice in the *Boulder Daily Camera* stated he had lived in the county (Boulder) for fifteen years however the census records do not agree with that.

Gestina must have moved to Salt Lake City (Salt Lake) Utah as according to her death certificate she died on 24 March 1912 from apoplexy/arteria sclerosis and was buried a few days later (27 March 1912) in the Salt Lake City Cemetery with no tombstone.

ROBERTSON, A. W. "Archie"

Birth: 05/18/1866
Death: 05/20/1892
Cemetery Location: F2

Father: unknown Mother: unknown; Wife: unmarried; birth location unknown but might be Canada and died at age 26 years, 2 days- mining accident in the Dinah shaft in Long Gulch near Raymond (Boulder) Colorado; original cemetery records have wrong birth year 1856

Boulder Daily Camera 20 May 1892:

"A TERRIBLE FALL-A Gold Hill Miner Takes a Plunge Down a Shaft—Yesterday afternoon the body of a Gold Hill miner named Barber was found in the bottom of an 80 foot shaft in Long Gulch. The man was still alive, but unconscious and his body covered with blood. Barber was working in the mine which belongs to Chris Esslinger, and some of the miners working in the drifts heard him start to go up, early in the afternoon. About 2:30 a visitor Charley Pughe coming down found him at the bottom of the ladder when he had evidently fallen. Barber was a young man of 26 years of age and has a mother in the east, whom he had been supporting. No one knows how the accident occurred. The body was carried to Gold Hill and Dr. Trovillian is doing all he can for the victim, but there are little hopes of his recovery."

Boulder Daily Camera 21 May 1892:

"Robertson is Dead. Archie Robertson was a barber, as well as a miner, hence our informant last night gave the name of Barber as the man who fell down the Long Gulch shaft.

Archie Robertson died at Gold Hill at 3 o'clock yesterday morning, not having recovered consciousness. The Long Gulch shaft is over 100 feet deep and Charley Pugh was working in the bottom level. He heard a noise about 5 o'clock Thursday afternoon and saw some dirt and rock falling. He called to his partner, Robertson, and received no reply, only a candle light glimmering in the shaft.

It appears that the unfortunate miner was coming down the shaft and every fair conclusion is that some rock fell upon him in the course of his decent, as his head was crushed in near the ear next to the wall. He fell bruised and bleeding upon the shaft stulling nine feet below the 80-foot level and, as Pugh ascended to where he discovered the prostrate form. Robertson lay with an unbroken alarm clock in one hand and his candle burning. These facts were convincing proof that his fall had been a short one. A rock had fallen and the blow was sufficient to inflict a fatal wound.

Pugh carried the man painfully up to the level, lay him upon some timbers and started out for town in search of help. Robertson was unconscious to the last, Dr. Trovillion expressing no hopes from the first. W.H. Thomas came to Boulder yesterday to procure a casket and telegraphed to Robertson's parents in Canada and a brother in California. Deceased was 26 and single and well liked among his fellows. The funeral will, probably, occur at Gold Hill tomorrow."

Interview with Tim and Pearl (Pughe) Walter (Courtesy of Lynne Walter)

(Pearl) "My father was working with a man, what mine wat that, Tim? The Seven Thirty? No, it was out in the vicinity of the Yeager's property."

(Tim) "Down over the hill almost to Long Gulch, right straight down from Yeager's."

(Pearl) "They had come up to eat their lunch. They were the only two that were working there, and they had to crawl up and down the ladder. My father [Charles Pughe] went down first, and he waited and waited for Archie to come down and he didn't come and finally Dad looked up and he saw the light—the candle up there and discovered it wasn't moving and he went up...am I telling this right, Tim?"

(Tim) "Well, he hollered up and got no answer, so then he went up. Archie had his arms hooked through the rungs of the ladder and was just hanging there unconscious. A rock had come down and hit him on the head. He'd stuck both his arms through the rungs of the ladder."

(Pearl) "Dad got a rope and tied him to the ladder and then he came to town for help. I'm not sure, I don't know whether Archie was dead when..."

(Tim) "No, he lived a few days. But he roped him to the ladder then he run for help."

ROMARINE/ROMAURINE/ROUMAURINE, Kathy Sue

(Incorrectly listed as being buried in the Gold Hill Cemetery)

Birth: 07/14/1941
Death: 11/29/1941
Cemetery Location: N/A

Father: Laurence Romarine; Mother: Virginia R (*Painter*); died at age 4 months, 15 days-pneumonia; buried in the Fairmount Cemetery, Denver, Colorado

Boulder Daily Camera 01 December 1941:
"Kathy Sue Romarene [sic], four and one half months old daughter of Mr. and Mrs. Laurence Romarene of the Salina star route, died Saturday evening at Community hospital, where she had been taken with pneumonia. Funeral services will be at Olinger mortuary in Denver at 16th and Boulder streets, at 10 o'clock Tuesday and burial will be in Fairmount Cemetery."

ROMIG, Athalia (*Neville*)

Birth: 06/1836
Death: 01/10/1901
Cemetery Location: C2

Father: Joseph Neville; Mother: Mary M. "Polly" (*Buckmaster*); Husband: John Felix Romig; born in (Holmes) Ohio; died at age 64 years, 7 months (approximately); some records has birth year 1838; see ROMIG, John Felix; see ROMIG, Elizabeth Athalia; see ROMIG, John William; see **About the Romig Family**

Boulder Daily Camera 10 January 1901:
"Mrs. Athalia Romig, mother of John F. Romig, died at 3 o'clock this afternoon, after a long illness with heart trouble. The funeral will be from the Baptist church at 10 a.m. Saturday. Interment will be at Gold Hill. All members of the Baptist church are requested by Rev. E.G. Lane to attend the ceremonies."

Boulder Daily Camera 11 January 1901:
"Mrs. Athalaia Romig, whose death occurred in this city yesterday afternoon, was one of the pioneers of Colorado, having emigrated from Iowa to Denver with her husband, John F. Romig, in 1861. During the Indian troubles they lived on Cherry creek, above Denver, and the Hungate family, who were murdered by the Indians, were their nearest neighbors. Mr. and Mrs. Romig with their infant daughter were not molested by the Indians, but with other survivors of the massacre moved to Denver until the Indians troubles were over, after which they returned to their ranch on Cherry creek, where they continued to reside until the great flood, which swept away their dwelling, house with all their household goods, Mr. Romig, after riding all night, having reached the house in time to rescue his wife and daughter just before the house was washed away. They then moved to Black Hawk where Mr. Romig engaged in mining, and later removed to Boulder county where they have resided for the past thirty years, most of the time in Gold Hill. Mr. Romig died in 1891, since which time Mrs. Romig has resided in Boulder. Her son, John W. Romig, is the only surviving

member of the family, the daughter Elizabeth having died in 1875.

The funeral service will take place at the First Baptist church of this city tomorrow morning at 10 o'clock, after which the remains will be taken to Gold Hill and laid to rest beside her husband and daughter."

Boulder County Herald 11 January 1901:
"MRS ATHALIA ROMIG
Mrs. Athalia Romig, whose death occurred in this city yesterday afternoon, was one of the pioneers of Colorado having imigrated [sic] from Iowa to this state with her husband, John F. Romig, in 1861. During the Indian trou-

"God chasteneth whome He loveth Mother"

233

bles of the early days they lived on Cherry Creek above Denver, and attributed their escape from the massacre of the whites in that vicinity to the friendship of one of the Indian chiefs. Their nearest neighbors were the Heingate family, all of whom were killed. The removed with the other survivors of the massacre to Denver, and after the Indian troubles were over returned to their branch on Cherry Creek, where they resided until the flood, which did great damage in Denver and along Cherry Creek, carried away their dwelling and household goods, Mr. Romig having ridden all night and reached his home just in time to rescue his wife and daughter from the flooded house. They then moved to Black Hawk and from there to Boulder county [sic], where they have lived for 30 years, most of the time at Gold Hill. Her husband died in 1891, since which time she has resided in and near Boulder. Her son, John W. Romig, survives her. The funeral services will be

held tomorrow morning at 10 o'clock at the First Baptist church of this city, after which the remains will be taken to Gold Hill and laid to rest by the side of her husband and daughter. Mrs. Romig has been in poor health for several years, which finally culminated in the fatal attack of heart trouble about a month ago."

ROMIG, Elizabeth Athalia

Birth: 03/06/1858
Death: 03/27/1875
Cemetery Location: C2

Father: John Felix Romig; Mother: Athalia (*Neville*); Died at age 17 years, 21 days, 0 months; tombstone states death at 16 years, 9 months, 21 days; earliest known burial with a tombstone; see ROMIG, Athalia (*Neville*); see ROMIG, John Felix; see ROMIG, John William; see **About the Romig Family**

ROMIG, John Felix

Birth: 01/18/1829
Death: 12/01/1891
Cemetery Location: C2

No tombstone engraving in reference to Athalia;
only John and daughter Elizabeth

Father: John/Johannes Romig; Mother: Martha Amelia Emilie (*Fenner*); Wife: Athalia (*Neville*); died at age 62 years, 10 months, 13 days; veteran of the Civil War; see ROMIG, Athalia (*Neville*); see ROMIG, Elizabeth Athalia; see ROMIG, John William; see **About the Romig Family**

Boulder County, Colorado Deaths and the Insane 1859-1900 by Mary McRoberts:

"Romig, John F. d 1 Dec 1901 Gold Hill of pneumonia. "Old and highly esteemed resident of Gold Hill." Age 62 years 10 months 14 days. Undertaker Neginnes sent up casket 2 Dec 1891. He came to Colorado from Iowa in 1862. He lived on a ranch west of Gold Hill for 18 years. Leaves widow, age 53, "in feeble health," a son and 2 adopted daus. Dau Mary and son John in Boulder public schools. First Baptist Church member of Boulder. Large funeral 3 Dec at school house with Rev. S.C. Davis. Bur Gold Hill cem."

ROMIG, John William

> Birth: 07/30/1872
> Death: 11/24/1939
> Cemetery Location: C2

Father: John Felix Romig; Mother Athalia (*Neville*); Wife: Ersula "Zula" (*Reedy*); born north of Gold Hill (Boulder) Colorado and died in Boulder (Boulder) Colorado at age 67 years, 3 months, 25 days-carcinoma of buccal mucosa; see ROMIG, Athalia (*Neville*); see ROMIG, John Felix; see ROMIG Elizabeth Athalia; see **About the Romig Family**

Boulder Daily Camera 24 November 1939:

"John W. Romig Of Gold Hill Dies In Boulder

John W. Romig, resident of Boulder county nearly all of the sixty-seven years of his life, died at 3:30 this morning.

He and Mrs. Romig moved to 1324 Euclid, in Boulder, a month ago for her health, after Mrs. Romig had suffered a heart attack. Mr. Romig, who had been under a physician's care for some time, became seriously ill a few days ago.

Mr. Romig was born on a ranch six miles north of Boulder July 30, 1872. His parents moved to Gold Hill when he was a child and most of his life was spent there. In his younger days he mined considerably and during the tungsten boom of 1914-18 operated tungsten property at Lakewood. Since then he had been ranching.

Survivors are the wife, Zula Reed Romig, a daughter, Miss Ellen Romig, who teaches at Gold Hill; a son, Paul Romig, who is engaged in carpenter work in Gold Hill, and another son, John D. Romig, whose home is in Cedar Crest, N.M.

Funeral services will be at Howe mortuary, Sunday afternoon, at 2:30. Rev. E.E. Habig, pastor of English

"Short is my pilgrimage.
Heaven is my home."

"Asleep in Jesus"

Lutheran church, will officiate. Interment will be in Gold Hill cemetery."

Boulder Daily Camera 27 November 1939:

"John W. Romig—Services were held Sunday afternoon at 2:30 at the Howe mortuary. Rev. E.E. Habig, pastor of English Lutheran church, officiated. Mrs. Wm. Morris sang and Mrs. A.R. Peebles played the organ. Pallbearers were E.P. Dommond [sic], Charles Gustafson, Sammie Lee, Peter Slatendale, C.B. Utterback, Clarence Jacobson and Clyde Reedy. Interment, Gold Hill."

About the Romig Family

John Felix Romig was born 18 January 1829 in Tuscarawas (Tuscarawas) Ohio; the son of John/Johannes and Martha Amelia Emilie (*Fenner*) Romig. His parents married 20 December 1827 in (Tuscarawas) Ohio. To their union two known children were born:

John Felix: born 18 January 1829 Tuscarawas (Tuscarawas) Ohio and died 01 December 1891 Gold Hill (Boulder) Colorado; buried Gold Hill Cemetery, Gold Hill (Boulder) Colorado; married Athalia Neville; see ROMIG, Athalia (*Neville*); see ROMIG, Elizabeth Athalia; see ROMIG, John William

Lydia: born 27 September 1891 Uhrichsville (Tuscarawas) Ohio and died 01 December 1910 Gnadenhutten (Tuscarawas) Ohio; buried Gnadenhutten-Clay Union Cemetery, Gnadenhutten (Tuscarawas) Ohio; married Samuel Luethi

In the 1850 census John Felix was living in Warwick (Tuscarawas) Ohio where he was a farm laborer in the household of Joseph Rehmel. Six years later John moved to Spring (Buchanan) Iowa where he was again a farm laborer in the household of "Braze" (aka Bridge/Breeze) W. Ogden. (Spring (Buchanan) Iowa is actually Ginther Spring Township which on 07 March 1857 became known as Sumner Township and B.W. Ogden was among the first township officers elected that year.)

On 16 August 1857 John Felix Romig married Athalia Neville in (Buchanan) Iowa. Athalia was born June of 1856 (some records state 1858) in (Holmes) Ohio; the daughter of Maryland native Joseph and Pennsylvania native Mary M. "Polly" (*Buckmaster*) Neville; see ROMIG, Athalia (*Neville*). Athalia had several siblings:

Sarah: born 03 April 1818 Millersburg (Holmes) Ohio and died 29 August 1903 Byron Township (Buchanan) Iowa; buried Fremont Township Cemetery, Winthrop (Buchanan) Iowa; married Isaac Shidler and John Clark

Wilson: born 05 August 1821 Hardy Township (Holmes) Ohio and died 30 November 1897 (Cherokee) Iowa; buried Pleasant Hill Cemetery, Aurelia (Cherokee) Iowa; married Rebecca Wilson

Hannah: born 09 July 1823 (Wayne) Ohio and died 15 June 1894 Independence (Buchanan) Iowa; buried Wilson Cemetery, Independence (Buchanan) Iowa; married Robert Downs

Sophia: born 09 July 1823 (Wayne) Ohio and died 30 January 1883; burial unknown; married James Harvey/Henry Tidball; 1880 census has her living in Berlin (Holmes) Ohio

Elizabeth: born about 1824 (Wayne) Ohio-death unknown; burial unknown; married George Markley

Josiah: born 07 February 1827 (Holmes) Ohio and died 14 August 1899 Independence (Buchanan) Iowa; buried Wilson Cemetery, Independence (Buchanan) Iowa; married Elizabeth Jane Logan

Margaret: 1830 Berlin Township (Holmes) Ohio and died 09 August 1884 Norton (Norton) Kansas; buried Lenora East Cemetery, Lenora (Norton) Kansas; married William Boone

Edward V.: born about 1831 (Holmes) Ohio-23 May 1863 Black River Bridge at Vicksburg (Hinds) Mississippi; burial unknown; married Mary Margaret Robertson; Civil War casualty

Joseph L.: born 11 February 1833 (Holmes) Ohio and died 04 May 1926 Norton (Norton) Kansas; buried Norton Cemetery, Norton (Norton) Kansas; married Louisa Calhoon

Rachel K.: born 25 February 1836 (Holmes) Ohio and died 03 April 1898 Gold Hill (Boulder) Colorado; buried Gold Hill Cemetery, Gold Hill (Boulder) Colorado; married Henry "Albion" Wallick; see WALLICK, Rachel K. (*Neville*)

Amelia Malinda: born 05 March 1841 (Holmes) Ohio and died 26 February 1889 Winthrop (Buchanan) Iowa; buried Fremont Township Cemetery, Nyman (Page) Iowa; married Alfred Uhl

The union of John Felix Romig and Athalia Neville brought forth two known children:

Elizabeth Athalia: born 06 March 1858 Sumner Township (Buchanan) Iowa and died 27 March 1875 Gold

Hill (Boulder) Colorado; buried Gold Hill Cemetery, Gold Hill (Boulder) Colorado; never married; see ROMIG, Elizabeth Athalia

John William: born 30 July 1872 north of Gold Hill-on the property of Colorado Mountain Ranch (Boulder) Colorado and died 24 November 1939 Boulder (Boulder) Colorado; buried Gold Hill Cemetery, Gold Hill (Boulder) Colorado; married Ersula May "Zula" Reedy; see ROMIG, John William

The 1860 census shows John Felix, wife "Alhalice" and their daughter, Elizabeth, living in Sumner (Buchanan) Iowa where John was a farmer. It is interesting to note that John's farm was next door neighbor to "Breeze" Ogden of whom John worked for in 1856 in Spring (Buchanan) Iowa (Ginther Spring Township that became Sumner (Buchanan) Iowa).

Ten years later the family was living in (Gilpin) Colorado where John Felix was a carpenter and by 1872 they were living north of Gold Hill (Boulder) Colorado on a farm ranch which now is the location of the Colorado Mountain Ranch swimming pool (north side of County Road 52, west of Gold Hill). Their son, John William Romig was born on this farm ranch and about three years later their beloved daughter, Elizabeth Athalia, died on 27 March 1875. Her burial at the Gold Hill Cemetery is noted as the earliest known burial with a tombstone.

John Felix not only farmed but also obtained several mining claims in the Gold Hill Mining District of which some were:

Small Hopes Lode
Harbour Lode
Daisy Lode
Grand Welcome Lode
Sunnieside Lode
Dixon Lode
May Bee Lode
Valleyview Lode

In 1880 they were still living on their farm just outside of the town of Gold Hill and in the 1885 Colorado State census Katie Winters and Mary "Bangstaw" were living in the household.

Katherine/Catherine Tabitha "Katie" Winters was born 19 April 1883 Boulder (Boulder) Colorado was the daughter of Daniel David and Telitha Sarah (*Bowers*) Winters. Katie was adopted by the Romig family after her mother, Tabitha "Telitha," died. It appears that her father, Daniel, traveled to Skamokawa (Wahkiakum) Washington. Katie married Stanton Nathan Crouch on 16 September 1900 (Boulder) Colorado. She died 10 April 1971 (Monterey) California; burial unknown.

As for Mary Bangstaw the last name was really Bengston. She was listed in the 1885 Colorado State cen-

sus as a daughter to John Felix Romig which actually was John's adopted daughter. Mary Elizabeth Bengston was born 15 July 1872 in Angelstad (Kronoberg) Sweden, the daughter of Salomon and Maja Lisa "Mary" (*Petersdotter*) Bengston. After Salomon died in Sweden his widow, Maja Lisa "Mary/Maggie," and family came to the United States and traveled to Colorado.

It isn't certain of how she ended up in the Romig household in 1885 but on 09 October 1892 Mary Elizabeth Bengston married Charles Christian Luethi in (Boulder) Colorado. Her mother, Maja Lisa "Mary/Maggie," was living in Loveland (Larimer) Colorado in 1900 when two years later she died 15 March 1902 in Fort Collins (Larimer) Colorado; ashes given to either family or friend. It is interesting to note that in this census record it is stated that she had no children. Her daughter, Mary Elizabeth Bengston Luethi, died 23 February 1969 in Columbus (Franklin) Ohio and is buried in the Green Lawn Cemetery there.

On 01 December 1891 John Felix Romig passed away from pneumonia. His son, John William Romig, received the bulk of the estate at the young age of 19 years old:

Boulder County Estate Files Part 1 1862-1904 Compiled by Lois Westcott, Indexed by Ruth Ratliff:
"File 881 ROMIOG [sic], John F. of Gold Hill died 1 Dec 1891. John W., heir, ae 19 on 30 July 1891 inherited mining claims valued at $1000. Mother, Athalia, gdn." [guardian]

By June of 1900 his widow, Athalia, and Katherine Winter were living on Pearl Street in Boulder (Boulder) Colorado.

Shortly after the marriage of Katherine, Athalia died on 11 January 1901 in Boulder (Boulder) Colorado. Her remains were taken to the Gold Hill Cemetery to lay at rest beside her husband, John Felix, and their daughter, Elizabeth Athalia.

About eight months after the death of his mother, John William Romig married Ersula May "Zula" Reedy on 02 September 1901 in Boulder (Boulder) Colorado. She was born 22 April 1880 in Gold Hill (Boulder) Colorado; the daughter of David McGinley and Mary Ellen (*Wright*) Reedy.

It is interesting to note that David McGinley Reedy was quite the prominent mining man of Boulder County. He died 18 February 1935 in San Diego (San Diego) California and buried at the Green Mountain Cemetery, Boulder (Boulder) Colorado; see REEDY, Mary Kerr (*Rankin*)

Boulder Daily Camera 19 February 1935:
"D.M. Reedy Dies In San Diego...
D.M. Reedy, for many years a miner in the Left Hand

district, died at San Diego. A message was received today by Milo McAllister, secretary of Columbia Lodge No. 14, but gave no particulars. Mr. Reedy was a member of the Boulder lodge. Mr. Reedy operated a mill and mines in Boulder County."

Boulder Daily Camera 20 February 1935:

"D.M. REEDY WAS FATHER OF GOLD HILL RESIDENT...

The funeral of D.M. Reedy, prominently identified with mining in Boulder County for 36 years, was held in San Diego today where he died the first of the week.

Mr. Reedy was the father of Mrs. John Romig of Gold Hill—the only member of the family in Boulder County. His first wife, mother of his children, was Mary Ellen Reedy and she died April 30, 1915. Since going to California in the fall of 1916 he remarried.

Mr. Reedy was born in Maringo, Ill., Jan. 1, 1855, and came to Boulder County in 1880. He located at Gold Hill and lived there until 1894 when he moved to Boulder.

He was secretary and manager of the Illinois Gold Mining Company which has mines and a mill in Left Hand Canon [sic] not far from Gold Hill.

Surviving children are David F. Reedy, residing in Spokane; Mrs. W.E. Burch and Miss Myrtle Reedy, residing in San Jose, Calif. His second wife survives. There are seven grandchildren and three great grandchildren."

To the union of John W. Romig and Ersula May "Zula" Reedy three known children were born:

John David: born 19 June 1902 Gold Hill (Boulder) Colorado and died 18 August 1976 Fort Myers (Lee) Florida; burial unknown; married Mildred Elizabeth DeKraker

Paul Neville: born 03 July 1903 Gold Hill (Boulder) Colorado and died 19 December 1963; buried Green Mountain Cemetery, Boulder (Boulder) Colorado-no grave marker but next to Ersula May "Zula" Reedy; married Katherine Ross

Ellen Rosellia: born 30 September 1907 Gold Hill (Boulder) Colorado and died 01 January 1982 Boulder (Boulder) Colorado; buried Gold Hill Cemetery, Gold Hill (Boulder) Colorado; married James Dussart Regnier; see REGNIER, Ellen Rosellia (*Romig*); see REGNIER, James Dussart

In the 1910 United States census record the family is living in Gold Hill where John William Romig was a miner but by 1920 he turned to the grain and feed industry, farming. The family continued to live in Gold Hill until shortly before his death when he moved to Boulder (Boulder) Colorado, living on Euclid Street where he died on 24 November 1939. He is buried in the Gold Hill Cemetery, Gold Hill (Boulder) Colorado however when his wife, Ersula May "Zula" died on 12 November 1948 she was buried in the Green Mountain Cemetery, Boulder (Boulder) Colorado.

RYDER, George Leif

Birth: 10/24/1915
Death: 12/18/1985
Cemetery Location: F1

Father: George Odleif Rytterager; Mother: Sigrid Fernanda (*Prydz/Prydy/Prynd*); Wife: Violet Natalie (*Lyczkowski*); born in Boston (Suffolk) Massachusetts and died in Los Angeles (Los Angeles) California at age 70 years, 1 month, 0 days; U.S. Army 1943-1945; parents born in Norway; see RYDER, Violet Natalie (*Lyczkowski*)

About George Leif Ryder

According to Ancestry.com George was born 24 October 1915 in Boston (Suffolk) Massachusetts; the son of George Odleif and Sigrid Fernanda (*Prydz*) Rytterager (maiden name of Prydz spelled many different ways on records).

George Odleif was born on 9 July 1879 in Christiania Norway; son of Nicolas Rytterager (mother unknown). George was an electrician by trade when he arrived in the Port of New York about 26 years of age in 1898. By 1900 he was living in St. Paul (Ramsey) Minnesota. On 21 May 1914 he petitioned for naturalization in Boston (Suffolk) Massachusetts. In the same year on 20 November he married Sigrid Fernanda Prydy in (Kings) New York. She was born 17 December 1883 in Moss (Ostfold) Norway; daughter of Ferdinand and Berta Kathinke (*Finnemann*) Prytz. To their union two known children were born:

George Leif: born 24 October 1915 Boston (Suffolk) Massachusetts and died 18 December 1985 Los Angeles (Los Angeles) California; buried Gold Hill Cemetery, Gold Hill (Boulder) Colorado; married Violet N. Lyczkowski; see RYDER, George Leif

Robert Prydz: born 07 May 1919 Philadelphia (Philadelphia) Pennsylvania and died 18 March 1998 (Lake)

Florida; burial unknown; married Berit M. Palmroos

George Odleif's World War I draft registration card of 12 September 1918 states he and his wife, Sigrid were living in Philadelphia (Philadelphia) Pennsylvania. A year later their last name of Rytterager was changed to Ryder in the Court of Common Pleas of Philadelphia County, Pennsylvania on 27 February 1919. In 1920 their residence was Brooklyn (Kings) New York where he was an electrician and naturalized as a citizen of the United States. George and Sigrid remained in (Kings) New York until his death in July 1963; burial unknown. No other records have been located for Sigrid.

Their son, George Leif lived in his parents' household in New York (Kings) New York until he decided to marry Violet Natalie Lyczkowski on 31 December 1941 in Brooklyn, New York City (New York) New York; see RYDER, Violet Natalie (*Lyczkowski*). According to Ancestry.com their union brought forth four known children however information on three:

Mark: born 1955 (Bergen) New Jersey and died 1957 (Bergen) New Jersey; buried Maryrest Cemetery, Mahwah (Bergen) New Jersey; meningitis

Paul: no further information

Ken: no further information

About a year and a half later he joined the United States Army on 12 August 1943 where it took him to Anchorage, Alaska. He was released from duty on 27 November 1945. By the early 1950s the family was living in New Jersey with documented New York passenger list 08 August 1961 as Paramus (Bergen) New Jersey their place of residency.

Their last residence being Ventura (Ventura) California George Leif died on 18 December 1985 and his wife, Violet, died on 26 May 2014.

RYDER, Violet Natalie (*Lyczkowski*)

Birth: 08/06/1918
Death: 05/26/2014
Cemetery Location: F1

Father: Lyczkowski; Mother: unknown; Husband: George Leif Ryder; born Brooklyn (Kings) New York and died Ohai (Ventura) California at the age of 95 years, 9 months, 20 days-cause of death unknown; see RYDER, George Leif

S

SAILER, Julia (*Kliker*)

> Birth: 11/12/1856
> Death: 11/26/1886
> Cemetery Location: D5

Father: Mr. Kliker; Mother: unknown; Husband: John Sailer; died in (Boulder) Colorado at age 30 years, 14 days-cause of death unknown

About Julia (*Kliker*) Sailer

There is very little information located for Julia however she lived in Ward (Boulder) Colorado and at the age of 28 years old she married John Sailer on 01 July 1884 (Boulder) Colorado. There seems to be no listing for them in the Colorado State census record of 1885.

Her husband, John, was born April 1853 in Alsace, Austria. He immigrated to the United States in 1882 and was naturalized on 15 April 1892 at the District Court in Boulder (Boulder) Colorado.

Unfortunately no children blessed their two and a half years of marriage while living in Ward (Boulder) Colorado. Julia died on 26 November 1886 and was buried

"Moge Ihre Seele in Frieden Leben"
German for
"May her soul rest in peace."

in the Gold Hill Cemetery. The inscription on her tombstone reads, "Moge Ihre Seele in Frieden Leben;" translated from German: "May her soul rest in peace."

John married again on 31 July 1893 in Denver (Arapahoe) Colorado to Isabelle Auer. She was born January 1860 in Germany; parents unknown. Two known children blessed their marriage:

Joseph F.: born 04 December 1895 Ward (Boulder) Colorado and died 29 April 1920 Boulder (Boulder) Colorado; buried Green Mountain Cemetery, Boulder (Boulder) Colorado; never married

Isabella A.: born 23 October 1899 Ward (Boulder) Colorado and died 17 November 1986; buried Green Mountain Cemetery, Boulder (Boulder) Colorado; married Leo Brehm

After many years of mining John Sailer moved to Boulder (Boulder) Colorado where he died on 14 January 1925 at age 72 years from failing health and is buried in the Green Mountain Cemetery in Boulder (Boulder) Colorado along with his wife, Isabella who died 19 January 1940. Their son, Joseph is also buried there as well as their daughter, Isabella.

Boulder Daily Camera 14 January 1925:

"JOHN SAILER DIED EARLY THIS MORNING...
John Sailer of 2055 Bluff street passed away at 1:15 o'clock this morning, aged 72 years. He had been in failing health for some time. He was a retired miner, coming here a number of years ago from Alsess [sic], Austria. He is survived by a wife and daughter. The body is at the Howe Mortuary and will be taken from there to the Sacred Heart church Friday for services at 9 o'clock. Interment will be in Green Mountain cemetery."

SCHIELDS/SHIELDS, Alice

> Birth: About 07/1885
> Death: 08/19/1886
> Cemetery Location: Unknown

Father: Charles Schields/Shields; Mother: Margaret "Maggie" (*maiden name unknown*); born and died in Gold Hill (Boulder) Colorado at the age of 13 months-overdose of morphine; twin to Mary Shields; no tombstone; see SCHIELDS/SHIELDS, Mary; see **About Charles and Margaret "Maggie" Schields/Shields**

SCHIELDS/SHIELDS, Mary

Birth: About 07/1885
Death 08/19/1886
Cemetery Location: Unknown

Father: Charles Schields/Shields; Mother: Margaret "Maggie" (*maiden name unknown*); born and died in Gold Hill (Boulder) Colorado at the age of 13 months-overdose of morphine; twin to Alice Shields; no tombstone; see **About Charles and Margaret "Maggie" Schields/ Shields**

Boulder County Herald Weekly 25 August 1886:

"ACCIDENTAL POISONING. The Shields Twins the Victims of Morphine.

Dr. King, coroner of this county, returned from Gold Hill Friday evening, having been summoned to investigate the cause of death of the two Shields children, the twins, Mary and Alice, aged thirteen months. A HERALD reporter met the Dr. Saturday and from him obtained these particulars, they being elicited at the coroner's jury trial.

Chas. Shields, the father, had been suffering with neuralgia and was given by Dr. Wells four morphine powders on Wednesday evening. On Thursday morning Mrs. Shields went to see a neighbor, Mrs. Boundy, and appearing very much alarmed told Mrs. B. that her husband had given the twins some medicine to go to sleep. Mrs. Boundy and another neighbor, Mrs. Welch went to the house and noticed that the children had a very queer appearance and they asked what was the matter. Mr. Shield replied that he had given them some morphine to put them to sleep that they were all right and would wake up soon. He did not want any doctor nor anybody else to attend to them. Doctor Wells was however sent for and just as he stepped in the door one of the children breathed its last. He diagnosed the case as being the result of opium poisoning, and immediately went to work trying to save the other one, using all the known antidotes, but in twenty minutes the other child died. Before the jury on oath, Mrs. Shield denied having told the neighbors mentioned that her husband had given the children medicine, and Shields denied having given o having said he gave the children morphine. The children having died from the effects of morphine, the coroner's jury returned a verdict that death was caused by the administration of opium poison by Chas. Shields, he being ignorant of the fact that an infant could not stand as large a dose as an adult."

Boulder County Herald Weekly 01 September 1886:

"Shields Jailed.

Chas. Shields, of Gold Hill, who gave his children an overdose of morphine, was tried before Justice Piper Saturday on a charge of murder. Mrs. Boundy swore Shields had told her he had given morphine to the children and Dr. Wells testified the children died from the effect of opium poison. There was no testimony for the defense and Justice Piper was hence obliged to send Shields to the jail to await the actions of the grand jury."

According to the Boulder County Herald Weekly article of 20 October 1886 Charles was accused of manslaughter but acquitted. About a week later Charles and his wife had left for Canada:

Boulder County Herald Weekly 27 October 1886:

"Chas. Shields and wife left Wednesday for Canada, and the scene of his misfortunes will know him no more."

About Charles and Margaret "Maggie" Schields/ Shields

Charles was born about 1850 in England; parents unknown. He married Margaret "Maggie" (maiden name unknown) who was born 1861 in Ireland; parents unknown. To the union of Charles and Margaret seven known children were born with records on four:

Alice: born about July 1885 Gold Hill (Boulder) Colorado and died 19 August 1886 Gold Hill (Boulder) Colorado; buried Gold Hill Cemetery, Gold Hill (Boulder) Colorado; twin to Mary; see SCHIELDS/SHIELDS, Alice

Mary: born about July 1885 Gold Hill (Boulder) Colorado and died 19 August 1886 Gold Hill (Boulder) Colorado; buried Gold Hill Cemetery, Gold Hill (Boulder) Colorado; twin to Alice; see SCHIELDS/SHIELDS, Mary

Anna Louise: born 1887 Lyons (Boulder) Colorado and died 1921 Lyons (Boulder) Colorado; buried Lyons Cemetery, Lyons (Boulder) Colorado; never married

Albert H. or T.: born 25 May 1890 (Boulder) Colorado and died 28 November 1901 Lyons (Boulder) Colorado; buried Lyons Cemetery, Lyons (Boulder) Colorado; never married; gravestone has 1886 as birth year

In the Colorado State census Charles (age 35) and Maggie (25) were living in Gold Hill (Boulder) Colorado where he was a miner. A few weeks after this census was taken their twins, Alice and Mary, were born only to die about a year later from an accidental overdose of morphine.

Charles Shields supposedly moved to Canada shortly after this incident but returned to Colorado where he and Margaret lived in Lyons (Boulder) Colorado.

Charles died 29 December 1895 and was buried in the Lyons Cemetery in Lyons (Boulder) Colorado.

Boulder News 02 January 1896:

"A man Chas. Shields died at Lyons Sunday and was buried at the expense of the county."
(former Gold Hill miner)

Digging Up Dirt

His wife, Margaret "Maggie" continued to live in Lyons (Boulder) Colorado until the end of 1934:

Lyons Recorder 28 December 1934:

"Margaret Shields Taken to Boulder...

Mrs. Margaret Shields, for a number of years in a feeble condition and suffering from hallucinations, was deemed this week unfit to care for herself and Sheriff George Richart came over and transferred her to the county home, where she is being cared for.

Mrs. Shields has the small home where she, herself, resided and another cabin which she rented. She has been regarded as too feeble to remain alone for a year or more, but clung steadfastly to her home here, and her transfer to the county home has been delayed for this reason."

Lyons Recorder 04 January 1935:

"Mrs. Shields Is Contined to Bed At County Home...

"Mrs. Margaret Shields, taken last week to the county farm, has refused to eat and lies in bed in one of the rooms with two other old ladies. Mayor C.L. Drage called on her Monday, and found her overjoyed to see anyone from Lyons. Old time people whom she has known since early days should call on her when in the county seat."

About a week later Margaret "Maggie" died 12 January 1935 and also was buried in the Lyons Cemetery.

Death records are very confusing as the tombstone for Charles states he was born 26 February 1828 which would make him 66 years old at the time of death however the 1885 Colorado State census record states his age as

Photo by Dina C. Carson

35 thus making his birth year 1850; Margaret's age was stated as 25.

It does seem to be reasonable to believe that the dates engraved on the tombstone are incorrect especially in relationship to the *Lyons Recorder* newspaper article of 04 January 1935 above (tombstone has death year as 1895).

Margaret's birth year is listed as 1861 so it's hard to imagine Charles was 32 years older than Margaret at the time of his death when he was only about 11 years older in 1850!

SCHIFF, William Leslie

Birth: 09/11/1945
Death: 10/25/1991
Cemetery Location: D6

Father: William "Dee" Schiff; Mother: Marion (*Frint*); Wife: Lynne Yvonne (*Walter*); died at age 46 years, 1 month, 0 days-extended illness; Vietnam veteran

Boulder Daily Camera 30 October 1991:
"William Leslie Schiff—William Leslie Schiff of Gold Hill died Friday, Oct. 25, at the Veteran's Administration Hospital in Denver after an extended illness. He was 46.

He was born Sept. 11, 1945, in Milwaukee, the son of William "Dee" Schiff and Marion Frint Schiff. He married Lynne Walter on April 24, 1989, in Boulder.

He graduated with a bachelor's degree in business administration from Iowa State University. In 1968, he was commissioned an ensign in the U.S. Navy. He served with the 6th Fleet aboard the USS Little Rock.

In 1970, he worked as a stockbroker for Dean Witter in Denver. In 1971, he formed the High Street Investment Co. and was successful in the real estate business.

He was a member of the Parachute Club of America and was a history buff.

Survivors include his wife of Gold Hill; his mother of Winter Park, Fla.; two brothers, Michael Schiff and Richard Schiff, both of Denver; three sisters, Margaret S. Schmalfeit and Jean S. Burns, both of Wisconsin, and Ann C. Schiff of Winter Park, Fla.

He was preceded in death by his father.

A service will be held Friday at 4:30 p.m. at the Gold Hill Cemetery with the Rev. Tom Woerth officiating.

Howe Mortuary is handling arrangements."

SCOGLAND, Helen Margaret

Birth: 01/14/1897
Died: 03/21/1903
Cemetery Location: B3

Father: Claus Albert Scogland; Mother: Maude Oleana/Oline (*Colvin*); born in Rowena (Boulder) Colorado and died in Boulder (Boulder) Colorado at age 6 years, 2 months, 7 days-heart disease; some records have Albert Claus Scogland

Boulder County News 10 March 1903:
"Gold Hill...Little Miss Helen Scogland is quite seriously ill."

Boulder County News 24 March 1903:
"Helen, the little daughter of Mr. and Mrs. Albert Scogland died here on Saturday, March 21st, of heart disease. Her death is a sorrow to the entire town, for her sweet face and winning ways made her a general favorite. The bereaved parents have sincere sympathy of all."

About the Scogland Family

Claus Albert Scogland was born 23 November 1869 in Ljungby Smaland (Kronoberg) Sweden; the son of John Scogland (mother unknown).

The 1920 United States census states immigration year for Albert was 1880 but the 1930 census states the year was 1873. However Albert was naturalized 18 April 1900 at the District Court in Boulder (Boulder) Colorado.

On 23 December 1893 Claus Albert Scogland married Maude Oleana Colvin in Jamestown (Boulder) Colorado (however marriage certificate states Boulder (Boulder) Colorado). Maude was born 22 December 1876 in Marshalltown (Marshall) Iowa; the daughter of Alva Dewite (Maude's obituary states Dwight Dwayne) and Margaret G. "Maggie" (*Arbuthnot*) Colvin. To the union of Claus Albert and Maude Oleana six known children were born:

Albert Dowite: born 29 March 1895 Gold Hill (Boulder) Colorado and died 18 November 1929 Boulder (Boulder) Colorado; buried Green Mountain Cemetery, Boulder (Boulder) Colorado; married Rose Kostansky and Ada A. (*Reedy*) Carpenter

Helen Margaret: born 14 January 1897 Rowena (Boulder) Colorado and died 21 March 1903 Boulder (Boulder) Colorado; buried Gold Hill Cemetery, Gold Hill (Boulder) Colorado; never married; see SCOGLAND, Helen Margaret

John Colvin: born 03 May 1904 Rowena (Boulder) Colorado and died 19 May 1968 Boulder (Boulder) Colorado; buried Green Mountain Cemetery, Boulder (Boulder) Colorado; married Thesta Kennedy McClendon

Carl Leroy: born 13 July 1907 Rowena (Boulder) Colorado and died 14 April 1957 Boulder (Boulder) Colorado; buried Green Mountain Cemetery, Boulder (Boulder) Colorado; married Lillian May Beason

Glenn Oren: born 15 July 1909 Rowena (Boulder) Colorado and died 24 June 1960 Denver (Denver) Colorado; buried Green Mountain Cemetery, Boulder (Boulder) Colorado; married Gladys Viele and Eloise Adda Robinson

William B.: born 23 April 1916 (Boulder) Colorado and died August 1986 San Manuel (Pinal) Arizona; burial unknown; married Lillas Irene Gregory and Janey Stringer; there is another William B. Scogland with the same birthdate who died September 1983 Shreveport (Caddo) Louisiana and Janey Stringer Scogland died there and buried in Forest Park West Cemetery, Shreveport (Caddo) Louisiana.

"*FOR LIFE IS BUT A WINDOW
AND WE ARE THE LIGHT
WHICH PASSES THROUGH
IN ALL DIRECTIONS,
COMING, BEING, AND GOING...*"
–William Schiff

The family spent many years living in Rowena (Boulder) Colorado but by 1910 they were back in Gold Hill (Boulder) Colorado where Albert was a miner. Ten years later he moved down to the plains where he farmed, living in Niwot (Boulder) Colorado along with his wife and family.

The 1930 census record is interesting as Albert, wife Maude and their son, John Colvin, were living at 3175 10th Street in Boulder (Boulder) Colorado. Their other sons, Carl Leroy, Glen Oren and William B., were living in the household of Floyd D. O'Connell (listed as Floyd's sons) at 3038 10th Street which apparently doesn't exist anymore.

Claus Albert Scogland died on 06 October 1930; dying from silicosis carcinoma of the stomach (the most common type of cancer) at the Colorado General Hospital in Denver (Denver) Colorado and was buried in the Green Mountain Cemetery in Boulder (Boulder) Colorado.

Boulder Daily Camera 07 October 1930:
"A.C. Scogland Pioneer Boulder Resident Dies...

Albert C. Scogland, 60, well-known pioneer resident of the county, died at 10 o'clock last night in Colorado General Hospital following an operation. He had been ill several weeks with stomach trouble.

Mr. Scogland had been caretaker of the Country Club grounds for three years. He and his family have been living at 3175 Tenth.

Mr. Scogland came to Boulder County about fifty years ago from Sweden. He was a miner for many years and was superintendent of the Mugget Mine and Milling Co., at one time. He was in the laboratory of the Utah Copper company when its big mines in Utah were developed.

For a while he farmed near Longmont and later bought several tracts near Boulder.

He was a member of the Mt. Sinai commandery, Knights Templars, and of Boulder Lodge No. 45 of the Masons.

These organizations will be in charge of the funeral. The arrangements are not yet completed. The body is at Howe Mortuary.

The widow and four sons, J.C. and Glen Scogland, of Rayne, La., and Carl and William Scogland, of Boulder survive.

Another son, Albert D. Scogland, died last November while on a visit here."

Boulder Daily Camera 08 October 1930:

"ALBERT C. SCOGLAND...

Funeral services for Albert C. Scogland, who died in Denver October 6th, will be held at the Howe mortuary Friday afternoon at 2:30 o'clock. Boulder Lodge No. 45 of the Masonic order will have charge of the services.

Interment will be in Green Mountain cemetery."

His widow, Maude Oleana (*Colvin*) Scogland lived a good thirty years longer, dying on 16 May 1964 in Boulder (Boulder) Colorado at the age of almost 87 ½ years old. She was buried beside her husband, Albert Claus.

Boulder Daily Camera 16 May 1964:
"Maude Scogland Died Friday...

Mrs. Maude O. Scogland, a long-time resident of Boulder County, died Friday at 8:40 p.m. in the Mesa Vista Sanitorium [sic].

She was born Dec. 22, 1876, in Marshalltown, Iowa, to Dwight Dwayne and Margaret A. Colvin, and moved to the Altona district with her parents when she was a child.

On Dec. 23, 1893, she was married in Jamestown to Albert Scogland, a miner in Jamestown, Left Hand and Gold Hill areas. He died in October of 1930. Also preceding her in death were three sons and a daughter.

Surviving are two sons, John C., Scogland of Boulder and William Scogland of Tennessee; seven grandchildren and one great-grandson. There are two sisters, Mrs. Myrtle Mayor of Boulder and Mrs. Claude Washburn of Baker, Ore.

Funeral services will be Monday at 3 p.m. at the Howe Mortuary. Interment will be in Green Mountain Cemetery."

Boulder Daily Camera 17 May 1964:
"Maude O. Scogland—Services were at 3 this afternoon at the Howe Mortuary with Rev. Wm. O. Byrd of the First Methodist Church officiating. Organist was Mrs. Howard Ashton and soloist Kenneth Stone. Pallbearers were Charles Reader, Richard Leiber, Harold Gunning, Edward Potter, Robert Smith and Perry Frazier. Interment was in Green Mountain Cemetery."

SHEA, Daniel

Birth: 1842
Died: About 1890
Cemetery Location: D3 (possibly)

Father: unknown; Mother: unknown; Wife: Ellen Elizabeth (*McGlaughlin*); born in Massachusetts and died in (Boulder) Colorado at about 48 years-cause of death unknown; no tombstone; see BENNETT(S), Mary Ann (*Shea*)

About Daniel Shea

Daniel Shea was born about 1842 in Massachusetts; Irish native parents unknown. He married Ellen Elizabeth McGlaughlin. She was born 01 December 1841 (1843 according to the mortuary record) in Ireland; the daughter of Ireland natives Mr. (first name unknown) and Kate (possibly Catherine) (*McDermott*) McGlaughlin. She immigrated to the United States in 1867 where she met and married Daniel Shea. To this union ten children were born (according to the obituary of Ellen Elizabeth (*McGlaughlin*) Shea) with information on seven:

William John: born 01 February 1868 Colorado and died 25 July 1946 Los Angeles (Los Angeles) California; buried Forest Lawn Memorial Park, Glendale (Los Angeles) California; married Hattie Barbara (*Berger*) Merstetter

Mary Ann: born 18 April 1869 Colorado and died 12 April 1899 Gold Hill (Boulder) Colorado; buried Gold Hill Cemetery, Gold Hill (Boulder) Colorado; married James Bennett(s); see BENNETT(S), Mary Ann (*Shea*)

Daniel: born September 1871 Colorado and died 12 July 1912; buried Sunshine Cemetery, Sunshine (Boulder) Colorado; married Bridia (maiden name unknown)

Frank: born 20 November 1874 Colorado and died 15 August 1908 (Boulder) Colorado; buried Sunshine Cemetery, Sunshine (Boulder) Colorado; never married

Nellie E.: born September 1876 Sunshine (Boulder) Colorado and died 13 March 1905 Cripple Creek (Teller) Colorado; buried Sunshine Cemetery, Boulder (Boulder) Colorado; married Frances Henry Berger; mortuary record states death date 12 March 1905

Maud E.: born July 1884 Colorado and died 27 March 1905 Boulder (Boulder) Colorado; buried Sunshine Cemetery, Sunshine (Boulder) Colorado; married Oscar Bernard Lagerlund

Harry: born 1885 Colorado and died 20 December 1897 Sunshine (Boulder) Colorado; buried Sunshine Cemetery, Sunshine (Boulder) Colorado

During or about the year of 1890 Daniel Shea died as per the estate affidavits filed in Boulder County on 22 January 1908. Even though listed as buried in the Sunshine Cemetery in Sunshine (Boulder) Colorado he was actually buried in the Gold Hill Cemetery in Gold Hill (Boulder) Colorado assuming by his daughter, Mary Ann (*Shea*) Bennett(s), who died in 1889; see BENNETT(S), Mary Ann (*Shea*).

Tragedy struck the family in 1897 when the youngest son, Harry, was accidentally shot and killed by a playmate at the tender age of 12 years:

Boulder Daily Camera 21 December 1897:

"Word was received by Coroner Trezise last night announcing that Harry Shea, the twelve-year-old son of Mrs. Dan Shea, an old resident of Sunshine, was accidentally shot and killed by a boy named Snively, of about the same sage, at that place yesterday afternoon. A party of boys went out to get evergreens for Christmas decoration, taking a gun along. Young Snively picked up the gun and asked his companion if it was loaded. On being told that is was not, the lad playfully snapped it at the Shea boy who was sitting in the wagon."

Tragedy again struck the family in 1905 when two daughters, Nellie E., and Maud E., died from the same fate as their older sister, Mary Ann (*Shea*) Bennett(s) who died in 1889. It appears that all three daughters suffered from blood poisoning following childbirth; see BENNETT(S), Mary Ann (*Shea*) for newspaper article.

Three years later their brother, Frank, was killed in the Ingram mine explosion:

Daniel Shea is believed to have buried in the area of Annie (*Bennett(s)*) & Edwin David "Ned" Goudge tombstone and Mary Ann (*Shea*) & James Bennett(s) tombstone

Original burial photo of Edwin D. Goudge which depicts a small tombstone to the upper left: might be the grave of Daniel Shea. FYI: Upon the death of Annie Elizabeth (*Bennett(s)*) Goudge the tombstone was turned (see photo left).

Digging Up Dirt

Boulder Daily Herald 17 August 1908

"A TERRIBLE ACCIDENT OCCURRED AT Salina in the Ingram mine Saturday afternoon and as a result three men were instantly killed and all of them were careful and popular miners. Just how the accident happened will never be known as the victims were the only ones present and their lips are sealed in death. The three men Frank Shea, Ole Broughton and Frank Cullacotte were at work in the stope of the 245-foot level. Several holes had been drilled preparatory to being loaded with powder. It was the intention to fire these and by Monday morning the fumes of the powder would have cleared away so as to permit further working. The holes were never charged. After they had been drilled Shea went to the drift and got from 40 to 50 pounds of dynamite. He had gotten back into the stope when by some means the powder exploded and all of the men were killed instantly. Shea had part of his face blown off, his right arm was torn off and his body was otherwise lacerated. The other two had their faces badly burned but not torn like Shea's, in fact, the latter was unrecognizable. Both the others had their bodies so torn that death must have been instantaneous.

As soon as the explosion took place, other miners at work could tell by the sound that the holes had not been fired, and since the men had not come out of the stope they feared the men must have been killed as proved to be the case. Ed Demmon tried to get into the stope but the fearful smoke kept him back. He finally did get as far as Shea's body and seeing the effect retired. It was impossible to go further and if the other two had not been killed by the explosion they would have been smothered to death. Word was sent to Corner Buchheit in this city, who immediately went up and gathering up the remains in burlaps, etc., brought them to Boulder. The body of Shea was found in one part of the stope, the other two in another part.

It is believed that in fixing the fuses Shea got too close to the powder, though this is simply a surmise.

The three men are well known in Boulder.

Frank Shea made his home with his brother in this city and was one of the best miners in the county. At the miners' drilling contest in Central City on July 4, he and Art Collins took the first prize in double-hand drilling. He was 33 years old and was unmarried. The funeral will be held tomorrow morning at 10:00 o'clock in Buchheit & Holley's parlors. He left an insurance policy of $2,000 in favor of his mother."

About four years later another brother, Daniel, died on 12 July from fibroid phthisis (tuberculosis).

Boulder Daily Camera 13 July 1929:

"Daniel Shea, aged 41 years, a pioneer mining man of Boulder County, died Friday afternoon at his home at 513 University Avenue. Services will be conducted from the Sacred Heart church Monday morning at 8 o'clock. Interment will be made at Sunshine, the Woodmen of the World, of which the deceased was a member, having charge of the services at the grave. He is survived by a wife and two children."

The influenza epidemic of 1918 claimed the life of Ellen Elizabeth (*McGaughlin*) Shea:

Boulder News Herald 18 October 1918:

"Influenza Claims 6 Boulder Victims In Past 24 Hours...

Six deaths have resulted from influenza in Boulder during the past twenty-four hours. Two of these occurred so late in the day that the undertaker who had charge of arrangements was unable to furnish their names to the press. The other four were:

Mrs. Ellen Shea, 70, of 2130 Twenty-second street; Herbert Palmer, 37, 1818 Walnut street; Charles S. Fairhurst, 42, Forth Twenty-sixth street, Richard C. Brown."

Boulder Daily Camera 19 October 1918

"MRS. ELLEN SHEA'S REST WILL BE BESIDE CHILDREN IN CEMETERY AT SUNSHINE

Mrs. Ellen Shea, whose death Thursday at her home, 2130 Twenty-Second Street, was recorded, will rest beside seven of her ten children in the cemetery at Sunshine after the funeral tomorrow.

This esteemed lady was mother of ten children, only one of whom survives, Will Shea, well known miner. Her husband [Daniel Shea] lies in a grave at Gold Hill.

She came to Sunshine in 1875 and lived there until 14 years ago when she moved to Boulder. Her son Will left here some years ago for Cripple Creek and came from that place a week or more before his mother's death and was at her bedside during her illness."

SHEARER, Florence (*Humphrey*)

Birth: 12/05/1889
Died: 06/05/1961
Cemetery Location: E3

Father: Reamer A. Humphrey; Mother: Lulu (*Massie*); Husband: David Homer Shearer; born in Kansas City (Jackson/Clay/Platte/Cass) Missouri and died in Boulder (Boulder) Colorado at age 71 years, 6 months-cerebral hemorrhage

Boulder Daily Camera 05 June 1961:

"Florence Shearer, Gold Hill Resident, Dies—Mrs. Florence Humphrey Shearer, of Kansas City, Missouri, a summer resident of Gold Hill, died at 11:30 this morning at Community Hospital. She was 71. She was the widow of David Homer Shearer, who died in Kansas City in 1918 and the mother of David Shearer, at present at the Holiday Inn. She was a sister of Miss Edith Humphrey of Gold Hill and of Miss Imogene Ragan of Dumas, Texas. There are four grandchildren and two great-grandchildren. Her parents, Reamer and Lulu Massie Humphrey, to whom she was born at Kansas City, Mo., Dec. 5, 1889, are deceased. Graveside services will be held in the Gold Hill Cemetery at 3 Tuesday afternoon. Rev. Robert Hempfling, pastor of the First Christian Church, will officiate."

Boulder Daily Camera 06 June 1961:

"Florence Humphrey Shearer of Kansas City, Missouri, who died at the Community Hospital on June 5th. Graveside services were held at Gold Hill this afternoon at 8 p.m. Here for the funeral were her son, David H. Shearer of Kansas City and her daughter, Mrs. Eloise Cella of St. Louis. Mrs. Shearer's husband died at Kansas City in 1918 and she had been spending summers at Gold Hill for many years. Rev. Robert Hempfling officiated. Howe Mortuary was in charge of arrangements."

Boulder Daily Camera Focus 01 November 1981:

"One of Gold Hill's more wealthy residents was Florence Shearer. Gertrude Jones was one of her cronies. She says of Florence: "When you got up in the morning you never knew what she was going to be up to. She had a house in Kansas City, one in Florida, and one in Gold Hill. We used to play gin rummy half the night, getting one-tenth of a cent per point. One time Florence invited me to 'go wooding.' I had never cut wood in the mountains so I got out my saw and my gunny sack. She said, "Where do you think you're going? You can just break the aspen up here into stove-lengths over a stove."

On foggy days she'd put on a big pot of soup. By the time she'd made it down Main Street she'd have invited all the summer people to lunch. She didn't worry. She'd laugh and say 'I'll just add more water!'"

(article by Laura Sickenberger)

SHELLEY, Daniel "Dan"

> Birth: About 1860
> Death: 04/19/1901
> Cemetery Location: Unknown

Father: unknown; Mother: unknown; single; born in Pennsylvania and died in Gold Hill (Boulder) Colorado at 41 years of age (approximately)-burned to death; possible burial; no tombstone

Boulder County Herald: 19 April 1901:

"DRUNKEN MINER BURNS TO DEATH…

Dan Shelley, a miner, was burned to death in his cabin on Gold Hill at 5 o'clock this morning.

He had gone home in an intoxicated condition, and it is supposed that in lighting his candle he set it where it set fire to the wall, and then rolled late bed [sic] and went to sleep without discovering his danger.

A newspaper carrier, passing by, discovered smoke from the cracks of the building and heard groans coming from the inside. He kicked open the door and attempted to enter, but the smoke drove him out. He then gave the alarm, but by the time the department could respond the cabin was a mass of flames.

The body was burned to a crisp, and the position in which it was lying testified in the horrible agony the man had suffered.

Shelley was a single man and had lived in the district a number of years. He has a sister living in Aspen."

About Daniel "Dan" Shelley

Little is known about Daniel Shelley except that he was listed as living in Leadville (Lake) Colorado in the U.S. City Directories for the years 1882 and 1885 and the 1885 Colorado State census record.

It is not certain that he was actually buried in the Gold Hill Cemetery as there wasn't much left of him to bury.

SHERWOOD, Charles Ray

> Birth: 12/20/1881
> Death: 08/17/1883
> Cemetery Location: Unknown

Father: Clifford Edson "Ted" Sherwood; Mother: Elizabeth "Lizzie" (*Chambers*); born in Gold Hill (Boulder) Colorado and died in Summerville (Boulder) Colorado at age 19 months, 28 days-congestion of the brain (bleeding in the brain which creates congestion and pressure on brain tissue); no tombstone; see SHERWOOD, Infant Son

Boulder County News 17 August 1883:

"Charles, the 18 months-old son of Mr. and Mrs. Edward [error] Sherwood, of Summerville, died of congestion of the brain, last night, and will be buried at Gold Hill at one o'clock to-morrow afternoon."

About the Sherwood Family

Clifford Edson "Ted" Sherwood was born 06 March 1849 in Muscatine (Muscatine) Iowa; the son of William and Susan Carolyn Ray (*McCloud*) Sherwood.

By 1865 the family was living in (Gilpin) Colorado and by 1880 they were living in Nederland (Boulder) Colorado where William was a jeweler. His son, Clifford, however, was living in (Weld) Colorado Territory in 1870 where, at the age of 22 years, he was a farmer.

Clifford married Elizabeth "Lizzie" Chambers on 04 September 1876 in Sunshine (Boulder) Colorado. According to her death certificate Elizabeth was born 22 November 1852 in Westmoreland (Westmoreland) Pennsylvania; the daughter of Benjamin Franklin and Nancy (*McCartney*) Chambers. To this union eight known children were born:

Infant Son: born 16 June 1877 Gold Hill (Boulder) Colorado and died 16 June 1877 Gold Hill (Boulder) Colorado; buried Gold Hill Cemetery, Gold Hill (Boulder) Colorado; see SHERWOOD, Infant Son

William "Willie" Benjamin: born 26 July 1878 Gold Hill (Boulder) Colorado and died 14 March 1943 Wilder (Canyon) Idaho; buried Wilder Cemetery, Wilder (Canyon) Idaho; married Esther A. Perrin

Edison Frank: born 26 February 1880 Gold Hill (Boulder) Colorado and died 09 March 1957 Rock Springs (Sweetwater) Wyoming; buried Heber City Cemetery Heber (Wasatch) Utah; married Mary Miama "Merle" (*Boulden*) Jeffs and Hallie Chloe Ross

Charles Ray: born 20 December 1881 Gold Hill (Boulder) Colorado and died 17 August 1883 Summerville (Boulder) Colorado; buried Gold Hill Cemetery, Gold Hill (Boulder) Colorado; see SHERWOOD, Charles Ray

Lillian Caroline: born 27 October 1883 Summerville (Boulder) Colorado and died 07 July 1959 Los Angeles (Los Angeles) California; burial unknown; married Charles D. Cramer

Robert McLeod: born 07 December 1885 Sunshine (Boulder) Colorado and died 09 August 1936 Milford (Beaver) Utah; buried Milford City Cemetery, Milford (Beaver) Utah; married Leah Hutchings and Bertha Frances Davidson

Alice "Allie" May: born 30 July 1888 Boulder (Boulder) Colorado and died 03 April 1921 Pocatello (Bannock) Idaho; buried Mountain View Cemetery, Pocatello (Bannock) Idaho; married Charles B. Still

Helen Adair: born 22 December 1892 Boulder (Boulder) Colorado and died 09 December 1974 Caldwell (Canyon) Idaho; buried Wilder Cemetery, Wilder (Canyon) Idaho; married John Calvin Young and Horace Milliner

Clifford's mother, Susan Carolyn Ray (*McCloud*) Sherwood, died 15 June 1889 in Boulder (Boulder) Colorado at the age of 62 years from paralysis (stroke) and was buried in the Columbia Cemetery there.

Boulder News 20 June 1889:
"Mrs. Wm. Sherwood, a lady well known and highly esteemed, in this community died Saturday afternoon, aged nearly sixty-two years. She was waiting on her husband who was suffering with paralysis when she two [sic], was stricken with the same disease. She was assisted to her room and the doctor called but it was thought she need rest and sleep, and so they left her. When her son looked in an hour or two later it was found that she had peacefully entered into that restful sleep that knows no waking in this world. The funeral services were held in the Baptist church on Wednesday at 10 a.m. conducted by Rev. Hayden, after which the remains were deposited in the city cemetery."

William Sherwood, father of Clifford, died nine days later on 24 June 1889.

Boulder News 27 June 1889:
"Wm. Sherwood, an old pioneer and good citizen, breathed his last Monday afternoon and was buried from the Baptist church Wednesday. He died of paralysis, his wife having died of the same disease but a week previous. He was so ill that he was unconscious at the time and never knew that his companion had preceded him to the better world. Mr. Sherwood was one of the original discoverers of silver in the state, and with his sons has done much to develop the mineral resources of this and other counties, and the death of such a man is a real loss to the community as well as to immediate friends."

Unfortunately Clifford and Elizabeth divorced.

Boulder News 07 September 1893:
"Mrs. Elizabeth C. Sherwood was on Tuesday granted a divorce from C.E. Sherwood on the grounds of desertion and non-support. She was also granted the custody of the children."

Later that year Clifford died in Cripple Creek (Teller) Colorado:

Boulder Daily Camera 29 December 1893:
"Death of Fred [sic] Sherwood...P.J. Werley just received a dispatch afternoon from Cripple Creek announcing the news of the death of C.E. Sherwood, better known as Ted Sherwood. There were no particulars with the telegram. Mr. Werley sent back word to ship the remains to Boulder. His wife, recently divorced, and five children live in East Boulder. The remains will arrive tomorrow."

Boulder News 04 January 1894:

"Mr. C.E. Sherwood, so long a resident of Boulder and well known to almost everybody here, died at Cripple Creek last week. Willie and Eddie, his two little boys, attended the funeral through the assistance of friends here and the Midland railway, which furnished them passes."

Clifford Edson "Ted" Sherwood was buried in Columbia Cemetery, Boulder (Boulder) Colorado.

Elizabeth "Lizzie" (*Chambers*) Sherwood then married Edvin Edholm (*Sjoman*) on 11 February 1898 in (Arapahoe) Colorado however in the 1910 census Edvin is listed as divorced, living in Sugarloaf (Boulder) Colorado where he was a miner. It is believed he died on 28 November 1932 in Kingman (Mohave) Arizona from chronic myocarditis at the age of about 72 years; buried in the Mountain View Cemetery, Kingman (Mohave) Arizona. According to the death certificate he was "single."

Elizabeth moved to Utah where she died on 10 October 1914 in Milford (Beaver) Utah and is buried in the Milford City Cemetery, Milford (Beaver) Utah under the Sherwood name. Interesting to note that on her death certificate she is listed (rightly so) as a "widow."

SHERWOOD, Infant Son

Birth: 06/16/1877
Death: 06/16/1877
Cemetery Location: Unknown

Father: Clifford Edson "Ted" Sherwood; Mother: Elizabeth "Lizzie" (*Chambers*); born and died in Gold Hill (Boulder) Colorado-probably stillborn; no tombstone; see SHERWOOD, Charles; see **About the Sherwood Family**

SIMMONS, William Robert

Birth: 10/20/1925
Death: 12/03/1996
Cemetery Location: H2

Father: Henry Thomas Simmons; Mother: Ines Ione (*Palmer*); 1st Wife: Mora Elizabeth (*Henderson*); 2nd Wife: Claire (*Richards*); 3rd Wife: Karen Eva (*Dare*); born in Auburn (Cayuga) New York and died in Boulder (Boulder) Colorado at age 71 years-cancer; Auburn (Cayuga) New York was the closest hospital to their home in Skaneateles (Cayuga) New York

Boulder Daily Camera 06 December 1996:

"William Robert Simmons of Boulder died Tuesday, Dec. 3, 1996. He was 71.

He was born Oct 20, 1925, in Skaneateles, N.Y., to Henry Thomas Simmons and Inez Ione Palmer Simmons.

He lived in Skaneateles until he entered the U.S. Navy in 1943. He was a second-class radio telegrapher in the South Pacific during World War II.

After the war, he worked at the first television station in Syracuse, N.Y. After moving to California in 1953, he earned a degree at Pomona Junior College. He moved to Boulder in 1957 to attend the University of Colorado. He earned a bachelor's degree in engineering physics and then a master's and a doctorate in physics at CU, finishing in 1965. He was elected to Tau Beta Pi, Sigma Xi, and Sigma Pi Sigma honor societies.

After a post-doctoral fellowship at the University of Hawaii, he moved back to Boulder to work on laser research at the National Bureau of Standards, now called the National Institute of standards and Technology, where he helped develop a device to measure the power output of a laser.

Beginning in 1970, he worked on the acoustic echo sounder program at the National Oceanic and Atmospheric Administration. In 1975, he began working for the Physics Department at the University of Colorado at Denver, where he remained an associate professor until his death. Engineering students elected him Teacher of the Year nine times in his 21 years, principally based on his "no notes, no calculators, just open minds" teaching philosophy.

Survivors include his wife, Karen E. Simmons of Boulder; a son, Greg Palmer Simmons of Lakeville, Minn; and three daughters, Cathy E. Wilder of Barton, Vt., Lynn D. Baxter of Louisville and Kelly A. Knauer of Westminster; 10 grandchildren; and a great-granddaughter.

A brother, Henry Palmer Simmons, preceded him in death.

Services will be at 1 p.m. Saturday at Howe Mortuary, 2121 11th St., Boulder. A burial service for family and close friends will be held at Gold Hill after the funeral service. A wake will be held at 4 p.m. Saturday at the Gold Hill Inn to celebrate Mr. Simmons' life.

Contributions may be made to the William Robert Simmons memorial fund at the Skaneateles Library, 49 E. Genesee St., Skaneateles, N.Y. 13152."

Digging Up Dirt

Memorial Handout:

"Most of us knew Bill as a researcher or as a teacher, and we all knew how much he relished his life. But before he became the teacher recognized for his excellence, he served his country in World War II.

When he was 18, Bill joined the Navy, and it opened the world to him. From Skaneateles, Bill went to boot camp on Long Island [corrected below to Samson Navy Training Station in West New York] and to radio school in Florida. From there comes one of Bill's favorite recollections.

In 1943 citrus fruits were rare in upstate New York, and in Florida Bill discovered grapefruit. He also figured out that the mess hall lines were long enough that he could eat one grapefruit in line and arrive again at the fruit station to collect another one. Now, we don't know how many times Bill made it through the line, but we do know he loved grapefruit because, years later, he still delighted in receiving part of the harvest from Karen's father's grapefruit trees.

He also loved being a sailor and was proud to serve during World War II. His service in the Navy took him to the South Pacific-Ulethe, Guam, Okinawa, Lyte, and Saipan. He was in the second battle of the Philippines, and his ship, the ATR, was the first American ship to enter Wakayama, Japan. He saw the world, just as promised.

Then, the Navy allowed him to go to school, and Bill, whose grandfather could not write, earned a doctorate in physics.

Today, let us remember Bill's achievements, his warmth, and his exuberance."

William Robert Simmons
October 20, 1925-December 3, 1996

(Submitted by Karen Eva (*Dare*) Simmons)

"Bill's family lived in the eastern most Finger Lake town of Skaneateles, New York. His grandfather, William M. Simmons, had emigrated from Somerset England to raise teasels [biennial plant] and Bill's father, Henry Thomas Simmons, worked in the felt mill north of town. Bill's mother, Ione Inez Palmer Simmons was a member of the Palmer clan that had come on the Mayflower in the 1600s.

Bill was born in Auburn, NY (the closest hospital) on October 20, 1925. He spent his young life in Skaneateles where he had a small boat on Skaneateles Lake. He fished and was a strong swimmer; he could swim the mile and a quarter across the lake, was a life guard at the lake's beach, played clarinet in the high school band and was a tackle on the high school football team. He enjoyed going off with his brother, Henry Palmer Simmons, in Palmer's roadster and had a sweetheart (Mora Elizabeth Henderson) in Marcellus, NY when World War II broke out. Palmer became a fighter pilot but Bill had trouble getting into the service due to his poor eyesight. Mrs. Wainright was a member of his church and while she waited for her General husband to be freed she was able to recommend the US Navy accept Bill into service. That was June 16, 1943 when he was a junior in high school. So off he went to Sampson Navy Training Station on the east shore of Seneca Lake. (Note, I was incorrect in the memorial handout when I said he went to Long Island boot camp.) Bill's unit received a "Rooster" award for being the best marching unit at camp that session, he was very proud of that honor. After boot camp he went on to the Miami area radio training station; it was here that he was introduced to something he'd rarely had in Skaneateles: grapefruit. Many years later he loved to visit with Karen's parents in Arizona and bring home boxes from their grapefruit trees.

From radio school it was by troop transport train across the nation that he was to defend but had never seen. Arriving in Stockton California he was assigned to the construction of the ATR 51; ATR stands for Auxiliary Transport Rescue, mostly they transported material around the Pacific but they were also a fire fighting ship and were used in the Leyte Gulf battle to fight fire on a torpedoed oil tanker. (This action is in his Radio Shack logbook.) It was while the ATR was being built that the little dog on the next construction ship gave birth to pups. The ATR crew adopted their little mascot who was given the name Khaki. (During a typhoon Khaki was swept overboard and Bill, the excellent swimmer I mentioned earlier, went overboard to rescue him. The skipper was going to mark him AWOL but instead gave him a glass of brandy. Yes, that was during a typhoon at sea! This is in his log too. (The picture of their boat returning to San Francisco has Bill, holding Khaki, and his fellow radio operator and friend Frankie Audia at the rail.)

When the ship was ready it sailed down to Treasure Island in San Francisco Bay where it was fitted with armament and commissioned June 22, 1944. During that period he was assigned to clean the heads at a commandeered hotel that was an officer's barracks in San Francisco. Every day when that was done he was free to roam the city. He retained that love for SF and every trip we made there was a memory walk for him; once when staying at the Sheraton Palace on Market Street for a conference I was attending he noted that it sure looked familiar. Yep, that was where he cleaned the heads! After commissioning, the ship headed to Long Beach for additional maneuver training out of San Pedro. Again during leave he was able to roam Los Angeles although he said it was a pretty rough area around San Pedro.

Then it was off to the Pacific where WWII was still raging. His log describes the traditional celebration when they crossed the Equator. In his old wallet there still has his commemoration card from that. The ATR transported ammunition and other items, mostly from Guam to other fighting fronts. After the signing of the peace with Japan (on the USS Missouri, which I later worked on at Ford's Island in Pearl Harbor, next to the sunken Arizona, with the Elderhostel Program) Bill's ship went to Wakayama Japan as the first American occupation force. There he learned the new skill of what became SCUBA diving while they cleaned the harbor of sunken hardware from the war. He had fascinating stories to tell about meting Japanese families, communicating through magazine pictures and bringing toothbrushes, candy, etc., to them-whatever the ship could spare. Years later we were supposed to go back to Wakayama, but he died just months before the trip. I went anyway and found people that still remembered him. We all cried.

On the ship's return to San Francisco in 1946, they stopped at Pearl Harbor. Except for one other occasion, it was the first time the crew had been off the ship since leaving San Pedro in 1944. The one thing they had missed the most onboard was ice cream. Bill and his Radio Shack buddy Frankie Audia went into town for ice cream. Bill said he ate SEVEN banana splits and then got two one-gallon jugs and proceeded around town with one jug full of milk and the other whiskey. They ended up in the brig that night! He returned to Hawaii later, with his second wife (Claire Richards) to teach and I am sure the stories were fascinating. Bill's three years Tour of Duty ended April 1, 1946 in San Francisco. He wondered if it was going to be an April fool's joke but he was released.

He wanted to stay and go to school in California where tuition was free but regulations said you had to return to your original location. Returning to Skaneateles he enrolled in a Syracuse school where he finished his high school education and in 1947 married the sweetheart that had sustained him with her letters during the war, Mora Elizabeth Henderson (Simmons Saunders). They went to Kansas City Kansas where he attended an advanced radio school; he wanted to be an airline navigator. Their daughter Cathy Elaine was born there. Unfortunately shortly after graduating the airlines decided they no longer needed navigators. Upon returning to Skaneateles he found a job with a new startup business in Syracuse: television. His radio licenses were useful there.

Both Bill and Mora related that the married life did not suit the young man that had spent his 'sowing wheat' years on a ship in the Pacific. He left to 'take the cure' in Reno Nevada during which time he made lifelong friends with the man who managed the Mapes Hotel, Bill Bowman, where Bill was a dishwasher. Returning to Skaneateles he met and married Claire Richards (b: Sept. 26, 1929, m: 1953; Mechling, Parker). While traveling on their honeymoon in 1953 they visited Los Angeles where Bill had wanted to stay after WWII. He applied and got a job at an airplane company. To fulfill some job relat-

ed work he went to Pomona Junior College for a calculus course, got a Junior of Arts degree and decided he would quit his job and go to school full time. He was accepted at University of California Los Angeles but they would not give him a student teaching stipend so he enrolled at CU in Boulder where he earned a BS degree in Engineering Physics, then a Masters and a PhD, both in Physics. He was elected to the scholarship honor societies of Tau Beta Pi Engineering, Sigma Xi Physics and Sigma Pi Sigma. While at CU his three children Lynn Diane, Greg Palmer and Kelly Ann were born.

Bill's PhD research was in atmospheric Nitric Oxide, a key atmospheric constituent. He had built an ultraviolet spectrometer to be flown from a rocket from White Sands, New Mexico. The rocket pointing mechanism failed, as did the parachute to return the instrument to the earth; it formed as molten metal over a white sand dune augmented with his tears, so he finished his research thesis on data he had collected while testing the instrument at the National Bureau of Standards facility in Boulder. (NBS is now called NIST). Upon graduation in 1965 he accepted a one-year post-doctoral position with the University of Hawaii Honolulu to manage a fellow rocket borne atmospheric researcher's project. Returning to Boulder he took a position in the new LASER technology lab at NBS where he help develop a devise to measure the power output of a laser. He was divorced from Claire during this period. When the laser division was moved to Bethesda, Maryland during a reduction in government workforce, Bill wanted to stay in Boulder so he quit NBS.

He then found work on the Acoustic Echo Sounder project at NOAA in Boulder. He married again, to Karen Eva Dare (b: March 04, 1944, m: March 14, 1969). He also began teaching Physics part time at the University of Colorado Extension Center in Denver. The NOAA funding dried up and we briefly went to San Jose, California with a new spectrometer startup company financed by General Electric, the same company that owned the TV station back in Syracuse many years earlier. When GE pulled out we were back to our off-the-grid-home near the Snowbound Mine east of Gold Hill after just 7 months. For a number of years Bill worked for a friend in the tire business in Boulder while he again took up teaching at CU Denver (the new name for the CU Extension Center). In 1975 he was granted a tenured faculty position in the Physics Department after a group of his students went to the Dean of Arts and Sciences to protest their excellent teacher having been denied tenure.

With a permanent teaching position in hand and having survived seven years of wind, kerosene lamps for light, cutting seven cords of woods for heat and below freezing temperatures (which froze the coffee on the table one night), we finally decided to purchase a small house in Boulder. It was on University Hill. That made it easy for Bill to walk to the bus to Denver to teach and for Karen to walk to her job on the Boulder campus. But we kept the house at Snowbound on Sunshine Canyon and delighted escaping Boulder in the summers. He was granted a sabbatical in the 1982-3 term; we went to Reno, Nevada where his old graduate school buddy, Jim Kliwer, was Physics Department chairman. They worked on some high-energy physics experiments and managed a published paper for the year. He returned to teaching at UCD for the fall 1983 term.

Bill continued teaching at UCD until his death at age 71. In his 21 years there he received nine Outstanding Engineering Teacher of the Year awards and was runner up for the school wide Outstanding Teacher Award. He was a very dedicated teacher and took great care in preparing his students for their futures. Many of his students reciprocated by returning; describing their success and thanking him personally. I have tried to carry on his dedication to his students by having a scholarship in his name available to UCD students in Physics, Mathematics and/or Engineering.

Bill was a tall man at 6 feet 4 inches. He was always trim, except in his college days, and loved handball and golf and he worked out regularly. He always had a ready laugh, enjoyed his friends and family and made new friends easily. He played the washtub, harmonica and 4-string banjo in what became the Gold Hill Jug Band 1970.

Bill died December 3, 1996 in Boulder, Colorado. He is buried in the Gold Hill Cemetery."

SIMMS, Horace Ridgly II "Dode"

> Birth: 06/15/1921
> Death: 12/30/2016
> Cemetery Location: C1

Father: Horace Simms; Mother: Margrett Grace (*Pease*); Wife: Katherine (*Lemen*); born in Racine (Racine) Wis-

consin and died in Longmont (Boulder) Colorado at age 95 years-natural causes

Boulder Daily Camera 08 January 2017:

"Horace Ridgly Simms II, a 95-year-old veteran of WWII passed away Friday, December 30, 2016. Horace was born in Racine, Wisconsin on June 15, 1921 to Horace and Grace Simms. He joined the US Army Air Corps on December 12, 1941. In November of 1944, 2nd Lt. Simms's s [sic] plane "The Easy Way" was shot down during a bombing mission over Germany. He was wounded and spent the rest of the war as a prisoner of war in Stalig Luft 1, in Northern Germany.

He married Katherine Lemen on February 11, 1951, and together they had one daughter. He and his wife taught at Albuquerque High School until 1960 when he returned to school, earning his Master's degree at the University of New Mexico, and his Ph.D. from the University of Colorado, specializing in Mycology. He became a Professor of Biology at Eastern Washington University and notably, stated the Red Barn Project where he encouraged his students to return to organic farming, and reinforced sound environmental practices for the preservation of our mother earth.

After retirement, Horace became an antique dealer, taking great joy in traveling throughout the Southwest, collecting antiques. It was in retirement that he wrote about his POW experience, a book he titled "Indelibly Etched."

He continued his interests in environmental science, and in his long held belief in a life without war. He was an active in the Veterans Against the War [and] he was also a member of the Union of Concerned Scientists, as well as the president of his Teacher's Union at EWU.

Horace is survived by his loving wife Katherine, his daughter, Maggie Simms, his adopted daughter, Linda Zobrist, his son-in-law, David Brigham, and his one grandson, Sean Simms Brigham.

In lieu of flowers, consider a donation to any of the following: The Environmental Defense Fund, The Red Cross, or 350.org.

A celebration of life will be in the springtime of 2017. Share condolences at www.howemortuary.com."

SIMMS, Katherine Gladys (*Lemen*)

> Birth: 04/11/1921
> Death: 02/01/2019
> Cemetery Location: C1

Father: Otes Lemen; Mother: Margaret (*Braas*); Husband: Horace Ridgly "Dode" Simms II; born in Seattle (King) Washington and died in Boulder (Boulder) Colorado at age 97 years, 9 months, 21 days-old age

Boulder Daily Camera 03 February 2019:

"Katherine Gladys Lemen Simms, born on April 11, 1921 in Seattle, Washington, passed away peacefully on February 1, 2019. She is survived by her daughter, Margaret Simms, her son-in-law David Brigham, her grandson Sean Brigham, her niece Linda Zobrist and several great nieces. She was preceded in death by her husband, Horace R. Simms. Katherine grew up the daughter of a Seattle fire chief and the secretary to the mayor of Seattle. She lost both her parents at an early age, then lived with her sister, Ethel, until she graduated from the University of Washington and subsequently moved to Boston. It was there she worked as a technical illustrator for the military and was partially responsible for drawing the first concepts of radar for World War II. She moved to New Mexico in the early 1940s, and became an art teacher at Albuquerque High School. She met her husband, Horace R. Simms (Dode) in 1952, and married in 1953. Together they had one child, Margaret and soon bought and renovated a 100 year-old Adobe in southwestern Albuquerque. The renovation reflected their mutual love of southwestern art, history and lifestyle. The family of three moved to Boulder in 1961 so that Dode could pursue a Ph.D. at the University of Colorado. Katherine spent the next 30 years teaching art and painting the vistas of her Colorado home. Katherine was smart, vivacious, rebellious and beautiful. She had a wonderful sense of humor and a true zest for life. She was an avid feminist and believed in protecting the earth and treasuring nature. A celebration of her life will take place in the summer of 2019. In lieu of flowers, donations may be made to Planned Parenthood: planned Parenthood Action Fund, Inc. P.O. Box 96771, Washington DC 20090-6771."

Katherine Gladys (*Lemen*) Simms will be laid to rest beside her husband Horace

SMITH, Clara

Birth: 1890
Death: 01/18/1897
Cemetery Location: Unknown

Father: Thane Doran Smith; Mother: Francis "Fannie" Elizabeth (*Eddy*); born (Boulder) Colorado and died Gold Hill (Boulder) Colorado at age 6 years-diphtheria; might have been born in the town of Sunshine or Gold Hill; no tombstone; see SMITH, Mary May; see **About Thane Doran and Francis "Fannie" Elizabeth (*Eddy*) Smith**

Boulder Daily Camera 18 January 1897:

"Another little casket was sent by Mr. Trezise to Gold Hill today, a second child of the Smith family having died from diphtheria. Mrs. Smith is a daughter of C.C. Eddy of this town. Other children of the family are afflicted with the same terrible disease."

Boulder Herald 20 January 1897:

"Mr. and Mrs. T.D. Smith of Gold Hill have been called upon to bury another child, the victim of diphtheria. Little Clara, aged 6 years, succumbed to the terrible disease last Monday and was laid to her rest that afternoon. The family has the sympathy of many friends."

About Thane Doran and Francis "Fannie" Elizabeth (*Eddy*) Smith

Thane Doran Smith was born December 1856 in Cincinnati (Hamilton) Ohio; the son of New York native Charles Wright and Ohio native Charlotte W. (*Brown*) Smith.

The 1870 United States census has the family still living there with Charles being an iron merchant. Five years later the family was living in Indiana and by 1880 the family was in Sunshine (Boulder) Colorado with Charles employed as a mine superintendent.

Both Charles and Charlotte lived in Sunshine until their deaths. Charles died 1901 and is buried in the Sunshine Cemetery in Sunshine (Boulder) Colorado alongside his wife, Charlotte, who died in 1910.

Thane Doran Smith married Francis "Fannie" Elizabeth Eddy on 01 January 1879 in Denver (Denver) Colorado. She was born September of 1859 in (Marquette) Michigan; the daughter of Vermont native Cullen Clement and New York native Omelia F. (*Bishop*) Eddy. Cullen came to Salina (Boulder) Colorado in 1875 and a year later his family joined him in Salina (Boulder) Colorado.

Cullen died on 18 November 1907 in Rosedale (Pierce) Washington and was buried in the Tacoma Cemetery in Tacoma (Pierce) Washington alongside his wife, Omelia, who died on 18 February 1912 in Bellaire (Larimer) Colorado.

To the union of Thane and Francis "Fannie" six known children were born:

Ella Eddy: born December 1881 Sunshine (Boulder) Colorado and died 05 August 1920 (Whatcom) Washington; buried Enterprise Cemetery, Ferndale (Whatcom) Washington; married Bert E. Williams and Robert Kuster

Francis Marion: born December 1883 Summerville (Boulder) Colorado and died 18 June 1948 Colorado; buried Crown Hill Cemetery, Wheat Ridge (Jefferson) Colorado; married Ida M. Drake and Rose Marie (Meis) Goodhue

Lotta Omelia: born October 1885 (Boulder) Colorado-death unknown; burial unknown; married Nathan Louis "Lew" Woolery; last known address (Park) Wyoming

Mary May: born 1889 Gold Hill (Boulder) Colorado and died 07 January 1897 Gold Hill (Boulder) Colorado; buried Gold Hill Cemetery, Gold Hill (Boulder) Colorado; see SMITH, Mary May

Clara: born 1890 (Boulder) Colorado and died 18 January 1897 Gold Hill (Boulder) Colorado; buried Gold Hill Cemetery, Gold Hill (Boulder) Colorado; see SMITH, Clara

Arthur Mellville: 19 May 1891 (Boulder) Grand Junction (Mesa) Colorado and died 10 December 1947 Colorado; buried Crown Hill Cemetery, Wheat Ridge (Jefferson) Colorado; married Elizabeth Setzer

By 1900 the family lived in Cripple Creek (Teller) Colorado on a farm where Thane was a painter. About 8 years later Fannie divorced Thane and married Perry Teeters/Teters, living in Bellaire (Larimer) Colorado. Unfortunately their marriage was short-lived as Perry died 30 August 1913 in (Larimer) Colorado and was buried in the Grandview Cemetery, Fort Collins (Larimer) Colorado in an unmarked grave.

In 1910 Thane Doran Smith was living in Boulder (Boulder) Colorado with his brothers: Lander, Alwyn and Minor. It appears five years later he was living in South Dakota, listed as a widower in the 1915 state census but his residency didn't last long as by 1920 Thane moved to Denver (Denver) Colorado and lived with his son, Francis Marion and family where he was a painter and a grocery man at the age of 64 years, listed as divorced.

Thane died 1928 in (Boulder) Colorado and was buried near his father, Charles Wright Smith, in the Sunshine Cemetery in Sunshine (Boulder) Colorado.

Frances "Fannie" Elizabeth married again on 19 March 1919 to Rodney W. Shattuck in Lewiston (Nez Perce) Idaho. They spent their married life in Ferdinand (Idaho) Idaho but by 1922 Fannie was a widow, living in Fort Collins (Larimer) Colorado, making her living as a nurse. She married her fourth husband, John H. Kelly and they lived with Fannie's son, Frances Marion and family, in Denver (Denver) Colorado in 1930 where John was a barber.

John Kelly died 05 October 1933 and was interred in the Fairmount Cemetery in Denver (Denver) Colorado. Fannie died a few years later on 01 February 1937 and was cremated on 02 February 1937 at the Riverside Cemetery in Denver (Denver) Colorado however her ashes are not interred there-records do not indicate where the ashes went.

SMITH, Dorthea (Dorothy) "Dorris/Dora" (*Christian*) Walsted Grover

> Birth: 05/25/1856
> Death: 06/24/1920
> Cemetery Location: C3

Father: Mr. Christian; Mother: unknown; 1st Husband: Nels/Nils Jacobsen Walsted; 2nd Husband: Lafayette L. Grover; 3nd Husband: William Henry Smith (his second wife); born in Norway and died in Boulder (Boulder) Colorado at age 64 years, 0 months, 30 days-gall stones; see WALSTED, Nels/Nils Jacobson; see GROVER, Lafayette L.

Boulder Daily Camera 24 June 1920:

"DEATH OF MRS W.H. SMITH CAME WHILE SHE SLEPT

The wide circle of friends of Mrs. Dora Grover Smith will be shocked to hear of her death which occurred at ten o'clock this morning of gall stones. She and her husband W.H. Smith and Mr. and Mrs. C.G. McWhorter, who are

visiting them from Bennett, attended a political meeting last night at the court house. Shortly after retiring at 10:30 she began having severe pain and at twelve suffered horribly, but with first aid remedies she grew easier and slept until 5 a.m. when she again had great cause to be awakened. She was born in Norway and for 46 years had made her home in Boulder County being 18 years of age when coming here. Until ten months ago she made her home at Gold Hill and Ward when she married Mr. Smith since which time they have lived in their cozy home, 2225 Fifteenth Street (The Oaks home.) Besides the husband two sons survive, Jake Walstead of Denver and Ed Walstead who is in Klondyke. The funeral will take place Saturday at 12:30 from the home and remains taken to Gold Hill for interment."

About Dorthea/Dorothy "Dorris"/Dora" (*Christian*) Walsted Grover Smith

Dorthea was born 25 May 1856 in Norway; the daughter of Norwegian parents with father's name being Christian (according to the mortuary record). She first married Nels/Nils Jacobsen Walsted and by 1880 they were living in Gold Hill (Boulder) Colorado with their two sons:

Jacob Cristian: born 10 February 1874 Colorado and died March 1933 Colorado; buried Crown Hill Cemetery, Wheatridge (Jefferson) Colorado; married Clara D. Henderson; interesting to note on legal documents last name is spelled "Walstead"

Edward: born 08 December 1876 Colorado and died 21 June 1938 Seattle (King) Washington; buried Wright Crematory & Columbarium, Seattle (King) Washington; married Grace King; interesting to note on legal documents last name is spelled "Walstead"

Nels/Nils Jacobsen Walsted died on 03 December 1890 at the age of 51 years and was buried in the Gold Hill Cemetery in Gold Hill (Boulder) Colorado; see WALSTED, Nels/Nils Jacobsen.

Dorthea then married Lafayette Grover on 12 January 1893 in Boulder (Boulder) Colorado. No known children blesed this marriage. Lafayette Grover died on 18 June 1912 in Ward (Boulder) Colorado and was buried in the Gold Hill Cemetery in Gold Hill (Boulder) Colorado; see GROVER, Lafayette L.

Dorthea married her third and final husband, William Henry Smith, on 25 August 1919 in Boulder (Boulder) Colorado.

William was born 21 July 1846 in (Cedar) Iowa; the son of Albert G. and Anna (maiden name unknown) Smith. His first wife was Eliza M. Tout who he married about 1875. Eliza was born 1837 in Indiana, the daughter of Benjamin and Martha Ann (*Moberly*) Tout. She died in 1917 in Sutton (Clay) Nebraska; buried at the Sutton City Cemetery. No known children blessed this marriage.

Dorthea was about 63 years of age at the time of her marriage to William which lasted less than a year as Dorthea died on 24 June 1920 in Boulder (Boulder) Colorado and was buried in the Gold Hill Cemetery in Gold Hill (Boulder) Colorado.

William Henry Smith then married a widow, Elizabeth (*Brown*) James; see SMITH, Elizabeth "Lizzie" (*Brown*) James.

William Henry Smith died on 18 April 1928 and was buried in the Downey Cemetery in West Branch (Cedar) Iowa.

SMITH, Elizabeth "Lizzie" (*Brown*) James

Birth: 06/19/1852
Death: 11/24/1925
Cemetery Location: E3

Father: James Brown; Mother: Margaret (*maiden name unknown*); 1st Husband: William Thomas James; 2nd Husband: William H. Smith; born in Pennsylvania and died in Boulder (Boulder) Colorado at age 73 years, 5 month, 5 days; mortuary record states birth year 1856

Boulder Daily Camera 24 November 1925:

"WIFE OF W.H. SMITH DIED THIS MORNING

Mrs. Elizabeth J. Smith, wife of William H. Smith, died this morning, aged 73 years, at her home, 2225 Fifteenth Street. She had been ill and failing for some time. Friday of last week she suffered a stroke of paralysis, since which time she has been in an unconscious state, quietly passing to her last, restful sleep. She had been a resident of Boulder county for the past forty years, most of which had been spent in Gold Hill where her former husband, Thomas James, a mine foreman, died several years ago. She was a member of the W.R.C. and had many friends both in Boulder and Gold Hill.

Lawrence James of Denver and Elinore James of Nevada, grandchildren, and two sisters, Mrs. Martha Drake of Denver and Mrs. Emily Brown of Arthur, Okla., and the husband, W.H. Smith, survive.

The body is at Howe mortuary awaiting funeral arrangements."

Boulder Daily Camera 25 November 1925:

"FUNERAL OF MRS. W.H. SMITH WILL BE HELD SATURDAY—The funeral of Mrs. William H. Smith will be held from the residence 2225 Fifteenth street Saturday at 12 o'clock. Rev. J.H. Skeen will officiate. The body will be taken to Gold Hill for burial."

Boulder Daily Camera 28 November 1925:

"FUNERAL OF MRS. SMITH HELD FROM LATE HOME—The funeral of Mrs. Elizabeth J. Smith was held from her home, 2245 Fifteenth Street, at noon today.

Mrs. Adams Weber sang several selections. Members of the W.R.C. attended in a body [sic]. The remains were taken to Gold Hill for burial, members of the G.A.R. being pallbearers."

About Elizabeth "Lizzie" (*Brown*) James Smith

Elizabeth "Lizzie" Brown was born on 19 June 1852 in Pennsylvania; the daughter of James and Margaret (maiden name unknown) Brown.

In 1860 the Brown family was living in Oskaloosa (Mahaska) Iowa where James was making a living as a plasterer while Margaret raised their six known children and about three years later their last known child was born:

Mary J.: born about 1841 Pennsylvania and died before November 1925; burial unknown; spouse unknown

Sarah: born about 1843 Pennsylvania and died before November 1925; burial unknown; spouse unknown

Martha A.: born 23 November 1845 Greenville (Mercer) Pennsylvania and died 02 June 1935 Denver (Denver) Colorado; buried Riverside Cemetery, Denver (Denver) Colorado; married George W. Drake

Margaretta: born 1849 Pennsylvania and died 15 July 1851 Pennsylvania; buried Pulaski Cemetery, Pulaski (Lawrence) Pennsylvania; died in infancy

Elizabeth "Lizzie": born 19 June 1852 Pennsylvania and died 24 November 1925 Boulder (Boulder) Colorado; buried Gold Hill Cemetery, Gold Hill (Boulder) Colorado; married William Thomas James and William Henry Smith; see JAMES, William Thomas

James H.: born about 1857 Iowa and died before November 1925; burial unknown; spouse unknown

Emily/Emma T.: born August 1863 (cemetery has 1862) Iowa and died 21 February 1934 Denver (Denver) Colorado; buried Riverside Cemetery, Denver (Denver) Colorado; married Samuel C. Brown

By the late 1870s the family was living in Colorado where Elizabeth married William Thomas James on 31 March 1879 in (Arapahoe) Colorado; see JAMES, William Thomas. To their union one known child was born:

James Rowe: born 31 May 1883 Gold Hill (Boulder) Colorado and died 02 July 1914 Gold Hill (Boulder) Colorado); buried Gold Hill Cemetery, Gold Hill (Boulder) Colorado; married Ida Mae Pughe; see JAMES, James Rowe

The family lived in Gold Hill (Boulder) Colorado where William Thomas was a miner where he located several mines in the Gold Hill Mining District.

Unfortunately William Thomas James didn't live to a grand old age as he died from pneumonia on 26 March 1891 in Gold Hill (Boulder) Colorado and is buried in the town's cemetery. It has been said that William Thomas was a veteran, having served in the Civil War.

His widow, Elizabeth, continued living in Gold Hill (Boulder) Colorado along with her son, James, and his wife and family; see JAMES, James Rowe.

After the death of James in 1914 Elizabeth moved to Denver (Denver) Colorado to live with her nephew, Milton P. Givens and family.

Between 1920 and 1925 she married widower William Henry Smith and moved to Boulder (Boulder) Colorado to 2225 15th Street where she died on 24 November 1925 from apoplexy at the age of age 73 years, 5 month, 5 days (mortuary record states birth year 1856). She was buried in the Gold Hill Cemetery in close proximity of where her first husband, William Thomas James, was buried.

About two and a half years later William Henry Smith died on 18 April 1928 and was buried in the Downey Cemetery, West Branch (Cedar) Iowa.

SMITH, Infant

> Birth: About 1892
> Death: 12/16/1892
> Cemetery Location: Unknown

Father: Rev. Smith; possible burial; no tombstone

Boulder Daily Camera 21 December 1892:
"Rev. Smith's baby, after a short illness, seemed to get better but had a relapse and died last Friday."

Boulder Daily Camera 21 September 1892:
"GOLD HILL...Mr. Smith, the new minister, delivered his first sermon to a large household Sunday night"

No further information.

SMITH, Mary May

Birth: About 1889
Death: 01/07/1897
Cemetery Location: Unknown

Father: Thane Doran Smith; Mother: Frances "Fannie" Elizabeth (*Eddy*); born in (Boulder) Colorado and died in Gold Hill (Boulder) Colorado at age 8 years from diphtheria; no tombstone; see SMITH, Clara; see **About Thane Doran and Francis "Fannie" Elizabeth (*Eddy*) Smith**

Boulder Daily Camera 09 January 1897:
"In response to a telephone message from Gold Hill received last night, Mr. Trezise sent up teams and a man to manage the funeral of the infant child of Mrs. Smith of that place."

Boulder Daily Camera 11 January 1897:
"Gold Hill is afflicted with diphtheria of a virulent form, according to a Boulder physician. Mary Smith, age eight, daughter of T.D. Smith and granddaughter of C.C. Eddy, was buried Saturday and three more of the six children of the family are down with it. It is popularly known as the "black diphtheria," almost universally fatal disease."

Boulder Herald 13 January 1897:
"May, the 8-year old child of P.J. [sic] Smith and wife of Gold Hill, died of diphtheria Saturday and was buried Sunday. When the child first took sick Dr. Trovillion was called in and he pronounced the case diphtheria and doctored accordingly. Dr. Smith of Sunshine, father of P.J. [sic] Smith later called in and he pronounced the case tonsillitis and Dr. Trovillion's medicines were put aside. Dr. Trovillion then no longer attended the case. When the child died, word was sent to C.C. Eddy of this place, father of Mrs. Smith, asking him to come to attend the funeral. Mr. Eddy took Dr. Kirkpatrick up with him yesterday and he pronounced it a malignant form of diphtheria. Three other children are suffering with the same trouble, Lottie, aged about 11 being very ill."

Boulder News 14 January 1897:
"Diphtheria has broken out again at Louisville and also at Gold Hill. At the former place a little son of Herman Kluge died and at the latter an eight year-old daughter of T.D. Smith, and several other children of the same family are afflicted."

Boulder News 21 January 1897:
"Another child of the Smith family at Gold Hill died of diphtheria Monday."

SMITH, Paul Edward

Birth: 10/10/1948
Death: 08/17/2010
Cemetery Location: F1

Father: Paul Marshall Smith Sr.; Mother: Evelyn Teresa (*Fee*); Wife: Kathleen (*Gilgannon*); born in Needham (Norfolk) Massachusetts and died in Gold Hill (Boulder) Colorado

Obituary Handout:
"Paul Edward Smith

October 10, 1948-August 17, 2010
Paul E. Smith—Father of Kialah Smith of Boulder, Mountain Jack Smith of Gold Hill, and Earthstar Jai Smith of Vancouver, British Columbia, Canada—passed away on August 17, 2010, after an incredibly courageous battle with cancer.

Paul was a musician, songwriter, photographer, film-maker, luthier, fine carpenter, and a brilliant mind. What he loved above all of these things was his three fine sons. His adult life was dedicated to them.

Some will remember Paul from "back in the day" when he had his instrument repair shop in the lower level of Folk Arts on Broadway in Boulder. Others will know him from his little shop in Putney, VT. Many will still see him in spirit drinking coffee in the Gold Hill General Store, writing about or developing his most current brainstorm. All who knew Paul, even casually, will remember him as a kind, gentle soul: a man with a great mind and a huge heart."

SOSNOWSKI, Josephine Maria (*Ludeman*)

Birth: 12/22/1894
Death: 02/01/1983
Cemetery Location: B5

Father: Joseph John Ludeman; Mother: Martha Maria (*Jenkins*); Husband: Michael Sosnowski; born in Raymond (Montgomery) Illinois and died in Denver (Denver) Colorado at the age of 88 years, 1 month, 10 days; see **About Michael and Josephine Maria (*Ludeman*) Sosnowski**

SOSNOWSKI, Michael

Birth: 08/09/1890
Death: 12/28/1978
Cemetery Location: B5

Father: unknown; Mother: Tatiana (*Vlasevna*) Kolonitskaya/Kolonitski; Wife: Josephine Maria (*Ludeman*); born in Vilna, Russia and died in Apache Junction (Pinal) Arizona at the age of 88 years, 4 months, 19 days; social security death index as birth year 1891; see **About Michael and Josephine Maria (*Ludeman*) Sosnowski**

About Michael and Josephine Maria (*Ludeman*) Sosnowski

Michael Sosnowski was born in Vilna, Russia on 09 August 1890; the son of Tatiana (*Vlasevna*) Kolonitaskaya/Kolonitski, father unknown.

He graduated from the Vilna Imperial School of Music. He studied under Malkin, a famous teacher who also taught Jascha Heifetz.

The United States census of 1920 states he immigrated in 1897 along with his first wife, Natalie (maiden name unknown). Together they had one known child:

Grace: born 19 February 1920 on the China Sea and died 22 December 1969 in Kamalo on the island of Moloka'i (Maui) Hawaii and buried in the Saint Joseph Church Cemetery there; married John Campbell McCorriston

Michael served as staff sergeant in the American Army (World War I) from 01 December 1919 to 27 December 1920 with a Military Petition on 04 March 1921.

His future wife, Josephine, was born on 22 December 1894 in Raymond (Montgomery) Illinois; the daughter of Missouri native Joseph John and Illinois native Martha Maria (*Jenkins*) Ludeman.

By 1900 the family was living in Beatrice Ward 1 (Gage) Nebraska where Joseph was a traveling salesman and by 1910 they were living in Ottumwa Ward 2 (Wapello) Iowa. Ten years later they returned to Illinois, living in Butler Grove (Montgomery) Illinois were Josephine left her home on an impulse.

There is a Josephine M. Ludeman in the 1920 census living in Canon City (Fremont) Colorado as a boarder in the household of William Hopper where she is a music teacher. Further records show that this Josephine M. Ludeman married S.E. Livingston on 01 June 1921 in Canon City.

Josephine traveled to Honolulu (Honolulu) Hawaii where she met Michael in a Honolulu music shop when she was an organist accompanist for the Princess Theatre silent movies and he was a concert master for the Honolulu Symphony Orchestra. They were married on 27 June 1928. No known children blessed this marriage.

Josephine's parents, Joseph and Martha Maria, also came to Honolulu in 1928 and lived there until their deaths: Joseph John Ludeman died 04 March 1935 and Martha Maria (*Jenkins*) Ludeman died 1941. They are both buried in the Diamond Head Memorial Park Cemetery in Honolulu (Honolulu) Hawaii.

After witnessing the attack on Pearl Harbor they returned to the main land where they both accepted positions at the Japanese Relocation Center near Poston (La Paz) Arizona. They came to Boulder (Boulder) Colorado in 1943 where Josephine gave a concert at Macky Auditorium on the University of Colorado campus as her thesis for her Master's Degree in Music in 1945.

For many years they spent their winters at 969 12th Street in Boulder (Boulder) Colorado but summered in Gold Hill (Boulder) Colorado in their home "Twin Pines" located on Dixon Road, around the bend from the Gold Hill Cemetery where they gave free outdoor music concerts for many years.

Boulder Daily Camera 14 July 1948:

"Sosnowski Musicals Will Begin Sunday...

Professor and Mrs. Sosnowski are announcing the first of their outdoor Sunday afternoon musicals, to be given this Sunday at 4 p.m. at their summer place in Gold Hill.

Originally, the Sosnowskis had intended to start their Sunday musicals earlier, but were unable to obtain necessary materials to build the outdoor platform for the piano until later. The platform is completed now, and beginning this Sunday each week Prof. and Mrs. Sosnowski will be hosts to their University, Boulder, and Gold Hill friends at informal outdoor musicals.

These Sunday programs, beginning each week at 4 p.m., will continue through Sunday, August 22."

Boulder Daily Camera July 1950:

"Sosnowskis To Again Entertain At Series of Outdoor Concerts...

Music lovers will be pleased to learn that another series of outdoor Sunday afternoon musicals are to be given by Michael Sosnowski, Violinist, at his summer home "Twin Pine," in Gold Hill. The first concert will be next Sunday and in it he will have the assistance of Peter Klaisle of Denver, an accomplished pianist.

The concerts will be given at 4 and all interested are invited. The concerts in other summers have drawn large numbers and there has been a demand for Mr. Sosnowski to again entertain.

On Sunday, July 30, he will be assisted by Miss Rachel Morgan, pianist of Boulder, who holds a master of music degree from the University. At the concert, August 6th, ending the series, the assistant will be Howard Waltz, of the piano department at the University.

In each of the concerts, Mr. Sosnowski will be accompanied on the piano by his wife, who has a master's degree in piano from the University of Colorado."

Boulder Daily Camera 04 August 1978:

"M. Sosnowskis Celebrate 50th...

Mr. and Mrs. Michael Sosnowski of Phoenix and Gold Hill will observe a belated 50th wedding anniversary Saturday evening at the Harvest House.

The couple, both former faculty members at University of Colorado departments of language and music, were married June 27, 1928, in Honolulu, Hawaii.

The former Josephine Ludeman of Illinois and Ottumwa, Iowa, and Michael Sosnowski met in Honolulu, where she was an organist accompanist for the Princess Theatre silent movies and he was a concert master of the Honolulu Symphony Orchestra.

The couple performed professionally as concert violinist and piano accompanist both in concert and with a radio program.

For the past 30 years the Sosnowskis have summered at Gold Hill, often treating neighbors and friends to informal classical music concerts at their home.

Those who have enjoyed the Sosnowski performances have included Mischa Mischakoff, former Detroit Symphony Orchestra concert master, Yasha Heifitz [violinist whose career extended over 65 years] and Yehudi Menhuin [had one of the longest and most distinguished careers of any violinist in the 20th century].

Joining the Sosnowskis at Saturday's dinner will be lifelong friends, Ruth and Jack Sever of Cold Creek

Digging Up Dirt

Canyon; Mr. and Mrs. Stanley Schmidt (a niece) of Oxnard, Calif.; a nephew and his wife, Shelby and John Williams of Troy, Mich., and their grandniece and her family, Dr. and Mrs. John Goff and daughter of Denver."

Michael Sosnowski died a few months later on 28 December 1978 in Apache Junction (Pinal) Arizona. Josephine moved to Denver (Denver) Colorado where she died 01 February 1983. They are both buried in the Gold Hill Cemetery in Gold Hill (Boulder) Colorado.

Courtesy Richard Dussart Regnier:
"Jim Kessler went on to tell of a picnic that they had out at Mount Alto Park on the old Switzerland railroad trail. As Jim begins to tell me what happened he starts laughing and said, he, my dad (Jim Regnier) and Bob Knapp laughed so hard at the story that Michael Sosnowski told them that they almost lost their lunch. A lot of it was due to the Russian accent Michael had, but, also the way he told it.

It seems that Michael Sosnowski had been born and raised in Russia, and times were hard. His family decided to send him to the United States. Now in his country each state had a different type of costume that represented them and was worn to let others know where they were from, so he started checking around to see what kind of costume was worn to represent the United States. One day as he was looking in some magazines he saw the picture of Uncle Sam. He rounded up the best looking Uncle Sam outfit he could find.

He got on the boat and headed across the Atlantic for the United States. When he saw the Statue of Liberty he hurried down to his cabin and changed into his Uncle Sam suit. When he came up on deck everyone stared at him. One of his friends told him he'd better get that thing off before they docked or they'd send him back to Russia. So, he went back down to his cabin and took it off.

My dad, Bob Knapp and Jim are doubled over by now, and Michael waits for them to stop before he continues. He was only in the United States a few days when he was invited to join the Army. He could speak no English and all he had was an English/Russian dictionary. He saw a sign that read "In case of fire break glass." So he looked up case, and it meant box. So he figured that the sign meant, "If there is a fire in a box he should break the glass." That made no sense at all to him.

When he went out to the rifle range he wasn't doing too good. He couldn't understand what the instructor was telling him. He kept telling him to look through the sights. Well, he looked up the word "sight" and it meant look. So he figured it out to mean "Look through the look," which again made no sense. But the instructor finally got through to him what he meant and he (Michael) became an expert marksman. But this created a problem.

When he became an expert marksman they made him an officer!!

Being an officer he now had men under him, but he couldn't speak English. When marching the men he knew what "Forward march" meant, but "About face" he didn't understand. Once more he went to the dictionary and looked up "about." He discovered that the word "about" meant "something," so "About face" meant something about the face. When he marched his men across the drill field, when they got to the other end he would halt them and tell them to turn around. On day another officer gave him the order, "About face," and he (Michael) stood there looking at his face, which made the other officer mad.

He (Michael) told them that he was smart enough to know that expert marksman meant that they ended up on the front line, so he knew he needed to change his job. He noticed they had a band on base and they needed a tuba player. He didn't know how to play the tuba, but he learned real quick.

When they got the orders to ship overseas they sent him and the band to Siberia. Russia was an ally during the First World War It was so cold in Siberia that the instruments wouldn't play.

He then told them that he knew how to run a mess hall but he still didn't know much English. He discovered one of the sergeants who ran a mess hall liked to drink so he (Michael) supplied the man with booze, and he ran the mess hall for him.

Next Michael told them about how the dough-boys (American soldiers) didn't have anything to do over there in Siberia but drive the horse-drawn sleighs. But they had a problem. When they said "Whoa" it sounded like "Go" in Russian, and the horses would go twice as fast.

Later in Siberia they made him an interpreter because he spoke Russian. But the dialect in Siberia was different than what he spoke, and he now didn't understand either side.

But through quick thinking, Michael Sosnowski told them, he managed to make it through the war without serving on the front line.

Michael and his wife, Josephine, were living in Hawaii when Pearl Harbor was bombed. They were playing in the Hawaiian Symphony at the time. Michael was first chair concert master, and she was a concert pianist.

In Gold Hill the Sosnowskis lived in the white house on the bend just before you reach the cemetery. They fixed up a small amphitheater in their yard so people could come and sit and listen to them play. Michael would play his violin and Josephine would move their piano over next to the door and they would give concerts for all who came."

(Unfortunately their house was completely destroyed in the Four Mile Canyon Fire in 2010)

Boulder Daily Camera Focus "Gold Hill Women" by Vicki Groninger (Camera Staff Writer) 01 November 1981:

"A world traveler in the Gold Hill group was Josephine Sosnowski, a professional organist. She and her husband, Michael, lived in Honolulu where he was concert master of the Hawaiian Symphony Orchestra for 18 years. They came to the U.S. mainland on 24 hour notice when the Japanese attacked Pearl Harbor. Both taught school in Nederland after they came to Colorado.

For a number of years after they purchased their place in Gold Hill they had the amphitheater, formed by the sloping hollow on one side of their property, lined with rows of improvised seats composed of strips of lumber supported by logs. Here people could sit and listen to the free concerts which the Sosnowskis gave every Sunday afternoon. The road in front of their house would be lined with cars with licenses from many states. Michael would stand in front of their open doorway and play classical music on his violin while Josephine accompanied him on the piano just inside the door..."

(Article by Laura Sickenberger)

ST. CLAIR, Joel Fuller Turrell

Birth: 09/12/1841
Death: 07/12/1913
Cemetery Location: D4

Father: Charles Northrup St. Clair; Mother: Elmina Baldwin (*Turrell*): 1st Wife: Mary H. (*Baird*); 2nd Wife: Margaret "Maggie" J. (*Stuchell*); 3rd Wife: Emma Lydia (*Stoapes/Stoopes*); born in Barre (Orleans) New York and died in Denver (Denver) Colorado at age 71 years, 10 months; see STUCHELL, Margaret "Maggie" J.

Boulder Daily Camera 16 July 1913:

"DEATH OF J.T. ST. CLAIR PIONEER OF GOLD HILL—Friends of Joel St. Clair, an old timer of Gold Hill but who has been living in Denver for some years, will be sorry to hear of his death, which occurred in Denver Sunday. The remains will be brought to Gold Hill for interment."

Denver Post 18 July 1913:

"ST. CLAIR—Funeral services of Joel F. St. Clair will be held from Olinger's mortuary Saturday at 2:30 p.m. Interment Gold Hill, Colo. Members of Crocker Relief Corps. No. 40, are requested to attend."

About Joel Fuller Turrell St. Clair

Joel Fuller Turrell St. Clair was born 12 September 1841 in Barre (Orleans) New York; the son of Canadian native Charles Northrup and New York native Elmina Baldwin (*Turrell*) St. Clair.

Joel lived his early years in Barre (Orleans) New York and on 03 August 1862 he enlisted in the 151st Infantry, Company A with the rank of corporal to serve in the Civil War. He was mustered out on 26 June 1865 at Washington, D.C., with the rank of sergeant.

A few years later met Mary H. Baird and married her on 20 August 1867 in (Orleans Parish) Louisiana. She was born 26 August 1848; believed to be the daughter of Scottish natives John and Mary (*Breckinrig*) Baird. To their union five known children were born:

Isabella Elmina: born 04 December 1868 Albion (Orleans) New York and died 12 December 1868 Albion (Orleans) New York; buried Mount Albion Cemetery, Albion (Orleans) New York; died in infancy

Mary Isabella: born 30 October 1870 New Orleans (Orleans) Louisiana-death unknown; burial unknown; married Henry W. (John Henry) Miller and William MacKellar/McKellar; 1940 census in District of Columbia (District of Columbia) Washington

Helen Elmina: born 23 August 1871 New Orleans (Orleans) Louisiana and died 26 July 1940 Pasadena (Los Angeles) California; burial unknown; married George Henry Noble and Samuel Arthur Bixby

Lelia Rose: born 09 May 1873 Louisiana and died 07 November 1906 Newport (Giles) Virginia; buried Mount Albion Cemetery, Albion (Orleans) New York; married Robert Hatfield Osborn; appears to be a twin to Charles Francis

Charles Francis: born 09 May 1873 and died 05 August 1873; buried Mount Albion Cemetery, Albion (Orleans) New York; appears to be a twin to Lelia Rose

Joel's wife, Mary H. Baird St. Clair died on 01 August 1874 in Albion (Orleans) New York and was buried in the Mount Albion Cemetery there. Joel continued to live in Albion with his three daughters, Mary Isabella, Helen Elmina and Lelia Rose until he moved to (Boulder) Colorado where on 28 November 1878 he married Maggie J. Stuchell. She was born 12 August 1850 in East Mahoning (Indiana) Pennsylvania; daughter of Jacob Stuchell and Margaret (*Johnston*) Stutchell (second wife of Jacob). To this union two known children were born:

Ida May: born 18 April 1875 Gold Hill (Boulder) Colorado and died 30 December 1948 Punxsutawney (Jefferson) Pennsylvania; buried Circle Hill Cemetery, Punxsutawney (Jefferson) Pennsylvania; married William H. Fetterman; interesting to note that Ida's death certificate states a birth year of 1875 with "Rebecca" Stuchell as mother however other documents do state Margaret "Maggie" J. Stchell as mother; Joel didn't legally marry Maggie J. Stuchell until 1878

Clara Elizabeth: born 06 April 1882 Gold Hill (Boulder) Colorado-death unknown; burial unknown; last known location: Tampico (Tamaulipas) Mexico

Unfortunately Maggie J. (*Stuchell*) St. Clair died on 08 November 1885 in Gold Hill (Boulder) Colorado from consumption at age 35 years, 2 months and 27 days and was buried in the Gold Hill Cemetery in Gold Hill (Boulder) Colorado. Interesting to note that her tombstone has her maiden name of Stuchell and not her married name, of St. Clair—see STUCHELL, Maggie J.

When Joel was about 47 years of age he married his third wife, Emma Lydia Stoops in 1888. Emma was born May of 1855 in Pennsylvania, the daughter of William and Mary Elizabeth (maiden name unknown) Stoops. No children blessed this marriage.

Emma was first married to William F. Granlee on 11 January 1877 in Trenton (Grundy) Missouri but by the 1880 United States census she was listed as divorced, living with her parents, William and Mary, in Trenton (Grundy) Missouri at the age of 25 years old.

In the 1900 census Joel and Emma were living in Gold Hill (Boulder) Colorado along with Emma's brother, Charles Stoop, and his daughter, Goldie.

Ten years later Joel and Emma were living on Meade Street in Denver (Denver) Colorado where he died on 12 July 1913 at the age of 71 years and 10 months.

Emma continued to live on Meade Street in Denver (Denver) Colorado. In the 1940 census she is living with her sister, Ellen F. "Nellie" Breecher, at the age of 84 years. The trail seems to grow cold from this point however there is an Emma L. St. Clair who died 22 April 1947 and buried in the Grandview Cemetery in Johnstown (Cambria) Pennsylvania. Perhaps this is where Emma is originally from. There is another Emma L. St. Clair with a birth date of 1869 and death date of 1949 in the Fairmont Cemetery, Denver (Denver) Colorado.

STEBBINS, Bruce Richard

Birth: 11/14/1942
Death: 07/27/1967
Cemetery Location: B5

Father: Dean Waldo Stebbins; Mother: Florence Jane (*Buchner*); Wife: Marilyn (*Linderoth*); born in San Antonio (Bexar) Texas and died in Denver (Denver) Colorado at age 24 years, 8 months, 13 days-overdose of morphine following deviated septum surgery (malpractice)

Courtesy John Clark 18 January 2001:

"Bruce Stebbins died July 27, 1967; he was buried the first week of August. Five or six of us got together to dig Bruce's grave; we went with our picks and shovels and pry bars to the location selected by his wife, Marilyn, in the Gold Hill Cemetery. Digging was not easy and when we got down about 5 feet we were scraping solid rock. It looked like we would need to blast so we went to someone with experience. There were two miners living in Gold Hill at the time: Joe Weaver and Tommy Lyle, we happened to consult Tommy. Tommy was in his eighties, about five feet tall and suffering from emphysema but he was vigorous and excited to help. He instructed us what to get. We bought dynamite, caps and fuse at Valentine's

hardware at Broadway and Pearl in Boulder,; we rented a compressor, drill and steel and headed for the cemetery. Tommy went with us and showed us where to drill and how deep: about 18 inches deep, diagonally down, from each corner, in the middle of each side, and straight down in the center. Tommy cut the dynamite sticks into individual charges and set them with cap and fuse, the fuses all cut to the same length. He pushed the charges into the holes with a piece of broomstick he had brought, taped the ends of the fuses in a bundle and proceeded to light the fuses with a kitchen match.

Whoosh! A cloud of smoke camped up and everybody ran. Just as I turned to go I heard a voice behind me, "Hey Johnny." I turned around and saw Tommy's eyes looking over the edge of the grave and he said, "Ya wouldn't leave an old man in the hold with his powder, would ya?" Well, I stepped back and gave him my arm and hauled him out. He said, "What's wrong with tem boys? Them's three minute fuses." There was a "Whump!" and some rocks flew straight up in the air. All that was left for us to do was to shovel the rubble out and Bruce's grave was ready."

STEPANEK, Antoinette (*Farnham*)

Birth: 03/14/1917
Death: 07/26/2004
Cemetery Location: C4

Father: Charles Farnham; Mother: Antoinette (*Brett*); Husband: Joseph E. Stepanek; born in New Haven (New Haven) Connecticut and died in Lafayette (Boulder) Colorado at the age of 87 years, 4 months, 12 days-ovarian cancer

Boulder Daily Camera 29 July 2004:
"ANTOINETTE FARNHAM STEPANIC... Antoinette Farnham Stepanic [sic] of Boulder died of ovarian cancer Monday, July 26, 2004, in Lafayette. She was 87.

The daughter of Charles Farnham and Antoinette Brett Farnham, she was born on March 14, 1917, in New Haven, Conn. She married Joseph E. Stepanic on June 10, 1942, in New Haven.

She graduated from New Haven High School.

Mrs. Stepanic was involved in many organizations around the world and was the founder of the Jakarta International School in 1952. She lived in Boulder County off and on since 1945. She and her husband lived abroad most of the time.

Mrs. Stepanic enjoyed poetry and languages and published several books including "Asian Highways," "A Town Called Shaoyang: Witnessing Dynastic Changes in China" and Farnham Families in America."

Survivors include her husband of Boulder, two sons, Joseph F. Stepanic of Boulder and James B. Stepanic of Connecticut; and two daughters, Antoinette Stepanic Shaller of Massachusetts and Debra Stepanic Johnston of Texas.

A memorial service will be at 11 a.m. Aug 7 at Unitarian Universalist Fellowship, 1241 Ceras Drive, Lafayette. The Rev. Catherine Harris of the church will officiate.

Darrell Howe Mortuary is in charge of arrangements."

STEPANEK, Joseph Edward

Birth: 10/29/1917
Death: 01/31/2008
Cemetery Location: C4

Father: Joseph A. Stepanic; Mother: Leona M. (*Wilson*); Wife: Antoinette (*Farnham*); born in Dillon (Summit) Colorado and died in Boulder (Boulder) Colorado at the age of 90 years, 3 months, 2 days

Boulder Daily Camera 24 February 2008:
"Joe Stepanek had many loves in life: his wife and family, his ranch in Gold Hill, Yale, and China. They pulled him away from Colorado when he was only 21, and occupied him utterly throughout his long and productive life. At the age of 90, Joe passed away at the Boulder Community Hospital Thursday, January 31, 2008, at 8:10 a.m., four years after his wife Toni.

A retired chemical engineer and industrial strategist, Joe was married to Antoinette Farnham Stepanek of New Haven, CT, for 62 years. During World War II he worked

in the Texas oil fields as a petroleum design engineer, then as an industrial strategist in China, Indonesia, Burma, India, Ethiopia, Colombia, and in 20 other countries before his retirement. Back in Boulder he spearheaded the drive in the 1960s to build the Pearl Street Mall, and in the 1970s to promote Colorado-China business ties. Each summer the Yale Club of Colorado met at Joe's mountain ranch above Boulder, "ten miles west and one mile up."

Joe was the son of Joseph A. Stepanek and Leona M. Wilson, who was born in Dillon. He and Toni wrote a history of his mother's family, and seven more books about the Stepanek, Farnham, and Brett families. Though his family's roots were deeply planted in Colorado, Joe Stepanek thought he was "born to travel." After graduating from CU in 1939 and from Yale in 1942 he met and married the daughter of a Yale professor who shared his passion for travel and adventure.

For the next 30 years, Joe advised governments on industrial development strategies. In China in 1946-49 Joe Stepanek ran an industrialization center in Hunan Province under the United Nations Relief and Rehabilitation Agency. "We were pioneers in this project," he said. "The interior of the country was literally in the Stone Age." Joe recruited dozens of American-trained PhD's to live in China and apply the latest technology in the service of small-scale, labor-intensive industries that made cement, acids, fabric, fertilizer, and food products—a movement later dubbed in the west as "walking on two legs," referring to the development of small plants to complement giant industries. This was the first attempt by the fledgling United Nations to introduce modern production methods to the countryside.

After China, he was sent to newly independent Indonesia, where he worked for the ministries of industry and of finance in 1950. "It was very exciting to see a new government take shape," he said. While there, Toni began a small school in her children's bedroom that became the Jakarta International School, the largest international school in the world.

"Luck and circumstance" led Joe to Burma and then to India, where he was asked to advise on the development of private industry. Joe discovered it required more than engineering and management skills to accelerate industrial development. His insights led to the creation of the Hyderabad school of business to teach entrepreneurship to small businesses. "I think we had a little hand in making India a very exciting place," he said. By then his international reputation led to a posting in Vienna in 1968 as deputy director of UNIDO, the UN's Industrial Development Organization.

Joe was employed by the World Bank, US Government, Ford Foundation, and a host of UN agencies, initiating projects not directly related to his degrees in engineering—a BS from CU Boulder and a Ph.D. from Yale.

But his profound knowledge of engineering influenced all he did. While driving across the flat expanse of south India he would point to a village cement plant, saying "They seem to be using the same tube mill technology we pioneered in China in 1946." The car would stop, manager found, and after warm toasts to lifelong friendship, it would turn out he was right.

Joe's retirement party lasted 10,000 miles, and is written up in a book by his wife, Asian Highways, that recounts their drive across Europe, Turkey, Iraq, Iran, Afghanistan, Pakistan, and India in a little Peugeot, finally arriving in Bangkok in 1973. One description of a hotel reads: "Acquainted ourselves with a motorcyclist's den, mosquitoes and misery...spending the night with the very bandits whose clutches we had hoped to escape."

In retirement Joe Stepanek made 12 visits to China with Colorado's then Lieutenant Governor Nancy Dick and Commerce Representative Henry Strauss, among other Colorado business leaders, to establish state-to-province relations with Hunan and sister city relations with Kunming, In addition, Joe has served on the boards of several academic, scientific, and business organizations and has won honors, including the Yale Engineering Association Award for the Advancement of Science and CU's prestigious Norlin Award.

Joe leaves behind his sister Betty Lambert of Denver, and four children: Joseph, James, Antoinette Shaller (born in China), and Debra (born in Burman); and nine grandchildren, and four great grandchildren.

A memorial service is planned in June at Joe and Toni's Gold Hill Ranch. Please contact his son at jamesstepanek@msn.com or daughter at tonis@earthlink.net, for details."

STOCKTON, James Monroe

Birth: 06/26/1845
Death: 07/23/1874
Cemetery Location: F4

Father: James Lowry Stockton; Mother: Louisa Mayfield (*Daniels*); Wife: Jennie Victoria (*Jones*) born in Tennessee and died in Gold Hill (Boulder) Colorado at age 27 years and 27 days-kidney disease

About James Monroe Stockton

James Monroe Stockton was born 26 June 1845 in Tennessee; the son of Ohio native James Lowry and Kentucky native Louisa Mayfield (*Daniels*) Stockton. James was one of eight known children born to their union:

Washington Irving: born 29 October 1841 Burlington (Des Moines) Iowa and died 05 March 1879 Burlington (Des Moines) Iowa; Aspen Grove Cemetery, Burlington (Des Moines) Iowa; married Mary J. Barnhill; some sources state death as 26 January 1878 with unknown burial

William E.: born about 1842 Tennessee; 1880 census has birth about 1858 Ohio; no further information

James Monroe: born 26 June 1845 Monroe (Livingston) Tennessee and died Gold Hill (Boulder) Colorado; buried Gold Hill Cemetery, Gold Hill (Boulder) Colorado; married Jennie Victoria Jones; see STOCKTON, James Monroe

Chalmers "Doc": born 05 March 1848 Nashville (Davidson) Tennessee and died 12 December 1925 Greeley (Weld) Colorado; buried Linn Grove Cemetery, Greeley (Weld) Colorado; married Sarah Wilson

Alice Cary: born 26 August 1852 Missouri and died 26 January 1876 Gold Lake (Boulder) Colorado; burial unknown; married Silas Thomas Tumbleson who is buried in the Jamestown Cemetery, Jamestown (Boulder) Colorado

Francis "Fannie" Annie Jane: born 09 January 1857 Macomb (McDonough) Illinois and died 04 April 1941 Boulder (Boulder) Colorado; buried Valmont Cemetery, Valmont (Boulder) Colorado; married Benjamin Franklin Morton and Henry Clay Wilson

John William "Will": born 12 September 1860 Missouri and died 17 July 1945 Denver (Denver) Colora-

do; buried Linn Grove Cemetery, Greeley (Weld) Colorado; married Hattie M. Homes

Hugh Cameron: born 10 June 1866 Iowa and died 03 April 1898 Pancost Lake-one mile east of Valmont (Boulder) Colorado; buried Valmont Cemetery, Valmont (Boulder) Colorado; married Maud A. Gordon

In the 1860 United States census James Monroe Stockton was living with his family in Monroe (Livingston) Missouri and four years later at the age of 18 years he enlisted in the Company F, Iowa 45th Infantry Regiment on 25 May 1864 with the rank of private. He was mustered out on 16 September 1864 at Keokuk (Keokuk) Iowa.

About 1867 he married Jennie "Jane" Victoria Jones. She was born September 1847 in Wales; the daughter of a Mr. Jones (mother unknown). Jennie and her family immigrated to the United States in 1850.

The union of James Monroe and Jennie "Jane" Victoria (*Jones*) Stockton produced four known children:

Edward L.: born about 1868 Burlington (Des Moines) Iowa and died 20 October 1931 Eugene (Lane) Oregon; burial unknown; married Anna D. (maiden name unknown)

Guy Cameron: born 23 April 1871 Iowa and died 15 December 1942 Long Beach (Los Angeles) California; buried Linn Grove Cemetery, Greeley (Weld) Colorado; married Beryl Ida Jones

James L.R. (Leroy): born 12 July 1873 Burlington (Des Moines) Iowa-05 January 1942 San Diego (San Diego) California; burial unknown; married Edith M. Burgess

Albert Clare: born 1876 Burlington (Des Moines) Iowa and died 13 September 1920 Murray (Alameda) California; buried Mountain View Cemetery, Oakland (Alameda) California; married Margaret "Maggie" Riordan; some records has birth year of 1874 and birth place of Colorado

In the 1870 United States census James Monroe and Jennie "Jane" Victoria (*Jones*) Stockton were living in Burlington Ward 6 (Des Moines) Iowa

It seems the family moved to Colorado where James Monroe died in Gold Hill (Boulder) Colorado on 23 July 1874 from kidney disease at the young age of 27 years old.

His widow, Jennie "Jane" Victoria, was living in Greeley (Weld) Colorado with her four sons in the 1880 census. Her in-laws (James Leroy and wife, Louisa) were living just a few household away from them. Fourteen years later James Leroy Stockton died on 14 January 1894 and was buried in the Linn Grove Cemetery in Greeley (Weld) Colorado. His wife, Louisa, died less than a year later on 06 December 1895 and was buried beside her husband.

Jennie married Knute Nelson on 20 February 1881 however the exact location of this marriage wasn't noticed in the Colorado records but assuming it was Greeley (Weld). Knute was born 1837 in Norway; parents unknown. To their union three known children were born:

Alvord Carl: born 15 July 1881 Greeley (Weld) Colorado and died 18 January 1944 Sacramento (Sacramento) California; buried Linn Grove Cemetery, Greeley (Weld) Colorado; never married

Louisa Pearl: born 30 January 1883 Greeley (Weld) Colorado and died 10 June 1949 Greeley (Weld) Colorado; buried Linn Grove Cemetery, Greeley (Weld) Colorado; married Colonel A. Taylor

Ole M.: born March 1885 Greeley (Weld) Colorado and died 24 October 1938; buried Linn Grove Cemetery, Greeley (Weld) Colorado; married Esther Marsh Madden

In 1910 Jennie moved to St. Johns Ward 2 (Multnomah) Oregon where she lived with her son, Alvord Carl Nelson. Ten years later she was back to Colorado, living with her daughter, Louisa Pearl, and family in Kersey (Weld). She died six years later on 22 April 1926 and was buried next to her husband, Knute Nelson, in Linn Grove Cemetery in Greeley (Weld) Colorado.

STOOP(S), Mary Elizabeth (*Snyder*)

Birth: 02/1830
Death: 11/13/1914
Cemetery Location: Unknown

Father: Peter Snyder; Mother: Lydia (*Row*); Husband: William Stoop; born in Pennsylvania and died in Denver (Denver) Colorado; no tombstone

Denver Post 13 November 1914:

"STOOPS—-Mrs. Mary Elizabeth, late of 4904 Meade street; Mother of Annie M. Wade, Emma L. St. Clair, Allen [Ellen] Beecher, Charles W. Stoops and D. R. Stoops. No flowers. Funeral services will be held from Olinger's chapel Saturday 4 p.m. Interment, Gold Hill, Colo."

About Mary Elizabeth (*Snyder*) Stoops

Mary Elizabeth Stoops was born February 1830 in Pennsylvania; the daughter of Pennsylvania natives Peter and Lydia (*Row*) Snyder. Mary was the wife of William Stoops who was born about 1820 in Pennsylvania; the son of Pennsylvania natives. Together they had ten known children with information on nine:

David R.: born 07 July 1850 Pennsylvania and died 19 July 1930 Lansdale (Montgomery) Pennsylvania; buried Woodlawn Cemetery, Export (Westmoreland) Pennsylvania; married Mary L. Mcgaughey

Emma Lydia: born about 1856 Pennsylvania; death unknown; burial unknown; married William F. Granlee and Joel St. Clair; 1940 census has her a widow in Denver (Denver) Colorado at the age of 84 years living with her sister, Ellen "Nellie" F. Breecher; see ST. CLAIR, Joel Fuller Turrell

Matthew H.: born about 1858 Pennsylvania; death unknown; burial unknown

Ellen "Nellie" F.: born February 1860 Pennsylvania; death unknown; burial unknown; married Franciscum "Frank" Haverium Breecher; 1940 census has her a widow in Denver (Denver) Colorado at the age of 80 years living with her sister, Emma L. St. Clair

Lydia: born 01 April 1863 Pennsylvania and died 23 December 1925 Boyne City (Charlevoix) Michigan; buried Maple Lawn Cemetery, Boyne City (Charlevoix) Michigan; married William H. Arbuckle

Anna "Annie": born May 1864 (tombstone states 1866) Pennsylvania and died 1949 (Morgan) Colorado; buried Riverside Cemetery, Fort Morgan (Morgan) Colorado; married Michael J. Ryan and Augustus Earl Wade

Gertrude J.: born about 1866 Pennsylvania and died before 1880 census

Charles W.: born August 1868 Pennsylvania and died October 1918 (WWI-disease)

Mary Violet: born 1869 Missouri and died before 1880 census

William and Mary were married in Pennsylvania where all of their children were born except Mary Violet where it appears they moved to Missouri about 1869. They were living in Somerset (Mercer) Missouri in the 1870s census where William was a farmer. Ten years later he was living with his family in Trenton (Grundy) Missouri, still farming.

On 06 October 1889 William died and was buried in the Maple Grove Cemetery in Trenton (Grundy) Missouri. Eleven years later his widow, Mary Elizabeth (*Snyder*) Stoops was living with her daughter, Annie Ryan in Denver (Arapahoe) Colorado.

In 1906 Annie married Augustus Wade and moved to Cripple Creek (Teller) Colorado while her mother, Mary Elizabeth, remained in Denver, living with her widowed sister, Ellen (*Stoops*) Breecher.

The Denver Post on 13 November 1914 stated the death notice of Mary Elizabeth Stoops with burial in the Gold Hill Cemetery, Gold Hill (Boulder) Colorado. Her burial wasn't listed in any previous Gold Hill cemetery records however. It is speculated that she is buried in an unmarked grave near the grave of her son-in-law Joel Fuller Turrell St. Clair.

STROUP/STROPE/STRUPE, John W.

Birth: 02/01/1857
Death: 06/26/1893
Cemetery Location: E2

Father: Stephen Stroup; Mother: Mary A. (*Carter*); Wife: Lydia "Lillie" M." (*Copson*); born in Ohio and died in

Gold Hill (Boulder) Colorado at age 36 years, 4 months, 25 days-pneumonia

Boulder Daily Camera 28 June 1893:

"Johnny Strope [sic] died at Gold Hill Monday afternoon with pneumonia. He was a well-known miner. The decease leaves a wife and three [error] children. The funeral will take place tomorrow afternoon in Gold Hill."

Boulder News 29 June 1893:

"John Stroupe, a well-known miner of Gold Hill, died Monday of pneumonia after only a few days illness. He leaves a wife and several small children."

Boulder News 06 July 1893:

"John W. Stroup of Gold Hill died at his home after a few days illness of pneumonia. He leaves a wife and three [error] children to mourn his loss."

About John W. Stroup

There are records of a John W. Stroup, son of German native Stephen and England native Mary A. (*Carter*) Stroup; born on 01 February 1857 in Batavia (Clermont) Ohio. It has been said that John W. Stroup was a veteran but not confirmed.

At 24 years of age John W. Stroup married a young 22 year old Lydia M. "Lillie" Copson in Boulder, Colorado on 25th August 1881. She was born September 1858 in New York; possibly the daughter of Ephraim and Jane (maiden name unknown) Copson.

To their union four known children were born:

Olive "Ollie" Mary "May": born 02 July 1883 Gold Hill (Boulder) Colorado and died 26 November 1959 Tulsa (Tulsa) Oklahoma; buried Crown Hill Cemetery, Wheat Ridge (Jefferson) Colorado; married James Alfred Shaw and Eli Pierce Harmon

Nancy J. "Nannie": born 05 October 1884 Gold Hill (Boulder) Colorado and died 29 November 1972 Oakland (Alameda) California; burial unknown; married Theodore Charles Ballou

Ralph John: born 27 October 1888 Gold Hill (Boulder) Colorado and died 1955; buried Evergreen Cemetery, Saint Edward (Boone) Nebraska; married Minnie Daigh

William Earl "Willie": born 22 November 1893 Gold Hill (Boulder) Colorado-interred 29 November 1949; buried Crown Hill Cemetery, Wheat Ridge (Jefferson) Colorado; married Gladys M. Campbell, Josephine Clementine Jordan, Esther Mabel (maiden name unknown) and Caroline P. Brown

In 1885 the family was living in Gold Hill (Boulder) Colorado where John was a miner. A mere eight years later he died from pneumonia and was buried in the Gold Hill Cemetery in Gold Hill (Boulder) Colorado. His widow, Lydia, married William Cowell on 05 November 1898 in Boulder (Boulder) Colorado; see COWELL, William. To this union one child was born:

George Elmer: born 19 June 1899 Gold Hill (Boulder) Colorado and died 01 September 1983 Denver (Denver) Colorado; burial unknown; married Ruby C. Thompson and Jacqueline Marie (*Moser*) Pollard

Lydia died while taking a nap at her home in Denver on 06 March 1929 and was buried in the Crown Hill Cemetery in Wheat Ridge (Jefferson) Colorado alongside her son, William Earl "Willie" Stroup.

STUCHELL, Margaret "Maggie" J.

Birth: 08/12/1850
Death: 11/08/1885
Cemetery Location: D4

Father: Jacob Stuchell; Mother: Margaret (*Johnston*): Step-Mother: Patience (*Doty*): Husband: Joel Fuller Turrell St Clair; born in East Mahoning (Indiana) Pennsylvania and died in Gold Hill (Boulder) Colorado at age 35 years, 2 months, 27 days-consumption; maiden name of Stuchell on tombstone; see ST. CLAIR, Joel Fuller Turrell; see **About Joel Fuller Turrell St. Clair**

Digging Up Dirt

Herald Weekly 11 November 1885

"Death of Mrs. St. Clair...

    Maggie J. Stuchell, wife of Joel T. St. Clair, died at their residence in Gold Hill, Nov. 8th at 1:15 a.m. aged 35 years, 2 months, and 27 days. The deceased has been for years a great sufferer with consumption, but bore her troubles with Christian spirit and patience, never complaining about her lot or condition. Sixteen years ago she united with the Presbyterian Church and has lived a true, conscientious and consistent Christian life. She faced death with fortitude and resignation, and the peace and calm which greets the believers was hers when the end was known to be nigh. A true Christian, a loving wife, and a fond mother has gone to the reward. The hearts of a devoted husband and two children are weighted down with irreparable sorrow at their irreparable loss. To them the sympathies of man friends are extended."

About Margaret "Maggie" J. (*Stuchell*) St. Clair

Margaret "Maggie" J. Stuchell's father, Jacob, was born 15 September 1801 in White Township (Indiana) Pennsylvania; the son of Christopher and Elizabeth (*Lydick*) Stuchell.

    Jacob first married Margaret "Peggy" St. Clair on 22 May 1828 in (Indiana) Pennsylvania. She was born 26 February 1803 in McKeesport (Allegheny) Pennsylvania; the daughter of Pennsylvania natives James and Jane "Jennie" (*Slemmons/Slemons*) St. Clair. To the union of Jacob and Margaret two known children were born:

    Samuel: born 17 August 1829 (Indiana) Pennsylvania and died 16 December 1904 Marion Center (Indiana)

Pennsylvania; buried Gilgal Cemetery, Marion Center (Indiana) Pennsylvania; married Phebe Doty

    Joseph St. Clair: born 20 August 1835 (Indiana) Pennsylvania and died 12 October 1875 Pittsburg (Allegheny) Pennsylvania; burial unknown; married Josephine Martin

    Margaret "Peggy" (*St. Clair*) Stuchell died 17 May 1841 in East Mahoning (Indiana) Pennsylvania. Her widowed husband then married Margaret Johnston on 23 November 1843 in (Indiana) Pennsylvania. She was born 18 May 1814; parents unknown. To this union five known children were born:

    Christopher D.: born 12 September 1844 (Indiana) Pennsylvania and died 21 January 1879 Leadville (Lake) Colorado according to Ancestral File, Church of the Latter-day Saints (FamilySearch) however the original burial record of the original Leadville Cemetery states "Charles" D. Stuchell; spouse unknown

    John J.: born 1847 (Indiana) Pennsylvania and died 04 January 1895 Brockway (Jefferson) Pennsylvania; buried Gilgal Cemetery, Marion Center (Indiana) Pennsylvania; married Sarah E. Donahue

    Sarah Elizabeth: born 02 June 1847 (Indiana) Pennsylvania and died 11 February 1893 East Mahoning Twp. (Indiana) Pennsylvania; buried Gilgal Cemetery, Marion Center (Indiana) Pennsylvania; married John M. Byers

    Margaret "Maggie" J.: born 12 August 1850 East Mahoning (Indiana) Pennsylvania and died 08 November 1885 Gold Hill (Boulder) Colorado; buried Gold Hill Cemetery, Gold Hill (Boulder) Colorado; married Joel Fuller Terrell St. Clair; see STUCHELL, Maggie J.; see ST. CLAIR, Joel Fuller Terrell

    Jacob T.: born 1853 (Indiana) Pennsylvania and died 02 June 1881; burial unknown; married Alice M. Donahue

    When Margaret "Maggie" J. was about six years old her mother, Margaret Johnston Stuchell, died 02 May 1856 in (Indiana) Pennsylvania. Jacob then married his third and final wife, Patience/Prudence Doty, on 11 August 1859 in (Indiana) Pennsylvania. She was born 15 September 1819 in Derry (Westmoreland) Pennsylvania; the daughter of Jonathan and Sarah (*Hartley*) Doty. To this union no known children were born.

    In the 1860 and 1870 United States census the family was still living in East Mahoning (Indiana) Pennsylvania where Maggie's father, Jacob, was a farmer. He died from apoplexy on 10 September 1871 there and was buried in the Gilgal Cemetery in Marion Center (Indiana) Pennsylvania alongside his 3rd wife, Patience, who died very suddenly (cause unknown) about a year later on 21 August 1872 in East Mahoning (Indiana) Pennsylvania.

Margaret "Maggie" J. Stuchell made her way to Gold Hill (Boulder) Colorado where she married widower Joel Fuller Terrell St. Clair on 26 November 1878; see ST. CLAIR, Joel Fuller Terrell. To this union two known children were born:

Ida May: born 18 April 1875 Gold Hill (Boulder) Colorado and died 30 December 1948 Punxsutawney (Jefferson) Pennsylvania; buried Circle Hill Cemetery, Punxsutawney (Jefferson) Pennsylvania; married William H. Fetterman; interesting to note that Ida's death certificate states a birth year of 1875 with "Rebecca" Stuchell as mother however other documents do state Margaret "Maggie" J. Stuchell as mother; Joel didn't legally marry Maggie J. Stuchell until 1878

Clara Elizabeth: born 06 April 1882 Gold Hill (Boulder) Colorado-death unknown; burial unknown; last known location was Tampico (Tamaulipas) Mexico

Unfortunately Maggie J. (*Stuchell*) St. Clair died on 08 November 1885 in Gold Hill (Boulder) Colorado from consumption at age 35 years, 2 months and 27 days and was buried in the Gold Hill Cemetery in Gold Hill (Boulder) Colorado. It is interesting to note that her tombstone has her maiden name of Stuchell and not her married name of St. Clair.

T

THOMAS, John B.

Birth: 11/20/1868
Death: 01/15/1922
Cemetery Location: E2

Father: John Thomas; Mother: Jane (*Bennet*); never married; born in Camborne (Cornwall) England and died in Boulder (Boulder) Colorado at age 53 years, 1 month, 26 days-complications; brother to William Henry Thomas; see THOMAS, William Henry; see BENNETT(S), Jane (*Bennet*) Thomas; 1881 (England), 1900 and 1910 census lists his birth as December 1865; tombstone has birth year of 1867; mortuary record has date of birth 20 November 1868

Boulder Daily Camera 16 January 1922:

"JOHN B THOMAS DIED AT A LOCAL INSTITUTION WAS GOLD HILL POSTMASTER

John B. Thomas, former postmaster at Gold Hill, died at a local institution last night of complications. He had been a resident of Boulder for thirty-eight years, coming

from England where he was born. He was a resident of Gold Hill for about twenty years. He mined there and later conducted a general store and post office.

Mr. Thomas had been an invalid for sixteen years with leakage of the heart. Because of failing health he moved to Boulder several years ago and had been living at 2044 Marine Street with his mother, Mrs. Jane Bennett, and sister, Mrs. Charles H. Walter. The funeral will be held from Howe's mortuary Wednesday. Interment will be in Gold Hill cemetery."

About John B. Thomas

John B. Thomas was born in Camborne (Cornwall) England; the son of Cornish natives John and Jane (*Bennet*) Thomas; see BENNETT(S), Jane (*Bennet*) Thomas. There are quite a few discrepancies in the records of exactly when he was born. The last census record (1920) has the birth year of 1867 and thus that date was engraved on his tombstone.

Immigration records vary also. The 1900 United States census states 1888 immigration year for John. There is a record of a John Thomas, born 1868 that arrived at the Port of New York on 29 September 1888 but not totally verified that this is the correct John B. Thomas. The U.S. and Canada Passenger and Immigration Lists Index, 1500s-1900s states John B. Thomas was naturalized on 26 September 1893.

About 1898 Johnny B. Thomas owned and operated a general store and post office on Main Street in Gold Hill where he let the town's women use US postage stamps to buy their supplies.

Boulder County Miner & Farmer 19 December 1907:
"Say, girls, have you looked in J.B. Thomas' window? He has a fine display of face powder and paints and other toilet articles. Come early and avoid the rush."

Three years later in 1911 John B. Thomas was still busy with his general store endeavors.

Boulder County Miner & Farmer 19 January 1911:
"J.B. Thomas of Gold Hill is in the city today on his return from Greeley where he has been attending the State Retail Grocers' convention, of which he is vice president."

(George Cowell Interview by Bob Gibson, Courtesy The Gibson Family for Historic Gold Hill, Inc.)

"John B. Thomas...He run [sic] the post office. I remember that well, because my brother went in, and John B. Thomas was 'the old merchant,' we called him. He was a little dried up Englishman. My brother went in and asked for a quarters worth of stamps one day, and he (John B. Thomas) told him the government wouldn't allow him to have that many. He'd only sell him two or three, he wouldn't allow him to have a quarters worth."

Unfortunately John became ill:

(Pearl Walter Interview, circa 1972, Courtesy of Lynne Walter)

"John B. Thomas shut down the store. He got sick and swore me [Pearl Walter] in as post-mistress for Gold Hill."

John died at the Boulder hospital (assuming Boulder Community Hospital) from complications on 15 January 1922 and was buried in the Gold Hill Cemetery alongside his brother, William Henry and his mother, Jane (Bennet) Thomas Bennetts.

THOMAS, William Henry

> Birth: 06/20/1869
> Death: 09/28/1911
> Cemetery Location: E2

Father: John Thomas; Mother: Jane (Bennet); Wife: Stella (*maiden name unknown*); born in Camborne (Cornwall) England and died in Gold Hill (Boulder) Colorado at age 42 years, 3 months, 8 days-pulmonary tuberculosis; brother to John B. Thomas; see THOMAS, John B.; see BENNETT(S), Jane (*Bennet*) Thomas

Boulder Daily Herald 29 September 1911:
"John [error] Henry Thomas, brother of Postmaster J.B. Thomas of Gold Hill, died at that town yesterday afternoon of miner's consumption. He was 42 years of age. For the past seven years he had been residing at Globe, Arizona, where he was seized with the fatal illness. He leaves his mother, one sister and two brothers [error]. The mother, Mrs. Jane Bennett and the sister, Miss Bessie Walters, live at Gold Hill. The funeral will take place at Gold Hill Sunday afternoon."

Boulder Daily Camera 29 September 1911:
"FORMER BOULDER MINER DIES AT GOLD HILL—Wm. Henry Thomas died at Gold Hill yesterday afternoon at 4 o'clock at the home of his mother, Mrs. Jane Bennett. The deceased has been in Gold Hill for the past fifteen days, coming from Globe, Ariz., where he has been employed in mining. He formerly worked as a miner in this county and is well known by miners of all the camps in the metaliferous district. Funeral services will

be held at Gold Hill at 2 o'clock Sunday. The deceased was a brother of J.P. [sic] Thomas, postmaster at Gold Hill and of Mrs. Becky Walter, also of Gold Hill."

About William Henry Thomas

William Henry Thomas was born on 20 June 1869 in Camborne (Cornwall) England; the son of Cornish natives John and Jane (*Bennet*) Thomas; see BENNETT(S), Jane (*Bennet*) Thomas.

According to the 1900 census he immigrated to the United States in 1890. He married Stella (maiden name unknown) in 1895. She was born May 1871 in Illinois; parents unknown but her father was born in Germany and her mother born in England. It is believed no children blessed this marriage.

By 1900 William and Stella were living in Gold Hill (Boulder) Colorado where William was a miner and Stella a housewife. From this point the trail grows cold until the death of William where he was living in Globe (Gila) Arizona. Interesting to note that the mortuary record listed him as single and the obituary mentioned nothing of a wife. No primary evidence has been located on what happened to Stella.

William Henry Thomas died on 28 September 1911 in Gold Hill (Boulder) Colorado from pulmonary tuberculosis (miners' consumption) and was buried in the cemetery there.

THOMPSON, "Judge" James Henry "Jay"

> Birth: 06/1834
> Death: 12/27/1901
> Cemetery Location: Unknown

Father: unknown; Mother: unknown; Wife; Narcissus Crittenden (*Knight*) Broughton; born in Virginia and died in Pueblo (Pueblo) Colorado at age 67 years, 6 months (approximately)-insanity; no tombstone

Boulder Daily Camera 30 December 1901:
"JUDGE THOMPSON DIES SUDDENLY—Sheriff Sipple received a telegram from Pueblo Sunday notifying him of the death in the insane asylum of J.H. Thompson, formerly of Gold Hill. He died of apoplexy quite suddenly. "Judge" Thompson as he was called, having been a justice of the peace at Gold Hill, was adjudged insane last fall. A few months before his brother, John, had mentally weakened and was sent from here to the insane asylum. "Judge" Thompson was quite feeble and well advanced in years. He was a miner in the Slide and other Gold Hill mines for many years. Interment was at that place today."

About "Judge" James Henry "Jay" Thompson

Jay Henry Thompson was born June 1834 (other source states January 1835) in Virginia; parents unknown but were Virginia natives.

Jay enlisted to fight in the Civil War. There is a James H. Thompson who some relatives believe this is Jay who enlisted in April of 1862 in Yorktown, Virginia, serving in Company F out of Tennessee. Captain Thompson was captured at Gettysburg 03 July 1863 and was able to rejoin his post on 25 June 1864. Other relatives believe "James Jay Henry Thompson" enlisted 26 April 1861 at Winchester, Tennessee in First (Turney's) Infantry with the rank of 1st Lieutenant.

Jay married Narcissus Crittenden (*Knight*) Broughton on 04 July 1875 in Boulder (Boulder) Colorado. She was born 09 September 1855 in Barbourville (Knox) Kentucky; the daughter of Dudley and Elizabeth (*Brown*) Knight.

It appears that Narcissus' parents died before she reached adulthood. The 1870 census has her living in the household of John Morrison Steele in Lebanon (Cooper) Missouri at the age of 15 years old however this census record is under the name of "Crittenden Knight."

Narcissus first married John Broughton in 1871 Missouri. Their marriage produced a son:

Oley C.: born 31 July 1872 Missouri and died 15 August 1908 Salina (Boulder) Colorado; buried Columbia Cemetery, Boulder (Boulder) Colorado; married Dora Gertrude Atteberry and Florence Emma Daniels; was one of three miners killed in the Ingram Mine explosion; see SHEA, Daniel

According to the 1910 census Narcissus had a total of nine children with six living; Oley C. Broughton was the fourth and the last five were of her marriage to Jay Thompson:

Frances "Fannie" Evelyn: born 19 April 1876 Gold Hill (Boulder) Colorado and died 01 November 1972 Casper (Natrona) Wyoming; buried Columbia Cemetery, Boulder (Boulder) Colorado; married Joseph Barnett

Virginia: born 17 March 1878 Gold Hill (Boulder) Colorado and died 09 May 1933 Boulder (Boulder) Colorado; buried Green Mountain Cemetery, Boulder (Boulder) Colorado; married Edwin Palmer Demmon

Howard Fielding: born 1880 Gold Hill (Boulder) Colorado and died 21 January 1961 Loveland (Larimer) Colorado; buried Highland Cemetery, Casper (Natrona) Wyoming; married Margaret McClelland

Robert Lee: born 30 September 1883 Gold Hill (Boulder) Colorado and died 30 September 1927 Reno (Washoe) Nevada; buried Highland Cemetery, Casper (Natrona) Wyoming; married Maude Searl

Merritt: born 31 May 1885 Gold Hill (Boulder) Colorado and died 29 September 1934 Colorado Springs (El Paso) Colorado; buried Columbia Cemetery, Boulder (Boulder) Colorado; never married

Earl Joseph: born 07 January 1889 Gold Hill (Boulder) Colorado and died 16 November 1938 Casper (Natrona) Wyoming; buried Highland Cemetery, Casper (Natrona) Wyoming; married Hazel Jacobine Elsasser

On 11 September of 1877 Jay Henry Thompson was one of three men sworn in to "honestly and faithfully discharge the duties of Registrar of Election Precinct Fourteen [Gold Hill] in the County of Boulder and State aforesaid, according to the law and to the best of my skill and ability, so help me God." The other two men were Horace A. Wolcott and John A. Hitchings; see HITCHINGS, John A.

Jay sold his Gold Hill property (Block 11, Lots 1,2,3 which included a 16' X 20' frame house with building) on 27 July 1878 to James H. Guise.

Through the years in living in Gold Hill Jay affectionately became known as "Gassy" because he loved to talk. He was an engineer at the Cold Springs Mine for 14 years and also the town's postmaster and Justice of the Peace.

Unfortunately through the years Jay was showing signs of insanity:

Boulder Daily Camera 05 November 1901:
"Complaint was sworn out today for insanity against, "Gassy" Thompson, formerly a Justice of the Peace at Gold Hill and a resident here for several years. Mr. Thompson's brother John was sent to the insane asylum from this county several weeks ago. He was a well-known miner and went off mentally by degrees. Now the "Judge" as he is known, is claimed to be unbalanced. Both are good men and are men of more than average mentality. Is it heredity?"

A few days later it was determined poor "Gassy" was insane:

Boulder Daily Camera 08 November 1901:
"GASSY IS INSANE.
James H. Thompson, a well-known miner of Gold Hill for a quarter of a century, but a resident of Boulder for some years, has followed his brother John to the insane asylum, a jury having pronounced him insane yesterday. Having been a Justice of the Peace at Gold Hill, Mr. Thompson was playfully called "Judge." He had no enemies, but was given to talking which earned him the sobriquet of "Gassy." John Thompson, his brother, was sent to the asylum last summer and has grown rapidly worse. The "Judge" is violently insane at this writing."

Family Letter from Greg Thompson to Dode Simms; postmarked 21 October 1996:

"Dear Dode,
Enclosed is the negative of the photo I have of Gold Hill. There is no date on the back. Since my grandparents, father & aunt left Gold Hill 1911. I assume the photo pre-dated their departure.

I just had dinner w/ my aunt, who lives in Loveland but was born in Gold Hill in 1909. She says my great-grandfather, Jay Thompson, was buried in the G.H. cemetery w/o a stone. Jay came to G.H. from Kentucky after fighting in the Civil War.

My grandfather, Howard T. was born 1880 in G.H. and worked in the mines, married Margaret McLelland (who came to G.H. with her father as young child from Toronto).

My Aunt Peg Steffens, of Loveland, knows of other people in Loveland with history in G.H...My grandparents lived in the house in the far NW corner of Gold Hill.

Regards,

Greg Thompson"

Jay Henry "Gassy" Thompson didn't last long in the Pueblo asylum as he died on 27 December 1901. His body was laid to rest in the Gold Hill Cemetery in an unmarked unknown location.

By 1910 his widow, Narcissus, had moved to Boulder with her sons Robert, Merritt and Earl, living on Pearl Street. Boulder City directories have Narcissus living in various locations in Boulder for the next ten years with her last address being 2233 21st Street.

She started to develop complications with her arm which became so severe that an operation was performed on 07 March 1921 to amputate it. Unfortunately the surgery was just too much for her heart as she went into shock and died. She was buried in the Columbia Cemetery in Boulder (Boulder) Colorado.

Boulder Daily Camera 08 March 1921:

"Mrs. Narcissus C. Thompson, who made her home with her daughter, Mrs. E. Demmon of 2331 21st street, died at a local institution Monday night. She had been an invalid for 2 years. She is survived by four sons, Howard, Robert, Merritt, and Earl, all of whom are at Casper, Wyo., a daughter, Mrs. Jos. Barnett, who is also at Casper, and the daughter, Mrs. Demmon of this city.

The deceased was a member of the Christian church of this city and of the Ivy Rebecca lodge. The funeral is to be held Thursday afternoon at 3 o'clock with Rev. Harris of the Christian church officiating. The surviving relatives are expected tomorrow.

Mrs. Thompson was born 65 years ago in Kentucky. She was a widow."

THOMPSON, John G.

Birth: 1853
Death: 10/16/1906
Cemetery Location: Unknown

Father: unknown; Mother: unknown; never married; born in Virginia and died in Boulder (Boulder) Colorado

at age 53 years (approximately)-insanity and pneumonia; no tombstone

About John G. Thompson

John G. Thompson was born about 1853 in Virginia; parents unknown. It is believed he was never married.

Information on John is next to none however according to the mortuary record he came to the Gold Hill area about 1900 and was a miner. He was the brother to Jay Henry Thompson; see THOMPSON, "Judge" James Henry "Jay." He was committed to the Pueblo insane asylum in the fall of 1901 and five years later he died from pneumonia at the Boulder County Poor Farm in Boulder (Boulder) Colorado. He was buried in an unmarked unknown location in the Gold Hill Cemetery in Gold Hill (Boulder) Colorado.

TREMBATH/TRENBATH/TRINBATH, Edwin/Edmond "Edney"

Birth: 01/1850
Death: 06/16/1908
Cemetery Location: Unknown

Father: unknown; Mother: unknown; Wife: Grace (*Victor*) Noye/Noy; born in England and died in Gold Hill (Boulder) Colorado at age 58 years-cardiac incompetence and complicated asthma (pneumonia); no tombstone

Boulder Daily Herald 16 June 1908:

"DEATH OF MR. TRENBATH [sic]

Edwin Trenbath [sic], of Gold Hill, died at his home there this morning at six o'clock, of pneumonia. Mr. Trenbath has been ill for a long time and the Foresters of America have for some time been doing all in their power to aid him and his wife, and their kindness is most sincerely appreciated. Mr. Trenbath [sic] is survived by a widow. He had lived in Boulder County for the past twenty-five years and was well and favorably known.

The funeral will take place from the church in Gold Hill, tomorrow afternoon at 3:00 o'clock, interment being in the Gold Hill cemetery, the Boulder Undertaking company having charge."

TREMBATH/TRENBATH/TRINBATH, Grace (*Victor*) Noy/Noye

Birth: 11/16/1820
Death: 02/12/1911
Cemetery Location: Unknown

Father: Edward/Edwin Victor; Mother: Mary (*Gillard*); Husbands: William Noye/Noy and Edmond/Edwin "Edney" Trembath/Trenbath/Trinbath; born in St. Just in Penwith (Cornwall) England and died in Boulder (Boulder) Colorado at age 90 years, 2 months, 27 days –arteriosclerosis; other sources state birth year 1822; no tombstone

Boulder Daily Camera 13 February 1911:

"DEATH OF MRS. TRENBATH PIONEER OF COLORADO—Mrs. Grace Trenbath [sic]of Gold Hill died at a local institution Sunday night of old age. She was brought from Gold Hill last week for medical treatment. Mrs. Trenbath was a pioneer of Colorado, having resided in various parts of the state for the past 35 years. She made her home in Gold Hill for 15 years prior to her death. Funeral arrangements await word from her two daughters, Mrs. Noys of Black Hawk and Mrs. Eddy of Nevadaville."

Boulder Daily Camera 14 February 1911:

"The remains of Mrs. Grace Trembath, who died at the age of 90 years at 6 o'clock Sunday evening, will be taken to Gold Hill tomorrow at 8 a.m. by Mr. Ben Holley. Mr. and Mrs. Richard Eddy of Central City, the later a daughter of Mrs. Trembath, will accompany them. The funeral will be held at 2 o'clock."

Boulder Daily Herald 15 February 1911:

"The remains of Mrs. Grace Trenbath [sic] were taken to Gold Hill by Howe and Holley, undertakers today. Interment was had there this afternoon."

Boulder News 16 February 1911:

"Mrs. Grace Trembath, and old and highly respected resident of Gold Hill, died at University hospital Sunday night of old age, she being 94."

Boulder County Miner and Farmer 16 February 1911:

"Mrs. Trimbath [sic], who has been sick at University Hospital for the past week, passed quietly away Sunday night. Her son and daughter, who reside in Central City, have been notified. Interment will probably be held in this camp."

Boulder County Tribune 17 February 1911:

"DEATH OF MRS TRENBATH PIONEER OF COLORADO...

Mrs. Grace Trenbath of Gold Hill died at a local institution Sunday night of old age. She was brought from Gold Hill last week for medical treatment. Mrs. Trenbath was a pioneer of Colorado, having resided in various parts of the state for the past 35 years. She made her home in Gold Hill for 15 years prior to her death. Funeral arrangements await word from her two daughters, Mrs. Noys of Black Hawk and Mrs. Eddy of Nevadaville."

About Edwin Edmond "Edney" and Grace (*Victor*) Noye/Noy Trembath/Trenbath/Trinbath

Edwin Edmond "Edney" Trembath was born January 1850 in England (some records states St. Just in Penwith (Cornwall) England); parents unknown. He might be related in some way to Elizabeth Jane (*Trembath*) Wolcott Williams; see WOLCOTT, John

According to the 1900 census he immigrated to the United States in 1872 where he located in (Gilpin) Colorado working the mines of that area.

In the *Veteran-Cemetery Records of Boulder County, Colorado, Transcribed 1839-1940 by NSDAR Arapahoe Chapter, Boulder, CO.,* he is listed as a veteran but no real primary evidence yet to be located.

He married Grace (*Victor*) Noye/Noy on 09 October 1893 at Quartz Hill (Gilpin) Colorado. She was born 16 November 1820 in (Cornwall) England, the daughter of Edward/Edwin and Mary (*Gillard*) Victor. Her siblings were (according to Ancestry files):

Edward: born 01 August 1819 Sancreed Parish (Cornwall) England and died 03 April 1877 Scranton (Lackawanna) Pennsylvania (according to Ancestry Family Trees); buried unknown; married Caroline Polkinhorne/Polkinghorn

Mary: born about 1821 Sancreed (Cornwall) England-death unknown; burial unknown; married William Semmons

Eliza: born 1826 (Cornwall) England-death unknown; burial unknown; married Henry Blackwell

Kitty: born 1828 (Cornwall) England-24 April 1905 Falmouth (Cornwall) England; burial unknown; married George Thomas

John Edward: born 1831 (Cornwall) England and died June 1852 Penzance (Cornwall) England; buried St. Just-in-Penwith (Cornwall) England; spouse unknown

Elizabeth Ann: born 1833 (Cornwall) England-death unknown; burial unknown; married Thomas Glasson

Nicholas: born 1835 (Cornwall) England-death unknown; burial unknown; spouse unknown

She married her first husband, William Noyes/Noy on 20 January 1849 in St. Just in Penwith (Cornwall) England. He was born about 1830 in St. Just in Penwith (Cornwall) England; the son of Robert and Loveday (*Reynolds*) Noye. According to the census records and Ancestry trees this union brought forth 16 children with possible records on 10 children:

Elizabeth: baptized 12 October 1849 Pendeen (Cornwall) England and died 19 October 1910 Hughesville (Gilpin) Colorado; buried married Thomas Bennetts and John Warren

William: born 10 September 1851 St. Just in Penwith (Cornwall) England and died before 12 February 1911 United States; no reference to him in his mother's obituary; might have married Mary Ann Collins (Jefferson) Colorado; not listed in the immigration record of 1873

Nathaniel John "Hy": baptized 19 June 1852 St. Just in Penwith (Cornwall) England- died before 12 February 1911 United States; no reference to him in his mother's obituary; married Elizabeth; 1885 Colorado State census living in (Gilpin) Colorado; some ancestry trees have Nathaniel J.V. and John Hy as two separate children

Grace: baptized 01 March 1856 Saint Just in Penwith (Cornwall) England-buried 08 January 1871 St. Just in Penwith (Cornwall) England

Henry: baptized 05 July 1857 St. Just in Penwith (Cornwall) England-burial date 08 December 1857 St. Just in Penwith (Cornwall) England

Thomas: born 02 February 1863 St. Just in Penwith (Cornwall) England-03 November 1914 Nevadaville (Gilpin) Colorado; buried Bald Mountain Cemetery, Nevadaville (Gilpin) Colorado; married Molly Cochran and Grace V. Nichols; there is a Thomas Noy who married Lavina Collins in Boulder (Boulder) Colorado 1893)

Grace: baptized 14 August 1864 Pendeen (Cornwall) England (not listed in the 1871 census or the immigration record of 1873); there is a Grace Noy who married Victor Lindberg Denver (Denver) Colorado 1925

William Henry: baptized 04 November 1866 Pendeen (Cornwall) England; not listed in the 1871 census or the immigration record of 1873

Martha Jane: baptized 03 November 1867 St. Just in Penwith (Cornwall) England and died between 1885 and 1888; in 1882 married Thomas Henry Rowe Jr., who later married Martha's sister Katey/Kattie in 1888

Katey/Kattie: born January 1868 St. Just (Cornwall) England and died 01 December 1937 Nevadaville (Gilpin) Colorado; buried Golden Cemetery, Golden (Jefferson) Colorado; married William Trezona, Thomas Henry Rowe Jr., and Richard Eddy

Records are a little confusing as there is another Noy family with parents of William and Grace with some of the children sharing the same name but living in Morvah (Cornwall) England.

In the 1873 immigration record five children came to the United States with William and Grace: Elizabeth, Nathaniel John Hy, Thomas, Martha Jane and Katey/Kattie.

By 1880 the family was living in Nevadaville (Gilpin) Colorado and continued to live there until the death of William on 02 February 1892 in Central City (Gilpin) Col-

orado. No cemetery record has been located where William was buried but might be Bald Mountain Cemetery, Central City (Gilpin) Colorado.

Less than two years later Grace married Edmond/Edwin Trembath on 09 October 1893 (Gilpin) Colorado. By 1900 Edwin and Grace were living in Gold Hill (Boulder) Colorado.

Early Days in Gold Hill by George Cowell (as told to Chuck & Doll Rowan and Bob & Shirlee Gibson; Transcript by Lynne Walter):

"There was someone who lived in a house by the school that had an interesting history. Didn't he leave home every so often?" [Shirley]

"Yea, that was Old Lady Trumbath [sic]. Old Man Trumbath he took care of the rink down there and did little odd jobs. He was crippled and he couldn't walk much. Old Man Edney and this O'd Lady Trumbath they were married and first thing you know she'd be throwing all of his clothes right out in the middle of the street and he'd pick them all up and go hobbling down to the rink. Next door to the rink there was an old room there, an old shanty, just a little place where he could stay and he'd go down there and 'batch' and Old Lady Trumbath wouldn't have a thing to do with him. He'd probably lay down there and 'batch' maybe a month. Then Old Edney would get sick so Old Lady Trumbath would fix up a big tray of food and take it down to poor old Edney and feed him and get him well and bring him back home. They would live happy for a few months till Old Edney's clothes would go out in the middle of the street again and Old Edney would pick them up and back down he'd go to the rink and live down there." (George)

On 16 June 1908 Edwin/Edmond "Edney" Trembath died of cardiac incompetence and complicated asthma (pneumonia) in his Gold Hill home. He lived to be about 58 years. He was buried in an unmarked grave (unknown location) in the Gold Hill Cemetery in Gold Hill (Boulder) Colorado.

His widow, Grace, never remarried and spent the rest of her life in Gold Hill until she was taken to the University Hospital in Boulder (Boulder) Colorado where she died on 12 February 1911. She, too, was buried in an unmarked grave (unknown location) in the Gold Hill Cemetery in Gold Hill (Boulder) Colorado.

U

UMBERGER, Susan Theresa (*Brown*)

> Birth: 04/07/1943
> Death: 05/27/2011
> Cemetery Location: B2

Father: Gilbert Lewis Brown; Mother: Barbara (*Heaton*); Husband: John David Umberger; born in Vallejo (Solano) California and died in Sheboygan (Sheboygan) Wisconsin at age 68 years, 1 month, 20 days

Sheboygan Press 29 May 2011 and *Lafayette Journal & Courier* 29 May 2011:

"Beloved wife, mother, sister, aunt, and Grandmother Susan Theresa Umberger died Friday May 27, 2011, in Sheboygan, Wisconsin. Susan Theresa Brown was born to Barbara Heaton Brown and Gilbert Lewis Brown in Vallejo, California in 1943 but grew up, with her two brothers, in Denver and Gold Hill, Colorado, areas in which her family had deep roots. Susan attended Denver's East High School and the University of Colorado, Boulder, where she earned a degree in sociology. She married John David Umberger, Junior in 1966 in Minne-apolis, Minnesota. Susan and David raised their daughter and son in West Lafayette, Indiana and worked at Purdue University until 2007-8 when they retired and moved to Sheboygan, Wisconsin to live near their daughter.

Susan was known as a warm, bright, generous, loving and humorous woman who loved nothing more than being with family and friends. She took pride in her Colorado heritage, which traces back to the 1860s when family members settled in the foothills of the Rocky Mountains. Susan was deeply involved in the lives of her children, devoting her life toward the betterment of theirs. She loved reading and spending time in her garden and the wildflower fields of the mountains. Susan and David cultivated close and lasting friendships in their "gourmet group," which has thrived over the course of forty years.

Susan is survived by her husband, her children and families, her brothers and their families, and a treasured family of friends. She will be laid to rest in Gold Hill, Colorado with her family. Contributions in Susan's honor may be made to the Sheboygan County Cancer Care Fund, the Hera Women's Cancer Foundation, and the Gold Hill Museum."

Courtesy John David Umberger:

"The family drove to Marble, Colorado to find the perfect beautiful piece of marble-granite stone for Susan's grave in the Gold Hill Cemetery. Daughter, Leslie, planted wildflowers and each friend or family member in attendance placed a piece of quartz from a mine dump up near Rocky Point, just west of town. The piece of lake-polished basalt with the quartz inclusions in the center of her grave is from Lake Michigan near the Umberger's home in Wisconsin. Susan was a member of the Gold Hill Club as was her mother, Barbara. She will be extremely missed but never forgotten."

UNKNOWN GRAVES

According to the Colorado State Archives death records were not officially registered with the State until approximately 1908 however burial registers for Boulder County began in 1895 with coroner's reports in 1909. Even with these resources along with mortuary records (if any) the grave location within the Gold Hill cemetery was not recorded. And since early records did not list all of the cemetery's inhabitants these graves became the forgotten until accidently discovered when digging for a burial. My great grandfather, Edwin David "Ned" Goudge was digging his own grave in the cemetery when his shovel hit a coffin (might have been the grave of Daniel Shea) thus he had to adjust his future burial site.

Today caution is taken when there is a burial in hopes to avoid this issue. So, it is very important for the cemetery's visitors not to remove or relocate any rocks or disturb the ground in any way as it very well can desecrate these graves.

V

VANDERPOEL, John Cornelius

Birth: 05/08/1914
Death: 06/17/1987
Cemetery Location: G2

Father: Cornelius Vanderpoel; Mother: Marie (*Kunzman*); Wife: Ruth (*Roberts*); born in Chicago (Cook) Illinois and died in Boulder (Boulder) Colorado at age 73 years, 1 month, 9 days

Boulder Daily Camera 18 June 1987:

"John C. Vanderpoel—John C. Vanderpoel of 705 S. 44th St., Boulder, died Wednesday, June 17, at Boulder Community Hospital. He was 73. Mr. Vanderpoel was born in Chicago on May 8, 1914, the son of Cornelius and Marie Kunzman Vanderpoel. He married Ruth Roberts in Noblesville, Ind., on Dec. 27, 1941. He worked as a tool and gauge inspector for Western Electric for 30 years. He was a member of the Steamers Club and the National Railway Historical Society. He belonged to the Mount View United Methodist Church. Mr. Vanderpoel is survived by his wife of Boulder; a son, Lance Vanderpoel of Boulder; four daughters, Linda Mitchell of Greeley, Marie Brookhart of Lamar, Colo., Vyvian Sells of Waldorf, Md., and Grace Harper of Port Orchid, Wash.; one sister, Edith of Wright of Chicago; and five grandchildren. Memorial services will be held at a later date. Contributions may be made to the Boulder County Heart Fund, 760 Flagstaff Road, Boulder 80302."

VANDERPOEL, Ruth Vyvian (*Roberts*)

Birth: 12/12/1919
Death: 05/25/2009
Cemetery Location: G2

Father: Roger Sylvanus Roberts; Mother: Vyvian Estelle (*Heaven*); Husband: John C. Vanderpoel; born and died in Noblesville (Hamilton) Indiana at age 89 years, 5 months, 13 days

Quaker Life- Friends United Meeting-Nov/Dec 2009:

"VANDERPOEL—Ruth Vyvian Roberts Vanderpoel, 89, May 25, 2009, Noblesville Friends, Indiana. Ruth was born December 12, 1919, to Roger Sylvanus and Vyvian Heaven Roberts. After graduating from Noblesville High School, she worked in Mr. Cottingham's abstract office. She then left for business college in Lafayette and returned to Noblesville to work in the law offices of Roberts & Roberts with her father, grandfather and uncle. She then met and married John Vanderpoel of Chicago. The two moved from Milwaukee to Noblesville to Colorado, back to Noblesville, before finally settling in Boulder, Colorado. John preceded her in death in 1987. Survivors include her children, Lance Vanderpoel, Linda Meek, Marie (Don) Brookhart, Vyvian Vanderpoel and Greta Harper; nine grandchildren; three great-grandchildren; one great-great grandchild; three nephews; one niece; cousin, Joseph; and lifelong friends, Carmel and Betty Gerrard. Memorial contributions may be made to Noblesville Friends Church or Blatchley Nature Study Club."

VANDERPOEL, Vyvian Lea

>Birth: 06/15/1945
>Death: 09/25/2015
>Cemetery Location: G2

Father: John Cornelius Vanderpoel; Mother: Ruth Vyvian (*Roberts*); Husband: Van Stephen Sells; born in Noblesville (Hamilton) Indiana and died in New Braunfels (Comal) Texas at 70 years, 3 months, 10 days; no tombstone; no further information

W

WAGNER, Harold Frederick

Birth: 08/31/1916
Death: 08/31/1962
Cemetery Location: E2

Father: George Wagner; Mother: Ruth J. (*May*); Wife: Ethel E. (*Halley*); born Albion (Erie) Pennsylvania and died near Macon (Roosevelt) Montana at age 46 years, 0 months, 0 days-auto accident

Boulder Daily Camera 04 September 1962:
"Harold F. Wagner—Funeral services will be held Wednesday at 11 a.m. at the Lewellen Funeral Home in Longmont for Harold F. Wagner, who was one of three persons killed Aug. 31 in an automobile accident near Macon, Mo. Private cremation will follow. Mr. Wagner was a machinist in the mechanical engineering department at the University of Colorado. He was born in Albion, Pa., Aug. 31, 1916, and spent his early life in Erie, Pa. He graduated from the General Electric apprentice course in Erie. He and his family moved to Longmont in 1960 and for eight months he was assistant building inspector. At the time of the accident, he was en route to a national radio convention in Indianapolis. Surviving are his wife, Ethel; a son, Eric H. of Longmont; and his parents, Mr. and Mrs. George Wagner of Lake City, Pa."

WALLICK, Rachel K. (*Neville*)

Birth: 02/26/1836
Death: 04/03/1898
Cemetery Location: C1

Father: Joseph Neville; Mother: Mary (*Buckmaster*); Husband: Henry "Albion" Wallick; born in (Holmes) Ohio and died in Gold Hill (Boulder) Colorado at age 62 years, 1 month, 8 days- tuberculosis

Boulder Daily Camera 04 April 1898:
"Mrs. Wallach [sic], the aged mother-in-law of E.H. Reedy of Gold Hill, died at that place yesterday. The funeral will [be] conducted by Mr. Trezise tomorrow."

About Rachel K. (*Neville*) Wallick/Wallack

Rachel K. Neville was born 26 February 1836 in (Holmes) Ohio; the daughter of Joseph and Mary (*Buckmaster*) Neville. She had eleven siblings including her sister, Athalia who married John Felix Romig—See ROMIG, Athalia (*Neville*) and another sister who married Walter Lincoln Wallick, the brother of Henry Albion Wallick (husband of Rachel)

"The Way We Were" by Alethea Wallack [sic] McClain, Anundsen Publishing, 1977:
"Henry, great-grandfather, born 5 Mar 1836, Holmes Co., Ohio, died 123 Aug 1925 at Albion, Nebr., where he is buried in the Rose Hill Cemetery. Married 17 Jun 1858 to Rachel Neville, born 26 Feb 1836 in Comes Co., Ohio, daughter of Joseph Nevill [sic], Sr. She had been previously married and had a son, James Downing. She died 3 Apr 1898 of tuberculosis and is buried at Gold Hill Cemetery near Boulder, CO. Henry and Rachel went to Marengo, Powshiek [sic-Poweshiek] Co., Iowa where they resided for a time and then head westward again to Kansas in 1879 and homestead in Norton Co., Cans [sic-Kans], hear Lenora and Edmond. The homestead was located near the Soloman River. All the children learned to swim well and the daughters were said to have been excellent equestrians but it was noted they all rode with side saddles. Henry served in the Union Army during the Civil War."

(Alethea Wallack/Wallick McClain was the daughter of Austin Henry Wallick who was the son of Phillip Uhl Wallick, son of Henry and Rachel (*Neville*) Wallick)

To the union of Henry and Rachel nine known children were born:
Albert Marshall: born 30 May 1859 Millersburg (Holmes) Ohio and died 23 September 1930 Seattle

(King) Washington; buried Greenwood Memorial Park, Renton (King) Washington; married Flora Elnora King

Walter Lincoln: born 30 October 1860 (Holmes) Ohio and died 03 April 1921 (Buchanan) Iowa; buried Wilson Cemetery, Independence (Buchanan) Iowa; married Julia Josephine Neville

Mary Emelia: born 16 June 1863 (Marshall) Iowa and died 23 March 1951 Topeka (Shawnee) Kansas; buried Elmwood Cemetery, Beloit (Mitchell) Kansas; married David "Ed" Allen and Henry Lesher

Charles Edgar: born 05 January 1864 Jefferson Township (Poweshiek) Iowa and died 29 August 1937 Los Angeles (Los Angeles) California; burial unknown; married Cordelia Deliah Barholtz

Phillip Uhl: born 09 January 1865 Jefferson Township (Poweshiek) Iowa and died 18 March 1939 Jennings (Decatur) Kansas; burial unknown; married Aletha Ursula Bishop

William Michael "Willie": born 21 May 1870 Brooklyn (Poweshiek) Iowa and died 16 July 1928 Lenora (Norton) Kansas; buried Lenora East Cemetery, Lenora (Norton) Kansas; married Elizabeth Ann Pickering

Jessie Alma: born 08 May 1875 (Poweshiek) Iowa and died 15 May 1957 Albion (Boone) Nebraska; buried Rose Hill Cemetery, Albion (Boone) Nebraska; married Charles Andrew Walker

Martha Ann: born 21 October 1872 Victor (Poweshiek) Iowa and died 18 January 1952 Denver (Denver) Colorado; buried Gold Hill Cemetery, Gold Hill (Boulder) Colorado; married Edward Hagar Reedy; see REEDY, Martha Ann (*Wallick*)

Minnie Ellen: born 17 January 1876 Jefferson Township (Poweshiek) Iowa and died 24 September 1952

Long Beach (Los Angeles) California; burial unknown; married Alphus M. Smith and Montgomery McCall Crouch Jr.

In 1860 the family was living in Hardy (Holmes) Ohio where Henry was a farmer. By 1870 they were living in Jefferson Township (Poweshiek) Iowa. In the 1880 census there are two listings for these family just days apart in the census records: 14th and 15th day of June 1880 living in Soloman (Norton) Kansas and the 18th day of June 1880 living in Twin Mound (Norton) Kansas where Henry is listed as a farmer in both listings.

Five years later they were living in Modell (Norton) Kansas. After 1895 the family came to (Boulder) Colorado and settled in Gold Hill where Rachel died on 03 April 1898 from tuberculosis.

After Rachel's death Henry moved to Allison (Decatur) Kansas to live with his son, Phillip and family. There is no listing for Henry in the 1920 census but it is assumed he left the household for Albion (Boone) Nebraska where he died on 12 August 1925 and was buried in the Rose Hill Cemetery there.

WALSTED, George

Birth: About 1880
Death: 09/09/1889
Cemetery Location: C3 (assumed)

Father: Nels/Nils Jacobsen Walsted; Mother: Dorthea "Dorris" "Dora" (*Christian*); born and died in Gold Hill (Boulder) Colorado at age 9 years-inflammation of the bowels; sometimes name is spelled Walstead; see WALSTED, Nels Jacobsen (Nelse/Nils)

Inscription
"I know that my redeemer liveth, and that he shall stand at the latter day upon the earth: And though after my skin worms destroy this body, yet in my flesh shall I see God."
Job .19..25

Tombstone of Rachel K. (*Neville*) Wallick

Boulder Herald 11 September 1889:

"Geo. Walsted, aged 9 years, son of NJ Walsted of Gold Hill, died Monday of inflammation of the bowels, after an illness of four weeks. He was buried today. The parents have the sympathy of many friends in their loss."

Boulder News 12 September 1889:

"George, the nine years [sic] son of Mr. N. Walsted, died at Gold Hill Monday after a long and painful illness."

WALSTED, Hanse Jacobsen

Birth: About 1841
Death: 01/1881
Cemetery Location: C3 (assumed)

Father: Jakob Nilsen; Mother: Helle Karene (*Hansdatter*); never married; born in Norway and died in Gold Hill (Boulder) Colorado-illness; brother to Nels/Nils Jacobsen Walsted; no tombstone

Boulder County Herald 05 January 1881:

"Our people were startled a few days ago to hear of the sudden death of Hanse Jacobson (Walsted.) The deceased had been a constant sufferer for years, and his death was expected by those who knew him best. The funeral took place from the residence [Gold Hill] of his brother, N.J. Walsted, which was followed to the grave by a large number of friends. Mr. and Mrs. Walsted return thanks to the citizens of Gold Hill for their kindness."

WALSTED, Infant Twins

Birth: About 1886
Death: 08/1886
Cemetery Location: C3

Father: Nels/Nils Jacobsen Walsted; Mother: Dorthea "Dorris" "Dora" (*Christian*); born and died in Gold Hill (Boulder) Colorado in infancy; sometimes name is spelled Walstead; unmarked grave located below that of Nels Jacobsen Walsted; see WALSTED, Nels/Nils Jacobsen

Boulder County Herald Weekly 25 August 1886:

"Word comes that Mr. N.J. Walsted living near Gold Hill, buried the last of the twins last week. He desires through the medium of the HERALD to extend the sincerest thanks of himself and wife to the friends who kindly assisted during the illness and burial of the child. The HERALD extends its sympathy to the bereaved parents."

WALSTED, Nelia

Birth: About 02/1884
Death: 12/1884
Cemetery Location: C3 (assumed)

Father: Nels/Nils Jacobsen Walsted; Mother: Dorthea "Dorris" "Dora" (*Christian*); born and died in Gold Hill (Boulder) Colorado at age 10 months old-Scar Latina (Scarlet Fever); sometimes name is spelled Walstead; see WALSTED, Nels/Nils Jacobsen

WALSTED, Nels/Nils Jacobsen

Birth: 04/16/1839
Death: 12/03/1890
Cemetery Location: C3

Father: Jakob Nilsen; Mother: Helle Karene (*Hansdatter*); Wife: Dorthea (Dorothy) "Dorris/Dora" (*Christian*); born in Lier (Buskerud) Norway and died in (Boulder) Colorado at age 51 years (approximately); sometimes name is spelled Walstead

About the Walsted Family

Nels/Nils Jacobson Walsted was born about 1839 in Lier (Buskerud) Norway; the son of Jakob and Helle Karene (*Hansdatter*) Nilsen. He married Dorthea (Dorothy) "Dorris/Dora" Christian, who was born 25 May 1856 in Norway; parents unknown. There are no known Colorado records of when Nels married Dorthea but their marriage was blessed with six known children:

Jacob Cristian: born 10 February 1874 Colorado and died 07 March 1933 Denver (Denver) Colorado; buried Crown Hill Cemetery, Wheat Ridge (Jefferson) Colorado; married Clara D. Henderson

Edward (Edvard): born 08 December 1876 Colorado and died 21 June 1938 Seattle (King) Washington; buried Wright Crematory and Columbarium, Seattle (King) Washington; married Grace King

George: born about 1880 Gold Hill (Boulder) Colorado and died 09 September 1889 Gold Hill (Boulder) Colorado; buried Gold Hill Cemetery, Gold Hill (Boulder) Colorado; see WALSTED, George

Nelia: born about February 1884 Gold Hill (Boulder) Colorado and died December 1884 Gold Hill (Boulder) Colorado; buried Gold Hill Cemetery, Gold Hill (Boulder) Colorado; see WALSTED, Nelia

Infant Twins: born 1886 Gold Hill (Boulder) Colorado and died 1886 Gold Hill (Boulder) Colorado; buried Gold Hill Cemetery, Gold Hill (Boulder) Colorado; see WALSTED, Infant Twins

In the 1880 census and the 1885 Colorado State census Nels/Nils was listed as a ranchman. About a year later he was naturalized on 26 April 1886 in Boulder (Boulder) Colorado. Four years later on 03 December 1890 Nels/Nils died and was buried in the Gold Hill Cemetery.

Less than two years later his widow, Dorthea (Dorothy) "Dorris/Dora" moved to Ward (Boulder) Colorado.

Boulder Daily Camera 28 September 1892:

"Mrs. Walstead has bought the Cottage House at Ward and will move there about the thirteenth of next month. It is sincerely hoped by all her friends that she will do well, although they do not like to see her go."

Apparently Dorthea (Dorothy) "Dorris/Dora" met Ward resident Lafayette Grover and her agenda for operating the Cottage House changed as on 12 January 1893 they were married in Boulder (Boulder) Colorado; see GROVER, Lafayette L. There is no listing for the Cottage House in the 1896 POLK directory.

After the death of Lafayette in 1912, Dorthea married William Henry Smith 25 August of 1919 in Boulder (Boulder) Colorado; see SMITH, Dorthea (Dorothy) "Dorris/Dora" (*Christian*) Walsted Grover.

Dorthea (Dorothy) "Dorris/Dora" (*Christian*) Walsted Grover Smith died on 24 June 1920 and was buried in the Gold Hill Cemetery, Gold Hill (Boulder) Colorado.

WALTER, Albert Charles "Bud"

> Birth: 11/13/1921
> Death: 05/01/1998
> Cemetery Location: D6

Father: Albert James "Tim" Walter; Mother: Pearl Annabell (*Pughe*); Wife: Darlene Joan "Smitty" (*Smith*); born and died in Boulder (Boulder) Colorado at age 76 years, 5 months, 18 days-in his sleep; see WALTER, Darlene Joan "Smitty" (*Smith*)

Boulder Daily Camera 04 May 1998:

"Albert C. 'Bud' Walter—Lt. Col. Albert C. "Bud" Walter of Boulder died Friday, May 1, 1998, at home. He was 76.

He was born Nov. 13, 1921, in Boulder, to Albert James Walter and Pearl Pughe Walter. He married Darlene J. smith on July 1, 1946, in boulder.

He retired in 1969 from the U.S. air Force and worked for the Boulder County Assessor's office, and was a member of the Retired Military Officers Association in Boulder, the Air Force Association and the AARP.

He lived most of his life in Boulder County except for when he lived throughout the United States and abroad during his military service.

Mr. Walter was a graduate of Boulder High School and attended the University of Colorado and the University of Denver.

Survivors include his wife, Darlene J. Walter of Boulder; two sons, Robert D. Walter of Gold Hill and James M. Walter of Boulder; a daughter, Lynne Y. Walter of Gold Hill; a sister, Gertrude Hammil of Irvine, Calif, and four grandchildren. Contributions may be made to a charity of the donor's choice.

Services will be at 10 a.m. Wednesday at Crist Mortuary Chapel, 34th Street and the Diagonal Highway in Boulder, with Bob Howard, a deacon, officiating. Services will conclude in Gold Hill Cemetery with military honors by the U.S. Air Force."

WALTER, Charles Thomas

Birth: 03/1857
Death: 06/05/1909
Cemetery Location: D3

Father: William Walter; Mother: Ann (*Vanstone*); Wife: Elizabeth Ann "Bessie" (*Thomas*); born in Holsworthy, Sutcombe (Devon) England and died in Gold Hill (Boulder) Colorado at age 51 years-miners' consumption; see WALTER, Elizabeth Ann "Bessie" (*Thomas*); see **About Charles Thomas and Elizabeth Ann "Bessie" (*Thomas*) Walter**

Boulder Daily Camera 08 June 1909:

"The funeral of Charles Walters [sic] of Gold Hill, who died there Saturday of miner's consumption, was held this afternoon at 2 o'clock. Buchheit, Howe and Hickox had charge of the services. He was 51 years of age and leaves a wife and five children."

WALTER, Darlene Joan "Smitty" (*Smith*)

Birth: 08/01/1918
Death: 05/07/2016
Cemetery Location: D6

Father: Dale Languel Smith; Mother: Jane (*Darling*); Husband: Albert Charles "Bud" Walter; born in Louisville (Jefferson) Kentucky and died in Louisville (Boulder) Colorado at age 97 years, 9 months, 6 days; no published obituary; see WALTER, Albert Charles "Bud"

Gold Hill Townsite Community Digest 14 May 2016:

"DARLENE J. (SMITTY) WALTER

Lynne and Bob and Jim's mother, Darlene J. (Smith) Walter died Saturday night, May 14th at Balford. For those of us who loved her, here are the services:

Catholic Mass at 10 a.m. on Monday May 16th.
Immaculate Conception Catholic Church
715 Cabrini Drive
Lafayette
This church is located just east of Walmart (between Arapahoe and Baseline)

This is the more formal service and not a big deal for people to come unless they want to, according to Lynne.

THE BIGGY—
Gold Hill Cemetery
Saturday, May 21st 11am
Casual dress—Lynne said, "This is a celebration of life—NO SADNESS!!!""

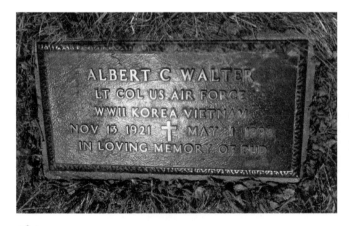

WALTER, Elizabeth Ann "Bessie" (*Thomas*)

Birth: 10/20/1857
Death: 12/27/1944
Cemetery Location: D3

Father: John Thomas; Mother: Jane (*Bennet*); Husband: Charles Thomas Walter; born in St. Blazey (Cornwall) England and died in Boulder (Boulder) Colorado at age 87 years, 2 months, 7 days-cerebral hemorrhage; tombstone has birth year 1858 and incorrect death year 1941; see BENNETT(S), Jane (*Bennet*) Thomas; see WALTER, Charles Thomas

Boulder Daily Camera 28 December 1944:

"Mrs. Eliz. Walter, Pioneer of Gold Hill, Dies at 87—Mrs. Elizabeth Ann Walter, widow of Charles Thomas Walter, died at her home, 2044 Marine, Wednesday night following a short illness. She was 87. Born in England, she came to Gold Hill 60 years ago and moved to Boulder 23 years ago. She is survived by three sons, Fred C. Walter and Albert Walter, both of Boulder, Harold Walter of Los Angeles, and by a daughter, Mrs. Mabel Spanner, whom she made her home at 2044 Marine. There are twelve grandchildren and five great-grandchildren. Body at Howe mortuary."

Boulder Daily Camera 30 December 1944:

"Elizabeth Ann Walter—Services were held this afternoon from the Howe mortuary at 1:30. Rev. Ellisworth Bradford, pastor of the Pillar of Fire church, officiated. Ben Walker sang, accompanied by Mr. F.J. Bartlett. Pallbearers were John W. Kirkbride, Merle L. Giles, George Cory, H.P. Doll and John Jones. Interment, Gold Hill cemetery."

About Charles Thomas and Elizabeth Ann "Bessie" (*Thomas*) Walter

Some records show that Charles Thomas Walter was born in January of 1857 and other records state February of 1860 and also March of 1857. According to the England & Wales, Free BMD Birth Index, 1837-1915 Charles Thomas

Walter's birth was registered in the year 1857, registration quarter of Jan-Feb-Mar; the son of William and Ann (*Vanstone*) Walter.

He immigrated to the United States in 1879, settling in Central City (Gilpin) Colorado where he was a miner. According to the 1900 census Charles married Elizabeth Ann "Bessie" Thomas in 1886 and in an interview by Pearl (*Pughe*) Walter, wife of Albert James "Tim" Walter; Charles and Elizabeth were married in Oregon.

Pearl (Pughe) Walter Interview by Lynne Walter (no date)

"They (Charles Thomas Walter and Elizabeth Ann "Bessie Thomas) knew each other in Wales, and were sweethearts, but Mr. Walter came to Oregon. She wasn't very old (Elizabeth). She came from England and across the country to Oregon..."

Elizabeth Ann "Bessie" was born 20 October 1857 in St. Blazey (Cornwall) England; the daughter of John and Jane (*Bennet*) Thomas; see BENNETT(S), Jane (*Bennet*) Thomas.

According to the 1900 census eight known children were born to Charles and Elizabeth with records on five:

Frederick Charles: born 08 October 1885 Central City (Gilpin) Colorado and died 14 January 1960 Boulder (Boulder) Colorado; buried Mountain View Memorial Park, Boulder (Boulder) Colorado; married Lela M. Kitto; conflicting birth years on WWI draft card and WWII draft card; obituary states 1895

Mable: born 02 September 1888 Central City (Gilpin) Colorado and died 05 February 1970 Boulder (Boulder) Colorado; buried Mountain View Memorial Park, Boulder (Boulder) Colorado; married Walter Victor Spanner

Albert James "Tim": born 27 April 1892 Gold Hill (Boulder) Colorado and died 20 August 1964 Boulder (Boulder) Colorado; buried Mountain View Memorial Park, Boulder (Boulder) Colorado; married Pearl Annabelle Pughe; built several structures in Gold Hill (Boul-

der) Colorado including the St. James Chapel and the Gold Hill Inn

Harold Thomas: born 13 June 1894 Gold Hill (Boulder) Colorado and died 28 August 1947 Boulder (Boulder) Colorado; buried Gold Hill Cemetery, Gold Hill (Boulder) Colorado; married Clara Mae (*Porter*) Gilmore and Ruth (*Averill*) McKenzie McGee; see WALTER, Harold Thomas

William Augusta "Willie": born 12 July 1897 Gold Hill (Boulder) Colorado and died 05 July 1936 Helena (Lewis and Clark) Montana; buried Gold Hill Cemetery, Gold Hill (Boulder) Colorado; married Mamie/Mayme Jodell Magor; see WALTER, William Augusta

About nine years later Charles died on 05 June 1909 from past injuries in a mining accident (death notice states miners' consumption) and was buried in the Gold Hill Cemetery in Gold Hill (Boulder) Colorado.

Interview Albert C. "Bud" Walter by Lynne Walter (no date)

"He (Charles Thomas Walter])had been mining down in Arizona. The family stayed here (Gold Hill) but he went to Arizona and mined. He was caught in a cave in and pressed some of his chest. I don't know how bad, but apparently severely. When he was able, he returned to Gold Hill and bought the stage [eventually became Walter Bros. Stage Line]. Your grandmother, Pearl (wife of Albert James "Tim"), says that the last time she saw Dad's father (Charles), she and grandma Pughe were coming up on the stage. It was a cold, snowy, miserable night and grandpa, my grandpa Walter, had a severe time trying to free the stage, and still trying to get the horse and team up the road with mother and grandmother. He went to bed and never got up again."

"He (Charles) was working, mining, and a slab fell on him in Bisbee, Arizona, and crushed his chest. He was never a well man after that. He quit mining and bought into the stage business. He died as a result of the long term injuries from the mine accident in Bisbee."

His widow, Elizabeth, remained in Gold Hill for a time, living with her sons, Fred, Albert, Harold and William. Her daughter, Mabel, was out of the household as she married Walter Victor Spanner on 28 November 1907 in Gold Hill.

By 1920 the household consisted of only one son, Frederick and by 1930 she was living on Marine Street in Boulder (Boulder) Colorado with her other son, Harold. At the time of her death Elizabeth was living with her daughter, Mabel Spanner at 2044 Marine Street. She died from cerebral hemorrhage and was buried in the Gold Hill Cemetery in Gold Hill (Boulder) Colorado.

WALTER, Harold Thomas

Birth: 06/13/1894
Death: 08/28/1947
Cemetery Location: D3

Father: Charles Thomas Walter; Mother: Elizabeth Ann "Bessie" (*Thomas*); Wife: Clara Mae (*Porter*) Gilmore; 2ⁿᵈ Wife: Ruth (*Averill*) McKenzie McGee; born in Gold Hill (Boulder) Colorado and died in Boulder (Boulder) Colorado at age 53 years, 2 months, 15 days; see **About Charles Thomas and Elizabeth Ann "Bessie" (*Thomas*) Walter**

Boulder Daily Camera 28 August 1947:

"Harold T. Walter, World War I Veteran, Dies This Morning—Harold T. Walter, native of Gold Hill and a veteran of World War I, died at Community hospital this morning of a heart ailment suffered a week ago. He was born June 3 [sic], 1894, a son of the late Mr. and Mrs. Charles Walter, pioneers of Boulder County. Enlisting for war service in 1918, Mr. Walter was assigned as a mail clerk to the base hospital at Cody, N.M. He was discharged at Camp Funston, Kan., in 1919. Surviving Mr. Walter are his wife, Ruth, and four children, Harold of 2044 Marine; Mrs. Inez Keating and William Walter of Los Angeles, and Jack McKenize, a stepson, Los Angeles. A.J. Walter of Gold Hill and Fred Walter of 1228 Mapleton are brothers; Mrs. Mabel Spanner, 2044 Marine, a sister. Funeral services will be held from Howe mortuary Saturday at 1:30 p.m. Rev. Ellis Steen, associate pastor of the First Presbyterian church, will officiate. Interment at Gold Hill."

Boulder Daily Camera 30 August 1947:

"Harold T. Walters [sic]—Services from Howe mortuary today at 1:30 p.m. with Rev. Ellis Steen, Associate Pastor of the First Presbyterian Church, officiating. Pallbearers were Carl Snively, Robert Nelson, Hyle Bradford, George Crawford, Charles Guhse and George H. Schadegg. Interment Gold Hill. Ben Walker sang, accompanied by F.J. Bartlett."

About Harold Thomas Walter

Harold Thomas Walter was born 13 June 1894 in Gold Hill (Boulder) Colorado; the son of Charles Thomas and Elizabeth "Bessie" Ann (*Thomas*) Walter.

In 1917 at the age of 22 years he was a mail carrier for the Gold Hill/Salina (Boulder) Colorado area until enlisting for war service in 1918.

He married Clara Mae (*Porter*) Gilmore whose first spouse was David Eric Gilmore. She was born 16 February 1901 in Kanwaka Township (4 miles east of Lawrence) (Douglas) Kansas; the daughter of William T. and

Mayme E. (*Richards*) Porter. Her first marriage brought forth a daughter:

Elizabeth Mae: born 18 March 1920 McPherson (McPherson) Kansas and died 25 July 2004 Reno (Washoe) Nevada; burial unknown; married Harry Neville and Raymond Henri Caulk

Clara's second marriage to Harold Thomas Walter was blessed with two known children:

Ines Lucille: born 01 May 1925 Colorado and died 07 December 2008 Moses Lake (Grant) Washington; burial unknown; married Edward Martin Keating

Harold Thomas Jr.: born 20 June 1926 Colorado and died 23 February 1978 Pagosa Springs (Archuleta) Colorado; buried Hilltop Cemetery, Pagosa Springs (Archuleta) Colorado; married Lucille L. Hurlburt

Unfortunately Harold Thomas and Clara Mae divorced. By 1930 Harold was living with his mother, Bessie in South Boulder. Clara and her daughter, Elizabeth, were living with her parents in Glendale (Los Angeles) California. For some reason Ines and Harold (the other children of Harold and Clara) were living with their Uncle Walter and Aunt Mabel (*Walter*) Spanner in Fort Collins (Larimer) Colorado.

Clara Mae (*Porter*) Gilmore Walter never married again. She died on 20 December 1990 in (Los Angeles) California and according to an Ancestry tree she is buried in a cemetery located in North Hollywood (Los Angeles) California.

Harold Thomas Walter, however, married again on 19 December 1936 in (El Paso) Colorado to Ruth (*Aver-*

ill) McKenzie McGee. She was born 04 October 1904 in Illinois; the daughter of John Howard Sidney and Minnie Mae Martha "Mayme" E. (*Choote/Choate*) Averill. From Ruth's first marriage to Blaine John McKenzie one child was brought into this marriage:

Jack: born 17 September 1924 Colorado; died 26 July 1986 Sonoma (Sonoma) California; buried Green Mountain Cemetery, Boulder (Boulder) Colorado

And from Ruth's second marriage to William McGee (who was about 15 years older than Ruth) a son was born:

Guy: born about 1930 (Boulder) Colorado and died 10 November 1946 Grand Junction (Mesa) Colorado; buried Green Mountain Cemetery, Boulder (Boulder) Colorado; never married; apparently Guy had mental difficulties and by the 1940 census he was an inmate at the Colorado State Home and Training School for Mental Defectives in Fruitvale (Mesa) Colorado

Ruth and her new husband, Harold Thomas Walter, were living in South Boulder (Boulder) Colorado in the 1940 census. Three children were also in this census record: Jack (stepson of Harold Thomas Walter), Harold Walter (stepson of Ruth; Clara was the mother) and a son:

William "Bill": born about 1934 Colorado and died between 1947-1963; last known address was Los Angeles (Los Angeles) California

Harold Thomas Walter and family were living at 2044 Marine Street in Boulder (Boulder) Colorado by 1947. He died at the city's Community Hospital on 28 August 1947 from a heart ailment. He was buried in the Gold Hill Cemetery in Gold Hill (Boulder) Colorado.

His widow, Ruth, married again to a Mr. Csonka and moved to Cloverdale (Sonoma) California where she died on 03 July 2000. Her burial is unknown.

WALTER, William Agusta/Augusta "Willie"

Birth: 07/12/1896
Death: 07/05/1936
Cemetery Location: D3

Father: Charles Thomas Walter; Mother: Elizabeth Ann "Bessie" (*Thomas*); Wife: Mamie/Mayme Jodell (*Magor*); born in Gold Hill (Boulder) Colorado and died in Helena (Lewis and Clark) Montana at age 39 years, 11 months, 23 days-chronic myocarditis

Boulder Daily Camera 08 July 1936:
"W.A. Walter—Word was received here today of the death of William A. Walter, 37, of Helena, Mont., son of Mrs. Bessie Walter, 2044 Marine street. He died suddenly July 5 and relatives here knew nothing of the cause of his death. Mr. Walter was born in Gold Hill, was educated

there and worked in the mines in that region until he left here for Idaho. He left Idaho for a position in a Montana mine only a few months ago. Surviving him are his widow, Mrs. Mamie Walter and three children, Elizabeth, Robert and James, His mother, three brothers, A.J., Fred and Harold, all of Boulder, and a sister, Mrs. Mabel Spanner of Ft. Collins. The body accompanied by the widow, will arrive here Friday. Funeral services to be held at the Howe mortuary have not been completed."

Boulder Daily Camera 10 July 1936:

"WILLIAM WALTERS [sic]—Funeral services were held at the Howe mortuary this afternoon, 2 o'clock. Rev. E.A. Bell officiated. Miss Marylee Copeland sang. Pallbearers were Wilbur Goudge, William Peterson, Fred Heitz, John Holman, Earl Snively and Everett Brown. Burial was in the Gold Hill cemetery."

About William Augusta "Willie" Walter

William Augusta Walter was born on 12 July 1896 in Gold Hill (Boulder) Colorado; the son of Charles Thomas and Elizabeth Ann "Bessie" (*Thomas*) Walter.

William enlisted on 14 October 1918 and was a private in the United States Army; honorable discharge on 11 December 1918.

He married Mamie/Mayme Jodell Magor on 01 May 1926 in Denver (Denver) Colorado. She was born 03 November 1907 in Gold Hill (Boulder) Colorado; the daughter of Frederick John and Myrtle (*Colvin*) Magor; see MAGOR, William John. To this union three known children were born:

Elizabeth "Betty" O.: born about 1926 Boulder (Boulder) Colorado-1940 census living in Murphys (Calaveras) California; no further information

Robert Leroy: born 07 September 1927 Boulder (Boulder) Colorado and died 13 May 1992 Grove (Washington) Oregon; burial unknown

James Lewis: born 16 May 1935 Idaho and died 20 November 1997 (Multnomah) Oregon; buried Willamette National Cemetery, Portland (Multnomah) Oregon

By 1930 the family was living in Nederland (Boulder) Colorado where William was working the quartz mines of the area. A few years later the family moved to Idaho where their last child, James, was born. A few months later the family moved to Jefferson City (Jefferson) Montana where William accepted a new mining position but before his career there could blossom he died on 05 July 1936 at the St. Peter's Hospital in Helena (Lewis & Clark) Montana from chronic myocarditis. His body was shipped to Boulder (Boulder) Colorado for the funeral with burial in the Gold Hill Cemetery.

In 1937 his widow, Mamie Jodell then married William S. Salmon in (Calaveras) California where they had a sheep ranch. He was born 09 September 1882 in Blue Ridge (Harrison) Missouri; son of James Frances and Rebecca (*Jones*) Salmon. He was first married Ruby Louella Wood in 1904 which ended up in divorce in 1919. His second marriage to Mamie only lasted about ten years when in 1947 he married Olive "Ollie" Lutt (*Wood*) Gillespie in (Clark) Washington. William died 03 September 1957 in McMinnville (Yamhill) Oregon and was buried in the Evergreen Memorial Park Cemetery, McMinnville (Yamhill) Oregon beside his first wife, Ruby Louella who died 12 July 1962.

The 1940 census has William Ellis and Mamie Jodell Salmon living in Murphys (Calaveras) California, a former gold mining settlement. Interesting to note the last name of the children is listed as Salmon and not Walter in this census record and all primary records from then on also have their last name recorded as Salmon.

It is from this point (1940) that the trail grows cold for Elizabeth "Betty" however Mamie and her two sons

ended up in Oregon where it appears she married Lawrence Lester Montgomery before her father's (Fred Magor) death in October 1960. Lawrence was born 07 May 1910 in Prineville (Crook) Oregon; the son of Joseph Perry and Julia Frances (*Newbill*) Montgomery. He died 22 October 1978 in Toledo (Lincoln) Oregon and was buried in the IOOF Cemetery and Mausoleum, Tillamook (Tillamook) Oregon beside his first wife, Winfred (*Sheepwash*) Montgomery who died 04 May 1939.

His widow, Mamie Jodell died 18 September 1987 in Newport (Lincoln) Oregon. There wasn't a funeral and her body was cremated. Bateman Mortuary stated that her ashes were picked up by her son.

WALTON, Annie Florence

Birth: 10/06/1870
Death: 08/26/1876
Cemetery Location: C3

Father: Leonard R. Walton; Mother: Elizabeth "Lizzie" Ellen H. (*Rule*); died at age approximately 6 years; according to the family Bible (information from Polly Westdal) Annie Florence Walton died on Aug. 26th, 1876 before family moved to Colorado; she is not listed in the *Cemeteries of Boulder County, Colorado, NSDAR, Arapahoe Chapter, Boulder Colorado* records; probably a memorial stone; see WALTON, Elizabeth "Lizzie" Ellen H. (*Rule*); see WALTON, Leonard R.; see **About Leonard R. and Elizabeth "Lizzie" Ellen H. (*Rule*) Walton**

WALTON, Elizabeth "Lizzie" Ellen H. (*Rule*)

Birth: 07/31/1848
Death: 07/27/1939
Cemetery Location: C3

Father: John Smith Rule; Mother: Amelia Aurelia (*Osborn/Osborne*); Husband: Leonard R. Walton; born in Schullsberg (Lafayette) Wisconsin and died in Boulder (Boulder) Colorado at age 90 years, 11 months, 27 days-myocardial degeneration; family genealogy states Elizabeth was born in Cornwall and came to Schullsberg (Lafayette) Wisconsin at the age of 2 years; mortuary record states location of birth as Schullsberg (Lafayette) Wisconsin as well as numerous census records; no tombstone but believed buried by her husband; see WALTON, Leonard R.; see **About Leonard R. and Elizabeth "Lizzie" Ellen H. (*Rule*) Walton**

Boulder Daily Camera 27 July 1939:
"Mrs. Ellen Walton, Pioneer Gold Hill Resident, Dies—Mrs. Elizabeth Ellen Walton, resident of Gold Hill for fifty-seven years and one of the most widely known residents of the mountain district of Boulder county, died early this morning. She was the widow of Leonard Walton whom she met at Shelleberg, Wis., and married there Mar. 8, 1866. She was born in Shelleberg, in 1848, and would have been ninety-one years of age had she lived until next Monday. Her maiden name was Rule. Mr. and Mrs. Walton came to Colorado in 1880 and located at Central City, moving later to Gold Hill, then to Rowena, and finally to Gold Hill. For the last thirty years she had made her home with her son, B.L. Walton, who is a custodian at the University gymnasium living at 921 Regent. She considered Gold Hill her home, however, and went there early each summer and remained until late fall. Mr. Walton, the husband, died at Gold Hill, Mar. 17, 1910. Of six children born to them all are deceased except the son named. Body is at Howe mortuary. Funeral services later."

Boulder Daily Camera 29 July 1939:
"Mrs. Ellen Walton-Old-time resident of Gold Hill. Service at 2:30 at Howe mortuary. Rev. C.S. Linkletter officiated. Eugene Hilligoss sang. Pallbearers were Herbert Cram, W. Cumow, John Ingold, Alex McLellan, Charles Gustafson and Clyde Bolton. Interment, Gold Hill."

Family Genealogy by Col. John Rule and Family Information courtesy Kathy Kautzman, Nancy Clark and Polly Westdal:
"Elizabeth Ellen Rule was born at Camborne, Cornwall on the 31st of July 1848 and when almost two years old came with her parents to the United States and spent the next few years at Shellsberg, Wisconsin. She met and married Leonared R. Walton at Shellsberg on the 8th of March 1866...he and Ellen moved to Colorado in 1880 and located at Central City, later moving to Gold Hill, then to Rowena in Left Hand Creek and finally back to Gold Hill.

Ellen became a fine dressmaker and her granddaughter Mrs. Leta Gray states that as a child she made all of her clothes and also made clothes for other people in the town. Her three boys, who grew to manhood, were her life. It is said that the entire town loved her and called her "Grandma." She worked very hard raising her family...She always had a good sense of humor and as she became older she made her home with her son and family, Bennett Walton at Niwot, Colorado and also spent part of the time with her son, Oscar and his family at Boulder, Colorado.

The winters in Gold Hill were too severe for her and now she was almost blind. She loved her home in Gold Hill and always looked forward to returning to it in the spring, until she was unable to live alone."

(Letter dated 27 July 1939)

WALTON, Glen/Glem

>Birth: About 10/1905
>Death: 12/11/1905
>emetery Location: Unknown

Father: Walter Rule Walton; Mother: Nancy Marie "Daisy" (*Pinkerton*); born and died in Gold Hill (Boulder) Colorado at the age of eight weeks-cerebral meningitis; no tombstone; see WALTON, Elizabeth "Lizzie" Ellen H. (*Rule*); see WALTON Leonard R.; see **About Leonard R. and Elizabeth "Lizzie" Ellen H. (*Rule*) Walton**

WALTON, John "Johnny"

>Birth: Unknown
>Death: Unknown
>Cemetery Location: Unknown

Father: Leonard R. Walton; Mother: Elizabeth "Lizzie" Ellen H. (*Rule*); died at 8 months old; no tombstone; see WALTON, Elizabeth "Lizzie" Ellen H. (*Rule*); see WALTON, Leonard R.; see **About Leonard R. and Elizabeth "Lizzie" Ellen H. (*Rule*) Walton**

According to Information from a family relative Polly Westdal with family genealogy by Col. John Rule (letter dated 27 July 1939) there was another baby born to Leonard and Elizabeth by the name of John "Johnny" who died at eight months old and was buried in the Gold Hill Cemetery however this baby wasn't noted in the family Bible and no further information has been found.

WALTON, Leonard R.

>Birth: 01/28/1838
>Death: 03/17/1910
>Cemetery Location: C3

Father: John R. Walton; Mother: Mary (*maiden name unknown*); Wife: Elizabeth "Lizzie" Ellen H. (*Rule*); born in Pennsylvania and died in Gold Hill (Boulder) Colorado at age 72 years, 1 month, 17 days-illness; see WALTON, Elizabeth "Lizzie" Ellen H. (*Rule*); see **About Leonard R. and Elizabeth "Lizzie" Ellen H. (*Rule*) Walton**

Boulder Daily Camera 17 March 1910:
"WITH THOSE WHO MOURN LOVED ONES GONE BEFORE—Leonard R. Walton, aged 72 years, died this morning at 8:30 at his home in Gold Hill. Besides the widow, three sons, Bennett, Oscar and Walter, survive, and five grandchildren. The deceased lived in Gold Hill for the past 40 years. The funeral will take place at 2 o'clock Sunday at the late residence. George Kirkbride, a close friend since 1878, will have charge of the service."

Denver Rocky Mountain News 18 March 1910:
"BOULDER, Colo., March 17.—Leonard R. Walton 76 years old and a resident of Boulder County for forty years, died today after an illness of several months. He was engaged in the mining business since coming to the state. He leaves three grown sons, with whom he was associated in mining."
[Error in age]

About Leonard R. and Elizabeth "Lizzie" Ellen H. (*Rule*) Walton

Leonard R. Walton was born on 28 January 1838 in Pennsylvania; the son of Welsh natives John R. and Mary (maiden name unknown) Walton.

Leonard R. Walton and Elizabeth "Lizzie" Ellen H. Rule were married 08 March 1866 in Schullsberg (Lafayette) Wisconsin. She was born 31 July 1848 in Schullsberg (Lafayette) Wisconsin; the daughter of (Cornwall) England natives John Smith and Amelia Aurelia (*Osborn/Osborne*) Rule. To this union seven children were born (according to the 1900 census record) with information on six:

Allie R.: born 28 April 1868 Schullsberg (Lafayette) Wisconsin and died 05 September 1888 Gold Hill (Boulder) Colorado; buried Gold Hill Cemetery, Gold Hill (Boulder) Colorado; married William Howard Patton; see PATTON, Allie R.; see PATTON, William Howard

Annie Florence: born 06 October 1870 Schullsberg (Lafayette) Wisconsin and died 26 August 1876 on route to Colorado; buried Gold Hill Cemetery, Gold Hill (Boulder) Colorado; probably a memorial stone; see WALTON, Annie Florence

Bennett Lewis: born 03 July 1873 Schullsberg (Lafayette) Wisconsin and died 11 July 1940 Boulder (Boulder) Colorado; buried Columbia Cemetery, Boulder (Boulder) Colorado; married Nellie Strock; some documents have Louis but family Bible has Lewis

Oscar Leonard: born 25 November 1878 Schullsberg (Lafayette) Wisconsin and died 16 May 1939 Boulder (Boulder) Colorado; buried Columbia Cemetery, Boulder (Boulder) Colorado; married Pearl M. Barnett; some documents have 29 November 1878 as birth date but family Bible has 25 November 1878

Walter Rule: born 29 July 1881 Gold Hill (Boulder) Colorado- 26 died February 1920 Denver (Denver) Colorado; buried Crown Hill Cemetery, Denver (Denver) Colorado; married Daisy Mae Pinkerton

John "Johnny": birth unknown; death unknown; buried Gold Hill Cemetery, Gold Hill (Boulder) Colorado; see WALTON, John "Johnny"

United States census records of 1850, 1860 and 1870 have the family living in Schullsberg (Lafayette) Wisconsin.

Excerpts from a letter to Richard Dussart Regnier from Polly Westdal (courtesy of Richard Dussart Regnier):

"My son, John Westdal spoke with you at Gold Hill regarding our Walton family who probably came to that area in 1877 or so. Leonard Walton was a miner. His wife, Ellen Elizabeth, is our actual relative. She was born in Cornwall, England, [other sources state Schullsberg (Lafayette) Wisconsin] the daughter of John Smith Rule and Amelia Osborne...The home of Leonard and Ellen Walton was at 14 Main Street (not Pine Street) and their son, Walter, lived at 25 Pine Street."

(He must have rented as there is no record of a Walter Walton living on Pine Street)

Family Genealogy by Col. John Rule and Family Information courtesy Kathy Kautzman, Nancy Clark and Polly Westdal:

"Leonard Walton was born on the 28th of January 1838 in Pennsylvania. Very soon after he and Ellen were married he went to the gold mines of California and did not return for three years. He then went to work in the lead mines at Shellsberg and as a result his health was injured, so he and Ellen moved to Colorado in 1880 and located at Central City, later moving to Gold Hill, then to Rowena in Left Hand Creek and finally back to Gold Hill."

In 1880 the family indeed was in Gold Hill (Boulder) Colorado where Leonard was a miner. The household included Bennet Osborne who was Elizabeth's uncle (brother of her mother Amelia Aurelia (*Osborn/Osborne*) Walton). At this time her parents (John Smith and Amelia Aurelia (*Osborn/Osborne*) Rule were living in Helena (Louis and Clark) Montana where John was a miner at the age of 63 years.

Five years later in the Colorado State census record Amelia was listed as a widow and living with Elizabeth

and Leonard in Gold Hill (Boulder) Colorado. It is assumed that John Smith Rule died in Helena (Louis and Clark) Montana and is buried in a cemetery there. The trail grows cold for Amelia as well. It is not known for certain when she died or where she is buried.

Leonard and Elizabeth continued to live in Gold Hill until he died on 17 March 1910 from a lingering illness at his home and was buried in the Gold Hill Cemetery. His widow, Elizabeth, stayed in Gold Hill until she died at Community Hospital in Boulder (Boulder) Colorado from myocardial degeneration on 27 July 1939. She was laid to rest next to her husband of about forty-four years in the Gold Hill Cemetery in Gold Hill (Boulder) Colorado.

WEAVER, William Tad "Bill"

Birth: 08/24/1945
Death: 11/06/2003
Cemetery Location: B6

Father: Joe C. Weaver; Mother: Carolyn E (*Lyle*); born in Boulder (Boulder) Colorado and died in Longmont (Boulder) Colorado at age 58 years, 2 months, 13 days-cardiac arrest

Boulder Daily Camera 08 November 2003:

"WILLIAM TAD WEAVER—William Tad Weaver of Longmont, formerly of Boulder and Gold Hill, died of cardiac arrest at Applewood Living Center in Longmont on Thursday, Nov. 6, 2003. He was 58.

Born Aug. 24, 1945, in Boulder, he was the son of Joe C. Weaver and Carolyn E. Lyle Weaver.

He attended school in the Boulder Valley School District and graduated from Boulder High School, where he was a star center/guard on the football team. He received a football scholarship to Mesa State College in Grand Junction but attended only a short time.

Mr. Weaver worked as a mechanic for Flatirons for more than 20 years.

He enjoyed collecting and restoring old cars and trucks, NACAR racing and collecting guns, and was an avid Broncos fan.

Mr. Weaver was a member of the Operating Engineer's Union Local No. 9 and the American Antique Truck Association.

He enjoyed being around his nieces and nephews. Bill's family would like everyone to remember him as: 'Bill Weaver, American,' his family said.

He was preceded in death by his parents.

Survivors include a brother, Joe Weaver of Arvada; and a sister, Phyllis Pfarr of Longmont.

Private memorial services will be held at a later date.

Contributions may be made in his name to the American Diabetes Association, Colorado Affiliate, 2480 W. 26th Ave., Suite 710, Denver, CO 80211, or the American Heart Association, 313523rd St., Boulder, CO 80304. Howe Mortuary and Crematory of Longmont is in charge of cremation arrangements."

WILLIAMS, Douglas James

Birth: 07/06/1957
Death: 04/05/1977
Cemetery Location: C1

Father: Richard Charles Williams Sr.; Mother: Verna Mae (*Regnier*); born in Longmont (Boulder) Colorado and died in Denver (Denver) Colorado at age 19 years, 8 months, 30 days-lengthy illness; see WILLIAMS, Verna Mae (*Regnier*); see WILLIAMS, Richard Charles "Dickie" Jr.; see REGNIER, James Dussart; see REGNIER, Richard James Dussart

Boulder Daily Camera 07 July 1957:

"Douglas Williams—Douglas James Williams, 10912 Lynne Ave., Lafayette, died Tuesday at St. Luke's Hospital in Denver after a lengthy illness. He was 19. He was born July 6, 1957, In Longmont to Mr. and Mrs. Richard C. Williams. In addition to his parents, he is survived by a brother, Richard C. Williams Jr., at home; six sisters, Diana Morrell, Lafayette, and Lee Ann, Debbie, Beth, Lynn and Shelley Williams, all at home; two grandmothers, Alice Barclay, Dacona, and Iris Diane, Austin, Tex.; and a step-grandmother, Ellen Regnier, Boulder. Funeral services will be held at 10 a.m. Friday at Henning-Howe Chapel in Lafayette First United Methodist Church officiating. Interment will be in Gold Hill Cemetery. Visitation at the Henning-How Chapel in Lafayette will be from 1 to 5 p.m. and 7 to 9 p.m. today."

WILLIAMS, Richard Charles "Dickie" Jr.

Birth: 05/26/1971
Death: 11/30/2013
Cemetery Location: C1

Father: Richard Charles Williams Sr. Wife: Verna Mae (*Regnier*); born in Boulder (Boulder) Colorado and died in Lafayette (Boulder) Colorado at the age of 42 years, 5 months, 6 days; see WILLIAMS, Verna Mae (*Regnier*); no tombstone yet but buried beside his mother; see WILLIAMS, Douglas James; see REGNIER, James Dussart; see REGNIER, Richard James Dussart

Hometown News 11 December 2013:

"Richard Charles Williams, Jr. (Dickie)
May 26, 1971-November 30, 2013

Dickie Williams was born in Boulder, CO on May 26, 1971 and passed away in Lafayette, CO on November 30, 2013.

He was a lifelong resident of Lafayette, and graduated from Centaurus High School.

Dickie is survived by his father, Richard Williams, and six sisters; Diana Hunt, LeeAnn Steele, Debbie Williams, Beth Van Dusen, Lynn Davis, and Shelley Eckenrode. He was a loving uncle to Jayme Steele, Jennifer Young, Ana Van Dusen, Callie Davis, Marissa Davis and Grand uncle to Savannah and Douglas Young. Dickie was preceded in death by his mother, Verna Williams and brother, Douglas Williams.

The rock grave marker for Richard Charles "Dickie" Jr. Williams will be replaced by a tombstone at a later date.

Dickie was much loved and will be greatly missed. He loved music, (he loved to play the bass guitar), the outdoors, bicycle riding and his pets, especially his dogs. He was a kind soul who was loved by his family.

Services will be held at the Darrell Howe Chapel in Lafayette, CO on December 19, 2013 at 10:00 AM. In lieu of flowers, please direct donations to the Bolder Humane Society, Birds of Prey Rehabilitation Center or Greenwood wildlife Center. Memorial Contributions can also be made to SAVE (Suicide Awareness Voices of Education) www.SAVE.org"

WILLIAMS, Verna Mae (*Regnier*)

Birth: 11/09/1936
Death: 09/03/1992
Cemetery Location: C1

Father: James Dussart Regnier; Mother: Iris Ruby (*Stogsdill*); Husband: Richard "Dick" Charles Williams; born in Erie (Boulder) Colorado and died in Longmont (Boulder) Colorado at age 55 years, 9 months, 25 days; see REGNIER, James Dussart; see REGNIER, Richard James Dussart

Boulder Daily Camera 05 September 1992:

"Verna Mae Williams—Verna Mae Williams of 10912 Lynn Ave., Lafayette, died Thursday, Sept. 3, at Longmont United Hospital. She was 55. She was born Nov. 9, 1936, in Erie, the daughter of James Regner [sic] and Iris Diane Stogsdill Regner [sic]. She married Richard Williams Sr. on Nov. 22, 1951, in Erie. She graduated from Erie High School and was a baker at King Soopers for 20 years. She belonged to the Lafayette First United Methodist Church, Friday Harbor Washington and the San Juan Island Museum. She loved whales. A son, Douglas

James Williams, preceded her in death. Survivors include her husband of Lafayette; her mother of Austin, Texas; a son, Richard Williams Jr., of Lafayette; six daughters, Diana Hunt of San Jose, Calif., Lee Ann Steele and Shelly Williams of Lafayette, Debbie Williams of Arvada, Lynn Williams of Boulder and Beth VanDusen of Edgewater; a brother, Richard Regnier of Mesa, Texas; a sister, Celia Regner of Longmont; a stepbrother Mike Adiano; a stepsister, Carol Frazier of Austin; and two grandchildren. Memorial service will be held today at 10:30 a.m. at First United Methodist Church of Lafayette, 200 E. Baseline Road. The Rev. Christine Zavier and Dale McArthur will officiate. Cremation will take place at Howe Mortuary in Longmont."

WOLCOTT, Edmond/Edmund

Birth: 08/10/1867
Death: 01/22/1923
Cemetery Location: Unknown

Father: James Wolcott; Mother: Elizabeth "Eliza" (*Thomas*); never married; born in (Cornwall) England and died in Boulder (Boulder) Colorado at age 55 years, 5 months, 12 days-pulmonary tuberculosis; brother to John Wolcott; no tombstone; see WOLCOTT, John

Boulder Daily Camera 25 January 1923:

"EDMUND WOOLCOT—Funeral services for Edmund Woolcot, veteran miner in the Goldhill district, who died, will be held Friday afternoon at o'clock from the Kelso & Tuttle mortuary. The Rev. H.M. Walters of the Episcopal Church will be in charge. The body will be taken to Goldhill on Saturday morning for burial."

Boulder Daily Camera 26 January 1923:

"EDMOND WOLCOTT—The body of Edmond Wolcott, who died Monday, was taken to Gold Hill this afternoon for burial in the Gold Hill cemetery, following funeral service at Kelso & Tuttle's mortuary. Rev. Father H.N. Walters officiated. Mrs. Waldo E. Brockway and Leslie B. Kelso sang. Mrs. B.M. Williams, of 2205 Twelfth Street, a relative of Mr. Wolcott, accompanied the body to Gold Hill."

About Edmond/Edmund Wolcott

Edmund was born 10 August 1867 in (Cornwall) England; the son of James and Elizabeth (*Thomas*) Wolcott. Never married, he came to the United States in 1891 and by 1900 he was living in Gold Hill (Boulder) Colorado with his brother, John and family, where he was a quartz miner.

Twenty years later he was living in Caribou (Boulder) Colorado along with his nephew Rowe J. where they both worked the mines.

Three years later on 22 January 1923 Edmund died at the County Sanitarium in Boulder (Boulder) Colorado from pulmonary tuberculosis. He was buried in the Gold Hill Cemetery in Gold Hill (Boulder) Colorado in an unmarked grave in an unknown location.

WOLCOTT, John

Birth: 07/1854
Death: 08/29/1908
Cemetery Location: Unknown

Father: James Wolcott; Mother: Elizabeth "Eliza" (*Thomas*); Wife: Elizabeth Jane (*Trembath*); born in (Cornwall) England and died three miles northeast of Nederland (Boulder) Colorado at age 54 years (approximately)-heart trouble; brother to Edmond/Edmund Wolcott; no tombstone; see WOLCOTT, Edmond/Edmund

Boulder Daily Camera 31 August 1908:

"John Wolcott of Nederland died at his home three miles northeast of that city Saturday night. Death was due to heart trouble. Funeral services will be held tomorrow from the Methodist church in Gold Hill. Wolcott, who was born in England, is survived by a wife, two children and several brothers."

Boulder Daily Camera 02 September 1908:

"INTERRED AT GOLD HILL...John Wolcott, a well-known miner of Boulder County, was interred at Gold Hill cemetery yesterday. The Foresters had charge of the funeral ceremonies, assisted by the Workmen and a numerous concourse of intimate friends from all parts of the county gathered in the little church to pay a last tribute to the memory of the departed. The floral offerings almost hid the casket from sight.

As his friends gathered around the grave, they sang the hymn, "Jesus, Lover of My Soul," with the sweetness that comes of human sympathy.

John Wolcott was born in England in 1855. In early boyhood he entered the mines, emigrating [sic] shortly after his marriage, to the United States, and settling in Colorado. He leaves a wife, son and daughter, who will henceforth make Gold Hill their home."

About John Wolcott

First of all the spelling of the last name has been varied ("Woolcock," "Woolcox," "Woolcot," "Wolcott," "Wilcox") thus quite a challenge to locate records believed to be correct.

John Wolcott was born July of 1854 in (Cornwall) England; the son of James and Elizabeth "Eliza" (*Thomas*) Wolcott. He married Elizabeth Jane Trembath in the year 1882. She was born about 1865 in (Cornwall) England; parents unknown. To their union two known children were born:

Annie Elizabeth: born 03 May 1883 White Haven (Cumbria) England and died 10 August 1950 Boulder (Boulder) Colorado; buried Columbia Cemetery, Boulder (Boulder) Colorado; married Otto Jay Cross; see CROSS, Rowe; see CROSS Walter; see **About The Otto Jay Cross Family**

Rowe James: born 29 February 1888 Gold Hill (Boulder) Colorado and died 23 February 1923 Boulder (Boulder) Colorado; buried Columbia Cemetery, Boulder (Boulder) Colorado; never married; tombstone has "Woolcock;" see **About the Otto Jay Cross Family**

John and his wife Elizabeth Jane (*Trembath*) Wolcott along with their two-year-old daughter, Annie, immigrated to the United States in 1887, settling in Gold Hill (Boulder) Colorado where their son, Rowe, was born.

In 1900 John was working the mines of Boulder County and soon moved his family near Nederland (Boulder) Colorado where he died at his home on 29 August 1908 from heart trouble. He was buried in the Gold Hill Cemetery with no tombstone, in an unknown location. Apparently his widow, Elizabeth Jane (*Trembath*) Wolcott, moved back to Gold Hill as per the 1916 Colorado Directory.

She married Benjamin Myrick Williams on 27 November 1917 in Boulder (Boulder) Colorado and they lived on the corner of Pine and Broadway. Today this location houses the Museum of Boulder in the old Masonic Lodge Temple building.

Elizabeth Jane died 17 November 1937 and was buried in the Columbia Cemetery in Boulder (Boulder) Colorado; see **About the Otto Jay Cross Family**.

X

There are no Xs.

Photograph by Dina C. Carson

Y

YERIAN, Dolores

> Birth: 09/10/1896
> Death: 03/16/1901
> Cemetery Location: F4

Father: William Frank Yerian; Mother: Ann "Anna/Annie" (*Weger/Wager*); born and died Summerville (Boulder) Colorado at age 4 years, 6 months, 4 days

Boulder Daily Camera 16 March 1901:
> "A child of Frank Yerian died at Summerville today, aged four years and a half."

About William Frank and Ann "Anna/Annie (*Weger/Wager*) Yerian

William Frank Yerian was born 02 December 1866 in Ohio; the son of William Franklin and Miriam (*Harvey*) Yerian. He was one of six known children born to William and Miriam:

Effie Amelia: born 24 July 1858 Liberty (Jackson) Ohio and died 30 May 1890 Liberty (Jackson) Ohio; buried Pleasant Grove Cemetery Jackson (Jackson) Ohio; married Charles Keeton

Iva Alma: born 23 December 1859 Liberty (Jackson) Ohio-11 January 1950 Rockford (Winnebago) Illinois; buried Fairmount Cemetery Jackson (Jackson) Ohio; married Albert Harper

Virginia Candace "Daisy": born 14 December 1862 Liberty (Jackson) Ohio and died 03 May 1970 Springfield (Clark) Ohio; buried Saint John the Baptist Catholic Cemetery, Hubbardston (Ionia) Michigan; married Bernard James Timlin

William Frank: born 02 December 1866 Liberty (Jackson) Ohio and died 07 November 1938 Jackson (Jackson) Ohio; buried Pleasant Grove Cemetery Jackson (Jackson) Ohio; married Anna Weger; see YERIAN, Dolores

Joseph Oscar: born 24 November 1868 Liberty (Jackson) Ohio and died 07 December 1932 Bishop (Inyo) California; buried East Line Street Cemetery, Bishop (Inyo) California; never believed married; interesting to note that on his World War I draft card birthdate is 24 November 1875 but all other records indicate either 1868 or 1869

Ira Edson: born December 1870 Liberty (Jackson) Ohio and died 24 August 1943 Liberty (Jackson) Ohio; buried Fairmount Cemetery, Jackson (Jackson) Ohio; married Margaret Alice Radcliff

All the Yerian children were born on a farm outside of Liberty (Jackson) Ohio and grew up there where their mother, Miriam (*Harvey*) Yerian died there on 24 January 1924 at the ripe old age of 89 years, 8 months and 20 days. She was buried in the Pleasant Grove Cemetery in Jackson (Jackson) Ohio. The patriarch and Civil War veteran of the family, William Franklin Yerian, died peacefully at the farm home about five years later on 01 January 1929 at age 94 years and 9 months. He, too, was buried in the Pleasant Grove Cemetery beside his wife of over 72 years of marriage.

William Frank Yerian traveled to Colorado where he married Annie Weyer [sic] on 01 July 1891 in (Boulder) Colorado. She was born 13 March 1871 in Illinois; the daughter of unknown parents. To their union five known children were born:

Percy Alden: born 17 December 1891 Summerville (Boulder) Colorado and died 24 February 1982 California; buried Rose Hills Memorial Park, Whittier (Los Angeles) California; married Susie Schiller

Hazel: born 1893/1894 Colorado; married Rice Williams; 1920 census living with mother (Anna) in Liberty (Jackson) Ohio with son Richard; there is a Hazel E. Wil-

liams born 1894 and died 1973 and buried in the Maple Grove Cemetery, New Haven (Huron) Ohio

Delores: born 10 September 1896 Summerville (Boulder) Colorado and died 16 March 1901 Summerville (Boulder) Colorado; buried Gold Hill Cemetery, Gold Hill (Boulder) Colorado; see YERIAN, Delores

Mearl/Mearle: born 30 October 1898 Summerville (Boulder) Colorado and died 11 April 1924 San Bernardino (San Bernardino) California; buried Victor (Teller) Colorado; married Jay Lorenzo Hitesman

Eileen Velma: born 10 July 1901 Colorado and died 13 June 1976 San Bernardino (San Bernardino) California; buried; married Lawrence O. McAleer and Arthur G. McDavitt

Olive/Oleva June: born 13 June 1906 Colorado and died 24 March 1998 (Riverside) California; burial unknown; married Cecil O. Eubanks; some sources have Hayden Eubanks

In the 1900 census Frank and Annie were living in Gold Hill (Boulder) Colorado with their children Percy, Hazel, Delores and Mearl along with a servant Ester Davis (born October 1882) from Sweden.

The Mining Camps: Salina & Summerville by M.M. Anderson, 2005, pg. 318:

"Frank Yerian lived in Summerville as early as 1892 and left the area shortly after the turn of the century. His four-year-old daughter, Delores, died two months before this accident on March 16, 1901 (see article below), and was buried in the Gold Hill Cemetery."

Boulder Daily Camera 16 May 1901:

"Two Miners on Victoria Narrowly Escape Death. Frank Yerian and Charles Shold, two miners on the Victoria, were injured by concussion by an explosion in the mine late yesterday afternoon and met with a miraculous escape. They had put in charge and lit the fuse and were ascending in the bucket in shaft No. 2 when the bucket caught. Engineer Fred Buckler, at the surface, reversed and lowered when the bucket caught again. They caught a ladder and began its ascent when the ladder broke under their combined weight and the men fell toward the very spot they had sought several seconds before to escape from. Sure death stared them in the face, had it not been that the ladder fell cross wise of a false plat sixteen feet above, over a manhole. Yerian was on top of the ladder when it broke and fell to the rocky bottom, jarred but sustaining no fractures. The men were considerably shaken up and all covered with mud. Their injuries are not thought to be serious. Had they fallen through the manhole, both would have been killed."

About ten years later they were living in Goldfield (Teller) Colorado which is now a ghost town but had a population of well over 3,000 when the Yerians lived there. The town was originally established in 1895 by the owners of the Portland Mine where Frank worked as a miner.

In the 1920 census record Anna is living with her children Olivia and Hazel Williams along with grandson Richard Williams in Liberty (Jackson) Ohio while Frank and Hazel's husband, Rice, were mining in Goldfield (Teller) Colorado.

It appears it was quite an interesting marriage for Hazel as she married Rice Williams 23 July 1911 in Goldfield but then divorced him 23 July 1914 (Teller) Colorado only to remarried him 03 July 1915 in Cripple Creek (Teller) Colorado.

Ten years later in 1930 Frank joined his wife, Anna, and lived in Liberty (Jackson) Ohio where Frank was a farmer at the age of 63 years. Unfortunately his health began to fail so they moved in the household of their daughter, Olive/Oleva June (*Yerian*) Eubanks where Frank died on 07 November 1938 and was buried in the Pleasant Grove Cemetery in Jackson (Jackson) Ohio.

Jackson Herald 08 November 1938: [Jackson County, Ohio]

"W.F. Yerian Dies Monday...William Frank Yerian, 66, widely-known Jackson man, died Monday at the home of his daughter, Mrs. Cecil Eubanks, on Parkview avenue, following an extended period of ill health.

He leaves his wife and two daughters, Mrs. Eubanks of Jackson, Mrs. A.G. McDovitt [sic], of San Fernando, Calif., and one son, T.A. [error should be P.A.] Yerian, of Los Angeles, California.

Funeral services will be held at 2:30 o'clock Wednesday at the Methodist church and burial will follow in the Pleasant Grove cemetery under the direction of C.E. Mayhew."

His widow, Anna, continued living with the Eubank family in Jackson (Jackson) Ohio until her death on 11 November 1949 at the age of 78 years. She was buried beside her husband Frank in the Pleasant Grove Cemetery in Jackson (Jackson) Ohio.

Jackson Herald 11 November 1949: Jackson (Jackson) Ohio

"Aged Resident Claimed Friday...Mrs. Anna M. Yerian Dies Suddenly In Eubanks' Home...

Mrs. Anna Meeker Yerian, 78, passed away in the home of Hayden Eubanks here Friday morning at four o'clock following a brief illness.

A native of Colorado, Mrs. Yerian was a member of the Methodist church.

She is survived by one son, P.A. Yerian of California; two daughters, Mrs. A.G. McDermott [sic] and Mrs. Cecil Eubanks of New Paris, Indiana and one sister who lives in Missouri. Her husband, W.F. Yerian, preceded her in death 11 years ago.

Arrangements are incomplete, pending the arrival of the children, but the body has been taken to the Clyde E. Mayhew funeral home. Burial will be made in the Pleasant Grove cemetery."

Z

There are no Zs.

Photograph by Dina C. Carson

The Gold Hill Cemetery shed that burned in the
Fourmile Canyon Fire

Photo by Shirley Ellis   August 2010

Botom two photos by Dina C. Carson

Fourmile Canyon Fire September 2010

On September 06 of 2010 the author was operating the Gold Hill Museum when one of the visitors caught her attention saying to come outside and "look at this!" Upon viewing the massive grey smoke in the southern sky she immediately told everyone to vacate the museum and head for Boulder; the museum was closed!

Reported at 10:02 a.m. this massive grey smoke came from a human-caused fire originating in Emerson Gulch. With just having a dry August it was quite a concern. Winds were blowing steadily that day (about 10-15 miles per hour with gusts up to what was reported at 41 miles per hour) so it didn't take a "rocket scientist" to know that this situation wasn't good.

The old church bell at the museum woke up and rang the warning to get the attention of all residents with volunteers going door-to-door for evacuation. The author was given one hour to pack up and leave. She used that hour filling her jeep with as many artifacts and museum items as it would hold. It was unbelievable how close the fire had come to the outskirts of the town in just sixty minutes!

This fire ravaged through the Gold Hill Cemetery after burning numerous homes in its path including the historical Pughe homestead. The town of Gold Hill itself was seconds away from being wiped off the map when a slurry bomber flew over the southern edge of the town releasing its red mass of fire retardant. This angel from God saved the town.

It's been over eight years since this catastrophe but definitely left its mark as one of the most devastating mountain fires in the state of Colorado.

INDEX

There is no death! The stars go down
To rise upon some fairer shore.
And bright in heaven's jeweled crown,
They shine for evermore.

—John Luckey McCreery (1835–1906)

Published in the
Boulder County Courier 27 September 1878

CPSIA information can be obtained
at www.ICGtesting.com
Printed in the USA
LVHW072310230519
618963LV00027B/1144/P